CHRISTIANITY

The Illustrated Guide to 2,000 Years of the Christian Faith

EARTH is an epic publishing feat never to be repeated, proudly created by Millennium House

This limited edition atlas—the world's largest modern atlas—is bound by hand in beautiful custom-dyed leather with silver-gilded pages for preservation and silver-plated corners for protection. *Earth* establishes a new benchmark in the world of atlases, with highly detailed mapping and comprehensive country profiles. With 580 pages, including 355 maps of 194 countries, more than 800 images, 4 breathtaking gatefolds, and information on every country, territory and dependency in the world, *Earth* will appeal to book collectors, libraries and institutions, map lovers, and anyone wishing to enjoy now, and preserve for the future, a record of our world today.

Earth can be ordered from all good book stores or contact Millennium House for your nearest supplier

www.millenniumhouse.com.au

CHRISTIANITY

The Illustrated Guide to 2,000 Years of the Christian Faith

Chief consultant
Ann Marie B. Bahr

MILLENNIUM HOUSE

First published in 2009 by Millennium House Pty Ltd
52 Bolwarra Rd, Elanora Heights, NSW, 2101, Australia
Ph: 612 9970 6850
Fax: 612 9913 3500
Email: info@millenniumhouse.com.au
Website: www.millenniumhouse.com.au

Reprinted 2010

ISBN: 978-1-921209-47-5
ISBN: 978-1-921209-36-9 (Cased)

Color separation by Pica Digital Pte Ltd, Singapore
Printed in Hong Kong

Photographs preliminary pages:
Page 1: *Madonna and Child Enthroned with Two Angels and Saints Andrew, Nicholas, John the Baptist, and James,* by Orcagna.
Page 3: A gargoyle in front of Notre-Dame Cathedral, Paris, France.
Pages 4–5: *Annunciation* by Benvenuto Tisi da Garafalo.
Pages 6–7: Christ the Redeemer statue, Rio de Janeiro, Brazil.
Pages 8–9: *The Four Doctors* by Jacob Jordaens.
Pages 10–11: Russian Orthodox icon, Moscow, Russia.

Publisher
Gordon Cheers

Associate publisher
Janet Parker

Art director
Stan Lamond

Project manager
Marie-Louise Taylor

Chief consultant
Ann Marie B. Bahr

Special adviser
Roland Boer

Editors
Monica Berton
Catherine Etteridge
Heather Jackson
Anne Savage
Marie-Louise Taylor
Dannielle Viera

Cover design
Stan Lamond

Senior designer
Jacqueline Richards

Designer
Ingo Voss

Map designer
Warwick Jacobson

Picture research
Kathy Lamond
Michael van Ewijk

Index
Tricia Waters

Production
Simone Coupland
Bernard Roberts

Production assistant
Michelle Di Stefano

CONTRIBUTORS

CHIEF CONSULTANT

Ann Marie B. Bahr is Professor of Religious Studies at South Dakota State University, USA. She served as the academic editor of the 11-volume *Religions of the World* series, writing two of the volumes: *Christianity* (2004) and *Indigenous Religions* (2005). Her articles have appeared in *Annual Editions: World Religions* (2002), *Encountering Faith in the Classroom* (2008), the *Chronicle of Higher Education*, and the *Journal of Ecumenical Studies*. Bahr is a member of Phi Beta Kappa, the American Academy of Religion, and the Society of Biblical Literature.

SPECIAL ADVISER

Roland Boer is a Research Professor at the University of Newcastle, Australia. He has four degrees in classics and theology from the universities of Newcastle and Sydney in Australia, and McGill in Canada (Bachelor of Arts, Bachelor of Divinity with Honours and University Medal, Master of Theology with First Class Honours, and a Ph.D. with Dean's Honours List). He has written numerous articles and books on theology, Biblical studies, and political philosophy, the most recent of which are *Criticism of Heaven* (2007), *Last Stop Before Antarctica* (2008, revised edition), *Political Myth: On the Use and Abuse of Biblical Themes* (2009), *Political Grace: The Revolutionary Theology of John Calvin* (2009), and *Criticism of Religion* (2009).

CONTRIBUTORS

Rev. Dr. Kyo Seong Ahn, a former missionary to Mongolia and mission practitioner, recently completed his doctoral studies at the University of Cambridge. He has taught at the Mongolian National Foreign Language Institute, Ulaanbaatar University, and Union Bible College in Mongolia, and he presently teaches at the Presbyterian College and Theological Seminary in Seoul, Korea. He wrote *The Church Which Lost the Disabled* (in Korean) and has authored numerous articles on Korean Christianity, Asian Christianity, Church history, mission history, ecumenism, and Bible translation (in English and Korean).

Austin Bennett Amonette, Ph.D., is Assistant Professor of Church History and Theology at Houston Graduate School of Theology in Texas, USA. His research specialization is American Christianity, particularly nineteenth- and twentieth-century evangelicalism. He has been published in the *Stone-Campbell Journal* and in the book *Baptist Identities: International Studies from the Seventeenth to the Twentieth Centuries* (2006).

Andreas Andreopoulos is Lecturer in Christian Theology at the University of Wales Lampeter. He founded and directs the postgraduate program in Orthodox theology there. He has written on Orthodox theology, the Greek Fathers, and Christian semiotics. His books include *Metamorphosis: The Transfiguration in Byzantine Theology and Iconography* (2005), *The Sign of the Cross: The Gesture, the History, the Mystery* (2006), and *Art as Theology: From the Postmodern to the Medieval* (2007).

Colin Barr is Associate Professor of History as well as Chair of the History Department at Ave Maria University in Florida, USA. A graduate of Cambridge University in the UK, he is a Fellow of the Royal Historical Society, and the author of *Paul Cullen, John Henry Newman, and the Catholic University of Ireland, 1845–65* (2003). His articles have appeared in *The English Historical Review, The Historical Journal, The Proceedings of the British Academy,* and *The Journal of Ecclesiastical History.*

Carlos F. Cardoza-Orlandi is Professor of World Christianity at Columbia Theological Seminary in Decatur, Georgia, USA. His research, writing, and work focus on history and theology in the non-Western world, intercultural studies, and interreligious studies. Cardoza-Orlandi's most recent work includes *A todas las naciones: una historia del movimiento misionero cristiano,* which he co-authored with Justo L. Gonzalez; and "The Future of Christian Mission in an Age of World Christianity," a chapter in *Chalice Introduction to Disciples Theology* (2008). His *Mission: An Essential Guide* (1999) is available in English, Spanish, and Korean. In 2008, Cardoza-Orlandi received the Building Bridges Award from the Islamic Speakers Bureau of Atlanta, Georgia, USA.

Howard Culbertson is Professor of Missions at Southern Nazarene University in Oklahoma City, USA. He is the co-author of *Discovering Missions* (2007) and the author of *Paul McGrady: Mr. Evangelism* (1969); *Rookie Notebook* (1976); *Pasta, Pizza and Pinocchio* (1980); *Mr. Missionary, I have a Question* (1987); *The Kingdom Strikes Back* (1990); and *Our Balanced Attack* (1991). He wrote chapters for *Living Out of the Mold* (1982) and *I Believe: Now Tell Me Why* (1994). His articles about global missionary work have appeared in several periodicals, including *Conquest, World Mission,* and *Holiness Today*. He is a member of the American Society of Missiology, the Evangelical Missiological Society, and the Midwest Fellowship of Professors of Missions.

Dr. Terence J. Fay is a Jesuit priest who authored *A History of Canadian Catholics: Gallicanism, Romanism, and Canadianism* (2002). He is a faculty member of the Toronto School of Theology at the University of Toronto, a former president of the Canadian Catholic Historical Association and a current member of its executive, a member of the Executive Council of the American Catholic Historical Association, and a member of the Historical Commission for the diocese of Pembroke for the beatification of Catherine de Hueck Doherty. He has published articles in Asia, Canada, Ireland, Italy, the USA, the UK, and Australia. His latest book is *The Unique Stories of Catholic Asians in Canada* (2009).

Lynda Garland is an Associate Professor at the School of Humanities, University of New England, Australia. She is an executive member of the Australian Association for Byzantine Studies (home.vicnet.net.au/~byzaus/) and contributes to *De Imperatoribus Romanis*, an online encyclopedia of Roman rulers and their families (www.roman-emperors.org/).

Gerard V. Hall is Associate Professor of Theology at St Paul's Theological College, Australian Catholic University, Brisbane. He is the founding and current editor of the *Australian eJournal of Theology*, co-editor of *Foundations of Christian Faith,* and author of articles on Christian theology, religious pluralism, and interfaith dialogue. Academic memberships include the International Academy of Practical Theology, the Association of Practical Theology in Oceania (president), and the Asia-Pacific Centre for Interreligious Dialogue. He has recently served on the international Spirit of Religion Project *(Foundazione Arbor),* directed by interreligious scholar Raimon Panikkar.

Dr. Erica C.D. Hunter is Lecturer in Eastern Christianity and Chair of the Centre of Eastern and Orthodox Christianity in the Department for the Study of Religions, School of Oriental and African Studies, University of London, UK. She has strong links with the Christian communities in Iraq and has recently edited *The Christian Heritage of Iraq* (2009). She currently holds an Arts and Humanities Research Council Large Grant (2008–2011) for her project "The Christian Library from Turfan," which explores connections between the patriarchate in Baghdad and Central Asia during the early medieval period.

Vivian Ibrahim completed her Ph.D. at the School of Oriental and African Studies, University of London, UK, where she is currently a Fellow in Middle Eastern History. Her work concentrates on the political, social, and religious mobilization of Copts during the nationalist period in Egypt. She is also features editor for the journal *Studies in Ethnicity and Nationalism,* and Seminars and Conference Chair for the Association of Studies in Ethnicity and Nationalism. Ibrahim is a member of the British Royal Historical Society and North American Middle East Studies Association.

Misoon Im is an Adjunct Professor at Memphis Theological Seminary, Tennessee, USA. Her research areas are the history of Korean Christianity, the history of mission, and Buddhism. Im is a member of the Association of Professors of Mission.

The Rev. Daniel Jeyaraj, Dr. theol. habil., Ph.D., D.D. (h.c.), is Professor of World Christianity, and Director of the Andrew Walls Centre for the Study of African and Asian Christianity, at Liverpool Hope University, UK. He is a pre-eminent scholar in the study of early eighteenth-century European missionary interaction with the peoples of South India. He has published several research monographs and essays in India, Germany, the UK, and the USA. He is the chief editor of *Dharma Deepika*, a South Asian missiological journal.

Steven Kaplan is Professor of African Studies and Comparative Religion at the Hebrew University of Jerusalem, Israel. His research concerns the religious and social history of traditional Ethiopia. He has written extensively on Orthodox Christianity, missions, and the dynamics of conversion. He is also a renowned expert on Ethiopian Jews, and has written several books and numerous articles on their history in Ethiopia and adjustment in Israel.

Anthony J. Kelly is Professor of Theology at the Australian Catholic University, a Catholic priest, and a member of the Redemptorist Order. He is the author of many books and articles, the most recent being *Eschatology and Hope* (2007) and *The Resurrection Effect* (2008). Currently based in Canberra, in 2004 he was appointed by Pope John Paul II to the International Theological Commission.

Ábrahám Kovács is Associate Professor of Dogmatics and Historical Theology at the Reformed University of Debrecen, Hungary. He is a graduate of the universities of Debrecen, Princeton (USA), and Edinburgh (UK); obtained his Ph.D. from Edinburgh; and studied at the University of Tübingen, Germany. He has degrees in History, Theology, and Comparative Religion. Currently he is the general secretary of the Hungarian Association for the Academic Study of Religion. His interests are comparative theology, interreligious dialogue, eschatology, and Jewish-Christian history in Central Europe.

Alastair Logan recently retired as Senior Lecturer in Christian Doctrine at the University of Exeter, UK. An expert on Gnosticism, he wrote *Gnostic Truth and Christian Heresy* (1996) and *The Gnostics: Identifying an Early Christian Cult* (2006), as well as numerous articles. He has also authored articles on Origen, Arius, and Marcellus of Ancyra, several of which were published in the *Journal of Theological Studies*, and he is presently researching early Christian art and architecture, particularly in Rome. He is a member and former secretary of the Society for the Study of Theology.

Andrew McGowan is Warden of Trinity College and Principal Research Fellow in Historical Studies at the University of Melbourne, Australia. He is the author of *Ascetic Eucharists: Food and Drink in Early Christian Ritual Meals* (1999) and of articles on eucharistic origins and other aspects of early Christian history, and also co-editor of *God in Early Christian Thought* (2009). He has taught at the University of Notre Dame Australia; the Episcopal Divinity School in Cambridge, Massachusetts, USA; and in the United Faculty of Theology at the University of Melbourne.

Felicity Harley McGowan is a Research Fellow in the Department of Art History at the University of Melbourne, Australia, and also an Adjunct Lecturer in the United Faculty of Theology. She has published on aspects of the development of Christian art in late antiquity, and lectures in the history of early Christian, Byzantine, and medieval art. She is currently preparing to write a book on the earliest images of the Crucifixion.

Janice McLean has just completed her Ph.D. at the School of Divinity, University of Edinburgh, UK. Her work concentrates on the construction and negotiation of ethnic and religious identities among West Indian immigrants in New York City and London. She also investigates the expression of various mission paradigms among majority world immigrant churches within the Diaspora. McLean is a member of the American Academy of Religion and the International Sociological Association.

Saneta M. Maiko is Adjunct Professor of African History and Religion at Indiana University–Purdue University Fort Wayne, USA. His articles have appeared in the *Journal of Youth Ministry* and the *Journal of Youth and Theology*. Maiko is a member of the American Academy of Religion, the Association of Third World Studies, and the Association of International Youth Ministry.

Peter Matheson began his academic life as a historian of the Catholic reformer Cardinal Contarini. He is the editor of *The Collected Works of Thomas Müntzer* (1988) and *Argula von Grumbach: A Woman's Voice in the Reformation* (1995), and the author of *The Rhetoric of the Reformation* (1998) and *The Imaginative World of the Reformation* (2001). He most recently edited *Reformation Christianity* (2006), part of the series *A People's History of Christianity*. He is Principal Emeritus of the Theological Hall of the Uniting Church, Melbourne, Australia, and Fellow of the Department of Theology, University of Otago, New Zealand.

Frank Mobbs, Ph.D. (Syd.), M.A. (Oxon.), M.Th. (Birmingham, UK), M.Litt. (UNE, Australia), is retired after 24 years of teaching history, philosophy, and theology in institutes of higher education in England, Canada, Australia, and Papua New Guinea. He has published 64 articles and two books.

Fr. Stelyios Muksuris, B.A., M.Div., M.Litt., Ph.D. 2009, is an independent scholar of liturgical theology and history. An active member of five academic societies, including the international *Societas Liturgica* and *Societas Orientalium Liturgiarum,* he has lectured at conferences and universities as a visiting professor. He has published several articles in academic journals, and is currently working on a book in his field. Fluent in several languages, he serves as Administrative Assistant to the Metropolitan of Pittsburgh, Greek Orthodox Archdiocese of America.

Thomas O'Loughlin is Professor of Historical Theology at the University of Nottingham, UK. He has written on the ways the transition from the Greco-Roman Mediterranean world to the Western European-centered, Latin Middle Ages affected Christian understanding and theology. He is the author of 18 books and over 100 articles in academic journals, and is the editor of the monograph series *Studia Traditionis Theologiae*.

Rev. Dr. James Dudley Perera, L.Ph., L.Th., L. S.S. (Rome); M.Th. (New York); Ed.D. (with special reference to Biblical Studies, Manila), has been Professor of Biblical Studies for 35 years in the undergraduate department of the Catholic National Seminary in Ampitiya, Sri Lanka. He is also Lecturer in Biblical Studies at the Protestant Theological College in Pilimatalawa, Sri Lanka, and Associate Professor in the Religious Studies Department at De La Salle University, Manila, Philippines. Perera has contributed articles of theological and Biblical interest to the premier magazine of theological studies, *Vidyajyoti,* in India.

Barbara Reeves-Ellington is Assistant Professor of History at Siena College, Loudonville, New York, USA. She is the author of "A Vision of Mount Holyoke in the Ottoman Balkans" (*Gender & History*, 2004) and "Gender, Conversion, and Social Transformation" in *Converting Cultures: Religion, Ideology, and Transformations of Identity* (2007). She is co-editor, along with Kathryn Kish Sklar and Connie Shemo, of *Competing Kingdoms: Women, Mission, Nation, and the American Protestant Empire, 1812–1960* (to be published in 2010).

Dr. Noel Keith Roberts, B.A., B.D., B.Sc. (Hons), Ph.D., was born and educated in Western Australia. At school he studied science, mathematics, Latin, and Ancient Greek. He obtained degrees in science, economics, and philosophy at the University of Western Australia, married and was appointed to the University of Tasmania where he obtained a Ph.D. in physical chemistry, rose to the position of Associate Professor, and studied at the Universities of Oxford and Munich. He is the proud father of five sons and two daughters. Upon retirement he obtained a degree in Divinity and taught New Testament Greek and Hebrew. Among his many publications in science and theology is *From Piltdown Man to Point Omega: The Evolutionary Theory of Teilhard de Chardin* (2001).

Patricia M. Rumsey lectures in monasticism, Celtic Christianity, liturgy, and Franciscan studies at the University of Wales Lampeter. She has published articles on these topics in *Worship*, the *American Benedictine Review, New Blackfriars, Anaphora,* and the *Irish Theological Quarterly.* Her most recent publication is *Sacred Time in Early Christian Ireland* (2007). She has lectured in England, Ireland, and Scandinavia, and is currently researching early Irish martyrologies.

Angel Santiago-Vendrell is Assistant Professor of Mission Studies at Memphis Theological Seminary, Tennessee, USA. His articles have appeared in the *International Review of Mission Studies, The Journal of Pentecostal Theology, Perspectivas, El Interprete,* and *Apuntes: Reflexiones Teológicas desde el Margen Hispano.* Santiago-Vendrell is a member of the American Academy of Religion, the Association of Missiology, and the Association of Professors of Mission.

Karen E. Smith teaches Church History and Christian Spirituality at South Wales Baptist College, and Cardiff University, Wales, UK. She has written many scholarly articles and contributed to numerous books. She is the author of *Christian Spirituality* (2007) from the *SCM Core Text* series.

Susan Smith is an adjunct faculty member of the School of Theology at the University of Auckland, New Zealand. She has co-edited three Accent publications: *He Kupu Whakawairua Spirituality in Aotearoa New Zealand: Catholic Voices; Land and Place, He Whenua, He Wahi: Spiritualities from Aotearoa New Zealand;* and *Nourished by Eucharist: New Thoughts on an Ancient Theme.* In 2007, her book *Women in Mission* was published. She is an Associate Editor of Mission Studies and a member of the International Association of Mission Studies.

Dr. Scott W. Sunquist is Professor of World Christianity at Pittsburgh Theological Seminary, Pennsylvania, USA. He is the editor of *A Dictionary of Asian Christianity* (2001), co-author with Dale Irvin of *History of the World Christian Movement* (2001), and co-editor with his daughter, Caroline Becker, of *A History of Presbyterian Missions* (2008). He previously taught at Trinity Theological College in Singapore.

Dr. Emma Wild-Wood is Director of the Henry Martyn Centre for the Study of Mission and World Christianity, Cambridge, UK. She has taught in Anglican colleges in Congo and Uganda and written on Christianity in east and central Africa, including "Saint Apolo from Europe or What's in a Luganda Name?" in *Church History* 77 (2008), about a Ugandan priest and Church Missionary Society (CMS) evangelist. Her most recent book, titled *Migration and Christian Identity in Congo (DRC),* was published in 2008.

CONTENTS

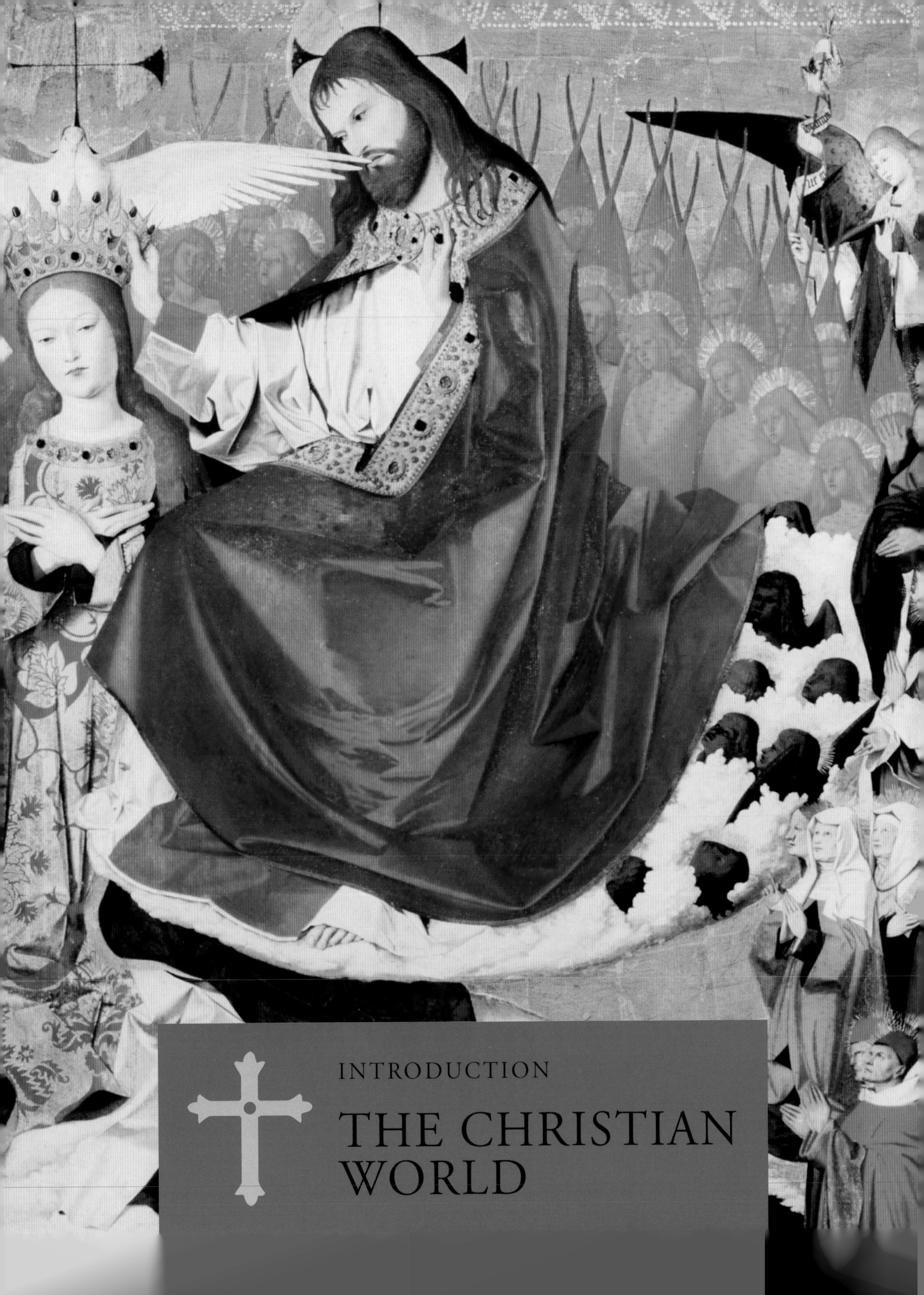

INTRODUCTION

THE CHRISTIAN WORLD

THE CHRISTIAN WORLD

Previous pages: The contract for *The Coronation of the Virgin* (1454) by French painter Enguerrand Charonton famously specified that an identical God and Jesus be depicted crowning the Virgin Mary, reflecting the *filioque* doctrine.

Below: Painted by German artist Albrecht Dürer in 1511, this single-panel altarpiece shows prophets, kings, martyrs, clergymen, and laypersons honoring the Holy Trinity—including the Holy Spirit represented as a dove.

This book tells the story of Christianity, the world's largest religion, in stunning pictures and captivating prose. The storytellers, who live in various parts of the world, provide a truly global perspective on the two millennia of Christian history.

Beginning in Jerusalem, the good news that Jesus of Nazareth was the Christ who brought salvation spread in all directions—from city to city, country to country, continent to continent—until at present one in every three people consider themselves Christian, and Christians live in every country in the world.

Although all Christians share similar basic beliefs, Christianity is one of the most variegated of the world's religions with respect to practice, style of worship, and cultural expressions. As you savor these pages, you will encounter these differences. You will learn of the theological and political struggles within and between different types of Christians, as well as the battles between Christians and non-Christians. You will meet the people, male and female, famous and forgotten, who lived the lives that made this story what it is.

You will also encounter the ideals and the failures of Christians. This book presents the ordinary people and the all-too-human institutions that told the world about the Love and the Power proclaimed by Christianity, a Loving Power which Christians believe we encounter in Jesus the Christ.

Divine mystery

Christianity has a unique perception of the Divine Being. The profession of faith in a transcendent yet personal God, who has revealed himself and his purpose to humankind within human history, is shared by Jews, Muslims, and Christians alike. The difference, however, which is absolute and nonnegotiable for all Christians throughout the world, rests on the belief that the one true God is a perfect and eternal union of three Persons—Father, Son, and Holy Spirit—known as the Holy Trinity.

Consequently, God exists as one Being, not as three, but all three Persons share the same divine essence. Each Person dwells mutually in the other two, but they are not confused with each other. They are bound together in perfect love. As a "community" of Persons, equal and eternal, the Trinity is the ultimate model of true personhood. It shows us the freedom to love, move, and act always in a relational manner with the created cosmos.

For Christians the triune God has made himself known in creation and throughout the course of human history, as noted in both the Hebrew Bible and New Testament. He is both creator and sustainer of the natural universe, of material and spiritual realms. According to the scriptures, God reveals himself and enters into a personal relationship first with the Jews and then, through them, to the rest of the world in the person of the long-awaited Messiah. For Christians this Messiah is none other than Jesus the Christ, God's son. Jesus is the very cornerstone of the Christian faith, God's own plan of salvation for humankind.

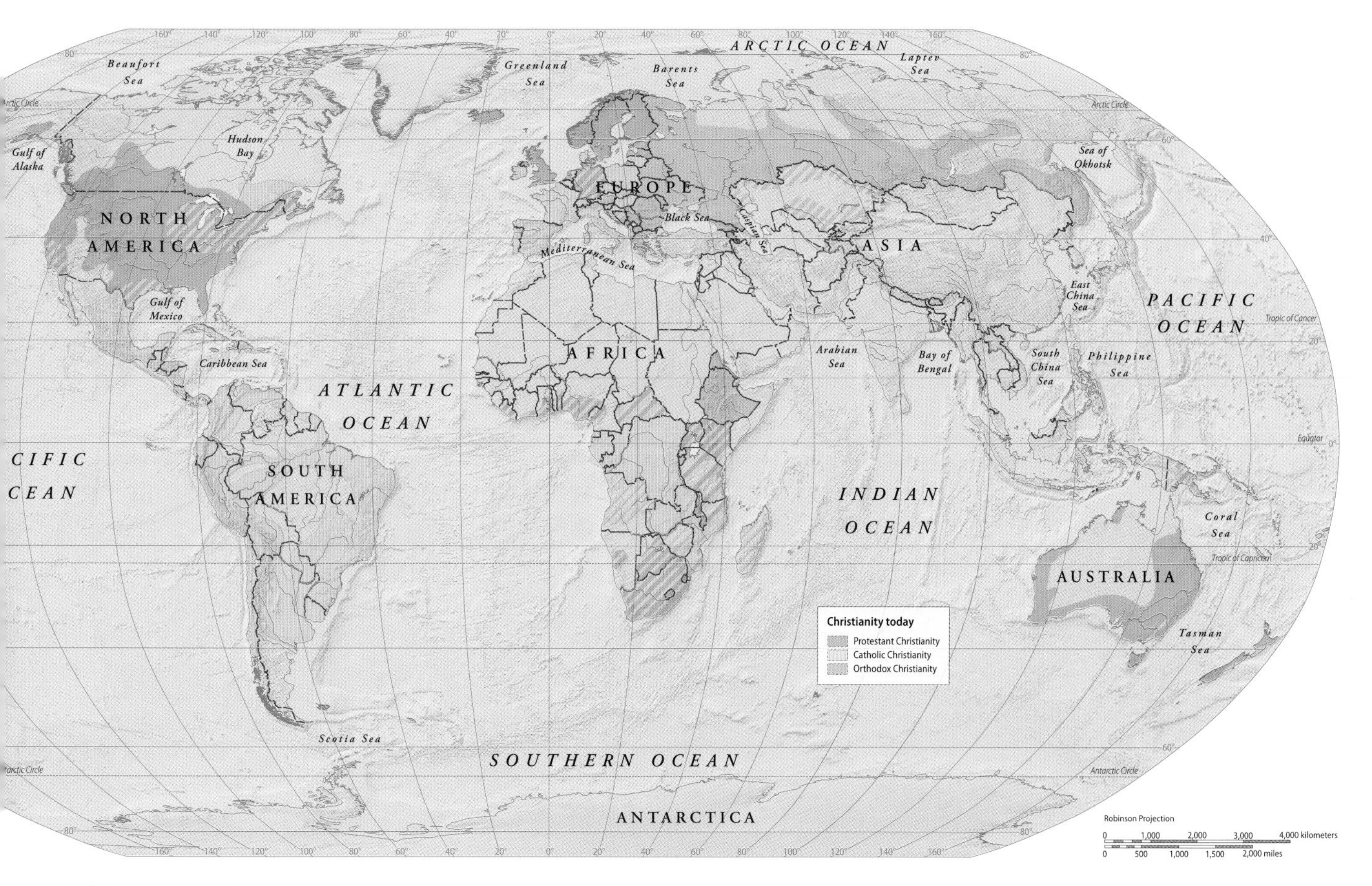

In the beginning: Creation

Christianity professes the belief in creation *ex nihilo*—meaning that the created universe came into being "out of nothing." There was no pre-existing material that God manipulated. Even more, creation—which is completely dependent upon God—is a selfless act of God's free will and love; it is not the result of some accidental or uncontrolled cosmic automation. The Christian teaching of creation is not concerned with a chronological starting point for the material world; it focuses on the affirmation of the created world's origin and reliance upon God.

As the absolute *summum bonum*, or "highest good," God fills the created cosmos with his own goodness. Genesis 1:31 says: "God saw all that he had made, and it was very good." This natural goodness in humanity is supplemented by the Christian belief that humanity is created not only to resemble God in his attributes and to possess the potential for life in God (image), but also to be driven internally to realize this potentiality (likeness; see Genesis 1:26). Consequently, Christianity holds that humanity does not exist for himself or herself as a "stand-alone" creature but for communion with God. To be added is the vocation of responsible stewardship over creation, avoiding its exploitation and working toward its return (theologically its "sanctification" and "redemption") to God.

The problem: Sin, evil, and the Fall

One key attribute shared by human beings with God—and the one that eventually resulted in humanity's fall—is free will, the capacity to live and make decisions freely without external pressure or influence. Here is a paradox: the "risk" God took in creating human beings as free included the possibility for wrongful choices, but God gave that freedom out of true love! Christianity teaches that humanity is neither evil by nature nor a source of evil. The origination of evil occurs as a double rebellion, a disobedience to God's law within the angelic and human worlds, the result of free will

Below: Women worship at the Fifth Station of Jerusalem's Via Dolorosa, at a chapel in honor of Simon of Cyrene, who helped Jesus to bear the burden of his cross.

having gone bad on both planes. Sin (the action of evil) is a conscious movement away from and rejection of God. That rejection set into motion cosmic forces in the universe responsible for the disorder, corruption, and destruction of all that God designated as "very good." Thus, evil possesses no reality of its own but is clearly the absence of God due to sin—a distortion of good, a parasitic condition rooted in the voluntary abuse of free will by any rational and free being.

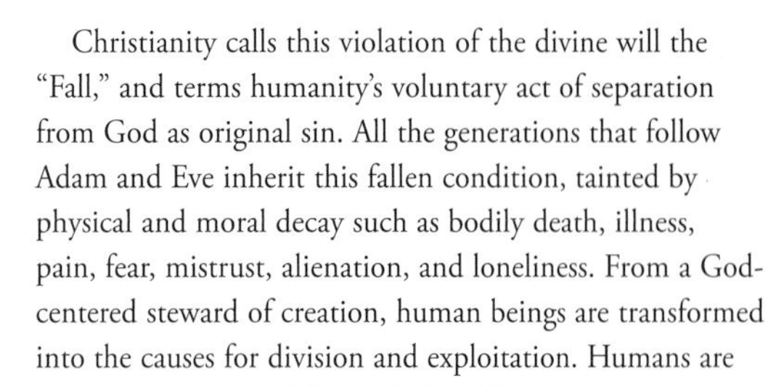

Christianity calls this violation of the divine will the "Fall," and terms humanity's voluntary act of separation from God as original sin. All the generations that follow Adam and Eve inherit this fallen condition, tainted by physical and moral decay such as bodily death, illness, pain, fear, mistrust, alienation, and loneliness. From a God-centered steward of creation, human beings are transformed into the causes for division and exploitation. Humans are separated from God and from each other, but also are inwardly fragmented and incomplete.

Below: The archangel Michael is often shown in religious art vanquishing Satan—particularly with a sword—because Michael is traditionally seen in Christianity as Satan's most powerful enemy.

At once blatant perpetrator and wounded victim, human beings alone could never have salvaged or renewed this relationship with God by themselves. This reality prompted the advent into the world of God himself in the second Person of the Holy Trinity: Jesus Christ.

The solution: Incarnation, atonement, resurrection

The initiative taken by God to bridge the chasm between himself and humankind took the form of the incarnation. According to this key doctrine, God the Son "becomes flesh," taking on human form and all the qualities and conditions characteristic of human existence—except sin. As perfect God himself, Jesus remained perfect man throughout his life, thus becoming the exemplar *par excellence* of authentic and wholesome living. His virgin birth from his mother Mary and the Holy Spirit denotes not only a true human birth but also affirms Christ's heavenly and eternal origin as God. Thus, no "new" being comes into existence; rather the pre-existent God is "materialized" in space and time.

Jesus' teaching and healing ministry on earth prepared his followers for his definitive act of self-sacrifice, called the "atonement" (or "at-one-ment") by which God erases humanity's offenses against him and ransoms humankind from evil and the consequences of sin. Hence, the "God-Man" Jesus Christ suffered and died a true death on the cross as mortal man but not as the transcendent and eternal God. Jesus' self-sacrifice is interpreted by the Christian Church as the supreme manifestation of love and forgiveness in a fallen world.

According to Christian theology, the indignity of a death by execution led Christ's soul into hell, into the depths not of a place but into the absence of God that is "inhabited" by Satan and the demons. Here, Jesus identifies himself with human anguish and alienation from God. By assuming humanity's fallen state completely, Christ ultimately heals it too, thus re-establishing once again full communion between God and man—just as it was in the beginning with creation.

Above: The Annunciation is the revelation to Mary that she would soon give birth to Jesus, the Son of God: "He will...be called the Son of the Most High" (Luke 1:32).

The bodily resurrection of Jesus on the third day following his sacrificial death is the touchstone of the Christian faith (1 Corinthians 15:14). It confirms the victory of God's love over evil and sin. Christians believe that, like Christ, they too will be raised bodily at the end of the age, experiencing the reunification of their souls not with the same corruptible body of their earthly life but with a transformed and holy body fully permeated by God's grace and never again susceptible to suffering and death. Jesus' death and resurrection then do not mean we will avoid suffering; they actually infuse that suffering with meaning. Christ's passion does not provide a pathway *around* suffering but *through* it. Hence, Christ's victory is the Christian's victory, and Christianity is for the Christian the profession of real joy in God.

In the end: The Second Coming and the Eschatological Age

Following Christ's resurrection and ascension into heaven, the first Christians celebrated Pentecost, the official "birthday" of the Church. This was the moment when the Holy Spirit descended upon the disciples of Jesus, converting them to apostles, and empowered them to preach the Gospel of love to the ends of the earth. Christians believe that God the Holy Spirit continues to live and dwell among men and women of faith and within the worshipping ecclesial communities throughout the world—forgiving, healing, illuminating, transforming, and saving humankind. These acts of grace uniting us with God allow for participation in the divine life, actualized in part within history, and to be fully realized in the finalization of God's eternal kingdom at the end of time. In the Holy Spirit, Christ inaugurates the kingdom of God, not a place but a state of God's continuous presence in our lives, radiating perfect joy and peace.

In another sense, Pentecost also ushers in the "end times," which may be understood in two senses: The present historical age, in which the cosmos advances toward its final consummation; or as the eventual establishment of God's reign in the universe following the world's end. The end of time will involve the Second Coming, which is when Christ returns in glory to earth. This extraordinary event involves the final judgment of all humanity from the creation onward, the conclusive defeat of the powers of evil, and the redemption and deification of the entire created order, fully permeated by the presence of the triune God.

Below: This *mola* (traditional costume) of an indigenous Kuna woman from Panama portrays Adam and Eve. Christianity arrived in Panama with the Spanish conquistadors in the sixteenth century.

THE CHRISTIAN BIBLE

Above: Comprising 250 leaves of vellum, the Lindisfarne Gospels is an illuminated manuscript dating to around 698 CE. It was created in honor of St Cuthbert by Eadfrith, Bishop of Lindisfarne.

The word "Bible" comes from *biblia*, the plural of the Greek word *biblion*, meaning "book." The title "The Books," with no other qualification, tells us the important place this text holds in Jewish and Christian traditions. It also suggests the Bible is a collection or an anthology, a library if you like, and in fact it comprises many literary forms, including poetry, narrative, history, and fiction. The books of the Bible are often called "sacred" or "holy" scriptures, implying that they were written under divine inspiration or guidance. They are also called "canonical," meaning they are included in an official list of sacred books called a canon (in both the Jewish and Christian traditions).

Variations in number of books

The Jewish Bible or Tanakh is also called the Hebrew Bible because the 24 books it contains in its three sections—The Law, The Prophets, and The Writings—were written in the Hebrew language. "Tanakh" is an acronym for Torah (Law), Nevi'im (Prophets), and Ketuvim (Writings). The Christian Old Testament contains all the books in the Hebrew Bible, but because Tanakh sometimes groups several writings into a single book, the Old Testament contains 39 books but Tanakh has only 24 books.

Therefore, the Christian Bible includes the books of the Hebrew Bible, composed roughly between the eleventh and second centuries BCE, as the Old Testament, and the specifically Christian books, written in the first and second centuries CE, as the New Testament. The 27 books of the New Testament include four gospels, 20 letters, one history book, one sermon (Hebrews), and the Apocalypse of John (also known as Revelation).

Below: Originally neither the Jews nor the Christians had a fixed canon for the books of the Bible. Agreement on the canon was most likely reached by the fourth century CE.

The three major Christian traditions in the world today—Catholic, Orthodox, and Protestant—vary among themselves in the number of books in the Old Testament. Protestant Bibles contain the same writings as Jewish Bibles, but in a different order. The Catholic and Orthodox traditions follow the Septuagint, the earliest Greek translation of the Hebrew Bible, made in Alexandria between the third and the first centuries BCE. It was commissioned because the descendants of the many Jews who had left Palestine

for business and other reasons over the centuries and had settled in other lands around the Mediterranean (Greek *diaspora*, "the Jews in dispersion") spoke only Greek and could no longer use the Hebrew Bible for worship and private prayer. Because some of the books included in the Septuagint were not included in the final canon of the Hebrew Bible, Orthodox and Catholic Bibles have more books than Protestant Bibles.

The Protestant canon contains 66 books (39 in the Old Testament and 27 in the New Testament). The Roman Catholic Church recognizes 7 additional books as well as additions to Esther and Daniel. The Orthodox Church recognizes all the books of the Roman Catholic canon, plus between 3 and 10 additional books depending upon which branch of the Orthodox Church is being considered.

Varieties of interpretation

The history of Christian interpretation of the scriptures begins with Paul of Tarsus, who used allegorical interpretations of the Jewish scriptures in his letters. For example, in Galatians 4:21–26, Paul reads the story of Sarah and Hagar (Genesis 16) as a tale of two covenants. Throughout the New Testament, the Old Testament is read as a prefiguring or "type" of a first-century event, an interpretive method known as typology.

During the Patristic period (approximately the first five centuries), the School of Alexandria favored symbolic interpretation. Its rival, the School of Antioch, favored a historical and more literal interpretation. A long-lived style of interpretation, which began in the Patristic period and continued through the Middle Ages and on into the contemporary period, featured four different levels of meaning: Literal, allegorical, tropological (moral), and anagogical (eschatological). For example, the city of Jerusalem is a literal city, but Biblical references to Jerusalem could also be interpreted as an allegory of the community of believers (the Church). The tropological meaning of Jerusalem might be the individual human soul as it journeys through life. In its anagogical meaning, Jerusalem points to the community of the blessed in heaven.

The modern period saw the development of two new forms of Biblical interpretation. The historical-critical method studies the process of formation of a text and its historical context in an effort to better understand its meaning. The text becomes a window into the times and ways of thinking when the text was composed. Fundamentalist interpretations begin with the assumption that the Bible contains scientific and historical facts, and then proceed to attempt to show the accuracy of Biblical statements when so interpreted (as scientific or historical facts).

Above: The additional books of the Hebrew Bible found in the Greek Septuagint and rejected by Jewish authorities are called "deuterocanonical," meaning the second canon.

Center: A monk from one of the twenty monasteries of Bahir Dar reads a Bible in Amharic, an ancient form of Ethiopian. The Bahir Dar monasteries are located on sacred islands in Lake Tana.

ORTHODOX AND EASTERN CHRISTIANS

Above: Orthodox Christmas celebrations on January 7 in Bethlehem's Church of the Nativity attract hundreds of the faithful every year. The church is reportedly built over the site of Jesus' birth.

The main division between Orthodox Christians and other Eastern churches occurred during a series of ecumenical councils that took place between the first and seventh centuries. Most of the discord arose out of debates surrounding linguistic misunderstandings in a doctrine that is highly complex and often difficult to follow.

The Church of the East

At the third Ecumenical Council in Ephesus in 431 CE, Christ's personal unity as both man and God was debated. While the Alexandrian School stressed the importance of the unity of Christ's person, the Antiochene School argued that this did not give enough stress to Christ's human nature; they argued that it was necessary to uphold Christ's manhood and were wary of any view which may imply that Christ's humanity was swallowed up by his Godhead. This theological split was also partly exacerbated by the fact that the Antiochene School was in the Persian Empire and not in the Eastern Roman Empire. This ultimately gave rise to the Church of the East, which is often known as the Syriac (Assyrian, Chaldean, and Nestorian) Church. Originally framed by the Tigris and Euphrates rivers, the Church had by the seventh century reached as far as China, but is now almost extinct with a membership at most of 50,000 people. In recent years, the Assyrian and Chaldean Orthodox churches, which boast up to 300,000 followers, have been frequently targeted in Iraq. This has led to many fleeing over the border to neighboring Syria.

Oriental Orthodox churches

The main split between what are more commonly known as the Eastern Orthodox Christians and the Oriental Orthodox churches occurred during the Chalcedon Council in 451. There were differences of opinion regarding whether Christ was to be acknowledged as having two natures in one person and one substance. Those who rejected this discourse became known as non-Chalcedonian or Miaphysite because they followed Cyril of Alexandria in describing Christ as "one nature," that one nature being both divine and human in character. Today, there are five separate non-Chalcedonian churches, but they are best known as the

Left: Founded in the seventeenth century, the Monastery of Ostrog in Montenegro is a place of pilgrimage for followers of the Serbian Orthodox Church.

Above: A priest of the Coptic Orthodox Church in Cairo, Egypt, is shown wearing the traditional headdress. Women are barred from the priesthood in the Coptic Orthodox Church.

Oriental Orthodox churches. The Coptic Orthodox Church of Egypt is the main Christian Church in Egypt, and has between six and eleven million followers. Most Copts live in Egypt although the Church also has around one million diaspora members in Australia, the UK, and North America. The Ethiopian Orthodox Tewahedo Church, which has been autonomous from the Copts since 1959, has approximately 38 million followers in Ethiopia alone. The Syrian Orthodox Church, also known as the Jacobites, has approximately 300,000 followers in the Middle East and another 50,000 in America. Thomas Christians in India placed themselves under the Syrian Orthodox Church in the seventeenth century, and followers are currently estimated at one million. Finally, the Church of Armenia has over three million followers across the Middle East and a further half a million in America.

Eastern Orthodox churches

Like the Oriental Orthodox churches, the Eastern Orthodox Church believes that it is the continuation of the true Church, while the others have fallen into heresy. The word "Orthodox" takes its meaning from the Greek words *orthos* and *doxa,* which literally mean "right belief." In 1054 a schism occurred in Christianity, resulting in the Eastern and Western churches. Eastern Orthodoxy represents the majority of Eastern Christianity and, compared to Western Christianity, it is more mystical and less legalistic. Today, the main difference that Western observers note is the relationship between Church and state; most Orthodox churches have not enjoyed the luxury of being able to challenge governments, although they often wield great national power. The nominal head of the Eastern Orthodox churches is the Patriarch of Constantinople, although he is only "the first among equals" and has no real authority over churches except for his own Greek Orthodox Church of Constantinople. Instead, the Eastern Orthodox churches include 15 autocephalous bodies in communion with one another, and number between 226 and 300 million people worldwide. Most of these churches are in the former Soviet bloc and include the patriarchates of Constantinople, Alexandria, Antioch, and Jerusalem, and the Orthodox churches of Russia, Serbia, Romania, Bulgaria, Georgia, Greece, Czech lands and Slovakia, Poland, Cyprus, and Albania. The Patriarch of Constantinople is ranked first among equals in Eastern Orthodoxy. However, from time to time disputes over jurisdiction arise, especially between Moscow and Constantinople—most recently in relation to Estonia and the Orthodox Church in the USA.

Below: Ethiopian women follow the men in a procession through an early morning mist to celebrate a special pre-millenium mass at an Orthodox church in the northern city of Axum, Ethiopia.

CATHOLICISM

Right: A large crowd gathered to welcome Pope John Paul II to Nigeria in 1982. Before Benedict XVI's election as pope in 2005, Nigeria's Cardinal Francis Arinze was considered a likely successor to John Paul II.

Jesus of Nazareth gathered around him a group of followers who traveled with him, witnessing his deeds and hearing his teaching. Their collective remembrance of these events is found mainly in the four Gospels, which bear witness to the belief that Jesus was not only God's messenger but also stood in a relationship of total unity with God. Twice the Gospels mention an *ekklesia* (Greek for "assembly") without an explanation of its nature.

In his final days on earth Jesus commanded that each of the eleven apostles should go out and teach in his name. But for how long? He never gave a clear answer, but his followers soon showed they understood him to have commanded them to teach all succeeding generations, for they passed on their authority to others by "the laying-on of hands" and in other ways.

In Catholic belief, that group of disciples and its successors in each following generation is collectively known as the Catholic Church. It has always existed since the time of Jesus and is the only church authorized by him. It was first given the name "Catholic" by St Ignatius in about 107 CE. Commonly it was used to name the "great" Church, as distinct from sects. In official documents, the Church has rarely used the name "Roman Catholic." Catholics almost always use "Catholic."

Below: Venerated by the Catholic Church, St Stephen became the first Christian martyr when he was falsely accused of blasphemy and stoned to death in about 35 CE after preaching in Jerusalem.

Beliefs

The Catholic Church holds that God has revealed the most important truths about himself and his plans for humans in the person of Jesus the Christ. This revelation he has entrusted to the Church to transmit to all generations with his guarantee that he will guide the Church so as to prevent it teaching error. John Henry (Cardinal) Newman expressed this belief: "The common sense of mankind…feels that the idea of revelation implies a present informant and guide… an infallible one…A revelation is not given if there be no authority to decide what is given." The revelation is passed on in the scriptures (Bible) and in tradition, whose contents the bishops are authorized to determine. Further, the Catholic Church teaches that the bishops have been given authority to govern Christians.

From time to time the body of bishops has solemnly defined a doctrine as being contained in revelation, thus binding Christians to believe it. These doctrines are contained in the creeds and in decisions of ecumenical councils, such as the Council of Trent.

VATICAN CITY

The headquarters of the Catholic Church is Vatican City, a tiny sovereign state of 110 acres (44 hectares) forming an enclave in Rome. Established in 1929, it is governed by the pope, who resides there. The state's economy is supported by contributions from Catholics; the sale of publications, postage stamps, and souvenirs; and museum admission fees. Its own bank, the Vatican Bank, even has an ATM with instructions in Latin. The Holy See has diplomatic relations with 177 states.

Gradually, the authority of the bishop of Rome (pope) came to be widely acknowledged, though with reservations from the Eastern churches who were, nevertheless, viewed as Catholics by the Western Church until about 1200. So, a few items of Catholic belief have been determined by popes.

Organization

The Catholic Church is distinguished by its unity. All members are subject to a bishop: "Those, indeed, who belong to God and to Jesus Christ—they are with the bishop," wrote Ignatius about 110 CE. All bishops swear obedience to the pope. This has ensured unity, though not uniformity.

Present condition

The unity of the Catholic Church helps account for the fact that it is the largest single religious body in the world today; the 1.2 billion baptized Catholics constitute 17.2 percent of the world's population. The number of Catholics is increasing by about 15 million each year, mainly in Africa. Around 50 percent live in the Americas. All are subject to the authority of the pope. The Catholic Church consists of 23 churches: The Latin Church (which contains 98 percent of Catholics) plus 22 Eastern churches, such as the Ukrainian Greek Catholic Church and the Maronite Church, each with its own ways of worship, form of government, and code of law.

A bishop rules members of a geographical area or of a group, such as the armed forces. There are about 2,800 dioceses. Most are divided into parishes headed by a priest, of whom there are about 407,000. Some 115,000 people are preparing to be priests. Many are members of religious orders, such as the Jesuits and Franciscans. Approximately 55,000 religious brothers (non-priests), 750,000 nuns, 29,000 members of secular institutes, and 33,000 deacons also serve the Catholic Church. Except for deacons, the numbers in all these categories are declining rapidly. The Catholic Church operates the world's largest non-government school system, with 2.2 million pupils, and is in charge of a vast charitable network.

Above: Priests being ordained in the 800-year-old Cathedral of Notre-Dame in Paris. A priest is available each day at the cathedral, to offer spiritual guidance and/or confession.

PROTESTANT CHRISTIANS

Above: Reverend Gideon Byamugisha of the Anglican Church of Uganda was the first priest in Africa to declare his HIV-positive status. He heads the HIV/AIDS program in the Namirembe Diocese.

Below: A panoramic view of Wittenberg, Germany, includes the twin towers of the fourteenth-century Marienskirche (St Mary's Church), the parish church where Martin Luther often preached.

Protestants today number approximately 500 million people worldwide and may be found in 233 countries. They are concentrated in northern Europe, the North Atlantic, North America, and in parts of South America, southern Africa, Australia, New Zealand, Papua New Guinea, the Pacific Islands, and South Korea.

This diversity goes back to a single source, the Reformation in sixteenth-century Europe. The main figures involved were the German monk Martin Luther (1483–1546), the French lawyer John Calvin (1509–1564), and the Swiss priest Ulrich Zwingli (1484–1531). Each wanted to reform the Church from within and restore it to what they saw as its original, Biblical form. To their surprise, they soon gave birth to mass movements for change.

Challenge and change

What were the positions of these reformers? First, the only path to salvation is through faith, which is a gift from God. Since we are utterly sinful, we can do nothing to save ourselves; good works certainly won't get us to the gates of heaven. Second, the only authority is the Bible (which must be read in one's own tongue), and anyone who claims to represent God is mistaken. Finally, since no-one is better than anyone else, all believers are equal before God. These positions fundamentally challenged the Church of the day. Pope and priest were suddenly out of a job. Almost all Protestants rejected saints, monasticism, celibacy, confession, images, and the meaning of the sacraments. Such a challenge was too much to change the Church from within, so Protestantism became a new movement.

Had Luther, Calvin, Zwingli, and other reformers lived a century earlier, they would have met a swift end at the stake. But the time was ripe for change and they were fortunate to have powerful protectors. For Luther it was Prince Frederick III of Saxony who kept him out of harm's way in Wittenberg; for Calvin, Geneva offered a safe haven; and for Zwingli, the town council of Zurich ensured that he could continue to preach, write, and organize. Political leaders who liked their ideas also saw the potential for independence from distant overlords (in England, Henry VIII's break with the pope in 1529 fits into this category). Filling one's empty coffers with the proceeds of confiscated monasteries and churches also helped. The reformers astutely targeted the ruling classes, with a good deal of success.

Radicals in the ranks

The ruling classes were not the only ones to take up the new beliefs. The common people were also swept up, sensing the challenges to power. The claim that each person could read the Bible on his or her own and that one's faith depended on a direct relation with God was a radical break. One could read the Bible, pray, and worship God in the

humblest peasant cottage, in the field, or in a small fishing boat. This simplicity also led to austere church designs. Without images, paintings, statues, and distractions, people were to focus on God alone. Even more important, the statement that the most exalted ruler, up to the pope or king, was as much a sinner as the lowly peasant, resonated deeply with those used to being downtrodden. As a result, some took the reformers' ideas further. There was a sense of change in the air: Economies were shifting to capitalism; politics was in turmoil; and beliefs changed with them. There were revolts—the largest one by the peasants in Germany (1524–1525), led by the one-time student of Luther, Thomas Müntzer. Those known as Radical Reformers took the new ideas much further. Their main difference was believer's baptism, or Anabaptism (baptism again), as it was called. Only a person conscious of their faith should be baptized, and that in effect meant adults, not children.

Variety and global power

Two important features of Protestantism are worth noting. To begin with, since each person could read the Bible on their own, interpretations from person to person were always going to vary. This has led to the appearance of a large number of different Protestant groups today—at least 30,000 of them. Further, Protestants have repeatedly found themselves in the seats of global power, most obviously in the USA. This is a direct result of colonial expansion by Protestant empires in Europe: The German, Dutch, Danish, and especially British empires ensured that Protestants ended up in those places that would become the major powers in the world today.

WHAT IS THE ORIGIN OF THE WORD "PROTESTANT"?

The name "Protestant" comes from a minority statement by reforming delegates at the Diet (conference) of Speyer (a city in Germany) in 1529. Faced with a majority Roman Catholic position that sought to roll back the Reformation, this minority made a "Protestatio" (protest) against the majority. The name stuck.

Below: An Amish woman at her sewing machine. The Amish form a religious group under the Mennonites; they are heirs of the Radical Reformers who took the ideals of the Reformers much further.

Left: The Easter morning mass at the Church of Hope (Pengharapan), a Protestant church in Jayapura, Indonesia, starts at 4:30 AM, with various processions beginning as early as 2:00 AM from the suburbs.

NONDENOMINATIONAL MOVEMENTS

Above: An all-female congregation of Waldensians sits quietly in church in the Italian village of Prali. Like most Protestant churches, Waldensians have only two sacraments—baptism and the Lord's Supper.

Much of the growth of Christianity, especially in Africa, South America, and among indigenous people, is due to nondenominational or parachurch movements. "Nondenominational" means they don't fit within traditional church denominations, while "parachurch" indicates that they spread across denominations. It is difficult to put an exact number on nondenominational Christians, since they are found within many churches, but they account for one-third to one-half of the two billion Christians worldwide.

Patterns of revival

These nondenominational movements are due to cycles of revival, which have been a feature of Christianity since its origin. Revivals have religious reasons (such as stagnation in the churches), social causes (often taking place during periods of dislocation and disruption), and economic reasons, especially during difficult economic times. Revivals are also emotionally charged affairs, bringing people to a vivid, personal experience of God. In addition, they follow a pattern. Initially they break with power structures in the Church, drawing on the disaffected and disillusioned. Church rulers then either try to absorb them or expel them. Soon the intense revival peters out and power relations return to the status quo. Some converts fall away, others rejoin their churches, and yet others form new groups, which consolidate into churches, such as the Assemblies of God, the Vineyard Movement, and the International Circle of Faith (ICOF) today. Sometimes, if there is extensive social and economic unrest, revival movements become revolutionary and threaten the social order (for example, the Peasants' War in 1524–1525 in Germany).

Colorful separatists

There are two types of nondenominational movements: One that breaks away to form a new group (separatists), usually following a charismatic leader; and the other that spreads across the existing denominations.

The separatists have had all manner of colorful names. During the Middle Ages there were the twelfth-century Waldensians, who still exist today in Piedmont, Italy, and believe in the model of Christian communism found in the Acts of the Apostles. The Lollards stressed personal faith, divine election, and the Bible, and were involved

in a series of uprisings between 1414 and 1431. The Taborites were a fifteenth-century religious movement that championed asceticism, communal living, and the establishment of the kingdom of God by force of arms. Then there was the Bohemian Brethren, who lived a communal life and influenced Czech literature through their Bible translation. In eighteenth-century England we find the Moravians, Seekers, Universalists, Quakers, Fifth Monarchy Men, Philadelphians, French Camisards, Sandemanians, Hutchinsonians, Sabbatarians, Seventh-Day Men, Thraskites, Adamists, Brownists, Tryonists (vegetarians), Salmonists, Heavenly-Father-Men, Children of the New Birth, Sweet Singers of Israel, and Muggletonians. Separatists often form a single congregation—a one of its kind for a mix of political, personal, and religious reasons.

Conservative and progressive

The other type of nondenominational movement exists within current structures. They act as bridges between mainline churches, linking like-minded people together. Today they include the Charismatics, who believe that the power of the Holy Spirit has been neglected in traditional Christianity. Worship often takes the form of speaking in tongues, faith healing, prophecy, and the ritual of laying on of hands in order to pass on the Holy Spirit. Fundamentalists also may be found in most churches in smaller or greater numbers. They share a belief in the inerrancy of the Bible, and a suspicion of modern science (especially evolution) and modern education when they conflict with a literal interpretation of the Bible. Fundamentalists have become powerful political lobby groups in some countries. Many nondenominational groups have millennial beliefs—they believe that the world will soon end and that Christ will return in the not-to-distant future.

Not all of them are conservative, however. Ecumenism (which literally means "the whole inhabited earth") is a movement that seeks understanding and cooperation across all Christian churches. The idea is as old as Christianity (the early Church councils were called ecumenical), but in its modern form it dates from the twentieth century and is embodied in the World Council of Churches. Slightly earlier forms of ecumenism were the Bible translation societies, which have now consolidated as the Wycliffe Bible Translators and the Bible Society, and the missionary movements, the most famous of which was the London Missionary Society, which sent missionaries into all parts of the world and is now part of the Council for Mission. Two other nondenominational movements are feminism and the green movement. Over the last century many churches have struggled to come to terms with the need for equality between the sexes in both church membership and leadership. More recently there has been a growing awareness that the idea of God's creation and a sustainable environment go hand-in-hand, and that churches may provide leadership in this area.

Above: In 1937, Samuel Ademola II, chief of Abeokuta in Nigeria, visited the Methodist Missionary Society in London. Modern British missionaries have met with reasonable success in Nigeria.

Opposite: People imbued with the Holy Spirit lie down at a religious meeting in Tulsa, Oklahoma, USA. In 2008, one quarter of Protestant churches in the USA claimed to have a Charismatic congregation.

PART ONE

IN THE BEGINNING TO 500 CE

CHAPTER ONE

JESUS OF NAZARETH

The Gospel of Matthew (Matthew 2) leads scholars to believe that Jesus was born in or before 4 BCE, the year Herod the Great died. Jesus grew up in Nazareth, a village in Galilee. Little is known about his childhood, but as an adult he developed a hugely successful itinerant teaching and healing ministry. This ministry lasted between one and three years, being cut short when his words and deeds caused conflict with those in power. He was crucified on charges of insurrection by the Roman authorities and leaders of his own people. The exact year of his death is as uncertain as the year of his birth—from the Gospels, it may have been 27 or 30 or 33 CE. Within a few days of his death, word began to spread that he had risen from the dead. Today, Jesus of Nazareth has more followers than any other political or religious leader in history.

Who was this Jesus, who died so young and so horribly, who today so many believe not only is alive but also gives eternal life to those who believe in him? No-one has ever been able to answer that question to the satisfaction of all. The early Church tried to define Jesus through councils and creeds in response to controversies about his nature. They succeeded in defining orthodox belief, but not in fully defining Jesus. The experiences of Christianity continued to give rise to new insights, and as time passed, Jesus was seen as a sacrificial victim, a king, a priest, an ascetic, a warrior of the last judgment, and more. Each of these images answered to its own time and place, but not to all times and places.

Modern Biblical scholars have tried to wrest a portrait of the historical Jesus from the literature of the New Testament, painstakingly working backward through layer after layer of testimony. This endeavor forms the basis for the way in which Jesus is presented in this book.

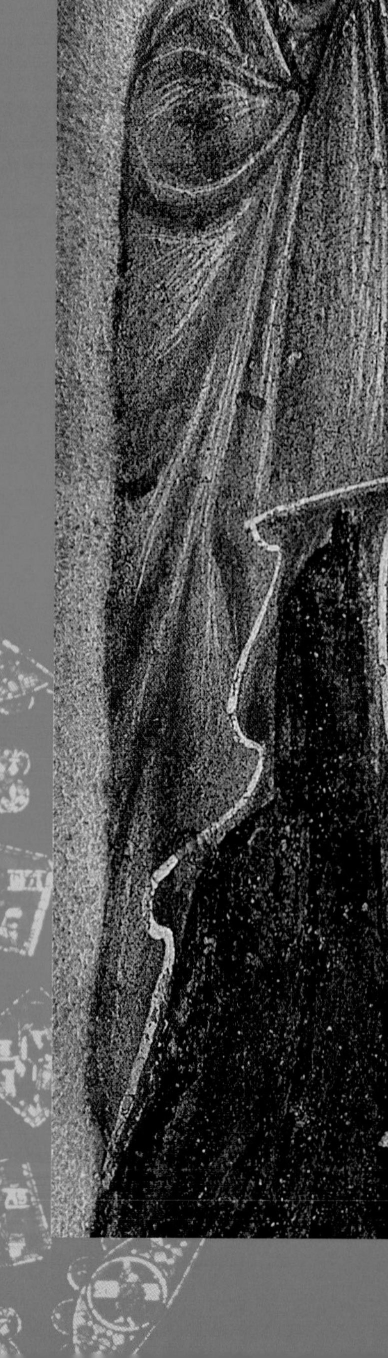

Previous pages: Mattia Preti's painting *Baptism of Christ* illustrates one of Christianity's most important sacraments. Baptism initiates new members of the Church, "washing away" their sins.

Right: Following Jewish custom, Mary and Joseph presented their firstborn son at the Temple in Jerusalem. There, the infant Jesus was dedicated to God.

RELIGION IN THE TIME OF JESUS

Nearly everyone in the Roman world believed in at least one god, and many believed in a number of gods. There was widespread agreement that the gods intervened in the affairs of the visible world, and that miracles were to be expected.

Greco-Roman religions

In the polytheistic Greco-Roman religions, worship was a matter of offering sacrifices to find favor with the gods. People believed that there was a close relationship between a peaceful and properly ordered society and the goodwill of the gods. So rituals, prayer, and sacrifice played a large role. These religions did not focus on how people lived their daily lives, for ethics was the concern of philosophers. People did not practice a religion in order to secure a happy afterlife but in hopes of securing the blessings of the gods in the present life.

Judaism

First-century Judaism shared with Greco-Roman religions a belief in miracles and the intervention of the divine, as well as a concern with rituals, prayer, and sacrifice. The major difference of the Jews was that they did

Below: Augustus' Altar of Lares (household gods). Rome's first emperor, Augustus set about restoring the state's traditional religious beliefs, claiming the gods were angry because they had been neglected.

Left: Jesus taught, preached, and performed miracles in the region of the Sea of Galilee, Palestine. Some say he chose this place because of the range of people living on its shores.

not have hundreds of gods and temples. Judaism was strongly monotheistic. A popular saying spoke of the "one Temple for the one God."

Orthodox Judaism was not focused on an afterlife. Heaven was not the expected reward for living a good life. Instead they expected a future kingdom of God on earth—God would bring an end to the rule of evil by establishing his kingdom. At that moment good Jews who had died would be resurrected in order to enter the kingdom.

Judaism was a highly ethical religion, but Mosaic Law included more than ethics. For as long as the Temple stood in Jerusalem, its rituals and sacrifices remained the focal point of Jewish life; rituals and sacrifices were as much a part of the Law as the Ten Commandments.

Judaic schools of thought

Judaism at the time of Jesus encompassed four major schools of thought—those of the Sadducees, the Pharisees, the Essenes, and various Jewish resistance groups such as the Zealots and the Sicarii.

The Sadducees (the "righteous ones") were the traditionalists. Although never numerous, they formed the priestly aristocracy based in Jerusalem, included a number of High Priests, and were politically very influential. They accepted only the Written Torah (Law) and for that reason did not hold to the resurrection of the body, judgment in the afterlife, or in the existence of angels and spirits—all of these beliefs they regarded as innovations.

Opposed to the Sadducees were the Pharisees (the "separated ones"). They were the innovators, making Judaism relevant for the people and working among them. In order to do so, they argued that alongside the Written Torah there was also an Oral Torah, passed down by word of mouth. That oral tradition allowed for reinterpretation and adaptation in different situations. As a result, they believed in the need to be pure, the resurrection of the dead, judgment in the next world, angels and spirits, human freedom, and God's guidance in everyday life.

The Essenes' concern for a pure and holy community was more radical than that of the Pharisees. They separated from society and formed a highly organized and monastic community at Qumran near the Dead Sea. The Essenes were an apocalyptic sect—they believed that the present evil age would be overthrown by God when he established his kingdom, that God would not allow evil to prosper and the good to suffer forever.

In the great tumult of first-century Palestine, many groups offered armed resistance to Roman rule. The most well known are the Zealots, who agreed with many of the Pharisees' teachings but wanted to be rid of the Romans. The Sicarii attempted to assassinate their opponents and held off the Romans at the battle of Masada in 73 CE, the last place of Jewish resistance after Jerusalem fell in 70 CE. All these groups saw God as their only leader and master.

Below: A Jewish man leans over a Torah as he reads from his prayer book. He is at the fortress of Masada in Israel, which symbolizes resistance for many Jews.

JESUS AND FIRST-CENTURY JUDAISM

Jesus' teachings did not conform to the beliefs of any known schools of thought in Judaism, which probably contributed to his vulnerability to those who conspired against him. Did Jesus believe what Jewish apocalyptic thinking taught—that evil ruled in the time in which he lived, but that God would overthrow that evil and establish the kingdom of God? The evangelists used apocalyptic imagery in their teaching, but talk of the overthrow of evil and the arrival of the kingdom of God was already present in their times.

POLITICS

Above: The people of Syria and Judea saw much physical evidence of Roman occupation, including aqueducts and roads. The Aqua Claudia in Rome is one of the greatest aqueducts ever built by the Romans.

Syria and Judea (Galilee and Palestine) became part of the Roman Empire in 64 and 63 BCE respectively. The three major cities of the region were Damascus and Antioch, both in Syria, and Jerusalem in Palestine. The city of Jerusalem had a turbulent history under Roman rule.

Roman rule

Rome looked with favor on the wealthy Judean family of Herod the Great, who practiced Judaism. The Herodians were not descended from any of the tribes of Israel, however, being Idumaeans, they were descendants of the Edomites of the Hebrew Bible. The family's Hellenistic cultural leanings led some to doubt the sincerity of their Judaism.

Herod ruled Palestine from 37 to 4 BCE. He was a violent man who killed his favorite wife, Mariamne I (he was married ten times), and five members of her family in a fit of jealousy. He was also a great builder, responsible both for Caesarea, destined to become the capital of Roman Palestine, and the rebuilding of the Temple in Jerusalem.

Judea was placed under direct Roman rule in 6 CE, and was thereafter administered by a series of Roman governors or procurators, of whom Pontius Pilate was one. A son of Herod the Great, Herod Antipas, was in charge of Galilee.

The Roman occupation was everywhere in evidence: In the aqueducts and other building projects, the roads and the soldiers who traveled on them, the coins imprinted with the emperor's image, the taxes—and the crosses that were positioned near the entrances to cities, on which accused insurrectionists were crucified. They signaled servitude to Rome, for Jews did not practice crucifixion; their form of capital punishment was stoning.

Jewish identity was maintained through worship in the Temple in Jerusalem and obedience to the Law of Moses. The Temple and the Law were the two primary centers of authority in first-century Judaism.

Above: Roman rule in Judea began during the reign of Augustus. His portrait appears on this ancient Roman coin.

THE SANHEDRIN

The Sanhedrin, which met in Jerusalem, was a Jewish council composed of 71 members approved by Rome and responsible for much of the internal government of Judea. The high priest convened the body and acted as its president. The Roman procurator appointed the high priest, who was a member of the priestly oligarchy, the Sadducees. The power of the priestly party was curbed by the presence of the Pharisees, the other main party in the Sanhedrin.

Right: This fresco by Fra Angelico depicts St Stephen preaching (left) and the Sanhedrin engaged in a lively debate (right).

SOCIETY

Palestine in Jesus' time was mostly agricultural and rural. Farmers raised sheep, cattle, and goats, and grew vegetables, fruits, olives, dates, and grains. They lived in small villages and walked daily to the surrounding fields. Almost the entire rural population was Jewish. In cities such as Caesarea, founded by Herod the Great and expanded by succeeding rulers, Gentiles (Romans, Greeks, and others) lived among the largely Jewish population.

Taxation

The Jewish populace suffered under a dual tax structure. The Mosaic Law included a system of tithes set up to support the priests, the Temple, and the poor, which added up to about 20 percent of a farmer's production. Rome also levied taxes, at least another 15 percent of production. To this the usually deservedly unpopular tax collectors added money for themselves, since they were paid according to how much they collected.

Rome had the power to collect its taxes by force. The tithes were not voluntary either, but the Temple had no way of physically coercing payment. Those who could not afford to pay both taxes generally opted to pay taxes to Rome and not to the Temple, economic duress thus rendering them "nonobservant." Even while Rome maintained an official policy of religious tolerance, its tax structure was undermining the observance of Jewish religious law.

Faced with both political and economic threats to their religiously based way of life, Jewish leaders reacted by reinforcing the walls of separation between observant Jews and the Gentiles and sinners. The purity laws articulated a holiness code designed to separate the faithful from anything that would render them unclean or impure. These laws dominated the social structure of first-century Palestine. "Impure" or "unclean" elements of society were barred from having contact with the "pure" or "clean"—so the righteous did not socialize with sinners and Gentiles, males did not socialize with females, and the diseased were barred from the community of the healthy.

The Temple was the administrative center of the purity system, and the priests were its administrators. Jesus seems to have angered elements among both the Pharisees and Sadducees by refusing to stay within the boundaries that had been erected by the purity system.

Below: This model shows Rome c. 300 CE. Over three centuries, Christianity changed from being a movement of people who followed one teacher, to being the official religion of the entire Roman Empire.

JESUS AS TEACHER

Right: *Suffer the Little Children to Come Unto Me,* by Juan Urruchi. The painting's title comes from the Gospel of Mark (10:13–14) in which Jesus urges people to bring their children to him to be blessed.

Jesus was called *rabbi* ("teacher") by friends and foes alike. Although he had no rabbinical training, the Gospel of John records that even the Temple police were astonished at his teaching: "Never has anyone spoken like this!" (John 7:46).

Wisdom teacher

Jesus did not speak in the style of the great prophets of Israel, men like Isaiah or Amos. His speeches were not punctuated with the formulaic "says the LORD," nor filled with promises of political blessing or disaster. Nor did Jesus adopt the style of the Pharisees: His teaching was not peppered with Biblical citations. The proverbs and parables that make up his teachings indicate that he taught in the simple style of a wisdom teacher from the country.

Wisdom teachers speak out of their experience and their observations of life. Jesus talks about shepherds and sheep, a woman searching for a lost coin, a farmer sowing seeds, rich men and poor men, Samaritans and Levites, laborers and landowners, camels and needles, yeast and bread, his teaching evoking a canvas of ordinary life. These were the realities of everyday peasant life. One gets the sense that Jesus saw the hand of God etched more clearly there than in the halls of power in Rome or Jerusalem.

The substance of Jesus' teaching revolved around the nature of the coming kingdom and how to be ready to enter it. His words and deeds pointed to a benevolent God who showers blessings without regard to a recipient's worthiness. When Jesus is said to have compassion for an individual or a throng of people, it is always because of their needs—they are sick, or hungry, or like sheep without a shepherd—never because they deserved it. He does not demand a confession of sins before he helps someone, although he sometimes pronounces forgiveness afterward. The only sins he inveighs against are hypocrisy, and the sinfulness of those who "load people with burdens hard to bear, and...do not lift a finger to ease them" (Luke 11:46).

Below: The parable of the Prodigal Son is illustrated in this nineteenth-century painting. Jesus' parables are contained in the Gospels of Matthew, Mark, Luke, and John.

Above: Samaritans belong to a version of Judaism alternative to the mainstream. Today Samaritans number about 700; they live in Kiryat Luza (pictured) on Mt Gerizim near Nablus (West Bank), and in Holon (Israel).

A society demarcated along lines of "the righteous and the holy" on the one hand, and "sinners and outcasts" on the other—precisely the social order established by the holiness code—does not mirror the kingdom as described by Jesus. Jesus' kingdom includes "the lost," the prostitutes, and even the despised tax collectors.

Mercy and generosity

Jesus points to God as the exemplar for his mercy. It is God who feeds the birds of the air, clothes the lilies of the field, and makes the sun to rise and the rain to fall on both the righteous and the unrighteous. Some of the parables point to the same overflowing generosity: The farmer who broadcasts his seeds without care for whether they fall on good or bad soil, the father of a disrespectful and dissolute son who welcomes him home with open arms, the vineyard owner who pays all his workers a full day's wage even though some had only worked a few hours (Matthew 20:1–16).

Jesus' stories did not follow moral stereotypes. A "good Samaritan" was an oxymoron in Jesus' day. Samaritans, members of an alternative Jewish cult, were so hated that most Jews would walk a considerable extra distance not to have to pass through their territory. To a large degree, the Samaritans' offense was religious: They worshipped on Mt Gerizim instead of in Jerusalem, which in orthodox eyes cut them off from contact with God. Yet in a now famous parable, Jesus creates such a powerful image of a Samaritan who did the right thing that the words "good" and "Samaritan" were forever after linked.

In a society in which wealth was taken to be a sign of God's favor, Jesus tells a story of a rich man who ends up in Hades because of his lack of compassion for a poor man while the poor man ends up in Abraham's bosom (Luke 16:19–31). Another parable tells of a farmer who has earned great wealth (by legal means), and decides to retire to savor the fruits of his labors (Luke 12:16–20). He dies that very night, undermining the assumption that hard work should have its just rewards. In many of Jesus' stories, the "wrong people" made it and the "right people" did not.

While many of his listeners were presumably of lowly status, coming from villages outside the cities, these stories challenged everyone to think hard about the nature of God, ethics, and morality, a task usually reserved for the religious elite. Jesus assumed that everyone—priest or peasant, literate or not—was capable of moral insight.

Above: A Samaritan waves the Samaritan Torah to celebrate Pentecost on Mt Gerizim. It was here, they believe, that Abraham offered Isaac in human sacrifice (Genesis 22:2–14).

JESUS AS HEALER

Jesus was a healer; so successful a healer that, according to the Gospels, multitudes constantly pressed upon him seeking a cure. He healed by means of a power that flowed out from him (Mark 5:30), a power identified as the power of the Spirit of God (Matthew 12:28 and Luke 4:18—"The Spirit of the Lord is upon me").

An alternative view of the world

Specific mention is made of Jesus healing fevers, leprosy, paralysis, a severed ear, a withered hand, a bent back, blindness, deafness, muteness, and persistent hemorrhage—illnesses that were difficult to heal without modern medicine. There was an occasion when he exorcized demons. Several incidents are recorded in which he brought someone back to life. In addition to this, the Gospels record other miracles such as the multiplication of the loaves and fishes, walking on water, and the calming of a storm. To a world in which everything has a scientific explanation, these things may seem a bit excessive and fanciful, but in those times not even Jesus' opponents questioned whether they actually occurred. The healing stories may best be seen as part of an alternative understanding of the way the world worked, an understanding shared by everyone. Therefore, the question was not whether they happened, but rather which spiritual power enabled them.

In ancient Israel, kings were anointed with the power of the Spirit of God, and so were priests. Prophets spoke by means of the same power. Although spirit-filled persons were not considered divine, they were seen as conduits through which the power and wisdom of God entered the earthly realm. The power belonged to God, but the person

Below: Jesus twice miraculously fed a multitude: The first time he changed five loaves and two fishes into enough to feed 5,000 people; the second time he provided food for 4,000 followers.

was anointed with it. The Gospels place Jesus squarely within this ancient understanding.

The oddity is that there were very few healers in the Hebrew Bible. God's anointed ones ruled (for example, David), offered sacrifices (for example, Samuel), and prophesied (for example, Isaiah), but no king, priest, or writing prophet was singled out for his ability to heal. The only personages to perform deeds of power with any degree of similarity to those performed by Jesus were Elijah and his successor Elisha, who are both associated with miracles involving the multiplication of food and the raising of the dead. There was a persistent belief that Elijah would return before the coming of the Messiah, and some people identified Jesus as Elijah based on these similarities.

Jesus offends the Jewish religious leaders

Jesus' healings attracted disapproval from many religious leaders—Pharisees, Sadducees, scribes, and others. They noted that he had healed on the Sabbath (John 9:14, Matthew 12:9–13). While it was permissible to heal on the Sabbath in order to save a life, it was not permissible to heal something that could have been left until the next day. The healings of a paralytic, a blind man, and a withered hand fell into the latter category. Jesus had also allowed his disciples to pluck grain on the Sabbath (Matthew 12: 1–2), which was duly noted by his detractors. Food consumed on the Sabbath had to be prepared ahead of time, since it was unlawful to perform work on the Sabbath, and plucking grain from the fields ran foul of that prohibition.

A perceived laxness in purity observances also seemed to place Jesus outside the Law. He was interrogated about the fact that his disciples ate with unwashed hands (Matthew 15:1–2; Mark 7). Jesus was known to have touched those whom the purity system deemed unclean—lepers, women, corpses, sinners—and to have allowed them to touch him. A recurrent complaint was that he ate with tax collectors and sinners, the impure. He talked to people who were beyond the pale: Gentiles and Samaritans, for example.

It was acts like these—healing and allowing work on the Sabbath, disregarding the purity code's rituals and social divisions, rather than his miracles—that put Jesus at odds with the religious and political leaders. When he lashed out against the institutional center of the purity system, the Temple itself, by challenging the way business was carried on there (Matthew 21:12–13, Mark 11:15–17, Luke 19:45–46), in essence he was proclaiming that the center of purification was itself impure. Such challenges to the highest religious and political authorities could only lead to disaster. The charges mounted: Jesus, they claimed, had been subverting Rome, opposing payment of taxes to Caesar, and claiming to be a king (Luke 23:2). Each was a crime of sedition, and they gave Pilate, the Roman governor, additional political reasons to orchestrate his downfall.

Above: King David was the God-ordained second ruler of the united kingdoms of Judah and Israel. Jesus is said to be descended from this brave and righteous king.

Below: Mark 8:22–26 describes Jesus healing a blind man in Bethsaida. Although this particular event is not mentioned in the other Gospels, Jesus does heal other blind men during his ministry.

JESUS AND WOMEN

A Jewish wisdom teacher named Jesus Ben Sira lived about two centuries before Jesus of Nazareth was born. A collection of his sayings (called Ecclesiasticus) made its way first into the Septuagint, the Greek version of the Jewish scriptures, and later into the Roman Catholic and most Orthodox Bibles. It is also one of the additional or deuterocanonical books of the Protestant Bible. Although Ecclesiasticus is not included in the Jewish Bible (Tanakh), Ben Sira expressed the dominant view of women at the time.

Below: Chapter 4 of John details Jesus' journey to Samaria. He meets a Samaritan woman at Jacob's well and asks her for some water; Jesus subsequently "washes away" her sins.

The traditional place of women

Ben Sira encouraged fear of God, respect for one's parents, and charity toward the poor. His advice was addressed only to men. He warns against keeping company with harlots, feasting one's eyes upon the beauty of a woman, or sitting at a table with a married woman (Sirach 9:3–9). Wine and women will corrupt a man's reason (19:2). Although he knows of good wives (26:1–4), he associates women with evil: No wickedness approaches that of a woman (25:19), and since sin began with a woman, we all must die because of a woman (25:24). Women being lusty, daughters are an unending source of worry for a father:

> Keep strict watch over a headstrong daughter,
> or she may make you a laughingstock to your enemies,
> a byword in the city and the assembly of the people,
> and put you to shame in public gatherings.
> See that there is no lattice in her room,
> no spot that overlooks the approaches to the house.
> (Sirach 42:11)

Ben Sira's notions about men, women, and their interactions outlived him. In the first century CE, pious Jewish men still kept their distance from all women, and especially harlots. Women were sequestered and kept under the supervision of fathers or husbands, because they were thought to lack moral discipline or the rational capacity to be instructed in it. The Gospel of John narrates an incident in which Jesus speaks to a woman when he is alone with her at a well. This behavior occasions great consternation on the part of his disciples (John 4:27), for chaste men and women were expected to act differently.

Jesus and the purity laws

The purity laws circumscribed a woman's presence in public. Either gender was rendered unclean by an emission of bodily fluids, but women spent more time in a state of impurity because of their menstrual cycles. Leviticus mandated seven days of impurity (15:19), and at some point the rabbis tacked on an additional seven days after the flow of blood ended. Anyone in a state of impurity had to separate themselves from others because impurity was transmitted by touch. Jesus' interactions with women frequently diverged from these prescriptions.

We know of no other Jewish teacher or prophet who had female followers, but both men and women followed Jesus (Luke 8:2–3, Mark 15:40–41, Matthew 27:55–56). Jesus even visits a woman's home when only she and her sister are present (Luke 10:38); one of them sits in rapt attention at his feet as he teaches.

One of the most frequent complaints against Jesus was that he ate with tax collectors and sinners (Mark 2:16; Luke 5:30). Tax collectors often trafficked in prostitutes, making it likely that prostitutes could be present at a meal hosted by a tax collector. Literature from this period

describes banquets where prostitutes were a part of the revelry. Women who held to the Law usually ate separately. For these reasons, it is often assumed that the woman who brought a jar of expensive ointment to a dinner and poured it on Jesus' head (Mark 14:3) was a prostitute. Luke's version of the encounter heightens the tension between the host, a Pharisee, and Jesus by having the woman touch Jesus' feet (7:36–40).

The Gospel of Mark contains side-by-side healing stories involving women. The woman with the hemorrhage (Mark 5:25–34) was continuously unclean due to her flow of blood. Because it was against the Law for her to touch anyone, she sneaks up behind Jesus and touches his garment. According to the Law, Jesus should immediately have washed his clothes, bathed, and followed the rules for the unclean until nightfall (Leviticus 15:27). He does none of those things, nor does he rebuke the woman. Instead, he proceeds to Jarius' house where he grasps the hand of the man's dead daughter, commanding her to rise (Mark 5:41). Touching a corpse meant an additional layer of impurity, and added to the complaints of the orthodox against him.

Above: When an adulteress was brought before him, Jesus said to her accusers, "Let anyone among you who is without sin be the first to throw a stone at her" (John 8:7).

Left: In this detail from a 1435 painting by Fra Angelico that depicts the deposition of Jesus, Mary Magdalene is shown tenderly kissing Jesus' feet as a sign of repentance.

JESUS AND THE GENTILES

Opposite: Jesus is linked to the Gentiles from birth. The "wise men"—priests or sages—that visited him in the stable are said to be "from the East" (Matthew 2:1).

The word translated in English as "Gentiles" actually means in the original Greek "the peoples." A better translation would be "foreigners"—everyone who was not a Jew. In the Gospels, Jesus interacts with a few Gentiles, and makes reference to Gentiles in his words. In the way these interactions were recorded we can see the effects of the later experiences of Christians, especially as Christianity grew beyond its home in Judaism to become a religion of the "foreigners." These experiences were projected back onto the stories in the Gospels. It is likely that Christian assessment of Gentiles grew increasingly positive as more and more Gentiles were baptized. Eventually Christianity became an overwhelmingly Gentile religion, spreading throughout the Roman Empire.

Jewish–Gentile relationships

Gentiles lived in Galilee during the lifetime of Jesus in significant numbers. Some of them would have come from the ancient Near East—from Egypt, Babylon, Syria, and further afield. However, the Greeks and then Romans in Palestine tended to live in the cities, which were modeled on those back in Greece. These cities represented the presence of an invading and occupying power—that of Rome. The paradox is that in the Eastern Roman Empire, of which Galilee and Judea were parts, the dominant culture was Greek. It was the language spoken, especially in the cities, and Greek culture dominated. For this reason it is called "Hellenistic" culture.

Due to the imperial presence of Hellenistic culture, the prevalent Jewish attitude toward Gentiles during the first century was a mixture of disdain and fear. We find this attitude expressed in the Gospels. For example, Matthew, Mark, and Luke all refer to "rulers of the Gentiles who lord it over them" (Luke 22:25, Matthew 20:25, Mark 10:42), and they express a fear of being handed over to the Gentiles (Matthew 20:19, Mark 10:30).

Below: Despite the fact that she is not of the "house of Israel" (Matthew 15:24), Jesus heals the possessed daughter of a Canaanite woman because the woman shows great faith.

Jesus' contacts with Gentiles

In some of the Gospel texts Jesus seems to share these views. So we find that Gentiles apparently had a reputation for empty talk (Matthew 6:7, 32). In a demeaning phrase, Jesus asks, "Do not even the Gentiles do the same?" (Matthew 5:47), and he associates Gentiles with tax collectors (Matthew 18:17). These sayings may be understood as expressing opposition to the imperial power of Rome and Hellenistic culture. Yet, when Jesus encounters individual Romans, he treats them fairly. So the Roman centurion with the sick servant (Luke 7:1-10, Matthew 8:5-13) is praised by Jesus for having faith beyond those in Israel.

However, when Jesus speaks favorably of Gentiles, he does so in reference to those from other parts of the known world. For example, he mentions the "sign of the prophet Jonah" (Luke 11:19–32 and Matthew 12:38–42), referring to a story from the Hebrew Bible (Old Testament) in which the hated and feared Gentiles of Nineveh heed God's word and repent. He speaks of the Gentile "queen of the South" who came to Israel seeking wisdom. And in Luke (13:22–29) Jesus envisions Gentiles from every point on the compass entering through the narrow door into the kingdom of God. In a sermon situated in the synagogue at Nazareth, Jesus points out that Elijah's miracle during a time of great famine was performed for a widow of Sidon rather than a widow in Israel, and that the leper cleansed by Elisha was a Syrian, not an Israelite (Luke 4:25–27).

Jesus' journeys take him beyond Galilee and Judea to the Decapolis (a league of ten Greek cities around Lake Galilee), to Idumea, Tyre, and Sidon, and "beyond the Jordan." We are also told that people from all those areas came to him in great numbers (Mark 3:8). The man with the legion of demons whom Jesus healed (Mark 5:1–20, Luke 8:26–39) was a Gentile.

Matthew's Gospel goes furthest in assigning a positive role to Gentiles. Contrary to the usual Jewish genealogies which mention only males, Matthew's genealogy of Jesus (1:1–14) mentions four women: Tamar, Rahab, Ruth, and "Uriah's wife" (Bathsheba). Each is morally unsavory by conventional standards (Tamar played the prostitute while Rahab really was one, Ruth was a Moabite, and Bathsheba was involved in an adulterous relationship with King David), but Matthew uses them as examples of genuine righteousness. Surprisingly, these four unconventional but truly righteous ancestors of Jesus are all Gentiles. The magi, the wise men who seek the infant Jesus, are Gentiles, and the place of safety from Herod's order to slaughter the infants is in Gentile territory (Egypt).

bosch

THE DEATH OF JESUS

Above: Prior to Jesus' crucifixion, Roman authorities flagellated (whipped) him using ropes or twigs. Many religious orders later prescribed self-flagellation as a form of penance.

In the end, Jesus came into conflict with both the Temple and the Roman overlords of Palestine. The high priest handed him over to the Romans, who crucified him as a political revolutionary. Jesus' teaching about the kingdom of God may have been read as critical of both Jewish and Roman power—it implied that both were lacking by comparison.

The deadliness of Jesus' death

Over time, various words have been used to refer to Jesus' death. The most common are Christ's "Cross" or "Passion" (from Latin *passio*, "suffering"). It also appears as the visible symbol of the crucifix. The Cross is a symbol with many meanings: It can designate suffering and despair, abandonment and loss, but it is also a symbol of hope and love. For Christianity it is, paradoxically, a symbol of God's love for the human race. Ever since, the day of Jesus' death has been known as "Good Friday."

It is difficult to imagine that Friday when it was far from "good," given the brutal reality of crucifixion. It was an obscene and tragic event, commonly used by the Romans for political rebels. The Jews preferred to execute the death penalty with stoning; the Romans used crucifixion. All Jesus had lived and worked for ended in hopeless failure. He was condemned by both the religious and secular authorities, betrayed by a chosen disciple, abandoned by his followers, and rejected by his own people.

Mark's Gospel depicts Jesus' sense of intense isolation. The one in whose name he had come, whom he had called his "father," is now completely absent. This experience wrings from the dying Jesus the agonized prayer, "*Eloi, Eloi, lema sabachthani?*" which means "My God, my God, why have you forsaken me?" (Mark 15:34). "Then Jesus gave a loud cry and breathed his last" (Mark 15:37). Watching from a distance were several of Jesus' women followers, including Mary Magdalene.

In death Jesus is stripped, as it were, of everything that had meaning. Crucifixion was a cruel business. It often, as in the case of Jesus, began with a flogging that would sometimes kill (a mercifully quick end). The idea of crucifixion was a slow and public death. Nailed to a cross, it would take many days. Usually, groups were crucified at one time. On one occasion, after the slave rebellion led by Spartacus, the crucified rebels lined the roads out of Rome. People came to watch and mock those crucified. Death would usually come through dehydration and hunger. To add to the pain, the soldiers might break the legs of those crucified so they couldn't support themselves.

Interpreting the Cross

The significance of the death of Jesus for Christianity has led to a huge amount of interpretation. What do Christians make of this ignominious end? The Gospels provide the earliest known interpretations. So we find that it is a sign that Jesus relies completely on God: "yet, not what I want, but what you want" (Mark 14:36).

Other interpretations stress that through the Cross, God's character is revealed. God the "father" appears to the world only through his crucified son. Further, through the Cross comes forgiveness: As Jesus prays that those who have crucified him should be forgiven, so all may be forgiven.

We also find that the Cross means love: "Having loved his own who were in the world, he loved them to the end" (John 13:1). In the face of human selfishness, the Cross invites believers into a life of self-giving love: "Just as I have loved you, you also should love one another. By this everyone will know that you are my disciples, if you have love for one another" (John 13:34–35).

Reactions

The Cross of Christ so shocked religious, philosophical, and political sensibilities that, according to St Paul, it made God look "foolish." Proclaiming the crucified Jesus as the Christ had to be scandalous to the Jewish people (including his earliest disciples), who were waiting on the Messiah to come in glory and power. For the Greek philosophers, too, any notion that the infinite God could be revealed in a suffering human, let alone a crucified criminal, defied imagination (1 Corinthians 1:23). All this was subversive to Rome: Christians preached that God was revealed in this man whom the imperial authority had condemned and executed under Pontius Pilate. Still, Paul insists, through the Cross, God's power and wisdom are revealed, "For God's foolishness is wiser than human wisdom, and God's weakness is stronger than human strength" (1 Corinthians 1:25). In John's Gospel, Jesus, referring to his saving death, promises, "And I, when I am lifted up from the earth, will draw all people to myself" (John 12:32).

Above: Crucifixion was usually a long and painful death involving blood loss, sepsis, dehydration, and/or exposure. Jesus' faith ultimately sustained him: "Father, into your hands I commend my spirit" (Luke 23:46).

Left: After he had been crucified, Jesus was laid to rest by Joseph of Arimathea in Joseph's own tomb. A number of women, including Mary Magdalene, watched the proceedings from afar.

THE RESURRECTION OF JESUS

Below: The Resurrection of Jesus is seen as a symbol of hope by Christians; in his rising from the dead, Jesus reinstated the privileges lost to humanity by their sinful ways.

Without the Resurrection on that first Easter Sunday, there would be no grounds for understanding Good Friday as "good" or Holy Saturday as "holy." Christianity is defined by the death and resurrection of Jesus; without them, there would be no Christianity. Like the crucifixion, the importance of the Resurrection has led to much reflection and interpretation. Because of the Resurrection, everything is seen differently. St Paul underscores what is at stake: To deny the Resurrection would be to misrepresent God "because we testified of God that he raised Christ"; there would be no hope for the dead; sins would not be forgiven; faith would be futile; and the preachers of the Gospel would be "of all men most to be pitied" (1 Corinthians 15:12–19).

The appearances of the risen one

The risen Jesus appeared to the disciples precisely at the time they were suffering the grief and disillusionment that followed his condemnation and execution. Whatever hopes they had were buried with him in the tomb. And yet he comes back to them. St Paul gives a list of those to whom Christ had revealed himself (1 Corinthians 15:3–11), while the Gospels—apart from Mark—provide their respective accounts of how Jesus appeared to his disciples and was recognized by them.

The New Testament never pretends to describe the Resurrection, nor reports anyone claiming to have seen it. It tells of an empty tomb and a risen Christ who appears to Jesus' disciples. Whatever the inevitable dismay and

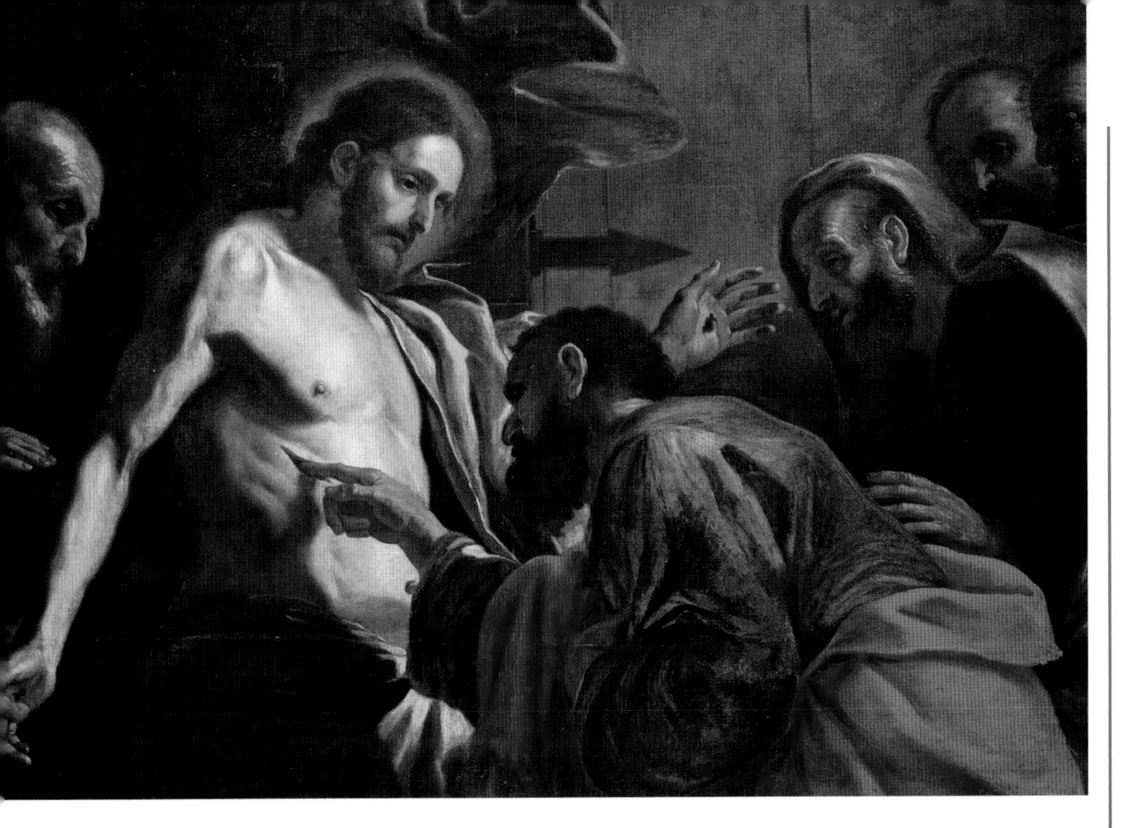

Left: Thomas would not accept that Jesus had risen from the dead until he had touched the wounds on Jesus' body. Because of this, he is now known as Doubting Thomas.

confusion connected with Jesus' return to his disciples, these early witnesses were utterly certain about Jesus' return from the dead. They experienced him in a way different from the visions, dreams, ecstasies, and miraculous resuscitations of the dead reported elsewhere in the New Testament. They were not meeting a ghost or inventing a myth (Luke 24:36–40; 2 Peter 1:16). They believed that something had taken placed that changed everything—even if words were hard to find for what was beyond all words and outside all previous experience.

The Gospels take care to stress that the risen one really is Jesus of Nazareth, even to the extent that he bears the marks of his crucifixion. Yet he is transformed—to become the source and assurance of new life for all who believe in him. In this risen existence, he freely discloses himself to his disciples, drawing them from doubt and hesitation to a moment of recognition. After that, they worship him and express unreserved commitment to him (John 20:16ff; Matthew 28:9, 17).

The layers of meaning are many. The Resurrection is felt to be the beginning of a new phase of human history, so much so that our system of dating turns on the figure of Jesus. It promises that love is at work, that God can overcome the powers of death and evil, that there is hope for the world, and that life will finally triumph.

The empty tomb

In each of the Gospel accounts of the Resurrection there is reference to the empty tomb. No-one denies that the tomb was empty, while there is an emphasis given to the women who first discover it. How then is the empty tomb related to faith in the risen Jesus? What is clear is that the overwhelming experience of the appearance of Jesus, who had been killed and was now risen, could never be reduced to the mere fact of finding his grave without a body in it. That would be ambiguous; however, there is no ambiguity in the disciples' conviction that Jesus had risen and that life thereafter was changed.

On the other hand, that emptiness has its place in the fullness of the Gospel narrative. It is a sign of the objective reality of the Resurrection, lifting the blank fact of the empty tomb out of its original ambiguity. It gives a concrete edge to Christian hope, making it more than a nice idea or a good feeling. Believing in the risen Christ is not the same as believing in an empty tomb. And a tomb containing his decaying corpse could hardly be a sign of God's transforming act, nor of Jesus' victory over death and sin.

The empty tomb, then, is a historical marker pointing to the fact that God has acted to raise up the crucified Jesus, and makes way for the fullness of Resurrection faith. This realism prevents the Resurrection being interpreted simply as way of saying that the cause of Jesus continues after his death. The central claim of Christian faith is that Jesus has been raised from the dead.

Left: A group of women are the first people to discover that Jesus' tomb is empty; an angel appears to them, instructing them to spread the glorious news of the Resurrection.

CHAPTER TWO

THE NEW TESTAMENT

Jesus of Nazareth was an itinerant preacher. There is no record that he put any of his teachings into writing, nor that the men and women who followed him on his journeys did so as they traveled. Jesus preached; they listened and remembered.

After Jesus was gone, those who believed in him passed on their memories of him as they spread his stories by word of mouth. Those memories also helped to shape the earliest sermons, debates with non-believers, and the words and actions of the baptism ceremony and the Holy Communion ritual. This period of oral transmission lasted for around 15 to 20 years.

Of the 27 books in the New Testament, the first to be written was a letter from Paul of Tarsus to an assembly of Christians in Thessalonica: 1 Thessalonians was written around 50 CE. In the decade that followed, Paul wrote additional letters that were later incorporated in the New Testament: Another letter to the Thessalonians; letters from prison to Philemon, the Philippians, the Galatians, and the Corinthians; and finally, near the end of his life, a letter to the Christians in Rome. The remaining books were written by other people. Most scholars believe that the last New Testament writings were completed by around 100 CE.

The 27 books in the New Testament are: Matthew, Mark, Luke, John, Acts of the Apostles, Romans, 1 Corinthians, 2 Corinthians, Galatians, Ephesians, Philippians, Colossians, 1 Thessalonians, 2 Thessalonians, 1 Timothy, 2 Timothy, Titus, Philemon, Hebrews, James, 1 Peter, 2 Peter, 1 John, 2 John, 3 John, Jude, Revelation.

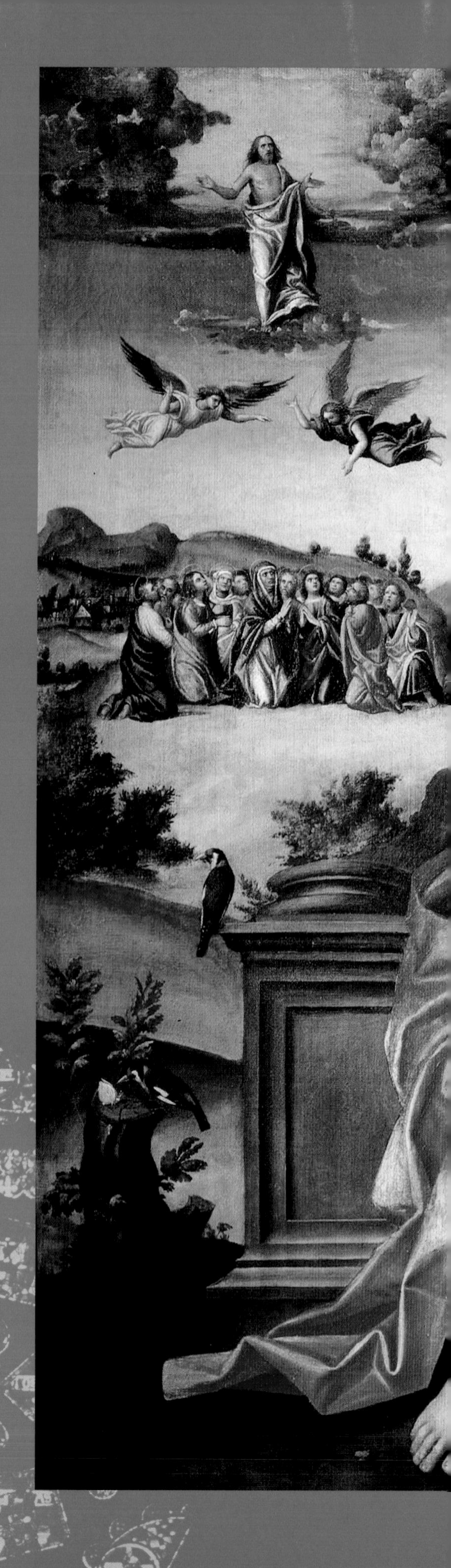

Right: Thomas, one of Jesus' 12 disciples, would not believe that Jesus had risen from the dead until he had put his finger "in the mark of the nails and [his] hand in [Jesus'] side" (John 20:25).

THE GOSPELS

Right: Although nobody knows who wrote the Gospels, Mark is often attributed to St Mark the Evangelist, who lived in the first century CE. Mark is shown here preaching in Egypt.

Not long after Paul's death, another form of writing—known as the gospels—appeared. "Gospel" comes from the Old English word *godspel,* literally meaning "good story." It translates the Greek *euangellion*, "*eu*" meaning good or happy, and "*angellion*" meaning announcement or proclamation. A gospel, then, is a joyous proclamation.

Mark and Matthew

If the Pauline letters are theological statements with a pastoral stance, the Gospels contain theology in story form. They are not biographies, although they contain biographical elements. Jesus' teachings were not reproduced word for word, nor were the descriptions of eyewitness accounts of miracles, for the Gospels were written 30 or more years after his death. By this time Jesus' words and deeds had undergone elaboration and interpretation through constant retelling in different situations. Each of the four Gospels provides, not a biography, but a theological answer to the question of Jesus' identity.

Below: The Gospels detail many facets of Jesus' ministry, including numerous examples where he heals the sick and injured, as well as those who are possessed.

The majority of scholars believe that Mark was written between 65 and 70 CE, making it the first of the four canonical Gospels. Like the other three, this Gospel is anonymous. The early Church added the names "Matthew," "Mark," "Luke," and "John," and the traditional names continue to be used for the sake of convenience. The Gospel of Mark portrays Jesus as the strong man who binds Satan; the many exorcisms in this Gospel provide evidence of his victory over Satan's legions. In the first half of the Gospel, Jesus' amazing words and his ability to heal win him large crowds of followers. Then, in the hinge section (8:22–10:52), Jesus three times predicts his suffering and death. Still blinded by the nonstop show of power, even his disciples fail to accept what he is saying. With the sole exception of several women who look on from a distance (15:40), Jesus dies abandoned, his followers hiding and silenced, unwilling to follow him as he steps out of the limelight and onto the cross. This first Gospel seems designed to show that salvation is present, in power and in suffering, despite the blindness of even those who believe.

The Gospel of Matthew portrays Jesus as a teacher of righteousness. For example, the Sermon on the Mount (chapters 5–7) challenges people to live a life of perfection (5:48) even as it blesses those whose lives seem least perfect (5:3–11). This Gospel also portrays Jesus as the fulfillment of the Law, since he alone of all human beings lived a life of perfect obedience to the will of God.

Luke and John

The Gospel of Luke portrays Jesus as the man who sets his face toward Jerusalem. In 10 out of 24 chapters (9:51–19:28) Jesus is journeying toward Jerusalem. Only in this Gospel, Jesus frequently teaches in Jerusalem, often inside the Temple. This Gospel alone opens in Jerusalem, with the story of Zechariah and Elizabeth, the parents of John the Baptist. In the Gospel of Matthew, the disciples are commanded to meet the risen Jesus in Galilee (28:7, 10); in the Gospel of Luke they remain in Jerusalem and meet the risen Jesus in its environs (chapter 24). The point is hardly historic or geographic. It is symbolic—Jerusalem was both the blessed city where God's promises were fulfilled and also the city destroyed because of sin. It was also the place of sacrifice for sin. Jesus sets his face toward Jerusalem because Luke portrays him as the fulfillment of the sacred destiny of that city.

The Acts of the Apostles is the second half of the Gospel of Luke. It portrays the spread of the Gospel, beginning in Jerusalem and ending with Paul approaching Rome, the seat of the empire's power.

The Gospel of John portrays Jesus as descending from the Father into the world (first half) and then reascending to the Father in heaven (second half). In this Gospel, Jesus is called the Word, and his descent and ascent is probably patterned on Isaiah's description of the word of God, which goes forth from God and does not return empty, but rather accomplishes the purpose for which it was sent (Isaiah 55:11).

Above: Each Gospel often describes the same event in Jesus' life in slightly different ways. Jesus' entry into Jerusalem is recorded in Mark 11, Matthew 21, Luke 19, and John 12.

CRISIS LITERATURE

The last book in the New Testament, the Book of Revelation or the Apocalypse of John, is widely referred to as "crisis literature;" in other words, literature that was written in a time of Roman persecution. It contains a wealth of symbolic material that was easily understood by Christians of the time, but which is relatively difficult to interpret from a distance of some 20 centuries. It also offered consolation to and the hope of a heavenly reward for those Christians who faithfully endured sufferings and even martyrdom for their faith.

Right: St John the Evangelist dictates the text for the Book of Revelation to Prochoros the copyist during his exile on the island of Patmos (now in Greece).

THE LETTERS OF PAUL

Right: Paul of Tarsus is also known as St Paul, Paul the Apostle, and Saul of Tarsus. He called himself "Apostle to the Gentiles" on his missions of evangelization.

The earliest surviving examples of Christian literature were written by Paul of Tarsus. Paul's missionary journeys resulted in the establishment of Christian communities throughout what is now Turkey and Greece. Inevitably, problems cropped up in some of these communities—problems concerning leaders, doctrine, and discipline—but because of his travels or due to imprisonment Paul could not return to solve the difficulties in person. In his place he sent delegates, often bearing letters addressing the problem or problems, which were read and reflected upon when the communities gathered together in worship.

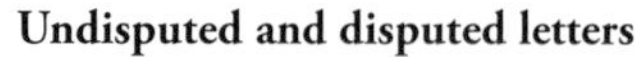

Undisputed and disputed letters

Thirteen New Testament letters are attributed to Paul, but it is doubtful whether he wrote all of them. As many as six may have been written in his name but not by him, most likely by followers of Paul's teaching who lived in the generation after him. Most scholars agree that seven letters—1 Thessalonians, 1 & 2 Corinthians, Galatians, Philippians, Romans, and Philemon—were written or dictated by Paul in 50–60 CE. These seven missives are often referred to as the "undisputed letters."

The letters written in his name but not by him are Colossians, Ephesians, 2 Thessalonians, 1 & 2 Timothy, and Titus. To determine whether a letter was written by Paul himself or by a later disciple or disciples in a Pauline school of thought, scholars look for the presence or absence of familiar themes (as determined by the seven undisputed letters), and for the degree of development or elaboration of those themes. They also consider whether the issues addressed in the letter reflect the decade between 50 and 60 CE or a later time period. Finally, they try to determine whether the style and vocabulary of the letter matches the style and vocabulary of the undisputed letters.

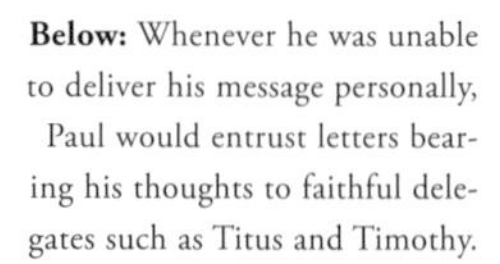

Opposite: After his conversion on the road to Damascus, Paul made three major journeys to spread the word of Jesus. On his second mission, he visited and preached in Athens.

Below: Whenever he was unable to deliver his message personally, Paul would entrust letters bearing his thoughts to faithful delegates such as Titus and Timothy.

Recurring themes

Paul's letters address specific issues that are pertinent to the situation of a particular community. Nonetheless, certain themes recur in his letters, and they allow us to sketch the outlines of Paul's thought. Paul, whose zeal for the Law had at one time led him to oppose the followers of Jesus, ultimately came to believe that people needed a savior more than they needed God to act as lawgiver, judge, and executioner. To divide the world into righteous versus sinners, Jews versus Gentiles, clean versus unclean, or holy versus unholy was pointless, for who among us, Paul asked, is truly righteous, truly a son of Abraham, truly holy? If God intervened in history as lawgiver, judge, and executioner, all would die, for all were sinners under the Law.

Paul believed that Jesus was God's provision for saving his creation, for giving it second birth rather than condemning and destroying it. Paul called the new humanity "the second Adam," and he called the renewal of the world "the new creation." Anyone who died to self to live in Christ became part of the "body of Christ," another name for the Christian community.

While the literal body of Jesus had ascended to heaven, the same Spirit that dwelt within Jesus now dwelt both in individual believers as well as in congregations as a whole, knitting them together in love and mutual service. Thus, Paul thought, had Jesus freed the world from its bondage to sin and allowed it to live as God intended; that is, in obedience to God's will as expressed in the Law but not fulfilled under the Law.

EXTRA LETTERS

The New Testament contains four letters in addition to the thirteen that comprise the Pauline corpus: James, Jude, and 1 & 2 Peter. The Letter to the Hebrews, once attributed to Paul, is neither Pauline nor a letter. It is a tightly argued sermon whose main contention is that Jesus is God's high priest, a claim made by no other New Testament document (although other writings use sacrificial themes in describing Jesus' death).

Reverendus pater D. Paulus Holgl · V · I · Doctor Canonicus Brixinen̄
et quondam A Divo Maximiliano Imp· reipublicæ Viennen̄ gubernaculis
admotus quo testaretur · et suam in Christum pietatem simul et fidem
Paulum Athenis concionantem in hac tabella adpingi curavit · q̄ Christu·
verbis magis graphice delineavit · quam possit ulla artis docta manus
Voluit aūt et D. Floriani de Waldenstain · I · V · Doctorem Canonicū brixine
simul ut amorem in se testaretur et illius

FORMATION OF THE CANON

Right: The Council of Trent comprised 25 sessions from 1545 to 1563. One of the main purposes of the council was to define the books of the Old Testament for Catholics.

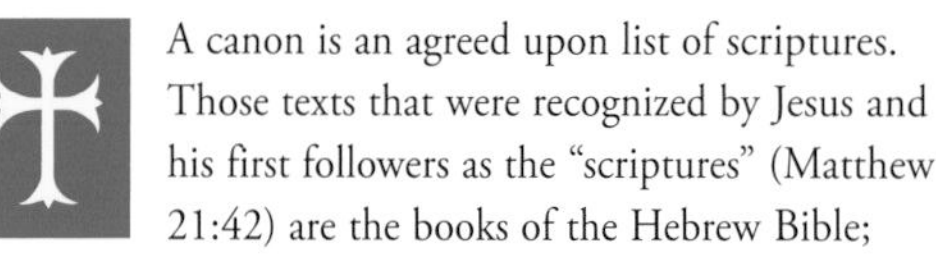

A canon is an agreed upon list of scriptures. Those texts that were recognized by Jesus and his first followers as the "scriptures" (Matthew 21:42) are the books of the Hebrew Bible; in time Christians would call this collection the Old Testament ("testament" here meaning "relationship with God"). The books written by Christians that eventually became canonical are called the New Testament. However, the terms "Old Testament" and "New Testament" were not in common usage until the end of the second century.

Birth of the New Testament

Within decades of the Resurrection there were numerous preachers traveling through the eastern Mediterranean recounting episodes from the life of Jesus. The stories they told were written down in Greek and became known as "gospels." Paul and other missionaries wrote letters to the communities they had founded or visited, clarifying issues of theology or practice. Other writings described the journeys and actions of various apostles. There were apocalypses, works describing cosmic events in a style similar to that found in the Book of Revelation. Initially none of these writings was singled out as canonical. They simply circulated among Christian communities and were read aloud at gatherings. In a short period of time some writings—for example, those of Paul—were considered scriptural. But they did not belong to a canon because there was no agreed upon list of scriptures.

The first stage in making such a list was to collate the various writings. This process began some time early in the second century with the Letters of Paul. The earliest lists contain 10 letters. Later, 1 & 2 Timothy, Titus, and Hebrews were added. By the end of the second century, this list of 14 was widespread.

Below: John the Baptist's deeds appear in many of the scriptures that now form part of the New Testament. Matthew 11:11 states "no one has arisen greater than John the Baptist..."

So many Gospels had been produced that it was hard to see the common story of Jesus behind the diversity of texts. In 170 CE Tatian tried to produce a unified story by harmonizing Matthew, Mark, and Luke. By the end of the second century, the Gospel of John had elbowed its way in despite hesitations caused by its popularity with the Gnostics, and a fourfold Gospel—Matthew, Mark, Luke, and John—had become generally accepted.

Although the Letters of Paul and the four Gospels were well established by the end of the second century, there was still no agreement regarding the rest of the New Testament. 1 Peter and 1 John gained canonical status in the second and third centuries, while the other Johannine letters, James, 2 Peter, and Jude still struggled.

In the fourth century several lists appeared. Some had more books than today's New Testament, while others omitted 2 & 3 John, Hebrews, 2 Peter, Jude, and/or Revelation. Some of the lists contained the same 27 books that we have in the New Testament today, but those lists did not have universal acceptance at that time. We do not know the date of universal acceptance. We know that there was widespread agreement by the fourth century, but we also know that Revelation was not accepted in the East until the tenth or eleventh century.

How big is the Old Testament?

There was no universal agreement regarding the canon of the Jewish Bible by the time of Jesus. Among the Greek-speaking Jews of the Mediterranean world the scriptures included texts composed in Greek in addition to the five

books of the Law and the books of the Prophets. The Jewish scriptures in Greek (known as the Septuagint) contained about 50 writings, while there were only 39 or 40 (depending on how you count) in Hebrew. Following the fall of the Jerusalem Temple in 70 CE, a movement arose within Judaism that called for an explicit determination of the writings to be included in a definitive canon. The religious authorities opted for only those that they believed were originally written in Hebrew, rejecting those originally written in Greek.

Christians continued to use the Greek version of the scriptures, which was longer than the emerging Jewish canon of 24 books. In 382, Pope Damasus I asked his secretary, the historian and later saint Jerome (345–420), to make a new Latin translation of the Bible (the Vulgate Bible) from the Greek New Testament and the Septuagint Old Testament. Jerome decided to translate the Old Testament books directly from the Hebrew where such a text existed. When he encountered the post-70 CE Jewish list, he argued that it must be the genuine list. His position was rejected by Augustine (354–430), who held that it was not what language a book was written in, but its long-term usefulness within the Church, that must be the basis of canonicity. So, despite Jerome's objections, the Latin Church continued with the lengthy Septuagint canon. (The Orthodox and other Oriental canons are even longer.) A thousand years later, the Reformers opted for Jerome's position, rejecting anything in the Old Testament canon that was not on the post-70 CE Jewish list, while the Catholics at the Council of Trent (1545) opted for Augustine's position. Thus it is that today the Protestant Bible has 39 books in the Old Testament; the Catholic Bible has 46; the Eastern Orthodox Bible has 49; and the Ethiopian Orthodox Bible has 52 Old Testament books.

Above: In 70 CE, the Romans under Titus besieged Jerusalem, razing the Temple and many other buildings. Despite this setback, Jewish leaders began establishing their canon.

CHAPTER THREE

COUNCILS AND CREEDS

Essentially, Christian faith is the unreserved acceptance of God's self-revelation in Christ. However, to explain that transforming event the early Christian pastors and theologians had to draw on vast resources of language and human thought. The saving significance of Christ's life, death, and resurrection had to be communicated in a variety of situations.

The most obvious example of this is the composition of not one Gospel text, but of four. The basic Christian "gospel" or "good news"—that God provided salvation for humans in Christ Jesus—has been told in a number of ways. We have four distinct tellings of this single belief in the four canonical gospels: Matthew, Mark, Luke, and John.

The Gospel of Mark, probably addressed to the early Christians of Rome after a period of intense persecution, emphasizes the radical character of discipleship. Matthew's Gospel underlines the continuity between the faith of Israel and that of the first generations of Jewish Christians, stressing the role of Jesus as the true teacher in a time of confusion. It seems that Luke's Gospel was designed to remedy the loss of conviction and missionary energy after the first generation of eyewitnesses had died out. It stresses the outreaching character of the Christian vocation and the loving mercy of God. The Gospel of John dramatically emphasizes the wonder of God's self-revelation in Jesus Christ.

As early Christians read and pondered the Gospels, they had to keep articulating the meaning of faith in order to hand it on. Inevitably, questions arose regarding the nature of God, human destiny, the origin and end of creation, the issue of evil and suffering, and hope beyond death.

Right: A fresco shows an ecumenical council in progress. It was at these gatherings during the early history of the Christian Church that bishops discussed and decided upon matters of Church doctrine.

THE HOLY TRINITY CONTROVERSY

Basic questions emerged in regard to the Christian confession of the One God and the three divine persons—the Father, Son, and Holy Spirit. The early Christian pastors and theologians had to articulate the Christian sense of "threefoldness" of God in such a way as to be faithful to Israel's confession of the One, True God. In addition, they had to avoid giving the appearance of relapsing into some form of the old mythological polytheism from which the great Greek philosophers had tried to break free.

Here, the challenge was to avoid reducing the three divine persons to temporary "aspects" or "modes" of God appearing in different times (Modalism). At the same time, orthodox faith had to avoid any impression that the concept of the Trinity implied "three gods" in some sense. Moreover, the usual philosophical idea of God being infinitely remote from the world had to be transformed. The distinctiveness of Christian faith turned on the recognition of the hitherto unimaginable closeness of God in Christ—right to the extreme of sharing in the human condition of suffering and death.

Below: Disputations—formalized theological debates—on the complex nature of the Holy Trinity occupied ecclesiastics, scholars, and philosophers for hundreds of years.

An early problem dealt with the genuineness of the humanity of Jesus. However, there remained some who could not accept this, referred to as Docetists (from *dokein*, "to appear"). They could not see how the exalted divine Word or *Logos* could suffer such an abasement as to become human, with the suffering and death that this implied. To them, Jesus was more an "appearance" of God in human form than actual flesh and blood.

Faith and culture

The first missionary expansion of the Church was in the Greco-Roman world, which gave Christian teaching access to great intellectual resources. The Greco-Roman culture's philosophical systems would enable the early Church to clarify its essential truths, and in doing so break free of mythological distortions. In addition, the two major literary languages, Latin and Greek, with their rich and subtle vocabularies and traditions of rhetorical and logical skills, aided the task of clarification.

The questions that arose, especially those dealing with the Trinity and the Incarnation, would take centuries to answer in clear terms. It should be remembered, nonetheless, that throughout that time the living faith was not reduced simply to solving doctrinal questions. That would be the main preoccupation of the early Councils of the Church (such as Nicaea in 325, Constantinople in 381, Ephesus in 431, and Chalcedon in 451). In the meantime, Christian life went on: New generations were baptized in the name of the Father, Son, and Holy Spirit.

Lead-up to the Council of Nicaea

The clarification of Trinitarian doctrine arrived at by the first Council of Nicaea in 325 was the outcome of a long and complex process. Arius, a priest in Alexandria in the early decades of the fourth century, had asked: Is Jesus Christ truly divine? Or does he belong to the realm of creation? Arius seems to have presupposed an unbridgeable gap between the infinite, changeless character of God and the changing, limited reality of the world, and that because of Christ's sufferings and exposure to human limitations he must belong to the created sphere. And so, a knockdown issue for the Church emerged. It permitted no middle ground: Does Christ possess a divine status, or is he merely a human creature, however noble and exemplary?

Before the Arian crisis, influential thinkers had begun to address this problem, with the intention of affirming Christ's divine status, but without undermining faith in the One God. Tertullian (died c. 223), a master of forceful Latin expression, coined a precise doctrinal formulation, "three persons" and the "one underlying reality." His theology, however, fell substantially short, since he seems to have imagined the Godhead as the one infinite, material reality

concentrated, as it were, in the three divine persons. In the East, the great theologian Origen (died c. 254) employed a much more sophisticated philosophical approach (Middle-Platonism), which envisaged gradated emanations from the one supreme Source.

By the time of Arius, Christian faith was confronted with a Yes/No alternative. In essence, the question was: Is God truly, personally, and compassionately involved in the salvation of the world, or is this God radically uninvolved with us, and acting only through a created representative?

The Council of Nicaea's response

The Council's response, an early form of the Nicene Creed, is as follows [emphases added]:

> We believe in **one** God, **the Father almighty**, **maker** of all things, visible and invisible. And in one Lord Jesus Christ, the Son of God, begotten of the Father, **only begotten**, that is, from the substance of the Father, God from God, light from light, true God from true God, **begotten not made**, of one substance with (**homoousion**) the Father, **through whom all things** came into being…who, because of us and **our salvation**, came down and became incarnate, **becoming man, suffered and rose again**…

This creed resolved that the Father is the creative source of everything outside of God. In addition, the Father eternally "begets" the only Son within God. This is not "making" but an act of generation of the Son by the Father, an eternal relationship between two members of the community of persons within the Trinity.

A new term, "of one substance" (*homoousion*), was used to emphasize that Jesus Christ as the Son of God belongs to the divine realm, and that within the divine unity there is a distinction and communion of persons. The phrase "through whom all things…" indicated that Jesus Christ, in receiving all from the Father, shares in the One God's creative power.

The focal point of the response, "…our salvation… becoming man, suffered and rose again," was that the true God is truly with us in the incarnation, suffering, death, and resurrection of Jesus Christ. This seemingly abstract definition and its (then) new terms were aimed at protecting the distinctiveness of the Christian sense of salvation.

Above: The first Council of Nicaea in 325 CE was the inaugural Ecumenical Council of the Christian Church. As well as formally rejecting Arianism, the Council adopted an early form of the Nicene Creed.

Left: A late fifteenth-century painting by an artist of the Novgorod School depicts Emperor Constantine I (reigned 306–337 CE) at the center of discussions during the first Council of Nicaea.

THE UNIQUE MYSTERY OF CHRIST

Above: The first Council of Ephesus in 431 CE was held at the Church of Mary, which now lies in ruins. The building was also called Church of the Councils.

Throughout these early centuries, the Word of God was preached, baptism administered, and the liturgy celebrated in the daily round of the Christian life. But in the intellectual culture of the day, new questions were being asked; and these had to be faced if the uniqueness of Christian revelation was to be preserved. The Council of Nicaea in 325 had clarified Trinitarian doctrine. But that gave rise to another consideration: If Christ were truly "one in being" with the Father, how can he be said to be "one in being" with us?

Different cultural contexts

Clearly, a new way of speaking was required to articulate the core message of the Christian faith. One difficulty was that different theological cultures were developing—not only between the Latin West and the Greek East, but also in the East itself, between the two great centers of Antioch and Alexandria. In general, Antioch tended to emphasize the humanity of Christ (which was somehow united to the divine Word) while Alexandria stressed the divinity of Christ (which somehow possessed and transformed his human nature). Moreover, while the Latin vocabulary for "person" and "nature" had been stable since the time of Tertullian, this was not the case in the Greek-speaking world: It took considerable efforts to give precise meaning to words like *hypostasis* ("person"), *prosopon* (also "person"), and *ousia* ("nature" or "substance"). Hence, confusion always threatened when words meaning "person" for some meant something like "nature" for others.

Two extreme positions

Within this context, two extreme positions emerged in the East. The first is attributed to Nestorius, a patriarch of Constantinople in the fifth century CE. Given his

Antiochene background, he stressed the human nature of Christ, both in body and in soul, so that the humanity of Christ is somewhat loosely connected to the divine Word. Nestorius argued strongly that we should not attribute to the divine Word what properly belongs to his human nature. For instance, he argued that Mary could not be said to be the *Theotokos*, "the Mother of God", but simply the mother of Christ in his humanity. The Council of Ephesus in 431 ruled that Mary could be termed the "Mother of God" because she was the mother of the person of the Word incarnate. This clarification opened the way to a deeper understanding of God-with-us in Christ.

In opposition to Nestorius' view, Cyril of Alexandria introduced the term "hypostatic union." It meant that there was a union of the two natures in the one person (*hypostasis*) of Christ. It aimed to maintain a sense of the unified identity of Christ, the incarnate divine Word who acts and suffers in a human way.

But then there was a wild exaggeration at the other end of the spectrum. Widely known as Monophysitism (= "one-nature-ism"), it is attributed to Archimandrite Eutyches of Antioch. This extreme view tended to see the human nature of Christ as somehow absorbed into his divine nature—like a drop of water in the ocean, or like molten iron in the fire. It gave the impression that the divine nature was somehow the soul of Christ's humanity, which left little room for his genuine humanness.

The Council of Chalcedon

The eventual definition of the 451 Council of Chalcedon threaded itself between these two extremes, and is exemplary in its balance. The Council is the pinnacle of a development that began with the *homoousios* or "one in being" of the Council of Nicaea in 325, and includes the *Theotokos* term of Ephesus in 431 [**bolding** indicates a correction to Nestorianism; and *italics* indicates the correction of Monophysitism]:

> ...**one and the same Son, our Lord Jesus Christ, the same** *perfect in divinity and perfect in humanity,* **the same** *truly God and truly man* composed of rational soul and body, **the same** *one in being with the Father as to the divinity, and one in being with us as to his humanity,* like unto us in all things except sin. **The same** *was begotten from the Father before the ages as to the divinity, and in the latter days, for us and our salvation, was born as to his humanity, from Mary,* the Virgin Mother of God.

The statement goes on to declare that the divine and human natures of Christ must not be confused or separated, so that "the character proper to each of the two natures is preserved as they come together in the one person."

Though these formulations appear very technical, the abiding significance of the Council of Chalcedon was to provide the Church with a way of speaking about the unique mystery of Christ, as God with us.

Above: Cyril of Alexandria (c. 375–444 CE) vehemently opposed any deviation from orthodox Christianity, and was supported by Pope Celestine I in his fight against the controversial ideas of Nestorius.

Left: Since the Council of Ephesus in 431 CE, Mary has been called the *Theotokos*, which is literally translated as "God-bearer" but is more commonly translated as the "Mother of God."

CLASSIC CREEDS

"The Nicene-Constantinopolitan Creed" (381), to give it its full name, is a classic statement of Christian faith. In its original Latin and Greek forms (despite the addition of the *filioque* or "and the Son" clause), what came to be known as the Nicene Creed has had a long history as a symbol of unity between the churches of the East and West, and is today the basis of a new era of Christian unity or "ecumenism."

Earlier forms

There were other and simpler creeds, usually employed in a baptismal setting. The one most known is the Apostles' Creed. But all creeds arise from the need for precision and brevity in articulating the core content of Christian teaching. For instance, as is clear in the New Testament, standardized "short formulae" were in existence from the earliest times. For example, Paul could say that he handed on what he had first received, "that Christ died for our sins in accordance with the scriptures, and that he was buried, and that he was raised on the third day..." (1 Corinthians 15:3–4). And another example:

Below: *Deposition of Christ* (c. 1800) by Antonio Canova features a neoclassical representation of the Holy Trinity. Theologians worked for centuries to define the mysteries of the Trinity.

He was revealed in flesh
vindicated in Spirit
seen by angels,
proclaimed among Gentiles,
believed in throughout the world,
taken up in glory (1 Timothy 3:16).

Such early formulations of faith were either sung or recited during times of worship or when new converts were instructed in the faith, even before the actual composition of the New Testament writings.

Shaping the Nicene Creed

However, the Nicene Creed took its final form only after several hundred years of theological reflection. It bears the mark of the clarifications of Christian doctrine that occurred in the early Councils of the Church, especially those of Nicaea (325) and Constantinople (381). The fact that this creed continues to be used sixteen centuries later,

Far left: Angels appear throughout the Bible and are most often seen as divine messengers from God, although in Hebrew the word for angel could refer to a celestial or mortal herald.

testifies to its enduring significance. Compared to other creeds, it is a comparatively complex and highly developed statement of Christian belief. Born of intense discussions over how best to formulate the mysteries of the Trinity and the Incarnation, it is not only a basic expression of Christian teaching, but also represents the considerable learning experience of the Church in those early centuries. Because this creed crystallizes agreement on key truths of faith, it comes down to us in the present as something like a resolution passed at the end of a long and difficult meeting.

Some key points

Let us note just a few points. As the creed begins by confessing "one God," it refers immediately to the Father, the source not only of creation, but of Trinitarian life. Moreover, belief in "the Father, the Almighty" demanded that the creed state, against the Gnostics (who were thought to demean the material world), that God was indeed the maker of everything, not just of spiritual reality.

Left: The Council of Nicaea held in 325 CE was convened by Emperor Constantine I. It sought to define and dismiss heretical theologies, and obtain a consensus on Christian beliefs.

Likewise, using the expressions of Nicaea, it had to assert against Arius (who had denied the divine status of Jesus Christ) that the Son of God was eternally "begotten, not made", and so "one in being" with the Father. Indeed, he is so one with the Father that he shares in the divine creative power: "through him all things were made". Yet the historical reality of his humanity is implied with the mention of two names: He is born of the Virgin *Mary*, and crucified under *Pontius Pilate*. After recalling the past events of Jesus' death and resurrection, the creed acknowledges that he now sits at the Father's right hand, and will come again in glory.

The third section of the creed acknowledges the full Trinitarian reality by affirming that the Holy Spirit is truly divine: "with the Father and the Son he is worshipped and glorified"—and, therefore, not just an impersonal creative or created force, as some tendencies regarded as heretical had suggested. But here there is contention. Where the original creed spoke of the Spirit "who proceeds from the Father", some centuries later in the Latin West, the phrase "...and the Son" was added. The Christian East resented this change in what had been a traditional sign of unity, and feared that it would undermine the sheer originality of the Spirit coming forth from the Father. The Latin West saw it as an advance, since it implied at least how the Holy Spirit was distinct from and related to the Son. Needless to say, theologians have long struggled to reconcile such different approaches so that this creed might continue to be a sign of unity in every respect.

DIFFERENCES THAT PERSISTED

The councils and creeds resulting from the theological ferment of the first centuries ultimately defined Christian belief for those in the Western and Byzantine churches. However, two important bodies of Christians in the East, the Nestorians and the Miaphysites/Monophysites, were not in full agreement with the Councils of Ephesus and Chalcedon. These Eastern churches became isolated from the Western and Byzantine churches, and were considered heretical. Nonetheless, they made important contributions to Christianity. The Nestorians (whose official name is the Church of the East) spread Christianity throughout Asia.

Below: Both Nestorians and Miaphysites/Monophysites continue to exist as distinctive Christian Churches today. These Ethiopian Orthodox Christians carry a portrait of the Virgin Mary and Child.

Church of the East

The theological position referred to as "Nestorian" held that Jesus had two distinct natures, one fully human and the other fully divine. In the early centuries, theological positions were often associated with geographic locations. The Church of the East accepted those who upheld the Nestorian position. The Nestorians were opposed by both the Church in Alexandria and by the Eastern Orthodox Church of the Byzantine Empire.

Nestorians reject the Orthodox doctrine of the *communicatio idiomatum* or "exchange of properties" where terms referring to Christ's humanity and his divinity could cross boundaries; for example, a term referring to Christ's humanity and his divinity (such as *Logos*) could be applied to his human nature, and vice versa. Modern opinion is divided as to how far Nestorian teachings are "heretical." Although he asserted two different natures and persons in Christ, Nestorius did affirm the oneness of Christ.

The excommunication of Nestorius, patriarch of Constantinople, at the Council of Ephesus in 431 dealt a mortal blow to Nestorian theology throughout the Byzantine realms. However, this form of theology not only survived but dominated in the geographic areas east of Byzantium. The Fourth General Synod of the Persian Church officially adopted Nestorian Christology in 486. Byzantine and Nestorian Christians were distanced not only geographically, but politically and culturally as well. Nestorians served in the Persian military against the Byzantine Christians when the two empires were at war. Whereas the Byzantine Empire used the Greek language, the Church of the East spoke Syriac.

Left: St Zeno (died c. 371 CE), the Bishop of Verona, performs an exorcism on the daughter of Emperor Gallienus. The practice of exorcism differs in Western and Eastern churches.

Nestorian theology was studied in various monastic institutions in northern Mesopotamia and spread along the Silk Road to Central Asia and other far-flung dioceses of the Church of the East, as far east as Chang'an, China's ancient capital. It was espoused in the debate between Timothy I, patriarch of the Church of the East, and the Abbasid Caliph Mahdi, that took place in 781–782 in Baghdad.

Today the Church of the East represents Christians in Iraq, Iran, Syria, and Malabar in India, as well as large diaspora communities in the USA and Australia.

Miaphysites/Monophysites

The Council of Chalcedon in 451 aimed to produce one indivisible, inseparable body of Christendom. The reality was precisely the opposite. Following the excommunication of Cyril of Alexandria, large swathes of Christians in Egypt, Syria, Armenia, and Georgia separated from the Byzantine Church to form what the Byzantines called Monophysite Churches (the churches prefer the label "Miaphysite"). These churches are also called non-Chalcedonian churches.

The Miaphysite/Monophysite communities in the Byzantine Empire were subject to pressure and competition from the Greek-speaking Orthodox Church and especially from Emperor Justinian, who was determined to have a unified church in his empire to ensure stability. Imperial agents hunted down members of the non-Chalcedonian clergy as enemies of the state and many were coerced, under pain of death, back into the Chalcedonian fold. Miaphysite/Monophysite bishops, including Severus of Antioch, were executed by Justinian. The untiring efforts of Jacob Baradaeus who galvanized the ailing Miaphysite/Monophysite Church and who received the secret support of Theodora, the wife of Justinian, ensured the survival of the Monophysite Church, which is sometimes referred to as the "Jacobite" Church.

Attempts were made to reach a compromise between the Chalcedonian and Miaphysite/Monophysite branches of Christendom, culminating in the Henoticon of Emperor Zeno, which was put forward in 482. It condemned the extreme positions taken by both Nestorius and Eutyches, receiving considerable support from both Miaphysite/Monophysite and Chalcedonian clergy alike, but failed because it was not countenanced by Rome. In a final bid at union, Heraclius produced in 624 the formula of "Monothelitism" that asserted two natures of Christ but only one mode of activity. However, it failed to gain the support of Sophronius, the patriarch of Jerusalem.

Today Miaphysite/Monophysite theology is represented by the Copts of Egypt, the Ethiopian Orthodox Church, the Armenians, and the Syrian Jacobites. The Ethiopian Orthodox Church is the largest of these churches, with between 40 and 45 million adherents. The Coptic Christians of Egypt, the largest Christian community in the Middle East, number between 8 and 18 million.

Above: Theodora, Emperor Justinian's wife, remained a Monophysite Christian despite her husband's Orthodox beliefs. She established a Monophysite monastery in Sykae, and often protected Monophysites accused of being heretics.

CHAPTER FOUR

THE FIRST CHRISTIANS

The Church in Jerusalem, led by James the brother of Jesus, was the first Christian congregation. Before the end of the first century, missionaries carried the Gospel to Damascus, Edessa, Asia Minor, Greece, Rome (the city), Egypt, Arabia, India, and Armenia. In the following centuries, churches were established in western North Africa, Ethiopia, Gaul, Spain, Britain, Ireland, Persia, Georgia, and among the Germanic tribes that invaded the Roman Empire.

Martyrs and monks—those who were willing to sacrifice all for Christ—were heroes. The death of a martyr was a public event in which the martyr, simply by refusing to renounce the faith, triumphed over his or her enemies. The martyr's death was seen as a victory, just as Jesus' death was portrayed in the New Testament as a victory rather than a defeat. Likewise, hermits and monks were viewed as victors over the world.

A growing Church needed a way to organize its worship, finances, charity, mission work, and instruction in the faith. Clergy—bishops, priests, and deacons—carried out liturgical and administrative functions. By the third century, they were distinguished from the rest of the congregants, who were called "laity." Bishops began to oversee entire regions rather than just individual churches. Metropolitans were appointed to significant cities, and the five principal sees of Christianity (Jerusalem, Antioch, Alexandria, Constantinople, and Rome) were recognized. The bishops of Rome issued their first claims to universal primacy in the fourth century.

Eastern and Western Christians both developed distinctive styles of Church architecture and their own unique liturgies. A Christian calendar emerged, commemorating events in the life of Jesus, the apostles, and the martyrs. The cult of Mary, the mother of Jesus, grew in popularity, culminating in the official designation of her as *Theotokos* (Mother of God) in 431 at the First Council of Ephesus.

Right: Following Jesus' crucifixion and resurrection, his disciples set out on missionary journeys in order to relate the story of his ministry and sacrifice for humanity to as many people as possible.

I·N·R·I·

JERUSALEM

When Jesus was born, Jerusalem was the capital of Judea. It was, at that time, ruled by the infamous vassal king, Herod the Great, as part of the Roman province of Syria. Herod rebuilt the Second Temple in an attempt to impress conservative Jews with his devotion, although the work was not completed until 62 CE. For Jesus, growing up in Galilee, Jerusalem was the "holy city" (Isaiah 52:1) and the center of the Jewish religious world, the place where God was uniquely present in the Temple.

Early Christian writings record that Jesus visited the city a number of times, but they also present his life as focused on meeting his destiny there. At Jerusalem he was crucified, near Jerusalem he ascended, and the Spirit came on the community, and here it was that the first preaching by the Church took place.

The Jerusalem Church

From the time of Jesus' death Jerusalem was an extremely important place, and his followers in the city multiplied. James, referred to in the New Testament as the brother of Jesus, led the Jerusalem Church for many years. According to the Jewish historian Josephus, James was widely known for his piety and strict observance of the law. Strict law observance would have made James an obvious choice for leadership of the Jerusalem Church because its members were Christians from Jewish backgrounds, many of whom undoubtedly continued to see themselves as Jewish. It appears that many of the Christians fled Jerusalem before Titus destroyed the city in 70 CE. By the time it was rebuilt as a major center, Judaism and Christianity had become distinctly separate religions.

Jerusalem as a symbol

To understand Jerusalem's symbolic power for the early Christian communities, we can look at the Gospel of Luke: Jesus' life begins (Luke 2:25) and ends there; the city links Jesus to his Jewish inheritance and is the place of his sacrifice. It is also the place from which the Gospel spread outward through surrounding areas to the ends of the earth (Acts 1:8) and which forms a link between all the churches (Acts 10:39). Jerusalem remains a holy site for Christian pilgrims, both as a place that is intimately linked with Jesus and as an important symbol in itself.

Below: The Madaba Map, a sixth-century CE Byzantine mosaic found in the Church of St George in Madaba, Jordan, features the oldest known cartographic representation of Jerusalem.

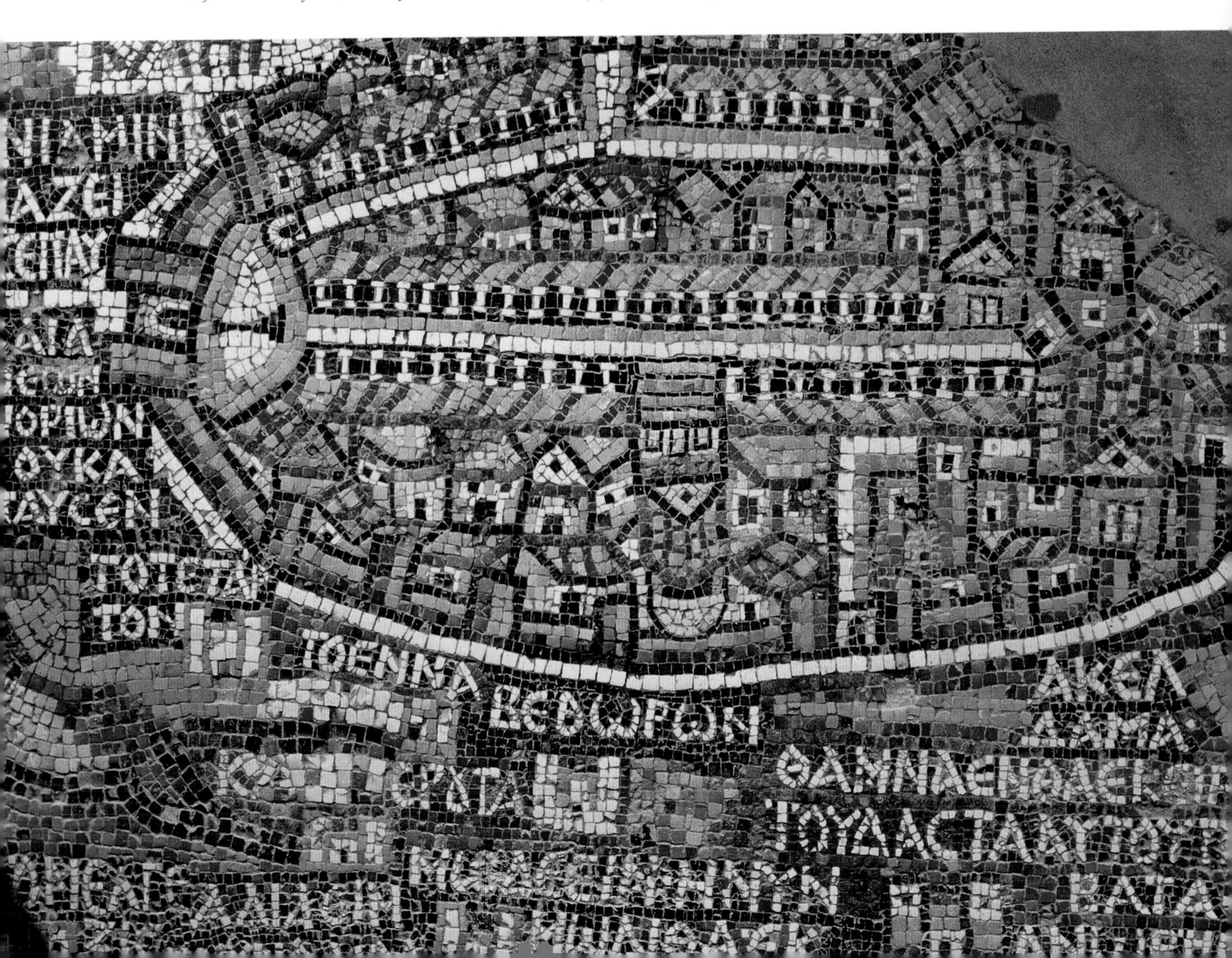

Left: In the fourth century CE, St Basil of Caesarea instructed anchorites to build a community at Göreme in modern-day Turkey. They hewed their buildings out of the region's soft volcanic rock.

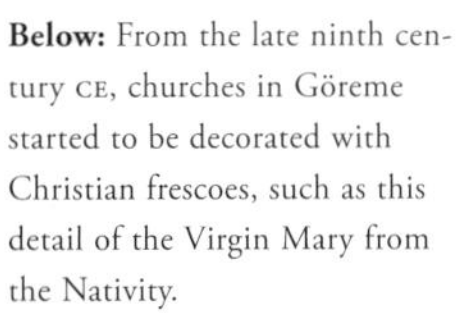

Below: From the late ninth century CE, churches in Göreme started to be decorated with Christian frescoes, such as this detail of the Virgin Mary from the Nativity.

ASIA MINOR AND GREECE

Christianity was born within the Hellenistic world, those regions surrounding the eastern Mediterranean, from Alexandria on the Nile, around through Syria, on through Asia Minor (roughly speaking, present-day Turkey) and into Europe (the lands we group as the Balkans). The Greek language and its urban culture made this area, once part of Alexander the Great's empire and now part of the Roman Empire, a single zone of easy commercial and cultural exchange. This in no small measure facilitated the growth of a small religious movement in Galilee into an empire-wide (literally, ecumenical) religion with pockets of adherents (called churches) found right across the region, with outlying pockets in Greek-speaking communities further afield.

A key part of Jesus' message was that the Father's love was to be made manifest to all humanity; from the very start his message, and the new Christian lifestyle, was being carried far and wide. Clearly this was easiest to accomplish in the Greek-speaking world, and the first stopping points of the missionaries were the Greek-speaking synagogues of Asia Minor and Greece. The significance of this move can be gauged by the fact that, despite Jesus having taught in Aramaic, all our early Christian documents (the letters, the discipleship guide called the *Didache*, and the Gospels) are written in Greek.

Paul's journeys

The most famous of the missionaries to the Greek world was Paul, a Hellenized Jew and Roman citizen from Tarsus in Asia Minor, who founded churches in Galatia (located in the central highlands of modern-day Anatolia in Turkey), along the western coast of Asia Minor, and in Greece, notably at Corinth. We have some of the letters he wrote to encourage and instruct these communities. By the late first century a whole network of churches in this region were communicating with each other, welcoming evangelists, and helping one another. We know their locations because Luke, writing in Acts, presented them as having all been founded by St Paul on three different journeys. Looking at the places Luke mentions shows how well established Christianity was in Greece and Asia Minor just fifty years after the Resurrection.

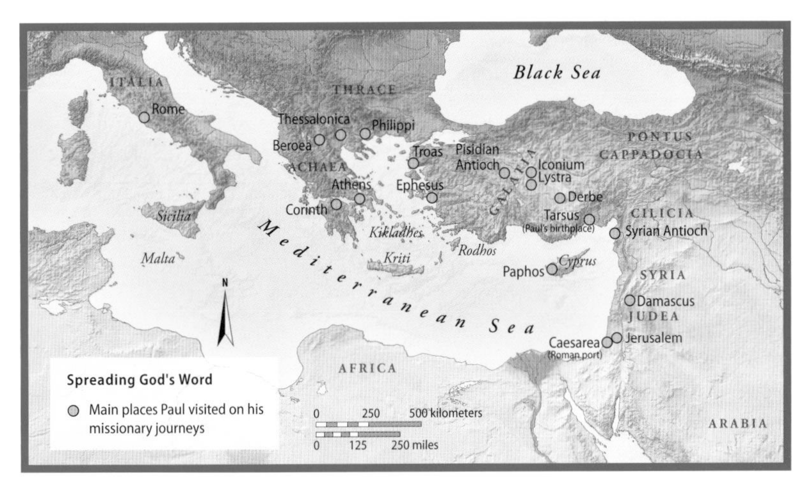

EGYPT

Above: Famed for its twin obelisks, which were transported to London and New York in the nineteenth century, Alexandria is also renowned as the heart of Egyptian Christianity.

The beginnings of Christianity in Egypt are shrouded in mystery, although most scholars believe that it probably arrived by the coastal route from Palestine. The Patriarchate of Alexandria—the nerve center of Egyptian Christianity—is one of the oldest and most venerable archbishoprics in the world. At the end of the second century CE the Coptic Church in Alexandria claimed that St Mark, the disciple of St Peter, had established it.

The type of Christianity that developed in Egypt was quite distinct, and has always been unique. Even today, the Coptic Church holds a Miaphysite/Monophysite position (believing that Christ's divinity and humanity are united in one nature without separation, confusion, or alteration). The Roman Catholic and Eastern Orthodox Churches considered the Copts to be Monophysites, a position that was formally condemned at the Council of Chalcedon in 451. The Egyptians were often the odd ones out at these Church councils, but they maintained their fierce independence and held to what they saw as the truth.

Independence of the Coptic Church

Egyptian Christianity's independence has a long history. Some of the earliest theologians, such as Clement (c. 150–215) and Origen (c. 185–254), came from Egypt, and a number of heretical movements grew up there, notably Gnosticism. In one of the major manuscript finds of the twentieth century, at Nag Hammadi in Upper Egypt, several Gnostic texts were uncovered. They focus on the evil world of matter and the need for secret knowledge (*gnosis*) for salvation. One of them, the Gospel of Thomas, contains a mix of Gnostic and non-Gnostic sayings, and is widely recognized as including a number of genuine sayings of Jesus not found in the Gospels of the New Testament.

Monasticism first arose in Egypt, with monks moving into the desert by the third century to follow an austere life devoted to prayer, poverty, chastity, and contemplation. At first they were hermits, but about 305 St Antony the Great emerged from the desert to establish the first simple community of monks on the Nile. Monastic communities had no private property and held all things in common.

NORTH AFRICA

T Africa was in many respects the powerhouse of the Christian Church in the first centuries. Some of the Church's greatest figures, such as Tertullian (c. 160–c. 222) and Augustine (354–430), came from North Africa.

Carthage, the major center in North Africa, was settled by those great sailors of antiquity, the Phoenicians from the cities of Tyre, Sidon, and Byblos in what is now Lebanon. Trading contacts along the North African coast were strong, so the first Christian missionaries would have arrived from Palestine and Syria by ship.

When Christianity arrived, it spread quickly, so quickly that by 200 CE Tertullian could write: "We are but of yesterday and we have filled all you have—cities, islands, forts, towns, assembly halls, even military camps, tribes, town councils, and palace, senate, and forum. We have left you nothing but the temples." Within a few years Christianity had spread across the whole of North Africa, which was at that time part of the Roman Empire, to Numidia and Mauretania (modern-day Algeria).

A dogma of austerity

The form of Christianity practiced in North Africa was austere. St Augustine is famous for presenting a view of Christianity in which sin was universal and inherited at birth, and believing that human beings could do no good without God. A little earlier, Tertullian had argued for Traducianism—the belief that one's soul was generated by one's parents rather than directly created by God, a belief that facilitated the concept of original sin. Tertullian eventually came to support the Montanists, a second-century breakaway group who believed the end of the world was nigh and that one needed to prepare with strict self-denial, a position labeled heretical by the Catholic Church.

A major issue for the North African churches in the early years was their response to persecution. They held that one should not flee persecution, buy indemnity, hand over the scriptures to the authorities, or be forgiven for lapsing. This explosive issue came to a head with the rigorous Donatists in the fourth century, who believed themselves, not the Catholic Church, to be the one true Church, the only Church whose sacraments were valid. Subjected to periodic persecution by the Catholics, the Donatists only disappeared with the Muslim conversions of the seventh and eighth centuries.

Above: As a student in Carthage, St Augustine lived a sinful life that he came to regret. He later returned to Carthage to teach rhetoric (the art of using language well).

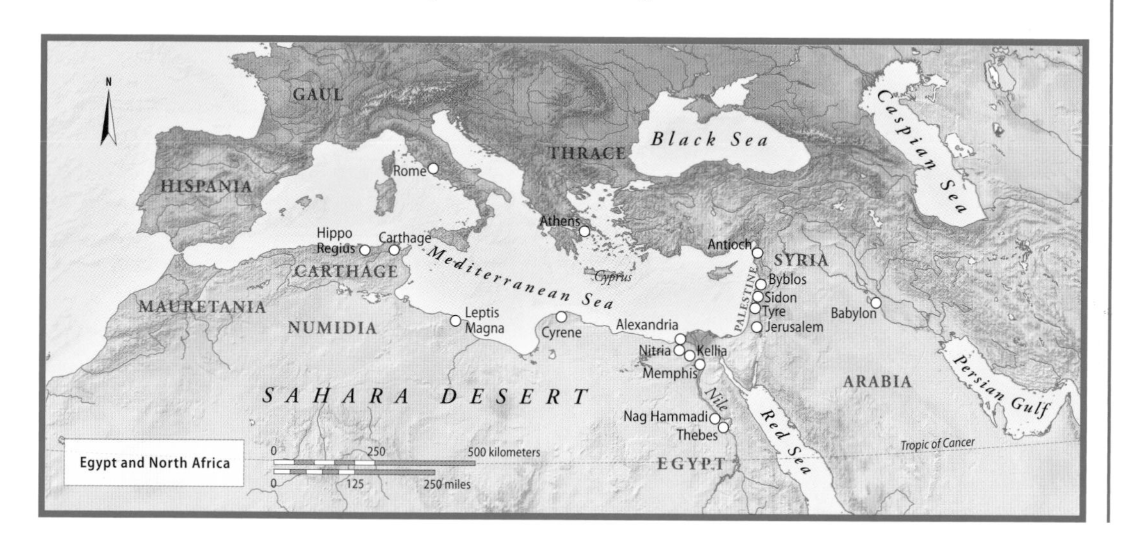

ETHIOPIA AND ERITREA

According to tradition, Christianity first reached Ethiopia through a royal official who is said to have been baptized by Philip the Evangelist (Acts 8:26–39). However, most scholars believe this story refers to the Nubian kingdom of Meroë, and date the Christianization of Ethiopia to the reign of Ezana, fourth-century CE ruler of the Ethiopian kingdom of Axum.

Historically, the Ethiopian Orthodox Church was intimately connected to the monarchy. The Emperor was the de facto head of the Church and often had a major role in determining Church policy, commissioning and even composing ecclesiastical literature, building and endowing churches. The political capital was an often important religious center. The first capital, Axum, was also the first sacred city, site of the important church of Maryam Seyon (Mary of Zion) and surrounded by several prestigious monasteries. Its successor, the twelfth-century highlands city of Lalibela, is famous for its rock-hewn churches, vivid expressions of an attempt to construct a symbolic replica of Jerusalem. Following an extended period during which the court was mobile, the seventeenth-century capital of Gondar became as well known for its churches as its royal palaces.

Self-governing status of the Church

From its establishment in the fourth century until 1959, the Ethiopian Orthodox Church was affiliated with the Egyptian (later Coptic) Church and led by a cleric appointed by the Patriarch of Alexandria. Following the liberation of Ethiopia from the Italian Fascist conquest (1936–1941), Emperor Haile Selassie I pursued a policy of achieving autocephalous status for the Church (meaning it could be governed by its own synod and appoint its own patriarchs). His success was greeted with joy in 1950, but local elected patriarchs have proved vulnerable to political upheaval. Changes of government in both 1974 and 1991 resulted in the replacement of reigning Church leaders.

Church and culture

Historically, the monastic clergy formed the vanguard of Ethiopian Christianity, with thousands of monasteries scattered through the country. These learned clerics were often active as missionaries, authors, artists, and teachers. Indeed, until the twentieth century virtually all education was carried out under Church auspices.

A striking aspect of the Ethiopian Church is its observance of a large number of practices that may be described as Biblical, Hebraic, or Jewish. These include abstinence from pork and pork products, circumcision of boys on the eighth day, and special observances of the Saturday Sabbath. The architecture of most Ethiopian churches mimics that of the Biblical Temple, with a tripartite division culminating in a "Holy of Holies" that holds an ark

Below: A seventeenth-century Ethiopian manuscript illustrates the ascension of Jesus' body to heaven following the Resurrection. It features the bright reds and yellows common to Ethiopian religious art.

(*tabot*) said to replicate the original Ark of the Covenant, brought to Ethiopia by Menelik, the son of King Solomon and the Queen of Sheba.

Throughout its history the sacred language of the Ethiopian Church has been Ge'ez, a Semitic language written in a distinctive syllabic script. Many of the religious texts written in Ge'ez, including the Bible, were translated from Greek and, from the thirteenth century onward, from Arabic. There are numerous original works by Ethiopian clergy, including hagiographic texts, hymns, poems, and royal chronicles, important sources for understanding the Church's veneration of foreign and local saints, the Blessed Virgin Mary, and other holy figures. Many of these works were composed to be read on Feast and fast days. Among the most important such occasions are Masqal (Feast of the Finding of the True Cross), Timqat (Epiphany), Fasika (Easter), and Ledat (Christmas).

The Ethiopian Church also made a crucial contribution to the development of the other expressive arts. Church buildings are among the most important architectural monuments, particularly in light of the rather limited extent of urbanization in Ethiopia. The visual arts, responsible for numerous murals, icons, and ceremonial crosses, were major vehicles for focusing the devotion of believers in a society in which most were illiterate.

The modern Ethiopian Church

The revolution of 1974 led to the disestablishment of the Church, as the Marxist military regime that held power

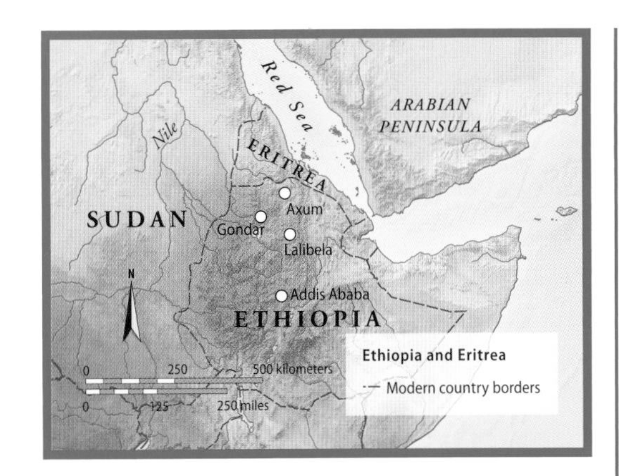

until 1991 sought to drastically curtail the role of religion. Active persecution of Orthodox Christians was comparatively rare after the first years of the revolution, but the Church lost its political clout and was deprived of its land as part of a broad policy of nationalizing land and urban property. It nevertheless developed grassroots support. The change of government in 1991 led to further disruptions when a new patriarch was chosen, his predecessor going into exile, claiming still to be the legitimate Church leader.

The province of Eritrea, which after a long struggle finally received independence in 1993, became the home of an independent Eritrean Orthodox Church. The more than one million Ethiopians who left their country in the twentieth-century diaspora have established dozens of churches in their new homelands.

Above: Ethiopia's Emperor Haile Selassie I, whose name means "Power of the Trinity," claimed to be descended from King Solomon and the Queen of Sheba. He was deposed in a 1974 military coup.

Left: The village inhabitants around Ethiopia's old capital, Lalibela, are almost all Ethiopian Orthodox, unlike other regions in Ethiopia that support non-Orthodox Christians as well as Sunni Muslims.

ROME, SPAIN, GAUL, AND BRITAIN

Above: This tapestry illustrates the struggle that took place between Christianity and paganism in Western Europe. The three figures to the right are ringing bells to frighten away evil spirits and pagan gods.

Christianity's rapid spread in Western Europe was facilitated by four important factors: The Roman Empire provided a political unity, fostering contact between cities; the Mediterranean acted like a highway in that travel to distant cities on its shores was easy; there were good roads (*viae*) between major cities; and there were many cities with existing Jewish communities, the first stopping points for those preaching "Jesus is the Christ." Christianity was an urban phenomenon: It spread from city to city, synagogue to synagogue, along the trading routes. Indeed, the countryside, the *pagus*, was seen as inimical to Christian community life, hence the later identification of non-Christians as *pagani*, "country people."

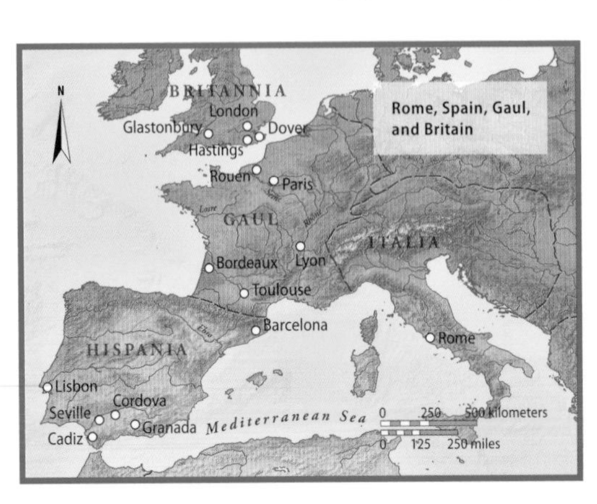

By 49 CE there were Christians in Rome among the Jewish community, and by the following decade, when Paul wrote to them, there were several churches; some of these churches were among the poor laboring classes. This Roman community drew together people from all over the empire and had easy contacts, likewise, with most places. By the first century's close it, like Jerusalem, was a focal center of Christianity. We have, from 96 CE, a letter from Bishop Clement of Rome urging the Corinthian church to continue its discipleship; we also have letters that Bishop Ignatius of Antioch wrote as he was brought as a prisoner to Rome to be executed in 110 CE: He asks the Christians of Rome to welcome him and support him with their prayers when he is martyred.

Christianity moves north and west of Rome

Paul had once thought of going to Spain, at the western end of the empire, to preach, but he never made the journey; exactly when Christianity actually arrived in Spain we do not know. It came first to Gaul in the Greek-speaking synagogues of the Rhone valley. By the later second century, the Bishop of Lyon, Irenaeus, tells us that there were many churches across Gaul, and that there were Christians in Spain and in Britain. This northwestern spread is confirmed by the fact that it was about this time that the first Christian documents appear in Latin, the normal language of the western part of the empire.

EDESSA, SYRIA, AND ARABIA

Edessa and Damascus were both important centers from which Christian missionaries departed. Missionaries from Edessa traveled east and evangelized many areas of eastern Mesopotamia and Persia. Missionaries from Damascus headed in all directions. Paul of Tarsus used the city as the starting point for a journey west.

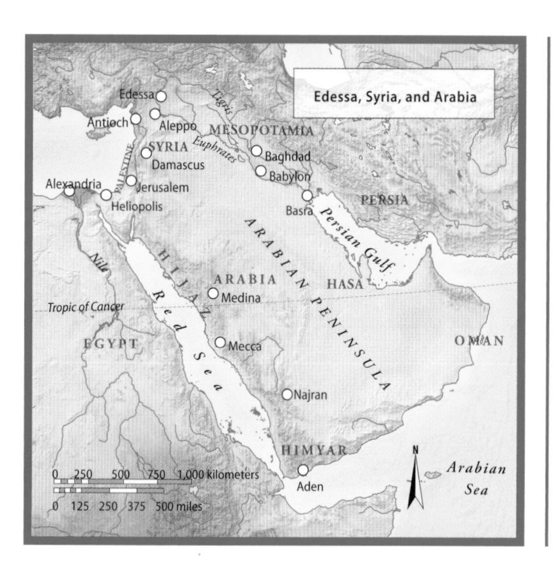

How did Edessa convert?

Legend clouds the conversion of Edessa, a Syriac town in northern Mesopotamia (modern-day southern Turkey), to Christianity. The best-known story comes from Eusebius' fourth-century *Ecclesiastical History*: King Abgar V Ukkama, who ruled Edessa between 9 and 46 CE, heard of Jesus' miraculous healings and not long before the crucifixion wrote to him, begging to be freed from a chronic illness. Knowing of the Jewish hostility toward Jesus, he offered his home as a safe dwelling place. Eusebius reports that Jesus replied, in his letter blessing the king but declining the invitation, promising that following his death and ascension a disciple would heal him.

Thaddaeus, one of the seventy disciples, is said to have been sent to Edessa where he healed King Abgar and soon converted him to Christianity. Other sources, however, confirm that the particular Abgar who embraced the Christian faith and under whom Christianity became the official religion was Abgar IX. By 190 CE Christianity was widespread in northern Mesopotamia, and Christian councils were held in Edessa as early as 197 CE.

Syria and Arabia

Syria also had a strong Christian following from the early years. The ministry of Paul following his dramatic conversion had a significant impact on the people of Damascus, which became a Christian stronghold and the starting point for Paul's second great missionary journey through Asia Minor and into Greece.

Paul of Tarsus and Bartholomew (one of the twelve apostles) both spent some time in Arabia. It is impossible to know whether they planted any Christian communities that survived, but it is clear there were Christian communities in both northern and southern Arabia by the third century. The northern communities, on the eastern border of the Roman Empire, may have been planted or nourished through commercial contacts. Southwestern Arabia, home of the Himyarite Kingdom, had commercial contacts with Alexandria, a city with many Christian inhabitants.

In the fifth century, several kings of Himyar converted to Judaism. A number of savage massacres took place as Jewish rulers called on Christians to abandon their faith and embrace Judaism. Eventually the whole of the Arabian Peninsula converted to Islam, though it is said that there are still some Christian communities in Najran where, according to Arab Muslim historian Ibn-Ishaq, Christianity first took root in Saudi Arabia.

Below: An eighth-century CE painting from St Catherine's Monastery on the Sinai Peninsula depicts King Abgar holding the Holy Mandylion or Image of Edessa, a cloth imprinted with the face of Jesus.

PERSIA AND INDIA

Acts 2:9 mentions the Parthians, Medes, and Mesopotamians among the witnesses to Pentecost. By the early third century CE Christianity was well established in Persia, with dioceses stretching from the Euphrates River to the Caspian Sea. Under the Sassanid Empire (226–651), Christians experienced alternating periods of toleration or persecution as suspected sympathizers with the Byzantine Empire. In 424 the Persian Church responded, declaring it would be governed by its own synod and appoint its own patriarchs.

Muslims came into contact with large Christian communities in Persia. During the eighth century, under the Abbasid caliphs, Syriac-speaking Christians were actively involved in the translation of Aristotelian philosophy from Greek into Arabic. After the Mongols sacked Baghdad in 1258, Christian communities were exposed to new ideas and cultures; under the Turko-Mongol rule of Tamerlane in the fourteenth century, they were reduced to an enclave in Kurdistan, near Urmia.

There are an estimated 300,000 Christians living in Iran today, who have representatives in the *majlis* (parliament): Two for the Armenians and one for the Assyrians.

Below: The National Shrine of St Thomas Basilica in Mylapore, south of Chennai (formerly called Madras), is reportedly built over the tomb of the apostle.

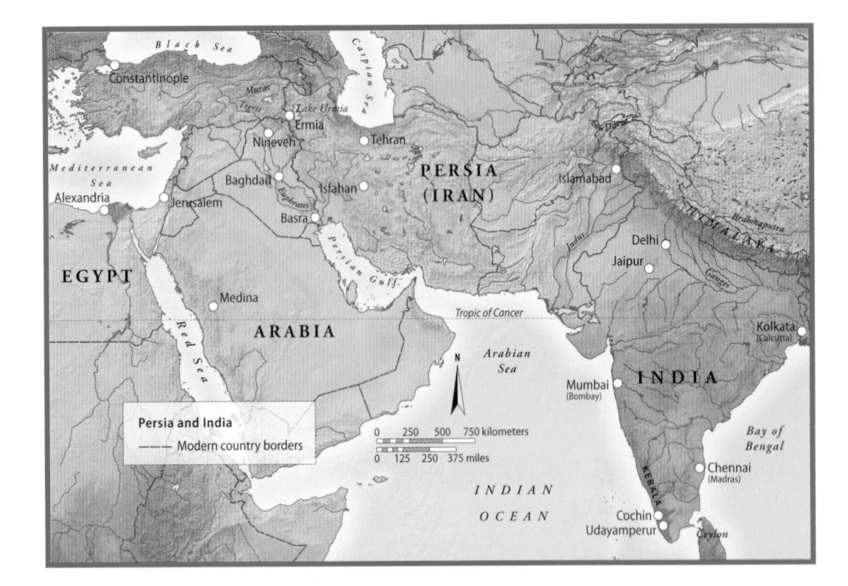

Thomas takes Christianity to India

Traditionally, the apostle Thomas introduced Christianity to India in 52 when he arrived in Kerala. He was martyred and Marco Polo visited his tomb, at Mylapore. Other early sources suggest that St Thomas came from Mesopotamia to build a palace for King Gondophares in the Punjab region. Some missionaries, including St Bartholomew, followed the spice route from Egypt. When Vasco da Gama arrived at the Malabar coast in 1498, he found well-established Christian communities that had adopted many Hindu customs, including abstinence from eating beef. During the sixteenth century, the Roman Catholic Church attempted to control the "heretical" Christians and at the 1599 Synod of Diamper (Udayamperur) demanded an unconditional surrender to the Holy See, burning the books and administrative records of the St Thomas Church. The Inquisition in India continued until the mid-sixteenth century.

Today Christians are largely concentrated in Kerala. Denominations include the Syro-Malabar Church (a Uniate Church), the Church of the East (the Metropolitan Mar Aphrem lives at Trichur), and the Malankara Orthodox, Syriac Orthodox, and Mar Thoma Syrian Churches. These churches all use Syriac in the liturgy, while Malayalam is the everyday language.

ARMENIA AND GEORGIA

Traditionally, St Thaddeus and St Bartholomew are the first "illuminators" of Armenia. St Bartholomew came to Armenia in 60 CE and was martyred eight years later. Tiridates III, who recovered his throne in 287, aided by Diocletian, persecuted Christians before he was converted. In 301, Armenia adopted Christianity as its official religion, and Gregory the "Illuminator" became its first patriarch. In 405, in a bid to bring the scriptures (previously written in either Greek or Syriac) to the populace, the Bible was translated into Armenian under the aegis of Mesrob, using the Armenian alphabet that had been specially created in about 387. The Armenians were not officially represented at the Council of Chalcedon (451) because they were being threatened by the Persian Empire. At the Second Council of Dvin in 551, the decisions of the Council of Chalcedon were officially rejected as being reminiscent of Nestorianism.

During the Ottoman Empire, Armenians were subjected to severe massacres between 1894 and 1923. Today, there is a large diaspora in the USA, as well as the community in Armenia with over 93 percent of the population belonging to the Armenian Orthodox Church.

St Nino's mission

According to a tradition that is no doubt embellished but appears to be based on a historical reality, Christianity was introduced to Georgia via a woman, St Nino. She first proselytized among the Jews who lived in Georgia, then cured the Georgian queen Nana. When King Miraim III was able to quell a storm by invoking Nino's God, he converted, as did his realm, in about 330. He built the cathedral of Svetitskhoveli at the ancient capital of Mtskheta. Georgian bishops met at the synod held at Seleucia in 419, but the country received its own patriarchate in the second half of the fifth century and a century later was ecclesiastically autonomous. Until the end of the sixth century, Christianity in Georgia moved hand in hand with Armenia, and a special alphabet was developed to write the scriptures. At the Third Council of Dvin in c. 608, the clash of the Patriarch of Georgia with his Armenian counterpart led to his excommunication. The Georgian Church was accepted back into the Chalcedonian fold where it remains today.

Above: The wedding at Cana, where Jesus "revealed his glory" by turning water into wine (John 2:1–11), is illustrated in this detail from a fourteenth-century Armenian manuscript.

GOTHS AND FRANKS

During the third century CE Germanic tribes, especially the Goths, had brought the Roman Empire to its knees. From then on they were always present, at times warlike and at times peaceful. Missionary work was slow to start, but when it did it went in an unexpected direction.

The great moment was the conversion of the Goths to Arian Christianity by Ulfilas (c. 311–383). Eventually condemned as a heretic, Arius (c. 260–336) had argued that Christ was second in status to God the Father, having been created by God and then made into the Son of God. Ulfilas' maternal grandparents had been carried off by the Goths in the third century, where he was then raised among them. He then turned up in Constantinople as a member of a Gothic commission. Here the emperor Constantius (317–361) happened to be Arian, as was his bishop, Eusebius. Under their powerful influence Ulfilas also became an Arian, and he was subsequently made a bishop in 341 CE. He was given a mission to work with the Goths in Moesia Secunda (modern Bulgaria), which he carried out with much energy—he produced the Gothic script, turned an oral language into a written one, and translated the Bible into Gothic.

The Goths became missionaries to other tribes, such as the Visigoths, Vandals, Sueves, Burgundians, Herals, and Ostrogoths. They all became Arian, which set them apart from Catholic Christians. It was an ethnic and religious marker: To be a barbarian invader meant being Arian; to be a Roman meant orthodoxy.

The Franks conquer Roman Gaul

Alone among these tribes, the Franks had converted to Catholic orthodoxy, especially at the direction of their leader, Clovis (c. 466–511). After his conversion in 506 CE he received the support of Catholic bishops and Roman officials and was able to conquer a large part of Roman Gaul. Renowned as a cruel and efficient ruler, Clovis defeated the Arian Visigoths in 507 CE and ensured their conversion to Catholicism. From then on the Visigoths in France and Spain, as well as the Burgundians and Sueves, slowly became Catholic.

But many remained Arian. By this time the Western Roman Empire was under barbarian control, with an Ostrogothic emperor based in Italy. Theodoric (c. 455–526) was Arian, but he tolerated during his long reign both Catholic and Arian Christianity. However, it was not to last, for Justinian (c. 483–565) from Constantinople eventually drove the Arian Goths out of Italy.

Right: Clovis I, King of the Franks, was baptized by St Remigius at Reims. His conversion was largely due to the influence of his wife, Clotilda, who was a Catholic.

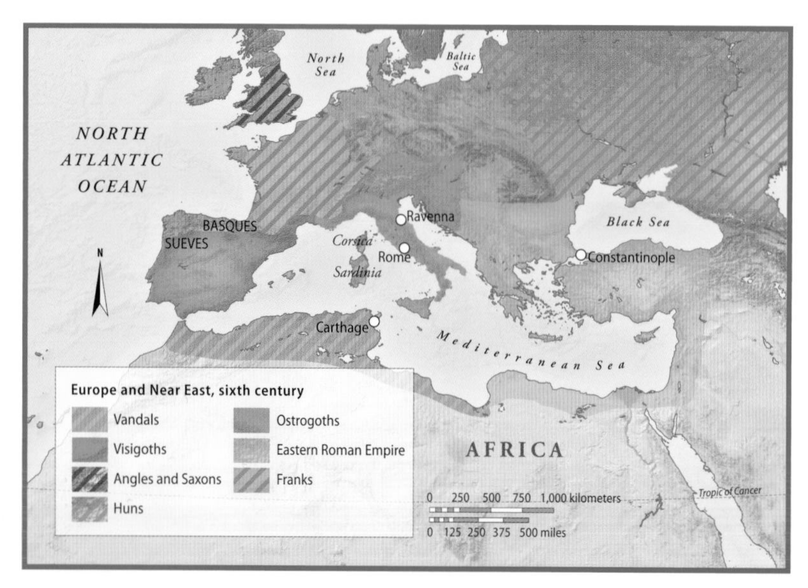

IRELAND

Ireland was never part of the Roman Empire, so Christianity arrived there by means other than those by which it spread through Gaul, Spain, and Britain. And in Ireland, for the first time in the West, Christianity was outside the Mediterranean/Roman matrix in which it originated.

The first Christians to come to Ireland were slaves captured from Britain, probably by those engaged in trade with Britain and the Continent. By 431 CE the Christian community was sufficiently large enough for Pope Celestine to send them a cleric named Palladius as their first bishop. No trace remains of his work in this foreign, nonurban land. But the early groups clearly were very successful, because by the middle of the sixth century there was a thriving Church with many monasteries, some of them even sending monks to parts of Europe now ruled by barbarian kings. Columbanus, for example, worked in eastern France, Switzerland, and finally Bobbio in Italy, just south of the Alps.

Ireland
Historic monastic sites
0 250 kilometers
0 125 miles
Shetland Islands
Orkney Islands
Outer Hebrides
NORTH ATLANTIC OCEAN
SCOTLAND
Iona
North Sea
Edinburgh
Belfast
Bangor
Lindisfarne
Newcastle
Armagh
Clonfert
Clonard
Clonmacnoise
Kells
Kildare
Irish Sea
Dublin
IRELAND
Glendalough
Cork
Ardmore
ENGLAND
N
WALES
Celtic Sea
Bristol
Isles of Scilly
Plymouth
London
Dover
Dunkirk
Calais
English Channel

St Patrick and Palladius

What happened in Ireland between these dates? We really do not know. All that has survived are two short documents by a bishop named Patrick, who was born in Britain. He certainly lived during this period: He came from a clerical family and was brought to Ireland as a captive aged sixteen, and later he preached where no-one else had yet preached. We know he fell out with the Christians around him over his doctrinal views, and that he condemned slave-traders who were Christians. Later, in the 680s, when the Irish wanted to write the history of those who converted the country, they had only two names, Palladius and Patrick, to work with, and only about Patrick did they have any records of preaching and baptizing. Since they needed a suitably great founder, Patrick was transformed into a great missionary who converted the country virtually single-handed and became the mighty saint of legend (Palladius was written out of the script). The work of those who presented Patrick as the great patron of Ireland was so successful that he became an icon of the country, and his feast day, March 17, a celebration of Irish identity.

Above: Legend states that St Patrick created the Celtic cross by overlaying the pagan circle symbol for the sun/moon with the Latin cross to show the pagans that Christianity had supplanted paganism.

Above: St Patrick has been credited with a number of deeds that are unlikely to have occurred, such as banishing snakes from Ireland and traveling with two ancient, mythical warriors.

MARTYRS

Right: Emperor Maximinus condemned St Catherine of Alexandria to the breaking wheel for her criticisms of his persecution of Christians, but the wheel broke at her touch. She was subsequently beheaded.

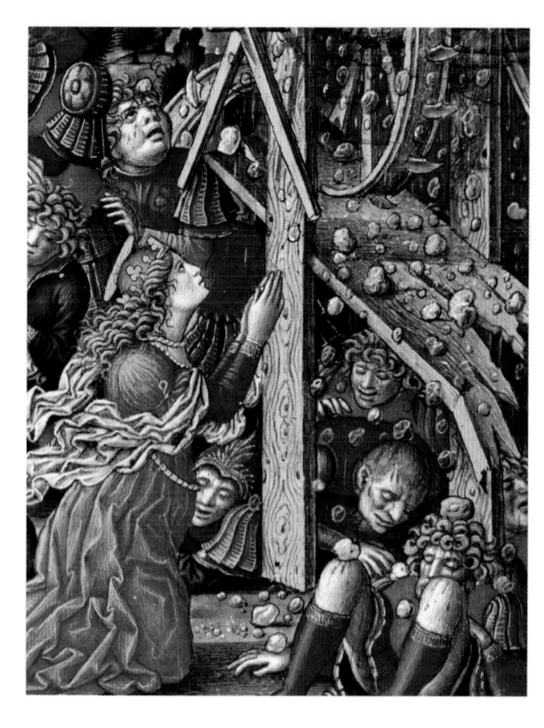

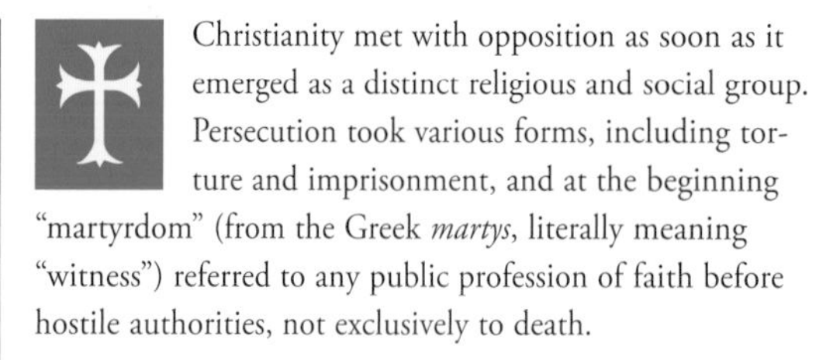

Christianity met with opposition as soon as it emerged as a distinct religious and social group. Persecution took various forms, including torture and imprisonment, and at the beginning "martyrdom" (from the Greek *martys*, literally meaning "witness") referred to any public profession of faith before hostile authorities, not exclusively to death.

The first martyrs

The first recorded executions of Christians (other than of Jesus himself) were those of Stephen, a leader among Hellenized Jews in Jerusalem, and of the apostle James. Although these earliest martyrdoms reflected tensions between Christians and (other) Jews, as well as with Roman authorities, in the centuries that followed martyrdom became primarily a symbol of the tension between the growing Church and the pagan empire.

The apostles Peter and Paul have traditionally been regarded as among the Christians massacred by Emperor Nero in an effort to shift blame for the great fire that partially destroyed Rome in 64 CE. Despite such specific outbreaks of institutional violence, there was no really systematic or ongoing large-scale violence against Christians in the first two centuries or so. Victims numbered in the dozens rather than thousands, and were often leaders like the aged bishop Polycarp of Smyrna (died c. 155), or converts like the respectable young mother Perpetua (died 203), whose visibility or symbolic importance made them attractive targets for authorities seeking to set an example and dissuade others.

These attacks were motivated by the religious exclusivity of the Christians. By refusing to take part in civic rituals with a pagan religious character, the Christians seemed to be antisocial, inviting misfortune on the community as a whole by not sharing in sacrifices. At a popular level, accusations of cannibalism, witchcraft, and perversion arose, which often occurs when a distinct ethnic or religious group is resented and its rituals are poorly understood. In some instances these popular suspicions spilled into mob violence, such as that connected with the martyrdoms at Lyon in 177 CE.

Only in the middle of the third century did a general threat emerge for the Christians in the Roman Empire, when Emperor Decius (who reigned from 249 to 251 CE) sought to impose universal observance of pagan sacrifice

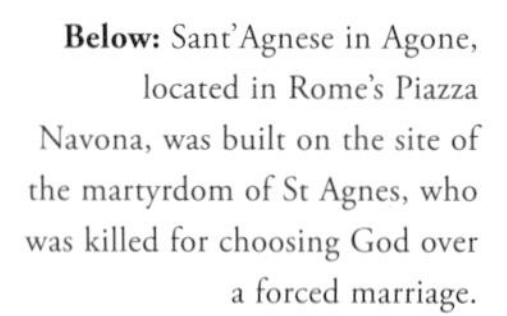

Below: Sant'Agnese in Agone, located in Rome's Piazza Navona, was built on the site of the martyrdom of St Agnes, who was killed for choosing God over a forced marriage.

Left: Not long after Jesus' crucifixion, St Stephen became the first Christian martyr. He was brought before the Sanhedrin, falsely accused and found guilty of blasphemy, then stoned to death.

for the safety of the empire. This new and more thorough imposition, which continued under Valerian between 253–260 CE, led not only to many martyrdoms, but also to apostasy and to divisions in the Church that would last for centuries. Victims of this decade included the Roman bishop Fabian and the African bishop and theologian Cyprian. In 303 CE the Emperor Diocletian launched the "Great Persecution," which led to the deaths of many hundreds of Christians, especially in the eastern part of the empire, whose stories have populated the calendar of saints ever since.

The accession of Constantine, a Christian convert, first as ruler in the West and then as sole emperor from 324 CE, saw the end of Christian martyrdom within the Roman Empire as such. However, the reversal of the relationship between the Church and the Roman state led to Christians outside the empire being viewed with a new suspicion—such as in Persia, where King Shapur II acted violently against the Christians in 341 CE—and thus to renewed opportunities for martyrdom.

Commemorating the martyrs

Although not huge in number, the ancient martyrs took on great importance for the life of the early Christian communities. While undergoing torture or imprisonment they were regarded as sources of supernatural power, already close to God even prior to death. Their examples served to inspire the many whose practice of Christianity may have been a risky but not fatal exercise. The parallel with Jesus himself was crucial to this understanding, since those who died were imitating their master and sharing his destiny.

The glory of martyrdom was attractive to some although frightening to others, for obvious reasons. Christian leaders and theologians ultimately advised following a middle path between excessive eagerness for martyrdom and cowardice or apostasy; however, choices were not always that clear. The church historian Eusebius of Caesarea records matter-of-factly the voluntary martyrdom of Christian women at Antioch whose chastity, as much as or more than their lives, was under threat from their persecutors.

The memories and examples of the martyrs were preserved in various ways. Narratives of their deaths were composed and read publicly, not unlike Biblical stories; their remains were preserved and venerated as precious relics, and the anniversaries of their deaths were celebrated as feasts. These are the origins of the cult of the saints as it has continued in Catholic and Orthodox Christianity; the martyrs were, in effect, the first saints.

Above: Refusing to worship idols and sacrifice animals for pagan gods during Emperor Diocletian's reign, St Dorothy was persecuted and then executed for her devotion to the one true God.

SOLITARIES AND CELIBATES

An ascetic form of Christian practice emerged in the fourth century in Palestine and Syria, and especially in Egypt. By venturing out into the desert, Christians were free from domestic, financial, and social obligations imposed by the empire, and also from the tithes, control, and increasing complexity of church life. In the desert, men and women were more nearly equal, and authority was granted to those who demonstrated wisdom and holiness, not to those who were priests, bishops, or theologians. Ultimately, however, desert Christianity was brought under the control of the bishops.

Celibate women, both widows and younger women who never married, played a role in Christianity from the beginning. By refusing to marry and have children, these women were rejecting the one social role available to women. Since the entire social order depended for its renewal on women who would bear and raise children, the threat to the established social order was plain. However, over time, virgins ceased to be symbols of the radical transformation of society, and became instead the symbol of perfect obedience to male authority. Although they were denied the ecclesiastic power of ordination, the charismatic power of their asceticism, holiness, and wisdom remained.

Communities of like-minded searchers for God gradually began to gather around reputedly holy men, such as St Antony, St Pachomius, and the great figures of the Desert Fathers—Abba Moses (St Moses the Ethiopian), Abba Lot (St Lot of Egypt), Abba Sisoes (St Sisoes the Great)—and women of the desert such as Amma Syncletica (St Syncletica of the Desert) and Amma Sarah (St Sarah of Egypt).

Below: During his time in the desert, St Antony was tempted from his spiritual path on several occasions by Satan, but he never strayed from his monastic life.

Influential monastic figures

Following the death of both of his parents, St Antony of Egypt (251–356) was inspired by the words of the gospel to leave all and follow Christ. After taking care of his younger sister's welfare, he lived the life of a hermit for many years, moving several times further and further into the desert as word of his holiness and wisdom spread and others came to seek his guidance. In his later years he became reconciled to the idea of guiding others and accepted those who came to him. His holy life and wisdom attracted many, both genuine disciples and curious visitors. The written account of his life by Athanasius influenced the spread of monastic life for generations.

St Pachomius of Egypt (c. 286–346) converted to Christianity as a young man, and he too lived as a hermit for some years before he heard the call to provide a religious life for many in a communal setting. He put his talents as an organizer and administrator to good use in setting up structures that provided community life for huge numbers of monks. His nine monasteries—seven for men, two for women—were like small towns, as they housed several thousand monks. The monasteries were divided into houses of thirty or forty monks who labored

WHAT IS A MONK?

Monasticism (from the Greek word *monachos*, "monk," which is derived from *monos*, "alone"), appeared in Egypt by the late third century. While it sometimes meant the equivalent of hermit or solitary, monasticism also referred to the monk's single-minded focus on God and the consequent marginality required in relation to the world, as well as the state of celibacy that has nearly always been linked to the monastic way for men and women. A monk lived alone in every sense, whether in an eremitical way or in a community.

Left: St Paul the Hermit escaped the Christian persecution being carried out by Emperor Decius by hiding in a mountain cave in the Theban desert until his death at 113 years of age.

Above: St Catherine of Alexandria was one of many women to devote their life to God. Her eloquent speeches on Christian piety induced many of her antagonists to convert to Christianity.

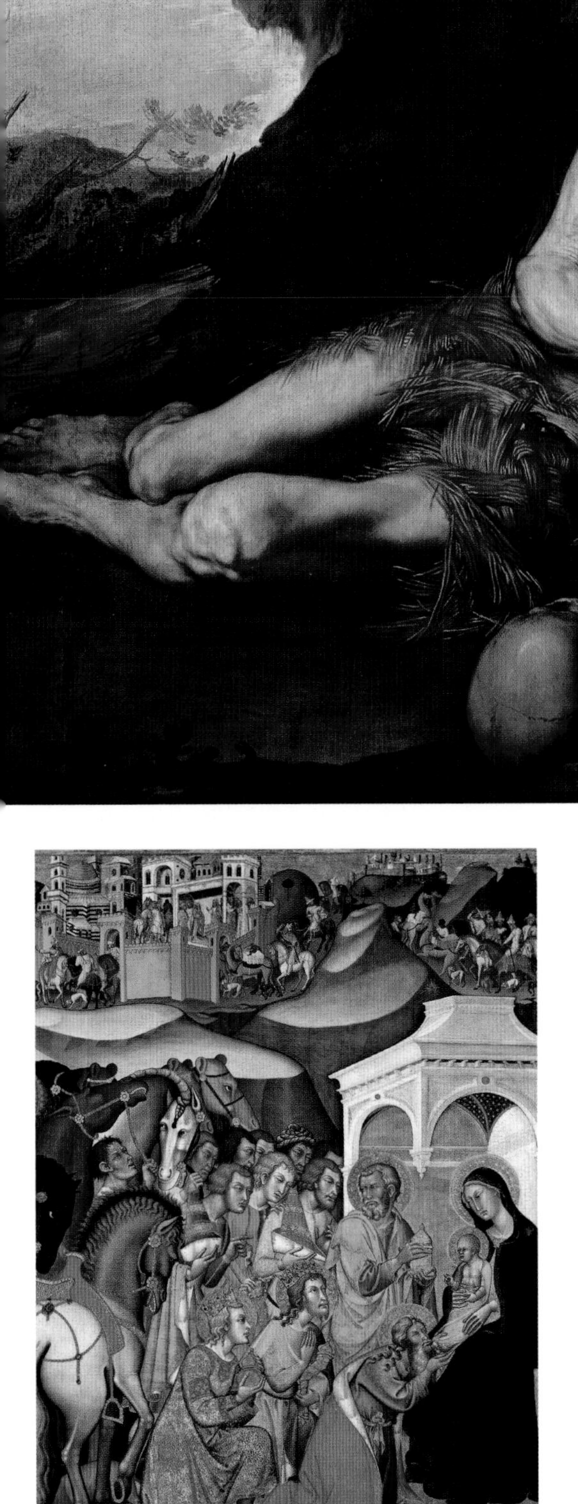

at their trades; the goods they produced were sold down the Nile in Alexandria to obtain funds and to help the poor. Religious life in Pachomian houses was hugely popular, and moderate in its demands.

St Shenout (St Shenouda the Archimandrite) (348?–453), both energetic and authoritarian, began a style of monastic life in reaction to Pachomius' more moderate approach. Characteristically, he demanded a solemn promise of obedience, and life in his monastery was austere and penitential.

St Jerome (c. 347–420) lived the monastic life in Syria and Bethlehem, and was responsible for monasteries of women, especially in Bethlehem. His writings, especially his *Life* of Paul the Hermit (St Paul of Thebes), helped to disseminate monastic ideals and practice, and his deep love of scripture and his translation work made further links between scripture and monastic life.

With St John Cassian (c. 360–435) we come to one of the major figures of early monastic life, largely responsible for bringing the spirituality of the deserts of the east to the Church in the west. About 415 he came to Marseilles and founded two monasteries, writing for them his *Institutes* and *Collationes*, which embody the fruits of his years in the desert. They became required reading for generations of monastics.

Left: Bethlehem, the holy city of Jesus' birth, was at the center of St Jerome's monasticism. One of his most important works, *De viris illustribus,* was written in Bethlehem in 392 CE.

CHURCH OFFICIALS

Above: Russian artist Ilya Repin's portrait depicts an ageing Orthodox Protodeacon. These particular deacons are married, and because of this they wear a burgundy skufia (soft, brimless cap).

Opposite: As bishops grew in importance within the Church, their clothing became more ornate. Most notable is the miter (liturgical headdress); the miter differs in shape and design in Eastern and Western churches.

Below: Fra Angelico's *Healing of the Deacon Justinian* depicts two saints, Damian and Cosmas, amputating Justinian's diseased leg and replacing it with the healthy leg of a dead Ethiopian man.

The first leaders of the Christian movement were authorized either by a personal connection with Jesus, or by an apparent inspiration directly from God. Of the first group, the traditions of many Eastern churches name one of the twelve apostles mentioned in the Gospels as their founder—for example Thomas in India, Philip in Ethiopia, Bartholomew in Arabia, and Thaddeus in Armenia. James, the brother of Jesus, seems to have led the Jerusalem Church on the basis of family ties. Paul the apostle is the most famous example of the other type—the "gentiles" or "nations"—who were considered not part of the Jesus movement initially but, after an intense religious experience, were endowed with a mission to the wider Roman world beyond Judaism.

The first leaders

Paul's letters attest to a further array of such charismatic leaders in the first generation or two of Christian history: Apostles, prophets, teachers, and others, who were regarded as divinely appointed to roles that were often itinerant. These roles played a vital part in establishing Christian communities around the Mediterranean world in the mid-first century; notably, each of these roles is focused on instruction or proclamation. Inspired speech featured prominently at Christian gatherings, originally held in the context of the communal meal (the Eucharist or Agape), as was typical for ancient associations or clubs.

The writings of Paul also refer to local leaders, with Greek titles such as *episkopos, presybteros*, and *diakonos*—words that literally mean "overseer," "elder," and "servant" or "steward" respectively, but which underlie the English words "bishop," "priest" (or "presbyter"), and "deacon." These titles suggest administrative functions rather than inspired teaching. There are parallels to such roles in Jewish synagogues and Greco-Roman associations. These local offices were to persist, while the more charismatic positions tended to disappear after a generation or two. Christian tradition has sometimes presented this change as a straightforward transition, with apostles "ordaining" or simply becoming the first bishops, but the reality was more complicated.

Although the terminology and tasks for these leaders varied in the first 50 years or so, *episkopoi* ("overseers") were individual leaders with executive authority, while the *presybteroi* ("elders") had more advisory roles and a collective mode of operating at first. The term *diakonos* was not restricted to servile or menial roles, and these "servants" had responsibility in areas such as finance, charitable works, and logistics. All were usually invested or ordained with prayer and other ritual, and had major roles in the formal leadership of Church gatherings, although other hosts and patrons featured too. Women certainly held both charismatic and institutional offices, with New Testament writings referring to women who were apostle, prophet, and deacon. Over time, however, men became increasingly likely to hold local offices exclusively, although one exception was a female version of the deacon's role, which later survived in Eastern but not Western Churches.

Evolution of the clergy

By the mid-second century, bishops (as we could now properly call them) had often become heads of the Christian community in a given city or region. There also continued to be different subgroups or communities associated with particular households or other meeting places, and monarchic governance did not emerge evenly or universally. Doctrinal, as well as other differences, led some Christians (such as those often called "Gnostics") to hold these authoritative structures at arm's length.

There were other leadership roles too. "Catechists," or instructors, had considerable importance in a movement still educating its own members and others about the meaning of the new faith. During and after times of persecution, "confessors" who had been imprisoned or tortured for their faith were regarded as a group like the presbyters, without the need for further authorization. Specific groups of women—virgins and widows—also had collective privileges and responsibilities. Further roles relating to worship and administration, such as readers and doorkeepers, began to emerge as defined functions and titles.

From around the third century bishops, presbyters, and deacons were seen as a distinct "clerical" group, or clergy, now distinguished from the *laos* or people of the Church generally (the "laity"). They began to be professionalized and salaried in some cases, and their offices were referred to as "orders," like those of the Roman equestrian and senatorial elites. When in the fourth century the Church was formally recognized, clergy sometimes received state support. By that time, the liturgical roles of these ordained persons were also well defined, with the bishop being the primary leader at most rituals, although presbyters could often preside at the Eucharist and some other assemblies. Deacons assisted them, and by tradition came to read from the Gospels to the congregation.

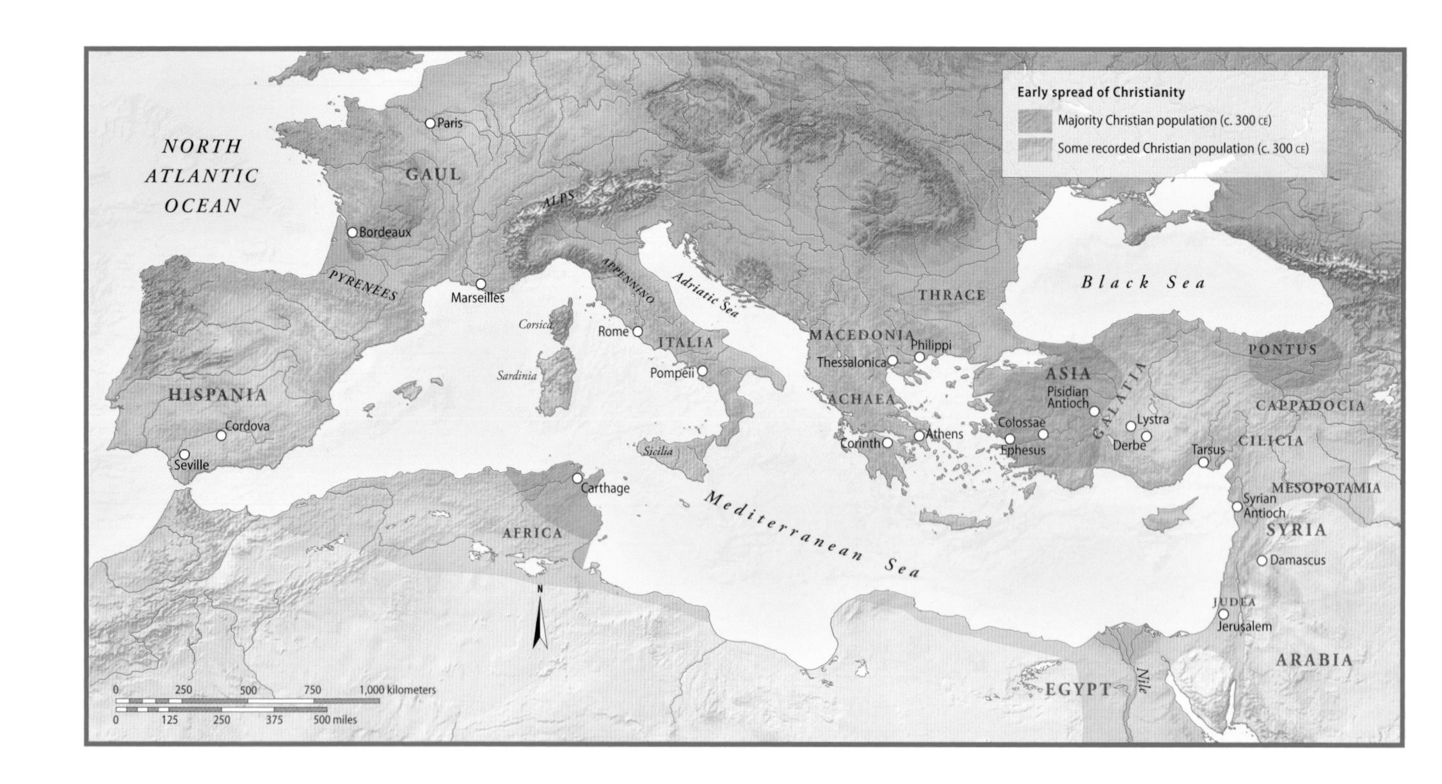

THE ROMAN EMPIRE PRE CONSTANTINE

Below: Pliny the Younger and his mother witnessed Mt Vesuvius erupt and bury Pompeii. Years later, as imperial governor (*legatus Augusti*) of Bithynia, Pliny ordered the execution of some Christians.

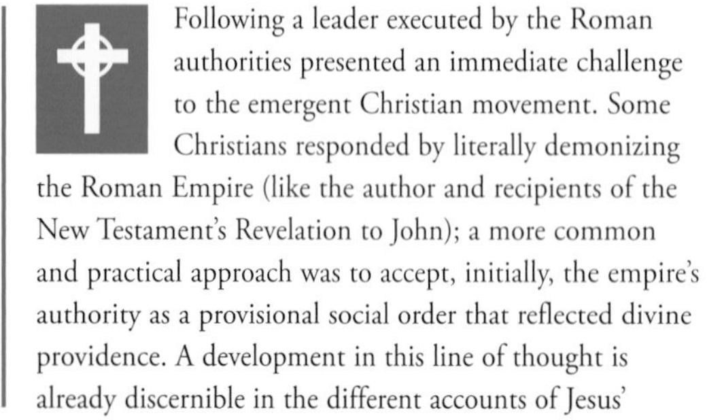

Following a leader executed by the Roman authorities presented an immediate challenge to the emergent Christian movement. Some Christians responded by literally demonizing the Roman Empire (like the author and recipients of the New Testament's Revelation to John); a more common and practical approach was to accept, initially, the empire's authority as a provisional social order that reflected divine providence. A development in this line of thought is already discernible in the different accounts of Jesus' trial: While the earliest Gospel version (Mark) allows the Roman governor Pontius Pilate to appear an indifferent tyrant, a later version (John) presents him as a sort of tragic philosopher, manipulated by Jews and onto whom responsibility for Jesus' crucifixion was increasingly shifted.

Spreading the Christian message

The *Pax Romana*, a period of peace and stability under Roman Imperial rule that characterized these formative first and second centuries, furnished a uniquely favorable environment for the missionary expansion of Christianity. The infrastructure necessary for upholding military networks, provincial administration, and commerce provided the means by which Christians could travel across land (utilizing road networks, canals, and bridges) and the Mediterranean Sea. Paul's letters reflect a pragmatic and even positive attitude to the benefits that this order afforded; his own claim of Roman citizenship (Acts 22) is a reminder that there were particular privileges extended to an elite group across this political and geographical structure.

Expansion of the Christian message was further aided by social networks of patronage and the support of some aristocratic converts. Adapting pagan practices, aristocratic Christian patrons in urban and rural settings provided meeting places and other forms of support for worshipping communities. Some powerful landowners erected purpose-built structures for liturgical use. In more private settings they continued, like their pagan contemporaries and predecessors, to build *mausolea* and domestic shrines, decorating them and household objects with Christian images.

Persecution of Christians

While Greco-Roman culture was relatively tolerant of new religious movements and cults, it expected them to leave room for the worship of traditional gods and the observance of religious rituals with civic significance. Sharing the absolute refusal of Judaism to countenance idol worship, Christianity clashed directly with this expectation. Whereas Judaism was largely tolerated, being an ancient (if idiosyncratic) religion and ethnically limited in the scope of its practice, Christianity was both novel and expansionist, and so was perceived as an intrinsically destabilizing influence within the empire.

Initially, persecution of Christians was sporadic rather than systematic. One revealing example is found in the correspondence between the Emperor Trajan and writer and statesman Pliny the Younger. While governor of Bithynia in Asia Minor from 111–113 CE, Pliny took action against the Christians, but was not encouraged to be particularly active or extreme. Later, general persecutions, such as those of Decius in 250 CE and Diocletian in 303 CE, were provoked by the success Christianity had in adapting to the conditions of the empire.

In response, a genre of Christian writing arose seeking to explain the practice and belief of the Church to the empire; issues of controversy were addressed theologically by "apologies" or defenses. Justin Martyr, writing in the mid-second century, addressed his work to Emperor Antoninus Pius, claiming the common ground of philosophy as a basis for understanding. Various apologetic writers attacked pagan religion, while also seeking to interpret Christian piety and virtue as natural and proper to Roman sensibilities. Against them, pagan Roman intellectuals like Celsus accused the Christians of appealing only to the so-called dregs of Roman society like slaves, unskilled workers, women, and children.

The tension between pagans and Christians was further sharpened with the rise of the Imperial cult, which often became a specific touchstone of conflict and persecution. While the conversion of the Emperor Constantine was a radical reversal of religious policy, the Church and the empire had both been changing in ways that made their eventual alliance relatively easy and logical. The Christians had grown greatly in number and had adopted ritual and organizational trappings in keeping with Roman society. The empire had been seeking for some time a unifying religion and ritual, through means such as the Imperial cult and monotheistic sun-god worship. Constantine's adherence to and tolerance of the Christians became the necessary link to allow these institutions to finally move from rivalry to alliance.

Above: The reign of Roman Emperor Antoninus Pius was a period of relative peace for the Christians, with very few suffering persecution and death for their beliefs.

Below: Before Constantine's conversion to Christianity, Romans throughout the empire maintained a polytheistic religion. Offerings were made to the gods to ensure their continued benevolence.

THE EMERGING PATRIARCHATE

The title "patriarch" only dates from the sixth century; it denotes the bishops of the five principal sees of Christendom: Alexandria, Antioch, Jerusalem, Rome, and Constantinople. Patriarchal jurisdiction was not confined to urban areas, but extended over adjoining regions, thus the bishop of Antioch included much of Asia Minor under his jurisdiction. Duties included ordaining metropolitans (bishops who have been given provincial powers) to principal sees, overseeing appeals, and making other judgments.

The first patriarchates

Rome laid a double claim to apostolic authority in the persons of St Peter and St Paul, the former reaching Rome in 42 CE. By 58 CE, a large Christian community already existed in the city. The period between the middle of the fourth century and the end of the fifth century saw a steady growth in the authority of the bishops of Rome as was recognized by the canons of the Council of Ephesus in 431 (later called the Third Ecumenical Council) and the Council of Chalcedon in 451 (later called the Fourth Ecumenical Council). During the eighth century, Rome's burgeoning authority and its increasing claim to primacy led to strained relations with Constantinople, which culminated over the interpolation of the *filioque* ("and the Son") clause into the Nicene Creed in the Latin West. Matters came to a head in 1054 and, despite a number of attempts to restore relations with Constantinople, the position of Rome was endorsed at the Council of Ferrara-Florence (1438–1445). In 1453, when Constantinople fell to the Ottomans, Rome remained the sole patriarchate that was not under Muslim dominion.

Alexandria was ranked second to Rome in the Roman Empire. Tradition ascribes St Mark as the apostolic founder, but the city's importance peaked in the fourth and fifth centuries, principally through the activities of its bishops—Athanasius, who was instrumental in combating the Arian

Below: Constantine the Great decided to make the ancient city of Byzantium his capital; he renamed it Constantinople. The city is now called Istanbul, and is in modern-day Turkey.

heresy, and Cyril, who secured Nestorius' excommunication. While the Council of Nicaea in 325 (later called the First Ecumenical Council) endorsed Alexandria's position, this was seriously damaged by the Council of Chalcedon since a sizable majority of the city's population espoused Miaphysite/Monophysite theology. Division between the

THE PATRIARCHATE OF SELEUCIA-CTESIPHON

In the territories of the Zoroastrian Sassanid Empire in Mesopotamia (modern-day Iraq), in what might be considered a shrewd political gesture, the Church, in 424, declared itself autocephalous of the pentarchy. Thus it established a patriarchate in the capital Seleucia-Ctesiphon that was independent of Byzantine influence. This patriarchate survives today as part of the Church of the East.

Chalcedonians and Miaphysites/Monophysites continued until the coming of the Arabs in 642, when the city passed from Byzantine control into Muslim hands, and effectively sealed its Miaphysite/Monophysite affiliation. Alexandria's standing was further debased in the tenth century when the Venetians pillaged the relics of St Mark and transferred them to their city. Today, the pope of the Coptic Orthodox Church is called the Patriarch of Alexandria.

Later patriarchates

At Antioch, c. 64 CE (the third-largest city in the Roman Empire), the disciples of Christ were first called "Christian." The city's claim to apostolic authority rests with the tradition that St Peter was the first bishop. Historical origins can be traced to the second century, with St Ignatius, whose letters still survive. By the fourth century, the bishop of Antioch was ranked third in authority after Rome and Alexandria, but the city's authority began to wane in the fifth century following the councils of Ephesus and Chalcedon. This process was exacerbated by the Islamic conquest of Syria that saw the city fall into Muslim hands. Today the Syrian Orthodox patriarch includes Antioch in his title, but lives in Damascus.

In 381, the Council of Constantinople recognized the new imperial city as second in authority, after Rome. Patriarchal status was conferred on Constantinople at the Council of Chalcedon. Canon 27 stated, "that the city which was honored with the sovereignty and the Senate, and which enjoyed equal privileges with the elder royal Rome should also be magnified like her, in ecclesiastical matters and be second after her." In doing so, the sixth canon of the Council of Nicaea, which insisted on "the preservation of the rights and privileges of the bishops of Alexandria, Antioch, and other provinces," was overturned. Constantinople's patriarchal authority was intertwined with the Byzantine Empire and over the centuries began to wane. The ecumenical patriarch of the Greek Orthodox Church still resides in Constantinople today.

The see of Jerusalem only assumed importance in the early fourth century following the visit of Helena, the mother of Constantine, in 326. Until the fifth century, Jerusalem was subordinate to the bishopric of Caesarea—this situation being due to the political turmoil in the first and second centuries. The Council of Chalcedon granted Jerusalem patriarchal status, but despite being the birthplace of Christianity, the city never rivaled the prestige and authority of Rome, Alexandria, and Antioch, all of which were Roman imperial cities. During the Frankish occupation of Jerusalem in the twelfth century, the Orthodox patriarch resided in Constantinople.

Left: In the fifth century CE, a priest named Lucian had a vision of the location of the lost tomb of St Stephen, and revealed it to the Patriarch of Jerusalem.

Above: Helena, the mother of Constantine the Great, reportedly found the cross on which Jesus was crucified, and instructed that the Church of the Holy Sepulchre be erected on the site.

BISHOP OF ROME

In Rome, unlike in other Christian cities, a single bishop emerged only in the later second century CE. The first claim to the primacy of the chair (*cathedra*) of Peter, popularly believed to have been martyred in Rome with Paul around 64 CE under Nero, was made by Bishop Stephen in the mid-third century, and was stoutly rejected by other bishops. Later that century, appeals were made from abroad to the bishop of Rome on matters of correct doctrine, but it was the conversion of Emperor Constantine (306–337) in 312, and his subsequent legalizing and favoring of Christianity, that began the transformation of the status of the bishop of Rome to head of the Church. Constantine built and endowed the Lateran basilica (St Giovanni in Laterano) for Bishop Miltiades (312–314). Constantine's choice of Miltiades to preside over a council in Rome intended to settle a doctrinal schism with the African Church was a failure, but the choice of bishop and city set a significant precedent.

In the latter part of the eighth century, the *Donation of Constantine* falsely associated Miltiades' successor, Silvester I (314–335), with Constantine's baptism and his construction of St Peter's and St Paul's, and, most famously, with Constantine's supposed donation of lands, ecclesiastical primacy, and jurisdiction to the bishop of Rome.

The rise of Roman claims to primacy

The forceful Julius I (337–352) was in fact responsible for the construction of St Peter's and St Paul's over the traditional site of the saints' remains. It was he who insisted, in the case of a dispute involving the bishop of Alexandria, that appeal should first have been made to Rome, the See of Peter. Damasus I (366–384), the first to refer to Rome as the "apostolic see," in 378 persuaded the emperors of the Eastern and Western empires to make Rome the ecclesiastical court of first appeal, to exclude the bishop of Rome from secular justice, and in so doing consolidated Rome's claims to primacy.

Below: Francesco Solimena's painting depicts Leo the Great meeting Attila the Hun. As well as Leo's persuasive arguments, a payment of gold may have encouraged the Huns not to attack Rome.

Julius' successor, Siricius (384–399), was the first bishop of Rome to issue decretals, directives in the style of imperial edicts and having the force of law, which, in the name of Peter, answered a series of questions about heresy, Church order, and discipline.

Innocent I (401–417), sometimes called the first pope, further consolidated the claims of Roman primacy in religious and political terms, issuing decretals on a range of disciplinary and liturgical matters that required that the Roman custom be the norm, intervening in Eastern theological disputes and seeking to keep the Balkans within his sphere of influence. When the African Churches appealed to him over the heresy of the British ascetic, Pelagius, Innocent referred to the "ancient tradition" that bishops everywhere should submit disputed matters of faith to the See of Peter, thereby fully enunciating the principle of Rome's supreme teaching authority. Innocent's seeking of a truce in the face of the onslaught of Alaric and his Goths, which led to the fall of Rome in 410, although unsuccessful, reflected the growing political influence of the papacy.

From Leo to Gregory the Great

Leo I, also known as Leo the Great (440–461), was deeply involved in both religious and political disputes. He was a

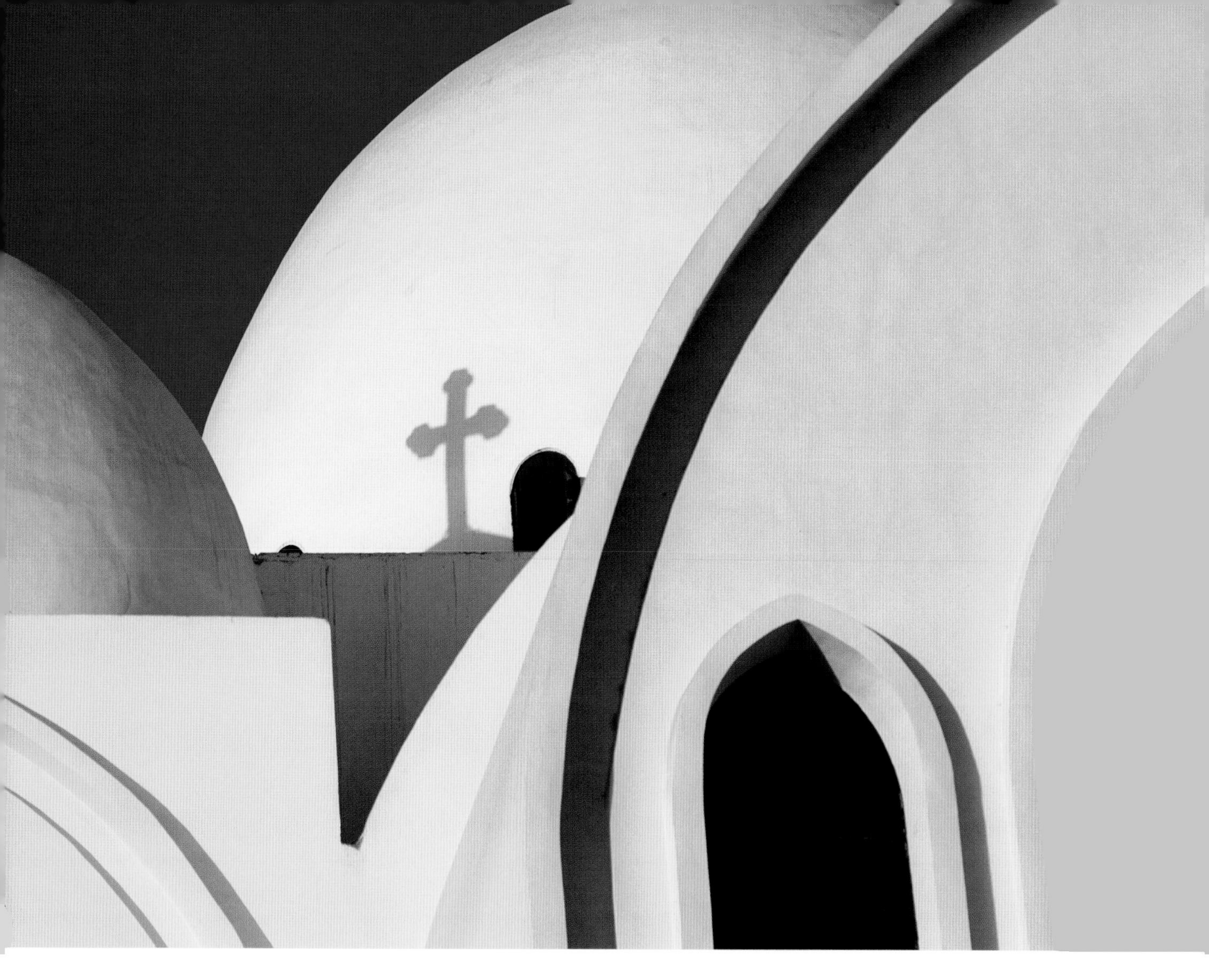

particularly forceful upholder of the primacy and universal authority of Peter, and he kept firm control of the Western bishops by correcting abuses and insisting on uniformity of practice. When called on for help by Archbishop Flavian of Constantinople, he issued a famous *Tome* (Letter) setting out the Western view of Christ's two natures as enshrined in the classic *Definition* of the fourth Ecumenical Council (Chalcedon, 451). The growing political authority of the papacy was exemplified in 452 by Leo's ability to persuade the infamous Attila the Hun, whose forces were ravaging north Italy, to withdraw, and in 455 by his success in dissuading the Vandal Gaiseric from setting fire to Rome and massacring its inhabitants.

Another notable fifth-century pope, Gelasius (492–496), was responsible for the later extremely influential theory of the two powers—the (superior) spiritual power of the pope and the (inferior) temporal power of the emperor. Early papal claims to power culminate with Gregory the Great (590–604), "the servant of the servants of God," who laid the foundations of the later papal state and acted as virtual civil ruler of Italy, coping with Lombard incursions while establishing effective oversight of the Western Church, evangelizing England, and maintaining claims to papal supremacy in the East.

Above: The simple white domes of the Coptic Orthodox Cathedral in Aswan, Egypt, are dazzling against the cloudless blue sky. From early times, bishops of Rome influenced the doctrines of the African Church.

Left: In the Eastern Orthodox Church, Gregory the Great is called Gregory the Dialogist because of his beloved writings on the life of the saints of Italy entitled *Dialogues*.

PATRIARCH AND EMPEROR

When Constantine pronounced his policy of religious freedom (the "Edict of Milan") in 313 CE and established Constantinople as his empire's capital city in 330, Christians now received patronage and protection instead of persecution and execution. Constantine took an active interest in Christianity and personally convened the Council of Nicaea (later called the First Ecumenical Council), but the intertwining of Church and state had created new problems. By the late fourth century, the Church had acquired great wealth, and ecclesiastical office had become an attractive public career attendant with power, influence, riches, and patronage. This was a far cry from the days of persecution and asceticism of a hundred years earlier.

Below: During his mid-twenties John Chrysostom lived the stark life of a hermit for two years in order to devote himself to studying and memorizing the Bible.

Patriarchs and the Byzantium court

The particular issues generated by wealth, and the profligacy of the Byzantine court and the decline in the moral standards of a society, came to a head in the person of John Chrysostom (347–407). In 398, against his wishes, he was brought out of monastic obscurity and made Patriarch of Constantinople. With a great concern for social justice, he immediately embarked on a campaign to reform a city that, in his opinion, had become complacent and corrupt. Chrysostom was a gifted and popular orator, earning him the nickname "golden-mouthed," but his sermons encountered the ire of Empress Eudoxia who interpreted his comments as personal criticism. The patriarch was removed from his see. Although he was soon restored, once again his enemies secured his banishment on the charge of unlawfully reassuming the duties from which he had been canonically deposed in 404. Despite his popularity among the people of Constantinople and the support of Pope Innocent I and the Western Church, Chrysostom was exiled first to Antioch, then to Pontus. Although he died impoverished, his patriarchy highlighted social issues in the Byzantine Empire.

Photius (c. 810–c. 895) was still a layman when he was elected as Patriarch of Constantinople in 858, following Emperor Michael III's deposition of the patriarch Ignatius. When Ignatius refused to relinquish his post, Photius and the emperor sent an embassy to Pope Nicholas I asking for the dispute of the two rival "patriarchs" to be decided by a synod. The pope's legates deposed Ignatius in 861, but two years later, at the synod of Rome, Nicholas I annulled the decision on the grounds of interference at Constantinople and proclaimed Ignatius once more as the patriarch. In 865 the emperor wrote to Nicholas I who promised to reopen the case; however, only the death of Ignatius in 877 led to Photius once more assuming the patriarchal office, this being supported by imperial decree. The papal legates approved Photius at a council held in Constantinople in 879–880, annulling the decision of the council of 869–870 in which he had been denounced. Photius resigned his see in 886, faced with internal opposition and the accession of Emperor Leo VI. His controversial career accentuated the conflict between the Roman claim to be the prime center for Christianity and the Greek conception of the five equal patriarchates, contributing to the deteriorating relations between Rome and the Byzantine Empire.

Gennadios II Scholarios

When Constantinople fell to the Ottoman forces in 1453, Sultan Mehmet II decided that he needed a reliable patriarch for the Christian Greeks of his empire. He chose Gennadios II Scholarios (c. 1405–c. 1472). Born and educated in Constantinople, Gennadios had been the leading theologian of his time and attended the Council of Ferrara-Florence in 1438–1439, where he supported the reunion of Constantinople and Rome. Later he was to take an opposing stance. In 1453 he was taken prisoner by the Ottomans and had become a slave of a rich Turk in Adrianople! The sultan ordered his release and, in January 1454, Gennadios became Patriarch of Constantinople, now

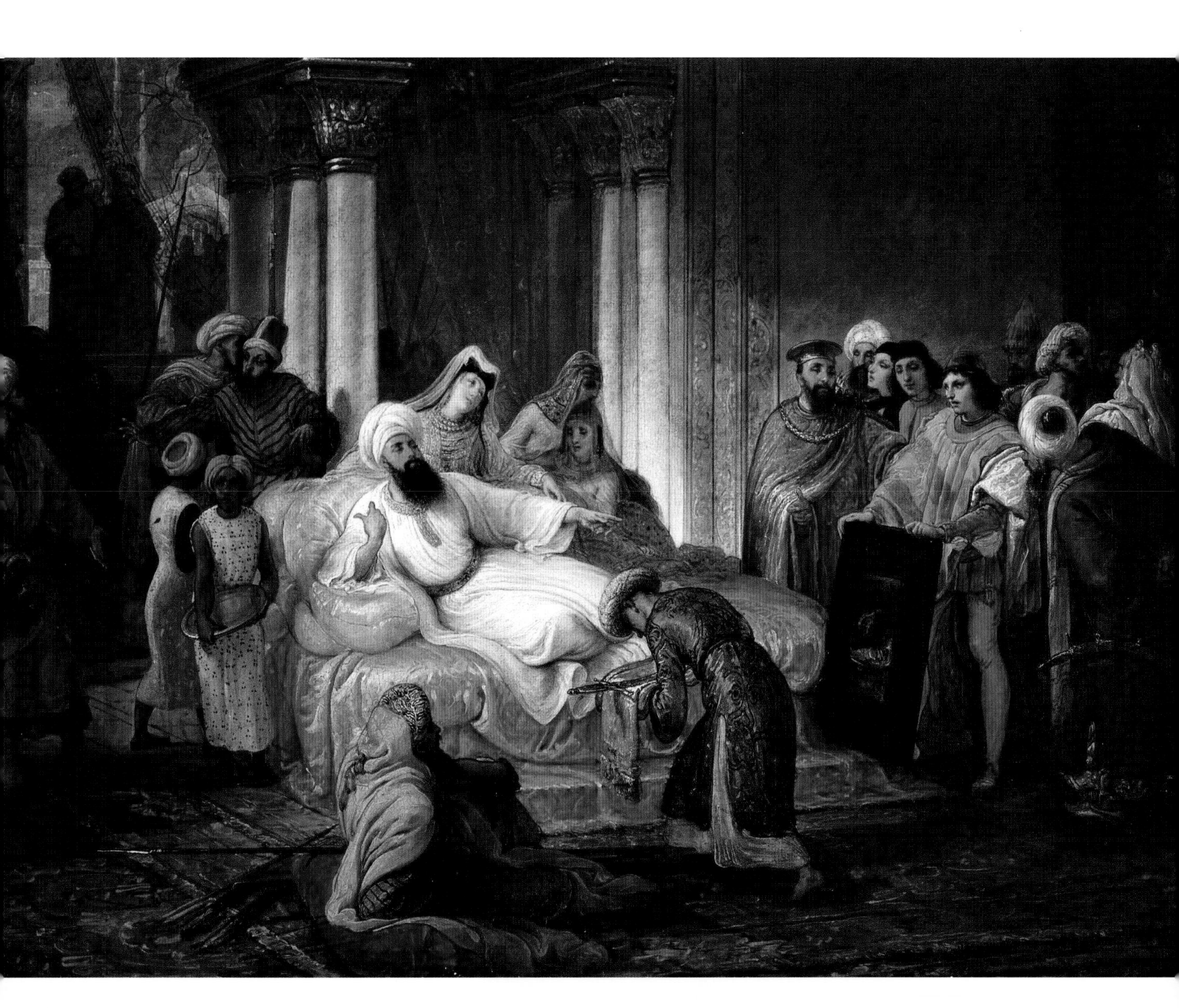

renamed Istanbul. He was invested with the pastoral staff, robe, and cross by Mehmet II at a ceremony that was held in the Church of the Twelve Apostles. This established an agreement that governed relations between the Orthodox Church and the Ottomans until 1923.

The patriarch now became the theocratic head of the Christian communities in the Ottoman Empire, responsible for order and good conduct. While the Christians ran their own welfare and educational systems, he taxed his flock on behalf of the Ottomans. But survival depended on enforcing the absolute loyalty of his Christian subjects to the Muslim sultan. Gennadios worked hard to defend the interests of the Christians under the Ottomans. He resigned after just one or two years in office, retiring to a monastery where he wrote a defense of Aristotelian philosophy and also translated works of Thomas Aquinas into Greek. He maintained communication with Sultan Mehmet II, who ordered him, on a couple of occasions, to resume his patriarchal office, which he reluctantly did, albeit for short periods of time.

Above: Sultan Mehmet II had a great respect for non-Muslims. As well as requesting that Christian texts be translated into Turkish, he commissioned Italian painter Gentile Bellini to paint his portrait.

Left: The Council of Nicaea (325 CE) devised several new canons, one of which acknowledged the supremacy of the sees of Alexandria and Jerusalem in their corresponding regions.

CHURCH ARCHITECTURE

Below: Giovanni Battista da Novara Ricci's seventeenth-century fresco re-creates the nave and aisles of the ancient Basilica of Constantine in Rome, which by Ricci's time lay in ruins.

Western and Eastern Christianity each developed characteristic forms of Church architecture. Behind the term "church" stands the Greek word *ekklesia* (gathering, assembly), found in the New Testament, particularly in Paul's letters, referring both to local communities, including house-churches, and the universal church. Only one uncontested example of early house-churches has been discovered, at Dura-Europos in Syria, a house converted in the 230s to include an assembly hall and decorated baptistery. Most house-churches would have been unconverted rooms in existing buildings. Rome provides one or two plausible examples of converted buildings. A complex of shops and houses under the basilica of St Giovanni and St Paolo near the Colosseum was apparently converted in the third and fourth centuries into a house-church with rooms on two stories and a small decorated private shrine. On this site the three-aisled apsed basilica was built during the fifth century.

Left: Richly decorated with a variety of frescoes, Emperor Constantine's imperial palace in Trier (in modern-day Germany) was built in 310 CE. It was later consecrated as a basilica.

The basilica

The basilica, originally a very common secular construction used for public assemblies, trade, justice, and so on, was probably not adopted as the prototype for Christian churches until the time of Emperor Constantine (306–337 CE). Constantine initiated a lavish building program in his Western half of the Roman empire, repairing, constructing, and endowing churches, which he continued in the Eastern half after becoming emperor there in 324.

Constantine's first influential church building was the Basilica of St John Lateran in Rome, an enormous five-aisled apsed basilica lavishly decorated with gold and marble, with a coffered wooden roof, brightly illuminated and richly endowed. Its principal altar was in front of the apse, which housed the seat (*cathedra*) of the bishop and benches for the presbyters. It had an adjoining baptistery and, able to accommodate 3,000 worshippers, was designed to impress as the seat of the Bishop of Rome, and as the parish church of Rome.

St Peter's in Rome

It seems, however, that Constantine was not responsible for the even more influential Basilica of St Peter's in the Vatican, a considerably larger, five-aisled apsed basilica with an enormous transept enclosing the shrine of the apostle. It was originally a cemetery basilica for pilgrims celebrating the festival of the apostle's martyrdom (June 29), housing the remains of those seeking burial near his relics, and accommodating funerary feasts in their honor. It was probably built by Constantine's youngest son, Constans, at the request of Bishop Julius (337–352), to undercut the joint martyr cult of Peter and Paul celebrated at a place usually called "ad Catacumbas" on the Appian Way. Here Constantine had begun a three-aisled ambulatory cemetery basilica, without altar or resident priests, now the church of St Sebastiano. This design had no future beyond Rome, however, and it was St Peter's, with its apsed transept and altar over the relics of the martyred saint and later a baptistery, which would eventually become the archetype of most Western churches.

Eastern churches

In the East, Constantine built memorial basilicas at sacred sites in Palestine associated not with martyrs but with key events in the life of Christ, such as the Basilica of the Nativity in Bethlehem, with octagonal shrine attached, and the Basilica of the Holy Sepulchre in Jerusalem, a five-aisled basilica adjacent to the circular Shrine of the Resurrection. In his new capital, Constantinople, he built palace basilicas, the churches of Holy Peace (Hagia Eirene) and Holy Wisdom (Hagia Sophia), and the church of the Holy Apostles, a circular imperial mausoleum with twelve pillars symbolizing the twelve apostles flanking his sarcophagus. In the end, however, it was the cruciform basilica attached to this church by Constantine's second son, Constantius II (337–361), that became a much more influential prototype for churches in both East and West.

Perhaps the most influential emperor in terms of Eastern Church architecture was Justinian (527–565). The major basilicas he built or rebuilt involved centrally planned structures with domes. His masterpiece is undoubtedly Hagia Sophia, still standing despite several earthquakes and changes of use, from cathedral, to mosque with four added minarets after the fall of Constantinople to the Ottoman Empire in 1453, and since 1935, by decree of Kemal Atatürk, a museum. Hagia Sophia has the largest unsupported dome yet built, galleries, and multicolored decorative mosaics. Since becoming a museum, a good deal of the plain or figurative plasterwork that Islamic principles decreed must overlay Christian iconography has been removed to display the original decoration.

In the West, in Ravenna in Italy, where Church architecture was considerably influenced by Constantinople, are perfectly preserved examples of both basilical and centrally planned churches, cruciform and octagonal.

Below: St Peter's Basilica dominates the skyline of Rome. It is the largest Christian church in the world, with room for more than 60,000 worshippers.

LITURGIES

Right: Liturgies (religious rites and rituals held in public) that occurred during Jesus' life are still performed today in both Jewish synagogues (like this one in Prague, Czech Republic) and Christian churches.

Jesus was born into a pious Jewish family in a liturgy-rich environment—and the legacy of those surroundings can still be found, if sometimes in a somewhat obscured way, in Christian liturgy. There was the liturgy of the Jerusalem Temple with its great feasts, in which Jesus took part (Luke 2:41), there was the weekly synagogue liturgy, in which he also took part (Luke 4:16), and there were the domestic liturgies of the Sabbath and other meals, daily prayers, and days of fasting. This all took place within a cycle of feasts such as Tabernacles, Atonement, Pentecost, and the Passover. We know that this pattern occurred in the community around Jesus and that the first Christian communities after the Resurrection adapted the pattern for their own liturgical life. We know that Jesus' followers in Jerusalem continued to go day by day to the temple, but "they broke bread at home" (Acts 2:46). The *Didache* (c. 50–60 CE), an early pastoral manual, tells us that Christians elsewhere had taken to having two fast days, and saying the Lord's Prayer three times each day. It also tells us about two other practices that have remained at the core of Christian liturgy: Baptism and what it calls "the breaking of the loaf."

Replacing circumcision

The decision to enter the Christian community was understood to embrace many things: The decision to be a follower of Jesus, the decision to turn away from an older life of sin, the decision to begin a new way of life, to become one with the Christ—to live "in the Christ"—and become a sister or brother in the Church. All this needed a significant event to mark the transition. Just as circumcision was understood as the mark of God's People before the coming of Jesus, baptism, or being buried in water ("baptism" literally means "plunged") and "rising to new life" became the mark of the Christian. It united Jew and Greek, slave and free, male and female, "for all of you are one in Christ Jesus" (Galatians 3:28).

Right: Some Protestant groups reject pedobaptism, the baptism of infants and small children, and believe only in credobaptism, the baptism of those who are capable of professing their faith in Jesus.

Above: *The Last Supper* by Juan de Juanes shows Jesus breaking bread with his disciples. Jesus entreated them to continue this tradition after his death: "Do this in remembrance of me" (1 Corinthians 11:24).

Sharing a loaf and cup

One of the characteristics of the way Jesus lived and taught was to gather people around a table to share a meal that would show them a new way of relating to the Father and one another, and be an image for the kingdom of God. Central to these meals were the notions of welcome and forgiveness, and the acts of praising and thanking the Father. The participants blessed God and ate a loaf broken so that each had a share; likewise, they shared a common cup. After Jesus died, his followers continued this meal practice as their central community meeting, believing that when they did this in Jesus' memory he was present at their "thanksgiving" (Greek *eukharistos*, from which we get the term Eucharist) to the Father. This prayer of blessing over a common loaf and cup—which could be shared by the very poorest—became the Christian replacement for the sacrifices in the Temple in Jerusalem. Not a little of the attraction of Christianity as it spread among the poor of the Roman Empire was this aspect of the liturgy: It was not an elaborate cult that required money or social standing. Some cults required the expenditure of much money for the animals necessary for sacrifice—but the Christians only needed a loaf of bread and a shared cup, ideally wine, although water was also used. This great act could be part of an ordinary meal and brought one into the divine presence. A Christian did not need to belong to a particular social stratum (as was the case with many of the mystery religions of the East); rich and poor shared what they had as the common children of the Father.

Early in the second century we know that Christians celebrated all their liturgy in their houses, they had an annual pattern of festivals, a weekly pattern of meeting for the Eucharist/common meal, days of fasting (Wednesdays and Fridays), a system of collecting for the poor at their common meals, and a pattern of daily prayer. In 112, one Roman governor described Christian liturgy thus: "On an appointed day they are usually met before daybreak and sang a hymn to Christ as if to a god...they then departed and met again to eat together, but it was ordinary and harmless food..." What looked so simple to the outsider meant so much more to those within the faith.

Following pages: As per the Law of Moses, eight days after he was born Jesus was circumcised; forty days after his birth, the infant Jesus was presented at the Temple in Jerusalem.

THE CHRISTIAN CALENDAR

Above: A bishop at the cathedral in Arkhangelsk, Russia, blesses the prepared foods during Lent. Lent is a forty-day period in which the faithful offer penitence and prayer before Easter.

Jesus of Nazareth himself, both by word and by example, gave the model for Christian prayer, formal and informal, in the synagogue or out in the hills in the early morning. The earliest Christians followed his example and took with the utmost seriousness the command to "pray without ceasing" (1 Thessalonians 5:16–18; Colossians 4:2; Ephesians 6:18; Luke 18:1). This prescription would be applied by later tradition to the formal liturgy of the Church, which has through the ages consisted of psalms, canticles, and hymns, and private and personal prayers and devotions. It was the need to coordinate prayer in relation to the various aspects of time that gave rise to the arrangements which we refer to as the "Christian Calendar."

Time and liturgy

The early thinkers of the Christian era saw all creation, including time, as sacred because it revealed the mystery of Christ. Time was a sacred element of life unfolding between two given points: It began at Creation (the Alpha) and will end with the Parousia (the Omega, the last or second coming of Christ).

Any formal arrangement of liturgical worship has complex relationships with the various cycles of the cosmos, which determine the rhythm of temporal existence. The day, based on the rising and setting of the sun, is the basic unit of time. The cycle of the seasons indicates the passing of a year, and the monthly waxing and waning of the moon produces a more easily visible intermediate unit of time. Calendars may be based on the movements of the sun (solar calendars) or on the movements of the moon (lunar calendars). The Christian calendar is a solar calendar; of all the Christian holy days, only Easter still retains a reference to the cycles of the moon.

Christian worship in the liturgical year celebrates the life of Christ, beginning in Advent, continuing to Christmas,

THE EMPEROR CONSTANTINE'S CONTRIBUTION TO THE CALENDAR

In the fourth century, in Christianizing Julius Caesar's basic calendar of 365¼ days arranged in twelve months, Constantine made three amendments that were to have the greatest significance for Christians: Sunday was prescribed as a holy day; Jesus' birth (Christmas) was to be observed on a fixed day; and the Resurrection (Easter) was to be celebrated on the Sunday after the first full moon after the spring equinox.

thence to Lent, Easter, and Pentecost. For Catholic and Orthodox Christians it also commemorates the regularly recurring festivals of the Mother of God and the saints, holy people revered as examples to be imitated, as intercessors before the throne of God.

Cycles of Christian prayer and worship

The progression of time from Creation to Parousia is linear, but we primarily experience time as cyclical. Within the great yearly cycle the lesser weekly and daily cycles each have an appropriate liturgical celebration. The Paschal and Christmas cycles are yearly, as are the annually recurring feasts of the saints and martyrs for Catholic and Orthodox Christians. The weekly cycle has from the earliest days of the Church perpetuated the memory of the Lord's Resurrection on Sunday, mainly by the celebration of the Eucharist. The Liturgy of the Hours in its different forms among Catholic, Orthodox, and Protestant Christians prescribes the cycle in which the various times of day and night are celebrated as sacramental and offered to God.

Thus within the overall linear structure from Creation to Parousia there are complex patterns of yearly, weekly, and daily cycles of liturgical prayer. According to the season being celebrated, these cycles can be joyous (Easter and Christmas), or somber and penitential (Lent, and to a lesser degree, Advent). Liturgical time alternates between stressed and unstressed, feast and fast, solemnity and festal, and "ordinary" time. It is the movement from one to the other, with the attendant periods of anticipation, celebration and fulfillment, ceremonies, ritual, and atmosphere peculiar to each feast or cycle of feasts, which creates liturgical dynamism.

The Christian liturgical calendar

The Christian calendar derived both its name and its basic form from the Roman pagan calendar (from *kalends*, the first day of the month by Roman reckoning). From early times the Christian calendar had as its essential components the commemoration of major events in Jesus' life—Christmas, Easter, and Pentecost—and the commemorations of the saints. These two festal rhythms are called the temporal and sanctoral cycles, respectively. All three traditional branches of Christianity—Protestant, Catholic, and Orthodox—celebrate the temporal cycle, but most Protestant denominations reject the sanctoral cycle. Jehovah's Witnesses, the Religious Society of Friends (Quakers), and many fundamentalist and American evangelical churches, however, reject both cycles.

Left: Initially a pagan springtime celebration of rebirth and renewal, Easter is now for the majority of Christians a time to commemorate and rejoice in the Resurrection of Jesus.

Below: This third-century CE pagan calendar features not only the Roman gods of the seven days (such as Saturn for Saturday) but also the signs of the zodiac, within a hexagram and hexagon.

THE CULT OF MARY

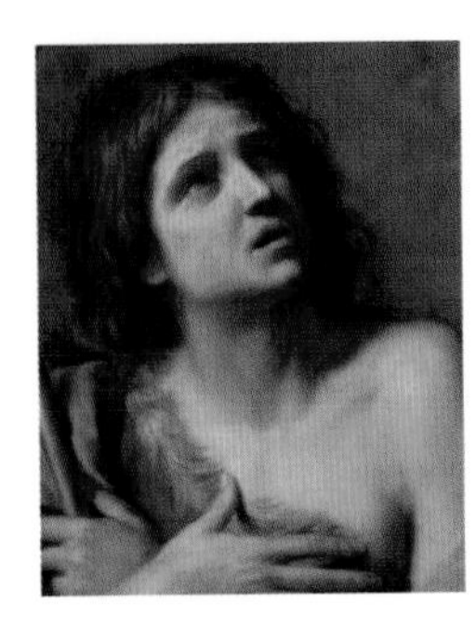

Above: John the Baptist was the son of Mary's cousin, Elizabeth. While both pregnant, Mary visited Elizabeth; at her greeting, Elizabeth "was filled with the Holy Spirit" (Luke 1:41).

Opposite: *Virgin of the Pillar* by Stefano da Ferrara was painted in the fourteenth century, with the stunning diadems being added sometime during the seventeenth century.

Below: The Gospel of Luke is the only place in the Bible in which the Annunciation—where the angel Gabriel reveals to Mary that she is to bear the Son of God—is recorded.

The cult of Mary, with prayers to her and honor given to her or her image, is a controversial part of Christian tradition. For most Christians—the Orthodox and other Christians of the East, and for Catholics—she is the all-holy, virgin Mother of God. She is placed first among the saints as the most holy member of the Church, and is the splendor of creation. Her image as *Theotokos* (literally, the "Mother of God") is a decorated focal point in all church buildings, usually with candles burning before it. For Protestant Christians, who trace their lineage to events in Western Europe in the sixteenth century, she is problematic. Some hold that any devotion to her is idolatry and earnestly reject her cult; others worry that prayer to her distracts from the Christ as the one mediator; and others, while honoring her as a holy model Christian, find her cult somehow "distasteful."

Curious origins

From what we can piece together from early Christian documents, Mary and Joseph were very pious Galilean Jews. They had a family of at least seven children, with Jesus being the eldest: "Is not this the carpenter's son? Is not his mother called Mary? And are not his brothers James and Joseph and Simon and Judas? And are not all his sisters with us?" (Matthew 13:55–6). (The traditional Catholic view, which stems from the Christian monk and scholar, St Jerome, claims that Jesus' "brothers" were actually his cousins. Jerome argued that the word that translates as "brother" has several different meanings in the Bible, one of which is "kinsman.") We know that the family lived in Nazareth, and that Mary was still alive at the time of the crucifixion because she stood beside the cross.

By the time the Gospel of Luke was written—sometime between 70 and 90 CE—Mary has been transformed into someone unique in the divine plan of salvation. To her is announced the Father's plan of Jesus' birth, her "Yes" (Luke 1:38) begins the new Age of the Lord; she is a virgin who conceived by the Holy Spirit; her cousin's unborn infant, John the Baptist, recognizes her as carrying the Christ; and Mary tells her cousin that "all generations will call [her] blessed" (Luke 1:48). Words from this Gospel (Luke 1:28, 42) became one of the commonest Christian prayers, the "Hail Mary" (*Ave Maria*); and the hymn that Luke placed on Mary's lips, the "Magnificat," has been a constant element in evening prayers since the third century.

Growing in renown

By the early second century the cult of Mary was developing rapidly. The Apocryphal text called the *Protoevangelium of James*, written before 150 CE, shows her life being celebrated as God's most wonderful creature. Her parents have been given names (Joachim and Anne), her own birth is miraculous, she is dedicated to the service of the Temple as a young girl. Jesus' brothers and sisters are not her biological children, but Joseph's from an earlier marriage, and there is a clear tendency to see her as ever-virgin. Many of the stories of the life of Mary as remembered by Eastern Orthodox Christians and Catholics are first found in this text, which was probably written to harmonize the nativity stories of Matthew and Luke.

We also know that prayer to Mary was developing: A third-century papyrus fragment from Egypt contains words ("We fly to thy protection, O holy Mother of God...") still used by Catholic and Orthodox Christians. Mary is seen not just as the mother of Jesus, but of the whole community, of the Church, and of each Christian; and for all these children she is seen as exercising a mother's care and protection in earthly dangers. As the saint-above-all-the-saints, she is presented as leading the Church in joining in the Christ's prayer to the Father for the salvation of Christians and the universe.

The full-blown cult

In 431, at a Church council held in Ephesus, whose aim was to defend the belief that Jesus was truly a human being and truly the Son of God, the assembled bishops opted for accepting the now long-established title *Theotokos* as expressing the mystery of who they believed Jesus to be. God cannot have a mother, but a human being must have one: In calling Mary "Mother of God" the tension within the mystery was preserved, yet its key elements were highlighted.

Devotion to Mary constantly took new forms: New feasts, new aspects of her life were highlighted. For those who approve of such honors, they draw Christians to a deeper awareness of the mystery of Jesus. For those who do not approve, they are human customs cluttering faith.

PART TWO

INVASIONS
501–1000 CE

MAXIMIANV

CHAPTER ONE

THE WESTERN CHURCH

After the Western Roman Empire collapsed in the fifth century, political disorder persisted for half a millennium. Invading tribes—Ostrogoths, Lombards, Visigoths, Burgundians, Angles, Saxons, Franks, Arabs, and finally Vikings—jostled for territory. Commerce and travel declined, cities shrank, and the system of Roman roads fell into disrepair. A feudal system of patchwork power prevailed.

The Church took over functions previously provided by the state. It protected the poor and the powerless. The papacy was able to increase the strength and the geographic extent of its power. Bishops had armies.

The greatest pope of the second half millennium was Gregory the Great. As a young man, Gregory endowed six monasteries with his inherited fortune, and gave the rest to the poor. As pope, he was an extremely able administrator who preserved the physical possessions (buildings and land endowments) of the Church of Rome, and made sure the poor were fed.

Monasticism spread. It was particularly vigorous in Ireland. There, abbots were more powerful than bishops. Monasteries were centers of learning, and of missions that extended throughout Western Europe. In Italy, Benedict of Nursia created a monastic discipline (the Rule of Benedict), which became standard in the West.

Abbesses (heads of women's monasteries) had the rare privilege of running an organization. They administered not only the monastery proper, but also associated land estates. Women who did not enter a monastery could gain status by bearing sons, but status did not entail autonomy. Women could find a modicum of self-rule only in religious life.

The Angles and Saxons of Great Britain were converted by missionaries from Ireland and Rome. Later, English missionaries from these very tribes played an important role in the conversion of what is now Germany and Holland. The last northern Europeans to be converted were the Saxons who remained on the mainland, and the Scandinavians.

Charlemagne, who ruled at the height of Carolingian power, was crowned Roman Emperor by the pope in 800 CE. Carolingian rule brought a measure of peace and order to western and southern Germany, the Netherlands, Belgium, France, Switzerland, Austria, and parts of Italy.

Previous pages: This detail from a Byzantine mosaic shows Emperor Justinian and his retinue. Justinian was a devout Christian ruler who built or renovated numerous churches, including the Hagia Sophia.

Right: Just before he was crowned Roman Emperor, Charlemagne supervised the construction of the magnificent Palatine Chapel at Aix-la-Chapelle (now Aachen, Germany), which was consecrated in 805 CE.

GROWING INFLUENCE OF THE PAPACY

Below right: Jesus said to Peter, "I will give you the keys of the kingdom of heaven" (Matthew 16:19). Roman Catholics use this statement as evidence of St Peter's primacy.

Below: Charlemagne's lavish golden casket features an effigy of the Frankish king enthroned between Pope Leo III (who crowned him Holy Roman Emperor) and Bishop Turpin.

By the mid-fourth century CE, the bishop of Rome was seen as having a "primacy" among all Latin-speaking bishops. He was both the bishop of the imperial capital and also the successor to St Peter, who was regarded as the leader of the apostles. This primacy in the West meant that the bishop of Rome was considered the senior bishop, the one who was to be appealed to in times of dispute and the only one who could settle any disputes among other groups of bishops. As the final referee, the bishop of Rome was from now on almost invariably called *papa*—a term that originally meant "father figure" and increasingly came to mean patriarch or "chief bishop."

Successor to St Peter

Gradually this position of being St Peter's successor meant that the popes saw themselves as having pastoral responsibilities, not just for their own dioceses but for all Latin-speaking Christians. The papacy, therefore, promoted missions to the new peoples who were entering the Roman Empire. Popes like Leo the Great (440–461) sought to determine matters of doctrine, while another pope, Gregory the Great (590–604), became a great promoter of monasticism. While bishops and clergy looked to Rome as a focal point for unity among all the Latin-speaking churches—and as such the pope was prayed for at every Eucharist—ordinary people regarded him as looking after "the keys" given to Peter and possessing special access to Peter's intercession (prayers in heaven on behalf of people on earth). Pilgrims to Rome did not imagine themselves going to see a city or meet the pope; they were visiting Peter who was now resting in his tomb.

Papal status

As a link with the apostles, and a link with the ancient capital city, the pope had unrivaled status: He could grant legitimacy to princes (for example, Pope Leo III crowned Charlemagne as Holy Roman Emperor in 800); his courts acted as courts of appeal; and his decisions given in letters to bishops were viewed as legislation. With every appeal to Rome, the papacy's power and significance increased. The papacy had a unique authority—not just in Church matters but in all Christian society—and provided a unique connection between heavenly and earthly realms.

ST GREGORY THE GREAT

Gregory was born into a wealthy family in about 540. He sold his inheritance to obtain the money to found monasteries, one of which he entered as a monk around 574. However, his background and skills led to the pope appointing him as one of Rome's administrators, and Gregory later represented the pope in the imperial court in Constantinople. It was while he was an official in Rome that he met two English (*Angli*) slaves and perceived the meeting as providential: To Gregory they were angels (*angeli*) sent to show him the need for missionaries to Britain. On seeing them Gregory famously exclaimed: *Non Angli sed angeli* ("they are not Angles but angels!").

The reluctant pope

After returning from Constantinople, Gregory—much against his will—was elected pope (590 CE) and his first task was to restore peace to the Italian peninsula. He also devoted considerable energy to the Church's "foreign affairs." Gregory sent Augustine and some monks to England as missionaries. He also sought better relations with Constantinople, although he strenuously refused to acknowledge that the patriarch there was entitled to call himself "ecumenical patriarch." At home, Gregory's achievements come under three headings. First, he promoted monasticism. His book *The Dialogues* created the image of St Benedict of Nursia as the great founder of Western monasticism. Second, Gregory wrote many books including *The Pastoral Rule*, a guide to the nature of pastoral care, in which he expounded the principle: "The supreme law is to save souls." Third, Gregory reformed the liturgy and reorganized the singing in Rome; hence "plain chant" is often called "Gregorian Chant" after him.

Gregory died in 604 and was immediately given the title "the Great"—a title that only Leo I (440–461) had held before him. He is considered to be the fourth of the great Doctors of the Church, and is one of the last Western saints honored also among the Eastern churches. The West celebrates his feast day on September 3, but in the East it is still celebrated on March 12, the date of his death.

Above: This detail from Peter Paul Rubens' Baroque masterpiece *Saint Gregory with Saints Domitilla, Maurus, and Papianus* shows St Gregory the Great in a moment of religious reflection.

IRISH MONASTICISM

Above: Lavishly illustrated, the *Book of Kells* (also known as the *Book of Columba*) contains a hand-written transcription of the four Gospels as well as other religious texts, and dates to c. 800 CE.

At about the same time as St Patrick's mission to Ireland, the concept of monasticism was spreading throughout the Western Church. It probably spread to Britain and Ireland from Gaul. St Patrick was very much aware of monasticism, even if he did not place great stress on it in practical terms. In his *Confessio* he cites the great numbers who were adopting the monastic way of life in response to his preaching as a proof for the genuineness of his mission. He attributes their taking up the monastic way of life to the inspiration of God. The Eastern ascetic ideals of the Desert Fathers were largely mediated to the West by the works of John Cassian, who was very influential in early Ireland, including *The Institutes* and the *Conferences*.

There were no physical deserts in Ireland so the monastic withdrew into the hills, the woods, or the mountains, or to one of the offshore islands—likened to a "desert in the ocean" by Adomnan, the abbot of Iona.

What attracted the Irish to monasticism?

Monasticism as a form of religious life held great attraction in Irish society, which was based on the clan with the chief at its head. Kinship and the personal rule of the clan leader were the common bonds. The monasteries were often associated with regional clans, but these deep-seated family loyalties resulted in a large number of Irish monasteries with few common bonds uniting them to each other. This strong familial spirit did have an effect in that monasteries founded by the same holy man tended to unite in a loose federation, for example, Iona, Kells, Durrow, and Derry, all founded by Columba of Iona (Colmcille). However, each founder had his own personal vision and ideal of monastic life that he lived himself and encouraged his disciples to do likewise.

There was very little written legislation in the early days. Two sources of information on early insular monasticism are the writings of Columbanus of Luxeuil (from the late sixth/early seventh centuries) and the Cambrai homily fragment (probably from the end of the seventh century).

"*Peregrinatio pro amore Dei*"

The Cambrai homily fragment speaks of "white," "green," and "red" martyrdom. "Red martyrdom" is the literal shedding of one's blood for Christ, and opportunities for this were not so common before the Viking incursions. However, "white martyrdom" ("where a man separates for the sake of God from everything he loves") is the *peregrinatio pro amore Dei,* the "pilgrimage for the love of God" much practiced by the early Irish monks. "Green martyrdom" ("when by means of fasting and labor he frees himself from his evil desires") refers to the monastic life of extreme renunciation and asceticism.

Peregrinatio, "journeying," was a phenomenon of Irish monasticism, and although the primary aim of the *peregrini* was ascetic—self-sacrifice in breaking ties of kinship—this

Right: St Patrick is the patron saint of Ireland, and his image appears prominently in religious buildings and private homes. This stunning stained glass window illuminates a church in Tipperary.

did not rule out other motives. There were many reasons besides the obviously religious one, for what Walahfrid Strabo called "the Irish fashion of going away." In modern terms such reasons could be classed under headings like scientific, colonial, or commercial, while still being religious in inspiration. Monks set off into the unknown in order to rely solely on God's providence; to sacrifice ties of home and family; to take the Gospel where it had never been preached before; or to fulfill a penance. This "pilgrim for Christ" would have had little hope of ever seeing his native land and his family and relations again, and this was a sacrifice he made for the love of God.

Another aspect of Irish monasticism was its austerity; Irish monks were famed for their penitential practices. Fasting, hard physical labor, silence, physical punishments, and the little sleep permitted broken to pray the nightly vigils, characterized Irish monasticism. There were also such practices as the *crossfigell* (praying with arms extended), as well as repeated genuflections and prostrations.

Below: St Martin of Tours (c. 316–c. 397) had an impact not only on Irish monasticism, but also on religious life in France, Hungary, and other places in continental Europe.

INFLUENTIAL MONASTIC FOUNDERS

St Martin of Tours was a crucial influence in Ireland. His disciple St Ninian built a monastery in his hometown of Whithorn in Galloway, Scotland, that attracted students from Ireland and some of them became well known. Among the students was Enda who founded his own monastery on Inis Mór in the Aran Islands off the coast of Galway, giving Ireland what was probably its first indigenous monastery. Finnian of Clonard founded a thriving monastery, Clonard Abbey. His students included Ciarán who founded Clonmacnoise; Comgall who founded Bangor; and Columba (Colmcille) who founded Kells, Derry, Durrow, and Iona. The period between approximately 540 and 615 CE was the age of the great Irish monastic founders.

BENEDICT OF NURSIA AND HIS RULE

In the latter half of the first millennium, Western monasteries had an array of Rules—collections of the wise sayings of the Church Fathers—they could choose to adopt. However, the Rule of Benedict eventually became the Rule of choice for most monasteries.

Benedict—Father of Western monasticism?

Many historians and monks now regard Benedict of Nursia (c. 480–547) as the founder of Western monasticism. However, during his lifetime Benedict's personal influence did not mark the Church as did that of Pachomius or Basil or Columbanus. Though Benedict was famed for his sanctity (and this was largely due to *Life*, written by Gregory the Great), he was simply the abbot of one of many Italian monasteries. According to the *Dialogues* of Gregory, Benedict was born in Nursia, around 480. He went to Rome to study, but the immorality of Roman society upset him so much that he retired to Spoleto where he lived as a hermit. Over the next twenty-five years, others came to join him. Eventually, as the result of monastic jealousies, he went to live on Monte Cassino, where he stayed for the rest of his life as abbot. He was buried next to his twin sister, Scholastica. His fame and place in history are due, along with Gregory's *Life*, to the Rule attributed to him, though modern scholarship now believes it is unlikely that he wrote this Rule as it now stands.

Below: St Columbanus (c. 543–615 CE) was an Irish monk who founded numerous monasteries on the European continent. His monastic Rules were relatively strict, and were later amended and improved by the Benedictines.

EARLY MONASTIC TEXTS

The earliest "wisdom documents" of Christian monasticism were the lives of the great founders. They include the *Life of St Antony* by Athanasius, which influenced almost every future Rule such as the *Apothegmata Patrum*; the *Lausiac History*, written by Palladius; and the *Historia Monachorum in Aegyptum*—all of them very influential texts. Another major text is anonymous: It is known simply as the *Rule of the Master*. It shows us a small community of twelve monks and their abbot, carrying out a round of psalmody, working, reading, and living a common life.

Above: A prolific theological writer, Athanasius of Alexandria (c. 293–373 CE) wrote not only a well-read biography of St Antony, but also treatises against Arianism and Macedonianism.

Rules for everyday monastic living

There were many different Rules, which may or may not have been written by the people whose names they bear, and it was quite common for a founder or an abbot to combine two or more Rules. A very popular combination was that of the Rule of Benedict and the Rule of Columbanus of Luxeuil. In seventh-century Gaul, whenever the Rule of Benedict is mentioned it is always coupled with that of Columbanus. Bede, in his *Lives of the Holy Abbots of Wearmouth and Jarrow*, tells of Benedict Biscop, the founder of Wearmouth/Jarrow, when he was dying. He urged the brethren, when they came to see him, to observe the Rule that he had given them. "For," he said, "you cannot suppose that it was my own untaught heart which dictated this rule to you. I learned it from seventeen monasteries, which I saw during my travels, and most approved of, and I copied these institutions thence for your benefit."

So it was quite acceptable for founders of new monasteries to shop around and take the best of what was on offer in various other houses. But by the year 800 the Rule of

Benedict was emerging as the dominant monastic Rule in the West. The Carolingians (that is, the reformers who worked with and under the emperor Charlemagne to bring about uniformity in all areas of Church life) championed it as part of the general campaign to reform the churches in the Frankish kingdoms and in Italy. Charlemagne wanted to apply Benedict's Rule as a unifying monastic principle throughout his dominions and, although he died before he had achieved this aim, it was taken up by his son, Louis the Pious. A monastery was founded near the imperial court at Aachen where Benedict of Aniane, a famous reformer, was abbot. Two monks from every European abbey were supposed to come there for "refresher courses" in monastic life. In their relentless drive for uniformity of practice in every aspect of religious life, from the design and layout of the standard monastery to the regulation of its everyday activities, the Carolingians successfully imposed a single Rule on the Western Church. This was the Rule of Benedict. It was so influential because it was practical; it was moderate in its demands and, compared to other Rules of the time, it was comprehensive. It sets out to provide a "school for those in the Lord's service."

Above: Benedict of Nursia blesses his disciple Maurus, a deacon who is considered the model of religious obedience. Benedict was canonized by Pope Honorius III in 1220.

POWER OF THE ABBESSES

Below right: St Thecla lived in the first century CE, and was a follower of Paul of Tarsus. In 1630 she reportedly assisted the community of Este, Italy, during a plague.

The information we have about early religious life for women is ambiguous and complex. It has filtered down to us through male authors, from a world in which the majority of saints and monastic figures were male. In this world the model of holiness was male, and only by adhering to this model could women become holy. To be more a saint was to be less a woman. This was a powerful philosophy in the late classical and early medieval times, and it seems to be the wisdom behind stories of women like Thecla, Pelagia, and others, who, in differing circumstances, are said to have donned the male habit and lived as monks, and who were only found to be female after their death. The implication was that they had to gain holiness by putting on the clothes of the male.

Slaves and queens

A slave woman had difficulty in becoming a nun, because her life was of such little value. Women from the upper strata of society, princesses, and queens, had the same difficulty, but for the opposite reason—as potential wives and mothers of kings and princes, they were social and political tools, so an extremely valuable resource. Society depended on them. Offered in marriage to princes and kings of potential allies, they could save the lives and the territory of their own tribes. They could win peace for tribes at war. They were far too valuable for their ability to bear sons who would be heirs and warriors, to disappear into a monastery and waste their lives unproductively. This was how medieval society saw its aristocratic womenfolk.

The power of the abbess

However, some women did brave parental opposition and leave the traditional structures of their society to enter religious life. For the very few who were chosen to be abbess, there was access to power and influence that was otherwise unavailable to women. They had the responsibility for the organization and carrying out of religious rituals, as well as the running and overseeing of farms and estates. They shared, even if only in a limited way, in the social and political roles of male clerics, and most of all they were able, up to a point, to direct their own lives by their spiritual and religious commitment. Religious life did succeed in providing an alternative lifestyle for women, but it was still very limited, even for those who risked social and familial disapproval. The freedom to arrange their own lives could never be absolute: Women relied on men for their access to the liturgical and sacramental life of the Church, and also for practical help with the heavier forms of labor.

Below: A Norman abbess addresses a priest and a monk or friar. Abbesses of the time had a certain amount of religious influence, and some chose to write theological texts.

Throughout the medieval world, women were were always seen as "belonging" to someone—father, husband, brother, son—or to the Church. Men had the power of life or death over their womenfolk (in fact, if not in law), whether they were wives or daughters. Women in this world had a hard and dangerous life. Marriage and childbearing were seen as their normal lot, and the percentage of maternal deaths in childbirth was high. The ability to bear sons was highly prized, and noblewomen in particular were precious commodities as potential tools for political and social alliances. Women's entry into the religious life was not encouraged, except in the case of widows whose childbearing days were over. Within religious life, even though empowered with a certain amount of freedom to order their own lives, they were still dependent on male clergy.

ORIGINS OF RELIGIOUS LIFE

In the writings of the Fathers of the Church, we find mention of women who chose to live unmarried, originally in their own homes, eventually in communities of like-minded women. Church teachers told the women they should dress in black, keep their hair cropped close, wear a black veil—given to them by the bishop at their consecration—and eat only one vegetarian meal a day, which they should share with some poor woman. They were to study the scriptures, rise during the night to pray, and gather in church to chant the psalms at the traditional hours. One of the earliest monastic texts is the *Lausiac History*, which was compiled by Palladius of Galatia in the early fifth century. It tells of several early monasteries of women in Egypt and includes, according to the text's preface, "memoirs of aged women and illustrious God-inspired matrons, who with masculine and perfect mind have successfully accomplished the struggles of virtuous aceticism...[and serve] as a model and object of desire for those women who long to wear the crown of continence and chastity."

Above: St Adelaide was a tenth-century German abbess renowned for her sanctity and the miracles she performed. In this 1845 stained glass window she is shown giving money to the poor.

MISSIONS TO NORTHERN EUROPE

Above: St Patrick's Day parades are held not only in Ireland's capital city, Dublin (seen here), but also in other countries far removed from Patrick's ministry, such as the USA and Australia.

During the second century CE, people in almost every corner of the Roman Empire came to have faith in Christ. Around 200 CE, a report surfaced of people having become Christian in Britain beyond Hadrian's Wall. At the same time missionaries were sent from Rome to establish a church in Paris. Clearly, Christianity had begun moving beyond the northern limits of the Roman Empire. In the middle of the next century, Ulfilas went as a missionary to present-day Romania, where he became known as the Apostle to the Goths.

The English slave who became an Irish saint

The name "St Patrick" often brings to mind Irish celebrations on March 17 and images of leprechauns, green-colored beer, and pots of gold at the end of rainbows. Those ways of celebrating a man named Patrick have little to do with what really happened.

In the early 400s, Irish pirates raided a village on the coast of England, pillaging it and carrying off several of the young people to be slaves. One of them, a teenager named Patrick, was forced to work on an Irish farm.

Although Patrick came from a Christian family, he was not a believer at the time of his capture. As a slave, however, Patrick turned to the Christian faith of his parents and grandparents. After about four years as a slave in Ireland, he had a vision that he believed was a divine message telling him to escape. Following the instructions given in the vision, Patrick managed to flee from his captors, get out of Ireland, and return home to England, only to feel after a short time that God was calling him back to the Irish as a missionary. Returning to the very people who had destroyed his home village, killed some of his family and friends, and enslaved him, Patrick gave thirty years of his life in ministry to them.

When he died, Patrick left behind a legacy of about seven hundred Christian churches in Ireland. A cleric named Palladius, who was sent to Ireland in 431 and became the first bishop, also played a part, but later historians gave Patrick all the credit for the conversion of

Below: The story of Elijah challenging Ahab and his pagan prophets (seen here) inspired the English missionary Boniface to try a similar tactic with the Germanic tribes that he was attempting to convert.

Ireland. The Irish Church became very influential, with Celtic *peregrini* carrying the Gospel to Scotland and England, the rugged hills of Gaul and the forests of Germany, the foothills of the Alps and the Rhine and Danube river valleys, and even to cities and remote valleys in Italy. The Celtic missionary movement was a remarkable grassroots one that operated independently of the bishop of Rome.

Chopping down the sacred oak tree

In the early 700s, Boniface, an English missionary living in what is modern-day Germany, felt he was seeing an inadequate response to his evangelistic efforts. He decided to set up a "power encounter" showdown that would mirror what the prophet Elijah did in Old Testament times when he challenged the Baal worshippers on Mount Carmel. To that end, Boniface announced that he was going to cut down a sacred oak tree dedicated to the pagan god Thor.

On the appointed day, many pagans gathered in the forest to see what would happen. Most felt that Thor would strike Boniface dead when he began to cut the sacred tree. When nothing happened to Boniface even after the tree came crashing to the ground, the Germanic tribes began turning to Christianity.

Keeping the faith

Further to the north, the Viking peoples of Scandinavia posed a tough challenge for Christians longing to see the Gospel spread to all the countries of Europe. Among other things, the Vikings were a warlike people who seemed to delight in terrorizing Christian communities, burning church buildings and enslaving church leaders.

In the early 800s, a missionary named Anskar went to Scandinavia and spent thirty years among the Vikings. Though Anskar is sometimes referred to as "the Apostle to the North," he had no visible, lasting results to show for decades of ministry in Scandinavia.

A more effective but much less visible form of conversion came through intermarriage. Vikings raiding the coastlands of countries further south often captured young women to take home to marry. Many of those young women were Christians who stayed true to their faith and witnessed (talked about what they had seen Christ do in their lives) within the family circles they were forced to create in their exile. Gradually, the Viking peoples were brought to faith in Christ by this way. Not long after the end of the first millennium, the Scandinavian countries were considered Christian countries.

Above: A stele from the early Christian period in Sweden is inscribed with an image of an embracing couple; the man is holding a crucifix.

THE HOLY ROMAN EMPIRE

Above: In conjunction with the French and English, Frederick I Barbarossa embarked on the Third Crusade in 1189. He drowned while crossing a river in Asia Minor just a year later.

Below: *Tree of Battles* is an allegorical illustration of feudal society, showing the discord between the different social classes. The king is separated from the trouble brewing below him.

Vast, colorful, and diverse, the Holy Roman Empire lasted for just over a millennium. On Christmas Day in 800 CE, the King of the Franks, Charlemagne (also known as "Charles the Great") was crowned Holy Roman Emperor by Pope Leo III. The empire finally ended after a long decline when Francis II (of Prussia) abdicated on August 6, 1806. Francis really jumped before he was pushed by Napoleon, who had just defeated him in battle.

Rise and fall

In between these two dates is a huge and turbulent history of rise, fall, rise, and fall again. For a time there was no emperor (between 924 and 962), at other times there was more than one claimant to the crown (1250–1273). The role of emperor was passed from dynasty to dynasty like a football: The Saxon, Salian, Hohenstaufen, and Habsburg dynasties all held on to it for a while. The emperor would often live in the region from which he came: Modern-day Germany, France, Italy, the Netherlands, and even Sicily.

Over its life the empire's borders fluctuated. Above all, however, it was a Western empire. The Eastern empire, based in Constantinople, reacted badly when Charlemagne claimed the title of Roman Emperor, so he didn't want to cause further trouble by actually claiming their territory. At times the Holy Roman Empire did extend its borders into southern Italy and Spain, and even at one point (with Frederick II in 1228) to Jerusalem. However, its core was modern Germany, France, Poland, Austria, Switzerland, the Netherlands, Belgium, and northern Italy.

Life of a serf

For the common people, the empire meant the long dominance of feudalism—a social and economic system often depicted as a pyramid. At the top was the king; then came the nobles, princes, clergy, and artisans; then the serfs. Largest in number, the serfs occupied the lowest position on the feudal "pyramid." If you had lived then, you would probably have been a serf (from Latin *servus*). The land on which serfs lived was not their own, since the lord (often a bishop) allowed the serfs to live on it. In exchange, the serfs gave the lord some produce, might serve as foot soldiers in periods of war, and gave up some labor time. For the rest, serfs lived by means of their own resources.

What was unique about the empire was that the emperor was not guaranteed the crown, although some tried to make it hereditary. Instead, the emperor was always elected, which depended on complex negotiations between different power blocks or "electors" (there were seven and then eight). Becoming emperor was a long and convoluted process; currying favor, bribery, promises, and the political maneuvering of the pope all played their part. Finally, the pope would officially recognize the new emperor. Such a loose federation was the secret to both its longevity and also its eventual decline. It provided protection for weaker states while allowing them significant autonomy, but it also tended to pull the empire apart.

Holy Empire versus sacred Church

Despite its name, the empire rarely included Rome. This was due to the temporal power of the pope, with whom the emperor often struggled. The last emperor to be crowned by the pope was Charles V in 1530. In the preceding centuries papal power had increased dramatically, especially with the "papal revolution" of the twelfth and thirteenth centuries. It was a time when the Church's autonomy was vigorously asserted, Church (or canon) law became a separate tradition, and the pope claimed significant temporal, or earthly, power. Needless to say, the pope came to see the emperor as a threat to his position and would often work with the princes and electors to undermine the emperor's power.

Nothing shows up the power struggle between pope and emperor better than the high point of the Holy Roman Empire under Frederick I Barbarossa (1122–1190) and Frederick II (1194–1250). Barbarossa insisted to Hadrian IV that the empire was not a gift of the pope but a "free crown" governed by ancient Roman law. Matters came to a head, and from 1159 to 1176 Frederick I supported a rival pope, Victor IV. Later, when Frederick II had included Sicily and large parts of Italy in his domain, the pope felt his power under severe threat. The response: Pope Gregory IX excommunicated him, not once, but twice.

If it was not based in Rome, why then was it called the Holy Roman Empire? It was considered "holy" because it claimed separate jurisdiction from the pope, and it was "Roman" due to the mythical claim to continue the legacy of the Roman Empire.

Holy Roman Empire c. 806 CE

- Empire of Charlemagne (c. 806 CE)
- Territories under Charlemagne's control
- Papal states aligned with Empire of Charlemagne
- Emirate of Cordova

North Sea
Baltic Sea
KINGDOM OF ENGLAND
English Channel
Boulogne
Hamburg
Bremen
ABODRITES
SAXONY
WILTZES
Münster
Elbe
Magdeburg
SORBS
Aix-la-Chapelle (Aachen)
FRANCE
Rhine
THURINGIA
Rouen
Seine
Mainz
BRITTANY
Rennes
Paris
NEUSTRIA
AUSTRASIA
Châlons
BOHEMIANS
Angers
Tours
EMPIRE OF CHARLEMAGNE
MORAVIANS
ALEMANNIA
Poitiers
Salzburg
Chalon
BAVARIA
Angoulême
AQUITAINE
BURGUNDY
RAETIA
CARINTHIA
Bordeaux
Lyon
Rhône
FRIULI
Cahors
Grenoble
Milan
GASCONY
LOMBARDY
Venice
Danube
Toulouse
PROVENCE
PYRENEES
Genoa
Modena
SEPTIMANIA
Bologna
Ravenna
CROATS
Pisa
Florence
Saragossa
SORABIA
Perugia
Corsica
Barcelona
PAPAL STATES
DUCHY OF SPOLETO
Adriatic Sea
Tortosa
Ligurian Sea
Rome
Valencia
Capua
DUCHY OF BENEVENTO
Alicante
Sardinia
Salerno
Tyrrhenian Sea
Mediterranean Sea
Ionian Sea
N
0 250 500 750 1,000 kilometers
0 125 250 375 500 miles
AFRICA

Right: Charlemagne was crowned *Imperator Romanorum* (literally translated as "Emperor of the Romans") by Pope Leo III on Christmas Day, 800 CE, in St Peter's Basilica, Rome.

CHAPTER TWO

BYZANTIUM

The Byzantine Empire was founded by Constantine the Great when he moved the capital of the Roman Empire from Rome to his new city of Constantinople (modern-day Istanbul), which was inaugurated in 330 CE. This new Christian capital, which became the center of the Eastern Orthodox Church, welcomed people of all races, as long as they could speak Greek and were prepared to accept the Orthodox religion. The wealthiest, most sophisticated, and cultured city in the world for most of its existence, with perhaps a million inhabitants in its heyday, Constantinople was finally to fall to the Ottoman Turks in 1453.

Constantinople was home to the Byzantine emperor and the patriarch, the head of the Orthodox Church and second only to the pope in Rome. It was believed that the city, or rather its predecessor, the small town of Byzantium, was founded by St Andrew, brother of St Peter, and thus of near equal status to Rome itself. It was a city of churches, of which the most important was the great cathedral, Hagia Sophia, and of monasteries, with some 300 or more in the capital, as well as the site of numerous church councils, which formulated Orthodox dogma. Protected by the huge walls erected in the early fifth century, the city was impregnable until the development of heavy artillery, and easily foiled the attacks of barbarians, Avars, Persians, and Arabs.

The Byzantines believed that as long as they followed Orthodoxy, God would protect their empire, whatever forces were amassed against them. They also believed that the emperor's main duty was to maintain the purity of the Orthodox faith. Even in the face of the Turkish threat, the populace resolutely refused to consider Church Union with the Catholic "Latins" of Western Europe because they believed that their faith would triumph, and the union was only reluctantly celebrated during the final siege in the hope of eliciting military help from the West—which never came.

Right: Originally a Christian cathedral, the Hagia Sophia was transformed into an Islamic mosque after Constantinople was captured by Mehmed II in 1453 and became the Ottoman capital.

حسن رضي الله عنه
علي رضي الله عنه

JUSTINIAN'S REIGN

Below: A mosaic in Ravenna's Basilica of San Vitale shows Empress Theodora, wife of Justinian, holding court. Unconventionally, she insisted that court attendees salute her as they would her husband.

Justinian succeeded his uncle, Justin I, as emperor of Byzantium (the Christian Roman Empire) in August 527 CE. Born of low origins in about 482 CE, he was destined to become one of the greatest Byzantine emperors, for he reconquered large areas of the West in North Africa, Italy, and southern Spain, which had been lost to the barbarians. He was also responsible for the revision and codification of Roman law, which is still the basis of civil law in many countries and which reconciled the law of old Rome with Christian ideals and standards. In these aims he was partnered by his ambitious and determined wife, Theodora, who was notorious for her past career as a mime (or striptease) actress in the Hippodrome and the fact that she had an illegitimate daughter prior to meeting Justinian. The were married in 525 after a special law passed by Justinian's uncle allowed the marriage of senators and actresses, which until then had been banned, while actresses had been denied the sacrament by the Church.

Justinian's battle for Orthodoxy

Both the emperor and empress were interested in theological debate, and supporters and patrons of churchmen and theologians. Believing that unity of faith was essential for unity as a whole within the empire, Justinian, early in his reign, brought about the suppression of many heretical groups and the forcible conversion to Orthodoxy of large numbers of pagans (some 70,000) who still remained in

Asia Minor. Paganism was outlawed entirely, even in private life. The rights of Jews were restricted, with the Hebrew language being forbidden in the synagogues. Heretics were executed: Justinian himself was present at the burning and drowning of prominent Manichaeans, while other groups who were deemed heretical, such as the Montanists who had women priests, committed mass suicide. Christians who lapsed into paganism were put to death, and pagans were banned from the public service.

Justinian's attempt to unite the empire under the umbrella of one faith was to be unsuccessful, despite the fact that he proclaimed that the emperor's word was law. His attempts to force his subjects to accept doctrinal compromises satisfied neither East nor West. The heresy Monophysitism (now called Miaphysitism), which taught that Christ had only one nature, which was divine (not a mixture of divine and human as in Orthodox doctrine), was prevalent in the eastern provinces of Syria and Egypt, despite having been condemned in 451. The empress Theodora was a fervent Monophysite, and the historian Procopius reports that the couple deliberately broadcast their religious differences to retain the support of all their subjects. It is notable that following Theodora's early death from cancer in 548, Justinian's attitude toward the Monophysites became more severe.

JUSTINIAN THE BUILDER

Justinian built or renovated some thirty churches in Constantinople alone, including that of the *Theotokos* (Mother of God) at Pege, where he believed he had been cured of a kidney disease. His most famous architectural achievement was the rebuilding of the Hagia Sophia, which had been burnt down during riots in 532 CE, following dissatisfaction with Justinian's officials and oppressive tax collectors. He used the opportunity of rebuilding the "Great Church" to showcase his reign, presenting himself as a builder rivaling the achievements of Solomon in his construction of the Temple at Jerusalem. Justinian also restored the Church of the Holy Apostles, the burial place of the imperial family, where he and Theodora were to be interred.

Right: Rebuilt by Justinian and consecrated in 550 CE, the Church of the Holy Apostles was demolished by the Ottomans in 1461 so they could build the Fatih Mosque.

Justinian as theologian

Justinian was genuinely and enthusiastically devout. He was one of the first emperors of Byzantium to be shown on his coinage bearing the cross, and he even wrote a number of theological treatises. He personally took part in dogmatic disputes and sponsored the Fifth Ecumenical Council in 553, though he was no respecter of churchmen who failed to agree with his theological definitions, on one occasion putting the pope under house arrest, when he visited Constantinople, for disagreeing with him.

Despite his persecution of Monophysites early in his reign, at the end of his life Justinian decided to adhere to the principles of the extreme Monophysite sect of Aphthartodocetists, who believed that Christ's divinity was such that even his body was incorruptible, not only after his resurrection but during his life on earth. Justinian, however, died (in 565) before his edict supporting these teachings was endorsed by the patriarch.

Justinian's reign was to be the turning point in late antiquity, when paganism finally received its deathblow. However, by the time of his death, compromise between Orthodoxy and Monophysitism was impossible, and there was an organized Miaphysite/Monophysite church and hierarchy in place, which still exists today.

Above: Justinian was a strict ruler, who would not tolerate opposition to his doctrines. Following the riots of 532 CE, he had 30,000 of the dissenters massacred in Constantinople's famous Hippodrome.

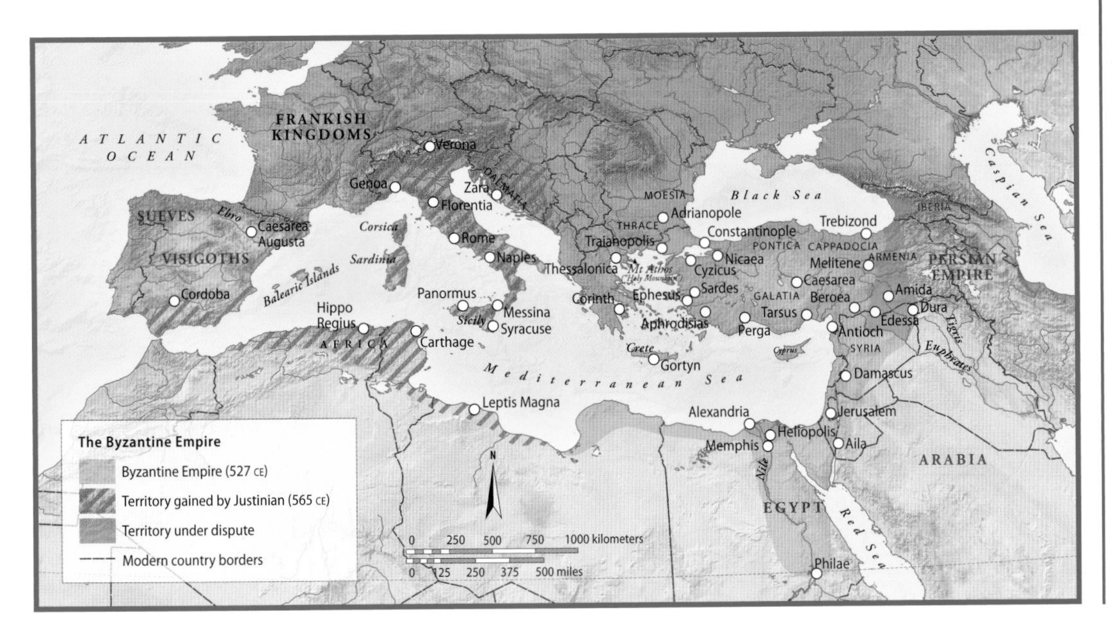

HAGIA SOPHIA

Right: In 1935, after more than 1,500 years of turbulent history, the Hagia Sophia was transformed into a museum by the Turkish president at that time, Kemal Atatürk.

The original church of "Holy Wisdom" (Hagia Sophia) in Constantinople was constructed by Constantine's son, Constantius II, and was the first of three structures to hold that name. The original church was inaugurated on February 15, 360, but was burnt down by the supporters of the patriarch John Chrysostom in 404. The church that stands in Istanbul today is the work of the Emperor Justinian, after the Hagia Sophia was again burned down in riots in January 532 that nearly cost Justinian his throne. This new "Great Church" was to be the most spectacular monument of Byzantine architecture and the seat of the Patriarch of Constantinople, and was to take 10,000 craftsmen five years to build. It was to remain the largest building in the world until 1520, when the Cathedral of Seville was completed.

Structure and design

The building itself is relatively square—256 by 236 feet (78 by 72 m)—with a dome 102 feet (31 m) in diameter over the nave. Forty windows surround the dome's base. The dome had to be restored and raised after an earthquake in 558 during which the main dome completely collapsed, giving the building its present height of 180 feet (55 m). The dome's weight is supported by four pendentives (triangular sections of masonry), which rest on four huge piers. Contemporary observers remarked that the dome appeared to be floating on air, and this innovative design was to have a far-reaching influence on Orthodox and Islamic architecture. After the Turkish conquest of Constantinople in 1453 the bells, 50-foot (15-m) iconostasis, and altar were removed and the mosaics were covered with plaster, while the Islamic features, such as the mihrab and the four minarets, were added.

Below: In the mid-nineteenth century, Sultan Abdülmecid ordered an extensive renovation of the Hagia Sophia, which took 800 workers around two years to complete.

The finest decoration

Marble from all over the empire was imported for the building's columns, the largest of which are some 60 feet (18 m) tall and weigh over 70 tons (64 tonnes). The interior walls and pillars are covered with marble slabs of magnificent green, white, and purple. Increasingly down the centuries, the church was decorated with glorious mosaics of saints, Christ, the *Theotokos* (Mother of God), and members of the imperial family, some inlaid with gold and adorned with jewels and precious stones. During the iconoclast controversy these icons were removed, and the apse mosaic of the *Theotokos* and Christ was put in place in 867 to celebrate the return of icons in the reign of Michael III. The finest of the Hagia Sophia mosaics is generally agreed to be the Deesis ("Entreaty") Mosaic in the upper gallery, completed to mark the return of the church to the Orthodox faith in 1261, after 57 years of Catholic use following the Fourth Crusade. In this depiction the *Theotokos* and John the Baptist are shown interceding with Christ on behalf of humankind on the Day of Judgment. The Hagia Sophia also contained fabulous relics, such as a stone from

Christ's tomb, the milk of the Mother of God, Christ's shroud, and the bones of numerous saints and holy men. Many of these are now in the West following the Fourth Crusade's capture of Constantinople in 1204.

Liturgy and ceremonies

Ceremonies in the Hagia Sophia were an important part of court life, and the upper gallery was reserved for the empress and her retinue who thus looked down at proceedings from above. Significantly, it is in this gallery that we see the impressive mosaics depicting members of the imperial family including the Empress Zoe and her third husband. At its southeast corner a passage connected the Hagia Sophia directly to the Great Palace so that the empress could enter the church privately.

The personnel involved in the running of Hagia Sophia was immense: Along with three other nearby churches, the Hagia Sophia was served originally in the sixth century by 425 clergy, but even these were not sufficient, and the number was later increased to 525. Imperial weddings normally took place in the palace, but it was customary for the emperor to be crowned in the Hagia Sophia and imperial baptisms could take place there too. When the violently iconoclastic emperor Constantine V was baptized in the church in 718, he defecated in the imperial font (so later Orthodox sources tell us), thus heralding his future as an icon-destroying heretic.

Left: In 1520, the Cathedral of Seville took the Hagia Sophia's place as the largest building in the world. It is still considered by some to be the world's biggest Gothic cathedral.

THE NATURE OF GOD

Right: St Elijah's Church in Cairo is just one of the many Melchite houses of worship in Egypt that derive from the Miaphysite/Monophysite churches of the past.

With the conversion of Constantine the Great in the early fourth century, Christianity became universally acceptable, though it was not imposed until the reign of Theodosius I in 381 CE. With the consequent surge of converts, wealth, and growth of a Church hierarchy, it became incumbent on the Church to clearly define the parameters of the faith. It was laid down at the Council of Nicaea in 325 that God has one "substance" in three "persons" and that the Father and Son therefore share the same "substance": They are consubstantial. The interrelationship of the Holy Trinity, and in particular the nature of Christ, was to be pivotal to many heretical debates and give rise to numerous sects in the early centuries.

Christological debate

Arianism was to remain the major theological and political problem of the fourth century, with immense popular debate around its issues, numerous councils attempting to reconcile both sides, and two emperors of the East being fanatic Arians, as were the "barbarian" tribes that settled in the West during the late fourth and the fifth century.

Opposite: The question of the role of icons in worship caused much heated debate—and occasionally violence—in the first millennium after Jesus' death. Icons are now revered in the Eastern Orthodox Church.

In the early fifth century Nestorius, Patriarch of Constantinople, objected to the term *Theotokos* (Mother of God) on the grounds that Mary was actually the Mother of Christ (*Christotokos*), thus stressing Christ's humanity rather than his divinity. He was demoted and exiled, though his adherents, the Nestorians, formed their own church that spread widely to Persia, parts of Syria and Arabia, India, and China. The question of whether he was a heretic is still under debate.

Below: Emperor Theodosius I united the Western and Eastern parts of the Roman Empire, and endorsed "Catholic Christianity" as the only officially sanctioned religion in the Empire.

Christ's divine nature

The next major heresy (which was never resolved) was that of Miaphysitism/Monophysitism, which tried to find another solution to Christ's relationship to the Father. The conclusion was that, while on earth, Christ's human nature was overshadowed by his divinity: The physical Christ was God rather than man. The provinces of Syria, Palestine, and Egypt were unremittingly Miaphysite/Monophysite, and the persecutions that had intermittently taken place against them made them supporters of the Arab invasions in the seventh century because under Arab rule they had freedom of worship. Attempts in the seventh century to propose compromise solutions such as monoenergism (that Christ had a single "energy") and monotheletism (that Christ had a single "will") failed dismally. The descendants of the Miaphysite/Monophysite church, who were independent of Byzantium after the Arab conquest, still exist today in the Melchite and Jacobite churches in Egypt, Syria, and Armenia.

The great icon debate

In the eighth and ninth centuries one of the greatest conflicts in Byzantine society was caused by the theological interpretation of icons—images of Christ, the *Theotokos*, and the saints—and their role in worship. Icons had been frowned upon as being pagan by the early Church, and the iconoclasts were reacting against the increasingly public use of icon-veneration from the sixth century. When Leo III in 726 ordered the removal of the icon of Christ above the gate of the palace it caused a riot including women and monks, who were always passionate defenders of icon-veneration. The clergy and army, however, favored removal, and the educated in general accepted that any attempt to depict Christ threatened to confuse or separate his two natures, since his divine nature could not be represented.

After some persecution, icons were again permitted under Empress Irene, ruling as regent for her son Constantine VI in 787. Even so, the army replaced an iconoclast ruler on the throne in the early ninth century and yet another empress-regent, Theodora, restored icons permanently in 843. It was not, however, until 867 that the first icons were publicly inaugurated in Constantinople.

ORIGINS OF HERESIES IN BYZANTIUM

Heresies may have arisen from a number of causes: The dissatisfaction of the poor; the wish to assert national identity, as in Egypt and Syria; and the continuation of pagan philosophies, especially in the East. Mainly, however, the motives lay within Christianity itself and the importance to the Byzantines of attempting to understand the nature of God and the way to salvation. Indeed, even when the Turks were at their walls in 1453, the Byzantines strongly believed that, whatever the forces ranged against them, God would protect "His" empire as long as it adhered to Orthodoxy.

LITURGY AND PRAYER

Above: In the Bible, Jesus often shares a meal with those he is teaching. This gesture is reflected in Byzantine liturgical practice, which saw Jesus present in the sacramental bread and wine.

The word "liturgy" (from the Greek *leitourgikos*, "ministering") means the order of service, which is symbolically modeled on the words and actions of Jesus in the New Testament and includes the sacraments, such as baptism and the Eucharist, that remind us of Jesus' life and his commands that we should keep these sacraments in his memory. Accordingly, liturgical practices in the Byzantine Church included a number of gestures performed by Jesus, such as blessing, bathing, touching, eating, and anointing, as well as the use of objects touched by him, such as bread, wine, water, and oil. The Eucharist, for example, is a replication of the words and actions described as taking place at the Last Supper.

The Byzantine rite

The Byzantine rite, or Rite of Constantinople, is used by all Eastern Orthodox Churches and the Greek Catholic Church and is the second largest in use today (after the Roman rite). It consists of the liturgies, canonical hours, sacraments, and prayers developed in the city of Constantinople, the capital of Byzantium and center of the Greek Orthodox Church. While there were originally alternative liturgies, from around 1000 CE the liturgy of John Chrysostom (Patriarch of Constantinople in the early fifth century) predominated. This liturgy consists of four parts: The preparation of the bread and wine; the introductory service of antiphons, litanies, and prayers; the "Liturgy of the Word" in which the texts to be read are carried from and to the altar, symbolizing the coming of Christ as the "Word of God"; and the liturgy of the Eucharist itself. However, the older liturgy of St Basil is still used on important days such as Christmas Eve, Sundays in Lent (though not Palm Sunday), and New Year's Day (which is also St Basil's Feast day).

PRAYER IN THE BYZANTINE CHURCH

Prayer in the Byzantine Church involves speaking in thought or word to God, Christ, the *Theotokos*, or the saints, in the form of petitions, thanks, praise, or confessions of faith. Prayer can involve the recitation of agreed formulae (such as the Our Father or Kyrie Eleison), or meditation, which should, if possible, focus on the life of Jesus. The ascetic life was thought to purify the mind and present the greatest possibilities of meditation, and the "Prayer of the Heart" (or "Jesus Prayer") was practiced in particular by the monks of Mt Athos, with hesychast or contemplative monks believing that through meditation and private prayer they could achieve communion with God.

Right: The monasteries of Mt Athos in modern-day Greece are famously linked to the Hesychast movement. Gregory of Palamas, an early follower of Hesychasm, was a monk at the Monastery of Vatopedi.

Above: Like most other Eastern churches, this Russian Orthodox Church in Florence, Italy, is elaborately decorated with numerous icons of Jesus, the Virgin Mary, and various saints.

Differences between the Roman and Byzantine rites include the use of unleavened bread in the Greek Eucharist, married clergy (but only for those below the rank of bishop; a priest had to divorce his wife if he wished to be promoted to a bishopric), a different Paschal (Easter) calendar, and a creed in which the Holy Spirit proceeds from the Father, not from the Father and the Son. It was this last difference that played the greatest part in the schism between the Churches, which is still in place today. Traditionally, in Byzantine practice, the congregation stands or moves around, and is separated from the sanctuary by an iconostasis; icons, music, architecture, vessels, and vestments unique to the rite have evolved over centuries. Most services are chanted rather than recited, and fasting laws are also stricter than in the West, with four fasting seasons, during which meat and dairy products, and sometimes fish and oil, are renounced.

The role of the priesthood

The liturgy is normally presided over by a minister, such as a priest or bishop, accompanied by a deacon who plays an important part in orchestrating the various actions, words, and gestures required of the congregation. Women, of course, were excluded from the priesthood, though in the early Church many women were allowed to become deaconesses so that they could assist in the baptism of women for reasons of decency.

Both court ritual and the prevalence of great monastic institutions influenced liturgical tradition. Imperial services were primarily enacted in the Hagia Sophia, although stational services were also an important part of the emperor's duties—increasingly, in Byzantine history, the entire city was seen as "liturgical space" and much of the emperor's time was taken up by processions to holy stations and buildings in the capital.

At the same time the powerful monastic institutions enriched the development of the Byzantine rite, especially in relation to music, iconography, hymns, and prayers. Byzantine music generally refers to the plainsong chant that accompanied the liturgy, and important churches and monasteries had large and imposing choirs.

EASTERN MONASTICISM

Monasteries (communities of monks or nuns) were established in Egypt and Syria from the late third century, the most famous instigator being St Antony the Great, who gave away all his possessions to live the solitary ascetic life. However, he was followed by many others interested in this lifestyle and, until his death in 356, had gathered around him in the Egyptian desert an extensive community. This trend was followed elsewhere: In the fourth and fifth centuries solitary hermits were common, who often followed very strict ascetic practices, living in caves, trees, and on top of pillars for periods exceeding 30 years. The Church, however, encouraged the growth of communities rather than the practice of individual asceticism, and from the sixth century the monastic establishment was the norm, in which a group of women or men devoted themselves to prayer and contemplation in search of salvation for themselves and for those for whom they prayed.

Below: Roussanou Monastery at Meteora, Greece, was built on the site of a hermitage in the sixteenth century. It was restored in the twentieth century, when a bridge was constructed to aid accessibility.

Monasteries

Monasteries could be of almost any size, from a minimum of three monks or nuns to the huge Stoudion Monastery in Constantinople, which housed over a thousand people. Monasteries were most prominent in Constantinople and on holy mountains such as Mt Athos; remote desert sites far from crowded cities were always popular in the East and Egypt. Many groups of monks felt more comfortable away from civilization, and from the fourteenth century at Meteora ("floating in the air") a group of monasteries was built on inaccessible rocky outcrops in northern Thessaly, Greece, some of which necessitated visitors and monks, as well as supplies, being drawn up on ropes.

There were no monastic "orders" as in the West, so monasteries were usually independent institutions reporting to the local bishop and only bound by their foundation charter, their *typikon*. Many of the smaller foundations belonged to specific families so that family members could retire there in old age or after the death of a spouse. This was common throughout the Byzantine Empire, and a high proportion of monks and nuns took their vows after a period of married life, as it was popularly believed that at death monastics went directly to Paradise instead of waiting in limbo for the Second Coming. There was even a tradition of double monasteries, which housed separate communities of monks and nuns under the direction of the same superior. While officially prohibited more than once, they still remained popular because families could remain together, with the husband and wife joining the community after their children had grown up. The practice resurged toward the end of the empire.

Architecture and organization

Typically, monasteries were housed within solid walls, along the inside of which were the dormitories, stables, workshops, refectory, and storerooms, with the main church (the *katholikon*) in the center of the complex. Some institutions included a bath and an infirmary. Most monasteries were governed by a superior (who in a family foundation could be a designated family member, with the role being transmitted from mother to daughter, or father to son), alongside a steward, sacristan, and officials who were in charge of the refectory, finances, and archives. Many monasteries, as on Mt Athos, could possess considerable holdings of land through bequests and donations, and it was customary for most monks and nuns to engage not only in prayer but also in manual labor, which might include tilling the fields, or in the case of nuns, spinning and weaving, so that the institution could be self-sufficient and a working community. There were very strict hours of communal prayer, which included the services of vespers, compline, midnight office, matins, and the hours (first, third, sixth, and ninth). The great members of the monastery of the Akoimetoi (the "sleepless" ones) in Constantinople performed their offices perpetually, with three choirs rotating in eight-hour shifts.

Left: St Antony the Great is considered the father of monasticism. His life of asceticism was recorded in the widely read contemporary biography by Athanasius of Alexandria.

Below: St Simeon Monastery (Anba Hadra) was founded in the seventh century CE on a hilltop in the desert near Aswan, Egypt. Abandoned in the thirteenth century, it is now in ruins.

The social role of monasticism

As well as providing a haven from the world for those people who wanted to follow the contemplative life, monasteries also performed valuable social services for nearby communities. They offered shelter to orphans and the elderly, took in the disabled and widows, and provided an alternative to prison for deposed emperors and unsuccessful rebels and their families. Many institutions also possessed guesthouses and hospitals, and distributed food and clothing to the poor. In Byzantium, monasteries seldom doubled as schools, except for the few children who had decided to enter monastic life, but they did possess libraries and scriptoria where manuscripts were copied, and perhaps half of all scribes were monks. Many monks were also hymnwriters or leading theologians, and monastics were fervent supporters of icon-veneration, with many institutions possessing famous miracle-working icons, which even today are the focus of pilgrimage.

THE HOLY MOUNTAIN

Right: While many monks on Mt Athos were uneducated, in the cenobitic monasteries there was great focus on intellectual pursuits, with scriptoria and large libraries of manuscripts.

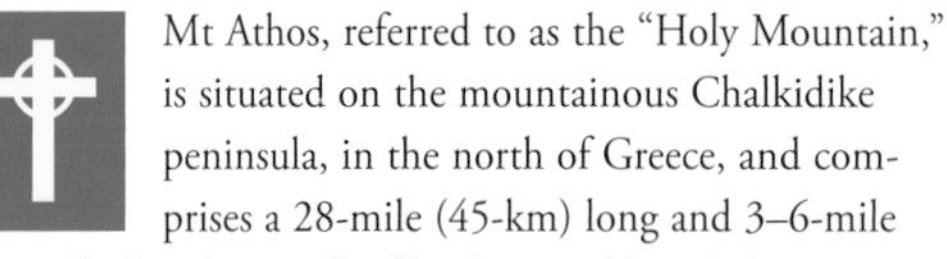

Mt Athos, referred to as the "Holy Mountain," is situated on the mountainous Chalkidike peninsula, in the north of Greece, and comprises a 28-mile (45-km) long and 3–6-mile (5–10-km) wide stretch of land accessible only by sea. While geographically part of Greece, it is an autonomous monastic state under the jurisdiction of the Patriarch of Constantinople, and home to 20 Eastern Orthodox monasteries. Known as the "Garden of the Mother of God," because Mary supposedly visited it on her way to Cyprus with St John, no other females are allowed to set foot on the peninsula, and traditionally even female animals were not permitted, except for cats to reduce the rodent population and hens whose eggs provide the yolk needed for the paint used in traditional iconography.

Settlement on Mt Athos

Attracted by the isolated nature of the area, monks began to settle on Mt Athos in numbers during the eighth or ninth centuries, initially living as solitary hermits. The first real monastic institution in the area was founded at nearby Kolobou in the mid-ninth century, while it was only in the mid-tenth century that institutions on Mt Athos itself came into being. The typical community was the Lavra, in which scattered monastic cells centered around a complex of church, refectory, and storerooms, with the monks living as solitaries during the week but assembling for worship at weekends. The Great Lavra was founded in 963 CE by (St) Athanasios of Athos and was to remain the most important institution on Mt Athos, while most of the other significant foundations took place before the end of the same century; that is, before 1000 CE.

Many of these foundations were established by different ethnic groups, most notable of whom were the Georgians (the Iveron Monastery), as well as the Italians, the Slavs, and the Armenians. From 885, emperors prohibited laymen or farmers from inhabiting the peninsula, which was to be open only to monks, with the mountain itself decreed an independent monastic state in 972 by Emperor John I Tzimiskes.

Below: Monasteries continued to exist in Thrace (in modern-day Greece), despite the Mt Athos community losing control of their land in the area after the arrival of the Ottoman Turks.

Government and organization

Initially, in the tenth century, the monks elected a Protos (or leader) who represented the whole community, but the abbot of the Great Lavra soon became the most authoritative figure. Increasingly the monasteries became great landowners of properties outside of the peninsula and engaged in the export of wood and agricultural products, such as fruit and wine. Emperors granted the monasteries stipends from the treasury or exemptions from taxes, as well as donating lands, and rulers from as far away as Serbia, Bulgaria, Wallachia, and Trebizond sent their own donations.

As the Byzantine Empire declined during the fifteenth century, communal monasticism also declined and many monks relocated because of the Turkish threat, while others returned to a more individualized or hermetic form of monastic life. Mt Athos remained autonomous under the Ottoman Turks, but the monasteries lost both their tax exemptions and their large estates outside the peninsula in Thrace and Macedonia.

Below: The Russian Orthodox Monastery of St Panteleimon near Mt Athos was founded in the eleventh century. Many Russian monks carried the information and culture they encountered on Mt Athos back to their homeland.

MT ATHOS TODAY

Currently there are over 1,500 monks settled on Mt Athos—both in the 20 monasteries and in 12 smaller, more isolated communities—many of whom are engaged in the work of cataloging and restoring the thousands of ancient manuscripts, icons, and ecclesiastical paraphernalia, such as vestments, which have been donated over the centuries. There are many monks of Russian, Serbian, or Bulgarian extraction; only males who are Orthodox and over 18 years of age are allowed to live on Mt Athos. The mountain is governed by the "Holy Community," which includes representatives of the 20 monasteries, with a civil governor in the administrative center at Karyes, and is today a UNESCO World Heritage site.

Right: The monks who currently reside on Mt Athos are responsible for a variety of tasks, including the repair and restoration of historical vestments (ceremonial attire worn by clergymen).

EASTERN CHRISTIANITY HEADS NORTH

Above: The tiny Church of Christ Pantocrator on the Nesebar Peninsula in Bulgaria was constructed around 400 years after Methodius' followers traveled to Bulgaria.

Although legend ascribed the Christianization of much of the area north of the Black Sea to St Andrew, brother of St Peter—a legend that allowed Eastern Christianity to challenge the primacy of the Roman Church—the effective conversion of the Balkans began in the ninth century and was a matter of conflict between the Roman and Byzantine churches, both of whom wished to extend their influence in this region. The greatest impact on the region, however, was effected by Byzantium, with much of the success being due to the brothers Cyril and Methodius.

Conversion of the Slavs

Saints Cyril and Methodius, the "Apostles of the Slavs," were brothers born in Thessalonica in the first quarter of the ninth century, who received an advanced education at Constantinople. There has been considerable debate on whether they might have been of Slavic descent, but there is no firm evidence on this point. When in 863 Rastislav of Moravia asked Emperor Michael III to send him missionaries, Cyril (more properly known as Constantine at this point), a philosopher who had already undertaken a mission to the Arab Caliph and the Khagan of the Khazars, was chosen for the role along with his brother. Rastislav was attempting to assert his independence from the Franks who had supported his claim to the throne, and turned instead to Constantinople in his wish to evangelize his kingdom. An expert linguist, Cyril was already acquainted with the language of the Slavs, and prior to the brothers' departure they invented the Glagolitic alphabet and the means of recording Slavonic texts in what is now known as Old Church Slavonic, as well as training assistants in this work of translation. Into this literary language Cyril and Methodius then translated the Gospels and psalms, as well as some liturgical books.

Below: A fresco of Methodius and Cyril adorns the wall of a fourteenth-century monastery near Skopje, Macedonia. The university in Skopje is named in honor of the brothers.

Conflict between Catholic and Orthodox churches

During their time in Moravia Cyril and Methodius organized a church, which used the native Slavonic language in its liturgy and worship. They also created, along Byzantine lines, the first Slavic civil code of law. However, their mission was viewed with suspicion by the Frankish (Roman) Church in the area and after some five years they were invited to Rome by Pope Nicholas I who had been alerted to the fact that they had come from Constantinople (at present in a state of schism with the Roman Church), and were preaching in Slavonic rather than Latin. Nicholas had died by the time the brothers arrived in 868, but his successor Adrian received them with respect and sanctioned their conducting the liturgy in Slavonic.

Methodius' mission

Cyril died in 869 while still in Rome (where he became a monk, under the name of Cyril, shortly before his death). The pope then sent Methodius to Pannonia and Moravia as archbishop. Shortly afterward, however, in 870, he was summoned to a synod of the Frankish Church, who were incensed at his holding the rank of archbishop, and put in prison. He was finally liberated after three years by the new Pope John VIII, who reinstated him to his diocese. Methodius continued to labor over the next few years to convert the Bohemians and Poles in northern Moravia and create a native church. Despite ongoing opposition, he used Slavonic in the Mass; this was one reason why he was made to return to Rome in 879 to prove his Orthodoxy. After a visit to Constantinople, Methodius and his disciples completed his translation of the scriptures as well as of numerous liturgical works and some Byzantine canon law.

THE LEGACY OF CYRIL AND METHODIUS

In 1980, Pope John Paul II proclaimed that brothers Cyril and Methodius were "patrons of Europe." They share the same saints' day, May 11, and in Eastern Europe they are popularly seen as the originators of Eastern European learning and education. They have been especially venerated by the Russian Orthodox Church, and even today they are celebrated in a variety of different festivals throughout Eastern Europe.

Following his death in 885, Methodius' disciples were forced to flee to Bulgaria where they established theological schools and devised the Cyrillic alphabet, a simplification of the Glagolitic. This spread through most of the Slavic world to become the standard alphabet, and thus the vehicle for the spread of Christianity through Eastern Europe; the Slavic sacred language spread to Bulgaria and from there to Serbia and the Kievan Rus, and thus Russia.

Below: Legend has it that St Andrew journeyed along the Black Sea coast, preaching as he went. Ukrainians believe he predicted the location of Kiev.

THE KIEVAN RUS

One of the most significant events in world history was the conversion of Grand Prince Vladimir of the Kievan Rus to Christianity in 988. The "land of Rus" was a mingling of Slav and Norse (Viking) cultures centered on the city of Kiev. As the Slavic tribes had been constantly at war with each other, they invited, so the *Russian Primary Chronicle* tells us, the Varangian Rus to rule over them and, as a result, three Viking brothers settled in Novgorod, the eldest of whom, Riurik, was the legendary ancestor of all Russian Tsars until the sixteenth century.

Riurik's successor Oleg chose Kiev as his new capital, and Kiev was to be the center of Rus culture until its fall to the Mongols in 1237. Between 945 and 956 Kiev had been ruled by Olga, who in 948 traveled to Constantinople and was converted to Christianity, with the emperor and empress as her sponsors. Her son Sviatoslav I, however, was determined to remain pagan, and in 978 his son Vladimir became Grand Prince.

Below: Named for Constantinople's Hagia Sophia, St Sophia Cathedral in Kiev was constructed in the eleventh century. The striking exterior is the result of renovations in the seventeenth and eighteenth centuries.

Grand Prince Vladimir

Prior to his conversion to Christianity, Vladimir is depicted in the *Russian Primary Chronicle* (a Christian source written c. 1113) as cruel and lecherous, with seven or eight wives and hundreds of concubines. At his accession he worshipped the pagan gods of the Slavic pantheon, and had statues of pagan gods set up at Kiev, the chief of whom was Perun, god of thunder and lightning. But Kiev was becoming surrounded by regimes that had converted or were converting to Christianity, and there already were a few Christians among the Rus, such as Olga.

After securing and expanding his territory, Vladimir pursued an alliance with the Emperor of Byzantium. This contact with Constantinople (known to the Rus as "Tsargrad"—the Emperor's City) was to result in conversion of the Rus to Orthodoxy and was to change the entire focus of their civilization and orient it from the steppe and paganism toward the south and Christianity. According to the *Russian Primary Chronicle*, Vladimir considered all four major religions in the region as possible options: Roman Catholicism, Islam, Judaism, and Orthodoxy. Islam was rejected because of the prohibition on alcohol, as drinking was "the joy of the Rus," and Judaism because the Jews no longer had their own state and nation showing that God had rejected them. A visit to Constantinople decided his envoys, who saw the Latin liturgy as feeble in comparison with Orthodox rite, and the magnificent Hagia Sophia as a veritable "heaven on earth, where God dwells among men."

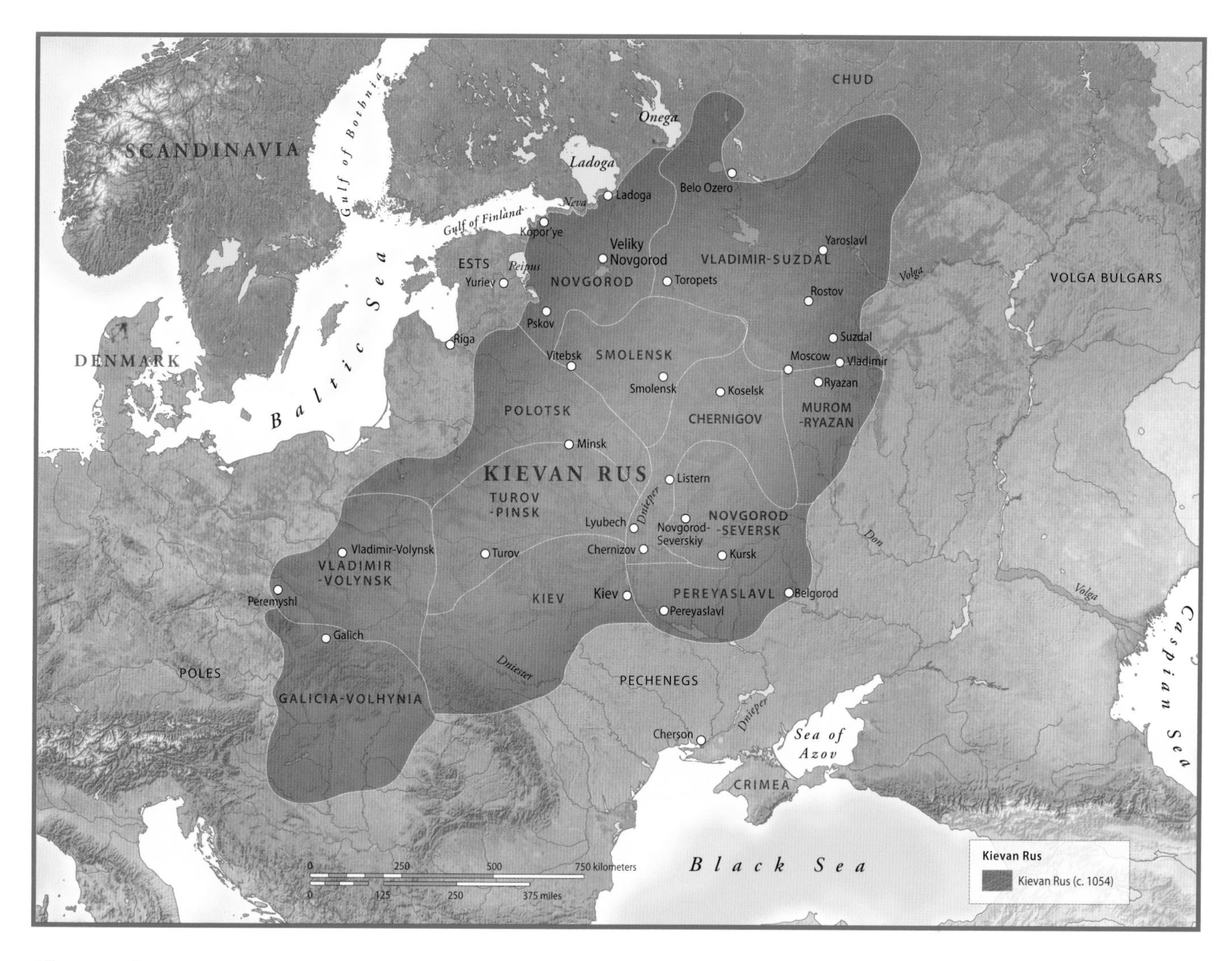

Alliance and conversion

The political context of his conversion was as follows: In 987 Vladimir assisted the Emperor Basil II in putting down a serious internal revolt, in the process taking the city of Cherson in the Crimea. In return he demanded that he be allowed to marry Anna, Basil's younger sister; his conversion to Christianity was a condition of this alliance. It was a heavy price, for this was the first "purple-born" Byzantine princess in centuries to marry a foreigner. A reluctant Anna, along with an entourage of officials and clergy, was dispatched to Cherson where Vladimir was baptized, taking the name of Basil in honor of the Emperor and returning Cherson to the Byzantines. Legend described that he had been struck with blindness, which was miraculously relieved when he underwent baptism.

Conversion of the Rus people occurred immediately and without discussion or argument. Vladimir set aside his other wives, destroyed the pagan idols he had earlier set up, ordered that all the inhabitants of Kiev be baptized in the Dnieper River en masse, and warned that all who refused to be converted would feel his personal enmity. Some pagan communities persisted, however, at least until the 1100s, and in many places pagan rituals were combined with Christian practices.

The benefits of conversion

The immediate benefits of conversion to the Rus included literacy and the introduction of written documents, including governmental records, while the Bible was translated into Slavonic, as was the liturgy. The people of Rus were thus able to worship in their own language, unlike the inhabitants of Western Europe, whose liturgy was in Latin. Early Rus cathedrals were designed by Greek architects, but a distinctive artistic style developed from the Byzantine, to become distinctively Russian, including the creation of Russian-style frescoes and icons.

A further benefit included the establishment of schools and ecclesiastical courts and the development of coinage, with gold and silver coins being struck depicting Jesus on the obverse and Vladimir on the reverse enthroned and wearing Byzantine regalia. In this way Vladimir was transformed into a Christian monarch with institutional legitimacy ratified by God himself, and Kiev was acknowledged as the "Rus Metropolis" or mother city. The Orthodox Church was for centuries to remain an intrinsic part of the Russian identity, even after the destruction of Kiev by the Mongols, after which Moscow became the "Third Rome," the successor of Rome and Constantinople and the center of the Russian Orthodox Church.

Above: Conversion of the Rus to Christianity paved the way for the development of a unique style of art, whereby stylized images ("icons") were painted on wooden panels.

CHAPTER THREE

UNDER MUSLIM RULE

Within a century of Muhammad's death in 632 CE, Muslim armies had conquered a broad swathe of territory including Spain, northern Africa, the Middle East, Central Asia, and northwest India. The Abbasid Dynasty assumed power in 750 and ruled from Baghdad for five centuries. Regional dynasties grew up under the Abbasids, including those in heavily Christian areas like Egypt, the Maghrib (western North Africa), and Spain. Though the Mongol invasions of the thirteenth century led to the loss of much of this territory, three new Muslim empires (the Ottomans, the Mughals, and the Safavids) reclaimed dominance after the collapse of the Mongol administration in the fourteenth and fifteenth centuries. Christians never again dominated in the Middle East after the Muslim conquest.

Under Muslim rule, Christians and Jews were allowed to practice their own religion, as long as they paid a head tax called the *jizya*. They were called *dhimmis* ("protected peoples") because the *jizya* was a payment for protection. In addition, because they were the landowners in newly conquered territories and Muslims were not, they paid taxes on their land and other property. Sometimes these taxes were so onerous that people converted to Islam to avoid paying them. On the other hand, many Muslim rulers did little to encourage conversions because they wanted the revenue from the taxes.

Additional laws developed requiring *dhimmis* to wear or avoid wearing certain clothing or colors, forbidding the carrying of arms or the riding of horses, and requiring special permission to build or repair places of worship. Some rulers enforced these rules and others ignored them. Over time, the majority of the population converted to Islam. However, Christian communities still exist in these areas, and their churches represent some of the oldest forms of Christianity on Earth.

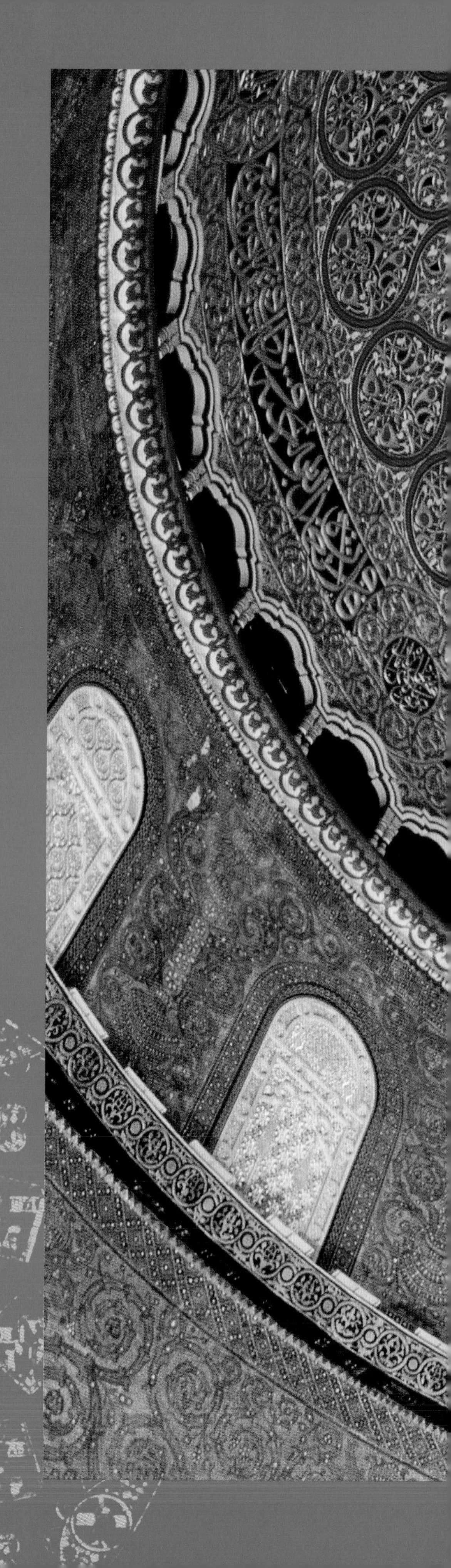

Right: The Dome of the Rock is an Islamic shrine in Jerusalem dating to 691 CE. The dome's interior is decorated with a red and gold mosaic, as well as inscriptions.

THE MUSLIM CONQUEST

Above: A late sixteenth-century illustration from the manuscript entitled *Zubdet-ut-Tevarih*, by Ottoman court historiographer Seyyid Lokman, depicts Jesus fleeing Damascus assisted by two angels.

Islam's first political expression emerged in 622 CE, when Muhammad assumed leadership of what is now the city of Medina in Saudi Arabia. His opponents controlled the city of Mecca, located 200 miles (322 km) to the south, until Muslim armies captured it in 630. Toward the end of his life, Muhammad concluded a peace agreement with the leaders of the local Christian and Jewish communities. They would be protected by the Muslims in exchange for payment of the *jizya*, a special tax on non-Muslims. Despite strong devotion to their polytheistic religions, the rural Bedouin converted to Islam before Muhammad died in 632, with virtually all of Arabia under his control.

Expansion of Muslim territory

The Bedouin people refused to give their allegiance to Muhammad's successor, Abu Bakr. This revolt, known as the *Ridda*, was rapidly crushed, but it convinced Bakr of the need to expand beyond Arabia to protect Muslim territory. Bakr died in 634, but the second caliph, Umar (who ruled between 634 and 644), implemented Bakr's intent to expand. He captured Syria and the city of Damascus from the Byzantines in 635. Jerusalem fell not long after, in 637. Umar instituted a policy of tolerance toward other religions, especially Jews and Christians, realizing that he needed the loyalty of his new subjects to secure his rule. He did, however, impose both the *jizya* and a tax on field productivity (known as the *kharaj*).

The Muslim army crossed the Sinai Peninsula and entered Egypt. In 642, the Byzantine Patriarch Cyrus surrendered the city of Alexandria. It was reconquered by the Byzantines in 645, but the Muslims recaptured it in 646.

After the first Muslim dynasty, the Umayyads, was established in Damascus in 661, a campaign to conquer the Maghrib (western North Africa) was launched in 663. Tripoli fell in 666, Tunisia in 670, and Carthage in 695. The Umayyads expanded into Spain and Central Asia in the early eighth century. Spain was ruled by the Visigoths (Arian Christians) and Central Asia was occupied by Turkish groups, most of whom were Buddhist. However, there had been a Christian presence since the late fifth century, and by the eighth century there were enough Turkish Christians to warrant their own metropolitan.

Christian reactions

At the time of the Muslim conquest, there were three main groups of Middle Eastern Christians: Chalcedonians, Miaphysites/Monophysites (including the Egyptian Copts and the Syrian Jacobites), and Nestorians. These three groups engaged in polemics against each other to prevent defections. Arabs were known for their raids, and initially Christians seemed to believe that the Muslim army was just another raiding party. They did not yet comprehend the magnitude of the invasion, nor did they realize that it had a serious religious aspect.

The Christian experience of the Muslim conquest varied with the time, place, and type of Christianity involved. One of the first Christian descriptions of what transpired comes from Jerusalem. Sophronius, the city's Chalcedonian patriarch, described the Muslim invaders as "godless" destroyers of towns, crops, churches, and monasteries. Nonetheless, he remained more concerned about his Christian opponents than he was about the Muslim invaders. A fellow Chalcedonian, Maximus the Confessor, was

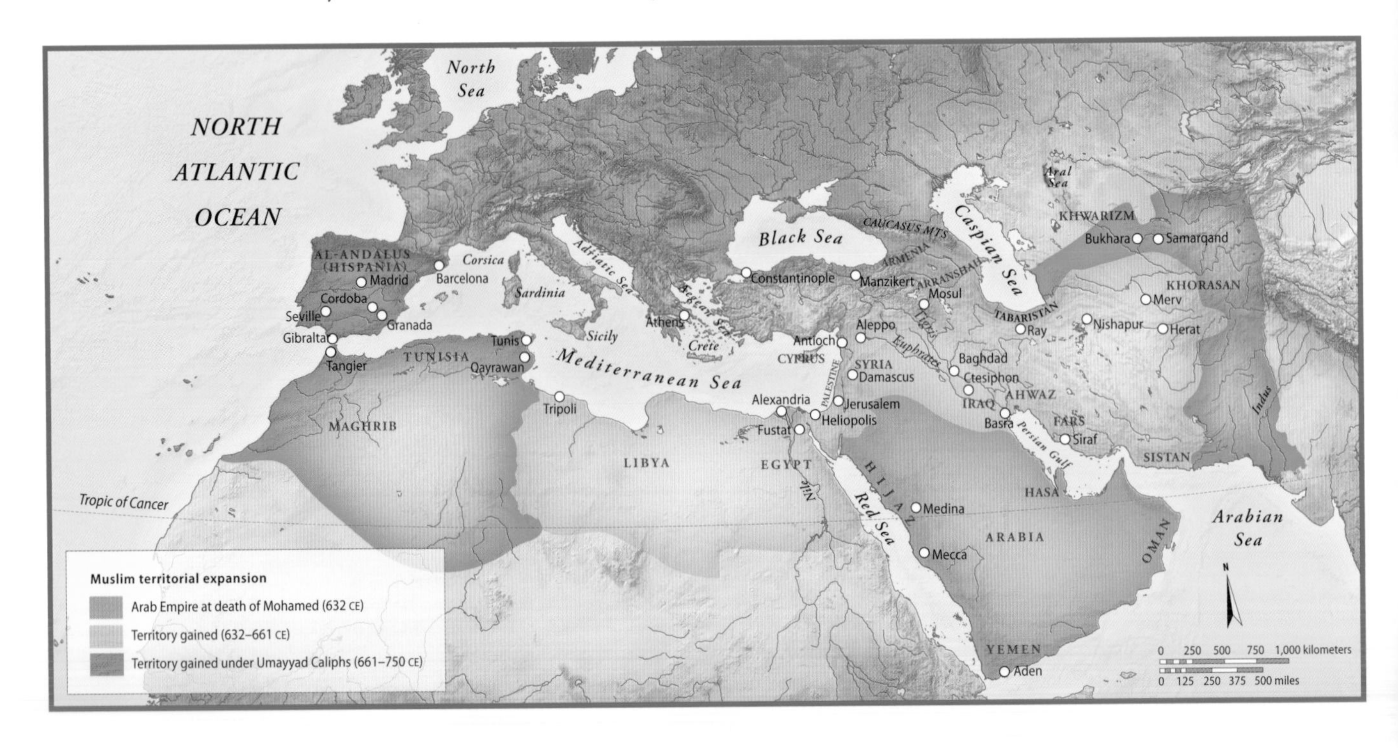

the first of many Christians to identify the religion of the invading Arabs as "Jewish." He described them as "a barbarous nation" comprised of "wild and untamed beasts" who were not truly human.

In northern Mesopotamia, a Nestorian patriarch named Isho'yab III (died 660) commented that the Arabs, like the Nestorians but unlike the Jacobites, considered God to be impassable and immortal. He said Muslims do not attack the Christian faith, and even confer benefits on churches and monasteries. He rebuked Christians for abandoning their faith when they were not forced to do so, but "merely" required to give up half of their possessions in exchange for remaining Christian.

In Egypt, Coptic Bishop John of Nikiu commented that the local population was dissatisfied with the Byzantine emperor and his appointed patriarch, which led to collaboration with the Muslim armies. He mentions the brutality of the invaders, but he also states that Christians who fled were permitted to return without harassment once peace was secured. However, their taxes were tripled. Some Christians were appointed to administrative positions, and Coptic Christians have continued to serve in the bureaucracy of Muslim Egypt ever since.

Above: Evening prayers at the Grand Mosque in the ancient city of Mecca can draw thousands of Muslims; the building can reportedly hold almost a million worshippers during important religious events.

JOHN OF DAMASCUS

The first Christian writer to demonstrate a detailed understanding of the religion of Islam, and to provide a Christian assessment of the portrayal of Jesus in the Koran (Qur'an), was John of Damascus (died c. 749). Unlike previous writers who had connected Islam with Judaism, John of Damascus saw a similarity to Christian Arians, since both denied that Christ and God existed eternally together.

NESTORIANS UNDER THE ABBASIDS

Above: Set among the hills near Gonbad in northern Iran is the Khalid Nibi shrine. Originally a site commemorating a fifth-century Nestorian Christian, today it is a place of Muslim pilgrimage.

After overthrowing the Umayyads in 750, the Abbasids built a new capital—Baghdad—on the Tigris River. The conquest had made Muslims the heirs of Greek science and philosophy. Caliph al-Ma'mun (813–833) founded the House of Wisdom in Baghdad, where scholars translated Greek, Persian, and Hindu texts into Arabic, and scientists engaged in the study of a variety of subjects such as engineering, optometry, and medicine. Baghdad was poised to become an intellectual and cultural center.

Right: Part of the Great Mosque of Samarra, built in the ninth century by the Abbasids in what is now Iraq, the Malwiya Tower is a spiral-shaped minaret 170 feet (52 m) high.

A favored group

Syrian Christians lived in Mesopotamia (present-day Iraq) prior to the Muslim conquest and remained there under the Abbasids. They belonged to one of the oldest Christian communities in the world, perhaps dating back to the very first generation of Christians; they were descendants of those shepherded by Isho'yab III during the Muslim conquest. Chalcedonian Christians considered these Nestorian Christians heretical. After suffering great persecutions in the fourth century, under the rule of the Persian Sassanids, the rule of the Muslims seemed mild by comparison. They were required to pay the *jizya*, refrain from building new churches, and not display crosses in public; and missionary activities were restricted. However, they were not physically harmed except during the reigns of Umar II (717–720) and al-Qadir (991–1031).

The Church of the East placed a high value on education, especially in the subjects of medicine, music, and languages in addition to theology. This prepared Nestorian Christians for their role in the Abbasid Empire, where they were favored above all other Christian groups. Only the Nestorian patriarchate was invited to move from Seleucia-Ctesiphon, the ancient center of Syrian Christianity, to Baghdad. The Arabs soon recognized that Nestorians were excellent financiers, builders, doctors, merchants, scientists, and teachers, not to mention translators. Most Nestorian scholars knew Syriac, Greek, and Arabic. Until the ninth century, almost all the renowned scholars in the House of Wisdom were Nestorian Christians. By the end of the eighth century, the Nestorian catholicos (patriarch) had more territory and probably a larger number of people under his direction than any pope prior to the sixteenth century. It was the Nestorians who were primarily responsible for transferring the knowledge of ancient Greece to the Arabs, from whence it was later transferred to Europe.

IN MUSLIM SPAIN

In 711 CE, when Muslim general Tariq ibn Ziyad led his forces north from the limestone promontory named after him (*Jabal Tariq* in Arabic, or the "Rock of Gibraltar"), the Iberian Peninsula was a Christian territory ruled by the Visigoths. By 720, all but the northernmost portions of the peninsula had become part of Dar al-Islam (the portion of the world that was ruled by Islam). The new Muslim territory was given the name al-Andalus, and Córdoba in southern Spain became its administrative center.

The last Umayyad outpost

Most of the Umayyad ruling family was slaughtered during the Abbasid Revolution that took place in 750; one grandson of the former caliph escaped to Spain. There, Abd al-Rahman I established the Emirate of Córdoba. This last outpost of Umayyad sovereignty continued for almost three centuries (756–1031), while the Abbasids and their affiliated regional dynasties ruled the rest of the Muslim world.

As Córdoba's population approached half a million, it became the most advanced city in Western Europe. Andalusian philosophers and scientists were an important influence on medieval European learning, and both Muslims and non-Muslims contributed to these achievements.

The life of a *dhimmi*

The three main religions in al-Andalus were Islam, Christianity, and Judaism. Most people were Christian, at least until the tenth century. Christians paid the *jizya* tax, with exceptions for the elderly, women, children, and those with disabilities. All Christians must accept Muslim superiority, refrain from trying to convert Muslims, and wear a special identifying badge. They had to abide by restrictions on clothing and the building of churches. A *dhimmi* (a Christian or Jew) could not give evidence in an Islamic court, own a Muslim slave, or marry a Muslim woman.

Despite differences in status between Muslims and *dhimmis*, the latter did have more rights than most subjugated populations at the time—they were not slaves, they were not forced to live in ghettoes, and they were not forced to convert to Islam, though there were economic and social inducements to do so. Although they often held jobs that were avoided by Muslims (like butchery or banking), they were not banned from any occupation. They could work in civil service jobs, but they could not be rulers. However, as Muslim power declined from the eleventh century, the position of non-Muslims deteriorated. There were pogroms against Jews and persecutions of Christians, with Christians forbidden to display any sign of their faith in public.

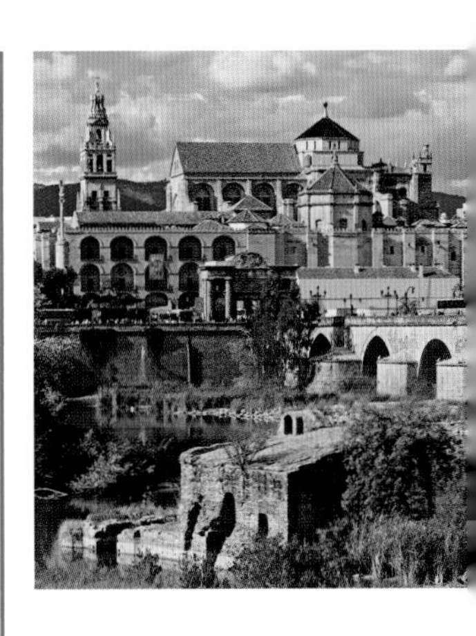

Above: Not long after the Muslims conquered the Iberian Peninsula, Emir Abd al-Rahman I ordered the construction of a mosque in Córdoba. The Mezquita was later consecrated as a Christian church.

Below: The Rock of Gibraltar is home to the Moorish Castle, built by Tariq ibn Ziyad in the early eighth century. The Moors occupied Gibraltar for over 700 years.

IN THE MAGHRIB

Right: An unusual baptismal bath dating back to the sixth century in a church near Kelibia, Tunisia, is covered with symbolic mosaics dedicated in honor of Bishop Cyprian.

Coastal colonies in the Maghrib (western North Africa) were an early center of Latin-speaking Christianity. Christianity spread mainly among the Italians who lived in urban areas; it made little headway among the indigenous Berbers.

Persecution of the Maghrib

The Maghribi church suffered episodic persecutions under Roman rule. Cyprian (died 258) was Bishop of Carthage during one of them. After the persecution ended, Cyprian had to decide what to do about Christians who had sacrificed to the Roman gods to escape death, but wished to be reinstated in the church. Since he believed there was no salvation outside the church, he allowed those who showed genuine repentance to rejoin the church.

The persecution of the Maghrib by the Roman emperor Diocletian, between 303 and 311, was the last, largest, and bloodiest. When Constantine legalized Christianity in 313, some North African church leaders refused to recognize priests ordained by bishops who had returned to the church after denying their faith under persecution. Donatus was a leader of the movement, and those who agreed with him were called Donatists. The Church in Rome rejected their position.

Decline of the Maghrib Christians

Christianity became the official religion of the Roman Empire by the end of the fourth century, but this did little to benefit most North African Christians because they belonged to the Donatists or other perspectives considered heretical by the official Church. This resulted in tension between the Maghrib and Rome.

In 429, the Vandals invaded the Maghrib. They followed an Arian form of Christianity, and therefore they opposed both the Donatists and the Roman Church. In 533, the Byzantine Empire drove the Vandals out and took control of the region. Once again, due to differences between Byzantine and Maghribi forms of Christianity, there was constant tension between them. Byzantine administrators often dealt harshly with Maghribis.

Muslim Arabs conquered the Maghrib region during the latter half of the seventh century. With the Byzantines soundly defeated, the Arabs turned to the conversion of the Berbers, and were successful. Islamization of the Christians of the Maghrib progressed slowly, but steadily. The Muslim rulers did not persecute the Christians, however; the Christians were required to pay additional taxes, and many found it too expensive to remain a Christian. Within a century, Christianity had declined precipitously. The last evidence of surviving Christian bishoprics comes from the tenth century.

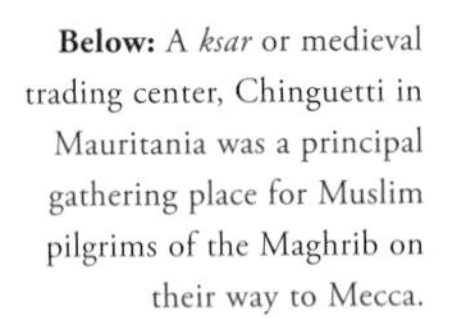

Below: A *ksar* or medieval trading center, Chinguetti in Mauritania was a principal gathering place for Muslim pilgrims of the Maghrib on their way to Mecca.

EGYPT UNDER THE FATIMIDS

The Fatimids were Ismailis, a branch of Shia Islam. In the tenth century, they became the dominant power in North Africa. They conquered Egypt, then a quasi-independent part of the Abbasid Caliphate, in 969, and ruled until 1174. The Fatimids were Egypt's only Shiite dynasty.

The Fatimids built a new capital in 973 called al-Qahirah ("the Victorious"), or Cairo. Under their rule, Egypt became a center of trade between the Atlantic and Indian oceans, and the center of a vast missionary movement. The newly established al-Azhar University served as the training center of an army of Shiite missionaries. Despite their missionary zeal, the Fatimids were very tolerant of other religions, perhaps learning from past experiences in which they had attempted to forcibly convert conquered populations only to reap a harvest of hostility. Sunni Muslims experienced the most restrictions, since they were suspected as possible supporters of the (Sunni) Abbasid Caliphate in Baghdad.

Treatment of Christians and Jews

Christians and Jews experienced unique opportunities in tenth-century Egypt. Muslims were still in the minority at this time, and it may have been considered prudent to avoid alienating the majority. For whatever reason, Christian Copts were able to dominate the financial administration, and both Christians and Jews served in large numbers in government positions. Imams (Muslim rulers) even visited churches and monasteries to observe Christian holy days like Epiphany. On occasion, this friendliness toward Jews and Christians aroused anger and resentment on the part of Sunni Muslims who retaliated with acts of violence toward Christians or Jews. However, with one exception, Imams did not persecute Jews or Christians.

The one exception was al-Hakim (996–1021), who was only eleven years old when he succeeded his tolerant and able father (al-Aziz) as caliph. Several thousand people were executed during al-Hakim's reign, many of them government officials. He forbade public display of the Christian cross, and almost immediately after ordered Christians to wear the cross in public. He was responsible for the destruction of thousands of churches and synagogues, most notably the burning of the Church of the Holy Sepulchre in Jerusalem.

Above: The al-Hakim Mosque in Cairo, Egypt, is named for al-Hakim bi-Amr Allah, the sixth Fatimid caliph, who oversaw its construction. During his reign al-Hakim persecuted the Christians of Egypt.

Left: A woman stands in the mihrab of the tenth-century al-Azhar Mosque in Cairo, Egypt. The mihrab is a niche in a mosque that indicates the direction in which Mecca lies.

CHAPTER FOUR

NESTORIAN CHRISTIANS IN CHINA

The Church of the East, commonly called the Nestorian Church, was located beyond the eastern borders of the Roman Empire. During the first millennium, this distinctive type of Christianity spread faster and farther than Roman Catholicism or Eastern Orthodoxy. Its earliest-known center was in the small independent principality of Osrhoene, located in the Euphrates valley on the present-day border between Syria and Turkey. The capital city, Edessa, was one of the oldest centers of Christianity in the world, and it produced the first translation of the New Testament.

Christianity soon reached another small kingdom, Adiabene, 400 miles (640 km) further east across the Tigris River. The capital of Adiabene, Arbela, was the launching pad for Christian missions in Central Asia. By the end of the second century, Nestorians had reached what is now northern Afghanistan, and by the seventh century, they had traveled as far as Chang'an (present-day Xian), the capital of China during the Tang Dynasty (618–907).

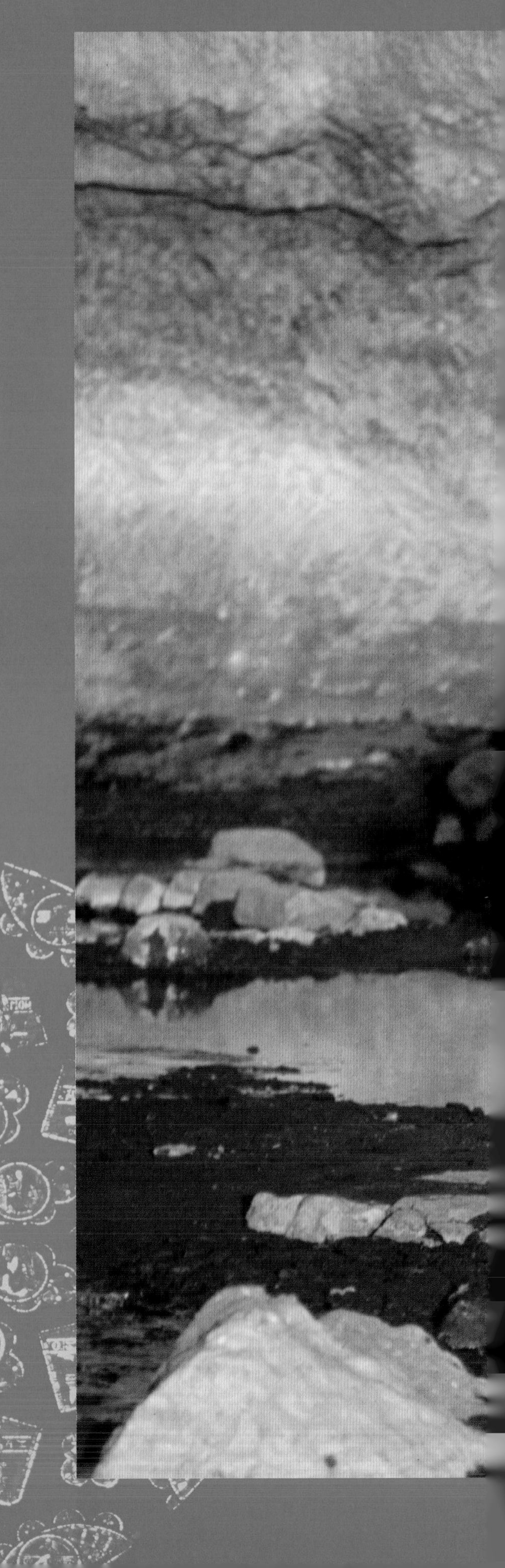

Right: The Tigris River has drawn settlers to the Middle East for millennia. The Adiabenians, who had converted to Judaism in the first century CE, inhabited an area east of the Tigris.

NESTORIAN MISSIONS

The Church of the East was distinguished by its extensive commitment to missionary journeys. Its strategy was to evangelize ethnic or cultural groups, beginning with the Jewish diaspora in Syria and Mesopotamia. Jewish communities had several characteristics useful to Christian evangelists: They were close-knit, respected by their neighbors, willing to ally with Christians against other religions, and well acquainted with methods of analysis based on the scriptures but adapted to their time and place.

Secrets of success

The Church of the East was also ascetic and monastic in structure. Nestorian asceticism was based on the idea of a covenant relationship with God. As a son of the covenant, bound to God by an oath, the true Christian was God's warrior against both the flesh and the devil. Herein lay the root of the monastic lifestyle that was the backbone of Nestorian missionary activity.

A final characteristic of Nestorian Christianity was its ability to adapt to different cultures. It received the Gospel in Greek, but brought it to Syria in Aramaic, the language of Jesus. Aramaic was chosen because it was the *lingua franca* of Syria and Mesopotamia. In Persia, Pahlavi was the language of mission work, even when Aramaic was retained as the liturgical language. This allowed missionaries to work in rural areas as well as in the Greek-speaking cities. Farther east, Nestorian missionaries created alphabets for Mongol tribes so they could read the Bible in their own language.

When the Nestorian missionaries to China reached the city of Chang'an, they encountered a flourishing Buddhist community. Christians borrowed concepts, terms, and literary forms from the Buddhists to aid in their presentation of the Christian Gospel.

The bishop and the emperor

In 635 CE, Alopen, a Christian bishop, traveled from Mesopotamia to Chang'an to head a fledgling Christian community. Taizong (599–649), one of China's most able monarchs, was on the throne at the time. Bishop Alopen was invited to the royal court to explain his teaching. The scriptures he had brought from Mesopotamia were translated and placed in the imperial library. In 638, Taizong declared Christianity to be a tolerated religion, and Alopen received permission to preach.

Over time, Christian monasteries were established in Chang'an and several other areas, Christian literature was produced in the Chinese language, and China received

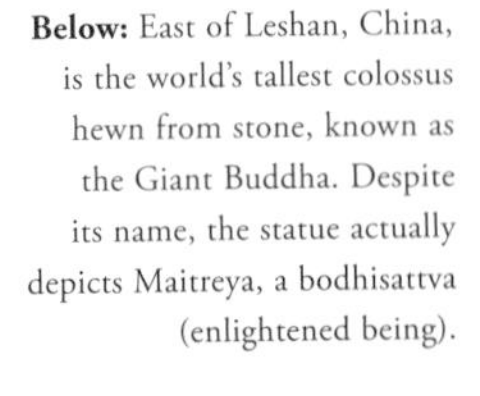

Below: East of Leshan, China, is the world's tallest colossus hewn from stone, known as the Giant Buddha. Despite its name, the statue actually depicts Maitreya, a bodhisattva (enlightened being).

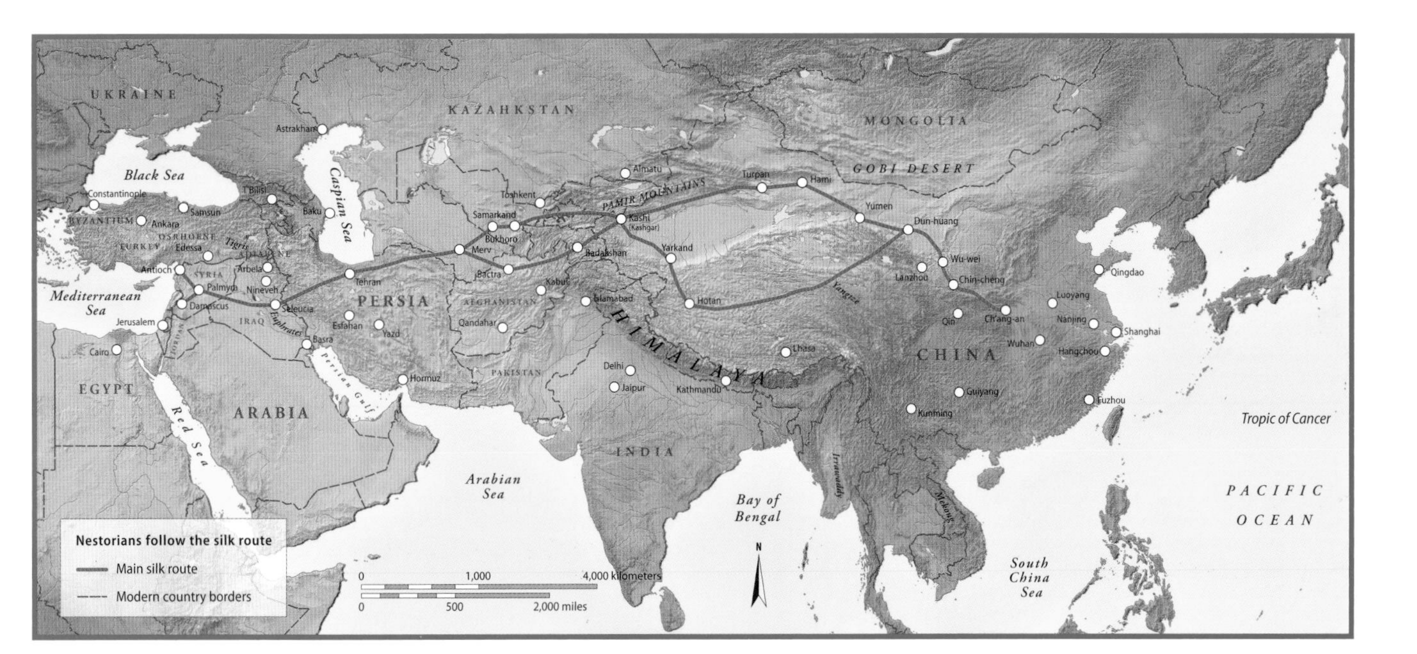

its own metropolitan (ecclesiastical head). Nonetheless, Christians remained a very small minority of the population. An imperial edict of expulsion in 845, which was directed primarily against Buddhists but included Christians, sharpened the decline in numbers, and the first Christian expansion into China virtually disappeared by the end of the Tang Dynasty.

Christians in Buddhist clothing

In his *Jesus Messiah Sutra*, Alopen described the Buddhist *dharma* (teaching) as the result of the work of the Holy Spirit. He used the *prajñā-pāramitā* (*Perfection of Wisdom*) literature and Nāgārjuna's concept of *śunyatā* (emptiness) to explain monotheism. He utilized the Buddhist description of the individual as a shifting aggregate of the five *skandhas* (aggregates), but added the Christian concept of the soul. He equated the Buddhist striving for liberation from sorrow with the Christian goal of salvation. In all of this, Alopen demonstrated an extensive knowledge of the Buddhist tradition.

Other Christians were struck by a similarity between Jesus and the Bodhisattva (divine being) of compassion, Guan Yin. Both came into the world to bring hope for the suffering and to show the mercy of the transcendent truth. The famous stele at Chang'an (modern-day Sian) was erected in 781 by one Yazedbouzid, whose father had been a priest in predominantly Buddhist northern Afghanistan. It includes this description of the Ascension: "He [Jesus] then took an oar in the Vessel of Mercy and ascended to the Palace of Light." While appropriate for its Christian purpose, the language reflects the cult of Guan Yin.

Yazedbouzid's son Adam helped Prajñā, a Buddhist monk from Afghanistan, translate a sutra on the *pāramitās* of giving, morality, patience, vigor, meditation, and wisdom into Chinese. In all of these examples, Christian actions demonstrated both a familiarity with and a respect for the ideas and beliefs of Buddhism.

Left: After meeting Alopen, Emperor Taizong decided to construct a church for the Christian bishop, known as the Da Qin Temple. Da Qin is the Chinese name for the Roman Empire.

WERE THEY HERETICS?

Nestorius (c. 386–c. 451) was accused of heresy because he claimed that "Mother of God" was a more appropriate name for Mary than "Mother of Christ." The conflict was part of the debate over the relationship between the divine nature and the human nature in Christ. Much of the theology of "Nestorian" Christianity was formulated before Nestorius was born, and even though the Church of the East does not follow Nestorius' theology but rather that of the later systematizer Babai the Great (c. 551–628), it has been given Nestorius' name. The Church of the East has also been stigmatized with the label of heresy. In reality, the early Church of the East's theology was no less orthodox than that of Rome or Byzantium in an age when orthodoxy was still being defined. In addition, recent discoveries have cleared Nestorius of many of his opponents' charges.

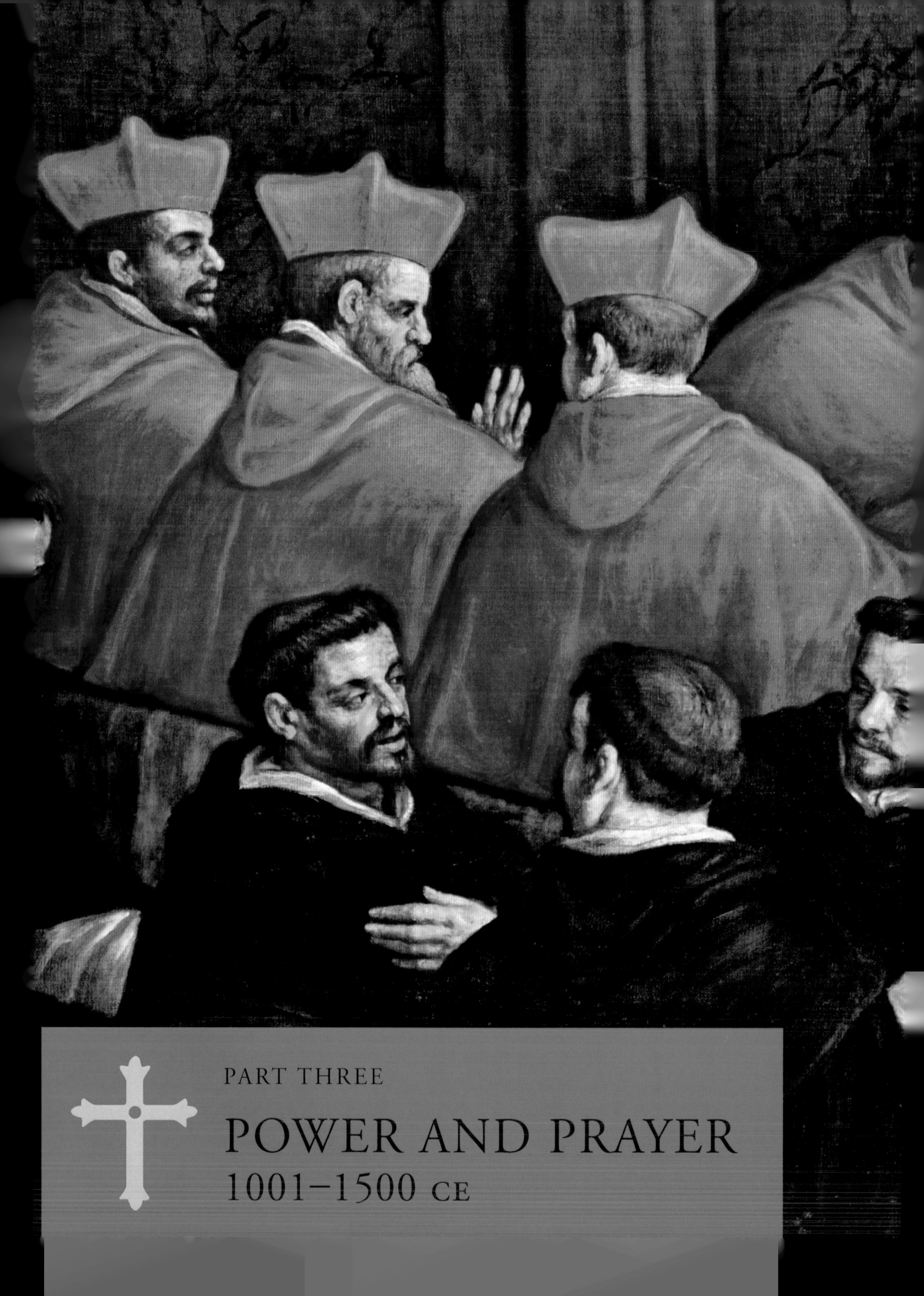

PART THREE

POWER AND PRAYER

1001–1500 CE

CHAPTER ONE

THE WESTERN CHURCH

After centuries of political disorder following the collapse of the Roman Empire, a dramatic upswing in papal power in the eleventh through the thirteenth centuries afforded Western Europe a greater degree of administrative unity. The local clergy, who were numerous, worked under a line of authority that extended all the way to Rome. In addition to overseeing the overtly religious aspects of life, the pope exercised political and military power. Papal legates oversaw the practices and rectitude of local clergy. Everywhere in the West, Christians had the same liturgy, sacraments, canon law (Church law), and rites. This unity, underlain by papal authority, led to unprecedented power in the Western Church. Popes became the ultimate patrons of the feudal system, dispensing favors and protection in return for allegiance, services, and tithes.

However, Rome by no means held absolute power. Popes excommunicated kings, but emperors deposed popes. Secular rulers and popes vied for final authority in any number of situations, including the right to levy taxes, control bishops, and make laws. While popes claimed that their authority came directly from Christ, emperors asserted their right to oversee the election and appointment of a pope.

Emperors were not the only papal critics. Universities, once established, were run by their teachers; thus they provided a platform for dissent. Monastic orders, though sworn to obedience to the pope, had much independence in the running of their own organizations. They may not directly confront a pope (as some emperors did) but, like a clever lawyer, they sometimes managed to find a way around a law without directly disobeying it. Lay movements like the Beguines and the Brethren of the Common Life operated outside most of the formal structures of the Church. These fissures in papal control eventually widened into cracks that fractured the unity of Western Christendom during the Reformation.

Previous pages: Papal power in the thirteenth century manifested itself in many ways. For instance, in 1216, Pope Honorius III was asked to approve the formation of the Order of St Dominic.

Right: In the 1370s, Catherine of Siena risked excommunication by approaching Pope Gregory XI in Avignon and insisting that the seat of the papacy move from Avignon back to Rome.

CATHEDRALS

Above: Two-thirds of the awe-inspiring windows of Sainte-Chapelle in Paris feature the original thirteenth-century stained glass, while the remaining third was restored in the nineteenth century.

In few other periods in history has devotional architecture matched the splendors of the achievements of the Western Church during the medieval period (1200–1500). The grand cathedrals of this historical period, built in Gothic style with thinner walls and more windows than the massive, Romanesque cathedrals of the previous era, are some of the most impressive houses of worship ever seen. Architecture reflected theology, with light flooding into the structure through large windows that extended to the very top—80 to 144 feet (24 to 44 m) above—so that the light, like God's grace, cascaded from the heavens and was directed onto the people below. Conversely, the long, linear lines of the building drew the people's eyes up to the source of the light that bathed them.

The heart of the community

Many cathedrals were enormous buildings that dominated the surrounding countryside and the towns in which they were built—some could hold most of the population of the town. People marveled at the breathtaking dimensions of these places of worship, as well as the colors, the carvings and statues, the tombs, and the rich furnishings (among them glorious tapestries). Series of carvings and stained-glass windows taught a mostly illiterate population stories from the Old Testament, and about the life of Christ, the Virgin Mary, and the saints.

These huge structures took time to complete, often more than a century. Those who designed a cathedral would not live long enough to see its finished form, and those who worshipped in it would never meet the pious

Above: A classic example of a Gothic structure, the imposing edifice of Chartres Cathedral has dominated the surrounding French town since it was completed in 1260.

visionaries who began the work. Thus, medieval cathedrals involved an impressive outlay of faith as well as finances.

Once finished, the cathedral would serve as the center of community life. A market would likely be located nearby. Open-air plays would be performed on its steps. The generations would arrive at its doors for coronations of rulers, investitures of bishops, and ordinations of priests, not to mention the lengthy procession of baptisms, confirmations, marriages, and funerals. The cemetery was usually located in the church grounds. Of course, the most important ceremony was the celebration of the Mass. The cathedral was the place where the people of a town were tied to God as well as to their neighbors, both living and dead.

Costs, construction, and maintenance

Building a cathedral was a huge and expensive undertaking. Kings and princes often donated money. Bishops of wealthy dioceses contributed from the proceeds of their estates. Very often church taxes (tithes) were diverted to fund the construction. Ordinary people also made voluntary donations. Many European towns grew rapidly in the thirteenth century, and they put their growing economic resources into building cathedrals. Because construction could take many years—more than a century in the case of the largest cathedrals—funds could be raised gradually.

Among the residents of the expanding medieval towns were merchants and bankers who helped with the financial aspects. The actual construction was done by migrant bands of builders, masons, and "masters." We do not know what percentage of the economy of the time was devoted to the building of cathedrals, but it must have been impressive. In just two centuries, more stone was quarried in France for the building of cathedrals than had been used in all the stone monuments of ancient Egypt.

There were two ways of staffing cathedrals: With chapters of monks (such as the Benedictines) and other religious men, or with secular canons. Both were required to chant daily the liturgical offices and to say Mass. Canons, who did not take the monastic vow of poverty, usually had a private income from the ownership of land. Cathedral clergy were not responsible for pastoral care, only for liturgical worship, so one frequently finds parish churches built near a cathedral, as at York in England.

Medieval cathedrals give witness to the profound Christian faith of the time, and the people's willingness to sacrifice their energy, creativity, and skills.

Below: Many cathedral statues are symbolic representations of revered Christian personages. This lifelike eagle, on the exterior of Orvieto Cathedral in Italy, emblematizes St John the Evangelist.

SACRAMENTS

Opposite: The sacrament of confirmation allows the baptized recipient—usually an adolescent in Western churches, but an infant in Eastern churches—to receive the gifts of the Holy Spirit.

Below opposite: The Baptistry of St John in Pisa's Piazza del Duomo was completed in 1363. Baptistries are rooms or even whole buildings that are constructed to hold the church's baptismal font.

Below: Jesus was baptized by John the Baptist in the Jordan River. The sacrament of baptism is still undertaken today as an act of spiritual cleansing and initiation into the Church.

According to the Gospels, Jesus engaged in baptism (he was baptized and asked his disciples to baptize others) as well as sharing food such as bread and wine.

At first there were two

In other Christian writings of the first century (Acts of the Apostles and the letters of Paul and Ignatius), these acts by Jesus came to be seen as "sacraments"—the word "*sacramentum*" means oath, which is a translation of the Greek "*mysterion*" or mystery. The earliest Christians accorded these sacraments the greatest importance. Baptism was the establishment of a "new covenant" leading to a new life between believer and God. The Eucharist (the meal of bread and wine) was the re-offering of Jesus' crucifixion; Jesus was present in the bread and wine, enabling the disciple to share in his resurrected life.

The significance of these rituals was gradually elaborated by the Apostolic Fathers in the first centuries. Baptism was deemed to be essential for becoming a Christian, and the Eucharist became the principal act of worship. For most Christians, their following of Jesus was repeatedly vivified by the reception of these sacraments. In medieval times these two sacraments chimed with reality: Things one could see and touch—water, salt, oil, bread, and wine—made God present in a powerful way to noble and peasant, man and woman, in an anxiety-ridden world.

From flux to certainty

By the turn of the first millennium there were increasing differences between the Eastern Orthodox and Western Catholic churches. Among the Orthodox they were called "mysteries," since they were hidden to unbelievers. For centuries the exact number of sacraments was undefined, and theories varied as to how many there might be. Some suggested there were three—baptism, Eucharist, and unction (anointing)—while others suggested six, now including ordination, monastic vows, and the funeral service. Others believed there were even more sacraments. The increasing tensions between the Eastern and Western churches, especially the effort by the Roman Church to control the Eastern Church at the Council of Florence (1439), led to the formulation of seven sacraments. While the Orthodox count seven, they also hold that acts such as funerals and monastic vows are "sacramental."

From Florence to Trent

The Western Church eventually decided on baptism, confirmation (chrismation in the Orthodox Church), the Eucharist, penance (confession), last anointing, marriage, and conferring holy orders. The first mention of the seven sacraments appears in Peter Lombard's *Sentences*, written between 1155 and 1158. Lombard and then Thomas Aquinas (1225–1274) argued that they had to have been established by Christ, although in some cases this was difficult to prove. So they argued that sacraments like ordination, confession, or last anointing were implicit in what Christ did or said.

The symbolic role of the number seven also played a role. This position was adopted by the Council of Florence (1439) and then elaborated at the Council of Trent (1547). By this time the Roman Catholic Church was responding to another challenge, this time from the Reformers, who restricted the sacraments to two—baptism and the Eucharist—since they argued that only these sacraments could be found in Scripture.

How do they work?

How did the churches see the sacraments? They all agreed that none was more important than baptism, which opened the gate to the other sacraments. In the Middle Ages it was commonly believed that salvation was impossible without it.

The Eucharist (or Mass for the Catholics) was the central act of worship, and while attending worship was obligatory on Sundays and feast days, attending it on other days was popular. People rarely received Holy Communion,

since they believed themselves too sinful and not in a state of grace. The Fourth Lateran Council of 1215 legislated that all must receive Communion once a year at Easter. Communion was taken in the form of bread, not wine, and involved long preparation through Lent.

As for the other five, common to the Orthodox and Catholics, a priest could confer marriage, confession, and last anointing, while ordination and confirmation were the domain of bishops. In confession a priest forgave sin in the name of God, and last anointing was administered by one or more priests to a sick or dying Christian by anointing and prayer. In exchanging vows, a Christian couple received the sacrament of marriage. Confirmation was always conferred by a bishop who anointed the recipient while invoking the Holy Spirit. A bishop conferred the sacred orders of bishop, priest, and deacon by imposing hands on a man's head with invocations and, in the case of ordination of a priest, handing him such things as a chalice and paten used in celebrating the Eucharist.

PARISH LIFE IN THE MEDIEVAL CHURCH

Opposite: One of the most important jobs for the parish priest in medieval times was to hear penitents' confessions, offering absolution to those who sincerely repented their sins.

In medieval times few people ever traveled further than 15 miles (24 km) or so from where they were born. They lived their Christian lives as members of a parish, the smallest administrative unit of the Church, and a very important social entity.

Parish size and staffing

Parishes varied in extent. In the sparsely inhabited rural regions of Sweden or Scotland, for example, they were large, but in towns they were often very small. On average a rural parish contained about 350 inhabitants, a city parish around 200 people. In Oxford in England, the presence of three parish churches about 200 yards (180 m) apart reflects this urban density. In addition to its church, a parish might also have a monastery, chapels, and shrines. City parishes were small because some 90 percent of the people attended church and the vast majority walked (a situation that continued until at least 1850).

Most parishes were staffed by at least one priest and several other clergy (other priests, deacons, and sacristans). "Clergy" was a loosely defined category, covering men in minor orders and even mere *clerici* (clerks). Throughout the Middle Ages there was an excess of priests in Europe, and many were unemployed. Bishops might ordain priests in batches of hundreds, with little or no examination, many such priests having no more education than some brief instruction in the administration of the sacraments. Few could preach effectively because of their ignorance of the Bible and of theology. Often their only books were liturgical books, which many found difficult to read. A priest might be a farmer with mud and cow manure on his boots, given a plot of land on which to earn an income, living as his parishioners did, plowing and reaping, and sharing their simple pleasures. Although Church law prescribed celibacy for priests, this condition was widely ignored, even more so in the countryside than in towns. Few could maintain celibacy when they had been given no preparation for living it.

Below: Medieval parish churches were often elaborately decorated to inspire devotion in the usually illiterate parishioners. This musical angel is part of the altarpiece of the parish church in Gries, Italy.

A priest was part of the everyday life of people, leading worship on Sundays and feast days, hearing confession, and performing baptisms, funerals, and masses for the dead. Since life was painful (aspirin had not yet been invented), disease was rife, plagues often swept through town, infant mortality was high, and life expectancy low, the priest was a vital link to the world beyond. The people would learn about Christianity from the pictures that covered the church walls (they could not read) and from the stories told by the priest. It was not uncommon for people to leave their meager pennies to the church in their will so that the priest would say masses for their souls after they had died.

Tithing

Buildings and clergy cost money. Churches were rarely built by voluntary donations from parishioners, often being endowed by lordly landowners, universities, and monasteries. Parishioners were usually responsible for the upkeep of part of a church's fabric, perhaps the roof. Some parishes neglected these duties, and their churches fell into ruin, but most cherished their church, which might be richly decorated and covered in paintings of stories from the Bible, a building that served as the center of town or village life and as a store of local history.

The great affairs of popes, bishops, and kings largely passed by the parish level. Not canon law, however, which permeated everyday life—in wills and bequests, sexual offences such as fornication and adultery, disputed marriages, failure to attend Mass, and offences involving clergy. Canon law also stipulated that all owners and tenants of land and operators of a trade or business were required to pay a tithe to the Church—nominally a tenth of gross income, generally in kind but sometimes in cash, but in fact at various rates established by tradition. Special barns were built to store the agricultural produce delivered in payment of tithe. Proceeds from tithing were meant to go to the upkeep of churches and payment for clergy, but often were siphoned off to monasteries or lords or cathedral chapters for private benefit.

Parishioners had no choice about paying tithes and other Church taxes, for defaulters were dealt with under canon law. Failure to pay was punished by the seizure of farm animals and produce, even the destruction of houses. This system continued in Europe for centuries. People grumbled at having to pay, often resenting it bitterly, but usually they accepted tithing as necessary. Like taxpayers today, they cunningly avoided paying when possible, however. Indeed, when the French Revolution began in 1789, there were before the courts 18,000 cases of failure to pay tithes.

Right: Parish churches in rural areas were responsible for a Christian community spread over a vast land area. The church often became the center of social life for its far-flung congregation.

QUORU
REMITTVNTVR EIS
Ioan. 20. n 3.

SAINTS AND THE BLESSED VIRGIN MARY

The Blessed Virgin Mary and the saints inspired through their holy lives, instructed through their example, and were believed to provide Christians on earth with the protection they asked for in their prayers.

Who is a Christian?

Ask someone today "Who is a Christian?" or "Who are the Church's members?" and you will get many answers: Mainstream Christianity would answer "Anyone who is baptized" or "Whoever believes in Jesus;" the more exclusive might answer "Whoever accepts Jesus as their personal savior" or even just "our denomination" or "our group." In every case, the respondent is thinking of people who are alive, those living around us now in the world. However, any medieval Christian would answer that the Church was, first and foremost, the saints in heaven—of whom the most eminent and holy was the Mother of God (this group was called "the church triumphant")—then those who had died in a state of grace, but still needed purification to fit them for glory (this was "the church suffering") and who were prayed for when someone said or wrote "R.I.P" or *Requiescat in pace* (may she or he rest in peace); and last, and least, those who are alive now ("the church militant"). These last were still being tested, and it was unknown, except to God, who from this "mixed body" would eventually join the complete, heavenly Church.

Rest in peace

These three groups were interconnected as God's family, and so, family-like, they helped each other. Living Christians asked help of the Virgin Mary and the saints to live this life, and for help at the moment of death, to become one of the saints themselves. We see this in the Hail Mary (known to every medieval Christian), which asks for Mary's intercession with God for help "now and at the hour of our death." The saints in heaven helped the Church on earth; and, in like manner, living Christians helped one another—people prayed for the hungry, for wisdom for rulers, and that their sisters and brothers would grow in holiness. This spiritual help for other members of the Church on earth is still widely accepted. However,

Below: The Madonna (the Virgin Mary) and Child (the infant Jesus) are shown at left with St Catherine and the Blessed Stefano Marconi in this painting by Ambrogio Bergognone (c. 1453–c. 1523).

what is not widely accepted now, except among Catholics, is that the Church on earth could help "the church suffering." Yet in the Middle Ages, praying for the dead and asking for prayers for oneself after death was an important aspect of life: Memorials were set up asking for prayers; religious houses were established to pray for their founders' repose. The three parts of the Church, thought of as one family with Mary as mother, were imagined as linked by bonds of mutual love and help: All the parts, they prayed, would be brought together in God's presence.

MORE THAN MODELS

In modern times, when we use the word "saint" we think primarily of someone whom we greatly admire and who therefore should be considered a role model. Medieval people, while appreciating the saints' function as exemplary disciples, thought that their help, interceding for living Christians with God, was far more important. One might study and admire a role model, and perhaps the curious might want to see where such a person lived and worked, but only if you truly believe that they are family and can help you now will you go so far as to celebrate the anniversary of their death (known as their feast day), build a cult at their shrine (the place where their body now rests awaiting the final resurrection), and treasure contact with them through such things as relics.

Global and local

Saints came in all shapes and sizes. There were those everyone knew: Mary, the Apostles, the early saints whose fame reached to every corner of the Christian world. There were saints known only in particular parts of the Church, be it East or West (for example, Western Christians have rarely heard of St Gregory Palamas, 1296–1359, widely venerated in the Eastern Orthodox Church). There were those known only in one country or region; even saints known only in one locality, whose memory might be preserved in the name of a single holy well. Every saint had their own special places, where they were connected to the Church on earth, and most had a special interest group—perhaps the inhabitants of a particular city (such as Saints Felix and Regula for Zurich), the members of a profession (St Luke for doctors), or those with a particular need (St Leonard for prisoners). Hence the idea of patron saints: Just as there were patrons on earth, so too among the saints.

Below: Medieval people believed in the power of prayer to help improve their lives. Even today, people pray to saints to help with health issues, moral dilemmas, and other everyday problems.

Left: The fifteenth Patriarch of Moscow and All Russia, Alexy II, visits the shrine containing the relics of the Grand Duchess Elizabeth and nun Barbara, at Moscow's Christ the Saviour Cathedral.

PILGRIMAGES

Above: Many sick people pilgrimage to Lourdes, France, in the hope that they will be cured by the water of the spring where St Bernadette saw the Virgin Mary in 1858.

Pilgrimages are journeys to special places which are not only significant in the history of a religion, but which are seen as holy places where one can encounter the spiritual world in a way not possible in one's ordinary location.

No early Christian pilgrimage

Pilgrimage is a phenomenon that is found in all the major religions, and was certainly common among Jews in the time of Jesus. Jews from all over Judea and Galilee, and from all over the Mediterranean world, came to the Temple in Jerusalem to encounter the divine presence and offer sacrifice—we have several stories of Jesus' family doing this (Luke 2:41). By contrast, the first Christians showed little interest in particular holy places, and even Jerusalem was ignored after its destruction in 70 CE by the Roman army (see John 4:21). The new religion celebrated the coming of Jesus as the Father's Anointed into creation, so everywhere was potentially holy, and Christianity's holiest place was in the midst of the community during the meal (the Eucharist): "But the hour is coming, and is now here, when the true worshippers will worship the Father in spirit and truth, for the Father seeks such as these to worship him" (John 4:23).

Discovering the holy places

By the end of the second century, however, Christians were traveling to Jerusalem to see the sites associated with Jesus so that the stories about him would become more real; this desire to see and touch and walk just where it all happened was the beginning of the Holy Land being the great center for pilgrims. The trickle became a flood when the Emperor Constantine, and his mother Helena, built special churches

Right: The Catacombs of San Gennaro in Naples, Italy, date to as early as the second century CE. Pilgrims come to pray to St Agrippino, who was once buried here.

at the sacred sites; still today one can see all the various kinds of Christians jostling with each other in these places. For many Catholic and Orthodox Christians it is openly a pilgrimage: They want to participate in the holiness of the place, that unique holiness imparted by the sacred events that took place there. For others, mainly Protestants and contemporary Western Christians, such notions may be either silly or repulsive. For them the emphasis is on how the land can illuminate the Bible, and they would rather say they were on a "Biblical field trip"—yet the desire to be photographed at the "actual spot" shows that the impulse to pilgrimage is deeply rooted in the religious imagination.

Tombs: Places of help and healing

As time passed, other places, almost invariably through their connection with the location of a saint's tomb, became centers of pilgrimage. There one could invoke that saint's heavenly protection and intercession; there one could do penance; there one could obtain healing and new hope. The tombs of Peter, Paul, and the early martyrs in the catacombs thus made Rome a special place of pilgrimage in the early Middle Ages: One was not visiting a city on the Tiber, but Peter in his tomb. Likewise, St James' tomb in Santiago de Compostela (northwest Spain) drew pilgrims from all over Europe. The tomb of St Thomas Becket drew pilgrims to Canterbury and was the backdrop to Chaucer's masterpiece, *The Canterbury Tales.* Significant holy places are those connected with the Virgin Mary, whose origin is usually linked to a special "appearing" of Mary to an individual or group. These places are now, after the Holy Land, the most important pilgrimage sites for Catholics. Lourdes in southwest France is an example: It attracts pilgrims from all over the world, but its fame rests on an apparition to St Bernadette in 1858.

Pilgrimage can be contentious

It was the belief that pilgrimage could be a source of grace that prompted a rejection of the notion and practice of pilgrimages by the Protestant theologians at the Reformation. And while there is now a general attempt by leaders of the Catholic Church to distance pilgrimage from what might seem magic or superstition, there is also a growing recognition that pilgrimage, which requires people to see the world from a new perspective, is a valuable spiritual activity. Pilgrimage has become, in recent decades, a key metaphor for the life of individuals and for the whole Church. So people see their own ups and downs, joys and troubles as disciples, as like the winding rough road to a sacred place in the distance. On a large scale, many groups (among them Catholics) now like to refer to "the pilgrim church."

Above: Proudly Catholic monarch Queen Isabella of Castile (1451–1504) was just one of the many famous historical personages to make the pilgrimage to Santiago de Compostela.

Above left: The patron saint of Spain, St James is reportedly buried in Santiago de Compostela, where his tomb draws thousands of visitors. He was one of the first disciples to follow Jesus.

THE RISE AND FALL OF PAPAL POWER

Right: During the medieval period, the feudal system saw merchants—such as those that made and sold fabric—situated in between the all-powerful pope and the lowly serfs.

Opposite: Pope Gregory VII is renowned for his successful reforms of the papacy. In 1584 he was beatified by Gregory XIII, and in 1728 he was declared a saint by Benedict XIII.

Below: Charlemagne was crowned as Emperor of the Romans by Pope Leo III in 800 CE, beginning the tradition whereby the pope reserved the right to bestow the imperial crown.

Over the period 1000–1500, papal power rose to undreamed-of heights, then began a long decline. The four key features of this period are relations between popes and kings; the rise of feudalism; the system of benefices and law; and the place of heretics and original ideas.

Unprecedented papal power

The rise of papal power was due to a new theory, energetic popes, European politics, and changing social landscapes. The theory drew on the forged *Donation of Constantine,* then believed genuine, and gave all power in Church and Empire to the pope. From Pope Gregory VII (1073–1085) on it was also asserted that the pope's power came directly from God. A series of energetic popes then put theory into practice. Through astute diplomacy they ensured they were indispensable to medieval society at every level, gathering around them multiple allies who extended their rule into all walks of life. The backward nature of Western European politics, compared to the sophisticated politics of the Byzantine Empire and the Muslim world, ensured that the popes were able to climb to the pinnacle of power. Warring princes, constant territorial conflict, and the perpetual search for strategic alliances meant that the pope became a useful ally for any prince seeking to increase his influence.

Eventually, however, it was precisely because the pope had become "one prince among many" that he fell foul of political maneuvering. When a pope was no longer useful for another prince's power games, his power began to wane.

Feudalism

A further factor was the nature of European society. From the time of Charlemagne (c. 742–814), the social and economic system known as feudalism, based on a complex system of mutual obligation, gradually made its way through Western Europe. Feudalism constructed a hierarchy with serfs at the base and kings at the peak; in between were nobles, clergy, craftsmen, and merchants. A superior could offer favors, protection and access to the courts; those lower down owed taxes, and their services and their allegiance, which was particularly important during times of war. The popes perfected the system in their favor, claiming to be the highest point of the social pyramid.

Benefices and law

They managed this by developing a highly complex system of benefices and a new legal system. To those who came to Rome and kissed the pope's feet were given an extraordinary range of benefits. It might be the legal claim to land for a monastery, order, or bishop; the confirmation of particular customs; freedom from the jurisdiction of a local lord; or honors such as the use of papal insignia. The popes showered their increasing numbers of supporters with material benefits and signs of status, thus ensuring an ever greater number of allies.

Further, the papacy created the most effective legal system of the Middle Ages. At its center was the re-institution of absolute private property, an idea forgotten after its invention by the Romans. By adapting Roman law to feudalism, the murky area of property was clarified. The popes of the eleventh to thirteenth centuries developed a system under which everyone sought the opinion of the papal courts. Land claims were cleared up, due process for every minute aspect of daily life was established, litigants streamed to Rome for decisions, the pope's legal representatives (legates) were everywhere, and papal power spread. This achievement of the "lawyer popes," often called the Papal Revolution, was the beginning of the legal system now dominant in the West.

Oppositional voices

It also meant that papal power became a victim of its own success. The sheer volume of legal business turned the popes into administrators devoted to keeping the system running. The machinery ground down the possibility of new ideas. For three centuries new ideas had been encouraged and had helped develop papal power, but by the fourteenth century new ideas no longer came from within, and the popes began denouncing one heresy after another. Added to this change were the increasing political machinations of the princes, and the growth of towns and a new merchant class. Whereas earlier princes would hand over heretics to keep favor with Rome, by the fourteenth century such freethinkers were useful allies in their struggles with the pope. Toward the end of this century, feudalism began to crack at the seams. The interests of the towns and commerce heralded the first glimmers of capitalism on the horizon. By 1500, Western Europe was beginning to change.

GIORGIO

SACRED VERSUS SECULAR POWER

Above: In addition to reigning as King of the Franks and Emperor of the Romans, Charlemagne was also coronated with the Iron Crown of Lombardy to become King of Italy in 774 CE.

On Christmas Day, 800, in St Peter's Basilica an event occurred which was to determine the political landscape of Western Europe for the next millennium: Pope Leo III crowned the Frankish (German) king Charlemagne Emperor of the Romans, an office that eventually became called "Holy Roman Emperor." The pope's hope was that he and his papal successors would control Charlemagne and his successors; in reality he had created not the position of deputy, but that of rival and often master.

The pope's viewpoint

As papal power increased, in theory and practice, through the eleventh to the thirteenth centuries, the pope came to see himself as God's mediator on earth. Through energetic holders of the office such as Gregory VII (1073–1085), Innocent III (1198–1216), and Boniface VIII (1294–1303), theory became reality. No longer was the pope merely the "vicar of St Peter"—he was the "vicar of Christ," which meant that even kings and emperors were his subjects. As Innocent III put it, "No king can reign unless he devoutly serves Christ's vicar." Under the feudal system, the pope was the highest lord, at the peak of the pyramid. Since he spoke God's word on earth, kings should obey him. Large papal armies ensured that this was no idle claim.

The King of the Germans was elected under a complex system, but should he prove not worthy of the title or should he not submit to the pope's will, the pope had the final say before crowning him Holy Roman Emperor. If a prince or king seeking to become emperor fell out with the pope, the pope would work behind the scenes to ensure he did not become emperor.

The problem was that kings and emperors repeatedly fell out of favor, whereupon the pope would excommunicate the ruler in question and absolve his subjects from obedience. The idea was to bring the ruler into line. If the ruler was weak, the condemnation would work, but at other times, stronger rulers would defy the punishment.

As a few examples in a very long list, we find that Gregory VII twice excommunicated Henry IV (1050–1106), the Holy Roman Emperor. In 1228 Gregory IX excommunicated the extremely powerful Frederick II. In 1303 Boniface VIII prepared to excommunicate Philip the Fair of France. And on it went.

The king's viewpoint

Looking through the king's eyes, we can do no better than to take the *Diploma Ottonianum* of 962, in which Emperor Otto I declared that the pope (who was, at that time, John XII) was permitted to control his Italian possessions, but that Otto would save "all things in our power and that of our successors." The message was clear: Hands off the Emperor. But Otto went further, asserting that he had the right to ensure that papal elections were carried out properly—which meant that no pope was to be appointed against the emperor's wishes.

Succeeding kings and emperors held to Otto's ideal, even if they didn't always achieve it. Being crowned by the pope was, in their eyes, a rubber stamp that could prove to be very useful for their own power struggles; however, it was to be ignored if it didn't suit them. When a pope asserted himself too strongly, some emperors called a council and deposed him. Or, like Philip the Fair with Boniface VIII in 1303, they sought to bring the pope to trial for interfering in their affairs. In 1084, Henry IV of Germany marched on Rome and captured Pope Gregory VII himself. The Holy Roman Emperors came to view themselves as the protector, overseer, and arbiter of the pope. Following 1530, the emperor ceased to bother with seeking the pope's approval and coronation.

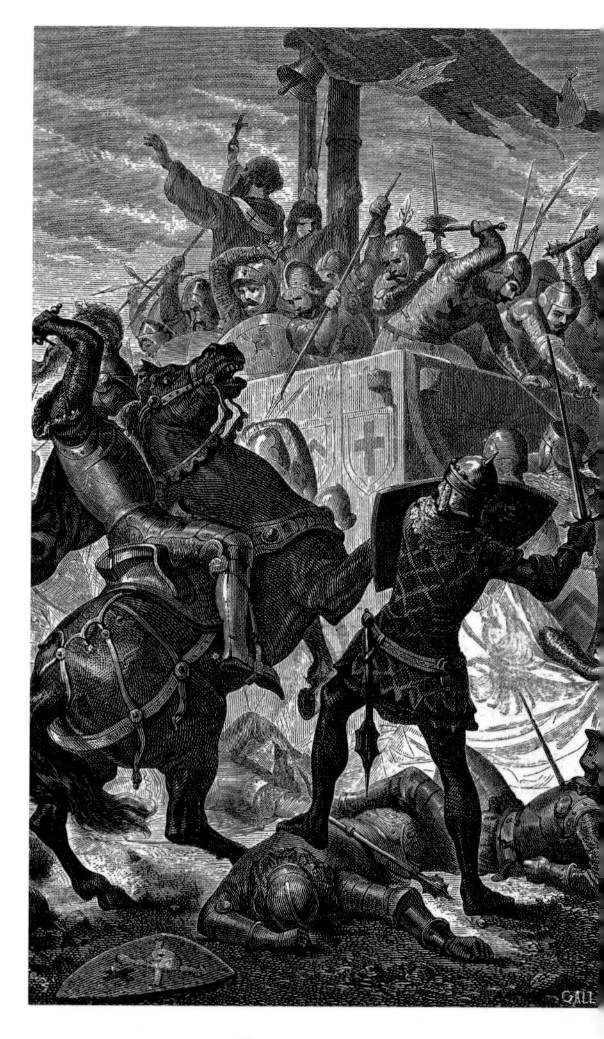

Right: Frederick II was excommunicated twice—in 1228 by Pope Gregory IX, and in 1245 by Pope Innocent IV. After the second excommunication, German knights fought the papal forces in a bitter civil war.

Below: Pope Innocent III aimed to improve papal power and influence throughout Europe and beyond, instigating both the Fourth Crusade to the Holy Land and the Albigensian Crusade in southern France.

Antipopes

Along with the number of kings excommunicated, the best evidence of this long power struggle comes from the large number of deposed popes and antipopes (improperly elected popes). The list of popes from 1000 to 1500 reveals no less than 12 popes deposed and the election of 20 antipopes. In each case the emperor had a hand in deposing the pope, and in each case the rival candidates to the papacy (sometimes there were up to 3 popes) were supported by a king or emperor. Needless to say, rival popes were more amenable to the emperor's wishes.

By the end of the thirteenth century papal power was on the wane. New currents of thought, opposition from intellectuals and townspeople, and the reality of new power structures meant that the princes, kings, and emperors had more to worry about than the pope's opinion and influence.

POPE GREGORY VII (1073–1085)

Below: This Baroque fresco by Giovanni Francesco Romanelli (1610–1662) depicts a young woman—perhaps a princess or a queen—receiving a blessing from Pope Gregory VII.

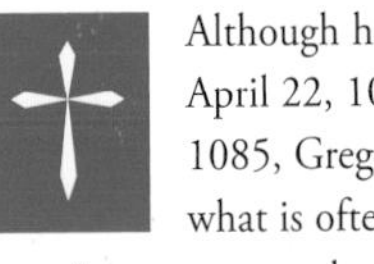

Although he was pope for only 12 years, from April 22, 1073, until his death on May 25, 1085, Gregory VII oversaw the beginning of what is often called the Papal Revolution, inaugurating an unprecedented period of papal power that was to last for two centuries before it began to decrease.

An austere monk

Who was Gregory? As is always the case with someone so important, legend is mixed with history. It used to be thought that he came from a poor family, but medical records suggest otherwise. The year of his birth is uncertain, probably around 1015, and the best guess for his place of birth is Sovana in Tuscany. What is known is that he had a very austere and rigorous view of the life of a priest or monk, which was to show up later in his campaigns against simony (the purchase of spiritual benefits or clerical office) and the immorality of the clergy. Gregory was himself a monk by profession, having entered the monastery of St Mary on the Aventine in Rome when very young to be educated. There he took the name Hildebrand.

Power and controversy

Hildebrand was no stranger to power. He first attached himself as chaplain to the deposed Gregory VI (reigned 1045–1046), even following the fugitive pope to Germany. On Hildebrand's return to Rome the new pope, the reforming Leo IX, quickly appointed him to the senior position of the patrimony of St Peter. Now Hildebrand was a real powerbroker, playing a great hand in the election of popes and cardinals. By 1073, he was the natural choice to replace Pope Alexander II.

Pope Gregory's years in office were engulfed in a whirlwind of reform, assertions of extraordinary papal power, struggles with kings and emperors, siege, capture, flight, and finally death in exile in 1085.

His major achievement was to claim independent power for the papacy. No longer would the pope's appointment and actions be determined by temporal rulers and their heavy artillery. The pope was independent of all that. The crucial move was to assert that the pope's authority came not from any earthly authority but from Christ alone. The pope was Christ's—and therefore God's—representative on earth. No-one, especially not the Holy Roman Emperor, would tell the pope what to do.

In his struggles at the local level, Gregory made great use of papal legates, who now had power over all other officers

BETWEEN GOD AND MAN

The pope can be judged by no-one;
The Roman church has never erred
and never will err till the end of time;
The Roman church was founded by Christ alone;
The pope alone can depose and restore bishops;
He alone can make new laws, set up new bishoprics,
and divide old ones;
He alone can translate bishops;
He alone can call general councils
and authorize canon law;
He alone can revise his own judgments;
He alone can use the imperial insignia;
He can depose emperors;
He can absolve subjects from their allegiance;
All princes should kiss his feet;
His legates, even though in inferior orders,
have precedence over all bishops;
An appeal to the papal court inhibits judgments
by all inferior courts;
A duly ordained pope is undoubtedly made a saint
by the merits of St Peter.

Gregory VII, Letters

of the Church (apart from the pope). Through them he sought to sweep away corruption and venal clergy. Given that many clergy had been secularly appointed to their positions, and frequently were members of propertied local families, this generated immense and often violent opposition, especially in Germany and France. Gregory demanded and sought submission from kings. Some gave it, such as William I of England and eventually Philip I of France. But others did not. His greatest struggle was with Henry IV of Germany, in line for the position of Holy Roman Emperor. Gregory excommunicated Henry (twice), Henry deposed Gregory in his turn and marched on Rome, capturing it and the pope in 1084 and planning to set up an alternative pope.

At the last moment the Normans came to Gregory's aid, freeing him from Henry, only to set about annoying and plundering the people of Rome. The people turned on Gregory, and he was forced to flee for his life to Monte Cassino and then Salerno, where he died. In a statement inserted in the collection of his letters, he left behind his legacy, an extraordinary expression of the papacy's claims to supreme power (see the feature box below).

Above: After losing favor with the people of Rome, Pope Gregory VII escaped to the monastery established by St Benedict at Monte Cassino, located 80 miles (130 km) southeast of Rome.

Left: Highly educated and very religious, Matilda of Canossa (1046–1114), Countess of Tuscany, was a close friend of Pope Gregory VII. She steadfastly supported his reforms and those of subsequent popes.

DEVELOPING THEORY OF PAPAL POWER

Above: One of Innocent III's first acts was to use his papal authority to call for the Fourth Crusade to the Holy Land, which eventually came to grief at Constantinople in 1204.

From the eleventh century through to the thirteenth, papal power in the worlds of politics, faith, and theory grew to enormous levels. The major steps in that growth are readily traceable.

Donation of Constantine

It begins as far back as the eighth century, with a forgery that expresses the dream of papal power—the *Donation of Constantine*. Although this document purports to have been written by Emperor Constantine—the first Christian Roman emperor—to Pope Sylvester I on March 30, 315, it was actually composed after 750.

Apart from speaking about Constantine's conversion and baptism, the *Donation of Constantine* offers the pope a number of things: Control over all churches, especially the great centers of Antioch, Alexandria, Jerusalem, and Constantinople in the East; the Lateran palace in Rome and the imperial insignia; and, finally, the transfer of all earthly power in Rome, Italy, and the provinces of the West. It may not have been a genuine document, but it laid out the basic ideas of the medieval papacy. Here we find the pope as universal bishop following in St Peter's footsteps, teacher and godfather of the emperor, Christ's agent on earth, and Lord of the West.

The ideal took quite a while to come to fruition. Until the eleventh century, the pope's limited power was based on the fact that people looked toward Rome and Peter's tomb; the pope did not actually exercise any power himself.

In theory, the claim to be in a direct line from St Peter should have given the pope massive power. Peter had died in Rome, appointed his successors, and his body lay in a tomb in the city. Pope after pope took care to remind everyone that they spoke in the name of Peter, who had the keys to heaven. But for three hundred years the unique power envisaged in the *Donation of Constantine* remained a dream rather than reality.

From St Peter to Christ

By the reign of Pope Gregory VII (1073–1085), all that was changing. Gregory asserted the independent power of the papacy in all areas of life: In law, the first independent body of Church (or canon) law developed; in politics, the pope strenuously asserted the right to appoint and depose rulers; in the Church, the pope's own agents (legates) had the final say over all clergy; in the everyday life of the common people, the pope became the ultimate feudal lord.

However, there was also a vital shift in the source of the pope's power. No longer did Vatican lawyers feel comfortable with the idea embodied in the *Donation* that the emperor had given the pope all that power. No earthly ruler could grant anything to Christ's representative on earth—only Christ could do that. Thus the theory of papal power was deepened and strengthened: His power came from none other than Christ; that is, God.

Vicar of Christ

Even with all these changes, the pope was still called the "vicar of St Peter," which for many centuries had been sufficient. But this title looked backward, tracing a direct line to the Apostle Peter and thereby to Christ, and the papacy was now looking forward—a new title became necessary.

Toward the end of the twelfth century, Innocent III (reigned 1198–1216) took on the title "vicar of Christ." As he put it, "We are the successor of the Prince of the Apostles, but we are not his vicar, nor the vicar of any man or apostle, but the vicar of Jesus Christ himself." This was an unambiguous claim to universal authority. Innocent stated that although he was lower than God, he was higher than any human being. He occupied a place between God and human beings and was the mediator between them. It was the high point of the theory of papal power. From there it was a long, slow way down.

Theory in practice

All this power could not be asserted merely on paper; power must be wielded in real terms, in real life. Popes did so by handing out benefits, which usually generated prestige and wealth; by devising an indispensable legal system; and by practicing astute diplomacy between warring princes—which meant that the pope could call on various princes and their armed forces to further his agenda. Hundreds of years later, when told that the pope thought he should stop repressing Catholics under his yoke, Stalin famously snorted, "The Pope! How many divisions does he have?" At the height of papal power the answer would have been: "Very many."

Left: For the first millennium after Jesus' death, Christians regarded the popes as mortal representatives of St Peter, the first Bishop of Rome, who is venerated at St Peter's Basilica.

Below: In 1209, Francis of Assisi and his small group of followers appealed to Innocent III for his approval of their religious order; the pope eventually gave it, and the men were tonsured (had their heads shaved).

DECLINE OF THE PAPACY

The climax of papal power was reached with Innocent III (reigned 1198–1216), after popes had struggled tooth and nail with kings and emperors to gradually assert universal control as the vicar of Christ. By the end of the thirteenth century that power was waning.

The trials of Boniface VIII

An excellent example is Boniface VIII, pope from 1294 to 1303. He modeled himself on Gregory VII and Innocent III, asserting his supreme spiritual and temporal power. But the times were changing. He set out with great hopes, wanting to pacify Europe and conquer the Holy Land. Neither aim was achieved. His great struggle was with Philip the Fair of France. Attempting to cut off Philip's funds for war with England, in 1296 Boniface banned the king from receiving extra taxes from the clergy. Philip halted the payment of gold and valuables to Rome, and Boniface caved in. A few years later, Philip put to trial a papal legate, Bernard de Saisset, seeking to strip him of his position. Boniface fumed, issuing bulls asserting the supreme power of the pope ("God has set popes over kings and kingdoms") and demanding Philip cease the trial. Philip ignored him and tried to bring Boniface himself to trial in 1303. Events moved quickly: Boniface prepared to excommunicate him; Philip's agent, Guillaume de Nogaret, captured the pope while he was at Anagni; Italian troops released him soon afterward; and Boniface died a month later a broken man.

Below: Nicknamed Philip the Fair, King Philip IV of France (reigned 1285–1314) was in perpetual disagreement with the Roman papacy, in particular Pope Boniface VIII.

Right: As a young man, Pope Boniface VIII was a canon of the cathedral at Anagni. During his papacy, he was captured by the king of France's men at his Anagni retreat.

A deep weakness

At the heart of the claim to secular power was a basic flaw. Boniface had stated, "He who denies that the secular sword is in the power of Peter does not understand the words of the Lord." But what he did not say was that the pope could wield the secular sword only indirectly. Therein lay the problem. The pope relied on deputies to carry out his secular aims, and these deputies were the princes and kings of Europe. He was the supreme commander and they must carry out his commands—or so he believed. The popes devoted immense energy to controlling the Holy Roman Emperor, for if they could not control him they had no hope of controlling other rulers.

That this system was held together by sheer willpower, along with a mix of benefits and the papal legal system, meant that the pope's physical power was in fact reliant on secular rulers. They provided the physical force, in terms of armies, that allowed him to enforce his will. The system worked if it suited the emperor or king in question. Papal approval and support meant a great deal in the perpetual struggle for power. But that support carried with it obligations with which the emperors did not always agree. Thus, if the pope became a liability, the emperor or king would simply ignore him or oppose him.

Increasingly the rulers of Europe began to see the pope as yet one more earthly ruler, to be obeyed if it suited them but to be opposed if it didn't. As the popes became political rulers, using their spiritual authority for earthly ends, they lost their unique status. Making alliances, waging war, and bringing recalcitrants to heel all contributed to the loss of the pope's superior position. When he began to see himself as the one to negotiate settlements between warring parties, this further weakened his influence. Added to this were the overuse of excommunication as a political weapon and the increasingly widespread use of indulgences (a guarantee of heaven). The overuse of excommunication cheapened it: Rulers and even towns found it inconvenient, but they carried on regardless. And the inflation of indulgences weakened the one power the pope still had: The keys of heaven.

Signs of the times

Boniface fought hard to maintain the glory days of the papacy, but by the fourteenth century a range of oppositional voices began to be heard. As the power of the papacy waned, the pope seemed to be surrounded by enemies and heretics. By the 1320s, John XXII seemed to spend all his time denouncing heretics: William of Ockham, Meister Eckhart, and Marsilius of Padua were all declared heretical. Their protector, the Holy Roman Emperor Louis IV (Louis the Bavarian), was excommunicated. Louis simply ignored the pope. At the end of the era, Pope Julius II (1503–1513) was still trying to lay claim to universal papal power in his struggles with the then Holy Roman Emperor, Louis XII of France. But such claims had long ceased to be effective.

Above: Pope Boniface VIII proclaimed the year 1300 as the first Jubilee of the Church, granting plenary indulgences to the thousands of pilgrims who visited Rome that year.

Above left: This Greek manuscript illustration shows Pope Leo IX excommunicating Michael Cerularius, Patriarch of Constantinople, in 1054. This action, taken in a time of great papal power, severed relations between Roman and Eastern churches.

THE CRUSADES

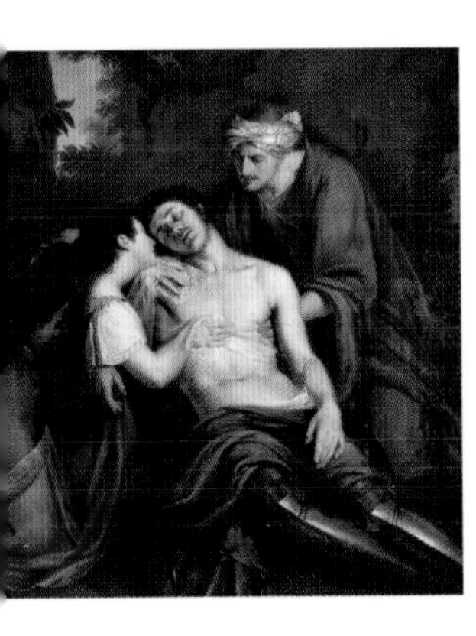

Above: Tancred, a Christian knight of the First Crusade, lies wounded after a duel. He was involved in numerous battles during the crusade, and subsequently became regent of the Principality of Antioch.

The word "crusade" brings to mind a single-minded focus on a particular goal. However, its origins lie in the military expeditions from Europe to recover the Holy Land from Islam from the eleventh century onward. At first they were called pilgrimages, but since the soldiers and pilgrims who went to Jerusalem wore a cross on their clothing, the word "crusade" (derived from "cross") became common.

Holy Land conquest

The initial wave of crusades captured and held Palestine for over a century. The First Crusade (1095–1099) was a well-organized military campaign involving several armies from France and southern Italy. Pope Urban II called for the crusade on November 27, 1095. His reasons for instigating the crusade were to drive back the Turks after their victory over the Eastern Roman Empire at Manzikert in 1071; and to recover the Holy Sepulchre, which had been under Muslim control since 638.

The First Crusade swept across Asia Minor (modern Turkey) and down the coast to Jerusalem, which was captured on July 15, 1099. The high point of the campaign was the proclamation of the King of Jerusalem—Baldwin of Bouillon—on Christmas Day of 1100. The success of the First Crusade led to a series of Western European states being established in Palestine and Syria—based at Jerusalem, Antioch, Tripoli, and Edessa to the east.

By this time the two special orders of military monks had arisen. The Knights Hospitaller and Knights Templar were established after the First Crusade. Originally dedicated to protecting pilgrims and, particularly in the case of the Hospitallers, the sick, they soon became the main military forces defending the Holy Land. The Templars, who had become wealthy and powerful, provoked a great deal of jealousy and were closed down in 1312. The Hospitallers survived much longer, eventually fading in the eighteenth century only to be transformed into the St John Ambulance Brigade in 1888.

The crusading spirit

As the Ottoman Empire expanded into Eastern Europe, many plans were hatched to drive the Turks out of Europe and also to recover the Holy Land. However, the armies were defeated at major battles at Nicopolis in 1396 and Varna in 1444. The Turks were there to stay.

The spirit continued with Portuguese and Spanish colonial expansion in the sixteenth century. Both were given the commission by successive popes to find a way around and drive the Muslims out of the Middle East and North Africa.

Why did the crusades happen? Devotion to Christ's earthly life in Palestine was on the rise; pilgrim numbers were increasing, and a sense grew that the Holy Land should once again be a Christian possession. Population pressures also played a role, so people sought new lands. Above all, with growing power, the pope could claim to rule over the whole earth. In order to sustain that claim, the need for military power became apparent—so much so that crusaders were granted indulgences, and those who died became martyrs.

Left: Guy de Lusignan, King of Jerusalem, surrenders to Saladin after the Battle of Hattin (1187). This stunning defeat of the Christians in the Holy Land led to the Third Crusade.

Far left: After a long and arduous journey, the First Crusaders reached Jerusalem on June 7, 1099. It is said that many of them wept for joy on seeing the holy city for the first time.

The crusader hold on the Holy Land was always precarious, and soon rising Muslim power threatened to topple the crusaders' gains. The eastern fortress of Edessa fell in 1144, and in response the Second Crusade was launched under the inspiration of Bernard of Clairvaux in 1147. It made little difference. Forty years later, the great Muslim military leader Saladin captured Jerusalem and overran most of the crusader territory. So the Third Crusade was launched (1189–1192) with the Holy Roman Emperor himself, as well as Richard I (Lionheart) of England and Philip II of France, taking part. They regained much lost territory, but failed to take Jerusalem.

To achieve that goal, the Fourth Crusade set out in 1202. It didn't even get close to the Holy Land. The Venetians persuaded them to attack Constantinople and take over from the despised Greeks. The result was a brief Latin rule in Constantinople, the union of Eastern and Western Churches for a time, increased bitterness, and a significant weakening of the Eastern Empire.

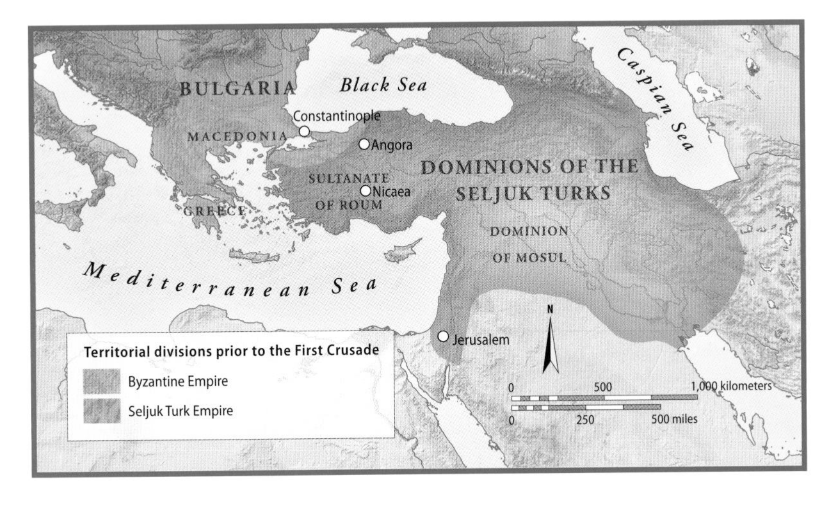

Crusades in all directions

Over the next phase of crusading (1204 to 1291), the crusader holdings in Palestine and Syria fell one by one. Waves of smaller and larger crusades tried to arrest the slide, even managing to recover Jerusalem through negotiation for 15 years (1229–1244). The two largest crusades were directed against Egypt, but in both cases promising starts came to a standstill.

By this time the crusading idea was losing focus. They seemed to go in all directions. With Palestine a futile cause, there were crusades against non-Christians in Europe—the Muslims in Spain or the unconverted Slavs. Heretics such as the Albigensians also became a target, as did political opponents of the pope such as Frederick II, the Hohenstaufen ruler of Sicily who had designs on Italy.

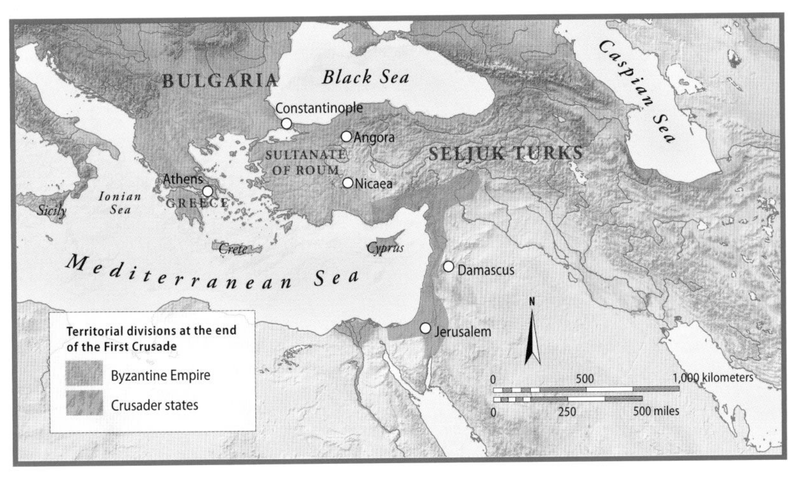

UNIVERSITIES

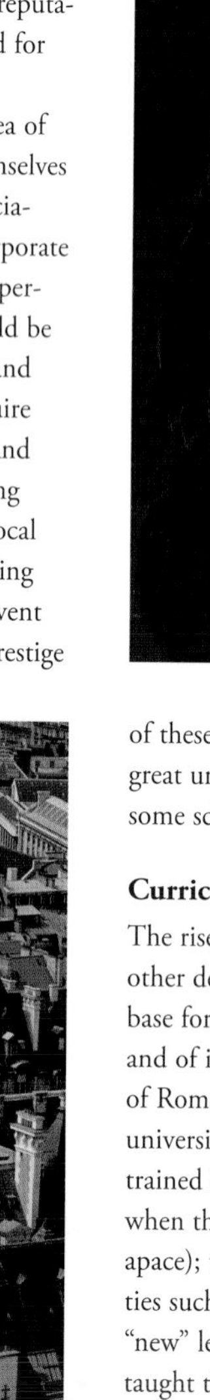

The university is one of the inventions of the medieval Latin Church that has survived and evolved to become the great educational and research institution we know today. The word *universitas*, although commonly thought to express the wide range of concerns studied in universities, actually means a "corporation." It refers to the fact that the "university" is a joint venture of the teachers in that place: They collectively own it, run it, control its library, and through it they could communally argue with cities, bishops, and princes. This notion was a revolutionary one in the late twelfth and early thirteenth centuries. Until the twelfth century, teaching—above the elementary level—was found mainly in monasteries, and this education, and the style of theology it produced, was seen as part of monastic life. To cope with the new cities of the twelfth century, cathedral schools came into existence but they were, for the most part, local affairs and depended on the local environment and its bishop, both for support and for students. However, already some schools, such as Paris, were growing in reputation both for the range of teachers they possessed and for their better-than-average quality.

By the beginning of the thirteenth century, the idea of a university had taken root: Scholars would join themselves together to form a corporation (or a guild or an association—this is the *universitas*), and then seek to get corporate rights to set themselves up as teachers. This required permission from the local bishop, whose chancellor would be head of the corporation, and it would require rights and exemptions from the state; and it would need to acquire property (such as a library) to carry on its business. And that business would be whole lives dedicated to writing and teaching. To insulate the group from too much local interference, they sought papal privileges from meddling by bishops, and general ecclesiastical privileges to prevent meddling by cities or princes. Indeed, such was the prestige of these guilds that cities courted them, and more than one great university (Cambridge, for example) was the result of some scholars breaking away from another place in protest.

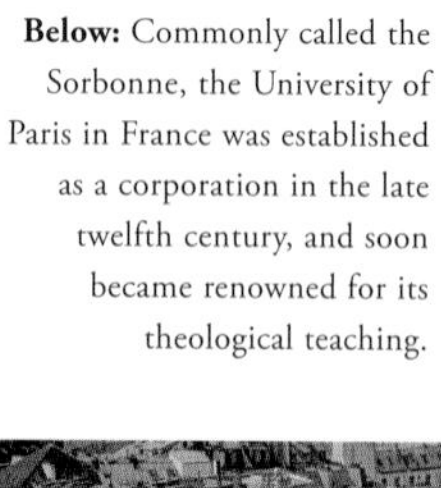

Below: Commonly called the Sorbonne, the University of Paris in France was established as a corporation in the late twelfth century, and soon became renowned for its theological teaching.

Curriculum and specialization

The rise of the universities coincided with a number of other developments: The rise of cities that could provide a base for such institutions (for example, the growth of Paris and of its university went hand-in-hand); the rediscovery of Roman law and the systematization of canon law (the universities, most famously Bologna, supplied the highly trained lawyers needed to run Church and state at a time when the infrastructure of European society was developing apace); the recovery of Greek and Arabic thought (universities such as Salerno were centers for the translation of this "new" learning, while the medical university of Montpellier taught the ancient medical classics such as Galen); and within theology there was the development of new methods

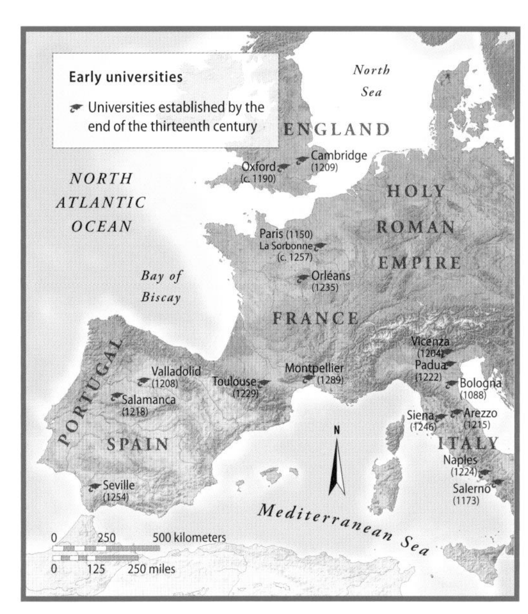

GETTING BETTER BY DEGREES

Most of the teachers in these educational guilds were clerics. Some were from the dioceses, but many were from the new city-based mendicant orders such as the Dominicans (who saw education as a key ministry) or the Franciscans, and there was often tension between the diocesans and the friars. But it is from the friars that the most famous teachers appeared: St Thomas Aquinas (1225–1274) and St Albert the Great (c. 1200–1280) were Dominicans; and St Bonaventure (c. 1217–1274) and Roger Bacon (c. 1214–c. 1292) were Franciscans. Moreover, the guilds organized themselves along clerical lines: As there were "grades" of clergy (deacon, priest, and bishop), so too were there "grades" in the university (bachelor, master, lector, and doctor). This is the origin of our degree structure.

of argument that presented doctrine in a manner not unlike the way evidence is presented in a court case—and Paris was *the* home of theologians.

The student was expected to become skilled first in the arts (language, reasoning, math, and philosophy), and then move on to one of the "greater" disciplines (medicine, civil law, and canon law), or to the highest specialty—theology—now more often seen as a formal body of knowledge rather than as a reflection on Christian faith.

The arrival of the universities had a major impact on the life of the Western Church, because the way that theology is studied and taught profoundly affects its values and emphases. The universities emphasized books and debate rather than the practices and experience of faith. This has left its legacy—theology today is often considered to be in opposition to Christian living; many Christians suspect that the "old-fashioned" formal theology has very little to do with "simple" believing.

Above: Medieval universities became centers of theological discussion and debate, which often eclipsed the notion of faith and the necessity of living a good Christian life.

Right: Roger Bacon (c. 1214–c. 1292) was a Franciscan philosopher and teacher nicknamed Doctor Mirabilis (Latin for "wonderful teacher"). He was one of the first champions of empirical scientific methods.

UNITY OF KNOWLEDGE

Above: Medieval universities taught the ideas of Classical Greek philosophers such as Socrates (pictured) alongside those of Christian thought as part of one large, interconnected web of knowledge.

For most people today, knowledge is a fractured business. On the one hand there is physics and math, about which people agree that they are for the most part correct and true. On the other hand there is human knowledge: History, psychology, and political theory. Here we assume that it is much harder to be certain about what is true and what is just a particular way of thinking. Lastly, there is philosophy and religion, and here we tend to think that these are private affairs far removed from "knowledge." These common attitudes make it difficult for us to imagine how medieval Christians saw all knowledge as an interlocking whole.

All wisdom is from God

There were several bases for this belief in the unity of knowledge, which, in turn, was seen to reflect the unity of the truth. The first pillar of the quest was Christian faith: God was the creator of all that is visible and invisible. This is part of the basic creed of medieval Christians, and since all things come from Him and are willed by Him, they must somehow fit together. The problem is that it is difficult for a limited and sinful human to see this unity. So what is discovered about human life by medicine must fit with what is revealed about human life in religion. When medieval Christians read the scriptures they found this vision of the unity of knowledge confirmed over and over again: "All wisdom is from the Lord, and with Him it remains forever" (Sirach 1:1) and "Wisdom is radiant and unfading, and she is easily discerned by those who love her, and is found by those who seek her" (Wisdom of Solomon 6:12).

Everyone can discover parts of the truth

The second pillar is this: If all creation is from God, it also bears witness to its maker and shows forth God's wisdom

Right: In the Middle Ages human knowledge and understanding was informed by the Christian belief that everything in the human domain was created by God and therefore shared a relationship with God.

and power. So every little scrap of knowledge about the creation must tell us something about every other part for they had a common artist, and by reflection must show some of the beauty and majesty of that artist. When medieval Christians read St Paul they found this view confirmed: "Ever since the creation of the world [God's] eternal power and divine nature, invisible though they are, have been understood and seen through the things he has made" (Romans 1:20), and so every human *can* see that creation comes from God and know there is a God and know something about God.

To break up knowledge was tantamount to breaking up the work of a great artist, or even to imagine that the artist was somehow defective and patchy in his work, or even worse to imagine that there were several competing artists. The desire to have unity of knowledge implied that all creation had an inner harmony and goodness. Since this could be known by all humans, true knowledge could be discovered by Christians, Jews, Muslims, or pagans.

Left: Medieval Islamic astronomers used information from the early Greeks and Indians in their studies of the stars; in turn, Islamic knowledge influenced later European astronomy.

No contradictions!

The third pillar was derived from the Greek view of how humans reason. Greek logic held that two statements could not contradict one another; both at the same time could not be equally true. If I say, "This pen is blue," then the one thing I cannot say at the same time and in the same conditions is, "This pen is not blue!" This was called "the law of contradiction." By making this principle the basis of all knowledge, one must accept the consequence that all true statements must be capable of synthesis into a single, coherent, whole body of knowledge. There can only be apparent or verbal contradictions, never real contradictions. Practically, this meant that the universities could study Greek philosophy, Islamic science, and Christian teaching side-by-side; confident that if they worked hard enough they would see that what is true in part of human knowledge must fit with every other part.

Medieval Christian scholars believed that each little piece of knowledge was capable of being related to every other little piece of knowledge. And all these true bits of knowledge would only finally be seen as a complete whole after this life when humans are in union with God. This is when a human being would fully appreciate truth. Today when we think of knowledge we think of a series of databases; these scholars imagined knowledge like all the interlinking arches of a Gothic cathedral or like the beautiful unity of bones, muscles, sinews, and mind of a human being walking.

Below: With its abundance of vines encircling the central threesome, Federico Zuccari's sixteenth-century fresco entitled *Wisdom* is a visual representation of the interconnectedness of all God-given knowledge.

AQUINAS VERSUS AUGUSTINE

Opposite: Reflecting his bringing together of knowledge from different times and cultures, St Thomas Aquinas is depicted standing between Aristotle and Plato and over the Islamic philosopher Averroes.

Above: One of the most influential figures in Western Christianity, St Augustine conceptualized the ideas of "just war," "original sin," and the Church as the "City of God."

Below: Rather than dismissing the knowledge that came out of the Islamic world as heretical and unworthy, St Thomas Aquinas saw this information as part of God's wisdom.

During the late twelfth and for much of the thirteenth century there was a revolution in Western Christian theology. This revolution is often referred to as "the rise of scholasticism" (a term emphasizing that the revolution produced a new theological style); at other times the revolution is presented as "Aquinas versus Augustine" (a term emphasizing that there were problems integrating new ideas with the beliefs long-held by Latin Christians). The older beliefs are represented by St Augustine (354–430), whose vast writings had been held in awe for centuries, while the new ideas and methods are represented by St Thomas Aquinas (1225–1274). But the reality was not as simple as a duel between the old and the new.

Revolutions are complex

The growth in the size of medieval cities such as Paris and Bologna saw the rise of the new educational organizations called universities, which adopted a very different view of learning than the one held by monasteries. Moreover, there were new kinds of religious orders in these cities—the friars—who could travel and devote themselves to teaching in a way that monks could not. Aquinas was a Dominican friar and spent his whole life teaching in universities or friaries, all located in bustling cities.

Another factor in the revolution was the rediscovery of ancient Greek philosophy—mainly the works of Aristotle (383–322 BCE)—whose philosophy had never before been an important influence on Christian thought. Greek philosophy posed new questions and showed new ways of looking at nature, which produced reactions from fear of the new to disdain of the old. Aquinas wrote many commentaries on Aristotle and used his works as the basis of his own thought. To some this was breaking with tradition (identified as "Augustine"); for others Aquinas was not nearly radical enough. One other development caused offence: Aquinas used a debating method to expound his thought, while his opponents preferred the older method more akin to sermons.

Along with the rediscovery of Greek philosophy came Islamic learning, which was also influenced by Aristotle. This Muslim learning seemed shocking to many people, yet Aquinas was prepared to engage with it and to use it within his Christian synthesis. He quoted the Muslim thinkers, along with Jewish philosophers like Maimonides, in his writings, because he believed that wherever some truth could be found would ultimately lead people toward the fullness of God's truth. Aquinas, like Augustine in his day, sought to find the best sources available so as to express more fully the Christian mystery for his day. Strangely, within a generation, the successors of those who disliked Aquinas and saw him as someone who advocated extreme views became his biggest supporters.

Conservatives like to freeze time

In any period of change there are those who like to imagine that new ideas are automatically threatening, and who would like to pretend that one can freeze time at a particular moment in the past and claim that that moment or thinker or book had all the answers. But human knowledge and questioning is always developing and changing. The conservatives in the thirteenth century imagined that Augustine had all the answers, ignoring the fact that there had been 800 years of growth and change in the West by Aquinas' time. However, for those who feared new ideas Aquinas was not someone grappling with the real problems, but someone who was "abandoning" the past—forgetting that Augustine had been writing about the problems he encountered in the last days of the Roman Empire. Part of the genius of Aquinas was that he engaged with the new without losing sight of the past, and he recognized that if Augustine was still to have value, then his thought had to be integrated with the new—and not simply repeated.

However, other members of the clergy allowed fear to conquer them and so they tried to deal with the problem by condemning the discussion of certain issues in the universities where they had influence—and some say these condemnations included Aquinas. The long-term effect of this perceived clash of "Aquinas versus Augustine" was to breed an attitude of suspicion of the new among many churchmen and a more widespread attitude that Christianity was always happier with established and accepted ideas. So while historians and theologians today deny that there was ever a real clash between Aquinas' thought and that of Augustine—some perceive the clash as a myth in the minds of conservatives at the time—we should not underestimate that myth, for it lies at the root of much modern fundamentalism.

SANCTUS THOMMAS DEACQ
VERITATĒ MEDITA
BITUR GUTT
UR MEUM ET
LABIA MEA
DETESTABUN
TUR IMPIU
PROVERBIOꝝ
MULTITUD
INIS USUS
QUE IN RE
BUS NOMI
NANDIS S
EQUENDU P
HILOSOPHU
CESET CŌMUNĒ
HIC
UMĒ
LESIE
HIC ADINVI
OMNEM VIĀ DISCIPL

CHRIST'S HUMILITY AND SUFFERING

Opposite: In the Middle Ages those who wished to "imitate Christ" followed his example by living a life of poverty, enduring the pain of suffering, and sometimes whipping themselves as Christ had been whipped before he was crucified.

When theology first started to develop its depiction of Christ from the New Testament stories, five major images emerged: The peaceful messiah, the prophet of the end of days, the wisdom teacher, the suffering servant, and the victorious Christ. The last two were the images that had the most appeal in the Middle Ages.

Christ the Victor

In the words of the Apostles' Creed, which was recited in the daily rituals of the medieval Church, we find the following statement:

... he descended to the dead.
On the third day he rose again;
he ascended into heaven,
he is seated at the right hand of the Father,
and he will come to judge the living and the dead.

This is the image of *Christus Victor*, Christ the Victor, which was so powerful from the time of Constantine the Great (died 337). One reason for Constantine's adoption of Christianity was that he felt Christ would help him in battle, especially the crucial battle of the Milvian Bridge (312), by which he won the empire. Christ was believed to be a powerful force, one who would guarantee victory. The reason was that Christ had conquered death and risen victoriously from the grave to take his place beside the Father—as the Apostles' Creed expresses so clearly.

Above: Constantine the Great was the first Roman emperor to convert to Christianity. After the conversion, he felt that he was chosen by God and assisted by Christ to rid the world of impiety.

As Christianity spread throughout Europe, a major appeal was the victorious Christ. Chieftain, ruler, and king decided one after another that Christianity offered a far more powerful force in life, death, and battle. For this reason we find the phenomenon of rulers as far as Scandinavia deciding to adopt Christianity and commanding their subjects to do so as well.

Suffering servant

Of the two major features of the story of Christ, *Christus Victor* focused on the Resurrection. The other emphasis was on his crucifixion, with all its attendant suffering. A little earlier in the Apostles' Creed it reads:

[he] suffered under Pontius Pilate,
was crucified, died, and was buried;

There are fewer words, and much less emphasis on Christ's suffering and humility. In time, however, this important theme would come to dominate views of Christ in the Middle Ages. It also drew from the picture of the "suffering servant" in the Old Testament book of Isaiah, which many felt was a prophecy of Christ. Here we find a figure who suffers in silence, is humiliated, beaten, tortured, and put to a slow and painful death. The point of this image is that he is God's anointed, but that the task he is given is to suffer for others. For many in the Middle Ages life was short and full of suffering; death was a terrifying process that could arrive at any moment from war, plague, or famine. In this context the suffering Christ came to mean far more.

Imitating Christ

The underlying theme in movement after movement was the imitation of Christ—*imitatio Christi*. If one was to follow Christ's example, then one must be humble and suffer.

This suffering Christ appears in many different forms. It appeared in the idea of sacrificing one's life for Christ. In the early Church this took the form of martyrdom during periods of persecution. Many wanted to imitate Christ's

Right: Before the battle of the Milvian Bridge, Constantine the Great claimed to have had a vision instructing him to fight under the sign of the cross, which would ensure victory.

own suffering, so they even volunteered for martyrdom. In the Middle Ages during the Crusades it took a different form. Those who died while trying to recapture the Holy Land were granted an indulgence and thereby direct access to heaven without passing through purgatory.

Another image of the suffering servant was found in the flagellants who began appearing in times of crisis such as the plagues, especially during the Great Plague of 1349. The flagellants first turn up in the thirteenth century in the towns, walking barefoot in groups, beating their backs with leather thongs to the point of drawing blood, and crying out in tears for God's mercy. Not only did they seek forgiveness for their sins, but they set out to imitate the sufferings of Christ. One notable example was the Red Knights, who felt that the blood they drew united them with the blood of Christ, and that the marks on their bodies were reminders of Christ's bodily suffering.

Most often the imitation of Christ took the form of religious orders and monasteries. Again and again people sought the path to salvation through self-denial and suffering. Some were strict, like the Cistercians, and others more open, like the Augustinian canons. Others expressed this desire in the denial of property and a life of begging, like the Franciscan friars.

NEW MONASTIC ORDERS

Previous page: In his 1223 bull entitled "Solet annuere," Pope Honorius III confirmed the Rule of St Francis, which even today continues to guide the lives of Franciscan friars.

Opposite: As his followers increased in number, St Francis felt it was necessary to create a written Rule for both the First Order of Friars Minor and the Second Order of Poor Ladies.

Below: Benedictine novices and nuns were expected to live a simple life following the 73-chapter Rule of St Benedict, preferring "nothing whatever to Christ" (Chapter 72).

Monastic orders in the Middle Ages followed a repeating pattern. Each one began as a desire for a new beginning in imitating the simple life of Christ. But with rare exceptions, each would succumb to the world against which it was protesting. Soon enough the new movement became established and worldly, and protests would arise again. Up until the eleventh century the Benedictines had provided the major form of monastic life. Their order had begun as a simple, austere, and well-organized movement, but by 1000 CE it was wealthy and involved in the power struggles of the time.

The inspiration of Augustine

A new current was found in the original and austere theology of St Augustine (354–430). One of his followers, perhaps with Augustine's assistance, wrote the popular Rule of St Augustine, which lay down a few simple guidelines for monastic observances and offered a reflection on the common life. The beauty of the Rule of St Augustine was its simplicity; one could take it in many directions. This rule was the inspiration for at least three new orders after the eleventh century, the Premonstratensian canons, Augustinian canons, and Dominican friars.

The Premonstratensians, established in 1120 at Prémontré in northern France, followed the Rule of St Augustine with extra severities. They drew in large numbers of women and recovered the old practice of having double houses. However, the usual suspicions of women returned, and the female part of the movement was suppressed.

The Augustinian canons were mostly devoted to service. They arose in obscurity, were low-key and relatively humble, but offered what many people needed: Religious services, prayers for illness, burial ceremonies, masses for the dead, and multiple everyday religious services. They were largely informal, requiring little money for establishment or maintenance, and their appeal lay in a simple, humble life.

Later on, in the early thirteenth century, the Dominican friars also drew upon the Rule of St Augustine. The dream of primitive Christian simplicity was important for the founder, St Dominic, but there was another factor: It set out to combat heresy through teaching and preaching. Dominicans soon played an important role in the towns and universities, where they became leading scholars of the age.

The inspiration of Benedict

Other orders that developed in the eleventh century were the Carthusians, Grandmont, and Cistercians. In their own way, each sought to recover the original purity and poverty of the Benedictines. The Order of Grandmont (the name of the mother house in Normandy) began with severe discipline, which became relaxed once the order was established.

Very different in nature were the contemplative Carthusians, founded in 1084 at a primitive monastery in Grande Chartreuse (hence the name). The discipline was extreme, and it never grew to be a massive movement. It was and is characterized by a vow of silence, mortification of the flesh, living in cells, devotion to mental prayer, and meeting for meals and services only on feast days.

For the Cistercians, simplicity meant living a rigorous and highly ordered life of self-denial away from civilization. They set themselves up in wild, uncultivated places, built around them a second level of worker monks, or *conversi*, and effectively colonized much of what was left of Europe. Their extreme discipline and poverty actually had the obverse effect: They attracted benefactors, bought up land, and within a century became wealthy. With this came the inevitable slackening in discipline.

Franciscans

The friars who followed the inspiration of St Francis took the ideal of humility and poverty to its extreme. Following the example of St Francis in the thirteenth century, they took literally Christ's command to sell everything, give to the poor, and forsake any glory, comfort, or organization. Utter poverty was the only way to imitate Christ. They lived as itinerant beggars, often drawing the poor into their ranks although they rejoiced when a noble joined them. However, as the bequests, wills, and other gifts poured in, the question of property became acute. The Franciscans simply set limits on such gifts, so they never became as wealthy as other orders. Like the Dominicans, the Franciscans were an order of the towns, where mendicant beggars could live in community. Again, like the Dominicans, they attracted scholars, rejuvenating theology, filling the universities, and producing some of the greatest minds of the age.

In each case we find simple beginnings, phenomenal growth, and then a flattening out as another order came to take the earlier one's place. And in each case the severity of the discipline was considered a mark of its purity.

TQVICVQ·HĀC·REGVLĀ·SECVTI·FVERĪT·PAX·SVP
SIGNA THAV SVP FRONTES VIRORV̄GEMĒCIV

LAY MEN AND WOMEN

Above: While clergymen such as bishops were concerned with performing religious rituals and other sacred duties, laypersons were more interested in finding God through a modest and unadulterated life.

The word laity comes from the Greek, *laos theou*, "people of God." At first it meant the whole congregation of Christians, but later came to mean all Church members who are not clergy. By the Middle Ages there was a sharp distinction between the laity and bishops, priests, monks, and nuns.

No more options

By the eleventh century, all bases of the religious life had been covered. If you wanted to be a Church leader, you could take the path of priest and perhaps bishop. If you wanted to be a lawyer, there was a Church position. If you wanted a contemplative life that valued manual labor, the strong Cistercian order was for you. If you aspired to a common life of poverty, celibacy, and obedience, there were the Augustinian canons. If you were interested in social work, scholarship, and art, the widespread Benedictines were there. If you were interested in preaching and study, the Dominicans would always welcome you. And if you were suspicious of collective property and wanted a life of absolute poverty sustained by begging, you could join one of the many other orders of friars. In short, every relationship with the world seemed to be wrapped up in terms of religious education, organization, and papal approval.

Lay brothers and sisters

Yet the people were not happy. In a time of poor diet, makeshift medicine, and the absence of decent painkillers, life was relatively short and often very painful. The end of the world always seemed close, whether in the form of an invading army, famine, or plague. A simple life in search of God and salvation had great appeal. But how was one to find that simple religious life without all the trappings of monasteries, organizations, hierarchies, and the daily rhythm of religious observances? In this context a number of lay movements arose, among them the development of lay brothers and sisters for the monasteries. They took on the manual labor as the monasteries became wealthier and the monks and nuns became more and more involved with ritual and Church business.

The desire for a simple religious life

Other lay movements were more innovative, among them the Beguines and the followers of Geert de Groote, who became known as the Brethren of the Common Life. (The Beguines are discussed later in this chapter.) De Groote (1340–1384) was the son of a cloth merchant from Deventer in Holland. Initially educated at Paris, he taught in Cologne for a time, living a luxurious lifestyle. But his life seemed increasingly empty, and in 1374 he decided he no longer wanted to become a priest, monk, teacher, or leader of the Church, vowing to live a simple, devout life in the service of God, outside the structures of the Church, free of the organization of religious life. He valued secular labor and encouraged others to do the same. For the last ten years of his life he preached in the Dutch towns of Deventer, Zwolle, and Kampen, his old gray cloak and patched clothes becoming legendary among his followers. He attacked the abuses within the Church, arguing that they blocked one's relationship with God. Many people were drawn to listen to him, his followers grew in number, and soon he was seen as a threat and banned from preaching. Nevertheless, small groups still met in his home.

He gave over his parental home in Deventer to a community of women. This was a significant move, since the established orders had become suspicious of women, who were increasingly depicted as evil, sensual, and out to tempt men, and the double houses (side-by-side religious communities of men and women) were falling away. In de Groote's house there were some rules, but they were simple. Its members were to belong to no religious order, to be laypersons subject to the secular courts, to take no vows and wear no habit, and to focus on their relationship with God. Small communities of men and women following these principles sprang up all over Holland, having everything in common as the Bible taught, doing what work they could to earn enough to live, especially by copying books, and later becoming active in secular education.

A century or two earlier, de Groote might have been excommunicated and his followers disbanded for their criticisms of the Church and refusal to join an order. But times had begun to change, and the search for other ways to be religious would eventually lead in the direction of the Reformation.

Right: Monks and nuns were obliged to follow the extensive guidelines set down by the founder of their order, while laypersons often had few if any official rules to control their relationship to God.

Above: Although medical knowledge improved throughout the medieval period, there were many illnesses and injuries that physicians could do little about. In a world where death was common, piety was important.

Left: Founded in 1170 by Herve de Montmorency, Dunbrody Abbey in Ireland was home to a group of Cistercian monks for almost 400 years before falling into disuse and ruin.

THE FRANCISCANS

Above: While praying on the mountainside at Verna in 1224, Francis was visited by a seraphim, a six-winged angel of God, after which the stigmata appeared on his body.

The Rule of St Benedict saw the personal poverty of the individual monk as vital to the true monastic spirit, but as Benedictinism developed in the later Middle Ages the monasteries as institutions could, and frequently did, own vast swathes of land and great quantities of possessions in huge monastic complexes. According to the vision of St Francis of Assisi (1181–1226), both the individual friar and the house he lived in had to be poor and simple, in imitation of Christ, who had nowhere to lay his head, who "for your sakes… became poor, so that by his poverty you might become rich" (2 Corinthians 8:9).

St Francis and the early friars

St Francis lived at a time of great social upheaval; the standards that underpinned the feudal society of the Middle Ages were being called into question, frequently with serious aggression. The aristocratic families, the *majores*, who had dominated the social and political structures, were being challenged by the *minores*, the lower classes, while an increase in commerce led to an emerging middle class of tradesmen who frequently built up great personal wealth, like Pietro Bernadone, the father of Francis. As a result of a vision, Francis came to react strongly against the greed and material acquisitiveness that he saw all around him.

An important anonymous early text, the *Sacrum Commercium*, describes Francis' commitment to a life of poverty and simplicity according to the chivalric language of the times, in terms of a romance with a beautiful but destitute lady, his "Lady Most High Poverty," to whom he considered himself betrothed. The Franciscan vision of poverty was inspired by the life of Christ, who was born poor in a manger, lived poor as an itinerant preacher, died in the total poverty of nakedness on the cross, and was buried in someone else's tomb. The radical poverty of Francis and the early friars was characterized by great personal devotion to the humanity of Christ and a desire to imitate his way of living. The friars wandered from village to village, preaching simply but effectively about the love of God and supporting themselves by manual labor, helping with the harvest, or nursing lepers in the leprosariums, and resorting to begging only when the work available was insufficient to provide them with life's necessities. While the order was still small, this worked well enough, but as its membership grew to number thousands and the new brothers knew Francis not personally, but only by hearsay, the vision of poverty began to dim.

The Lady Clare: St Clare of Assisi

Someone who truly understood and shared Francis' original vision for a simple life, and continued to live it long after his death, was Clare, the daughter of one of the noble houses of Assisi. Devout and pious from her early childhood, when still quite young she came under the influence of Francis, who greatly inspired her with ideals similar to her own—a desire to live the Gospel in a life of great simplicity and poverty. She ran away from home on the night of Palm Sunday 1212, and was accepted by Francis and his small band of like-minded young men. They escorted her to a local Benedictine monastery of nuns where she worked for a short while as a domestic, but "her soul was not at rest." Eventually, Francis found sanctuary for Clare and her younger sister Agnes, who had also incurred parental wrath by joining her, in the little monastery of San Damiano, outside the walls of Assisi. Here Clare lived in great poverty and austerity for the next forty years. Her reputation for holiness spread and she was consulted by bishops, cardinals, and popes. However, her lifelong battle was to have her *Forma Vitae*, with its vision of poverty, approved by the Church, a wish granted on her deathbed in 1253.

Above: Probably written after Francis' death, *Sacrum Commercium* chronicles Francis' search for the "Lady Most High Poverty," to whom God "had entrusted the keys of the kingdom of heaven."

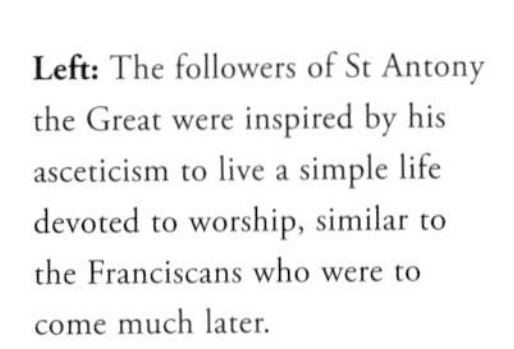

Left: The followers of St Antony the Great were inspired by his asceticism to live a simple life devoted to worship, similar to the Franciscans who were to come much later.

CHRISTIAN ATTITUDES TO POVERTY

The ideal of Christian living presented in the Acts of the Apostles describes the first Christians of Jerusalem living a life of communal sharing where no-one kept anything to themselves; in other words, where all things were held in common. For the Fathers of the Church such as St Basil the Great and St Augustine, this was the inspiration for the monastic vision that they set out in their writings. Complete detachment from material possessions in imitation of Christ became an important aspect of early monasticism, as lived by St Antony the Great and the Fathers and Mothers of the desert. This tradition came to the West with St Cassian, for whom renunciation from temporal things was crucial.

"ENEMIES OF THE CHURCH"

Above: A thirteenth-century Waldensian youth hides his vernacular Bible. Before the 1500s, Waldensians—who encouraged respect for religious differences—were persecuted as heretics.

The standard term of opprobrium to throw at an opponent in the Middle Ages was "heretic." The original Greek *hairesis* meant "choice"—choosing a different position in a debate. However, the definiton of heresy now included the specific denial of established Church doctrine and of what the Church saw as a revealed truth. In this time of questioning and challenging the status quo, the most powerful and influential groups ended up representing orthodoxy. Those who lost the struggle were branded heretics.

In the Middle Ages a number of heretical movements were born out of a desire to recover the simplicity of the early Church. The Church had become massive, highly structured and wealthy, and many people wished for a life of basic piety without all the trappings. The Church's reaction boiled down to either absorbing or crushing these movements for reform—a new order might be established, such as the Franciscans, so that there was room for the new ideas, or a movement's members would be excommunicated and condemned to death.

Bogomils and Cathari

One colorful example of a heretical movement is the Bogomils. Beginning in Bulgaria under the leadership of Bogomil in the ninth century, this Gnostic sect spread rapidly from the eleventh century and strongly influenced the development of the like-minded Cathari in Italy and France (also called Paterenes and Albigensians). In the thirteenth century the Cathari were such a threat to the Church that the word "heretic" specifically meant Cathari. Both Bogomils and Cathari believed in dualism: The world and the body were the work of Satan, only the soul was made by God; the New Testament and the Psalms were the only true Scripture; Christ had only the appearance of a human body; salvation meant the soul was freed from the evil body. Above all, they rejected the authority of the Church, and saw the sacraments as evil. Naturally, to them everyone else was a heretic; the Church treated them likewise. They were mercilessly persecuted for centuries.

Many other groups suffered the same fate, such as the Waldensians (who still exist in Italy); the Beguines; the followers of Geert de Groote; witches; and even sodomites (a term that covered same-sex relations and sex with animals). The Inquisition was established in 1232, to deal with these "enemies of the Church."

AQUINAS ON HERESY

"Heresy is a sin which merits not only excommunication but also death, for it is worse to corrupt the Faith which is the life and soul than to issue counterfeit coins which minister to the secular life. Since counterfeiters are justly killed by princes as enemies to the common good, so heretics also deserve the same punishment."
Thomas Aquinas, *Summa Theologiae*.

Jews and Muslims

By comparison, other "enemies of God" such as the Jews were relatively privileged. Jews were not to be converted by force, and their children could not be taken from them to be brought up as Christians. They could also practice Judaism as long as they did not try to convert anyone else. But that was all. They were permitted to live, but only in the barest of circumstances. Frequently reviled and attacked, they were accused of having "sinned" through their "unbelief," and also of having killed Christ and of bringing on the Black Death.

During the eighth century, Islam, another "enemy of God," had overcome many Christian lands—Palestine, Syria, North Africa, and Spain all fell under Muslim sway.

Right: Traveling in southern France in 1203, St Dominic was shocked to see how widespread the Albigensian heresy had become, and decided to devote his life to stamping it out.

Left: In places like Italy's Po River valley, aristocratic patronage of heretic groups in the Middle Ages aided not only their survival in the face of vehement Church opposition, but also the spread of their ideas.

After the Muslims (Moors) were expelled from Spain a few centuries later, the Spanish Inquisition was established in 1478, and in Portugal in 1536. The Inquisitors initially set out to deal with all heresies, but increasingly they turned their attention to the *moriscos* (converts from Islam) and the *conversos* (converts with Jewish ancestry), both perceived to be problems after forced mass conversions in the late fifteenth century, and who were executed if their conversions were found to be insincere.

The age of unrest

The harsh treatment of converts from Islam and Judaism was really a sign of wider instability from 1300 onward; another sign was the rise in condemnations of heretics. The growth of towns, the increasing strength of secular rulers, new economic developments from trade, the outpouring of new ideas, and the willingness of people to speak out were all parts of the change. The winds of change had begun to blow, and in this context a range of perceived enemies was denounced: Pope John XXII condemned the Franciscans for their vow of poverty, as well as Marsilius of Padua, William of Ockham, and many of the writings of Meister Eckhart.

Below: Following the expulsion of the Muslims from Spain, many Islamic items such as intricately decorated clothing and scholarly books were deemed heretical and destroyed by the Christians.

WILLIAM OF OCKHAM

One of the most influential figures condemned and excommunicated during the age of unrest (c. 1300–c. 1550s) was William of Ockham. In a rapid cascade of events, he was denounced for heresy (by the chancellor of the university of Oxford), then censured for 51 positions in his writing, then excommunicated, then expelled from his order (the Franciscans), and finally condemned to perpetual imprisonment—all between 1323 and 1331. He was never actually imprisoned, since he was astute enough to seek the protection of the Holy Roman Emperor, Louis of Bavaria, in 1328. Needless to say, he was regarded by the pope and leaders of the Church as a substantial threat.

The pope a heretic

Why was this man from the obscure town of Ockham, a day's ride to the southwest of London, such a threat? The main reason was that he was not afraid to state a controversial opinion, the most obvious example being his conclusion that the current pope, John XXII, was a heretic. He arrived at this position in the midst of a dispute over poverty while in Avignon (the pope's residence) in 1324–1328. The pope and Michael of Cesena, minister general of the Franciscans, were engaged in a heated argument over poverty, which all turned on the interpretation of how Jesus and the disciples had lived, according to the Gospels. Michael argued for absolute poverty; the pope disagreed. So Michael asked William of Ockham to study the issue by considering earlier papal statements, including those of the current pope. Ockham surprised himself by concluding that the pope's position was willfully, stubbornly, and persistently heretical, even after he had been shown it was incorrect. This was the worst type of heresy, meaning that the pope was no longer legitimate.

Below: The popes of the Avignon Papacy first took up residence in the city in 1309; it was in Avignon that William of Ockham proclaimed that Pope John XXII was a heretic.

Protection

The situation became a little precarious. Ockham, Michael of Cesena, and a few other Franciscans left Avignon in May 1328 and fled to the protection of Louis of Bavaria. Louis himself was in dispute with the pope and was inclined to protect other critics. There was no turning back; until his death in 1347, Ockham remained under Louis' protection and wrote polemical political works directed against the pope and in favor of the emperor. He became one of the first medieval authors to argue for a form of separation of Church and state (in which the emperor did not need to be validated by the pope and could depose him if he were found to be heretical).

Thought

This challenge would have been of no consequence had Ockham been a man of little intelligence—but he was one of the leading independent thinkers of his time, credited with beginning what is known as the *via moderna*, which opened the way to modern thought and the sciences. His writings fall into three major areas: Theology, philosophy, and politics. Within philosophy, he made major contributions to the important areas of medieval thought—logic, physics or natural philosophy, theory of knowledge, and ethics. His work is notable for a rigorous reassessment of earlier positions, especially those of Aristotle, but he was creative enough to develop them into striking new areas.

Ockham is most famous for his "razor," the principle that the explanation of any phenomenon should make as few assumptions as possible (sometimes called the law of parsimony). He was a deeply logical thinker and developed what is now known as formal logic. He also controversially attacked and dismissed the pervading idea of universals—the argument that something is, for example, big because it relies on a universal idea known as "bigness." Ockham argued instead that only individual things exist and that we come to know them directly with our minds—in other words, only individual big things exist.

His theological ideas were consistent with his philosophical ones. Ockham stressed God's absolute power, knowledge, and freedom. None of these should be limited in any way. This applies to creation—God does not make things following the pattern of universal ideas in his mind, since that would limit God's freedom. It applies to morals—God decrees our moral order and does not rely on any models to do so. And it applies to knowing—no arguments can prove God's existence, so we must rely purely on faith in God's revelation. It was a complex and formidable system of thought, put forward by a man not afraid to carry his views to their logical conclusion, and for these reasons he was a challenge to the status quo.

Above: Rather than dismissing the ideas of earlier philosophers such as Aristotle—seen here in a fifteenth-century fresco—William of Ockham studied the ideas then expanded upon them.

Below: Opposing the traditional Catholic view, Pope John XXII declared that Beatific Vision (the faithful immediately seeing the presence of God after death) did not occur; he later retracted his statement.

JOHN WYCLIF

Above: Often called "The Morning Star of the Reformation," John Wyclif (sometimes spelled Wycliffe) was one of the first theologians to challenge Catholic supremacy.

An underappreciated voice from a distant era, John Wyclif is nevertheless a compelling figure whose condemnation of a self-justifying and worldly Church provoked a theological and ecclesiastical upheaval whose final implications became apparent in the sixteenth-century Reformation.

An especially dismal era

In the fourteenth century, a sequence of disasters (natural and otherwise) created humanitarian, political, and ecclesiastical crises that were popularly seen to portend an apocalyptic conclusion. Between 1315 and 1322, thousands of northern Europeans died of starvation and infection when years of bad weather, with abnormally severe winters and cold, wet summers, caused harvest failures and animal deaths; this Great Famine anticipated the even worse catastrophe of the Black Death, a pandemic of plague that killed perhaps a third of the population of Europe in 1347–1351. A long and ruinous war erupted in 1337 when England's King Edward III claimed the French throne as his birthright, leading to over a century of Anglo-French hostilities usually called the Hundred Years' War.

Right: In 1410, John Badby became one of the first Lollard martyrs when he was placed in a barrel and burned to death at Smithfield, London, for his unwavering denial of transubstantiation.

In those and other late medieval calamities, the Church not only proved incapable of adequate theological clarification or pastoral consolation, it demonstrated a self-destructive tendency. From 1309 to 1377 the papacy surrendered much of its spiritual authority when Pope Clement V and his successors took up residence at Avignon in France. The situation worsened in 1378 when two claimants to the papacy, Urban VI and Clement VII, divided the loyalties of Western Christianity. The travesty of popes competing with antipopes was finally ended by the Council of Constance in 1417.

The life and opinions of a radical thinker

John Wyclif, born around 1330 in Yorkshire, studied and taught philosophy at Oxford before undertaking a study of theology. He gained the patronage of the king's son, John of Gaunt, who also patronized Geoffrey Chaucer, famed author of *The Canterbury Tales.* Wyclif and Chaucer shared anticlerical opinions that were, judging from the extant literature of the era, pervasive—but Wyclif's anticlerical ferocity countermanded Chaucer's genial journalistic acceptance of affairs.

Wyclif observed a worldly and self-aggrandizing Church populated by an ignorant horde of believers and governed by venal, stupid clergy. His egalitarian notions of divine election led him to reject the distinction between clergy and laity, which further led him to devalue clerical office and call for the divestment of ecclesiastical property. For Wyclif, the Bible mediated God, which meant that scriptural authority superseded ecclesiastical authority. Because the corrupted Church would not restitute itself, the dominion of the state was required to make amends.

As Wyclif's opinions became increasingly strident, he caught the attention of John of Gaunt who, leading the government's efforts in 1376 to raise money to sustain the French war, desired to institute taxation of the clergy. At Gaunt's behest, Wyclif preached his anticlerical views in London, which earned from Archbishop Courtenay of London a summons to account for himself at St Paul's Cathedral, where he appeared with Gaunt in support. The quarrel that ensued further increased Wyclif's notoriety, and culminated in Pope Gregory XI denouncing Wyclif's theory of dominion in 1377.

Wyclif's ideas were literally seen as revolutionary, as he was blamed for the Peasants' Revolt of 1381. Oxford condemned him that same year, and the next year, at the "Earthquake Synod" in London, Archbishop Courtenay led an official condemnation of his opinions. Suffering the effects of a stroke, Wyclif shortly afterward withdrew from public life to the rectorate at Lutterworth, where he died in 1384. In 1415

the Council of Constance posthumously condemned him as a heretic, and his remains were disinterred and burned.

After-effects of radical ideas

No other pre-modern heretic has enjoyed such a celebrated afterlife as John Wyclif. His spirit endured among the Lollards (possibly from the Dutch word *lollaerd*, "a person who mutters," because their prayers sounded like murmuring). The Lollards held to many of Wyclif's teachings, especially piety derived from the Bible and unmediated through the Church, and had contempt for Roman ideas such as transubstantiation. Lollardy existed as an extra-ecclesial movement until the English reformation. English nonconformity usually traces its origins to Wyclif through the Lollards.

Wyclif's views on scripture and dominion earned him a favorable reappraisal by the sixteenth-century reformers, who viewed him as an ally in their advocacy of "scripture alone" and the positive role of the secular government. His argument for scriptural supremacy motivated some of his followers to work on translating the Bible into English, a milestone for English-speaking Christians that gained common recognition of Wyclif's name to this day.

Above: St Bernard Tolomeo administers communion to victims of the Black Death in 1348. During this terrible time, the Church was criticized for its inability to console the faithful.

Left: Part of the Hundred Years' War, the Battle of Agincourt (1415) was a pitched battle in which the outcome was seen by the victorious English army as God's judgment on the French.

MARSILIUS OF PADUA

Above: Marsilius of Padua was one of the many students who attended the University of Paris. Although radical for his time, Marsilius' ideas have since seen him called the forerunner of the Reformation.

Opposite: A Catholic Ecumenical Council meets in the Vatican. Marsilius of Padua proposed that Church authority rest with a General Council rather than with the pope.

The most trenchant critic of papal power in the fourteenth century was Marsilius (or Marsiglio) of Padua. His challenge was breathtaking: He argued that the pope is a purely earthly leader; he is not appointed by God, and he does not represent an unbroken line from St Peter. (Indeed, Peter was never given such a leadership position by Christ.) As for the Church, it has no jurisdiction, whether spiritual or temporal. Up until this point, some had challenged the temporal or earthly power of the Church, but no-one had argued that it had no spiritual authority either. Marsilius also asserted that, like the pope, the Church is a human institution that is not entitled to any power or property except what the state might grant or lend it. Any authority in the Church resides not with the pope but with a General Council, which should be made up of a mix of clergy and laypersons.

Life of Marsilius

All of this was argued in a bombshell tract called *Defensor Pacis*, "Defender of the Peace," written in 1324. Realizing that it would cause trouble, Marsilius did not sign his name to the controversial work. It was to no avail, for in 1326 his authorship was discovered. He fled as soon as he was able to the protection of Louis IV of Bavaria, Holy Roman Emperor and protagonist of the pope, John XXII. The pope was unimpressed, condemned five of Marsilius' propositions and promptly excommunicated him in 1327.

But who was Marsilius of Padua? He was born in Padua around 1275, but his early life is a little obscure. It is known that he was an academic, had studied in Padua, and in Paris in 1311. His main interest was neither theology nor politics but medicine, and within a couple of years he was made rector of the University of Paris, the second-oldest university in Europe (the oldest is Bologna). Later, he studied in northern Italy and Avignon, returning to Paris around 1320. After he was discovered as the author of *Defensor Pacis*, he remained close to the protection of Louis of Bavaria. He followed Louis to Rome in the years 1327–1329, where he witnessed the crowning of the Holy Roman Emperor in the city of Rome by delegates of the people, and was made imperial vicar. His last years were spent in the safety of Louis' court in Munich.

Defender of the peace

If the pope and the Church no longer had any jurisdiction, then someone or something would need to take their place. For Marsilius the state was the great "defender of the peace." And the state gains its power and authority from the people, who may appoint or depose a ruler depending upon performance. The state also grants the Church any jurisdiction or power that it might have. As for property, that belongs to the state; any property the Church may wish to use is lent by the state but never actually given over. In short, it was an assertion of complete secular control over the Church. In practice, it meant that the leader of the state, the emperor—who was to be made ruler by acclamation of the people—would determine who was to be pope and who bishops, what property was to be lent, and what rights the Church might have. He could also withdraw them as he chose. In 1327–1329 Louis attempted to challenge the Church in this fashion, ruling in Rome, formally deposing the pope and seeking to replace him. In the end, he didn't succeed and retreated to Munich.

Towns and secular rulers

Marsilius of Padua was in his time the strongest voice of opposition to the pope's power. However, his was not merely an individual expression, for he voiced the increasing sense of independence of the commercial towns and of a growing sense of secular power in opposition to the Church. Louis found him useful, being himself engaged in a long struggle with the pope, who had excommunicated him in 1327 for harboring known heretics like Marsilius and William of Ockham. However, Marsilius' proposals threatened at their roots the sense of order of medieval society. Louis was not going to take things that far; all he was interested in was his own political power. It was to be another two centuries before challenges like those of Marsilius would tap a groundswell and become a movement that would shake the very foundations of the Middle Ages.

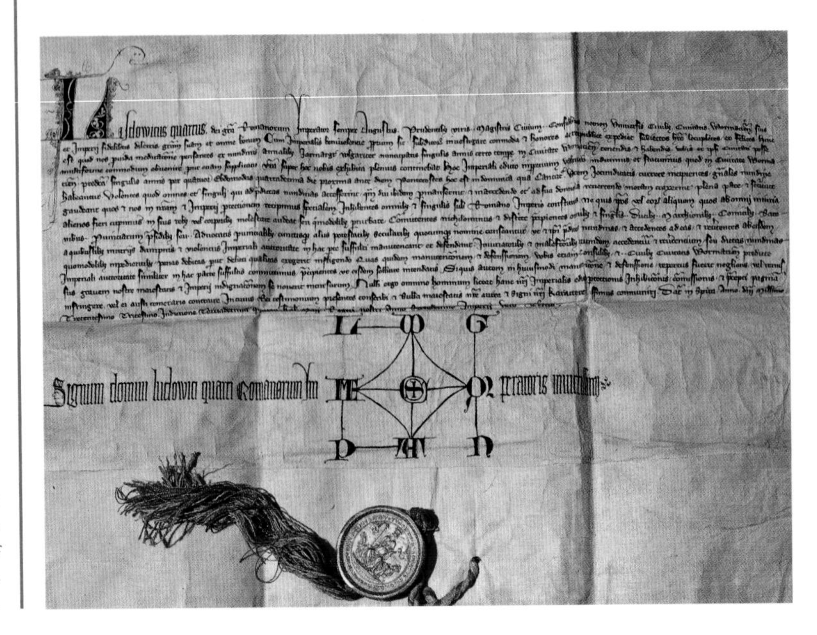

Right: This lengthy bull (a formal statement by the pope) features the seal of Louis IV of Bavaria, protector of Marsilius of Padua.

WOMEN'S RELIGIOUS ORDERS

There is a New Testament statement that had a deep impact on medieval society. It comes from St Paul: "To the unmarried and widows I say that it is well for them to remain unmarried as I am. But if they are not practicing self-control, they should marry." For women, Paul outlines two states—a higher one of celibacy and a lower one of marriage for those who can't control their passions. However, since there were few possibilities for medieval women who did not wish to be married, or who sought independence, the monastic life was the clear option.

Below: This book cover shows St Hildegard of Bingen and the Four Seasons. A German abbess, theologian, and visionary, Hildegard (1098–1179) also wrote on religion, medicine, and botany, and composed music.

Repression and resistance

For this reason there was constant pressure for monastic orders for women; with an upsurge in the seventh to the ninth centuries and then from the twelfth century onward. They may be seen as safety valves in a society where women were allowed little room. At the same time, these movements ran into another deeply held assumption: A woman was responsible for the first sin, and women were far more sensual and sexual than men. Continually, men opposed the rise of women's orders, trying, often in vain, to control or ban them. This tension accounts for the rise and fall and rise again of women's monastic orders.

The most systematic effort at control came with the reforms of Pope Gregory VII (1073 to 1085), when papal powers increased dramatically and a string of new orders began—Augustinians, Cistercians, Carthusians, and Premonstratensians, then later the Dominicans and Franciscans. Society was changing rapidly, the population shot up, and in response a new sense of order in all aspects of life became increasingly popular. The achievement of Gregory VII and those who followed him was to provide the legal and administrative guidelines for that order. New rules emphasized the role of properly qualified monks in leading religious life. In this situation, monasteries for women lost out.

On the margins

Yet, the desire for monastic life for women could not be contained. By the twelfth century nunneries were forming again, usually at the margins of the new orders. An excellent example is the double monasteries of the Cistercians.

The Cistercians (founded in the eleventh century) were known for their rigorous, highly ordered life away from human society. They were also the most male-oriented order of all, shunning contact with women, whom they saw as dangerous temptresses, and placing significant barriers to women's presence. However, when the Cistercians began establishing monasteries in remote areas of Europe, nunneries soon followed. In its official records, the order simply ignored the presence of women, yet time and again individual abbots of the male order would sponsor them and give them protection.

Without official recognition, these female houses grew up on the margins with a fair degree of freedom. For example, in Spain the aristocratic families that sponsored male monasteries also set up large houses for women. Into their fold the daughters of aristocratic families would go, following an old pattern where the daughters of such families found relief from the social and economic pressures of

Left: St Radegunda—a pious Merovingian queen who left her husband to become a nun—established one of the earliest monasteries for women in Poitiers in the sixth century.

Above: Benedictine nuns erected a wooden church and nunnery at Vilnius, Lithuania, in 1622. After the buildings burned down, they were reconstructed using stone, and dedicated to St Catherine.

marriage. Some of the abbesses became very powerful. Pope Innocent III was horrified to find that abbesses gave benedictions to their nuns, heard confession, and even preached—this was supposed to be the role of priests and monks.

From 1213 onward the Cistercian order finally tried to control the women. They imposed limits on their number and on the power of the abbesses, banned new nunneries, and ordered that only a priest could perform the role of confessor and preacher. But it was too late. In some countries such as Germany, Belgium, and Holland, female houses outnumbered the male ones by up to three to one. The combination of powerful aristocratic women and the marginal existence of the nunneries gave great scope for freedom.

THE WILES OF WOMEN

Conrad, abbot of Marchtal Monastery from 1089 to 1122, once said: "We and our whole community of canons, recognizing that the wickedness of women is greater than all the other wickedness of the world...and that the poison of asps and dragons is no more curable and less dangerous to men than the familiarity of women, have unanimously decreed for the safety of our souls, no less than for that of our bodies and goods, that we will on no account receive any more sisters to the increase of our perdition, but will avoid them like poisonous animals."

FIRST WOMEN'S VOICES

Above: Inspired by the intellectual and insightful nature of her writing, fellow French theologian Peter Abelard described Héloïse as *nominatissima,* meaning "most renowned."

Right: Controversy surrounds the last resting place of Héloïse and Peter Abelard. Pilgrims visit their tomb at Père Lachaise cemetery in Paris, but a Benedictine monastery near Troyes claims they are buried on their site.

Far right: The lyrical writings of Hadewijch reflected the songs sung by the court musicians of her time; however, their subject of human love was replaced with her more pious love of God.

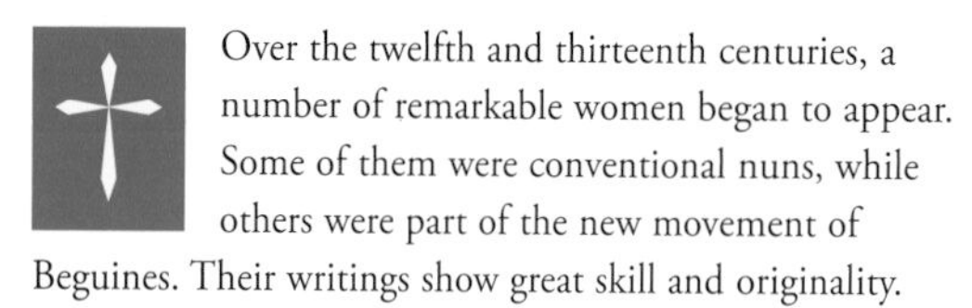

Over the twelfth and thirteenth centuries, a number of remarkable women began to appear. Some of them were conventional nuns, while others were part of the new movement of Beguines. Their writings show great skill and originality.

Héloïse (1101–1164)

Usually hidden behind the theologian Peter Abelard, Héloïse had a distinct and subtle theological mind. After their tumultuous affair, the birth of a child, secret marriage, and brutal treatment of Abelard at the hands of Héloïse's relatives (they castrated him), the couple settled in different monasteries as abbot and abbess. From this time (1125) they engaged in correspondence until their deaths. It is from these letters that Héloïse emerges as an independent theologian, equal to if not better than Abelard. She reveals a unique knowledge of Latin, Hebrew, Greek, and theology.

The letters begin with their troubled lives, expressing their love for one another, although Héloïse chides Abelard for his lack of communication over the years. After encouraging him to tell all and not spare her his feelings, Abelard insists that it was all youthful lust and that he had repented of his sin. From then on the letters concern theological and philosophical problems. Here Héloïse prods Abelard to think more deeply and poses difficult theological questions, collected in the *Problemata Heloissae* (*Héloïse's Problems*), as the following example shows:

> There is no doubt that the Lord, on behalf of the adulteress who was to be set free, replied to the Jews (John 8:7): "Let him among you who is without sin be the first to throw a stone at her," and so rescued her. Now since he did not permit her to be stoned except by someone without sin, he would seem to forbid anyone from using the rod of punishment, since no one is without sin, not even an infant having a single day of life upon the Earth.

Mechthild of Magdeburg (c. 1207–c. 1282)

Mechthild's book of seven mystical Revelations—called *Das Fließende Licht der Gottheit* (*The Flowing Light of the Godhead*)—is one of the most skillful and arresting collections of writings to have come from this period. Lost for centuries, the book was rediscovered in the nineteenth century. It opens as follows:

> This book is to be joyfully welcomed for God Himself speaks in it.
>
> This book I now send forth as a messenger to all spiritual people both good and bad—for if the pillars fall, the building cannot stand. The book proclaims Me alone and shows forth My holiness with praise. All who would understand this book should read it nine times.

Coming from a noble Saxon family, Mechthild had already experienced visions at the age of 12 and joined a community of Beguines in Magdeburg. Her life was full of illness, personal threats, disapproval from church officers, and repeated threats to burn her writings. Eventually she found safety in a community of Cistercian nuns at Helfta, where she met Gertrude of Helfta (1256–c. 1302), who was also writing mystical texts. In contrast to Gertrude's more conventional liturgical mysticism and her focus on the sacred heart of Jesus, Mechthild's writings are exuberant and passionate, full of dialogues with Jesus, mystical bridal union with him, and matters of theology and world's end.

Hadewijch (thirteenth century)

Apart from her writings, which were rediscovered in 1838, little is known of Hadewijch. Probably a member of a Beguine community, she wrote in the Brabant dialect of Middle Dutch and came from an aristocratic family, since at a time when learning was available to very few, she clearly knows her Latin Bible, theology, and secular French literature.

What is understood about Hadewijch is that she was an innovator. She took the poetry and language of courtly love and applied it to the relation between the soul and God in a striking new way. The result is a deeply sensuous and erotic literature of devotion, which includes *Visions*, letters, *Poems in Stanzas*, and *Poems in Couplets*. Her letters and some of her poems are didactic, focusing on different elements of the Christian life. But the most interesting poems employ the particular styles used by *trouvères* and *minnesingers*, court musicians in France and Germany who composed and sang songs about human love. Hadewijch replaces their content with the intense love of God, as this fascinating example shows:

What is sweetest in love is her tempestuousness,
Her deepest abyss is her most beautiful form;
To lose one's way in her is to touch her close at hand.
To die of hunger for her is to feed and taste.

THE BEGUINES

Above: Pope Clement V convoked the Fifteenth Ecumenical Council, the Council of Vienne, which declared the Beguines to be reprehensible for their refusal to form a proper religious order.

The Low Countries (Holland and Belgium) have been a source for new forms of spirituality for centuries. Here people sought a more authentic way of relating to God, never satisfied with the existing structures. The outward forms of prayer, buildings, and worship were not enough. This desire was not restricted to men; women emerged too, some of them becoming the first significant voices in Dutch literature, such as Hadewijch.

The Beguines begin

Restricted from involvement in churches and monasteries, women like Hadewijch became part of a popular movement in the Low Countries called the Beguines. The origin of the name is obscure—perhaps a derogatory term from their enemies or a name they themselves chose. They first emerged in the late twelfth century around the town of Liège, and spread through Holland, then Germany (many appeared in Cologne), France, and other European countries. The Beguines were condemned as an "abominable sect" by the Council of Vienne (1311–1312) and told to form themselves into a religious order, were persecuted during the thirteenth and fourteenth centuries, revived during the seventeenth century, and finally petered out by the eighteenth century. It was in the Low Countries that they were always the most numerous. A number of contemporary writers admired them immensely and held them up as the ideal of piety.

The Beguines were a popular movement of women who lived either alone or in groups. Rather than separate themselves from the world in closed monasteries, they remained within the world. They did not seek approval from the pope, they claimed no saint as their founder, there was no constitution, they did not bind themselves to a strict monastic Rule, and they did not seek the leadership or guidance of men—although they did make their initial promises (not

Left: The Eternal Father looks upon St Mary Magdalene and St Catherine in this painting by Bartolomeo della Porta (1472–1517). Mary has often been called the "virtual patron saint" of the Beguines.

Above: Catherine of Siena was one of the most influential mystics in medieval Europe. The Beguines also followed mysticism, seeking a more intense, personal, and direct relationship with God.

a vow) before the local priest to dedicate their lives to God. They did not give up their property as nuns were supposed to, but reserved the right to buy and sell property. Beguines might keep whatever profession they had (as far as women could) or they might engage in social work in hospitals and other places. Above all, they supported themselves through their own labor and did not rely on anyone else's labor. In order to be free from the expectations of marriage or of venal priests, they remained celibate, although they reserved the right to change their status and marry if they so chose. While they were Beguines, they would usually meet for communal prayer. However, they were not entirely separated from the existing monasteries; sometimes their communities—known as Beguinages—were close to Franciscan and Dominican friaries and they would cooperate with them.

Passionate piety

The Church authorities were suspicious of anything they couldn't control. Here was a spontaneous movement of women who refused to stay in one place and refused to join a regular order, or follow a recognized set of rules from such an order. Some detractors were annoyed at what they felt was a claim to be holier than everyone else. And there were always suspicions about women on their own. To add to the consternation of the authorities, the Beguines were passionate and enthusiastic about their spirituality, often expressing it in overtly sexual tones, and they sought a direct personal relationship with God that was not mediated by anyone else. Gradually they were pressed into recognized convents by the Council of Vienne, although groups continued outside such control.

Men follow suit

Noting the success of the Beguines, some men decided to follow suit, although the Beghards were never as numerous. The Beghards tended to be more monastic, giving up their property and using a common purse, and were often minor craftsmen, such as weavers, dyers, and fullers. They were more prepared to reform and become a recognized order when condemned at the Council of Vienne.

MYSTICS

Right: In around 1366, Catherine of Siena (1347–1380) underwent a "spiritual espousal" (mystical marriage) to Jesus, which she wrote about extensively. She was canonized by Pope Pius II in 1461.

Below: The seventeenth-century painting *Triumph of the Carmelite Order* shows the group's glories and legends. One of the most famous Carmelite nuns is the mystic Teresa of Avila (1515–1582).

By the twelfth century there was a growth in first-person accounts of visionary experience on the part of both men and women. The later Middle Ages saw a "new mysticism," heavily influenced by the Franciscans and Dominicans and their unwavering devotion to the humanity of Christ. Their approach was built on the earlier monastic tradition, but insisted that mystical experience was open to all Christians. For this reason, and because it was frequently expressed in the European vernacular tongues, rather than in Latin, the new mysticism was open to women, who soon became very enthusiastic participants.

Female spiritual expression

In this "new mysticism," women discovered a realm of spiritual expression that was widely accessible to them and appealed to their Christological vision. The reasons for this are complex. They include sociological and economic factors, such as increased opportunities for women to access education and so be capable of putting their visionary experiences into writing; the invention of printing, which rendered the written word more accessible; and the work of the mendicant friars, which brought mysticism out of the monasteries and into the marketplace. In order to do this, the friars popularized devotional practices such as the Stations of the Cross, the Rosary, and the Angelus—all of which enabled the devotee in his or her imagination to follow in the footsteps of Christ and share in the events of his life, Passion, and death.

A mysticism strongly influenced by personal devotion to Christ and expressed in sexually charged imagery characterized such female mystical writers as Mechthild of Magdeburg, Gertrude and Mechthild of Helfta, Clare of Assisi, Catherine of Siena, and Julian of Norwich. These are some of the many female visionaries who flourished from the thirteenth century onward. The Carmelite Order in sixteenth-century Spain produced one of the greatest women mystics in Western Europe in Teresa of Avila. Teresa's writings included her autobiographical *Life*, *The Interior Castle*, and *The Way of Perfection*.

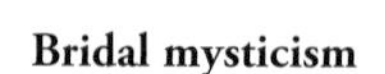

Bridal mysticism

The tradition of "bridal mysticism" has a long history, which reaches back into the Hebrew Bible. The rabbis interpreted the imagery of the Song of Songs (also called Song of Solomon) as expressing the closeness of the relationship between God and Israel. As a metaphor for the relationship between God/Christ and the Church it passed into Christian theology. Church Fathers wrote at length on the subject of consecrated virginity, using the same potent imagery. Bernard of Clairvaux famously preached a series of Sermons on the Song of Songs to his monks, and the erotic imagery became part of the Cistercian heritage, other abbots following in his wake. From then on, it gradually became common currency in the highly charged mysticism of the Middle Ages. Many women described their intense visionary experiences as a "mystical marriage." Clare of Assisi counseled Agnes of Prague:

> You took a spouse of more noble lineage, Who will keep your virginity ever unspotted and unsullied, the Lord Jesus Christ. When you have loved Him, you are chaste; when you have touched Him, you become more pure; when you have accepted Him, you are a virgin.

Even Teresa of Avila, described as "the saint of sound common sense, of sane good humor," could write such sensuously charged passages as the following in her *Conceptions of the Love of God:*

> But when this most wealthy Spouse desires to enrich and comfort the Bride still more, He draws her so closely to Him that she is like one who swoons from excess of pleasure and joy and seems suspended in those Divine arms and drawn near to that sacred side and to those Divine breasts. Sustained by the Divine milk with which her Spouse continually nourishes her and growing in grace so that she may be enabled to receive His comforts she can do nothing but rejoice.

The imagery here develops from that of nuptials into those of motherhood. It is characteristic of this form of mystical writing that the metaphors are drawn explicitly from natural functions, articulated in probably the only language these women had in which to describe their overpoweringly vivid sense of union with God. These women had little philosophical or theological training and were not normally familiar with scholastic language and concepts, so they used the homely language of the vernacular. Instinctively, they employed familiar images drawn from domestic life that appealed to them, and for which, in the world of their time, they were particularly responsible—courtship, betrothal, and marriage; nursing and motherhood. In these terms and with these images they could express the intimacy of their relationship with Christ.

Above: Throughout her life as a Carmelite nun, Spanish mystic Teresa of Avila experienced periods of religious ecstasy, whereby visions of Jesus and God became apparent in her mind.

CHAPTER TWO

THE EASTERN EMPIRE

At the beginning of the second Christian millennium, Byzantium was at the height of its power, little suspecting the turmoil that hovered on the horizon. The empire extended from Mesopotamia to the Balkans. Many Slavic peoples—Bulgarians, Rus, and Serbs—had been converted to Christianity in the tenth century. They were under the spiritual leadership of the patriarch of Constantinople, who was himself under the authority of the Byzantine emperor.

Monasticism flourished. Urban monasteries administered hospitals, orphanages, and homes for the poor. Monasteries in rural areas functioned as agricultural communes.

The First Crusade (1095–1099) was initiated by a call for help from Alexius Comnenus, the Byzantine emperor, to Pope Urban II. It captured Jerusalem and led to the establishment of a Latin kingdom in the Middle East. The Second and Third Crusades failed to stem Muslim conquests and win back territory that had been lost. After the Third Crusade (1189–1192) failed to retake Jerusalem, a Fourth Crusade was launched in 1202. These last Crusaders were diverted to Constantinople where they became involved in political intrigues. When promised resources failed to materialize, they besieged Constantinople in 1204 and sacked the city. The looting of Constantinople impoverished the Byzantine Empire and paved the way for its final demise.

Byzantine Emperor Michael Palaiologos took back Constantinople in 1261. However, in the following century the city was beset by major earthquakes and the bubonic plague. The emperor was forced to negotiate humiliating agreements with the pope in Rome and with the Ottoman sultan, but even this did not stave off the capture of Constantinople by the Ottomans in 1453.

After Constantinople fell, Russia assumed the leadership of Eastern Christendom. This seemed natural, since the power of the Russian state was waxing, and the metropolitinate of Moscow had already become independent of Constantinople.

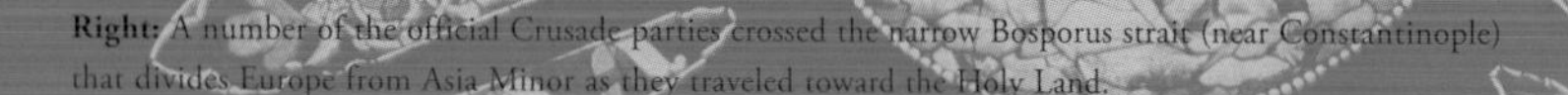

Right: A number of the official Crusade parties crossed the narrow Bosporus strait (near Constantinople) that divides Europe from Asia Minor as they traveled toward the Holy Land.

CAPTURE OF CONSTANTINOPLE

Above: Now called Istanbul, Constantinople was considered the gateway between Europe and Asia Minor, drawing thousands of merchants, scholars, pilgrims on their way to the Holy Land, and other visitors.

Top right: After the fall of Constantinople in 1204, four bronze horse sculptures were stripped from the Hippodrome and taken to Venice. Each horse weighs almost one ton (835 kg).

During the medieval period, Constantinople was the largest and richest city known to Europeans. This cosmopolitan city, whose population was ten times more than any other city in the West, was a vital center of commerce and trade. Its public buildings were splendid, and its cultural life was rich. The Library of Constantinople was one of the greatest repositories in Europe, containing countless treasures of Greek and Roman literature. Education flourished, with Greek medicine and mathematics being studied in various institutes of higher education.

The Fourth Crusade

The Fourth Crusade that set out from Venice in 1202 originally intended to sail directly to Egypt, but was diverted to Constantinople. The plan was engineered with the support of Alexius IV, the son of Emperor Isaac II who had been overthrown by his brother Alexius III. Alexius IV had been imprisoned in Constantinople, but was smuggled out by two Pisan merchants in 1201. In Europe, he met Boniface of Montserrat (who had been chosen to lead the Fourth Crusade) and persuaded him to help topple his uncle, Alexius III, and restore his father to the throne. Alexius IV promised in return 10,000 Byzantine soldiers, the payment of 150,000 silver marks owed by the Crusaders to Venice, and that the Byzantine navy would transport the Crusader army to Egypt. He also pledged to place the Orthodox Church under Rome's aegis. The Crusaders' initial motive was induced by much-needed financial and military support, since their supplies and finances were seriously depleted.

Upon arrival, the Crusaders made overtures to the citizens of Constantinople to restore Isaac II to the throne, but these were met with indifference and taunts, instead of the welcome that Alexius IV had promised. However, before turning their attention to Constantinople, in a show of strength the Crusaders sacked the nearby cities of Chalcedon and Chrysopolis. In July 1203, the Crusaders began the siege of Constantinople's walls and, although the armies of Alexius III vastly outnumbered those of the Crusaders, the latter's military superiority soon prevailed. The Byzantine army retreated and Alexius III fled. Alexius IV was elevated to the throne along with his blind father, Isaac II. However, a major fire in the city rendered many of the citizens homeless.

A city decimated

The new Byzantine emperors were unable to meet their commitments since the Byzantine treasury was depleted.

To do so, Alexius IV ordered the melting down of valuable icons, much to the consternation of his citizens, but he still could not raise the required sums. Alexius IV asked the Crusaders to stay on, but this diminished his standing with the citizens of Constantinople who despised his associations with the West. Alexius IV was murdered by one of his courtiers who then took the throne as Alexius V. The Crusaders and Venetians were outraged at his murder and demanded that Alexius V honor the promises that had been made. When he refused to do so, the Crusaders attacked the city on April 8, 1204.

Despite poor weather conditions, the Crusaders finally took Constantinople on April 12, 1204, and for three days indulged in a frenzy of looting and destruction. Much of the city was burnt and priceless treasures were stolen. The Library of Constantinople, together with its contents, was destroyed. Churches were not exempt—the Hagia Sophia, the patriarchal church of Constantinople, suffered much damage, including the smashing of the silver iconostasis. The Crusaders desecrated sacred vessels and seated a prostitute on the patriarchal throne. The total amount looted from Constantinople is estimated to have been about 900,000 silver marks. From this amount the debt of 150,000 marks was paid to the Venetians, and Venice also received many of the priceless treasures including the four horses from the Hippodrome of Constantinople that were installed on the terrace of the facade of St Mark's Basilica in 1254.

DISUNITY IN CHRISTENDOM

Pope Innocent III excommunicated the Crusaders when they stormed Constantinople instead of Jerusalem. But relations between Constantinople and the West had been strained for a long time. The "massacre of the Latins," which had taken place in Constantinople in 1182 against Roman Catholic merchants and families who dominated the maritime trade, had not helped matters. The siege of Constantinople in 1204 during the Fourth Crusade inflicted terrible damage on the city, which never recovered both physically and spiritually. From this point onward any notion of the unity of Christendom was shattered. If the doctrinal discussions had been the preserve of the priestly hierarchies of the Churches, the occupation and pillaging of Constantinople sowed an intense national hatred and indignation against Western aggression and sacrilege among its ordinary citizens.

Right: As well as instigating the ill-fated Fourth Crusade, Pope Innocent III also called for the Albigensian Crusade against the heretics of southern France after the murder of a papal legate in 1208.

RECAPTURE OF CONSTANTINOPLE

Above: The island of Lesbos (also known as Lesvos) was once part of the "Latin Empire of Constantinople." It features many historic churches constructed out of local stone.

Far right: This ninth-century Byzantine mosaic of the Virgin and Child still adorns the dome of the apse in the Hagia Sophia, having survived many sieges over the years.

Right: The Mamluk sultan of Egypt entered into a treaty with Michael VIII in 1263, just 13 years after the Mamluks had taken power in Egypt. The Egyptian Mamluk Dynasty ended in 1517.

The capture of Constantinople by the Crusaders in 1204 had led to the creation of six new Frankish states, dozens of minor dependent lordships, and a scattering of Venetian and Genoese colonies. The "Latin Empire of Constantinople" was to survive for 57 years. Originally the empire had territorial claims to Constantinople, parts of coastal Thrace, Anatolia, and the islands of Samos, Chios, and Lesbos. By 1225, however, these territories had shrunk and the empire basically consisted of the capital city. When Emperor Michael VIII reclaimed Constantinople in 1261 from the Crusaders, large areas of the imperial city were virtually abandoned and its citizens numbered only 35,000.

Michael Palaiologos reclaims Constantinople

Emperor Michael VIII, or Michael Palaiologos, was the scion of a great military family. He was a regent for John IV (1258–1261) who ascended the throne at Nicaea, the capital of the Greek Empire of Nicaea that had been founded after the fall of Constantinople in 1204, at the age of seven. In 1261, the troops of Michael VIII recaptured Constantinople from the last Latin emperor, Baldwin II. Shortly after his coronation, Michael (who was 36 years of age) ordered John IV (who was 11) to be blinded and incarcerated in a monastery. The patriarch of Constantinople, Arsenios, responded to the blinding of John by excommunicating Michael VIII—a ban that remained until 1268. Michael VIII was a consummate statesman, negotiating treaties and changing sides to bolster his position. In 1263 he signed a treaty with the Egyptian Mamluk sultan and the Mongol Berke Khan; he betrothed two of his illegitimate daughters to Mongol kings.

Despite his success, Michael's reign was still under threat from the deposed Latin Emperor Baldwin II. Michael VIII successfully staved this off by offering the possibility of an ecclesiastical union between Constantinople and Rome. This was realized in 1274 at the Second Council of Lyons, where a treaty between Michael VIII and Pope Gregory X included the recognition of papal primacy and also acceptance of the *filioque* ("and the Son") clause in the Nicene Creed, which had been a contentious issue between East and West for centuries. This "compromise" may have stopped an immediate attack by the Latins on Constantinople, but it destroyed Michael's credibility with his subjects who considered him to be a traitor.

The benefits of the Second Council of Lyons were short lived. Pope Gregory X died and was succeeded by Martin IV in 1281. The new pope considered that Michael's adherence to a union with Rome was both hypocritical and politically motivated, rather than being the result of real theological discussion. He dissolved the union and endorsed plans for a new crusade to retake Constantinople and place it once again under Roman Catholic control. He also excommunicated Michael from the Roman Catholic Church, and denounced him as "patron of the Greeks who are inveterate schismatics and fixed in the ancient schism." However, in March 1281 Michael VIII managed to defeat the forces led by Charles I (Angevin king of Naples and Sicily) and, aided by Sicilian rebels, torched the Latin ships in Palermo harbor, thus averting the proposed crusade.

Restoration of Constantinople's splendor

Michael VIII managed to restore some of the grandeur of Constantinople and precipitated a remarkable cultural

THE LEGACY OF MICHAEL PALAIOLOGOS

Michael VIII revitalized the moribund city of Constantinople; the cultural and building works breathed a new vitality. His bid to regain the glory of Constantinople, together with the rediscovery of the ancient cultural Hellenistic heritage, were bold attempts to restore the prestige of the Byzantine Empire. Despite all his achievements, and his military brilliance, the citizens hated him, rejoicing when he died in 1282. His perceived liaisons with the West, especially the union of 1274, were despised, and his policies alienated society at large, not the least because he had imposed very heavy taxes. However, the Palaiologian Dynasty, which he founded, would rule until the fall of Constantinople to the Ottomans in 1453.

efflorescence. He reconstructed the city walls that had been badly damaged by the siege during the Fourth Crusade, and he built several major monasteries. He even subsidized the construction of a new mosque, replacing that which the Crusaders had burnt, in a bid to cultivate political, military, and economic links with the Mamluks. Many of Constantinople's churches were refurbished, most notably the patriarchal church, the Hagia Sophia. The stunningly beautiful mosaics that can be seen in the Hagia Sophia today largely date from this time. Under imperial patronage, much literature was written and there was an increased interest in the sciences, mathematics, medicine, and astronomy. Many classical Greek works that had been previously considered to be lost were rediscovered. Hesychasm or mystical theology also flourished in this period, as evidenced by the works of Gregory of Palamas.

MYSTICAL THEOLOGY: HESYCHASM

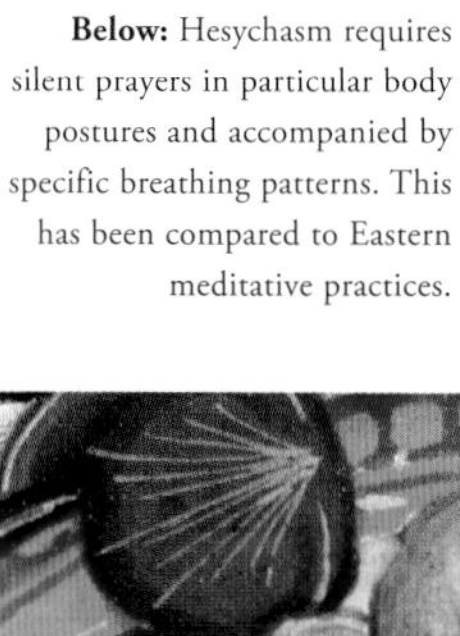

Gregory of Palamas (1296–1359) was a monk at Mt Athos, but left due to Turkish attacks on the monastery. He became part of a spiritual group that was influenced by the mystic Gregory of Sinai (1255–1345), a leading exponent of Hesychasm, a mystical theology that focused on a silent, monological prayer, often known as the "Jesus Prayer."

Early Hesychasts

The origins of Hesychasm are rooted in fourth-century Egypt. Ascetics in the deserts, following the example of St Antony, sought inner peace and spiritual insight while practicing contemplation and self-discipline. An influential proponent of Hesychasm was the Christian monk Evagrius Ponticus (345–399), who taught wordless, imageless prayer and the purification of the mind until it attained the sapphirine clarity of the sky. Silence was thought to be the only fitting way of addressing God. A key text was *The Ladder of Divine Ascent,* written by the seventh-century mystic John of Climacus. The twenty-seventh of its thirty "steps" was devoted to Hesychia or "silence," which had two levels: An outer (the door of the cell) and an inner (the door of the tongue).

Hesychasts advocated that the prayer should be recited in a specific position, with the head bowed and concentration focused on the heart and interior of the body. The saying of the prayer was to be synchronized with one's breathing, although this practice only probably dated from the early medieval period. The physical postures were not essential, but the prayer was never to be used without the elder's direction. Particular emphasis was placed on the direct teaching of a spiritual father or mother, with the aspirant disclosing to the elder all thoughts, especially those which may be demonically or divinely inspired.

Below: Hesychasm requires silent prayers in particular body postures and accompanied by specific breathing patterns. This has been compared to Eastern meditative practices.

Gregory of Palamas

Gregory maintained that God transcended understanding, being "above all essence" and "above all name." Man could not know God in his essence or inner being, but only in his energies or outward revelation. But he thought that man was able to have a direct knowledge of God's energies and a mystical union with God face-to-face. Gregory supported the claims of the Hesychast mystics to experience God and spoke of the Uncreated Light that transfigured Christ on Mt Tabor (Matthew 17:1–9). This light was non-imaginary and non-material, simultaneously invisible and visible, uncreated, and infinite.

Gregory came to the defense of the Hesychasts in a series of letters called the *Defense of the Holy Hesychasts* (c. 1338), which he exchanged with Barlaam of Calabria, a monk trained in Western theology who attacked the practices as superstition. Barlaam objected to the distinction in

PRAYER IN HESYCHASM

Hesychasm revolved around the repetition, at first ver bally and then internally, of the "Jesus Prayer." Its fundamental elements are the discipline of repetition, the emphasis on penitence, and the teaching of imageless and wordless prayer whereby the Hesychast no longer simply says the prayer, but is *in* prayer all the time. These elements, combined with a devotion to the holy name of Jesus, formed the "Jesus Prayer." Monological prayers such as "Lord Jesus Christ have mercy on me," or variations including "Jesus Christ, Son of God, have mercy on me, a sinner," were possibly inspired by 1 Corinthians 14:19. But the use of a specific formula probably only dates from the sixth or seventh centuries.

Hesychast theology that conceived God as a compound of essence and activity, maintaining that this distinction would destroy God's unity and simplicity. The conflict between Gregory of Palamas and Barlaam of Calabria, who was the poet Petrarch's Greek teacher, was between contemplative, conservative monks and emerging humanists who admired Greek classical philosophy and secular learning, which was being rediscovered. Because of the very precise posture and breathing that was required to execute the "Jesus Prayer," Barlaam of Calabria criticized Hesychasm as simply "navel gazing."

In defending Hesychasm, Gregory appealed to the concept of the Incarnation and referred to the transubstantiation of Christ's body during the Eucharist. His theological defense was endorsed by synods held in Constantinople in 1341, 1347, and 1351. His *Hagioritic Tome,* written in 1341, became the yardstick of Orthodoxy in spiritual theology, and the official doctrine of the Orthodox Church. In 1351 any opponents of Hesychasm were excommunicated and acclamations of Palamas were introduced into the liturgy of the Feast of Orthodoxy. After the fall of Constantinople in 1453 to the Ottoman Turks, Hesychast doctrines fell into relative decline with the destruction of the many monasteries that ensued. However, the eighteenth century saw a revival of the Hesychast tradition, and the use of the "Jesus Prayer," throughout the Eastern Orthodox Church.

Above: Gregory of Palamas began his ascetic life at the Monastery of Vatopedi on Mt Athos (in modern-day Greece). Four centuries later, Mt Athos was the site of a resurgence in Hesychasm.

Left: The Monastery of Aghiou Pavlou on Mt Athos features this Eastern Orthodox icon entitled *Christ Pantocrator* ("Christ Almighty"). Mt Athos is a center of practice of the "Jesus Prayer."

FALL OF CONSTANTINOPLE

Opposite: Benjamin Constant's 1876 oil painting depicts the dramatic moment when the Ottomans led by Mehmed II (also known as Mohammed II) triumphantly entered Constantinople on May 29, 1453.

The Palaiologian Dynasty, founded by Michael VIII in 1261, was still ruling when the city fell to the Ottomans in 1453. However, a series of circumstances combined to weaken the dynasty's strength and pave the way for the Ottoman victory. There had been several major earthquakes and, in 1347, the bubonic plague arrived. Ottoman strength was growing. In 1357 the Ottomans, who had already taken nearby Kallipoli (Gallipoli), reached the walls of Constantinople.

Rekindling the union with Rome

Faced by this ever-growing danger of occupation by the Ottomans, Emperor John V Palaiologos appealed to Pope Innocent VI for ships and troops, offering an ecclesiastical union in return. Innocent was unmoved. John had better success with his cousin, Amadeo VI of Savoy, who sailed from Venice and retook Kallipoli in 1366. The Byzantine Emperor eventually professed the Roman Catholic faith at the Hospital of the Holy Spirit in Rome on October 17, 1369. Three days later he publicly submitted on the steps of St Peter's Basilica.

When John V returned to Constantinople in 1371, he found that the power of the Ottomans had grown steadily. John decided to broker a treaty with Sultan Murad I that obliged Byzantium to convey regular tribute (*kharadj*) and contribute troops to the Ottoman army. In return, John hoped that the Turks would not attack Byzantine territory. Effectively, the emperor had become a vassal of the sultan, since the Byzantines had, in military terms, become a spent force.

John's last-ditch negotiations with Murad did halt the Ottomans, but the Turks continued to advance through the Balkans. Sofia was taken in 1385, and Kosovo in 1389. When the new emperor, Manuel II, decided to break with his father's long-standing policy of subordination to the Ottomans, refusing to pay the required tribute and to provide troops, the sultan considered this an act of rebellion. He launched an attack on Constantinople, which was to last for nearly eight years. He also sought to replace Manuel, but not to overthrow the dynasty.

Below: Sultan Murad I reigned from 1360 until his death at the Battle of Kosovo in 1389. During his rule the Ottoman holdings expanded greatly, and Constantinople's emperor became one of his many vassals.

Averting an Ottoman siege of Constantinople

In the face of these renewed threats from the Ottomans, Manuel II toured Europe and attempted to raise support, visiting Venice, Padua, Milan, Paris, and London, where he met Henry IV. He spent 18 months in Paris as the guest of Charles VI and wrote a lengthy treatise on the Orthodox view of the *filioque* ("and the Son") question. No appreciable military aid or commitment came out of this visit to Europe. He was still in Paris when the Mongol conqueror Tamerlane clashed with the Turks at the legendary Battle of Ankara in 1402, routing the Ottoman army. Sultan Bayezid I was captured and an Ottoman assault on Constantinople was averted. In the Byzantine viewpoint the Virgin Mary had intervened on their behalf.

As well as Constantinople being saved, the fortunes of the Byzantine Empire seemed to be on the increase. In 1403 Thessalonika, Mt Athos, and some of the Black Sea coast were recaptured from Turkish hands. But this winning streak was not to last. When Mehmed I died in 1421 and was succeeded by his son Murad II, Emperor John VIII resolved to incite an internal rebellion against the new sultan. It failed dismally, and the upshot was that in February 1424 he was forced to negotiate a settlement with Murad II whereby Constantinople once again paid tribute. The Ottomans now regarded its vassal as a liability.

In the 1430s John VIII renewed efforts to gain union with Rome, negotiating for a resolution of dogmatic differences at the Council of Ferrara-Florence (1438–1439). The emperor attended and a basis for agreement was found, with the Orthodox accepting the principle of papal primacy and conceding that the *filioque* ("and the Son") dispute was based on semantic confusion. Formal union with Pope Eugenius IV was celebrated in July 1439 in the cathedral of Florence, but the benefits of union were negligible for Byzantium. They did not evoke the much-needed Western sympathy. The people of Constantinople considered John VIII to be a traitor. Some even preferred the authority of the sultan to that of the pope!

The final assault on Constantinople

Murad II had kept to the treaty of 1424, but his successor Mehmed II "The Conqueror," who was only 19 years old when he came to power in 1451, adopted a very different attitude. When the new emperor, Constantine XI (the brother of John VIII, who had died childless), threatened a rebellion unless certain subsidies were provided, he supplied the pretext for Ottoman action. A siege commenced on April 6, 1453, and breached the walls of Constantinople on May 29 of that year. Constantine XI died in battle, and the core of the Byzantine state was lost forever. The sultan only allowed his troops one day to pillage the city, then immediately set about its redevelopment. The imperial cathedral of Byzantium, the Hagia Sophia, was transformed into a mosque. The Orthodox Church of Byzantium now became a subordinate religion.

MOSCOW'S RISE

Right: Commissioned by Ivan the Terrible, Moscow's Cathedral of St Basil the Blessed (also known as the Cathedral of the Intercession of the Virgin on the Moat) dates to the mid-sixteenth century.

In 1328, Metropolitan Peter of Kiev and All Russia decided to shift his base from Kiev and take up residence in Moscow, then a small and relatively unimportant town. Kiev had never fully recovered from its occupation in 1240 by Batu, the Mongol grandson of Genghis Khan, during which several Russian princes had been martyred for their faith. The move to Moscow transformed a relatively insignificant town into a major city, engaging the services of leading architects and artists. The first Dormition Cathedral was built between 1475 and 1479 (it was rebuilt in the fifteenth century by the Italian architect Aristotele Fioravanti), and the Annunciation Church was also rebuilt; its iconostasis was decorated by the renowned fresco and icon painters Theophan the Greek and Andrei Rublev. Italian architects were also responsible for the Kremlin Cathedral of St Michael the Archangel, which was constructed between 1505 and 1509.

Muscovite autocephaly

The Russian Church was founded between 1441 and 1448. The Grand Prince of Moscow, Basil II, had refused to accept the appointee of the Patriarch of Constantinople, claiming that the Russian Church should be able to exercise its right to elect a metropolitan by a local synod of bishops. This request for independence by the Russian Orthodox Church was in response to the Council of Ferrara-Florence in 1438–1439, because the concessions made between the Greeks and the Latins in the union had ramifications on liturgy and theology that the Russians considered unacceptable. The Russian Orthodox Church distanced itself from the Greeks and refused to receive metropolitans from Constantinople. In 1448 the synod of Russian bishops independently consecrated Jonas as Metropolitan of Moscow and All Russia. The Russian Church was now autocephalous (self-governing) and independent of Constantinople.

Kiev resisted, clinging proudly to its ancient prestige and traditional connections with Byzantium. Gregory, the Metropolitan of Kiev, wrote to Patriarch Dionysius I in Constantinople repenting his erstwhile support of the union at the Council of Ferrara-Florence. In return for this act of loyalty, Dionysius acknowledged Gregory as the Metropolitan of the whole Russian Church in 1461. To cement things further, Dionysius also forbade any communion with Jonas, Metropolitan of Moscow, seemingly unaware that he had died. Basil II reciprocated these acts by forbidding contact with both the Metropolitan of Kiev and the Patriarch in Constantinople.

Below: St Nicholas is one of the most revered saints in the Russian Orthodox Church. Often depicted with Jesus and the Virgin Mary, icons of this saint appear in churches throughout Moscow.

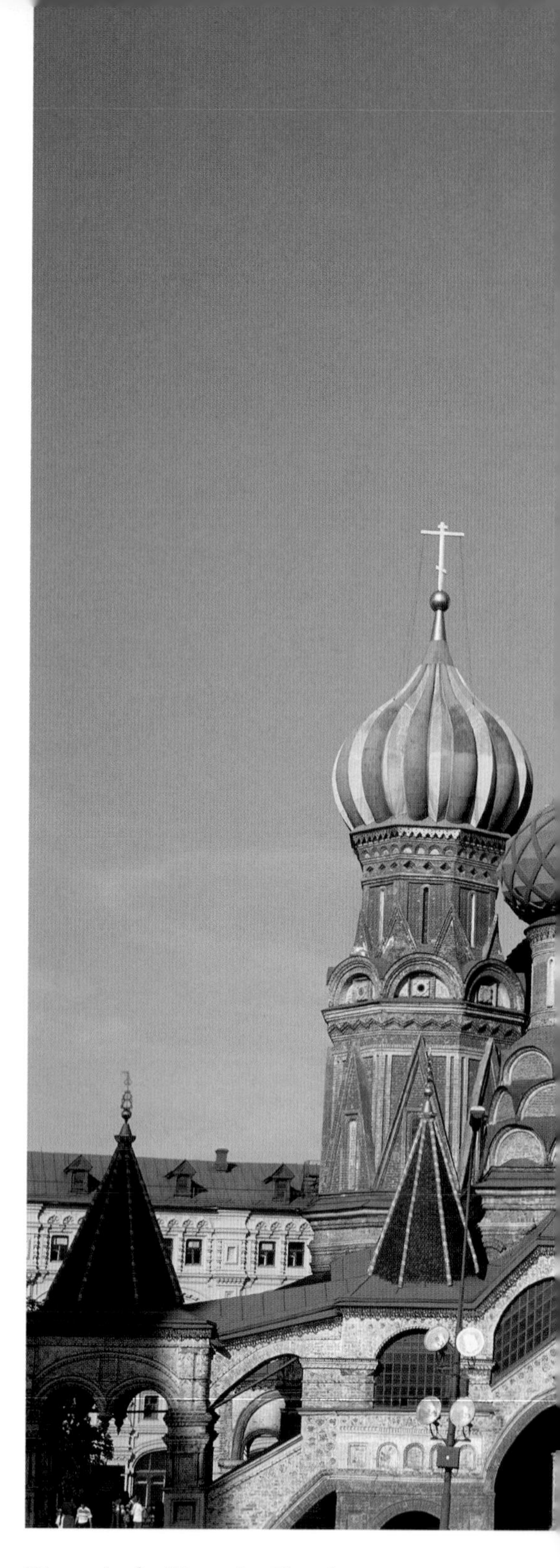

Dissent in the Muscovite Church

The independent Muscovite Church was established, but was wracked with internal dissent. The last three decades of the fifteenth century were preoccupied with wrangling between two rival monastic movements: The "Possessors" or "Josephites," and the "Non-Possessors." Both were influenced by mystical Hesychast movements and considered themselves to be the upholders of the purity of faith. They both sought to consolidate the standing of the Church in Moscow, but they differed dramatically over the question of secular power and ownership of land. The Possessors,

THE HUNDRED CHAPTERS

The Metropolitanate of Moscow had separated from Constantinople in 1448, but needed to have its own canon law in order to govern the affairs of the Church. The leader of the "Possessors," Joseph of Volokolamsk, already proposed this in 1503, but it was only realized in 1551 with the convening of the "Council of the Hundred Chapters." Acting in the capacity of an ecu menical council, this council attempted to implement a wide range of reforms. Russian independence, which had seen Ivan the Terrible crowned as the first tsar in 1547, was further consolidated with the creation of the Patriarchate of Moscow in 1589. Patriarch Job (1589–1605) was consecrated by the Patriarch of Constantinople, Jeremias II.

who owned vast tracts of land, sought a Church that was submissive to the state while the Non-Possessors, eschewing all possessions, strove to follow an ascetic, mystical path that was truly independent of secular influence. They also attempted to re-establish intellectual and potentially canonical dependence on the Greeks. Eventually the Possessors gained the upper hand.

Moscow was now positioned to become the most senior patriarchate in Christendom after the five apostolic patriarchates. With the fall of Constantinople to the Ottomans in 1453, Russia saw herself as the only nation capable of assuming leadership in Eastern Christendom. The growth of the Church went hand-in-hand with the might of the Russian state. The two were interpreted as a sign from God of Moscow's role as the "Third Rome," even though the Patriarchate of Constantinople had traditionally supported the metropolitans of Kiev. Between 1461 and 1589, the Russian Church was divided because both Moscow and Kiev had their own metropolitans. It was only in 1686, when the Kievan metropolitanate and the Muscovite patriarchy were finally reunited, that Moscow truly emerged as the primary seat of the Russian Orthodox Church.

Above: Often described as a cruel and despotic ruler, Ivan the Terrible was an intelligent and devout man who was prone to rages possibly as a result of mental illness.

CHAPTER THREE

CHRISTIAN MISSIONS TO THE MONGOLS

The Mongols were a formidable military force, sweeping across the Middle East and deep into Russia during the thirteenth century. They practiced shamanism, but the Khans who ruled the Mongol Empire adopted a policy of religious tolerance. They were open to Christianity, allowing churches to function without hindrance. The period of Mongol rule witnessed a marked increase in the prosperity of Christianity in the territories under their control, seen in both artistic and literary works.

The thirteenth century saw a series of remarkable missions initiated by popes Innocent IV and Nicholas IV to the Mongol courts. Intrepid Dominican and Franciscan friars, including John of Plano Carpini and William of Rubruck, traveled to Karakorum in Mongolia. In 1271, the young Marco Polo and his father and uncle went to China bearing gifts for Kublai Khan from the newly elected pope, Gregory X. Franciscan friar John of Monte Corvino was sent by Nicholas IV in 1289 to China, traveling by sea via India.

The Roman Catholics were not the first Christians to make contact with the Mongols, since they had had contact with the Nestorians for several centuries. Some female members of the Mongol royal family were Nestorian, including the mother of Kublai Khan, Mongke Khan, and her brother Hülagu Khan. At the Mongol court in Karakorum, Dominican and Franciscan friars met Nestorian clergy. The Mongols sent Nestorian emissaries to Rome. Rabban Bar Sauma, a Nestorian monk from Central Asia, was dispatched to Rome where he met Nicholas IV and celebrated communion with him. He also met with many European monarchs in a bid to arrange a Franco-Mongol alliance in order to consolidate the Mongol gains against the Muslim Mamluks. These diplomatic overtures were not realized, and when the Mongol Khans embraced Islam in the fourteenth century, the situation and treatment of their Christian subjects changed.

Right: Along with his father Niccolò and his uncle Maffeo, two successful traders who had already visited the East, Marco Polo sailed from Venice in 1271 on his famous journey to China.

CHAPTER FOUR

IBERIAN PENINSULA REGAINED

In 711 Muslims from North Africa entered the Iberian Peninsula across the straits of Gibraltar. Within three years the Muslims had defeated the Visigoths and taken possession of *al-Andalus* (the Arabic name for parts of the Iberian Peninsula) except for the extreme north. The tenth century was a "golden age" of enlightened relations between Christian, Jews, and Muslims, but internal rivalries weakened the caliphate in the eleventh century. In 1085, the capital Toledo fell to the army of Alfonso VI of Castile; it was the first Christian gain.

The Muslims did seize their territories back, but in 1212, a combined army of Christian forces including Castilians and Aragonese defeated them at the battle of Las Navas de Tolosa. This marked the beginning of a steady decline in Islamic power, with the only remaining Muslim stronghold being at Granada, the capital of the Nasrid Kingdom (1238–1492). Artists, scholars, and scientists contributed to Granada's reputation as a city of culture. Architecturally it was crowned by the Alhambra.

In 1492 Isabella I of Castile (1451–1504) and her husband Ferdinand of Aragon annexed the Kingdom of Granada following its surrender by Boabdil, the last Moorish ruler. Legend has it that Boabdil wept as he surrendered the keys of the Alhambra and left Granada forever. The treaty of surrender included clauses respecting the rights of the defeated citizens of Granada. However, many left with Boabdil. In the attempts to establish a unified Christian realm, many Muslims were converted by force and the Jews were expelled.

The actions of Isabella and Ferdinand had finally restored the Iberian Peninsula as a Christian dominion after a period of over 700 years of Muslim rule. The taking of Granada was seen as a counterblow to the fall of Constantinople in 1453 to the Ottomans. In recognition of their services to Christendom, Pope Alexander VI bestowed on Isabella and Ferdinand the title "the Catholic Monarchs."

Right: Located on a rocky hill above the town of Granada, the Alhambra is an imposing edifice that still stands today as a testament to Islamic art and architecture.

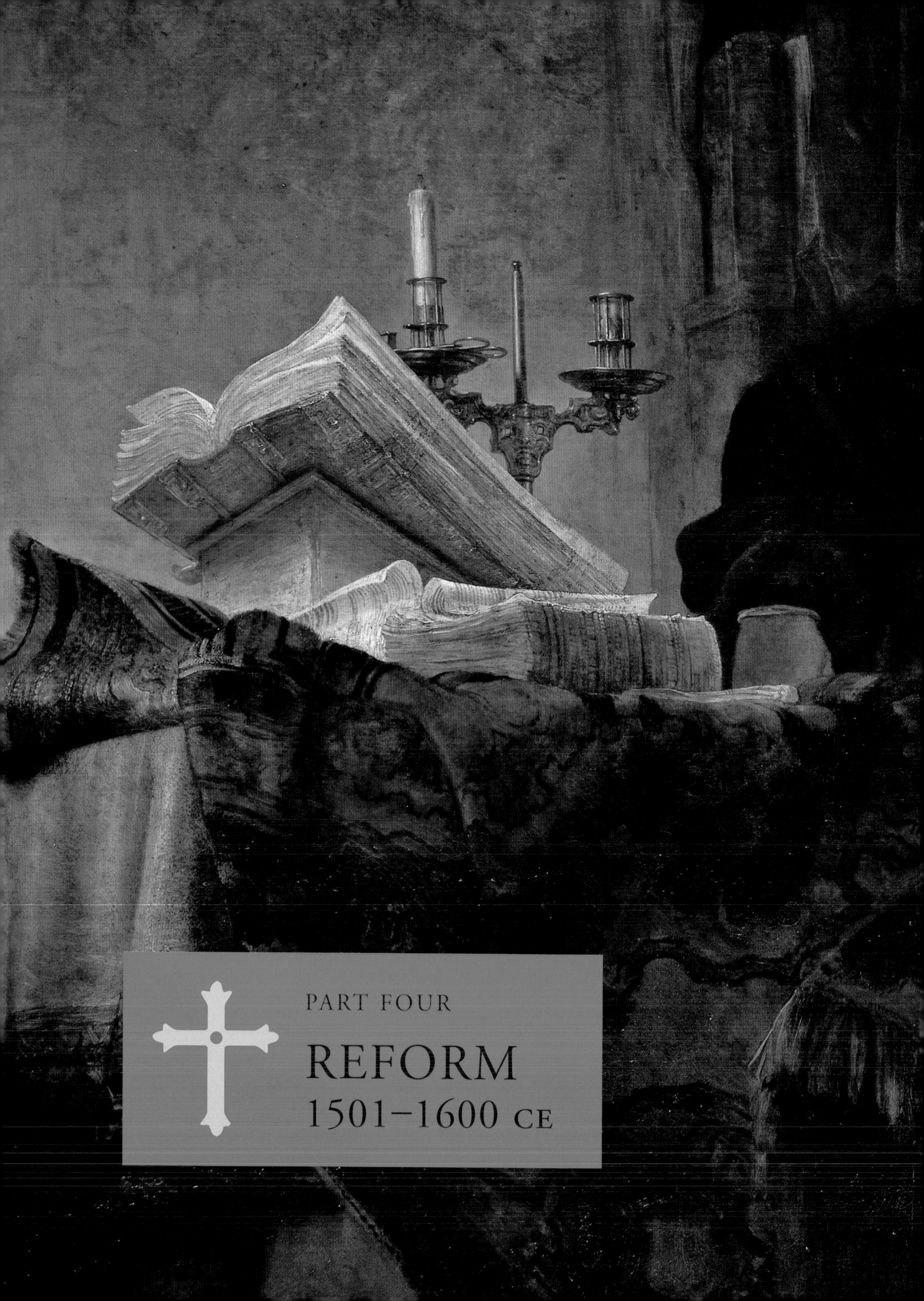

PART FOUR

REFORM

1501–1600 CE

CHAPTER ONE

A NEW CENTURY

The sixteenth century opened up new horizons for Christianity, both geographically and spiritually. Christian missions spiraled out into the Americas and the East; and adventurers, traders, colonizers, and missionaries explored what was for them an alluring new universe. Quite literally, the maps of the world had to be redrawn, and cultural and political expectations imploded. This geographical revolution was accompanied by the most radical shake-up the Christian Church had ever seen. A remarkable renewal of Church structures, spirituality, and theology got underway. On the heels of a startling renaissance of classical and early Church learning came one reformation after another: Catholic, Lutheran, Reformed, and Radical. The Bible, always so important in the Church's life and worship, now took center stage. Old authorities were challenged. Lay people experimented with secular patterns of discipleship and claimed new rights and responsibilities. "Reformation" is the word that sums all this up, or rather "reformations," for there were several.

Previous pages: *The Mennonite Preacher Anslo in Conversation with his Wife* by Rembrandt. The Mennonites represented a milder form of Christianity and followed the principle of "Love thy neighbor."

Right: French Jesuit missioneries settled in Siam (modern-day Thailand) to establish a French protectorate and to begin evangelizing the Far East. Here they pray during a solar eclipse.

EUROPE IN TURMOIL

Opposite: Erasmus of Rotterdam was an important humanist in his time. He wrote many books on humanism, translated the works of early Latin and Greek Church Fathers, and was first to publish the New Testament in Greek.

Below: The facade of Santa Maria del Fiore cathedral in Florence, Italy, was dismantled in 1587–1588 because it appeared dated by Renaissance standards. It was rebuilt in the nineteenth century.

✝ Politically, economically, and culturally the European world was in upheaval. Astrologers predicted strange conjunctions of planets in the sky. Nation-states such as France and England began to emerge, especially in the West, and with them subtly different loyalties and identities. Princely territories, such as Saxony or Bavaria, or Italian city-states, also built up a professional corps of administrators. Taxation systems were refined, a money economy became the norm, and in many cases written Roman law replaced ancient, unwritten customs and liberties. The feudal system, with its traditional hierarchies based on the land, was eroded. Key pillars of the medieval world, the Holy Roman Empire and the papacy, no longer seemed inviolable.

With the upturn in commerce, civic pride and self-confidence were manifested in spectacular architecture. Mining, manufacturing, and overseas trade required more substantial sources of capital, and banking firms such as those owned by the Fugger and Welser families burgeoned. Patrician merchants sent their sons abroad to see a wider world and develop useful contacts. Travel remained hazardous, inns were dirty and uncomfortable; however, networks of communication gradually improved.

The Venetians, who lived by their commerce, were the first to see the need for diplomatic outposts in faraway places. Geographically, the world might be growing larger, but culturally it grew closer. The new "republic of letters," consisting of artists, poets, and historians, crossed traditional

boundaries. By 1500 Erasmus of Rotterdam could boast correspondents from Hungary in the east to England in the west, from southern Italy to Sweden in the far north. He was, perhaps, the first truly international scholar.

The new printing press meant news and views spread faster. A growing number of lay people, including women, could now "pocket" new ideas and leapfrog the traditional guardians of truth. They could "study" for themselves in the privacy of their own homes and in the circle of their friends. City councils hired their own civic preachers to meet the lay demand for lively, relevant sermons. Universities had to upskill or lose out to informal groups of poets, writers, artists, and independent scholars who clustered round the royal or princely courts or the printing presses in the towns. Cheap pamphlets poured out in the vernacular. Graphic woodcuts adorned the walls of the local tavern. Nor was the countryside immune to new ideas. Most villages boasted at least one person who could read out aloud the latest news at the market cross.

The old world fades

Not everyone welcomed change, of course. These disruptions were accompanied by anxiety and pain as well as excitement and hope. Village communes fought hard against the erosion of their traditional rights, as did artisan guilds in the towns, and knights in their rat-ridden castles. Those in the Church and in high society, who were accustomed to unquestioning obedience, feared social chaos as centuries-old certainties were challenged. The venerable schism between Orthodoxy in the East and Catholicism in the West had seemed remote to most people. Now the conflict was within the heart of Europe itself. Who was one to trust: The traditional authority of the Pope and the Councils, or the critical voices of the poets and historians, the startling messages of Martin Luther or John Calvin, or even the radical Anabaptists?

None of this happened overnight. People did not wake up one morning to find the Middle Ages over! The routines of their lives remained the same, but gradually, as dramatic incidents upset the status quo, the old world disappeared.

Left: During the sixteenth century, the printing press spread rapidly throughout Europe and brought various translations of the Bible to the masses.

THE RENAISSANCE

Right: The gilded dome of Santa Maria del Fiore cathedral in Florence is a shining example of Renaissance architecture. It was the first octagonal dome ever built and remains the largest masonry dome in the world.

The Renaissance (the word literally means "rebirth") saw a wonderful flowering of art, architecture, poetry, philosophy, and history in Europe. We think of Leonardo da Vinci and Michelangelo, but also of political thinkers such as Machiavelli, Hebrew scholars such as Reuchlin, and the great classicist, Erasmus of Rotterdam. Many of its proponents had no particular religious motivations at all; they simply enjoyed good art, literature, philosophy, and history. Yet it was not an anti-clerical or anti-religious movement; indeed, many of its greatest patrons were popes and bishops. Humanism, in this period, simply means the love of humane studies, such as the classical languages of Greek, Latin, and Hebrew, the elegant style of Cicero, and classical literature and philosophy.

Birth of humanism

Christian humanism was by 1500 a widespread movement of writers and reformers, and included the likes of Sir Thomas More in England, Desiderius Erasmus in the Netherlands (Erasmus of Rotterdam), and Jacques Lefèvre d'Etaples in France, who sought to return the Church to its original sources: The Bible and the Early Church. They thought of the Church of their time as a muddy lagoon full of stagnant, brackish water, steeped in ignorance and superstition, and wanted it to return to the pure clear springs of living water, representing the prophets and apostles, the great scholars (such as Origen, Ambrose, and Augustine), and the so-called Early Church Fathers (the influential Christian writers and theologians of the time). They believed fervently in education and good scholarship, which should be made available to lay people, including women, and to the clergy. Their program was one of cultural and moral renewal.

Above: Thomas More was an eminent Renaissance humanist and writer. He was Chancellor during Henry VIII's reign, and executed for refusing to recognize Henry's break with Rome.

Exploiting the new printing press, the humanists produced new grammars and dictionaries of Latin, Greek, and Hebrew, as well as new editions of works by the Early Church Fathers. In 1516, Erasmus' Greek edition of the New Testament appeared, along with his new Latin translation. This proved hugely influential, challenging the orthodox Vulgate edition. By getting back, for example, to the original meaning of the Greek word for penitence, *metanoia*, an inward change of heart, the true meaning of the sacrament of penance could be recovered. Religion, in other words, was not an outward ritual but essentially an outflowing of inward faith into daily discipleship. The humanists promoted this as a commoner's religion, to be exercised in the home, at work, in human relationships, and, indeed, in politics. Holiness was no longer seen as a retreat from the world into celibacy or monastic life, but as love for one's neighbor, and as practical Christianity, following the example of Christ.

The Christian humanists poked fun at, and sometimes fiercely condemned, the abuses of the institutional Church, criticizing the wealth and worldliness of the hierarchy, and the superstitions associated with pilgrimages and relics, and devotion to the saints. They hoped to renew true piety and discipleship by education and example. Christ, as the great teacher, would show the way. Many of the clergy were among their most ardent supporters. In the nature of things, the humanists tended, with their love of good style and scholarship, to be a somewhat elitist group.

A complex cultural movement

The Renaissance was, then, a complex phenomenon. Like all great cultural movements, its origins are hard to trace. It drew to some extent on the release into the West of Byzantine scholarship after the fall of Constantinople to the Turks in 1453. It owed a debt to the Islamic world, which had kept alive the works of Aristotle. The revival of Platonic philosophy in Italy was another major influence on Erasmus and others. Italian cities such as Florence, Venice, and Rome provided a context in which great works of art could be sponsored and new ideas could be explored. German, Burgundian, French, and other European cities and princely courts soon followed suit.

Side by side, therefore, with the medieval cathedrals, monasteries, and universities (and often finding niches within them), new groups began to emerge, centered round the courts, schools, and printing presses. Individuals wrote elaborate letters to one another, cultivated friendships, and tended to promote a more secular view of life. The Renaissance is often associated with a more inward, even mystical understanding of spirituality, an affirmation and enjoyment of the material and external world, with an intense interest in exploration and science, the human body, and the human soul.

Above: The Renaissance was a rebirth of humanistic culture and an enhancement of education for all people. Its purpose was to rediscover the ancient Greek and Roman roots of European culture, renew society, and refresh religious belief and practice.

Left: Byzantine ideas and knowledge influenced the West; this illumination is of Jesus' parable about the Pharisee and the Publican, in Luke 18:9–14. The Eastern Orthodox Church read the story before the Great Lent.

CHAPTER TWO

REFORMATION

"What wonderful German Jesus speaks!" This naive statement by a layperson seeing for the first time the Gospels in his own language, expresses something of the excitement experienced by ordinary people in Europe in the early 1520s. There had, of course, been several vernacular versions of the Bible in the late Middle Ages. There had also been a series of reform movements: The Beguines, the Brethren of the Common Life, seeking a renewal of simple piety; widespread monastic reforms; and an outpouring of piety around the Dominican friar, Savonarola, in Florence in the 1490s.

Martin Luther was loyal to the Roman Catholic Church until well into middle age. He and other prominent reformers never dreamt of founding a new church. So, although the rupture brought about by the different reformations—Catholic, Lutheran, Reformed, and Radical—was to be massive, there was much continuity. The Bible, baptism, and Eucharist (Lord's Supper) stayed the same; the parish churches people attended and the moral codes they observed also remained familiar.

Yet this reformation was exciting. Church structures were shaken as if by an earthquake. In Protestant countries, the landscape of piety changed: Monasteries and nunneries, so often in the past powerhouses of mission work and piety, virtually disappeared; the papacy lost its primacy and legal authority; and the clergy were pruned and reinvented. Much of the Church's wealth and resources were redistributed. Even the more moderate Catholic reform, as seen in the Council of Trent, introduced for the first time seminary education for priests, modernized the role of bishops, and facilitated a sweeping commitment to overseas mission work.

Even more importantly, what had been basic Christian beliefs were overturned in Protestant territories: Hallowed traditions were questioned by the supreme authority of scripture; and the authority of popes, councils, and even the local bishop was relativized or rejected. Marriage and celibacy were seen in a new light. Seven sacraments became two, and the intercession of Mary and the saints fell by the wayside. The whole understanding of salvation came under scrutiny. The Roman Catholic Church, too, emerged after Trent with much greater clarity about the nature of justification and the relationship between scripture and tradition.

For the ordinary believer, however, the greatest changes may have been in the area of spirituality. In worship, the pulpit did not replace the altar, but in Protestant culture there was a move away from a visual or sensual piety to a more inward, word-centered one; from an ascetic ethic to a discipleship focused on daily living. Within Catholicism, a Baroque piety emerged, which gloried in dramatic worship and exuberant architecture.

Right: The Council of Trent was held between 1545 and 1563 at Trent in northern Italy. The council condemned the Protestant reformation and defined the Roman Catholic Church doctrines of scripture and tradition, original sin, justification, the sacraments, and the Eucharist.

THE LUTHERAN REFORMATION

That a reformation should be named after just one man was a sign of the times. No doubt about it, Martin Luther was a towering personality, with an Einstein-like intellect; he could cut through the heart of intricate theological and spiritual problems. He had a fine, earthy way with language, and the influence of his Bible translation on the German language is comparable to that of Shakespeare on the English language. His vernacular eye and ear enabled him to engage with ordinary people in their language. His hymns remind us of his great love of music.

Martin Luther—the man

Martin Luther could be rude, crude, and authoritarian, but he never lost the human touch. It was his little devotional writings that won him the heart of the German people. He had a sixth sense that enabled him to enter into the strange world of the psalms and the prophets, and of the Gospels and Paul. The Hebrew world was as much a part of his bloodstream as the New Testament.

Yet, it would be a mistake to imagine the Lutheran reformation was all his own doing. Luther was carried along by the stream of his time. Like the Swiss reformer, Ulrich Zwingli, the Hebraist Reuchlin and his disciple, Philip Melanchthon, Luther was greatly influenced by humanism. He owed much to his great mentor in the Augustinian Order, Johann von Staupitz, with his mystical emphasis on the love and grace of God. At the obscure University of Wittenberg in Saxony he worked with a superb team of linguists, and rubbed shoulders with creative artists such as Lucas Cranach.

Far beyond Wittenberg, too, he was part of a reformist network of preachers, scholars, and lay people in imperial cities such as Nuremberg and Augsburg. Without the support of princes such as Frederick the Wise of Saxony and Philip of Hesse, he would never have overcome the handicap of being an outlaw in the eyes of the empire, and a heretic in the eyes of the papacy. Above all, he rode a tidal wave of popular support. In the three decades after 1518, about six million pamphlets and books about the Reformation poured out, and just as important were tens of thousands of passionate sermons. It is a mistake to dismiss these as propaganda; they represented a new phenomenon in European culture—the emergence of public opinion as a key factor in social change.

Below: Zwingli was a Roman Catholic priest who became a Protestant reformer. Like Luther, he preached that salvation was by the grace of God and not by the works of man.

A gospel of grace

Lutheranism took root, then, because Luther's ideas gained scholarly, political, and popular support. As a preacher, priest, and confessor he became perturbed at the popular piety around what were known as letters of indulgence, which were "credits" handed out by Church officials—in their grosser forms they suggested that God's pardon for our sins could be bought with money. This morphed into a wider concern for the heart of the Gospels; as Luther saw it: God is above all a God of mercy and grace. When the hierarchy, including the papacy, lined up behind the letters of indulgence, he became convinced that the final authority in the Church lay in the living Word of God, which speaks to us directly through scripture. If the leaders of the

Left: Seen as the founder of the Reformation, Martin Luther's theology challenged the authority of the Roman Catholic pope by teaching that the Bible is the only source of divine knowledge.

Below: Martin Luther taught, translated, and preached from the Bible. The Luther Bible contributed to the development of the modern German language, and is a landmark in German literature.

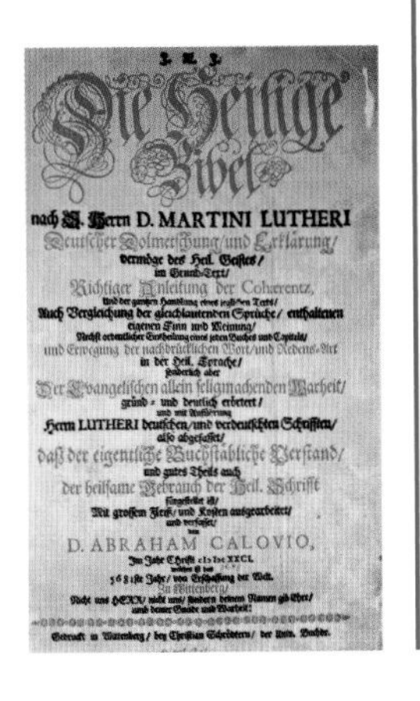
Die Heilige Bibel
nach S. Herrn D. MARTINI LUTHERI
Deutscher Dolmetschung und Erklärung
D. ABRAHAM CALOVIO.

Church persecuted those who supported this Gospel of grace, then they represented the Anti-Christ. This message of Luther's coalesced with much popular anti-clericalism.

Luther could robustly criticize particular rulers, princes, and magistrates, but they were given an almost episcopal role in governing the Church. Lutheranism tended to be socially conservative, treating the distinctions within society as God-given. When peasants and artisans rose up in 1524–1525 and claimed the support of scripture for their opposition to serfdom and other forms of injustice, Luther was outraged, especially when they resorted to arms to support their cause. The freedom of the Gospel must be understood spiritually, not politically.

The Lutheran movement, which emerged in the cities and princely territories of Germany in the 1520s, focused primarily on scripture, and on faith in God's graciousness. It had a high view of the individual conscience, and of the "priesthood" of the laity. All vocations, including secular ones, were holy. Preachers did not mediate salvation—they were no different from anyone else, but chosen for their gifts as interpreters of scripture. The Church was redefined in the famous 1530 Confession of Augsburg as believing people gathered around the preaching of the Word and the celebration of baptism and the Eucharist.

NATIONALISM AND RELIGION AS ONE

The reformations coincided with the rise of nationalism and state-building. Catholic and Protestant monarchs and princes, and even city magistrates, saw themselves as paternally responsible for the faith of their people. Except among Radicals such as the Anabaptists, it was taken for granted that uniformity of doctrine and worship must be ensured within each territory. National and religious identity came to be seen as almost synonymous, although local traditions continued to assert themselves against the power of the court and churches.

THE RADICAL REFORMATION

Since 1945, scholars have paid more attention to studying a varied grouping of people called the Anabaptists or Radicals. Although in comparison with the Catholic, Lutheran, and Calvinist reformations their numbers are relatively small, politically, socially, and theologically they offer a distinct alternative to the other forms of reformation. Some were of Swiss origin, with a strong emphasis on the New Testament call to nonviolence, and to a discipleship that separated the Christian from the values of the world. Others, in the wake of Andreas Karlstadt and Thomas Müntzer in Saxony, championed a religion of the spirit. Others, again, had pronounced apocalyptic views.

Rise of the radicals

The Anabaptists in southern Germany, with their vernacular translations of the New Testament, believed that ordinary members, often artisans, were quite capable of interpreting scripture themselves. Thomas Müntzer, like other Radicals, drew on medieval mysticism but gave it a popular touch. He broke with Luther, saying he was becoming a new pope, was too closely allied to the princes, and left no room for personal religious expression in faith. The Anabaptists had no professional clergy. Small groups of followers studied the Bible together, to solve practical problems such as: Should one ever use weapons; or baptize children; or drink in the tavern? Most of the Radicals felt that the commitment to discipleship was one only an adult could take, so infant baptism was wrong. They were impatient with pious words and suspicious of academics. A common proverb ran: "The more learned, the more perverted." The emphasis on costly, suffering discipleship is another hallmark of the Radicals. As Müntzer so succinctly put it, "If you will not taste the bitter Christ, you will eat yourself sick of honey."

The Radicals picked up the communal traditions of the medieval period and combined them with the Biblical theme of the covenant. They had a profound sense of

Below: Radical reformers took up some elements of the Calvinist reformation, like worshipping in the vernacular and encouraging everyone to read the Bible in their own language, but they went much further.

Left: Groups of radical Protestants emerged during the Reformation who rejected the doctrines of the Catholic and Protestant churches. As a result they were executed for seeking a truer form of Christianity.

brotherhood and sisterhood in Christ, for just as the bread of the Lord's Supper, which consists of many grains, is one, so are they. They could, however, be very censorious of those who disagreed with them. Those in the Hutterite tradition, which flourished for decades in Eastern Europe, saw the need to share all their possessions in common. In the later Mennonite version of Anabaptism, which became so influential in the Netherlands, and later in America, community discipline was all-important.

Persecution and repression

So, why were the Radicals so cruelly persecuted by the Catholic and Protestant authorities, often being drowned alive in mockery of their beliefs in adult baptism? Some were pacifists, but their break with Christendom and the idea that Church and society should have the same extent, was deeply offensive to the spirit of the time. Others had been caught up in the struggles of the Peasants' War (1524–1525), hoping to build a fairer and freer society, and were suspect because of that. Others, such as those involved in the attempt to set up a New Jerusalem in the city of Münster in 1534–1535, were apocalyptic dreamers, whose excesses and violence were used to tar all Radicals with the same brush.

Much of the fierce repression they encountered, however, stems from their courageous experimentation with new forms of community living, and their sturdy belief in their right to worship and live according to their own understandings of the faith. This was an affront to city magistrates and princes who sincerely believed that they were not only endangering their own salvation, but posed a threat to all authority in Church and state. They had, of course, to meet in secret to escape capture and this encouraged the widespread perception that they were a dangerous conspiracy. Fortunately, however, a remarkable number of their influential writings, accounts of their martyrdoms, and their hymns have survived. These documents testify not only to their personal heroism, but also to their understanding of discipleship, scripture, and society, which continue to intrigue many of us today.

THOMAS MÜNTZER

Thomas Müntzer was a former priest who became a follower of Martin Luther. As a pastor in the little Saxon town of Allstedt in 1523–1524, he translated the worship services into German to give his people access to the Bible and train them in the Christian way. Everyone, not just the elite few, was to be educated in the way of holiness. Rough, unsophisticated peasants, he believed, like Jesus' own disciples, were the most likely to respond to Christ's call and disclose His will. The elect of God, he believed, could also be found among the Jews and the Turks.

Right: Thomas Müntzer and his followers are usually labeled Anabaptists who took their utopian beliefs to the extreme. The Anabaptists were regarded with suspicion, and it was through the pacifist Mennonites that they later gained respect.

THE REFORMED TRADITION

Right: John Calvin's interpretation of Christianity influenced followers of Protestantism in Europe and North America. His theology is widely thought to have had a major impact on the formation of the modern world.

The Lutheran reformation was largely a German and a Scandinavian affair. Lutheran ideas did penetrate to the rest of Europe, even to far off places such as Scotland and Poland, as enthusiastic students came back from Wittenberg and brought Luther's Latin writings with them, but there was a need to translate them and to adapt Luther's thought to quite different situations. However, in Zurich and Basel in Switzerland, and in southern Germany, a more civic and less liturgical form of Protestantism had emerged—one that was freer from the authority of the princes. Swiss Protestantism had something republican about it, and was strongly influenced by everyday concerns.

For most of Western and Eastern Europe, and including Italy, it was largely in its Calvinist form that Protestantism spread. John Calvin (1509–1564) represented the second generation of the Reformation. He had been forced to flee Paris because of his reformist views—the movement which he founded in Geneva in the 1530s and 1540s was marked by the experience of exile and persecution, which he shared with many others.

A movement for and of the people

Calvinism was spare, tough, and determined. It had an international view, looking outward from Geneva to France, the Netherlands, the Rhineland, Poland, Hungary, and Italy. If Luther was the Karl Marx of the Reformation, Calvin was its Lenin—he was a masterly strategist. After the whirlwind of the 1520s, the alarm caused by the Peasants' War (1524–1525), and the religious divisions of the 1530s and 1540s, people craved certainty and order. Calvinism provided this. Not for nothing is Calvin often compared with his counterpart in the Counter-Reformation, Ignatius Loyola, the founder of the Jesuits.

In 1536, while still a very young man, Calvin wrote the *Institutes of the Christian Religion.* It went through many revisions, but remained essentially the same throughout his life, providing a comprehensive understanding of the Church and of theology. It was to prove one of the most influential books in European history. For Calvin, the Bible supplies not only the guiding spirit but an actual blueprint for the form of the Church: Teachers, pastors, lay elders, and deacons all working together in synods. Calvinism mobilized the enthusiasm of ordinary people in the governance of the Church. Not surprisingly, therefore, it attracted

Left: Days before his death, ministers of the Church came to visit John Calvin. He recounted his life in Geneva and the hardship he had endured. Calvin was buried in an unmarked grave.

professionals such as lawyers, teachers, magistrates, and nobles who were fired by a vision to reform society. Calvinism has been characterized as realistic utopianism. It was confident that God's sovereign will could be realized in human society. Western culture was to be lastingly stamped by its rational and programmatic character.

Calvin and his beliefs

Calvin was initially appointed as a lecturer on scripture and then as a pastor in Geneva, so it was only gradually, and after many long and bitter struggles, that the Council in Geneva came under his sway in the 1550s. He was an exceptional scholar, well versed in Greek and Hebrew. His commentaries, on 23 books of the Hebrew Bible, and all the New Testament ones except Revelation, are still read today. His authority derived from the way in which he related his Biblical and patristic scholarship to contemporary issues. Calvin's Biblical and historical arguments against the claims of the papacy and Church tradition convinced many. His main priorities, like the reformers Martin Bucer in Strasbourg and Ulrich Zwingli in Zurich, were in the educational and moral realm—the provision of catechisms and sermons for ordinary people, and the best Biblical scholarship for the pastors. The Genevan Academy became a training ground for missionaries to France, England, Scotland, Hungary, Poland, Italy, and elsewhere.

PURE DOCTRINE AND INTOLERANCE

Most controversial today, perhaps, are Calvin's high doctrine of predestination and his concern for communal discipline. While he could be remarkably flexible in many matters, he never tolerated dissent on matters he regarded as central—pure doctrine, respect for the office of the preacher, and the integrity of the Lord's Supper. Open sinners and libertines, he believed, were not only an unwholesome influence on their neighbors, they violated God's honor, and so endangered the entire community. He fought a long and successful battle for the right of the Consistory, the joint body of pastors and elders which enforced Church discipline, to excommunicate offenders. Thus Geneva became a magnet to many as a beacon of godliness, but others fled from it. The death of Michael Servetus at the stake in 1553 for denying the Trinity became a symbol of intolerance. Recent research has demonstrated that the bulk of the Consistory's work was in family disputes and was welcomed as positive, speedy, and just.

Right: For John Calvin, the Trinity was absolutely central to Christian belief and practice. He saw the essence of God as undivided; it belonged equally to a Father, Son, and Spirit.

THE ENGLISH REFORMATION

The English reformation was different. It came later than those on the Continent, proceeded by way of an abrupt succession of surges and reversals, and was very much dependent on monarchical initiative. Today it is indelibly connected with Henry VIII's many wives, but it would be unwise to discount its genuine religious content. The soaring beauty of the *Book of Common Prayer* is testimony enough to that.

How did it take hold?

The degree of popular support for the Reformation remains controversial. The Lollards (followers of John Wyclif) were few and scattered, but they combined with a more general anti-clerical dissatisfaction and the reformist concerns of humanists (such as John Colet), to ensure a receptivity for Lutheran and reformed views as they seeped into England along the trade routes and through reformers such as William Tyndale, who had spent time in Wittenberg.

Below: Anne Boleyn, Henry VIII's second wife, failed to give him a son. She was charged with treason and found guilty of adultery and plotting to kill Henry. She was beheaded in May 1536.

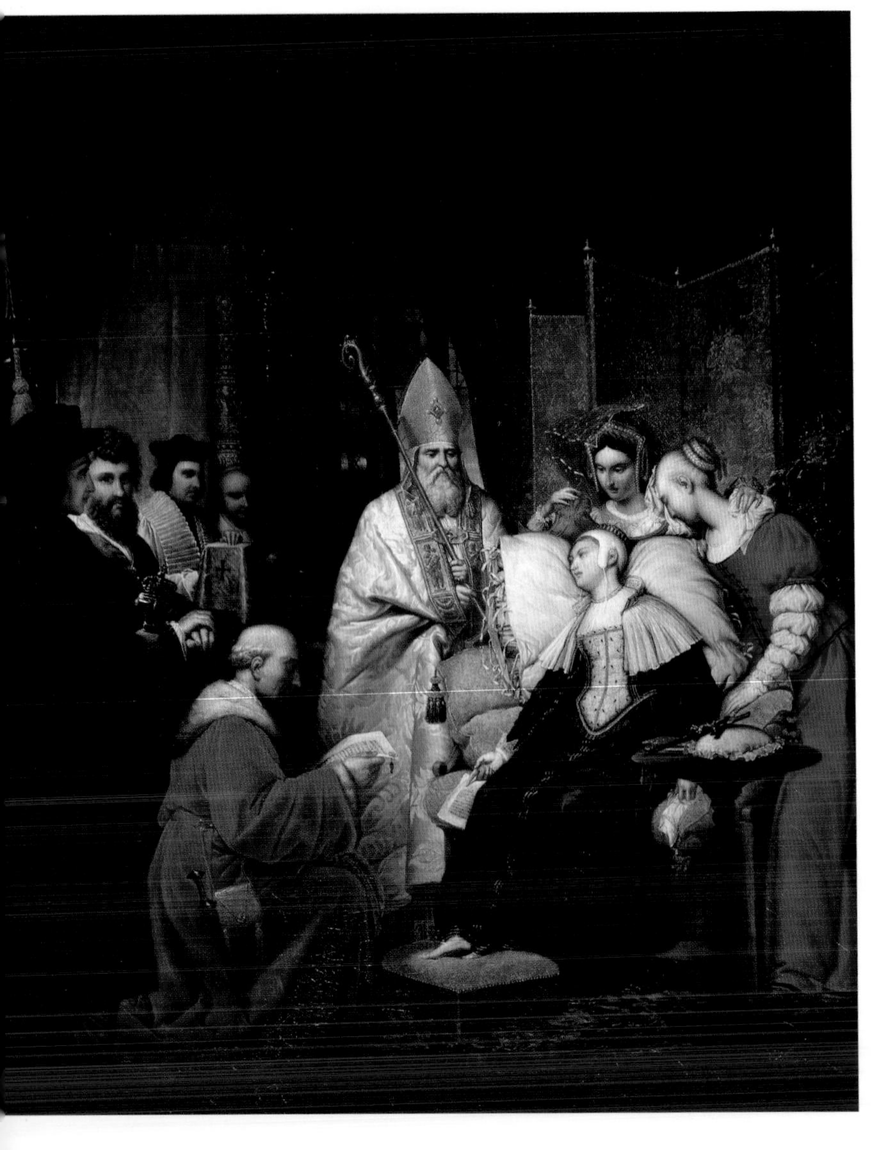

Catholic piety had flourished in the late medieval period, but so did the superstition around relics and pilgrimages so lampooned by the humanists, and the abuse of hierarchical wealth and power.

Henry VIII, who reigned from 1509 to 1547, was no theological radical. He made a name for himself as a defender of sacramental orthodoxy and was duly savaged for his pains in one of Luther's more vitriolic pamphlets. But when papal jurisdiction stood in the way of deposing Catherine of Aragon as his Queen and replacing her with Anne Boleyn, he broke with Rome and declared his own supremacy over the Church. England was an empire! The conscientious dissent of the Chancellor, Sir Thomas More, to this breach, as More saw it, with the Church universal, was rewarded with death. The monasteries and the chantries (which practiced Mass for the dead) were dissolved, and a cautious Biblical reformation was put in place. None of this could have happened without a considerable degree of popular support for the evangelical cause. Archbishop Cranmer's 1549 *Book of Common Prayer* ensured that this support would quietly build. Under Edward VI the sinews of reformed theology and practice were strengthened, and Mary Tudor's reign (1553–1558) was too brief for the Catholic recovery she attempted to take hold. As a matter of fact, the martyrdom of Cranmer and others, dramatically recorded in John Foxe's *Book of Martyrs* (published in 1554), rallied opinion against the Old Church.

Protestant England

The long reign of Elizabeth I (1558–1603) ensured the eventual triumph of Protestantism. As Henry's illegitimate daughter, in Catholic eyes, she was bound to steer a course away from Rome. The theological basis of the Elizabethan Settlement—the 39 Articles—have a Protestant, in places even Calvinist, ring, but the traditional episcopal structures, which encouraged a close connection between the Church and the court, were maintained, and Calvinist patterns of worship and discipline were not followed. Clerical vestments, crucifixes, and Church art and music were retained. The laity had seen so much chopping and

A NEW WORLD

Socially, the changes brought about by the reformations to family relationships, and the place of women, appear to have been limited. Yet the home life of the married Protestant pastor modeled a new set of ideals. In the 1560 Scottish *Book of Discipline* the poor tended to be regarded as a social, rather than an individual, responsibility, and the local school was given a much higher priority. The elan of the new Catholic orders, not least the Jesuits, in social work, education, and mission work abroad was equally impressive. No longer medieval, and not yet modern, a new world was in birth.

Left: Oliver Cromwell was a military leader in the many sieges and battles that would make England a republican Commonwealth. He ruled England as Lord Protector between 1653 and 1658.

Above: In the months following Elizabeth I's coronation, she re-established the Protestant Church in England, and became Supreme Governor of the Church of England to appease the Catholics.

changing that this stable course, based on a revised form of the *Book of Common Prayer* (the vernacular Bible), and the leadership of the Queen, appears to have been what most people wanted. The overwhelming majority of the clergy took the required oath of uniformity. One should not underestimate, however, the continuing strength of pockets of Catholicism or the determination of a Puritan wing, including some bishops, to promote godly discipline and Biblical preaching. It was a time of bitter religious conflicts and wars in the Netherlands and in France, and England was never insulated from them. Martin Bucer, the Strasbourg reformer, taught in Cambridge after the 1548 Interim forced him into exile. The advice and the books of reformed leaders such as Bullinger in Zurich and Beza in Geneva were influential. Also important were the links with Scotland, which from 1560 had moved to a Calvinist form of Churchmanship and piety.

The confrontation with the Spanish Armada that took place toward the end of Elizabeth's reign associated Catholicism with the national enemy, yet on the death of Elizabeth the unresolved tensions within the Church were still evident. On the one hand, under the Stuarts, the Authorized Version of the Bible appeared, and the aggressive policies of Archbishop Laud meant a distinct shift to High Churchmanship. Communion tables, for example, were replaced with altars. On the other hand, there was a burgeoning of "root and branch" Puritanism, and of congregational and Baptist tendencies, which had always been present, and which were to come together in the 1642 Civil War with the republicanism of the Army and Oliver Cromwell. With the Restoration of 1660, Anglicanism, as we know it today, finally emerged, yet the continuing existence of Catholicism and nonconformity reminds us of the varied nature of the English reformation.

Left: During the English reformation, stone altars replaced the wooden communion tables found in places of worship. This alone greatly changed the look and focus of church interiors.

VERNACULAR BIBLES

Opposite: Martin Luther translated the New Testament into German. The Luther Bible, as it is called, led to other Protestant versions being published in French, Dutch, and English.

There can be few more remarkable events in religious history than the way in which Bibles in French, German, English, and many other languages took Europe by storm in the sixteenth century. After all, the 66 books that make up the Christian Holy Scriptures, with their ancient law codes and histories of the Jewish people, their dark prophecies, their variant Gospels, and complex Epistles of Paul, seemed altogether remote from the experience of early modern Europe. Originally Hebrew and Greek in language, and, in their Latin form, traditionally the preserve of the literate clergy, it seemed altogether improbable that in their vernacular form they would be seized upon so eagerly by lay people as the pathway to salvation and godly living. Yet the scriptures of the Old and New Testaments bounded out of domestication like a wild animal and "ran free" through the cultures of Europe.

The Bible, of course, had always been central to the Church. The psalms had provided the strong backbone to the monastic liturgy. The familiar images of Adam and Eve, Lot's wife turned into a pillar of salt, Daniel in the lions' den, and, of course, the countless depictions of Jesus' birth, life, and death were vividly represented on tens of thousands of carvings and stained-glass windows. In England, the use of vernacular Bibles by the "heretical" Lollards had led to their prohibition, but that was not the case elsewhere, though the translations tended to be awkward and wooden. It was evident that the printing press was opening up a new accessibility of the Bible to lay people.

Below: Revered by scholars and Church historians as the "Father of the English reformation," William Tyndale translated and published the first modern English edition of the Bible from Hebrew and Greek texts.

Centrality of scripture

With the reformations, however, both humanist and Protestant, the scene was transformed. First of all, for the reformers Erasmus, Luther, and Calvin, scripture became the way back to the pure sources of the faith, uncluttered by pious but often dubious traditions. Allied to this quest for apostolicity was a stir of apocalyptic excitement. Through scripture the living Word of God was believed to speak immediately to the believer and point the way forward to the future. One should remember, though, that for most people—not much more than 5 percent of the population was literate at the time—the encounter with the Bible was not through the printed word but through the dramatic, spoken event of the sermon. From the little villages around Allstedt in Saxony, for example, people crowded in to hear Thomas Müntzer preach in 1523–1524. All over Europe this sort of thing happened. The literate met in little book clubs, as we would call them today, to ponder over the prophets or Paul's letters. The ordinary folk drank in the Biblical teachings and stories through reformist sermons, which held up a mirror against contemporary Church and society, and confirmed the gut feeling of the parishioners that something was badly wrong and reform was necessary.

A clutch of genial translators led the charge. Martin Luther argued that a translator, as well as knowing intimately the Biblical language and ways of thinking, needed an equally sharp ear for the way ordinary people spoke in his own time, in the marketplace, or at home—for two infinitely remote worlds have to blend. The ancient, uncompromising, and inspiring prophecies of Isaiah, for example, have to rasp against contemporary reality. A laywoman, such as the writer Argula von Grumbach, reading her way through scripture and relating it to her Bavarian context, could proudly proclaim that she spoke "with Jeremiah" or "with Paul."

This "unleashing" of scripture happened right across Europe. Luther's New Testament in 1523 developed into a lifelong commitment with his team of scholars to translate the entire Bible. This both gave scripture a "home" in the German language, and enriched the latter. The language used in the sanctuary would be that used in everyday life. The cultural significance of such an achievement is incalculable because the abyss between the sacred and the secular is bridged. Yet, by some miracle of good taste, the scriptural message was never vulgarized or trivialized.

The English Bible

William Tyndale's fine translation of the Pentateuch (the first five books of the Jewish and Christian scriptures) and the New Testament provided the basis of various English versions of the Bible. In 1536 in Brussels, Tyndale was burnt to death for his work. The scholarly Geneva version of 1560, with its marginal notes, was to become hugely influential. In 1611, an Authorised Version, commissioned by James I to counteract the Calvinist tone of these marginal notes, was to prove the crowning glory of the English translations. The 1610 Douai translation provided a rather Latinate version for English Catholics.

REFORMATION HYMNS

Above: Gregorian chants originated in the monasteries, and were sung nine times a day. Singing psalms was also part of monastic life, and smaller groups or soloists sang the chants.

Even in today's literate society, music imprints itself most deeply in the memory and the heart. How much more so in sixteenth-century society, when few could read and even fewer could afford a book! Yet at home, in the church, at the inn, or in the marketplace, the rhythms and rhymes of song were on everyone's lips. A hymn could be quickly learnt by heart and cost not a cent to buy. Popular folksongs were cherished not only in the villages and towns, but also in the schools, universities, and courts. Everyone loved a song.

The Lutheran reformation, in particular, was quick to realize this. Luther saw music as one of God's greatest gifts. He was often portrayed as the Wittenberg nightingale, or as a lute player, singing "a new song." He himself composed hymns, some of which, like "A Mighty Fortress Is Our God," are still sung today. He married new words in a genial way with medieval tunes, some of them secular ditties, some devotional songs to the saints, or to Mary. So reforming ideas could ride piggyback on melodies which had been familiar to countless generations, who had sung them on pilgrimages or processions or at home and work. From 1524 little collections of German hymns, written by Luther and others, began to appear in print. Together with the vernacular Bible, pamphlet, and sermon these Lutheran hymns, or chorales, proved one of the most potent means for spreading "the holy Gospel which now by the grace of God has risen anew" (Luther).

Hymns enter the church

A decisive step was introducing the vernacular hymns into church services. Previously the choirs of the cathedrals had sung beautiful polyphonic music in Latin, and singing required elaborate training and skill. In the normal parish church the Gregorian chant had been intoned by the priest alone; the congregation remained silent and listened. The contrast with the Reformation could not be greater. Now the congregation could sing hymns together in their own language—a powerful bonding experience. For song brings together mind and body, individual and community, in a unique way, and all ages can participate. At Christmas time children would sing Martin Luther's carol, "From Highest Heaven," after placing the baby Jesus on the altar.

Left: The Gregorian chant is music of great variety—from simple recitations to complex melodies requiring trained vocal skills. Singers often chant while holding a gradual, a collection of chants for Mass.

Hymns were central to the school curriculum as well, and not only in Lutheran schools. In 1586 a Jesuit teacher wrote to his superior: "For a whole year I have been laboring with our village boys but could not make them remember even the words of the Lord's Prayer. But now that I have taught them how to sing, they learn the Apostle's Creed and the Ten Commandments in a few hours."

Perhaps more important than their use in church and school was the way in which hymns were sung throughout the week, especially in household worship, which, strongly propagated by the reformers, was the responsibility of the father of the family. It was through these hymns that lay people could develop and maintain their own personal piety, sometimes contrary to the wishes of their clerical or secular authorities. Hymns were sometimes used as a form of symbolic protest to interrupt the Catholic Mass, and as differences hardened between Protestants and Catholics, countless hymns were written with a propagandist aim, rather like ballads, denouncing the other side. For the Anabaptists, hymns had a special role in providing consolation in the face of drowning, the stake, decapitation: "Love overcomes all things/water, fire, sword do not conquer it" as the preacher Hans Betz wrote. Each verse in one of the Anabaptist hymns has a different initial against it, giving us an insight into the way the whole lay group composed it.

Congregational psalms

Some Protestants, however, such as Ulrich Zwingli in Zurich, believed that the sensual nature of music was an unnecessary distraction from the pure word of God, and although he was a fine musician, he banned hymns from church services. The Calvinist tradition, too, was unhappy about the use of worldly music and limited the music sung in church to the biblical psalms. Arranged in metrical verses, with haunting or militant melodies specially composed for them, these psalms did, however, become a potent means of inculcating piety. Defiantly sung on street corners, they could also be a form of evangelism and protest. From Hungary to Scotland a lasting tradition of congregational psalm singing was firmly established.

Protestant worship moved away from the sacramental and the visual to the spoken word, though this process should not be exaggerated. Hymns sung in their own language ensured, certainly, that the imaginative world of the Bible and the depths of religious experience continued to resonate for believers and that the emotional vibrancy of piety and worship were not lost.

Left: The reformist Martin Luther believed music was an important part of worship. He wrote and had printed hymns that ordinary people could sing in church or at home.

CATHOLIC REFORM

Above: Ornate church interiors were viewed by Protestant reformers as evidence of corruption in the Catholic Church. In 1563, the Council of Trent published guidelines on art, asserting the importance of sacred images and their role in instructing the faithful.

Long before the Protestant reformations, a variety of reform movements within the "Old Church"—humanist, monastic, mystical, and institutional—were already under way, from Spain and England, to Italy and Germany. The Fifth Lateran Council of 1512–1517 foreshadowed significant moves to renew the episcopate, to raise the educational and moral level of the clergy, and to reach out to the laity. Catholic reform cannot be seen simply as a response to Protestantism; it would have taken place anyway. Initially, at least, reformers such as Luther had hoped to work from within Catholicism. Yet it is indisputable that it was the brutal shock caused by the Protestant break with Rome which galvanized lay Catholic leaders such as Emperor Charles V to demand with mounting impatience that the vested interests and corruption which stood in the way of a renewal of Catholicism should be tackled, and that a coherent doctrinal response be developed to meet the Lutheran and, increasingly, the Calvinist challenge.

The Council of Trent

Some influential Catholics, especially in Italy and Germany, including Cardinal Gasparo Contarini, believed that a reform of Catholicism might persuade moderate Protestants to return to the unity of the Church. Their own studies of Paul had led these "evangelical" Catholics to a degree of convergence with Lutheran views. However, these peaceful initiatives, which were met with skepticism both in Rome and Luther's Wittenberg, foundered at the Regensburg Conference in 1541. This left the way open for the Council of Trent, which met intermittently from 1545–1563, being convened by the reformist pope, Paul III. It had three main aims: To unite Christendom against

the Turkish attacks in the East; to reform the institutional life of the Church; and to clarify the teachings of scripture and tradition, justification by faith, and the sacraments.

The council's doctrinal decrees determined the stance of the Roman Catholic Church for centuries to come. It adopted a balanced position on scripture and tradition, seeing them as two streams of revelation, written and unwritten, both going back to the Apostles. The traditional Vulgate version of scripture was validated, and the Bible was to be interpreted according to the sense of Holy Mother Church. Salvation was not by faith alone, but yoked with love. By God's grace we could perform meritorious works. The traditional seven sacraments, which the Protestants had reduced to two, were reaffirmed.

Key reforms included the strengthening of the pastoral role of the bishops and the establishment of proper seminaries for the training of priests, though it would take decades before the necessary financial resources were found and resistance to reform was finally overcome. Gross abuses, such as the selling of indulgences, disappeared. The council did not achieve the longed-for unity of the Church, and some issues such as the supreme authority in the Church—papacy or general councils—were not resolved, but its lucid, carefully formulated decrees launched a new and positive era for the Roman Catholic Church.

Above: Pope Paul III convened the Council of Trent in order to formalize various decrees of the Catholic Church. He attended sessions in Trent and Bologna before passing away in 1549.

Spiritual renewal

Undergirding the reforms was a spiritual renewal of the Church. The lax, if broad-minded Renaissance papacy gave way to a succession of reforming popes. The Curia, the papal bureaucracy, was gradually purged and modernized, and the responsibilities of the cardinals were restructured. Bishops spearheaded a pastoral commitment of the episcopate to the educational and spiritual needs of the laity. Catechisms became widely available. Pluralism, nonresidency of clergy, and the purchase of clerical offices did not disappear overnight, but a new spirit was abroad.

For most lay Catholics, the great gains of the Catholic reformation lay in the improved preaching and pastoral care. Devotions to the Blessed Sacrament and to Mary breathed new life into the old medieval fraternities. Members would gather for Mass, participate in processions, distribute charity, and covenant themselves to daily prayer. In villages and towns these groups helped to unite communities in the love of God and communal service.

VISIONS AND POETRY

The mysticism of Teresa of Ávila (1515–1582) and St John of the Cross (1542–1591) is rightly seen as one of the supreme flowerings of the Catholic reformation. Both were cautious about sensationalist visions, and deeply loyal to the Church, though they had to cope with suspicions of heresy. The sublime poetry of St John of the Cross remains among the most beautiful of all spiritual literature: "That was the love, all else above/Of perfect peace, devotion deep."

Below: St John of the Cross was a major figure in the Catholic reformation. His poetry and studies on spiritual growth and prayer were highly influential. He was canonized in 1726.

THE INQUISITION

Even today, the very mention of the Inquisition makes us shudder. In view of the arbitrariness of many of its procedures, the networks of its informers, the use of torture, the failure to inform the accused of who was offering evidence against them, indeed the whole phenomenon of "thought control," this is understandable. Publicly staged "liturgical" executions of heretics in the so-called autos-da-fé (acts of faith) served to intimidate dissenters. The two presuppositions that underlay the Inquisition were that error has no rights, and that the Church, as the standard bearer of the truth, was duty bound to defend it. Doctrinal dissent, too, tended to be branded as immoral and criminal, and blasphemy, sexuality, and sorcery were specifically targeted. Punishment included confinement, physical abuse, and torture.

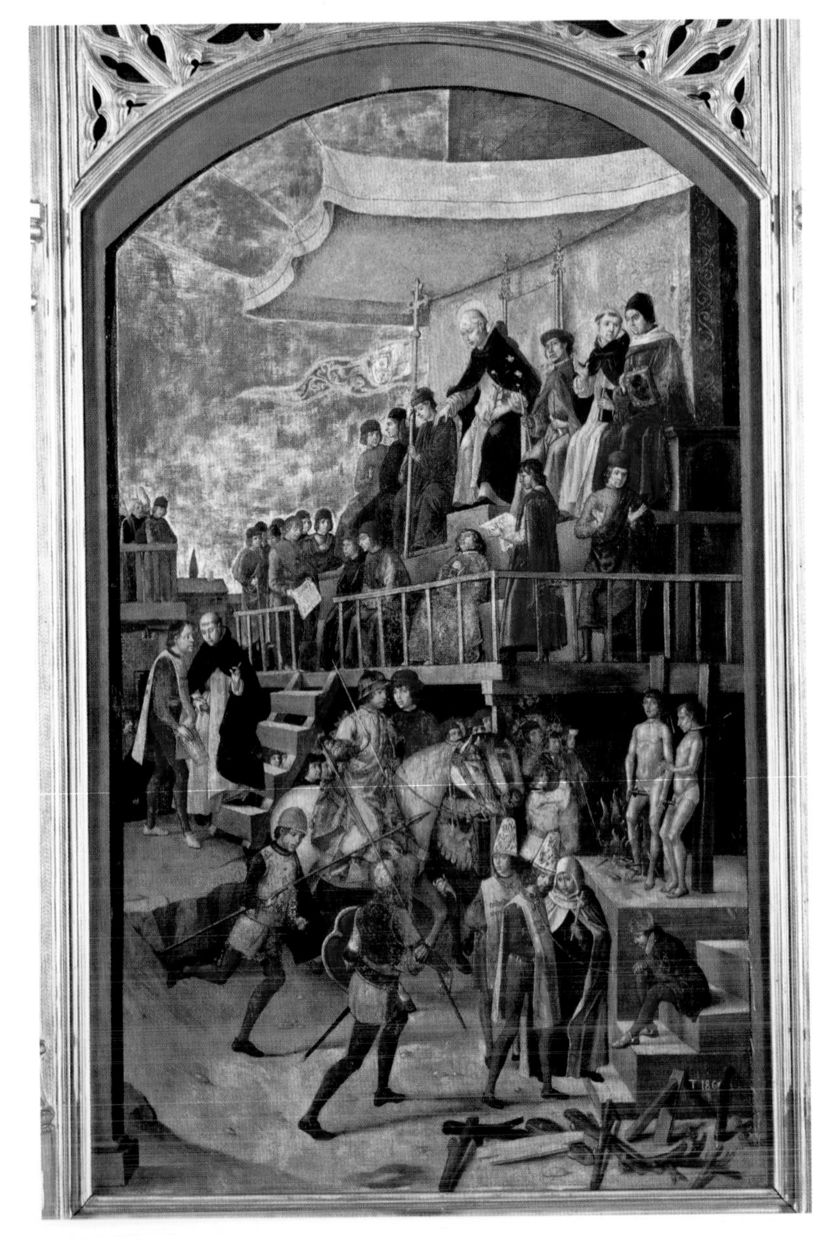

Below: The Inquisition was ruthless in its bid to banish heresy from Europe. Those who confessed to heresy were tortured; those who refused were burned alive at the stake.

Who were the inquisitors?

Historically, we have to be cautious both about numerical exaggerations and about misrepresenting the mentality from which the Inquisition sprang. A recent survey of heresy trials in Europe, both Catholic and Protestant, between 1520 and 1565, puts their number no higher than about 3,000. Inquisitors, and their supporters, tended to be people of high principle, crusaders and reformers, who firmly believed that what they did upheld the honor of God and was necessary for the salvation of humanity. There is no lack of evidence that on occasion inquisitors could show great patience and pastoral concern. Ironically, it tended to be the cynical and the indifferent who actually opposed the Inquisition.

The medieval bishops' inquisitions had been courts set up to pursue and eradicate heresy. The word "inquisition" simply means "enquiry." What was new in the sixteenth century was that social control was more effective as bureaucracies were professionalized and centralized; and that the need for uniformity appeared more urgent as religious divisions tore apart the seamless cloak of the body of Christ. Another complicating factor is that heresy and treason were almost inseparable in sixteenth-century minds. Religion, of course, was seen as the cement which held society together. On the whole, the secular arm was eager to support the Inquisition. In England and France most of the work of the Inquisition was done through secular courts. Queen Elizabeth I's *Act of Uniformity* in 1559, which tolerated no dissent from either Catholics or Puritans, was par for the course.

In Spain and Portugal the Inquisition was closely related to nationalist, monarchical, and even racial concerns to unite and purify the country, following pogroms against the Jews since the mid-fourteenth century and the completion in 1492 of the *Reconquista*, the military crusade against the Moors in the south. So tens of thousands of Moriscos and Marranos (converted Jews) faced accusations of heresy from the Spanish Inquisition when King Ferdinand II of Aragon and Queen Isabella I of Castile set it up in 1478 with the support of the papacy. Others caught in the net were mystics, visionaries, and Erasmians. Not until about 1560 were Protestants a serious factor.

The Roman Inquisition, founded in 1542 by Pope Paul III, had a different focus, being primarily directed against the emergent Protestant threat. Prior to the Council of Trent, of course, there had been considerable room for doctrinal debate about such matters as justification by faith or the sacraments. In Naples, Lucca, Venice, and elsewhere Protestant or crypto-Protestant groups had emerged, sometimes with the support of eminent clergy and laity, and sometimes inspired by popular preachers. But 1541 saw the collapse of the attempted reconciliation with the Lutherans at Regensburg, and the tide changed in a rigorist and repressive direction. Though the number of heretics executed in Rome was fewer than 100, humanist as well as

Protestant dissent was ruthlessly crushed. In the *Index of Prohibited Books of 1559* all of Erasmus' works were proscribed. The growing centralization and clericalism of the Catholic Church made the Inquisition particularly unsympathetic to popular culture and to women. In Venice, a whole world of artisan culture, centered around discussions and games in the taverns, disappeared.

Protestant intolerance

Within Protestantism there was more ambivalence about the right and necessity to enforce orthodoxy. In principle, Luther had argued that the conscience cannot be coerced, and influential reformers, such as the German theologian Johann Brenz (1499–1570), opposed the use of the death penalty for Anabaptists. The city of Strasbourg became something of a haven for dissenting views. French Protestant Sebastian Castellio's arguments in favor of toleration won over many. The fierce persecution, however, of the Anabaptists was justified on the grounds of their alleged blasphemies and socially disruptive behavior.

Yet tragic as the various manifestations of the Inquisition proved, on a cultural and spiritual as well as human level, they never approached the rigor of totalitarian control seen in modern times. Repression could be ferocious but it was intermittent. Intolerance was not the hallmark of society as a whole. In the end, the Inquisition helped spur the growth of Prostestantism in areas not dominated by the Catholics.

Above: King Ferdinand and Queen Isabella established the Spanish Inquisition in 1478 to maintain Catholic beliefs in the kingdom. It was not formally abolished until 1834.

Left: Those on trial during the Spanish Inquisition were forced to wear clown-like clothing, which included a dunce hat. The costume was designed to humiliate its wearer.

THE CAPUCHINS AND JESUITS

Above: The Jesuit missions in Trinidad and Jesús, Paraguay, feature some of the most impressive churches and sculptures ever built by the Jesuits. The ruins still survive today.

The Council of Trent, the new religious orders, and the Inquisition have traditionally been seen as the pillars of the Counter-Reformation. There is some truth to that. Yet the emergence of the Capuchins and the Jesuits had virtually nothing to do with a reaction against Protestantism; they were a result of inner-Catholic dynamics.

The "hooded brothers"

Reformist groups within the Franciscans, for example, sought to restore order to its original purity and poverty, and eventually secured papal approval in 1528 and 1534 to form the "hooded brothers" or Capuchins. The order spread with almost unbelievable speed, fanning out all over Europe, and by 1536 boasted 310 houses, each with about 10 members. Zeal for prayer and contemplation was married to a passion for preaching. The Capuchins made a name for themselves by their fearless devotion during outbreaks of the plague and by their solidarity with the poor. They dressed, ate, slept, and housed in exemplary simplicity. One learnt most, they said, from the "book of the Cross." They went where the need of ordinary people took them, and this impetus led, particularly in the seventeenth century, to missionary work overseas. Interestingly, one of their outstanding leaders, Bernardino Ochino (1487–1564), criticized the Inquisition, and went over to Calvinism, though he eventually broke with the latter, too, over predestination.

An intense discipline

As for the Jesuits, the dramatic story of the conversion of their founder, Ignatius Loyola (1491–1556), has often been told: The cannon ball that shattered his leg and his military career in 1517; the night vigil at Montserrat; the typically Spanish determination to devote his whole life to a crusade for God, originally with the Holy Land in mind. This gradually morphed into a determination to put a teaching order at the disposal of the pope; to create schools, colleges, and seminaries for boys; to develop specialist pastoral care; and to engage in mission "throughout the various parts of the world." A truly romantic story, yet one wedded to the most intense discipline.

Left: Ignatius Loyola founded the Jesuits (the Society of Jesus). He was elected General Superior of the society and served in that post until his death in 1556. He was canonized in 1622.

For two decades after 1517 Loyola, a late starter academically, toiled at acquiring a scholastic education, all the while gathering around himself like-minded friends. He drew on his own spiritual experiences, later formalized in the *Spiritual Exercises,* to advise them. The book featured meditations, prayers, and various mental exercises. At this time of global expansion the *Exercises* took the individual on an imaginary journey through time, back to the Fall of Adam and through to the consummation of all things. This Biblical pilgrimage, which involved all the senses, was accompanied by the most searching inner scrutiny. Those taking the *Exercises* were guided to see their own lives in the context of eternity and of the ongoing cosmic struggle between good and evil. The honor of God and the salvation of souls ceased to be abstract goals but were integrated into one's own life. Reason and imagination were deployed to free the will from "inordinate affections." The members of the new order, which finally obtained papal approval in 1540, were thus superbly equipped to be sent anywhere, on missions abroad, to schools, prisons, and to counsel the highest princes in the land. Freedom from the traditional liturgical obligations of the monastic orders meant, too, that they were unusually flexible. "The world is our house," as one of their early leaders, Jeronimo Nadal, put it.

Like the Capuchins, the number of Jesuits grew with remarkable speed. With their superior education they were at the forefront of the polemical engagement with the Protestants (and often urged the burning of suspect books), but their chief concern was positive: "To help souls;" to offer consolation to the faithful; and to build up the Catholic Church.

The privileges the Jesuits gained from the pope grated with other orders and some of the secular clergy, leading at times to denunciations and prohibitions, not least in France, but their cheerfulness, refinement, and graciousness appear to have been the qualities which stood out in most people's minds. Though only a minority were priests, preaching, teaching, and taking confessions were areas where they developed particular skills and sensitivities. They combined scholastic orthodoxy with the appeal of humanistic rhetoric, always with the aim of touching people's hearts. This was most evident in the hundreds of educational institutions, universities, seminaries, and schools they founded. They were the first religious order to make systematic provision of schools for any student who wished to make use of them. The influence the schools gave them on key groups in the wider society does much to explain the success of the Catholic reformation as a whole.

Below: The Capuchins sought a primitive way of life. They followed the Gospel and the spirit of St Francis (pictured), and took a vow of poverty, chastity, and obedience.

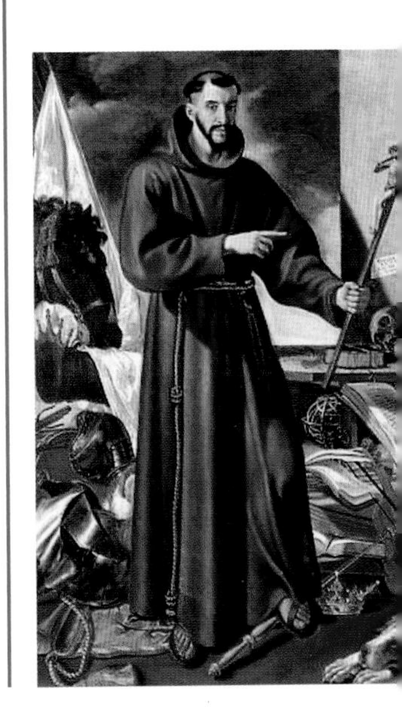

WOMEN'S VOICES

Only in recent decades has attention been given to the role of women in the reformations—how they contributed and how they, in turn, were affected by them. Many reference books still make no mention of 50 percent of the human race at this time. The balance, however, is beginning to be redressed, as today many historians are women, and there is a growing appreciation of gender issues.

A reformation for women?

How much the religious turmoil changed matters for women remains, however, a matter for debate. On the down side, the virtual abolition of nunneries in Protestant lands removed one area in which women had enjoyed a degree of autonomy and leadership; rigorist reformers within Catholicism also sought to limit the social and cultural outreach of women in religious orders into wider society, though recent research shows that the latter often resisted such controls. One should remember, too, the prominent role of women saints, not to mention the Virgin Mary, in late medieval piety. Again, in Protestant areas this modeling of feminine attitudes and virtues disappeared. The patriarchal squeeze on women's commercial and entrepreneurial activities was, quite simply, socially motivated. Highly contentious, however, is the effect of the religious controversies on the witch hunts, which were 90 percent

Above: The Virgin Mary was celebrated in medieval times and during the Renaissance, when women were taught to pray to the Holy Mother. This changed during the Reformation.

Right: *Punishing the Witch* by George H. Walker. The Reformation led to the persecution of women whom the Church deemed as "witches." The women were accused of having supernatural abilites and participating in Satanic rituals.

directed against women, and reached their height toward the end of the sixteenth century. Where the so-called witches were seen as engaging in a pact with the devil, and not just committing maleficent acts, the connection with theological anxieties about heresy is clearly evident.

On the plus side, humanism's emphasis on education undoubtedly provided both the rationale and opportunities for some women to read, write, learn, and teach—from Sir Thomas More's daughters to independent thinkers such as the Italian noblewoman Giulia Gonzaga. Printing also opened up access to new ideas to women. Elizabeth I of England is typical of many highly educated monarchs, but pauper women in Tours, France, were also quite able to argue their case and beliefs and could rely on strong female networks across the city.

Women theologians

Of special interest are the women, both Catholic and Protestant, who specifically used Biblical or theological arguments to bolster their opinions and push the boundaries limiting women to home and family. The mystical tradition, not least in Spain and Italy, had always encouraged the awareness that God could give special insight or revelations to those, such as women, whom society had marginalized. Teresa of Ávila (1515–1582) combined brilliant gifts of leadership and plenty of good common sense with the profoundest insights into the religious life and, like so many other women, had fine skills as a letter writer.

Then there is the noblewoman with the unusual name: Argula von Grumbach (1492–1556/7), who challenged, head on, the proud theologians of Ingolstadt University, the Catholic clergy, her Bavarian princes, and even her own husband, all in the name of Christian liberty. "I have always wanted to find out the truth," she said. She was the first Protestant woman writer whose publications became bestsellers. Within a year her first writing ran into 15 editions. All in all she wrote eight pamphlets, including a poem, reminding her readers of prophetic women in the Bible like Deborah, and arguing that all Christians, like the women around Jesus, had a duty to speak their mind: "I cannot and I will not cease/To speak at home and in the street."

Katharine Zell, wife of a Strasbourg pastor, was a true "mother of Israel," famous for her hospitality and care for the poor. But she also produced an impressive corpus of writings, based on scripture. In Geneva, the publications by Marie Dentière defended not only her Protestant beliefs, but also the right of women to teach and preach, with which, of course, the Calvinist preachers disagreed.

Far left: Giulia Gonzaga formed friendships with the humanists Juan de Valdés and Pietro Carnesecchi, who were at the forefront of the movement for Catholic reform in response to the Lutheran challenge.

Left: Teresa of Ávila founded many convents during her lifetime. She also wrote a number of works which represent important benchmarks in the history of Christian mysticism.

THE MARTYRS

It had always been the mother who imparted the first prayers or Biblical stories to young children, who arranged for their early schooling, and taught them the Christian way. Among the nobility, too, women had tended to be more literate and numerate than their men. During the Reformation there were many continuities here with the medieval period. What was new, among many of the largely lower-class Anabaptist women, was a heroic willingness to go to a martyr's death, like Soetken van den Houte, beheaded in Ghent in 1560, sadly farewelling her children but confident of the blessedness of her suffering. Such actions spoke volumes, and were remembered in hymns and accounts of their martyrdoms. The role of most women during this period, whether Catholic or Protestant, may still have been nurturing the faith in the family, but the challenge of some to traditional secular and religious restrictions crops up in many chronicles and anthologies.

Above: The historic town of Ghent in Belgium named its guilds after various saints. The important economic and social role the guilds played in society was to decline during the sixteenth century.

CHAPTER THREE

CHRISTIANS BEYOND WESTERN EUROPE

Even as Western European Christianity was fracturing into antagonistic factions, it began its first global expansion. Spanish and Portuguese explorers claimed territories in the Americas, the west coast of Africa, India, and the Far East. There they planted the Catholic form of Christianity found in their homelands through missionaries. It would be several centuries before the newborn Protestant churches would engage in a comparable global expansion.

Events in Europe shaped the Christianity that conquistadors, merchants, settlers, and missionaries carried with them to their distant destinations. The Iberian Peninsula emerged from the last vestiges of Muslim rule in the same year that Christopher Columbus made landfall in the Bahamas. It was also in 1492 that the Catholic monarchs of Spain issued the Alhambra Decree, which expelled Jews from the Kingdom of Spain and all its territories. Those who wished to remain were forced to convert to Christianity; even then, they were constantly under suspicion of falling back into their prior beliefs. The Spanish Inquisition functioned primarily to ensure Catholic orthodoxy among these recent converts. The Portuguese Inquisition functioned likewise. Spain and Portugal established the Inquisition in their new territories with the purpose of ensuring that there should be no backsliding among the newly baptized there; that is, among Native American converts.

In India, Portuguese explorers discovered already-existing Christian communities. These native Christians were not Roman Catholics like the Portuguese, but were associated with the Church of the East. Tensions between the two different forms of Christianity led to divisions among Indian Christians throughout the second half of the sixteenth century.

The Ottoman Empire reached its greatest extension in the sixteenth century, bringing Christian communities in southeastern Europe, the Middle East, Egypt, and western North Africa under its rule. The Ottomans followed the example of prior Muslim empires by giving its Christian subjects the status of *dhimmis*. They also established a new system that made religious communities like Christians and Jews semi-autonomous, known as the Millet system.

To the north of the Ottoman Empire, Russia remained independent. In the sixteenth century, the Russian Orthodox Church received its first patriarch and Moscow became an orthodox patriarchate.

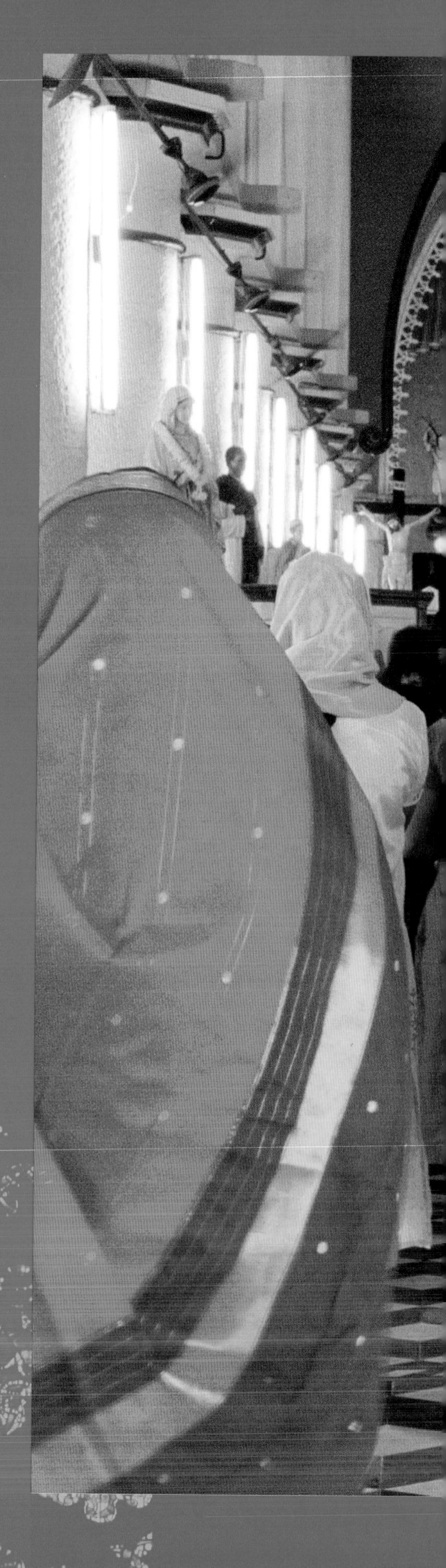

Right: Christianity is the third largest religion in India, with followers scattered throughout the country. It is believed St Thomas introduced Christianity to India when he arrived in Kerala in 52 CE.

SPANISH MISSIONS

Right: Granada Cathedral is a grand example of Spanish Renaissance architecture, complete with Gothic and Baroque influences. It houses the tombs of Ferdinand and Isabella, and took 180 years to build.

From about 790 to 1300, a period known as the *Reconquesta* or Reconquest, several Christian kingdoms on the Iberian Peninsula waged campaigns to retake the peninsula from the Muslims. After completing the *Reconquista* by defeating the last Moorish stronghold in Granada, Spain emerged as a unified kingdom with all the trappings of Roman law and a centralized government controlled by the monarchy in the later part of the fifteenth century. The "discovery" of America in 1492 by the explorer Christopher Columbus was, in reality, an event of conquest of the lands inhabited by the "Indians." Columbus believed that he had reached the Indies, whose inhabitants he called "Indians," but, in fact, he had reached the Caribbean. Placing crosses as a sign that the newly discovered territories belonged to the Spanish monarchs and to the Catholic Church, Columbus substituted the names of the islands for Christian names as a symbol of their baptism into Christianity. The Spanish monarchs instructed Columbus and his subjects to evangelize the natives, even by violent means.

Slavery, the *encomienda* system, and evangelization

The first phase of the evangelization and colonization of the New World centered on the Caribbean: Hispaniola, Puerto Rico, and Cuba in particular. In the second voyage, Columbus brought with him the first group of evangelists. Friar Bernal Boyl was appointed as apostolic vicar of the newly discovered territories. The first Mass celebrated was in November 1493 in the newly founded town of La Isabela in Hispaniola. Puerto Rico was colonized by Juan Ponce de León in 1508 and its first diocese was established on August 8, 1511, under Bishop Alonso Manso. The first cathedral was built in the initial capital Caparra, with the diocese consisting of two parishes in San Juan and San Germán. Christianity arrived in Cuba with the second voyage; however, it was not until 1522 that the bishopric of Baracoa was established there.

Below: Friars accompanied Christopher Columbus on his second voyage to the "Indies." Spanish artist Dioscoro de la Puebla depicts Columbus as the great colonizer and evangelist.

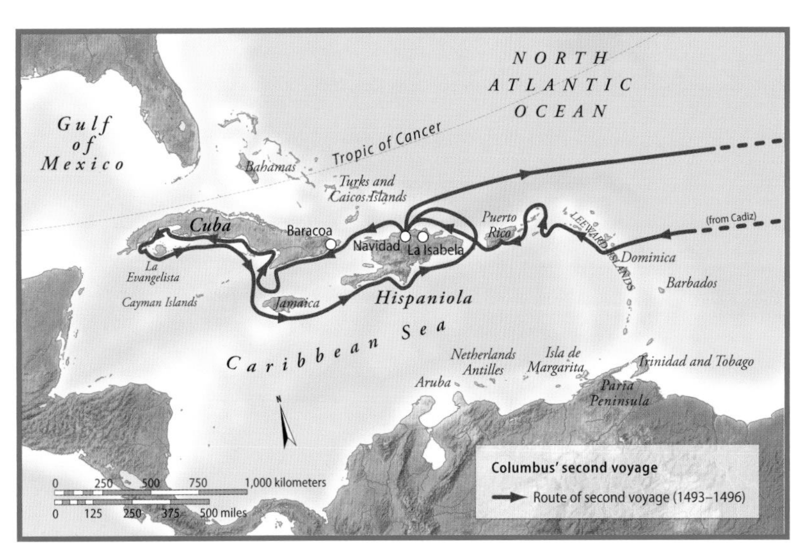

In 1503, Queen Isabella legitimized the *encomienda* system, under which a group of Indians was entrusted to Spanish colonists for instruction in the Christian faith in exchange for their services. The *encomiendas* became a form of legal slavery in which the natives were exploited, abused, and tormented by those who were supposed to be their teachers and mentors. The decimation of the Indian population posed the ethical question of how evangelization should be implemented across the New World. It was not until early in the eighteenth century that the *encomienda* system was legally abolished.

Prophetic voices of compassion

The first group of Dominican friars arrived on the island of Hispaniola in 1510. After witnessing the decimation of the natives, the Dominicans expressed their horror and astonishment, and denounced the abuses by the conquistadors. Headed by their superior, Pedro de Córdoba, they wrote a passionate sermon which was delivered to the colonists during the Advent of 1511 that would inaugurate the ethical controversy over evangelization. In that now famous sermon of 1511, the friar Antonio de Montesinos fervently preached to a large gathering of stunned colonists. "You are all in mortal sin!" he declared, "You live in it and you die with it! Why? Because of the cruelty and tyranny you use with these innocent people."

CHRISTIAN CHURCH AND SPANISH MONARCHY IN THE NEW WORLD

One constant in the whole process of colonization was how the Church and the monarchy acted as an indissoluble entity. In theory, the main purpose for taking possession of the newly discovered lands was the evangelization of the natives, but in practice the expansion and enrichment of the crown of Spain became the norm. The unequal encounter of cultures was won by the sword of the conquistador, but the cross of Christ was never absent from the New World. The irony of Catholic mission in the Age of Discovery under royal patronage and Christendom was that, despite the violence of the colonization, there were committed religious figures who dedicated their lives to the cause of the Indians, while the Indians received that message and made it their own.

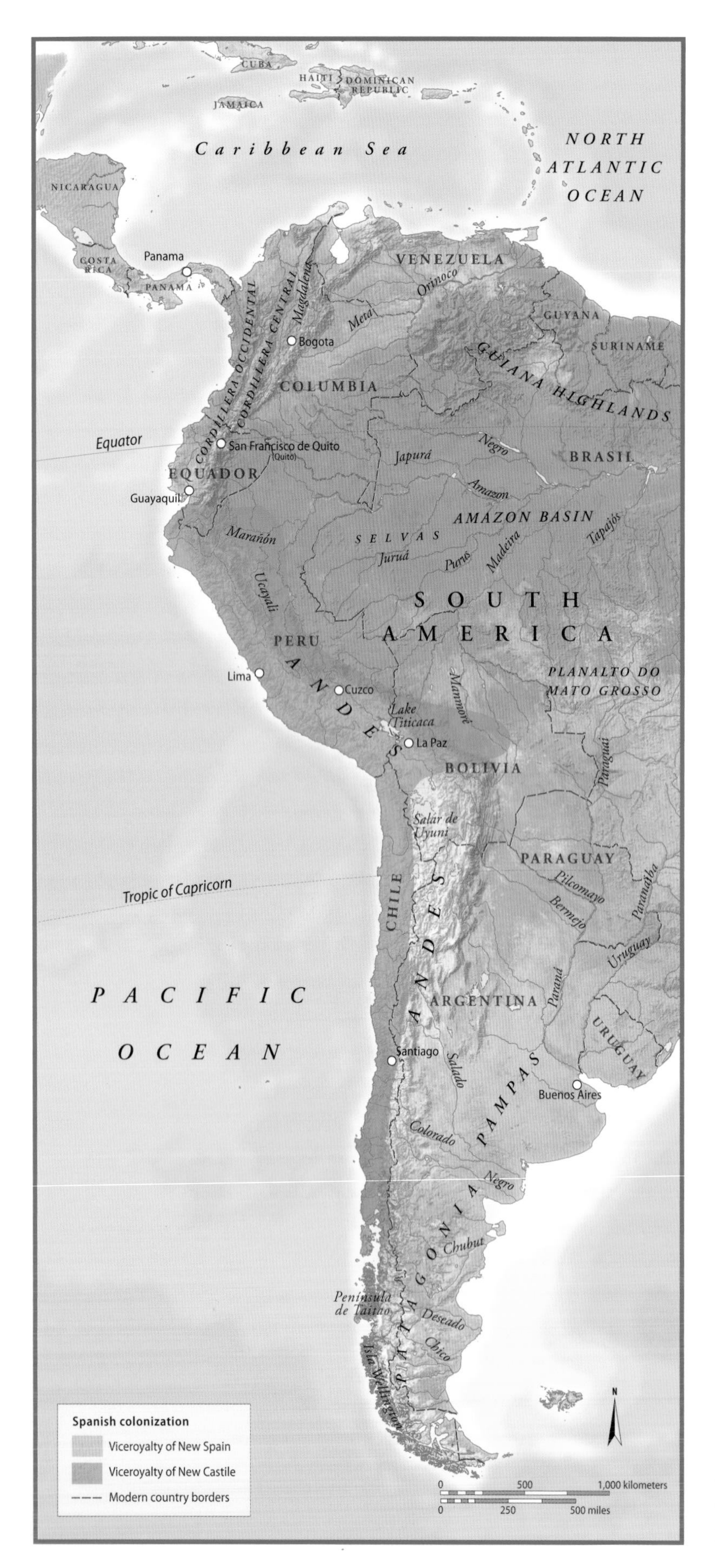

Central to the argument put forward by the Dominicans was the humanity of the Indians. If the conquistadors acknowledged the Indians as human beings, then they had to acknowledge that they were equals in the eyes of God. The conquistadors vehemently opposed the sermon, insisting that it was contrary to the papal edict (*Inter Caetera* of 1493) that granted the newly discovered lands to the monarchs of Spain. The crown responded by decreeing the *Capitulations of Burgos*, the first document with specific norms on how the Church should be established in the New World. Another fruit of Montesinos' sermon was that it touched the life of a young *encomendero* by the name of Bartolomé de las Casas, who later in his life decided to free his Indian slaves and join the Dominicans. De las Casas dedicated the rest of his life to the cause of the Indians who were fighting the *encomienda* system.

Colonization and evangelization from the Caribbean to South America

After Hernán Cortés defeated the army of Montezuma and conquered Tenochtitlán in 1519, he requested Franciscan friars to evangelize the Indian population. Cortés wanted to establish a new church in the New World. The evangelistic tactic of the Franciscans was to preach the Gospel to tribal

leaders while constantly denouncing the indigenous shrines as idolatrous. The Franciscans were especially committed to the evangelization of children since they believed that once children were converted to the Gospel, idolatry would stop. The first bishopric was established in Tlaxcala on October 11, 1525, with Juan Garcés as its first bishop, while the diocese of Mexico City was established in 1530 with Juan de Zumárraga as its first bishop.

In 1535, the Spanish explorer and conqueror Francisco Pizarro conquered Cuzco, capital of the Inca Empire in Peru. A Dominican priest, Vincente Valverde, and a "secular priest" (a priest who lives within a community), Juan de Sosa, accompanied Pizarro on this expedition. The diocese of Cuzco was established in 1537, with Vincente Valverde as its first bishop. The colonization process continued with Sebastián de Belalcázar, who established San Francisco de Quito in 1534. The first group of Franciscan missionaries arrived shortly after, followed by the Mercedarians in 1537, and the Dominicans in 1541. Under the command of Pedro de Mendoza, seventeen ships arrived in Buenos Aires in 1536. Accompanying de Mendoza were twelve "secular priests," four members of the order Hermits of St Jerome, and two Mercedarian friars who later came to be in charge of the evangelization of the natives.

Left: Francisco Pizarro defeated the Inca Empire and claimed most of South America for Spain. This opened the way for Spanish customs, language, and religion to dominate the continent.

Below: Machu Picchu in Peru was a ceremonial city for the Inca people. The Incas are thought to have abandoned the city after the conflict with Spain and the consequent smallpox epidemic the war brought.

PORTUGUESE MISSIONS

The realization that there was a vast world outside Europe came as quite a shock in the fifteenth century. Until then Europe had been cut off from the rest of the world, with Islam to the east and south and the Atlantic Ocean to the west. In the fifteenth and sixteenth centuries, as Portuguese sailors slowly worked their way down the African coast, around its southern tip, over to India, and even to Japan and China, they established trading posts. Small colonies followed, then missionaries, churches, and clergy.

Medieval missions

What was distinctive about medieval missions? The word "mission" was actually a new word in the fifteenth century. It meant that the Church saw the whole world as its parish and divided that world up into zones and sent representatives called delegates or "missionaries." They were tied to the Church in Europe, derived their authority from it, and were granted salvation on its behalf. Although there were bishops and even archbishops in the colonies, most missionary work was carried out by religious orders, such as the Franciscans, Dominicans, and Augustinians but above all by the Jesuits. Further, the Portuguese king was the "patron" of both the colony and missionary work. That meant that the king endorsed papal decrees and approved bishops before they went to the colonies. Finally, Roman Catholic theology relied upon the tradition of natural theology, which argued that some knowledge of God may be derived from the natural world and human reason apart from divine revelation. This meant that native beliefs may lead one partly to God, but Christianity provided the missing step of revealed theology. Conversion involved not so much a change of heart as a process of catechism and baptism, which was regarded as the mark that conversion was complete.

The Portuguese had been energetic in the fifteenth and early sixteenth centuries, especially after the two papal bulls—the *Inter Ceterae Divinae* of 1493 and the *Romanus Pontifex* of 1555—gave the Portuguese crown sole control over its colonies, along with the right to propagate the faith, combat Muslims, and enslave the local populations.

India and the East

After slowly introducing Christianity in many places along the African west coast such as Mauritania, Portuguese Guinea, Guinea-Bissau, Benin, Gambia, Senegal, Angola, and the Congo, the largest Portuguese center was in Goa, India. By 1557, Goa had its own archbishop, who is still known as the Patriarch of the East Indies and Primate of the East. Initially, the Portuguese did not enforce conversion or undertake mass baptisms; nor did they bother with

Below: The Church of the Immaculate Conception in Goa, India, was built in 1541. It is an amalgamation of Indian architecture and the Portuguese Baroque style. It has the second largest church bell in the world.

missionary work in inland areas. This task fell to the Jesuits, who arrived in 1542 under the leadership of Francis Xavier. Given a commission by the pope to evangelize the East, Xavier made Goa his headquarters and traveled to Travancore, the Moluccas, Sri Lanka, and Japan; he would have landed in China had he not died on his way in 1552. Making use of whatever means were available to him—preaching, use of government forces in Goa, the Portuguese Inquisition based in Goa, and persecution of competitors—Xavier established churches wherever he went. The paradox of the Church in India is that the arrival of the Portuguese and the work of Francis Xavier actually fragmented the existing Thomas or Malabar Christians.

Above: The Portuguese explorer Pedro Álvares Cabral is credited with discovering Brazil. On April 23, 1500, he landed on the coast at Port Seguro and treated the natives kindly by letting them board his caravel.

Brazil

In 1500, Pedro Álvares Cabral landed on the coast of what is now Brazil. He was supposed to be on his way to India with a large fleet, but the recent Treaty of Tordesillas of 1494 had allocated the Americas to Spain. Cabral's discovery led to a speedy claim of territory by Portugal and recognition by the pope. Cabral's mission on this voyage, given to him by King Manuel I, included conversion of those he encountered, by force of arms if necessary. The first Portuguese colonies were limited to the coastal strip, exploiting at first Brazilwood and its red dye, then sugar on vast plantations with slaves, and gold.

After a failed effort to colonize the interior by means of private, hereditary "captains," the colonial government was established by Tomé de Sousa in 1549. He also brought a group of Jesuits, who were the major source of missionary work and established what became São Paulo. Since they held to the tenets of natural theology, they worked hard at trying to understand the natives, learnt their languages, built churches and schools, and tried to limit the enslavement of the indigenous population. Instead, they supported African slavery. The Jesuits gathered people into communities or "reductions," putting them to work and converting them. The effect was controversial, since the European models disrupted the patterns of native life and hastened the breakdown of their social order.

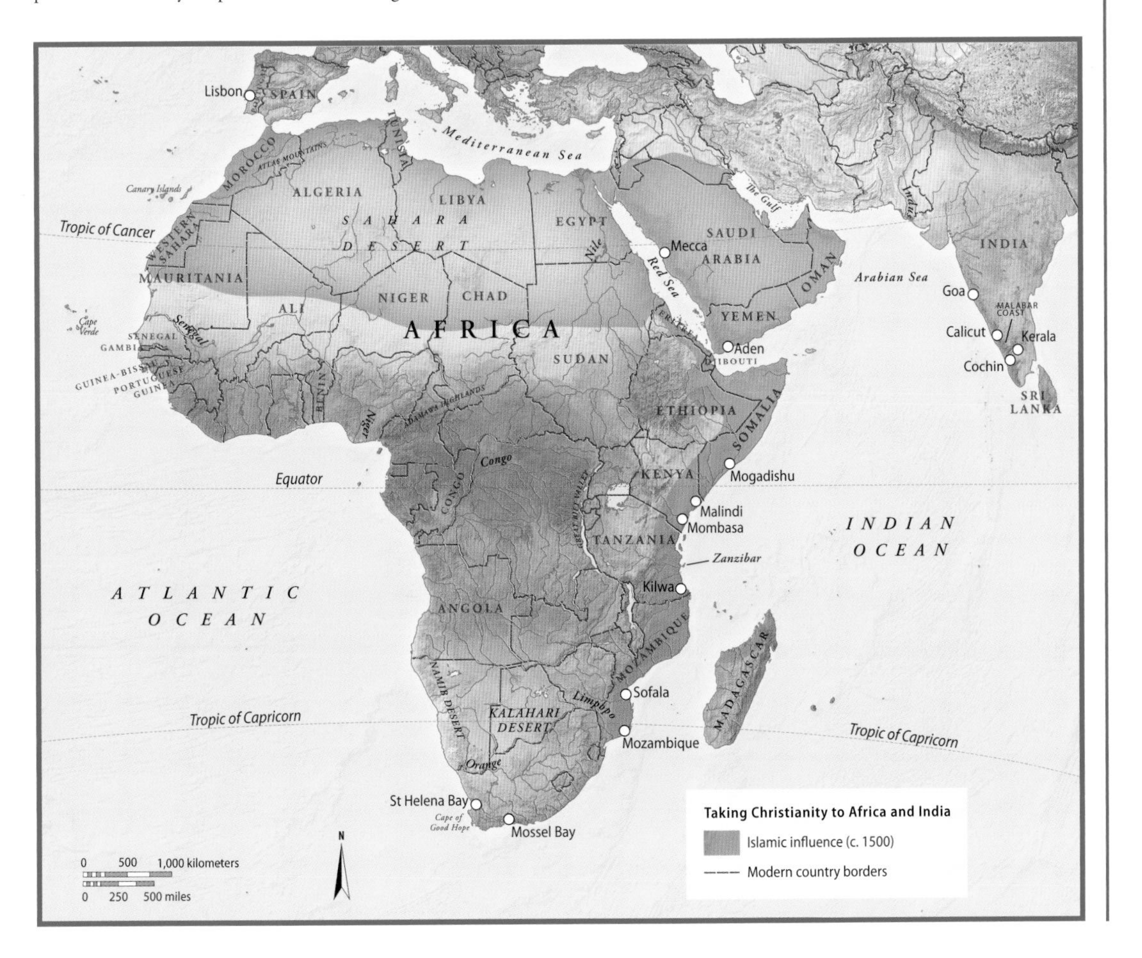

THE THOMAS CHRISTIANS OF INDIA

Above: In prayer, Thomas Christians see the Virgin Mary as the "mother of Christ;" not the "mother of God."

Opposite: St Thomas was the only apostle to travel outside the Roman Empire to preach the Gospel. He arrived in India in 52 CE and established seven churches in Kerala.

Below: Thomas Christians have existed on the southwestern coast of India, in the state of Kerala, since ancient times. They were in full communion with the Church of the East.

When the Portuguese arrived in Goa on the Indian west coast in the early sixteenth century, they found to their surprise that Christians were already there, especially in Kerala in southwestern India. The Thomas or Malabar Christians had been in India for over a thousand years.

Followers of St Thomas

The earliest evidence of Christianity in India comes from an Alexandrian merchant called Cosmas Indicopleustes or "Cosmas, the Indian Navigator." His 12-volume work from c. 547, *Christian Topography*, mentions the existence of Christianity in India. However, branches of Thomas Christians claim that Christianity had arrived in the first century with St Thomas the Apostle, who was then martyred near Madras. Evidence points to close connections and perhaps an origin in Syria (where Christianity was established from a very early date), because the Thomas Christians use Syriac as their language in worship and they follow variations on the Syrian rite. Further, their deacons and bishops used to be appointed by the patriarch of the Church of the East in Baghdad.

Here come the Europeans

When the Portuguese captured Goa in 1510 they also brought dissension among the Thomas Christians. The initial friendly approach of the Portuguese to the "Syrians" was not to last. The Jesuit Francis Xavier, who arrived in 1542, used what forces he could—the Portuguese governor, military troops, and the Inquisition—to counter the Thomas Christians and their connection with the Church of the East. The problem with the Church of the East, at least for Roman Catholics, is that it follows ancient theological traditions from Antioch, especially the thought of Theodore of Mopsuestia (who was posthumously associated with Nestorianism). Their differences relate to the nature of Christ within the Trinity and they disagree with some formulations accepted in Rome and the West. They also explicitly reject the doctrine that Mary is the "mother of God" and other decisions of the Council of Ephesus in 431. Above all, the Church of the East and therefore the Thomas Christians were not Catholic in either theology or practice, so Francis Xavier saw them as a threat.

Xavier was keen, with the help of the governor, to bring them over to control by Rome. Eventually some of them gave in, agreeing to give up their connections with the Church of the East and submit to Rome. All this took place in 1599, many years after the death of Xavier, at the Synod of Diamper (now Udiyamperūr), under direction by the archbishop of Goa. The new Church was called the Malabar Uniate Church, and it was heavily Westernized in theology and Church governance, although it was allowed to keep the ancient Syrian liturgy.

Disagreement and schism

Not everyone was happy. Some had not joined the new movement and had kept up their theological traditions and connections. The Portuguese governor tried to enforce the new agreement, and ruffled many feathers. By 1653, a large number had broken with Rome and latched onto the Syrian Orthodox Church, based originally in Antioch (but now in Damascus). Their theology is distinctly Miaphysite/Monophysite—they hold that Christ has one nature and not two, as is customary in Rome and among many Orthodox churches. Although some were brought back to Roman Catholic control by 1662, the Syrian group continued. The Portuguese still tried to interfere, blocking the appointment of bishops, but the Church persisted. Today the Thomas Christians form one of the largest branches of the Syrian Orthodox tradition. Over the following centuries there were more disagreements and splits, as is the way with Christian churches. So now there are groups who acknowledge the pope; others the Syrian Orthodox Church; others who have close links with the Church of England; and others who are independent. But they all recognize their common ancestry. They have also spread significantly through strong missionary activity.

Worship

What would a worship service be like? Still used is the liturgy or *Qurbana* of Addai and Mari (disciples of St Thomas who are traditionally attributed with founding Christianity in modern-day Iraq). One of the most ancient Christian liturgies in the world, it dates back at least to the third century and probably comes from Edessa, an ancient city in northwestern Mesopotamia. The most distinctive feature is the Anaphora, or prayer recited before Holy Communion, which addresses Christ directly rather than God the Father. During the Anaphora, Ghanatha (from *ghan*, meaning "bow"), or prayers of praise, are recited by the priest in a low voice. Hymns by the ancient St Ephrem are usually sung during the Communion. And a piece of dough from the bread is saved week-by-week in order to leaven the Eucharistic bread for the following week.

CHRISTIANS UNDER OTTOMAN RULE

Above: Egypt has seen many influences from different ruling empires—Abassid, Fatimid, Mamluk, and Ottoman. The Ibn Tulun Mosque was built during the Abassid Empire, but underwent extensive restorations during the Ottoman Empire.

On May 29, 1453, the Byzantine city of Constantinople fell under the leadership of the Ottoman ruler Mehmet the Conqueror. The Ottomans, whose empire is dated from 1299, continued to rule over much of the Middle East, Balkans, and North Africa until 1922, when the empire finally collapsed. The sixteenth century marked the expansion of the empire. Various Christian communities resided in its territories; some, like the Coptic Orthodox Church of Egypt, were already familiar with Islamic rule, having been previously ruled by a succession of Muslim dynasties. In contrast, new Christian communities who had been under Byzantium Christian rule were brought under Ottoman tutelage during the reign of Suleyman the Magnificent (1520–1566). The status of Ottoman Christians changed considerably over time, and particular treatment varied according to shifting situations in the Ottoman state. Overall, however, the relationship between the Islamic Ottoman Empire and Christians was largely secured by an Islamic legal framework which governed relations between Muslims, Christians, and Jews.

Religious and legal status under Islam

After the conquest of the Balkans, the Ottomans were faced with the challenge of having to rule over a territory which was largely Christian. The status of Christians in the Ottoman Empire was grounded in legal and religious traditions regarding religious minorities that had been practiced and inherited from early Islamic law. Islamic law was particularly keen to impart a special status on those who practiced monotheistic, confessional faiths—most particularly on the Jews and Christians. As so-called *Ahl al-Kitab* or "People of the Book," tolerance was encouraged toward Christians and Jews as inheritors of the Abrahamic faith. This semi-legal framework had its roots in early Islam when the prophet Muhammad made a treaty with the Christians of Najran in the seventh century after they promised to aid him. Under Islamic rule, Christians were obliged to pay the *jizya* tax—a poll tax for the maintenance of their integrity as a community. There were also some restrictions placed on gaining property and on Christians in lawsuits.

In the case of the Balkans, as well as in relation to other Christian communities living under Ottoman control, an

CHRISTIANS AND OTTOMANS IN THE NINETEENTH CENTURY: HATT-I HÜMAYUN

The Hatt-ı Hümayun, also known as the Imperial Edict, was implemented by Sultan Abdulmajid on February 18, 1856, as part of a series of reforms in the Ottoman Empire known as the "Tanzimat." One aspect of the Hümayun decree was directed toward religious practice: It granted and guaranteed freedom of religious worship. The Hümayun decree also held patriarchs and archbishops accountable to their communities by making them swear an oath upon entry into office. The decree also guaranteed the full right of Christians living in the Ottoman Empire to repair buildings of worship.

existing Islamic administrative practice was put into place: The Millet system. Although not formally recognized until the nineteenth century, the Millet system granted semi-autonomy to the respective Christian communities to be led through the Orthodox Patriarch. His role would be to secure all matters of personal law such as marriage, divorce, and inheritance within the confines of Christian doctrine. Similarly, the Patriarch was also responsible for the collection of taxation, including any *jizya* that was due. More importantly, the informal adoption of the Millet system had a fundamental impact on the power and authority of the patriarchate. The empowerment of the Patriarch of Constantinople, who had previously been "the first among equals," effectively sanctioned him as pope, arbiter, and power broker. Thus, the Church was reorientated from a previously decentralized religious organization into an administrative successor to the Byzantium state.

The army and expansion

Anatolia, also known as Asia Minor, remained an insecure territory for the Ottoman Empire as late as the fifteenth century. The unique experience with the Christian minority in the region resulted in the adoption of Christian elites and military men into the army as part of the expansionist doctrine of the empire. This served the purpose of a conciliatory policy toward Christians, making the conquest of new Christian territories easier. The positive attitude of the Ottomans toward Christians was also fuelled by a desire to create a dynastic power through the prestige of the Janissary Corps—an infantry unit which captured young Christian boys and shaped them into Ottoman elite soldiers. The Janissaries were paid soldiers in uniform who were an integral part of the empire until the corps was dissolved in 1826. While the recruitment of the Janissaries was a violation of Christian rights under Islamic law, it also provides evidence of the political pragmatism of the Ottomans.

Above: Mehmet the Conqueror was the seventh sultan of the Ottoman Empire. He is best known for conquering Constantinople and rebuilding it into a prosperous Ottoman capital, called Istanbul.

Above left: This Turkish manuscript features Suleyman the Magnificent, tenth sultan of the Ottoman Empire. Suleyman conquered the Christian strongholds of Hungary, Rhodes, and Belgrade and doubled the empire during his 46-year reign.

MOSCOW'S ORTHODOX PATRIARCHATE

Previous pages: Moscow's St Basil's Cathedral was commissioned by Ivan the Terrible. Its eight domed towers were built around a ninth spire, forming an eight-point star that symbolizes the Christian Church as a guiding light to humankind.

Anyone who has spent some time in Russia soon realizes that the unique and independent history of the country is a source of pride for its people. The same applies to the Russian Orthodox Church, although the final step in its independence took 600 years to achieve. In 988 Prince Vladimir I was baptized as a Christian and in 1589 the first independent Patriarch of Moscow, Job (or Jove), was appointed.

Path to independence

In between those two dates is a tumultuous history in which the Russian Church stepped ever closer to its prized independence. The first small step was the use of the local vernacular in worship services rather than Greek. This meant that there were less and less imported Greek-speaking priests who had to learn the language and an increasing number of local priests. The next great step was the Russian decision to support the Eastern Orthodox churches in the growing split with Rome. That took place during the so-called Great Schism of 1054 when Western and Eastern churches realized they could no longer see eye-to-eye and went their separate ways. However, this moment was the culmination of many frictions between them.

Almost 400 years later, a group of demoralized and desperate Eastern Orthodox leaders, under siege from the Turks and decimated from the wars, agreed to submit to Rome. It took place at the Council of Ferrara–Florence in 1438–1439 after the pope had offered the Eastern Church a stark choice: Submit (and gain help in the wars) or go under (it was to no avail, for Constantinople fell 14 years later). The Russians would have nothing to do with the agreement at Florence, rejecting the terms of the union. In response, the Patriarch of Constantinople deposed the metropolitan of Moscow, Isidore (called "the apostate"). A few years later, in 1448, the Russian bishops gathered in a council and elected their own metropolitan—Jonas—without reference to Greek authorities. The path to independence had become stronger. Moscow had become what is technically called autocephalous—with its own head.

A patriarch of their own

A century later the last step to independence was achieved. It happened through the famous Council of a Hundred Chapters, which gathered in 1551 to reform the clergy of the Russian Church. Their most important act was to create their own patriarchate, yet they were astute enough

Below: Eastern Orthodox churches vary in shape and complexity. The building itself is a symbol of the universe, the dome representing the open heavens. Its square or oblong base stands for the earth below.

Left: The Council of Ferrara-Florence met in 1438–1439 to negotiate Catholic reunification with several Eastern churches. All bar the Russian Church reached an agreement on papal primacy, pergatory, and the *filioque* (and the Son) clause of the Nicene Creed.

Above: Boris Godunov was the first elected Tsar of Russia. He conducted successful military campaigns, built numerous defensive towns and fortresses, promoted foreign trade, and assisted the head of the Muscovite Church to become patriarch.

not to antagonize Constantinople, where the Church had survived the Turkish invasion. So Jeremias II of Constantinople was persuaded to establish the Patriarch of Moscow on January 26, 1589. Independence had been achieved, and with recognition from the other patriarchates. They remain in full communion to this day.

The astute Job

Who was this first patriarch? Job (or Jove) was his official name, although his original name before he took monastic vows was Ioann. He followed the usual path to higher offices through a monastic life, moving all the way from his local monastery (Staritsa) to become the first patriarch. On his rise to the top, he passed through positions as abbot of monasteries in Moscow, bishop of Kolomna, archbishop of Rostov, and metropolitan of Moscow and All Russia before the final step.

For all his piety, Job was known neither for his intellectual prowess nor indeed his ability to read. He did realize that friends in high places always help one's cause. One was none other than Ivan the Terrible, who had initially assisted his rise to the position of abbot in his first monastery back in his home town. Another useful friend was the future Tsar Feodor I, Prince Boris Godunov. In return for supporting Godunov's own aspirations to the crown, Godunov gave Job a helping hand in his own rise. It was Godunov himself who persuaded the Patriarch of Constantinople, Jeremias II, to establish a patriarchate in Moscow. Who else would be appointed but Job?

Now there was no stopping Job. In the 16 years left until his death he revised the liturgical books for worship, built a spate of new cathedrals and monasteries, sent missionaries to the newly conquered areas of Siberia and the Astrakhan Khanate (a Muslim state near the mouth of the Volga), ensured that Godunov became Tsar in 1584, and glorified a number of Russian saints, including the intriguing Basil Fool for Christ. He was not impressed with Godunov's efforts to establish a university in Moscow, fearing it would introduce non-orthodox and heretical teaching by foreign professors, but in this matter he did not prevail.

Left: Bogolyubovo Monastery was established at the palace of Andrey Bogolyubsky in the mid-twelfth century. In 1570, some monks were accused of supporting Vladimir Staritsa (heir to the throne) and were punished by Ivan the Terrible.

PART FIVE

NEW WORLDS
1601–1700 CE

SCIENTIFIC REVOLUTION

Above: In his work, Roger Bacon detailed his applications of astronomy, optics, alchemy, and mathematics. He was also the first European to describe how to make gunpowder, and proposed flying machines and motorized ships.

Right: The Copernican System of astronomy was the first European theory that placed the sun as motionless at the center of the solar system with all the planets revolving around it.

Previous pages: Known as the Apostle of the East, St Francis Xavier was a Spanish missionary who visited India, Malacca, the Banda Islands, the Moluccas, Ceylon, and Japan, to convert the native people to Christianity.

Seventeenth-century Europe, which was predominantly Christian, witnessed an explosion of interest in the natural world. For hundreds of years perceptions of the natural world had been influenced by the philosophies of the ancient world (particularly Greece) in which matter was often regarded as evil and the rationality of the universe was considered doubtful. Even Aristotle's theological assumptions were inimical to the emergence of aspects of modern science, though much of his ethical thinking remains valid today.

The emergence of science as we understand it today was not simply a consequence of a developed society and more leisure; certain theological assumptions about the world were a prerequisite. Better instrumentation was one reason for the emergence of science, but on a deeper level it was a new way of thinking about the world and nature, fostered by Christianity, that gave rise to what is now referred to as "the scientific revolution."

First thoughts

Christian interest in the study of nature dates back to the English philosopher Roger Bacon (c. 1214–c. 1292), a man of wide vision, regarded by some as the father of experimental science. Bacon entered the Franciscan order in the belief that he would be free to pursue his studies. However, his *Opus Maius* was reportedly condemned by the general of the order for "suspect novelties" and "dangerous doctrine," and any real achievement has been lost in his imaginary mechanical inventions and flirtation with astrology.

Long before the telescope was first invented in 1608, Nicolas Copernicus (1473–1543) of the University of Padua, a canon in the Roman Catholic Church, proposed the heliocentric theory—that the Earth moves around the sun—contradicting the Egyptian astronomer Ptolemy. Copernicus' theory aroused little interest from the Catholic Church for fifty years; the most scathing condemnations came from Protestants, in particular Martin Luther (1483–1546). Initially there was a comparatively mild reception of Copernicus' views by the Catholic Church, which regarded his system not as a description of reality but as a model that enabled a simpler method of calculating the motion of the heavenly bodies than the Ptolemaic system.

Another reason for the initial mild reception of Copernicus' theory was that Copernicus was not a great practical observer; much of the argument in favor of his theory turned on its economy and mathematical appeal. The question of the movement of the Earth reached the stage of genuine conflict only toward the end of the sixteenth century.

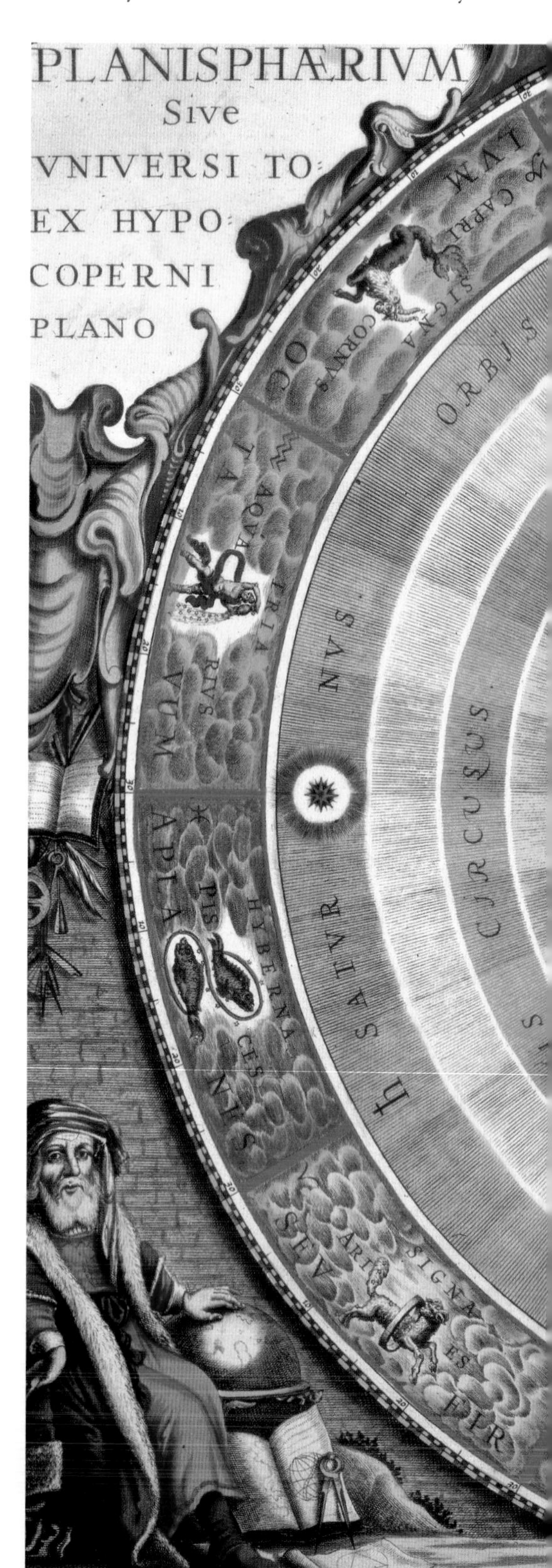

DIRTY WORK IN THE HEAVENS

The association between Johannes Kepler and Tycho Brahe was not a happy one: Although Brahe obstinately refused to share his observations, Kepler used many of them to construct his laws of planetary motion.

Recent forensic analysis, undertaken to determine the cause of Brahe's sudden death, found highly toxic levels of mercury in his hair and hair roots, and supports earlier suspicions that Brahe did not die a natural death. Circumstantial evidence gathered by the authors Joshua Gilder and Anne Lee Gilder in 2005 indicates that Kepler had the means, the motive, and the opportunity to murder Brahe, and they surmised that he probably did so in order to steal Brahe's celestial observations.

Beyond Bacon and Copernicus

At the dawn of the seventeenth century, on February 17, 1600, the Inquisition sentenced a Dominican priest, Giordano Bruno (1548–1600), to burning at the stake for heresy. Bruno was a disciple of Copernicus, and although his astronomical views had nothing do with his death sentence, they were seen to be the reason for his condemnation.

Johannes Kepler (1571–1630) studied theology at the University of Tübingen and became a Protestant minister. He attached himself to a flamboyant aristocrat, Tycho Brahe (1546–1601), who had spent forty years mapping the heavens with unprecedented accuracy but remained unconvinced of the Copernican hypothesis. By this time, resistance to the Copernican hypothesis was common to both Catholics and Protestants: In 1596, following the publication of his *Mysterium Cosmographicum*, Kepler was persecuted by the Protestant Faculty at Tübingen and so decided to take refuge with the Jesuits.

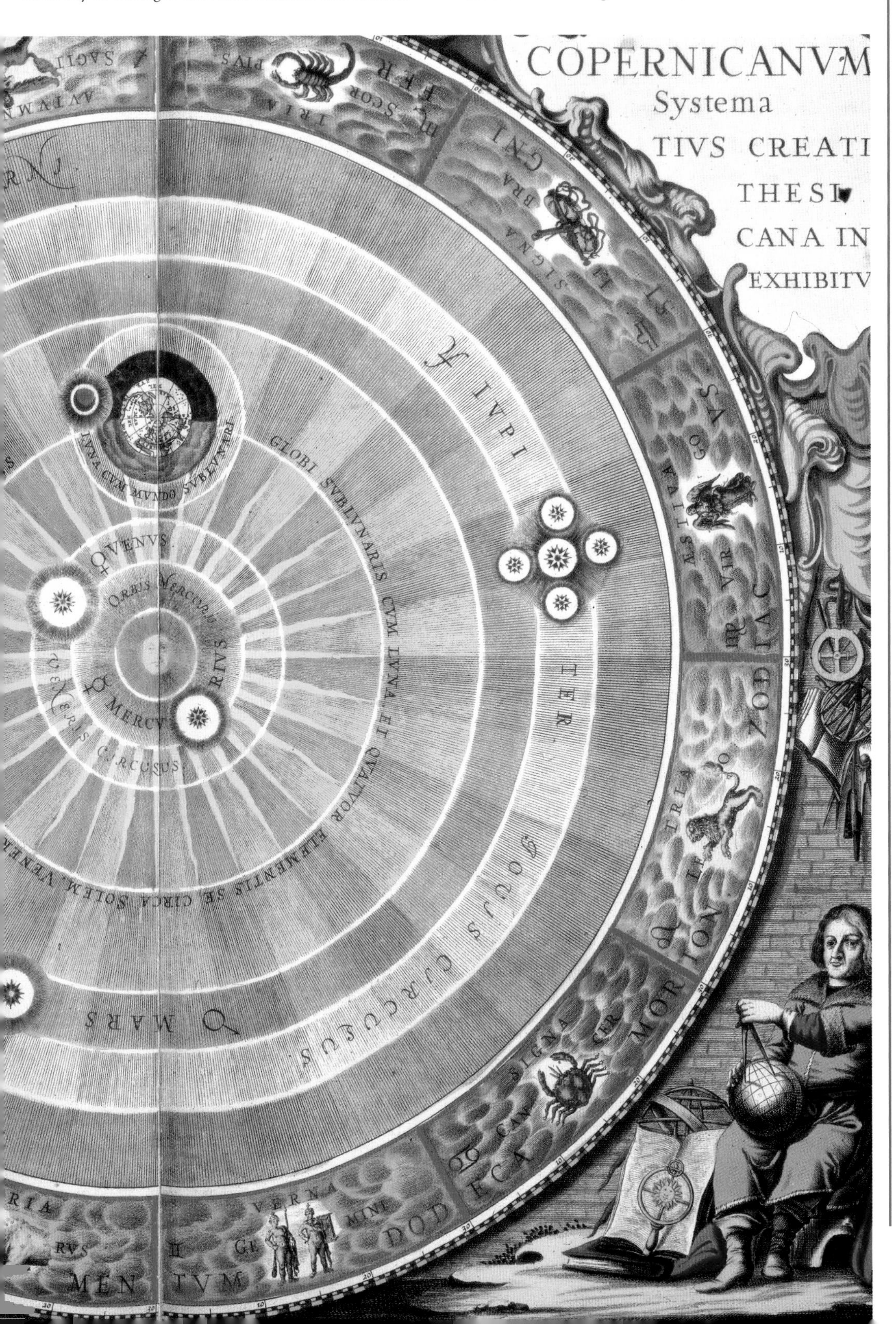

Above: Johannes Kepler was best known for his laws of planetary motion. Being a Lutheran, he incorporated religious zeal into all his work, and credited God for each discovery he made.

Above: Galileo Galilei devised the basic laws of falling bodies. He also constructed a telescope with which he studied lunar craters, and discovered the four moons revolving around Jupiter and the phases of Venus.

Theology and science

The Italian scientist Galileo Galilei (1564–1642) was a key figure in the scientific revolution of the seventeenth century. His work in physics, astronomy, and the methodology of science has earned him a well-deserved place in the annals of science. In theological circles he is also remembered for his clash with the Catholic Church over the interpretation of the Bible.

When Galileo and other astronomers of the time began to speculate about the universe—about its age, about whether it was eternal or had a beginning, about whether other universes existed, and about the place of Earth in the cosmos—some became concerned because many of these speculations seemed to conflict with scripture. It could have been said in reply that throughout the scriptures God had behaved in ways that defied human thinking, and science is a set of tools by which we manoeuvre in a world beyond our total comprehension.

An eventful life

After a brief period of study for the priesthood Galileo began a medical degree, but he did not complete it. He turned to mathematics and was appointed to the chair of mathematics at the University of Pisa and later to the chair at Padua. He accepted a non-teaching position of Mathematician and Philosopher to the Grand Duke of Tuscany, giving as his reasons for moving his heavy teaching load at Padua and his dislike of the wine in the region. Although he is popularly remembered as an astronomer, it was in the field of mechanics that Galileo made his greatest contribution to human knowledge.

Galilio never married, but he fathered two daughters and a son to Maria Gamba. Both his daughters, Virginia and Livia, entered a Franciscan convent near Florence at the tender ages of twelve and thirteen. Fortunately, we have 124 preserved letters from Virginia (Sister Maria Celeste of the Poor Clare Order) to her father up to the year 1633, the year of his infamous trial for heresy. Nowhere does she suggest that her father was a heretic, and she continued to support him and correspond with him until her death at the age of thirty-three.

Below: Galileo supported Copernicus' theory of planetary motion around the sun and was consequently convicted of heresy. He was sentenced to life imprisonment but, due to his age, was placed under house arrest.

Trial and recantation

The pope at the time, Urban VIII, was a friend of Galileo, and had even written a Latin ode celebrating Galileo's discovery of sunspots. However, in late 1632, after publishing *Dialogues on the Two Chief World Systems*, Galileo was ordered to Rome to be examined by the Holy Office of the Inquisition. This amounted to a charge of heresy, and he was called to repent. He was accused of teaching and defending the Copernican doctrine that holds that the sun is at the center of the universe and that the Earth moves around it. This doctrine had been declared heretical in 1616, and Copernicus' book had been placed on the Index of prohibited books. (Galileo's position was not helped by the fact that in *Dialogues on the Two Chief World Systems* he put in the mouth of a foolish character, Simplicius, an argument that the pope had once defended.)

The Inquisition argued that the Copernican doctrine was contrary to sacred scripture. For example, Psalms 93:1 and 96:10, and I Chronicles 16:30: "The world is firmly established, it shall never be moved;" Psalm 104:5: "[The Lord] set the earth on its foundations, so that it shall never be shaken;" Ecclesiastes 1:5: "The sun rises and the sun goes down, and hurries to the place where it rises."

Galileo was forced to recite and then sign the following formal abjuration:

> I have been judged vehemently suspect of heresy, that is, of having held and believed that the sun is in the center of the universe and immoveable, and that the earth is not at the center of same, and that it does move. Wishing however, to remove from the minds of your Eminences and all faithful Christians this vehement suspicion reasonably conceived against me, I abjure with a sincere heart and unfeigned faith, I curse and detest the said errors and heresies, and generally all and every error, heresy, and sect contrary to the Holy Catholic Church.

Galileo's imprisonment was commuted to house arrest, and in December 1633 he was allowed to retire to his villa outside Florence. During this time he completed *Discourses on the Two New Sciences.*

Galileo's defense

Galileo claimed that the doctrine of Copernicus was not at odds with scripture. In his *Letter to Castelli* he took a position reminiscent of Augustine's views on the interpretation of scripture: Not to take every passage literally, particularly when the scripture in question is a book of poetry and songs, rather than a book of instruction or history. The

Above: In 1592, Galileo became Professor of Mathematics at the University of Padua, where he remained until 1610. He mainly taught Euclid's geometry and astronomy to medical students.

S. ROBERTVS CARD. BELLARMIN
E SOC. IESV.

writers of scripture wrote from the perspective of the terrestrial world, and from that vantage point the sun does rise and set. While Galileo admitted that the Bible is, indeed, an inspired text, he held that two truths—Biblical and scientific—could not contradict each other. Consequently, if science achieved a true result then the Bible should be interpreted so as to accord with scientific truth.

Cardinal Robert Bellarmine, the most influential member of the Sacred College, and head of the Holy Office of the Inquisition, was willing to consider Galileo's position, provided that "a real proof be found that the sun is fixed and does not revolve round the earth, but the earth round the sun." Bellarmine conceded that "it would then be necessary, very carefully, to proceed to the explanation of the passages of scripture which appear to be contrary, and admit that we have misunderstood them rather than pronounce false what has been demonstrated." Bellarmine raised the very important question: What constitutes proof or demonstration of a scientific claim?—a question that is vigorously debated to this day.

A paradox

Ironically, Galileo had a better grasp of Biblical interpretation than did the Inquisition, while Cardinal Bellarmine had a better appreciation of what constitutes a scientific proof. Galileo thought he had the proof of the Earth's motion around the sun in his *On the Ebb and Flow of the Tides*, published in 1616, the year the Copernican theory was declared heretical, and later incorporated in his work *Dialogues on the Two Chief World Systems*. He argued that the motion of the Earth, diurnal and axial, was the cause of the tides. He was wrong, but even if he had been correct, the tidal argument does not deal directly with the annual motion of the Earth about the sun, nor with the central position of the sun.

SCIENTIFIC SOCIETIES

An important feature of the scientific revolution was the creation of scientific societies, in particular the Royal Society (founded 1645). We have a description of the Royal Society from a contemporary: "Our business was (precluding matters of theology and state affairs), to discourse and consider of philosophical enquiries, and such as related thereunto: as physics, anatomy, geometry, astronomy, navigation, statics, magnetics, chemics, mechanics, and natural experiments."

John Henry Newman (1801–1890), founder of the Oxford Movement, believed that these societies, because they specifically precluded all discussion of theology, ultimately had the effect of treating theological impli cations of scientific discoveries as irrelevant, and thus widened the gap between science and religion. In his Oxford University Sermon, *The Usurpations of Reason*, Newman warned that, "These bodies, many of them founded with no bad intention, have gradually led to an undue exaltation of reason."

Above: Isaac Newton is one of the greatest scientists of all time. He studied mathematics, physics, optics, chemistry, the early history of Western civilization, and theology, and formulated universal gravitation and the three laws of motion.

The clockwork universe

While some were studying the heavens, others were investigating terrestrial matters. William Harvey (1578–1657), famous for his work on the function of the heart, studied at the University of Padua, where both Copernicus and Galileo spent time. Just as the astronomers treated the heavens as a piece of delicate machinery, Harvey treated the human heart as "a piece of machinery in which though one wheel gives motion to another, yet all the wheels seem to move simultaneously." The mechanical picture of the human heart proposed by Harvey mirrored the clockwork picture of the heavens proposed by the astronomers.

Isaac Newton (1642–1727) was the most illustrious scientist of the seventeenth century, and one of the foremost scientific minds of all time for his work on optics, mathematics, and gravitation. His primary interest, however, was the interpretation of the Bible, and his writings on the subject were voluminous. His extremely heterodox views were not fully made public until the twentieth century. Newton believed that Christianity went astray in the fourth century at the 325 Council of Nicaea (later called the first Ecumenical Council), when it defined the doctrine of the Trinity, which is at the heart of Christian belief. Public denial of this doctrine would have led to a serious break with the Anglican Church. Nonetheless, he venerated the Bible and had a strong sense of God's guiding hand in nature.

The universe that found its final expression in Newton's law of universal gravitation (that every mass in the universe attracts every other mass) appeared settled and unalterable. God seemed no more than a clever watchmaker. Little did the scientific world realize that the universe would prove to be more complex than anyone could possibly imagine.

Opposite: Cardinal Bellarmine was involved in the early stages of the Copernican controversy. He admonished Galileo not to preach or teach Copernican astronomy, as it contradicted Holy Scripture.

BAPTISTS IN ENGLAND AND AMERICA

In England, during the sixteenth century, the Church of England was challenged by a spirit or mood for reform known as Puritanism. Puritans were those who were unhappy with the religious settlement made by Queen Elizabeth I and wanted to see the Church purified and cleansed of practices and rituals that, in their view, were not Biblically warranted. Often Calvinistic in their theology, they strongly emphasized preaching and personal devotion, and an adherence to a strict moral code of conduct.

Disappointed with the lack of religious reform, many Puritans decided to leave the Church of England; if they could not cleanse it from within, the only alternative, in their view, was to separate from it. Though forbidden by law, they formed Separatist congregations and began to meet regularly for worship.

Then in the seventeenth century, fuelled by social and political unrest and dissatisfaction with the Church, a number of sectarian groups emerged out of the Separatist movement. Among them were two groups of English Baptists known as the General Baptists (because of their belief in general atonement—the idea that Christ died for all people), and the Calvinistic or Particular Baptists (who believed that the saving work of Christ on the cross was only for the elect or those who were chosen by God).

Below: The Synod of Dort in 1618 was held to settle the controversy in the Dutch churches after the rise of Arminianism, which questioned the teachings of Calvin. The Synod rejected Arminian viewpoints.

Baptists and freedom

In 1608, fleeing from persecution, some English Separatists went to Holland. Among them was John Smyth, who came to believe a congregational form of Church government and believer's baptism was necessary for the true Church. In 1609, Smyth baptized himself most probably by affusion (pouring water over his head), and then baptized the other members of his congregation in the same way. (Baptists later adopted the practice of total immersion as the true mode of baptism.) Not long after the formation of this

Baptist congregation, Smyth discovered that a group of Waterlander Mennonites in the area also practiced believer's baptism. His decision to join them caused a rift among the Baptists and in 1612, led by Thomas Helwys, a small group returned to England and established the first Baptist church on English soil at Spitalfields, outside of London.

Shortly after their arrival in England in 1612, Helwys published a plea for religious toleration called *A Short Declaration of the Mistery of Iniquity*, in which he argued that all women and men must be free to choose to respond to God. Although Helwys made this bold plea for religious freedom, severe fines and sometimes imprisonment were inflicted upon Baptists and other dissenters until the *Act of Toleration* was passed in 1689.

Above: Boston was founded in 1630 by Puritan Protestants. The site was declared the capital of the Massachusetts Bay Colony, and became the largest British settlement in America.

English Calvinistic Baptists

While Helwys and his congregation were General Baptists, the first English Calvinistic Baptist congregation developed out of a Separatist congregation in the late 1630s. By 1644, a number of Calvinistic Baptist congregations had emerged and they published a Confession of Faith in London. While Calvinistic and General Baptists may have differed in their understanding of election and the work of grace, they shared similar views concerning believer's baptism, religious freedom, the Trinity, grace, evangelism and missions, complete separation of Church and state, and, most importantly, the Church as a "gathered" or covenant community of faith. This is the belief that congregations are drawn together by God in a covenant relationship.

Baptists in America

Religious toleration also proved to be a stimulus for the formation of Baptist congregations in America. In 1631, Roger Williams (1603–1683) went to Massachusetts where some Puritans had settled. He soon fell out of favor with many of the people in that congregation for his beliefs on liberty and religious freedom. To their dismay, he insisted that the land they occupied rightly belonged to Native Americans and should be purchased from them. He also suggested that religious belief should not be enforced by law, but was a matter of individual conscience.

Williams was forced out of the Massachusetts colony in the winter of 1635 because of his radical views. He was befriended by the native Narragansett people, bought land from them, and established the colony of Rhode Island in 1638. While he did not remain a Baptist, he is credited with founding a Baptist congregation in Providence in 1638. This small congregation, and others that formed in Rhode Island, included members with both Calvinist and Arminian (Protestant Christians who followed the Dutch Reformed theologian Jacobus Arminius) views. All, however, had complete religious liberty. This quite distinctive idea along with the notion of the authority of scripture, a regenerate church membership, baptism of adult believers, the autonomy of the local church, and the priesthood of the believer, were held by Baptists in both the British and American colonies.

Above: Roger Williams established the first Baptist church in America at Providence, Rhode Island. He served as governor of the new colony from 1654 to 1658, and sanctioned religious freedom for all people.

CONGREGATIONALISTS

Above: A churchyard in Devon, England. The first Congregationalists in England wanted to reform church structure from within the Church of England.

Right: The Congregationalists adopted Martin Luther's view that everyone is a priest, so there is no need for a higher human authority to make decisions about the Church.

"For where two or three are gathered in my name, I am there among them." This text from Matthew 18:20 provides the inspiration for Congregationalists, as well as their challenge to power. As the name suggests, the basis of this form of Christianity is the congregation, which is formed as soon as people gather to worship God. Each congregation is independent and autonomous in government; it is not subject to a higher authority, a sole leader, or even church councils. The congregation elects its officers, decides who will be minister, and makes its own decisions. This means that Congregationalists are deeply democratic, in the sense that all members have a right to speak their mind and vote.

The underlying belief of Congregationalists is that Christ is the head of the Church; no human being can fill this role. All church members are equal, since they are all "priests unto God." However, each individual congregation is part of the wider Church Universal—every Christian is part of this universal and single Church. And as with so many Christian movements, Congregationalism's original belief was that their church organization most closely reflects the nature of the early Church, and enables people to have a direct relationship with God.

It is an ideal that is sometimes hard to follow, but Congregationalists were devoted and fiercely independent, and worship was a simple affair. Although they were initially outside state control and therefore did not have access to education for their elected ministers, they came to be known as well educated in theology, literature, and the sciences.

Brownists and separatists

These days many Congregational churches have united with other churches, Methodist and Presbyterian most often, but in their early days they were a dissenting movement that originated in the Church of England. By the middle of the sixteenth century there were groups of men and women meeting of their own accord, listening to preaching, and administering baptism and communion without the direction of a Church of England parson. It was a strong challenge to the power of Church and state. They took Martin Luther's doctrine of the priesthood of all believers to its logical conclusion: Since everyone is a priest, there is no need of one appointed by a bishop or by the national Church.

The defining moment came in 1582, when the preacher Robert Browne published two booklets with the quaint titles *A Book which sheweth the Life and Manners of all true Christians* and *A Treatise of Reformation without Tarrying for Any*. Browne was a Puritan-influenced dissenter who had set up his own congregation in Norwich, had been imprisoned for doing so in 1581, and when released, had taken his congregation to the Netherlands. There he published the two books. Although Browne was a quarrelsome man and eventually ended up in the Church of England, these two works set the basis for Congregationalism. In fact, his influence was so strong that they were first called "Brownists." Browne argued that the "gathered churches" of the faithful few should not be under state control (as was the case with the Church of England), and that they should be able to govern themselves.

Above: Congregational churches have become widely established in the United States. They have communities in most states, even in remote areas of Hawaii.

Persecution and flight

By the late 1580s, Congregationalists were found everywhere, especially in southern England. As they grew they became more conscious of being part of a movement. This meant that the isolation of the original groups gave way to a sense of being part of a common understanding of the Christian faith and how church life should be ordered. Later, in the seventeenth century, they would form the Congregational Unions of Scotland, England, and Wales. However, these unions did not undermine the basic idea of the independence of each congregation.

Such wider organization could only take place once Congregationalists were tolerated. It was not so easy in the sixteenth century. The government and the Church of England hierarchy looked darkly upon such breakaway groups, and so a range of laws was enacted against them. They were persecuted, some were thrown into prison, and their meeting places were closed. So they fled both to the Netherlands, where there was a long tradition of religious tolerance, and then to North America, which provided another haven. They congregated in the New England area and came to influence profoundly the development of religious and political thought. Above all, they stressed the tradition of independence, participant democracy, and freedom from state control that had a deep effect on the way religion and politics were understood in the United States. These ideas, formed in the Massachusetts Bay Colony, were to become basic elements of the American Constitution.

ENGLISH AND AMERICAN PURITANS

Above: The Puritans were fervent believers in the writings and ideas of John Calvin. They saw the Geneva Bible as God's true law, and believed it provided a clear plan for living.

Emerging from the debris of the Reformation, the Puritans won great power in seventeenth-century England and an enduring legacy in the United States, where Puritanism is popularly thought to be part of the national character.

How Puritanism emerged

King Edward VI of England died in 1553, leaving his Catholic half-sister Mary Tudor as queen. Mary repealed the Protestant reforms of her two predecessors, renewed relations with the Catholic Church, and enforced new laws that designated Protestants as heretics guilty of capital crimes. Fear drove many committed Protestants into exile in continental Europe, with some of them sojourning in John Calvin's Geneva, where they discovered three principles that would influence Puritanism. First, through contact with Calvin's deputy Theodore Beza, these "Marian exiles" encountered a system of evangelical theology that would eventually gain prominence as "Calvinism." Second, they experienced the iconoclastic and simplified worship directed by Calvin, who avoided any "popish" liturgical expressions. Third, the exiles translated the Bible into English, adding interpretive marginal notes that were decidedly evangelical. In historical perspective, these influences appear to have been formative, particularly in view of the behavior of the exiles after their return to England.

To the relief of the exiles and other Protestants, Queen Mary died in 1558. Her successor, her half-sister Elizabeth, sought a compromise that all of her subjects, Protestant and Catholic alike, might find agreeable. Upon the return of the exiles, armed as they were with their new theological, liturgical, and scriptural influences, they found intolerable the form of Catholicism inherent in the "Elizabethan Settlement." They desired an evangelical purification of the Church of England with an imposition of the Geneva Bible, as the translation accomplished by the Marian exiles became called. Soon the scornful epithet "Puritan" was attached to the movement as a disparagement of the perceived naive arrogance of its adherents.

The Puritan ascendancy in Stuart England

After brooding through the Elizabethan era, the Puritans eagerly hailed the 1603 accession of the Scottish Presbyterian James Stuart, whom they believed would ally with their reformist agenda. Unaware that James loathed Calvinism, they sent him the Millenary Petition, a document stipulating their demands for reform. James agreed to meet with them at the Hampton Court Conference of 1604, causing Puritan hopes to surge in anticipation; those hopes collapsed when the king adeptly defended the Prayer Book, episcopal polity, and other contentious issues. However, he did authorize a new translation of the Bible into English—the Authorized or King James Version.

James I was succeeded in 1625 by his son Charles, who, with the Archbishop of Canterbury William Laud, oversaw an intensification of hostility between the Anglicans and Puritans. The king and "Arminian" archbishop antagonized the Puritans by enforcing and expanding Anglican policies; however, Puritan power increased throughout Charles' reign, until a sequence of events triggered civil war in 1642. The English Civil War, in which the Puritan Parliamentary "Roundheads" defeated the Anglican Royalist "Cavaliers,"

Below: The Salem witch trials occurred in Massachusetts in 1692. Among the hysteria, more than 200 people were accused of practicing witchcraft, of which 20 were executed.

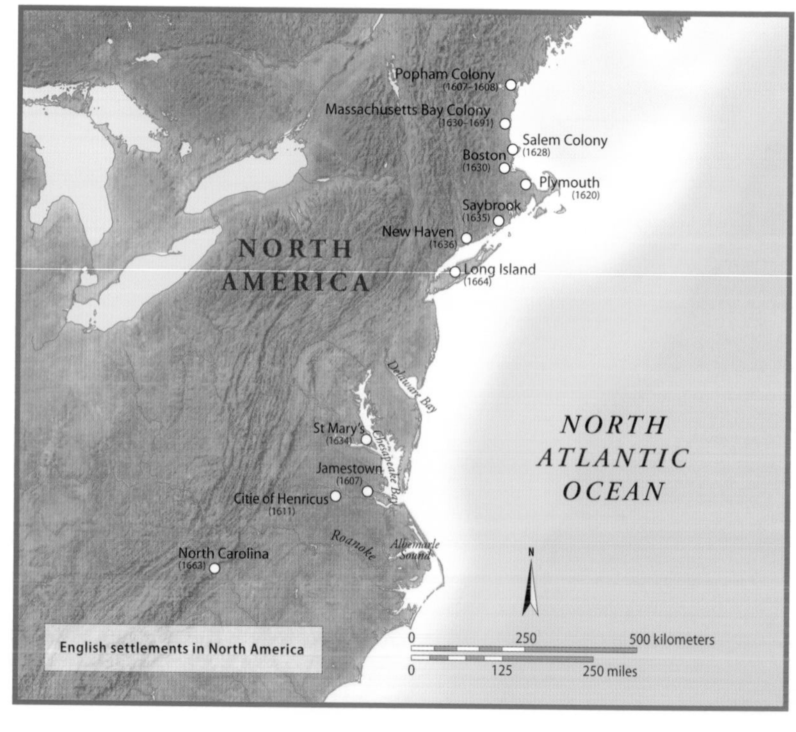

ended in January 1649, when the victors beheaded King Charles. Oliver Cromwell emerged as national leader and established the Commonwealth and Protectorate, which failed after his death in 1658. Antipathy to the Puritans caused the public to clamor to reinstate a monarch, and with the accession of Charles II in 1660, the Puritans lost all influence in politics and religion in the subsequent era known as the Restoration.

Puritan colonization of New England

Dejected by the regime of Charles I, some Puritans began despairing of the possibility that they might ever witness a purification of the Church of England, and they began seeking alternative means of achieving their goals. A migration to the New World seemed the best option for them. In 1630 an officially "Puritan" colony was established on American soil when John Winthrop led to Massachusetts Bay a group whose intention was to establish an ideal and pure but non-separated church. Another group, the "Pilgrims," had arrived in the region ten years earlier, but they were Separatists with a different ecclesiastical vision. The home government joined the two colonies in 1691 as a way of controlling potential sedition, which is exactly what developed in the following century.

The Puritans began creating a civilization out of the wilderness that they found, preaching to the Native Americans and establishing Harvard College in 1636. Despite many impressive successes and the brilliance embodied by individuals such as Cotton Mather and Jonathan Edwards, the Salem Witch Trials of 1692 discredited—permanently, in the eyes of many—American Puritanism. Puritanism expired as a significant factor in American life by the end of the eighteenth century, although traces of its former importance have persisted in American history to this day.

Above: In 1620, a group called the Pilgrims founded the colony of Plymouth in New England. They soon came into conflict with the local native Americans, who resisted the invasion of their land.

NEW FRANCE

Above: One of the first permanent French colonies of North America was at Port-Royal in Acadia, Nova Scotia. The area is known as the French Shore.

Below: The magnificent interior of Notre-Dame de Montréal, founded in 1657. The present-day church was built between 1672 and 1683, in the Baroque style.

During the seventeenth and eighteenth centuries, French colonists landed in Canada and promoted the Christian evangelization of its native peoples. The French Church, which inspired them, generated a mystical and heroic spirituality. The first recorded Indian conversions took place at Port-Royal in Acadia, Nova Scotia, in 1610. The French missionary, Líabbé Jessé Fléché, baptized Chief Memberton and his family and 140 Miíkmaq and Malecite converts. The following year, the Jesuits Pierre Biard and Énemond Massé replaced Fléché, studied the Indian languages, educated converts in their own language, and translated the catechism. The Jesuits began a program of methodical Christian instruction for the Indians.

French Catholics settled in three main locations in Canada: At the fortress of Quebec; at the remote sanctuary of Sainte-Marie Among the Huron Indians; and at Ville Marie (Montreal). Enterprising Catholic chaplains traveling with the fur brigades penetrated quickly to the heart of the continent at Michilimackinac (Michigan). Sharing the Gospel with the Indians as they went, they paddled their canoes down the Mississippi River to the Gulf of Mexico by 1687.

Quebec: A multipurpose center

In 1608, the layperson Samuel de Champlain founded Quebec by planting the French flag and evangelizing the Indians living nearby. He was followed by missionary volunteers—the Recollets, the Jesuits, the Ursulines, and the Brothers Hospitallers of St Augustine—who built churches, hospitals, colleges, and schools that dotted the Canadian riverbanks. Quebec was a multipurpose center for New France which included government administration, commercial trade, military contingents, and the seat of the new diocese, which stretched across North America from the Gulf of St Lawrence to the Gulf of Mexico.

As Quebec became the bedrock of French colonialism in North America, Jean de Brébeuf, Antoine Daniel, and Ambrose Davost boarded Huron fur canoes and began the torturous four-week journey up the St Lawrence, Ottawa, and Mattawa rivers to cross over the high land at Lake Nipissing and descend the French River into the open waters that led to Huronia. When they arrived in 1634, the three Jesuits initiated a mission to convert 25,000 Hurons. Five years later, near Midland, Ontario, Jerome Lalemant and his Jesuit companions built the historic Sainte-Marie Among the Hurons, which became the center for enculturation of the French Jesuits into Indian life.

Sainte-Marie: European enculturation

Their names ringing like church bells in Canadian ears, Jean de Brébeuf, Isaac Jogues, Gabriel Lalemant, Antoine Daniel, Charles Garnier, Noël Chabanel, Jean de Lalonde, and René Goupil began the long learning process of what is now called enculturation. They paddled and portaged as Hurons, they hunted and ate as Hurons, they lived in Huron longhouses and shared their harvest, and they learned with great humility to speak the Indian languages and respect Indian culture. The Hurons shared with the visitors their

corn, tomatoes, potatoes, beans, and squash, as well as their fishing and hunting methods. In turn, the Euro-Canadians brought from France chickens, pigs, and cattle to supplement the Indian diet. The Jesuits were the first to bring the Christian Gospel to the Hurons, making converts and forming Christian communities. Seventy Jesuits and donées (religious laymen who worked in return for food, clothing, and shelter) lived at Sainte-Marie Among the Hurons at its peak, and the compound became a place for Euro–Huron cultural exchange. Joseph Chihwatenha, Joseph Teondechoren, Paul Atondo, and other Hurons converted to Catholicism and were baptized. They evangelized their fellow Hurons, and soon founded Christian villages.

Ville Marie: Lay evangelization

As Quebec was a multipurpose center, and Huronia a place for European enculturation, so Ville Marie (Montreal) was a location for lay evangelization. Paul de Chomedey de Maisonneuve led the expedition of lay Christian missionaries up the St Lawrence River to the Indian fur markets at its juncture with the Ottawa River. Maisonneuve and his companions founded Ville Marie. Jeanne Mance opened the first hospital, and Marguerite Bourgeoys founded the first school and established the first uncloistered religious order in North America—the Congrégation de Notre-Dame. Unlike Ursuline nuns who lived within the cloister wall, the Congrégation de Notre-Dame left their convent daily to do apostolic ministry work throughout the countryside. The Sulpicians arrived in Montreal in 1657, to found the principal church, Notre-Dame de Montréal, and the Grand Séminaire de Montréal. In the midst of danger, the Christian faith was lived with a missionary intensity, and Montreal emerged as a center of lay evangelization—while Sainte-Marie stressed enculturation and Quebec City multiple functions. Francois de Laval, whose lineage can be traced back through the centuries to the first Christian Franks in the fifth century, arrived in Quebec in 1659 as its first missionary bishop. His assignment was to take charge of missionary endeavors, to direct the birth of the Canadian Catholic Church, and to create a local infrastructure.

Below: Father Joseph le Caron, accompanied by Samuel de Champlain, was one of the first Jesuit priests to travel to New France. He aimed to convert the Native Americans to Christianity.

BRITISH COLONIES IN NORTH AMERICA

With the 1607 settling of Jamestown, Virginia, the British colonization of America was permanently underway. In New England, Separatists (the Pilgrims) from the Church of England landed at Plymouth in 1620, and in 1630 Puritans established the Massachusetts Bay Colony. The aristocratic Calvert family founded the colony of Maryland in 1632 as a refuge for Catholics. Thus, between the Anglicans in Virginia, Calvinists in New England, and Catholics in Maryland, American colonization reconstituted the ecclesiastical triangulation in Tudor and Stuart England, a striking example of what the historian Mark Noll has called "the old religion in a new world." However, whereas the situation in the old country created violence and warfare, the American colonists coexisted generally without such hostilities.

A better Christian coexistence

The colonists were, if not less ideological, less confrontational than their compatriots in the motherland, and as the English Civil War ignited in the 1640s, if the Puritan New Englanders and Anglican Virginians wished to emulate their counterparts back in England, they refrained from invading one another. Given the bloodshed over religion not only in Britain but in all of Western Europe in the first half of the seventeenth century, the peaceable coexistence of the American colonists becomes all the more remarkable. Indeed, the more dangerous triangulation in North America was between Britain, Spain, and France—a trio engaged in a cycle of cold and hot wars, most conspicuously the global Seven Years' War from 1756 to 1763. In cases of Puritan zealotry, such as the expulsions of the theologian Roger Williams and Anne Hutchison in the 1630s, the New Englanders were enforcing discipline within their own group rather than imposing their beliefs on outsiders, as their English counterparts attempted before and during the Protectorate of Oliver Cromwell.

Colonial Americans negotiated survival strategies to manage the double triangulation described above and to avoid the havoc of Old World fanaticism. One strategy was restraint, as seen in the refusal of the colonists to recapitulate the civil war of the homeland. A second, nobler strategy was liberty: The Quaker William Penn established Pennsylvania on principles of toleration; and more radically, Rhode Island's founder Roger Williams argued for absolute religious freedom, even for non-Christians. A third strategy utilized was indifference, which was evident especially in the southern colonies, where the official Anglicanism mattered little to the hard-living Carolinians and Georgians. The American avoidance of anything like the ruinous European Thirty Years' War from 1618 to 1648 underscores the success of these strategies.

The surprising work of God

The colonists not only avoided conflict, they sometimes found unity. In Northampton, Massachusetts, from 1734 to 1735, the Congregationalist minister Jonathan Edwards observed astounding physical, emotional, and spiritual responses to his preaching, and wrote a book in 1737 about those events entitled *A Faithful Narrative of the Surprising Work of God*, which in retrospect showed that the Northampton revival was a precursor of an even more astonishing phenomenon—the transatlantic revival called the Great Awakening, the most noteworthy event of colonial Christianity. The sensational revival tour of George Whitefield from 1739–1741 was the linchpin of the Great Awakening. A preternaturally talented orator, Whitefield preached ardent sermons for conversion and disparaged the spiritual condition of the Church, both of which earned him much affection from ordinary people. When Whitefield personally visited Edwards in 1740, their meeting symbolized a summit of the greatest practitioner, Whitefield, and the greatest theorist, Edwards, directing the peculiarly American contribution to Christianity—revivalism. Many traditionalists, though, were hostile to the emotional excesses of revivalism and attacked preachers who encouraged the ecstatic signs exhibited by the worshippers.

The Great Awakening disrupted the patterns of colonial Christianity, and most groups faced massive upheavals: For

Below: In 1607, a large group of settlers from London landed at Jamestown, Virginia, to establish an English settlement and to find gold and a water route to the Orient.

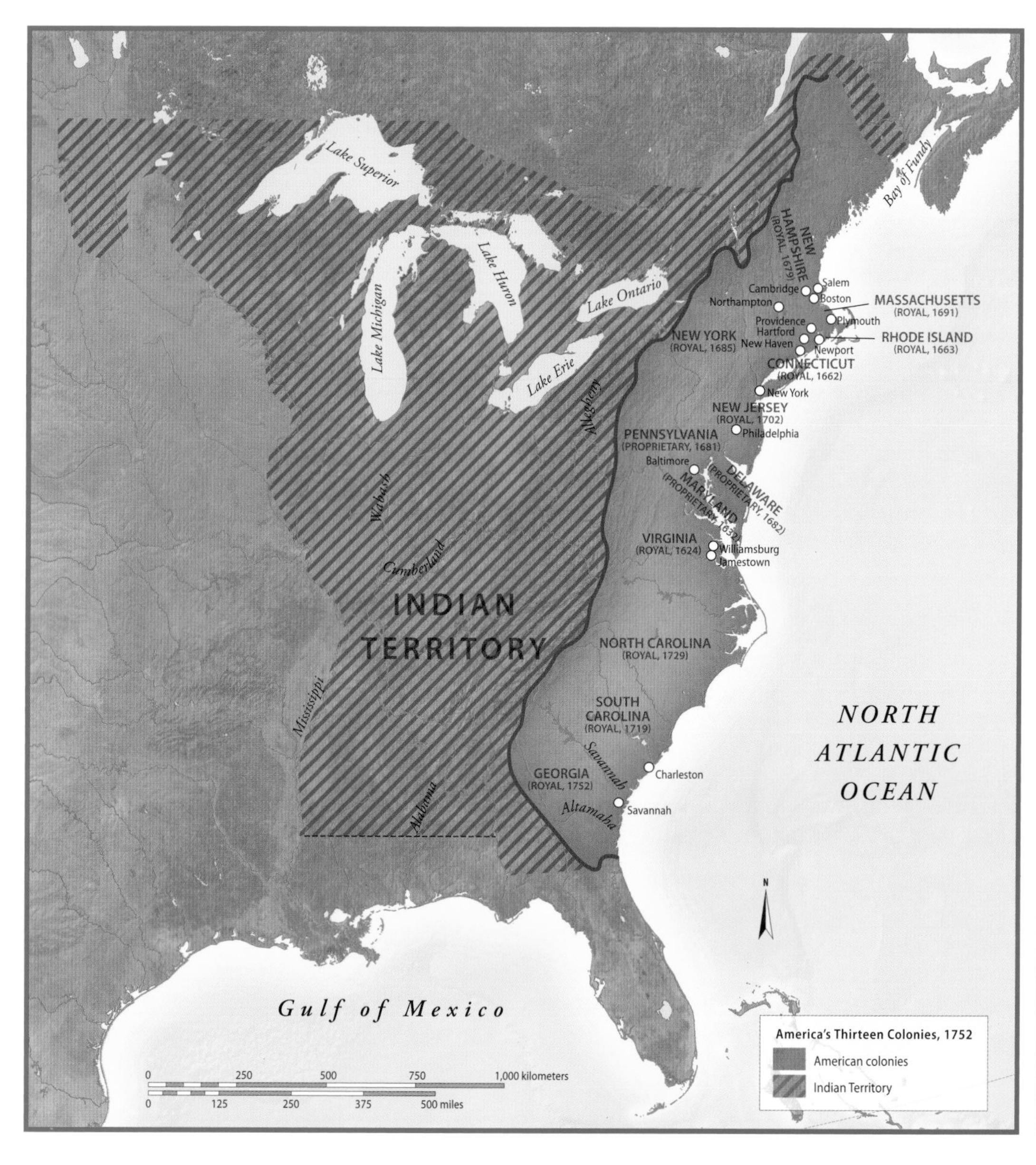

Above: William Penn was a proficient writer who expounded his theories on religious liberty and Quaker ideals in many books, essays, and pamphlets.

Below: Leader of the English Quakers and founder of Pennsylvania, William Penn, established friendly relations with the Native Americans during his visit in 1682.

instance, the Baptists were affected permanently. Shubal Stearns, who was converted by Whitefield's preaching and became a Baptist in 1751, moved to Sandy Creek, North Carolina, and, with his brother-in-law Daniel Marshall, started Sandy Creek Baptist Church in 1755. Within three years, the Sandy Creek church started two more congregations, and when the three churches formed the Sandy Creek Association, a pro-revivalist, less formal Baptist tradition began. Those who followed the Sandy Creek tradition became known as the Separate Baptists, who demanded that church members, who tended to be rural, poor, and uncouth, show evidence of conversion through the raucous preaching of their uneducated clergy. The appearance of the Separate Baptists created a schism in Baptist America (the lines of which remain discernible to this day), between the newer tradition and the older one: The Regular Baptists. In the aftermath of the split, the more energetic Separate Baptists were mainly responsible for the striking Baptist expansion that ensued over the next hundred years.

PIETISM

Pietism was a Protestant reform movement that began in Germany in the seventeenth century. The focus of Pietism was a desire for heartfelt piety revealed in disciplined devotion and purity of life. In the context of social and political turmoil in Europe after the Thirty Years' War (1618–1648), as well as a growing scholasticism in Protestant churches, Pietists called for spiritual renewal in the Church. In the years following Martin Luther's death in 1546, a number of theological debates among Lutherans had resulted in the development of new doctrinal formulations of faith. This Protestant scholasticism, according to Pietists, had moved away from genuine piety. They opposed mere intellectual assent to doctrine, as well as ritualism and formalism in worship, and stood for a practical, ethical, and vigorous outworking of Christian faith which stressed religious experience and growth in holiness.

Pious desires

The leader of the movement was Philipp Jakob Spener (1635–1705), pastor of a Lutheran congregation in Frankfurt, Germany, who wrote a work entitled *Pia Desideria: Or Heartfelt Desires for a God-pleasing Improvement of the True Protestant Church* (1675). In this treatise, Spener pointed to signs of moral decay in the culture and suggested that many Christians had neglected practical, experiential faith and devotion. Outlining specific proposals for reform, which included small-group Bible study and prayer, and a renewed emphasis on "conversion" and "new birth," Spener also called for changes in pastoral training which would place less emphasis on scholastic theology and more on the practice of devotion. While insisting that reforms were needed in the ways that pastors were trained, he likewise urged Christians to recover the notion of the "priesthood of the believer." This idea that every person is his or her own priest before God had been at the fore of Martin Luther's reforming efforts in the sixteenth century and became a focal point for Lutheran piety.

University of Halle

Spener was greatly influenced by the writings of Johann Arndt (1555–1621), a Lutheran theologian and mystical writer who published a work called *True Christianity* (1606), which stressed the work of Christ in the heart of an individual. In 1691, Spener went to Berlin, and on his recommendation, August Hermann Francke (1663–1727) was appointed as pastor and teacher at the newly formed University of Halle. Under Francke's direction, Halle became a center for the Pietist reforms focusing on personal devotion with a practical outworking of the faith. As a result of the work of Francke and Spener, a renewal movement spread throughout the Protestant Church in Germany, which emphasized Bible study and social action. They founded orphanages and hospitals, and embarked on a worldwide missionary endeavor. While their critics argued

that their insistence on personal piety at times drifted into a new legalism, their emphasis on reforming the Church through personal Bible study and ministerial formation would have a lasting impact on many Protestant groups.

Count Zinzendorf and the Moravians

Among the Protestants influenced by Pietism were the Moravians. At the invitation of Count Nikolaus Ludwig von Zinzendorf (1700–1760), a group of Bohemian Moravians established a settlement on his estate which they named Herrnhut ("the Lord's watch"). Shaped and influenced by Francke's teaching at Halle, Zinzendorf had a vision for Church renewal and reform with an emphasis on personal and heartfelt religious experience. Believing that they were to share the Gospel around the world, the Moravians established schools, embarked on social care, and sent missionaries abroad to teach and preach. John Wesley, the founder of the Methodist movement, was greatly impressed by the devotion of Moravian missionaries he met on his way to serve as an Anglican missionary in the North American colony of Georgia in 1735. In fact, it was a Moravian missionary who confronted Wesley with a question about the assurance of salvation, which he did not then know how to answer. The question troubled him, and when Wesley returned to England he met with Peter Böhler, a Moravian leader, who spoke to him of personal faith and assurance. Later, Wesley visited Count Zinzendorf at Halle in order to see firsthand the Moravians' work and witness. Wesley continued to draw inspiration from Moravian piety, though he distanced himself from some of the more mystical elements of their devotional practice.

Pietistic reforms spread across Europe and North America. Since Pietism emphasized experience over doctrinal confessionalism, it is credited with encouraging the union of Christian groups including the Lutheran-Missouri synod in America and the Lutheran Church of Australia.

Above: John Wesley was a preacher and founder of the Methodist Church. He preached about the social issues of the day to large crowds and spoke of Christian perfection as the "holiness of heart and life."

Opposite: The Thirty Years' War (1618–1648) was a series of complex military and political conflicts in central Europe. It was also, in part, a religious war between Catholics, Lutherans, and Calvinists.

THE PILGRIM'S PROGRESS

Above: John Bunyan was an English writer and a Puritan who wrote the novel *The Pilgrim's Progress* while imprisoned for preaching the Gospel in a non-sanctioned place.

The Pilgrim's Progress by John Bunyan (1628–1688) is one of the most well known devotional works in Christian history. First published in 1678, and now translated into more than 200 languages, this classic of English literature and Christian devotion has never been out of print. Written at a time when England was torn by religious and political strife, *The Pilgrim's Progress* was intended to call readers to greater self-awareness and urge them to turn to God. The story itself is steeped in scripture and is shaped by an emphasis on Godliness in life.

John Bunyan was born in the village of Elstow, about 2 miles (3 km) from Bedford in England. His parents were poor but sent their son to a local school to learn to read and write. Trained to follow in his father's footsteps as a "brasier" or tinker, when the English Civil War began in 1642, he joined the Parliamentary side. Led by Oliver Cromwell (1599–1658), a man with strong Puritan sympathies, Parliamentary forces defeated King Charles I's army and the king was beheaded in 1649. As Lord Protector, Oliver Cromwell declared religious liberty to all but Anglicans, Roman Catholics, and Antinomians. The period of relative calm would not last, however, for by 1658 Cromwell died and in the anarchy that ensued, Charles II (1660–1685) was invited to come and take the English throne. Although he published the Breda Declaration in 1660, which promised religious toleration, Puritans—John Bunyan among them—would inevitably suffer persecution.

Persecution and imprisonment

Bunyan had returned to Bedford after the civil war and married in 1647. Around this time, he went through a period of intense spiritual crisis lasting for four years, in which he saw himself as the "chief of sinners." During this time, in addition to reading the Bible, he was greatly helped by two books which his wife had given to him: Arthur Dent's *The Plain Man's Pathway to Heaven* (1601) and Lewis Bayly's *The Practice of Piety* (1613). Shaped by these Puritan writings and his desire to lead a holy life, by 1653 he joined an Independent (later Baptist) congregation in Bedford. He was recognized as a preacher in 1657 and soon became well known in the countryside around Bedford.

Following the restoration of Charles II in 1660, Bunyan was arrested for unlicensed preaching and spent most of the years between 1660 and 1672 in the Bedford jail. He used the time in prison to write extensively, completing over 80 different works, including *The Pilgrim's Progress* (1678) and his autobiography *Grace Abounding to the Chief of Sinners* (1666). Much of his work focused on the need for Christians to take seriously the idea that they were engaged in serious spiritual warfare in the world. At stake for him was nothing short of the salvation of sinners.

Pilgrim's journey

The Pilgrim's Progress was written as an allegory in two parts. The first part presents the Christian life as a journey, which begins at the "City of Destruction" and ends at the

Right: The Battle of Edgehill was the first conflict of the English Civil War. Charles I and his army fought Parliamentary forces near Edgehill; neither side won because they both withdrew troops due to exhaustion.

"Celestial City." In the second part Christian's wife, Christana, makes a similar journey. Part one was published first and stands as the best known of the two tales. Here, the main protagonist, Christian, is weighed down by a great burden of the knowledge of sin and struggles to make his way through temptations and trials. The many pitfalls of the journey are depicted as Christian makes his way through such places as the "Slough of Despond," the "Hill Difficulty," "Valley of the Shadow of Death," "Doubting Castle," the "Enchanted Ground," and "Vanity Fair." Along the way, there are also conversations with those who give advice or warning, such as Worldlywise, Pliable, and Obstinate, as well as Prudence and Faithful, to name a few. In addition to the plain, simple, and accessible style, this work is lauded for its thorough dependence on the Bible.

John Bunyan died in 1688, just one year before the *Act of Toleration* 1689 was passed, which would grant liberty of worship to all but Roman Catholics and Unitarians. However, he is remembered not only for his significant literary achievement in writing *The Pilgrim's Progress* and for his depiction of the Christian life as one of struggle, failure, and triumph, but also for his own willingness to suffer for his faith. A hymn written by Bunyan sums up his view of the Christian life as pilgrimage with the claim that: "There's no discouragement shall make him once relent his first avowed intent to be a pilgrim."

Above: Charles II (right) desired religious toleration, largely due to his leanings toward Catholicism. He made a number of attempts to formalize toleration of Catholics and Nonconformists, but was ultimately opposed by an Anglican Parliament.

SERMONS

Right: According to the Gospel of Matthew, Jesus began his Sermon on the Mount with the words: "Blessed are the poor in spirit, for theirs is the kingdom of heaven."

The Latin word *sermo* means a continued talk, often of a learned type. In the Christian Church a sermon came to mean an address by the minister or priest to the congregation. Although the ideal was a talk based on the Bible, sermons have varied as widely as those who have delivered them. Politics, the sins of members of the congregation, a vile competitor in the next parish—these and many others have been topics.

The model is often held to be the Sermon on the Mount in Matthew 5–7, which includes the Lord's Prayer and the Beatitudes. There have been noted preachers through the ages, such as John Chrysostom in the early Church, or Martin Luther, or indeed Billy Graham. However, it is agreed that a major high point in the art of sermonizing was in the seventeenth century.

Homiletics

The art of producing sermons is known as homiletics. This requires careful study of the Biblical text, preferably in the original languages of Hebrew and Greek, identification of the main points, their relevance for the congregation, and a desire to determine what God might want to say to the congregation. It also involves skill in public speaking: How to raise and lower the voice, how to project one's voice (amplification is a recent invention), how to use pauses, and how to ensure the main point gets through—say it once, say it again, and then once more.

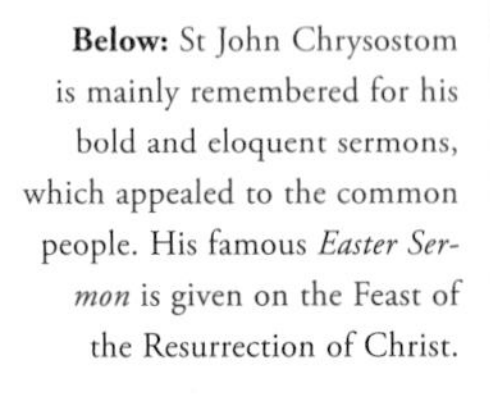

Below: St John Chrysostom is mainly remembered for his bold and eloquent sermons, which appealed to the common people. His famous *Easter Sermon* is given on the Feast of the Resurrection of Christ.

Sermons have not always been prominent in Christian history—there are many complaints concerning illiterate and uneducated clergy across the ages. The Church went through several long periods when there were just two or three sermons in the year at high points such as Easter and Christmas. However, during periods when the clergy were well educated, sermons improved. One such period was the thirteenth century, when Dominican and Franciscan scholars produced a high level of education among some priests. Another period followed the Reformation, which pushed both Protestants and Catholics not only to introduce regular sermons but also to improve their quality. Again education was a crucial factor, especially the training in original languages and the discipline of homiletics. By the seventeenth century, these changes began to have an effect.

John Donne

There is an old adage: If a sermon does not go over the congregation's head, then the people are disappointed. The idea was to lift the mind and heart to God. One of the great exponents of such sermons was John Donne (1572–1631). Once a poor, youthful, and agnostic writer of great love poems, he became, after lengthy theological training, the dean of St Paul's Cathedral in London (1621–1631). By all reports, Donne did not disappoint the old adage. His sermons were full of learning and were liberally sprinkled with references to the Church Fathers. The sermons employed images skillfully and were delivered to great effect. However, their appeal lay in Donne's focus on the inner life. Often he spoke of his life as a sinner, and of his forgiveness in light of God's great mercy. This resonated deeply with his audience, and he was much sought after. He preached at all the festivals of the Christian year in the church, and was on several occasions called upon to preach in the royal court to the king.

Above: John Donne was an English poet and a preacher of sermons. His work embraced a range of secular and religious subjects, including divine love, and the decay and resurrection of the body.

The hourglass

In many churches it was not uncommon for sermons to be preached every day of the week. In Rostock (Germany) the records state that 1,500 sermons were preached in one year, 1640. As another German Lutheran minister said at the time, "we preachers preach ourselves to death." This was not to unwilling congregations, for there was a great thirst for sermons in an age when not so many could read. So much so that the Puritan minister, Lawrence Chaderton (who was also one of the translators of the King James Version of the Bible), once decided to stop preaching after two hours since he felt that people were becoming weary. "For God's sake, go on," came the cry, "We beg you, go on." He preached for an hour more.

Gradually it became a custom to preach for an hour. In order to ensure that preachers stayed within the time limit, pulpits were decked out with hourglasses and even in some cases half-hourglasses. However, the makers tended to err on the side of the listeners, especially since some felt that the ear was the first of the senses to grow tired. One of these hourglasses, which still survives, completed the hour in just forty-eight minutes.

DEVELOPMENTS IN NEW SPAIN

By the seventeenth century the rapid conquest and colonization of the Americas and the Philippines had brought Spain a territory undreamt of a century before. It extended from the tip of South America to what is now southwestern USA (from Florida to California) and then across the Pacific Ocean to the Philippines. While the South American portions (with the exception of Brazil) became the Viceroyalty of Peru, the rest was administered as one political unit from Mexico City—the Viceroyalty of New Spain. It lasted in various shapes and extents from 1525 to 1821. In this vast empire the Spanish established a complex administrative system based around *misiones* (missions), *pueblos* (civilian towns), and *presidios* (military garrisons).

Arm in arm

The long, slow process of driving the Muslims out of the Iberian Peninsula (790–1492) had united Church and state in Spain in a strong bond. On top of opposition to Islam, the perceived threat the Reformation presented to law and order had brought the Catholic Church under the control of the Spanish crown. This same union crossed the Atlantic to the Americas in the sixteenth and seventeenth centuries. Missionaries accompanied the conquistadors and were instrumental in the spread of the empire, so much so that in some places the clergy were also imperial governors.

Following the New Testament command to baptize all nations (Matthew 28:19), the missionaries adopted the practice of mass baptism—accounts speak of up to 14,000 a day in some areas. The indigenous peoples were very willing to convert; however, they were just as willing to convert away again. In some instances they would simply add the Christian god—he had been responsible for the conquest—to their collection of other gods.

So the Catholic clergy undertook a rigorous program to eradicate the beliefs and structures of indigenous religions. The result was widespread destruction of religious and cultural artefacts, burning of religious books, persecution and execution of their religious leaders, banning of distinctive religious foods (such as amaranth, the "grain of the gods"), and demolition of many temples and statues.

The indigenous peoples strike back

The indigenous peoples of New Spain were decimated by new diseases (measles, smallpox, and typhus) and eventually struck back at the colonizers. By the later seventeenth century they took advantage of the Spanish concerns with the British, who were attacking the "Spanish Main" (the trading link) across the Atlantic and Pacific oceans. During the middle of the century, the Tarahumara, who had retreated

Right: In 1587, Englishman Sir Francis Drake occupied the Spanish port of Cádiz for three days, capturing six ships and destroying many others. The attack sidelined the Spanish Armada for a year.

Below: Completed in 1649, the Cathedral of Pueblo in Puebla, Mexico, features artistic works of great value in its altarpieces, seventeenth-century paintings, carvings, and overall structure.

to the Copper Canyon from the Chihuahua Mountains, attacked the Spanish (the athletic Tarahumara still live in this area to this day and maintain a traditional lifestyle). By 1670 the "Chichimecs," a conglomeration of semi-nomadic tribes in northern Mexico, attacked the Spanish, took the town of Durango, and drove out the governor and Spanish garrison. A decade later, a widespread revolt broke out across two dozen pueblos in New Mexico and many Europeans were slaughtered.

Part of the problem was that the indigenous peoples had been given the status of second-class citizens. With inter-marriage and the arrival of African slaves to make up for the massive reduction of local peoples, an effective caste system had come into being. In this mix, the indigenous peoples were declared to be legal minors under the jurisdiction of the Spanish crown. Despite efforts to train indigenous clergy, there was little success. It was not until 1679 that Nicolas del Puerto became bishop of Oaxaca, and even then native clergy were virtually nonexistent.

Inquisition

In 1571 the Mexican Inquisition, an extension of the Spanish version, was established in Mexico City; it closed only in 1820. Its presence was a sign of the Church's shift in focus. Up until then its concern was the conversion of indigenous peoples, but by 1650 there were new concerns. Most of the Inquisition's attention was focused on "negroes," "mulattos," and the "Crypto-Jews" who had also migrated to New Spain to escape persecution. The most dramatic moment was the arrest and trial of 109 "Crypto-Jews" in 1642. They were accused of secretly carrying on the Jewish faith or at least Jewish cultural practices; 13 of them were put to death. Sixteen years later 14 men accused of homo-sexuality were burned at the stake. The other major concern was the new scientific and political ideas stemming from the Enlightenment. Scholars were closely investigated for espousing scientific ideas, and an eye was kept on the influence of republican and democratic ideas from the French Revolution and War of Independence in North America.

Above: The Spanish encountered the Tarahumara Indians as they encroached on their territory in Mexico in the 1500s. The Jesuit missionaries followed, but had little success converting them.

DEVELOPMENTS IN ASIA

Right: The Sinulog Festival in the Philippines honors the child Jesus (Santo Niño) and features a colorful grand parade that commemorates the Cebuano people's pagan origin and their acceptance of Christianity.

The story of Christianity in Asia through the seventeenth century is one of success and failure, competition and schism, persecution and colonial domination. In some places (China and Japan) it petered out, but in others (the Philippines, Vietnam, India, and Sri Lanka) it survived and grew.

The Philippines

As part of Spain's effort to dominate the Pacific, Spanish explorers from Mexico colonized the Philippines in the sixteenth century. Christian evangelization only seriously began in 1572 in Manila, but by the beginning of the seventeenth century there were all kinds of Roman Catholic orders competing with one another: Franciscans (arrived 1578), Jesuits (1581), Dominicans (1587), and even the Recollects (1606). All of their missionary work was directly controlled by the Spanish crown. In order to reduce competition, the orders were granted monopolies in different regions. Given time, exclusive access (Protestants were not allowed), and even an archbishop by 1595, Roman Catholic Christianity spread throughout the Philippines over the late sixteenth but especially the seventeenth century. A university was established—the Dominican University of St Thomas—in 1611. With royal patronage, the orders gained immense wealth, particularly in land. Yet, even though large numbers of local people were baptized, the few indigenous priests held inferior positions.

Japan

The first touch of Christianity on Japanese soil came with the intrepid Francis Xavier in 1549. However, after some limited initial success the story is a rather brutal one for the seventeenth century. The Jesuits founded four Christian communities of 800 believers on Kyushu. Physician Luis d'Almeida built a foundling home in 1556 and a hospital the following year in Funai. Fortunes changed in 1587: After growing suspicion by Japanese authorities that the missions were preparing the way for colonial conquest, a decree was issued ordering missionaries out of Japan in 20 days. Christians largely ignored it and kept a low profile, but then Franciscans and Dominicans continued to arrive until 1596, when persecution began to rage.

Below: Christian missions first entered Japan in the sixteenth century. However, by 1640 Christianity was extinct, and it was not until the Meiji restoration, when religious freedom was again accepted, that Christianity saw a resurgence.

In 1597 a Spanish ship was seized, its cargo was confiscated and 26 Christians including clergy and laity were crucified. Persecution broke out again in 1613, and by 1640 many thousands had suffered due to their Christian convictions. For more than two centuries all foreigners were excluded from Japan under pain of death. However, when Roman Catholic missions re-entered the country after 1859 (when a treaty was signed with France allowing limited liberty of worship), they found thousands of Christians in small local communities who had passed on their faith without priests or education for over 200 years.

China

In contrast with Japan, the situation in China was one of continual conflict between approaches to mission. It begins with two famous Jesuits, Matteo Ricci and Michael

Ruggieri, who arrived in 1582. They followed a policy of adaptation, impressed Chinese scholars with their skill in mathematics and astronomy, and stressed the need for using Chinese religious terms and rituals in worship. By 1601 the missionaries were allowed to proceed to Beijing and to live at the imperial court. Learning Mandarin and other Chinese dialects, they translated the catechism and Ten Commandments into Mandarin and made converts among the Mandarins. Ricci published 20 volumes of Christian spirituality in Mandarin and the Confucian classics in Latin for Westerners.

These moves were not popular with other Catholics, so when the Franciscan, Dominican, and other missionaries arrived, they looked askance at the activities of the Jesuits. They complained to the pope, denouncing what was called "accommodation"—adaptation to altered circumstances. The struggle gave rise to the long-running Rites Controversy, which severely hampered the fledgling church in China. By the turn of the eighteenth century, Clement XI had condemned the Jesuit practices, and the Chinese emperor had become annoyed and issued decrees against Christianity. Split by tensions, Christianity petered out.

Left: The Jesuit missionary Matteo Ricci with the Chinese Ming official Li Paulus Xu Guanqi. In 1582, Ricci arrived in China as a missionary and introduced Western mathematics to the Chinese.

India

From the time Roman Catholicism came to India with Portuguese colonists and traders in 1498 and then Francis Xavier the Jesuit in 1542, myriad tensions arose that spilled over into the seventeenth century.

The first was with the Thomas Christians, who had been in India for a millennium. The Roman Catholic missionaries attempted to bring them over to Roman practice. A section disagreed, became disgruntled, and broke away, although an even smaller section stayed with Rome.

Another tension arose out of the different approaches to mission. Some, such as those who followed the line of Francis Xavier, preferred to baptize and establish churches under a Roman Catholic bishop and then an archbishop (from 1557). A different approach came with the Tuscan Jesuit Robert de Nobili, who arrived in South India at Madura in 1605. Noting the influence of the Brahmins in Indian society, de Nobili adopted the lifestyle of a Brahmin holy man in order to gain influence. Other missionaries objected, so de Nobili put pen to paper and wrote theological works in his defense. He then approached Pope Gregory XV, who approved his approach in 1623. Given a free hand, de Nobili had access to the highest levels of Indian society, leaving behind works in Latin, Italian, Portuguese, Sanskrit, Telugu, and Tamil. However, because he was an Italian noble and identified with the Brahmins, he did not associate with the Jesuits, who evangelized the *parangi* (the poor and low castes).

Tension also arose with the Portuguese colonial government, which asserted the right to appoint all bishops and missionaries to India. By 1600 it was clear that Portugal did not have the resources to fulfill these obligations, and in 1637 the central mission authority in Rome, the Sacred Congregation for Propagation of the Faith (*Sacra Congregatio de Propaganda Fide*), appointed an Indian Brahmin as Vicar Apostolic; he had special responsibility for an area, often in missionary fields, with direct responsibility to the pope. By century's end the practice of appointing an Indian to the position had lapsed, but there was an increasing number of apostolic vicars responsible to the pope.

For much of the seventeenth century, the Protestants kept a low profile in India. The English, Dutch, and Danish colonial trading posts had chaplains to care for their own people. There were only limited efforts at mission work.

Vietnam

Although Christianity arrived in the area now known as Vietnam in the 1580s, serious mission activity did not get underway until the Jesuits—escaping persecution in Japan—established the mission of Cochin China in 1615.

The most influential figure was the Frenchman Alexander de Rhodes (1591–1660). A stunning linguist, de Rhodes managed to produce a written script for Vietnamese using the Latin alphabet and five additional signs placed above the letters. It is his most lasting legacy, since his script has been used for writing Vietnamese ever since. De Rhodes followed the missionary practice of both Matteo Ricci and Michael Ruggieri in China, adapting Christian belief and practice to Vietnamese culture. Expelled in 1645, de Rhodes established in 1660 the *Missions étrangères de Paris*—the Paris Foreign Missions Society.

During the seventeenth century Rome became involved as well, with the Sacred Congregation for the Propagation of the Faith creating two apostolic vicars in 1658, one for the north and one for the south. A feature of Vietnamese missions was the early ordination of Vietnamese priests (1668) and a religious order of women (1690). However, by the end of the century persecution was at the door.

Sri Lanka

Originally, Christianity in Sri Lanka had come from India with the Thomas Christians. The Portuguese put an end to that, with at first the Franciscans in 1543 and then a flood of missionaries in the seventeenth century—Jesuits, Augustinian friars, and Dominicans. They adopted the simple but effective strategy of mass baptisms. It seemed to work, since despite concentrated Protestant efforts from 1658 onward (when the Dutch expelled the Portuguese), Roman Catholicism survived. Dutch Reformed missionaries and ministers worked very hard to bring the people over to Protestantism, and a good portion converted. Nonetheless, by the time the British in turn expelled the Dutch (1798) and abolished restrictions on Catholics (1806), the Catholic churches of Sri Lanka had survived.

Above: This fresco from Goa, India, depicts a saint holding a sword. The major centers of Christianity in India are Kerala, Tamil Nadu, Goa, Manipur, and Mizoram.

Left: This church in Old Goa, India, is a typical example of Portuguese colonial architecture. The Portuguese arrived on the Indian subcontinent at the end of the fifteenth century.

Opposite: Apart from being a religious building for Catholics, Notre Dame Cathedral in Ho Chi Minh City, Vietnam, was also designed to celebrate Christianity and the greatness of French civilization.

NATIVE AMERICANS AND CHRISTIANITY

Above: Spanish explorer Hernán Cortés brought Christianity to Mexico in 1519. Over the next five years Franciscan friars would convert numerous Aztec people to Christianity via baptism.

Christianity entered the Americas when the Spanish Dominicans and Franciscans settled in Mexico in the early sixteenth century and left their mark. The Jesuits joined the friars in the second half of the century and Christianity spread throughout Central America, the southern part of North America, and to South America. The Spanish faithful, emptying out monasteries and religious houses in Spain, sailed to this new frontier and moderated the harshness of the effects of the Spanish conquistadors on the indigenous people.

South America

An example of this moderating influence was the Paraguay Reductions (communities), founded by the Jesuits in 1615 and lasting until the nineteenth century. The Paraguay missions formed an extensive series of indigenous villages in the South American interior, providing the inhabitants with protection from the Portuguese Paulistas (residents of São Paulo in Brazil) who ravaged unprotected villages, stole possessions, and enslaved the people (30,000 were killed or enslaved in 1630). There were 30 Guarani villages and 11 mission towns among the Chiquito tribes; the Reductions became centers of learning and enterprise.

Many talented and dedicated Jesuits committed their lives to the rigors of mission, learning the indigenous languages, and showing the Native Americans how to construct schools and churches, make and play musical instruments, and forge military weapons for protection. Although the Reductions have been criticized for their harshness, the Paraguay Reductions were unusual in that the Jesuits did not force the Native Americans to adopt a European way of life but limited themselves to teaching Christianity and various practical arts. The apex of the Reductions was reached in 1717 with 121,168 inhabitants.

The success of the Reductions for the indigenous people became a concern for the secular colonial governments, and in 1767 they removed the Jesuits and dismantled indigenous villages. By a secret treaty in 1750 between Portugal and Spain, the Reductions fell into Portuguese hands. The Jesuits were expelled, and the indigenous people who dared to resist this injustice also endured the dismantling of their churches, schools, possessions, and economy.

Canada

An experiment similar to the Reductions began in New France in the early seventeenth century, when the Franciscan Récollets and the Jesuits began centers of indigenous evangelization near Quebec. An English military incursion in 1628 expelled the French for four years. The Jesuits returned to the colony in 1632 and three centers of evangelization were established: At Quebec for the French; at Huronia for the indigenous people; and at Ville Marie for the lay ministry to the indigenous people. Quebec became a military, economic, and religious center. From there, Jesuit missionaries began the treacherous canoe journey past Iroquois country to Huronia. They ate indigenous food, paddled birchbark canoes, and learned the indigenous languages. Because they needed to master the indigenous style of oratory used in the assemblies of chiefs, they constructed the settlement called Sainte-Marie Among the Hurons in 1639. It was a center for enculturating French Jesuits into indigenous culture and instructing the Huron people in Christianity. The Jesuits opened schools, hospitals, and churches to welcome the indigenous people and to prepare them for baptism. They perceived the strength of their culture and did not try to "gallicize" the people.

Sainte-Marie survived for ten years, until the Iroquois intensified the war by seizing control of the beaver trade and, in 1649, overwhelming the Huron villages. The Jesuits burnt Sainte-Marie, and the missionaries and the Hurons withdrew to Quebec. In 1642, Ville Marie at Montreal was founded at the geographical center of the indigenous fur trade so that zealous French laity, such as Paul de Chomedey de Maisonneuve, Jeanne Mance, and Marguerite Bourgeoys, could speed up indigenous conversions.

Above: In 1666, the missionary Jacques Marquette arrived in New France and spent two years learning various Native American languages. He "discovered" the Mississippi River in 1673 while on an expedition to evangelize the Native Americans.

British North America

While English colonists were establishing the thirteen colonies along the east coast of North America, Catholic missionaries traveled from Quebec to the American interior. Jesuits Claude Allouez and Jacques Marquette crossed the Appalachian Mountains to evangelize the Huron, Nipissing, and Illinois. Claude Allouez established mission posts, bringing the Gospel to some of the 23 tribes, and baptizing 10,000 people. Jacques Marquette ministered to the Algonquin at Sault Ste. Marie and then moved with the Illinois to Michilimackinac at the entrance to Lake Michigan. Marquette and Louis Joliet joined forces to paddle down the Mississippi River almost to New Orleans. The Jesuits preached to the nomadic nations, praying that they would adopt a sedentary Christian lifestyle.

In this period, English colonists along the east coast, including Roger Williams in Rhode Island and William Penn in Pennsylvania, purchased land from the natives and signed treaties. They were satisfied if the indigenous people moved west, and showed little interest in evangelizing them. However, Protestant missionary societies in England were formed to keep the reform tradition alive in North America among the members of the English-speaking world. Today most Native Americans continue to adhere to some form of Christianity.

Left: The first Guarani mission in Paraguay was founded by the Jesuits in 1615 in an effort to protect the Guarani people from Portuguese slave traders.

AFRICANS IN THE AMERICAS

The relationship between Africans in the Americas and Christianity is complex and indelibly linked to issues concerning colonization, the transatlantic slave trade, and slavery.

Christianizing the African

For the Africans, their introduction to the Americas, beginning in 1493, was as an alternative labor source that would help to preserve the indigenous population. For many Spanish and Portuguese colonizers, this enslavement was justified in the context of civilizing and evangelizing the Africans—it gave the Africans the opportunity to give up their idolatrous and pagan practices to become Christians. However, according to the Spanish writer, Carlos Dieve, the motive underlying the Christianization of the slaves was not just apostolic zeal, but a process which sought to easily perpetuate the physical subjugation of Africans while emphasizing the salvation of their souls. Under the Spanish and Portuguese, Christianization took the form of making sure that the slaves received Catholic instruction, and were baptized. This format was implemented in Spanish and Portuguese colonies in Central and South American countries, and the islands of the Caribbean.

Below: The island of Gorée, off the coast of Senegal, was a center for the slave trade for three centuries (1550–1850). Slave traders shipped native Africans primarily to America and the West Indies.

With the arrival and establishment of other European colonies in the seventeenth century, the importation of African slaves became an essential part of the transatlantic slave trade. This trade was comprised of three stages: Shipping manufactured goods from Europe to Africa, which were bartered for Africans; transporting native Africans to European colonies in the Americas; and returning to Europe with the tropical produce from the plantations.

Within the British and Dutch colonies, the established Protestant churches were highly dependent on and mainly served the needs of the white elite. Within such a context, any attempt to Christianize the slaves was resisted, and, more importantly, ignored. So although the 1696 British slave code stipulated that masters and mistresses should endeavor to instruct their slaves in the Christian religion as a means of facilitating their conversion and eventual baptism, it was never implemented.

In Catholicism and the non-conformist Protestant denominations, particularly the Baptists, Methodists, and Moravians, the slaves encountered a Christianity that resonated on several levels with their African religious heritage in terms of the veneration of saints, style of worship, and other beliefs. This enabled them to decode and understand the Christian Gospel through the interpretive framework of their previous religious experience. From this amalgamation emerged various Afro-Christian traditions such as an Afro-American spirituality called Winti, and during the twentieth century, Pentecostalism. These variant forms of Christianity provided the Africans and their descendants with an alternative lens through which they could see themselves, God, and their world.

The life they made

The majority of the slaves brought to the Americas originated from West Africa, specifically the areas of the Gold Coast (Ghana), Slave Coast (Togo, Benin, and western Nigeria), and the Windward Coast (Ivory Coast). For many of them, life on the plantation was extremely brutal. As a result, they developed several survival techniques, one of which was "losing" oneself. Through this form of passive resistance the slaves were able to subvert or undermine the plantation system by adopting complex hybrid personalities reflective of their daytime lives spent in their master's presence and the nighttime and weekend lives spent in the villages. Other forms of passive resistance included refusing to work, running away, and committing suicide.

Active resistance took three forms: Spontaneous rebellion, guerrilla warfare by the Maroons (runaway slaves), and planned rebellion. One unexpected feature noted among several of the planned rebellions was the prominent role that Christianity played. For although Christianizing the slaves was believed to make them obedient and more

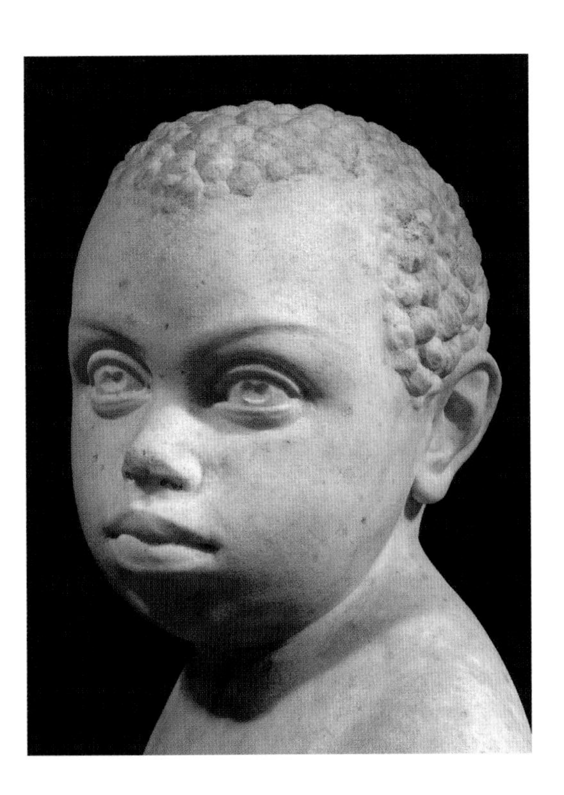

accepting of their place in society, it also brought them in contact with the doctrine of equality and the belief that personal liberty was the birthright of all people. Armed with such knowledge, several slaves sought to overthrow the tyrannical system that kept them in bondage. The slaves' interaction with the plantation system also gave rise to the creation of Creole dialects and various forms of music and dance which incorporated African and European cultural and linguistic elements.

The Christian legacy

Christianity and its denominational expressions continue to play a significant role in the lives of Africans and their descendants in the Americas. For many, the Church has been, and continues to be, a place that engenders the authentic expressions of their faith, while also providing them with a place of acceptance, empowerment, and belonging. Although certain aspects of Christianity have been, and continue to be, used to disempower and subjugate Africans in the Americas, it has also provided many with an active framework in which to interrogate and address various issues within society including racism, socioeconomic deprivation, and violence.

Above: Reverend William Knibb was a Baptist missionary in Jamaica who campaigned against slavery. He acquired land for settlements where emancipated slaves could live without fear of being evicted.

Top left: This statue of an African boy symbolizes the slave trade that took place in Nantes, France's largest port, during the eighteenth century. The city's wealth came from shipping slaves to the New World.

Left: In 1807, the British Parliament passed the *Slave Trade Act,* which abolished the slave trade throughout its dominions. It was a response to the anti-slavery campaign led by the Evangelical Protestants and Quakers.

PART SIX

REVOLUTION

1701–1800 CE

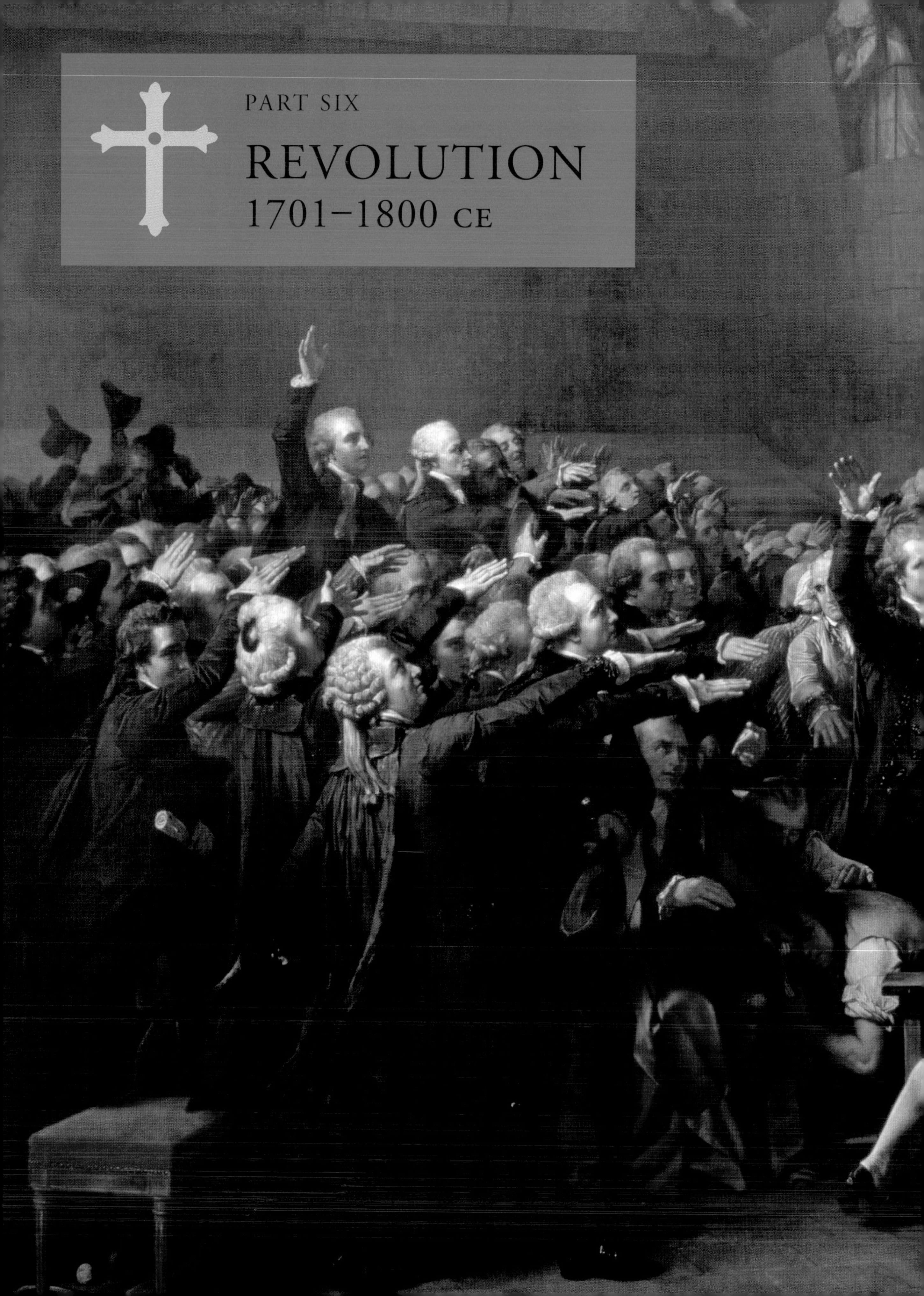

PETER I ABOLISHES THE PATRIARCHATE

Previous pages: During the French Revolution, members of the Third Estate, led by Abbé Sieyès and Mirabeau, signed a pledge called the Tennis Court Oath, that formed the National Assembly, the name of France's new primary legislative body.

For 42 of his 52 years, Peter I (Peter the Great) ruled Russia. He became joint emperor (with his brother Ivan V under the patronage of his sister Sofia) at the age of 10, then sole emperor in 1696. For the following three decades until his death in 1725 he undertook a massive and energetic reform of Russia, bringing it out of its isolation and turning it into a major European power. He was perpetually at war, often traveling, and when at home he followed through a bewildering array of reforms based on Western models.

Undermining power structures

Such achievements can only be carried out by someone with immense strength of will and determination. Peter brooked no rival. A major policy to cement power was to undermine the existing power structures that challenged and frustrated his work. One was the imperial service. Tradition had it that the boyars (nobles) were appointed to senior positions on hereditary lines. Peter abolished this practice and introduced a "Table of Ranks" in which positions in the imperial service were appointed on the basis of competent service to the emperor. In addition, Peter insisted, after returning from a long trip to Western Europe, that the boyars should adopt Western dress and shave off their massive beards. Those who refused to do so had to pay a beard tax of 100 rubles.

Another challenge lay with the Russian Orthodox Church. It had a knack of attracting many of the best and brightest among the nobility into its ranks, especially into the monasteries. So Peter devised a law that ensured he could make use of such talent instead. No male, he decreed, was to join a monastery before the age of fifty. Given that this age was the life expectancy of most people at the time, the monasteries were not only deprived of talent but they became old people's homes—should one make it past fifty.

Below: Russian Orthodox women shared common liturgical and iconographic practices. Orthodox rituals were a part of their daily life and defined the behavior, moral values, and social roles they displayed.

Peter strikes

Peter's major act during his reign was to abolish the patriarchate. Since 1589 Moscow had had its own independent patriarch. Although the Church was in full communion with other Orthodox churches, the Moscow patriarch was autocephalous—he was not subject to any higher authority. He was an extraordinarily powerful figure and Peter saw clearly an entrenched system of power distinct from his own. Peter set out to change this situation, although he was clever enough to avoid ousting the sitting patriarch.

Peter's chance came in 1700, when the Patriarch Adrian died, and Peter deliberately slowed down the process of appointing a successor. He could do so, since although the patriarch was elected by the bishops, the tsar had the final

say. For 21 years Peter allowed the patriarch's coadjutor to carry out the task. Finally, he instituted his "Spiritual Regulation," in which the patriarchate was abolished, including the coadjutor. In its place came the Most Holy Synod.

Most Holy Synod

The synod was made up of 10 then later 12 leading clergy. It included the metropolitans of St Petersburg, Moscow, and Kiev, as well as the Exarch of Georgia. But Peter was not going to let the synod out of his control, so he ensured that members of the Holy Synod could be appointed and dismissed by him at any time. Furthermore, a government official, the Chief Procurator, attended all the meetings and had a hand in all decisions. Its reach was extensive, covering every aspect of life in the Church, and indeed some outside the Church. A partial list of its responsibilities includes purity of the faith, conduct of worship, removal of superstition and heresy, publication of religious books, public religious education, Church courts, and even marriage. Although the structure was new, especially with imperial control, it was an extraordinarily clever move. The idea of a holy synod goes back to the earliest Church and has a very strong pedigree. Peter could argue that he was reinstituting an ancient practice while bringing the Church firmly under his control. Later, Greece and Egypt would also establish holy synods, based on the Russian model. The difference was that the patriarch remained in these places, although he is subject to the synod and does not have complete power.

As with many of Peter the Great's reforms, this new arrangement lasted for almost two centuries. Ironically, it was only after the February Revolution in 1917, when rule by the tsars came to an end, that a new patriarch—Tikhon—was elected by the council of bishops. The Patriarch of Moscow remains an office to this day.

Above: Patriarch Adrian was Patriarch of Moscow and All Russia from 1690 to 1700. He adhered strictly to Godliness and tradition, and opposed Peter the Great's reforms.

Left: The interior of a Russian Orthodox Church always features vibrant iconic art. Icons are filled with symbolism and follow a set methodology for how the saint should be depicted.

ENLIGHTENMENT IN WESTERN EUROPE

Opposite: The combined emphasis on reason, experience, and naturalism during the Enlightenment led to a skeptical attitude toward the resurrection of Christ and other miracles.

In his 1784 essay "What is Enlightenment?" Immanuel Kant wrote, "If we are asked, 'Do we now live in an enlightened age?' the answer is, 'No,' but we do live in an age of enlightenment." The Enlightenment, traditionally dated from the English Glorious Revolution of 1689 to the French Revolution of 1789, heralded modernity, and Kant's influential essay provides a scintillating review of the message of the *philosophes*, as the multinational group of thinkers and writers were known. Kant extolled freedom and progress, and exhorted his readers, "Have courage to use your own reason!" He blamed laziness and cowardice as the hindrances to enlightenment, and singled out clerical "religious incompetence" for particular scorn, calling it "not only the most harmful but the most degrading of all." In this opinion, Kant concurred with the other *philosophes*, who assailed Christianity as the worst purveyor of ignorance, superstition, and repression.

The major thinkers of the Enlightenment—Voltaire, Montesquieu, Denis Diderot, David Hume, Jean-Jacques Rousseau, Edward Gibbon, Adam Smith, Benjamin Franklin, Thomas Jefferson, and Kant—cultivated a united image, despite many fundamental internecine disagreements, frequently involving Rousseau. As a "family" of intellectuals, they hoped for progress despite the erratic historical record of it. They celebrated the dignity of the rational, autonomous individual and, like the Renaissance Humanists, found inspiration in pagan antiquity. They demanded attention, and by doing so invented modernity, particularly the liberal tradition within it.

Below: As a scientist, Benjamin Franklin was a significant figure in the Enlightenment. He was born into a Puritan family, but as an adult became a Deist, like many of his fellow thinkers.

A scientific method

The popular memory of the Enlightenment as the Age of Reason does not recall the complexity of the epistemological disagreement among the *philosophes*, who were divided between the Rationalists (who believed that knowledge derives from reason) and the Empiricists (who believed that knowledge derives from experience, and who did not value reason as highly as the Rationalists did). Toward the end of the Enlightenment period, Kant, in his 1781 book *Critique of Pure Reason*, was able to reconcile rationalism and empiricism by distinguishing between *a priori* knowledge from reason, which was not omnicompetent as the Rationalists claimed, and *a posteriori* knowledge from experience, which was always biased. Therefore, given the shortcomings of both epistemologies, the task of the philosopher was investigative and analytical rather than descriptive. Additionally, the *philosophes* were staunch adherents of naturalism, the argument that all phenomena are understandable according to laws ascertained methodically, as Isaac Newton had shown when he discovered his three laws of motion. The historian Edward Gibbon demonstrated the elasticity of naturalism when he explained the fall of Rome according to historical causes, not one of which was God's wrath.

Theologians found themselves in a bind. The Rationalists had demanded that theology be accountable to reason, the Empiricists had demanded that theology correspond to experience, and the Naturalists had demanded that theology be explicable by scientific theory, all of which meant a devaluation of faith and miracles. Moreover, the Kantian synthesis ruled impermissible any scholastic appeal to reason, which vitiated such longstanding theological projects as proving the existence of God. The dilemma for theologians was how to remain recognizably orthodox and adjust to the new intellectual atmosphere, in which, for instance, a belief in the resurrection of Christ—a miracle apprehended by faith—appeared naive and infantile. From that point onward, the theology that appeared in response to the Enlightenment attempted to adhere to the rules that the *philosophes* had stipulated.

Liberty from God and His obnoxious church

The *philosophes* identified Christianity in its various guises as a formidable enemy to be subdued, and they enlisted the classical pagans, who had created a progressive civilization before the appearance of the Apostles, in their service. The main problem with Christianity was not simply that it was irrational and therefore implausible, but that it impeded liberty. Voltaire for this reason was the sworn enemy of the Catholic Church, because it abhorred individual autonomy, which the *philosophes* esteemed most of all, as even reason was a means to autonomous ends. On the other hand, Rousseau, frequently at odds with Enlightenment thought, recognized the limits of autonomy, famously beginning *The Social Contract* with "Man is born free, and everywhere he is in chains." Rousseau also doubted his counterparts' adoration of reason, thus articulating a countertrend that would soon thrive as Romanticism.

If any form of religion was to be acceptable, it must place far fewer dogmatic demands on its adherents than orthodox Christianity, which is how Deism emerged as the preferred religion of the *philosophes*. English philosopher William Paley's analogy of God as a watchmaker and the universe as a watch illustrates apprehension regarding a personal, evangelical God, and thus noncommittal terms like "The Almighty" provided a tolerable alternative.

THE GREAT AWAKENING

Right: The Old First Church of Christ (Congregational) in Springfield, Massachussets, is the fourth church building to be erected on this site. The original church was built in 1645.

The Great Awakening was the name given to a period of intense religious enthusiasm and fervor in the 1730s and 1740s, primarily in North America but associated with the Evangelical Revival in Britain in the same period. The Congregationalist pastor Solomon Stoddard had laid the foundation for reform in Northampton, Massachusetts, between 1643 and 1729. Stoddard was succeeded as pastor of the church by his grandson, Jonathan Edwards, who claimed to have noticed a new enthusiasm for the Christian faith when in 1734 he began to preach a series of sermons on justification by faith—that a person can have a good relationship with God through faith in God alone rather than by doing good works or merely attending church services. This fresh response to the Christian Gospel lasted for three years, but seems to have been waning by 1737 when it was reported by Edwards in his *A Faithful Narrative of the Surprising Work of God.* These first signs of revival sparked great debate about the necessity and appropriateness of religious experience, with critics of Edwards claiming that he had blatantly appealed to the emotions of people. Edwards later believed that this emotional outpouring was the first expression of the much greater awakening that was to come.

George Whitefield

Edwards was correct in pointing out that the experience of his Northampton parishioners was not unique and certainly not an isolated experience. The Great Awakening, as it came to be known, was a much larger event that included a number of revivals that swept up and down the eastern coast of America between 1740 and 1743. The person responsible for fanning the isolated flames of revival into one great fire was the "Grand Itinerant" George Whitefield (1714–1770). Whitefield, a Calvinistic Methodist from

Below: George Whitefield was an enthralling preacher who is known to have held crowds of 20,000 spellbound at Moorfields and Kennington Common in London. He preached more than 18,000 sermons in his lifetime.

England, had been a member of the Oxford Holy Club, which had included the brothers John and Charles Wesley. While John Wesley concentrated his preaching for renewal on England, Whitefield crossed the Atlantic Ocean many times preaching tirelessly and enthusiastically about the necessity of an experience of faith. According to Whitefield, part of the responsibility for the decline in Christian churches could be laid at the feet of preachers who seemed to talk of an "unknown and unfelt Christ." Whitefield concluded that "the reason why congregations have been so dead is that dead men preach to them."

Urging ministers to take up the task of preaching for conversion, Whitefield convinced the Presbyterian Gilbert Tennent (1703–1764) and the more emotionally unstable James Davenport (1716–1757) to embark on an itinerant tour in order to "blow up the divine fire," which had already been kindled in various places in New England. They were followed by other lay and itinerant preachers who often preached using a flamboyant style, and looked for an emotional response from their audience, such as fainting, weeping, and shrieking. Characterized by these emotional outbursts and, sometimes, direct appeals for signs of conversion, the Revival preachers managed to stir up a great deal of opposition as well as support. Many condemned the direct and affective preaching for conversion as little more than emotional tactics. The overall result was to encourage a new evangelistic zeal among the people and a concern for vital Christian faith.

Above: Jonathan Edwards is recognized as one of America's most important philosophical theologians. His work expressed two themes: The absolute sovereignty of God and the beauty of God's holiness.

Revival unity and division

While the general excitement of the Great Awakening lasted only three years, from 1740 to 1743, the long-term result was that many regular ministers were shaped by this new emphasis on personal evangelism. While denominations divided into those who were in favor of Revival methods and those who were not (the New Lights and Old Lights respectively), among both groups there was a new enthusiasm and a sense of responsibility for proclaiming the Gospel message. Another outcome of the Great Awakening was to draw together people of a similar evangelical outlook, in spite of doctrinal difference or denominational affiliation. This kind of evangelical fellowship would later become a powerful force in American culture.

The Revival has never been satisfactorily explained. Some historians have pointed to social or psychological reasons, but can't explain why it seems to have included people of different social and intellectual backgrounds. The Congregationalist Jonathan Edwards, who later served as president of Princeton University and is acknowledged as the first American theologian, always maintained that the Revival was a sign of God's work among the people. He wrote analytical descriptions of the Revival, placing it in a theological context. He was opposed by Charles Chauncy, a minister in Boston, who wrote a treatise entitled *Seasonable Thoughts on the State of Religion in New England* (1743) and claimed that reason was just as important, if not more so, than emotional behavior. Edwards, nevertheless, maintained that "true religion, in great part consists of holy affections."

AMERICAN WAR OF INDEPENDENCE

Above: The death of General Warren at the Battle of Bunker Hill during the American Revolution in 1775. He played a role in the activities leading to the revolution and gave addresses venerating the Boston Massacre.

In retrospect, the American Revolution seems hardly inevitable. British forces won an impressive victory in the French and Indian War (1756–1763). The colonial militias bravely fought alongside the British regulars, and at the end of the war, the motherland and her colonies seemed quite united. However, ensuing British policies and taxes estranged many of the colonists, and the American Patriot Party moved in the direction of rebellion. A now-famous sequence of events provoked a crisis: The Boston Massacre (1770), when British soldiers fired into a jeering crowd, killing five; the Boston Tea Party (1773), when colonists disguised as Indians dumped tea into the harbor to protest the British tax on tea imports and the monopoly given to the East India Company; the "Intolerable Acts," in which Parliament attempted to reassert control; the skirmishes at Lexington and Concord (April 1775); and vicious battles at Breed's Hill and Bunker Hill (June 1775). The Declaration of Independence, written mostly by Thomas Jefferson and approved by the Second Continental Congress on July 4, 1776, framed the cause for independence as liberty conquering tyranny, which would produce many repercussions for American Christianity. The subsequent war arrived as a British invasion and occupation of the colonies of Boston, New York, and Philadelphia.

Christianity and the revolution

Many dissenters and Separatists from the Church of England colonized British America. They descended from the English Puritans who were after all the revolutionaries who aggravated the volatility during the reign of Charles I, victoriously prosecuted a war, and executed the king. In the next century, another British king, George III, discovered that more than one hundred years and transatlantic emigration had done little to allay the enthusiasm of the colonial descendants of the Puritans.

CHRISTIANITY AND AFRICAN-AMERICANS

With disgracefully few exceptions, colonial Christians did and said little about the abomination of slavery. In 1787, the Black Methodist preacher Richard Allen protested the abject treatment of his fellow Black Methodists, and eventually he established in Philadelphia the Bethel African Methodist Episcopal Church, which was the foundation of the African Methodist Episcopal Church. Also in Philadelphia in 1794, Absalom Jones, the first Black Episcopal priest, founded the St Thomas African Episcopal Church, the first Black Episcopal Church in America. These two events foreshadowed the development of a distinct African-American Christianity that would speak powerfully in American history and culture.

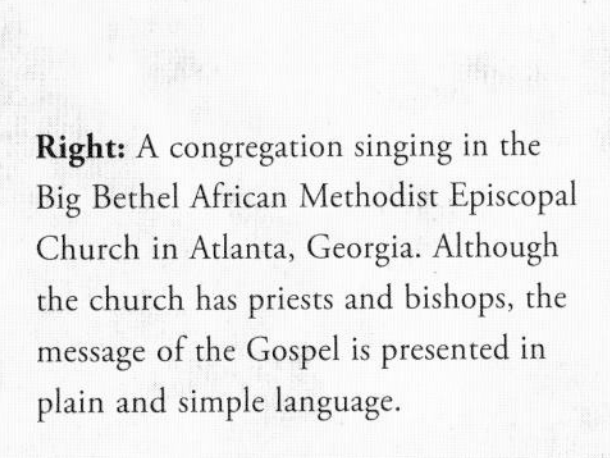

Right: A congregation singing in the Big Bethel African Methodist Episcopal Church in Atlanta, Georgia. Although the church has priests and bishops, the message of the Gospel is presented in plain and simple language.

None of the major revolutionary leaders—George Washington, Benjamin Franklin, John Adams, and Thomas Jefferson—practiced evangelical Christianity; they were more inspired by the radical thinkers of the Enlightenment than the preachers of the Great Awakening. However, their lack of "enthusiasm" did not vacate the place of Christian thought and culture in their minds. Their strong ideas about political morality derived as much from the debates of seventeenth-century British Christianity as from eighteenth-century philosophy, and they frequently appropriated theological language. They sought through prayer, and acknowledged in word, divine assistance in their cause.

The rhetoric that paved the way to the American War of Independence was replete with Biblical imagery and Christian symbolism. The Continental Army had chaplains in its service who led daily prayers and weekly worship, which George Washington attended. The chaplains would sometimes exhort the soldiers to fight courageously for the cause of liberty. Pastors engaged in pro-American partisanship, lending their support from the pulpit via readings of the Bible that saw the colonies as the New Israel, which through obedience to God would bless the world or through disobedience would receive God's curse. Many pastors became directly involved in politics, and some even joined the army to fight or to serve as chaplains.

New directions

In the aftermath of the war, much had changed for American Christianity, but two groups—Anglicans and African-American Christians (see box)—provide especially poignant stories of the new situation. Anglicans found themselves in a double predicament. First, how might they remain good Anglicans, given all the cultural and organizational implications thereof, while appearing to be good citizens of the United States? Second, conversely, how might they proceed as American members of the Church of England; that is, true to both Anglican and democratic principles? During the war, Loyalists such as Henry Caner, the Anglican rector of King's Chapel in Boston, had experienced tremendous anxiety for remaining devoted to the Church of England in tumultuous Boston. Although some committed Anglicans opted out of the problem by moving to Canada, those working toward a postwar solution discovered one by drawing upon both evangelical religion and democratic principles, particularly the employment of the laity in church polity. The American Church needing a bishop, and with the Church of England uncooperative, American theologian Samuel Seabury traveled to Scotland in 1783 to secure episcopal consecration from sympathetic Scottish bishops, and then in 1789, the new ecclesiastical body called the Protestant Episcopal Church was born in America.

Below: Thomas Jefferson was a powerful advocate of liberty who, after the American Revolution, went on to become the third president of the United States. He also founded the University of Virginia.

CONSTITUTIONAL LIFE IN AMERICA

Above: Anglican clergyman Sir Thomas Bray was established the Church of England in North America. He recruited missionaries and envisaged a library in each parish in America.

Below: The Abbey Church in Bath, England, was ruined after the dissolution of monasteries during the English reformation—an order by Henry VIII to strengthen the Church of England in that country.

"Congress shall make no law respecting an establishment of religion, or prohibiting the free exercise thereof." So begins the First Amendment to the Constitution of the United States of America. The first clause prohibits the establishment of any religion; the second protects the free exercise of religion.

Old habits linger in the New World

The Church of England had been established in several early colonies in North America, especially the southern colonies. Dissenters who fled the effects of an established church in England nonetheless set up their own form of Christianity in the northern colonies. The mid-Atlantic colonies were religiously plural, and a number of them (Pennsylvania, West Jersey, Delaware, and Rhode Island) had no established church. These middle colonies were laboratories for experimentation in freedom of religion.

The colonies with established churches followed the "Old World" model: "Dissenting" or "nonconforming" churches might be made illegal or denied places to meet. Individuals who belonged to a dissenting church could be barred from public office, or sentenced to weeks in prison and hefty fines for failing to attend the established church's worship services. While many of the first settlers arriving in North America came seeking religious freedom for their own beliefs, they did not at first understand that freedom for one meant freedom for all. It would take more than a century, and the efforts of trailblazers like Roger Williams and William Penn, before most colonists were willing to adopt the twin values enshrined in the First Amendment: Separation of Church and state (no religious establishment), and religious freedom (free exercise of religion).

Even after it was ratified on December 15, 1791, the First Amendment and the rest of the Bill of Rights only applied to the federal government. It was not until 1868 that the provisions of the Bill of Rights were made applicable at the state as well as federal level.

The task of interpretation

The Supreme Court, which interprets the Constitution, has ruled that the "establishment clause" of the First Amendment is intended to erect a "wall of separation" between Church and state. This does not mean that government is obligated to be hostile to religion, and the US Supreme Court has on several occasions recognized a need for a kind of benevolent neutrality between Church and state. The protection against "establishment of religion" is made more difficult to define with precision due to the equally compelling need to safeguard the right to "free exercise of religion." The Supreme

Court has emphasized for over three decades that a violation of one's protection against establishment of religion may occur when governmental actions have either a primary religious end or primary religious effect, or when government becomes excessively entangled in the affairs of religion.

The court battles have been fiercest in the area of state-funded education, where issues of Bible reading in classes, public prayer in schools and, most recently, efforts to have "Intelligent Design" (the theory that the universe exhibits intelligent design as opposed to random chaos) taught as a scientific alternative to evolutionary theory, have divided the nation. The courts have consistently ruled that Intelligent Design is a religious, not a scientific, theory, and therefore has no place in public schools. In 1963, the Supreme Court ruled that the Bible is not to be taught as a confessional document, but it may be taught as literature or for its value as an historical document. State-sponsored prayer is prohibited, but classrooms may be used for religious gatherings and prayer when classes are not in session. Finally, teachers may not proselytize in the classroom.

The "Establishment of Religion" Clause

"The 'establishment of religion' clause of the First Amendment means at least this: Neither a state nor the federal government can set up a church. Neither can pass laws which aid one religion, aid all religions, or prefer one religion over another. Neither can force nor influence a person to go to or to remain away from church against his will or force him to profess a belief or disbelief in any religion. No person can be punished for entertaining or professing religious beliefs or disbeliefs, for church attendance or non-attendance. No tax in any amount, large or small, can be levied to support any religious activities or institutions, whatever they may be called, or whatever form they may adopt to teach or practice religion... In the words of Jefferson, the clause against establishment of religion by law was intended to erect 'a wall of separation between church and State'." Supreme Court Justice Hugo Black, 1947.

Below: President Bill Clinton delivers his 1997 State of the Union Address. The system of federal government seen today in the United States derived from the Constitution.

THE FRENCH REVOLUTION

Above: On July 14, 1789, Parisians stormed the Bastille, a prison which represented royal authority. Along with old grievances, severe food shortages and extravagant spending by the monarchy had spurred the people to action.

Previous pages: Nuns from the Sisters of Our Lady of Charity of the Refuge, founded in Normandy, France, in 1641. During the French Revolution some people feared nuns might disrupt social order, and called for convents to be abolished.

The French Revolution had many causes: Economic, political, social. It also had religious origins. The religion of France was Roman Catholicism; and since the 1685 revocation of the Edict of Nantes and the expulsion of the Huguenots, most French people were Catholics. But over the course of many years, the French state had secured extraordinary control over the Church. These so-called Gallican liberties—of which both the French state and French Church were very proud—included the right to nominate bishops and almost total control over Church lands and revenue.

The Church in the Ancien Régime

The French state had been in decline long before the fall of the Bastille in 1789. This decay extended to the Church, which reflected the stratification and ossification of French society. The episcopate and the positions of the higher clergy were the near-exclusive preserve of the nobility; for much of the eighteenth century, not one bishop was commonborn. While noble birth was a requirement, piety was not. Some prominent bishops in the later part of the century were at best Deists, and made little effort to hide the fact. The religious orders were little better. The wealth of some of the larger abbeys was under the control of commendatory abbots—men appointed for family or political reasons who, although they received the abbey's income, were never resident and quite often laymen. The secular clergy, excluded from advancement, were often ill educated, disgruntled, and tempted by egalitarianism. In elite circles, the Church had long been the target of men such as Voltaire, who deployed sarcasm and scorn to withering effect. Socially, the Church's vast landed (and other) wealth was resented as unproductive and unearned. The French Church was seen as an integral part of an unpopular Ancien Régime.

Revolution and the First Estate

The decision to call the Estates-General (a kind of three-chambered parliament, based on social class) for 1789 was an important moment for the French Church. As the First Estate, the Church had an important role to play in any new political dispensation. Given its hierarchical nature, it might be expected that the Church's representatives would be devoted monarchists and reactionaries. This turned out not to be the case, largely because the decision was made that the electoral districts for the First Estate would not coincide with diocesan boundaries. This introduced an element of competition between bishops, and allowed the lower clergy a certain freedom of maneuver. Although a number of bishops, and a greater number of their candidates, were selected, many radical lower clergy found themselves in Paris.

Although the Estates-General began with a grand religious procession, the place of the Church quickly became precarious, and then collapsed altogether. In the meetings of the First Estate, the tensions between higher and lower clergy quickly broke into the open, and the lower clergy began to look to the Third (or common) Estate for allies. On June 13, 1789, three curés joined the Third Estate, more followed, and on June 17, Abbé Sieyès proclaimed the National Assembly. Two days later, the majority of the First Estate ratified this decision.

Break with Rome

The increasing radicalism of the National Assembly and its successors was felt by the Church: In July 1790, the Civil Constitution of the Clergy was passed. It suppressed sees, changed the territory of others to match political boundaries, and eliminated archbishops and the higher clergy without the "care of souls." All priests were to become civil servants, paid and controlled by the state. It was the triumph of the radicalized lower clergy, who gained a legal share in the administration of their dioceses. The laity gained the right to elect parish priests. It was a total rejection of the Council of Trent and as such was anathema not only to French traditionalists but also to the Holy See. The oath of obedience to the Civil Constitution demanded of all priests was resisted by most of the bishops and—a surprise—by the majority of the curés. The revolution had pushed too far, and left the bulk of the Church behind.

The terror

There were now two Catholic churches in France, the Roman and the Constitutional. In early 1791 the first Constitutional bishops were consecrated, formalizing the split. As the revolution passed into the hands of the Jacobins, Church lands became targets for seizure, and non-juring clerics candidates for the guillotine; hundreds if not thousands died. Maximilien Robespierre's short-lived Cult of the Supreme Being was only the most obvious manifestation of the Jacobins' hostility to Catholicism. Until Napoleon Bonaparte made his peace with Rome in 1801, the French Church remained implacably opposed to the revolution. Although many faithful Catholics had joined in the fervor of 1789, the radicalization of the revolution forced them to choose between their faith and their politics.

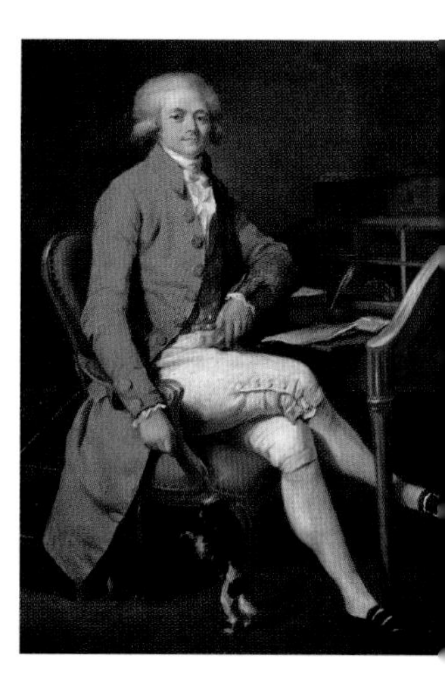

Above: Maximilien Robespierre. As a member of the Committee of Public Safety, he was part of the Reign of Terror in which many people opposed to the revolution were executed.

Below: A church is confiscated during the French Revolution. This was a time of great hostility toward Christianity because the Roman Church was seen as part of the earlier government.

METHODISM

Above: John Wesley founded Methodism. He formed societies in England, Scotland, Wales, and Ireland, and traveled widely throughout the Bristish Isles, often on horseback, preaching as he rode.

Methodism had its beginnings in eighteenth-century Anglicanism. The movement may be traced to a group known as the Holy Club, which formed in Oxford about 1729. They met regularly for prayer and Bible study and they engaged in acts of charity. Dubbed "Methodists" by their opponents because of their methodical approach to holiness of life, members of the group included the preacher George Whitefield (1714–1770), Charles Wesley (1707–1788), and John Wesley (1703–1791)—who was later recognized as the founder of Methodism.

An experience of faith

Brought up in a devout Anglican home, John and Charles Wesley were nurtured in Christian faith by their mother Susanna and father Samuel, a priest in the Church of England. After studying at Christ Church College in Oxford, John Wesley was ordained as an Anglican priest in 1725 and then went to Georgia in the American colonies to serve as a missionary. Restless and longing for an assurance of faith, en route to America he met Moravian missionaries. Impressed by their confident devotion to Christ, when John Wesley returned to London he continued his conversations with the Moravian leader, Peter Böhler.

In 1738, John Wesley went to a small-group meeting in Aldersgate Street in London where at last he claimed to have discovered an assurance of faith. At the meeting, as someone was reading from the preface to Martin Luther's *Commentary on The Epistle to the Romans*, Wesley said that he felt his "heart was strangely warmed." He wrote: "I felt I did trust in Christ, Christ alone, for salvation; and an assurance was given me that he had taken away my sins." This experience proved to be a turning point for Wesley, who went on to become a preacher and a leader of the Evangelical Revival in Britain.

Revival methods

The success of the Methodist movement may be attributed to John Wesley's organizational skills and the promotion of certain Revival "methods" such as field preaching and the formation of small-group meetings for prayer and Bible study. To oversee these small groups, Wesley appointed itinerant, non-ordained preachers who traveled widely, evangelizing and caring for people in the societies. Women as well as men were encouraged to take active leadership roles and to preach and exhort others in the societies. Hymn singing was another important part of the Wesleyan movement. John Wesley's brother Charles wrote many hymns that provided a way of teaching and summing up Christian doctrine. In addition to preaching and writing many treatises and sermons, John Wesley corresponded with other evangelical leaders, opened chapels, and established a school at Kingswood in Bristol.

John Wesley was opposed by many who felt that his methods were a threat to the Church of England and to

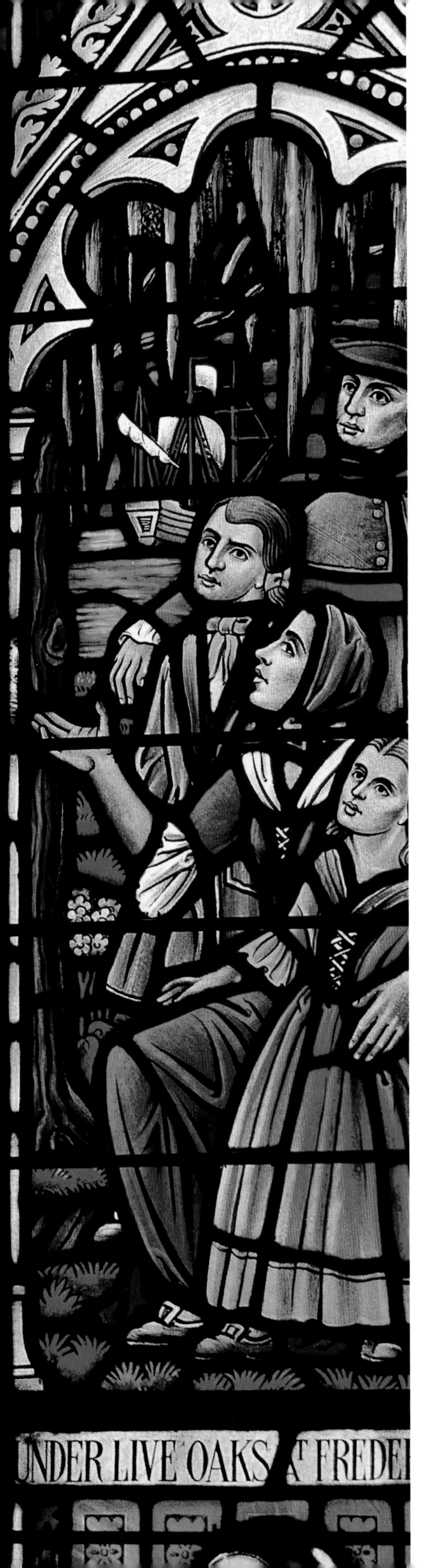

society as a whole. These adversaries felt that he should not encourage meetings for preaching without being ordained and licensed by the established Church. Yet, in spite of being castigated, ridiculed as fanatics, and at times even physically attacked for preaching, the Methodists continued to believe that it was necessary to use every means to call people to genuine repentance and faith.

Left: A stained glass window depicting Charles Wesley, who was a leader of the Methodist movement. He is renowned for his hymns, having published more than 5,500 in his lifetime.

The growth of Methodism

Although he is considered the founder of Methodism, to the end John Wesley claimed he had not intended to start a new denomination, and he considered himself to be a member of the Church of England. However, the fact that he ordained bishops for the Church in America in 1784 and, in the same year, set up the yearly Conference of the People called Methodists, meant that the Methodist movement would continue as a separate group after his death. By 1795, Methodists in Britain were clearly recognized as a group in their own right when they were legally able to conduct marriages and perform the sacraments.

John Wesley held to an Arminian theology (started by Jacobus Arminius) and believed that Christ's death on the cross was for all people. There were other Methodists who were Calvinistic in their outlook. They believed that Christ died only for "the elect" or those who had been chosen by God. Calvinistic Methodists enjoyed great success in Wales and were led by Howell Harris (1714–1773), Daniel Rowlands (1713–1790), and others who were connected to preachers associated with the Countess of Huntingdon, Selina Hastings (1707–1791). George Whitefield was also a Calvinistic Methodist who preached in England and crossed the ocean many times in order to encourage the evangelical awakening. Both Whitefield and John Wesley are credited with leadership of the Evangelical Revival, which became an international, indeed, intercontinental phenomenon in the eighteenth century.

Below: Lovely Lane Meeting House in Baltimore, Maryland, is considered the first Methodist church in America. In 1784, it held the famous Christmas Conference where the Methodist Episcopal Church was born.

BEGINNINGS OF CHRISTIANITY IN KOREA

Right: In 1592, the great Samurai feudal lord Toyotomi Hideyoshi sent Japanese armies to invade Korea. Hundreds of Koreans were taken prisoner and sent to Japan, where they became devout Catholics.

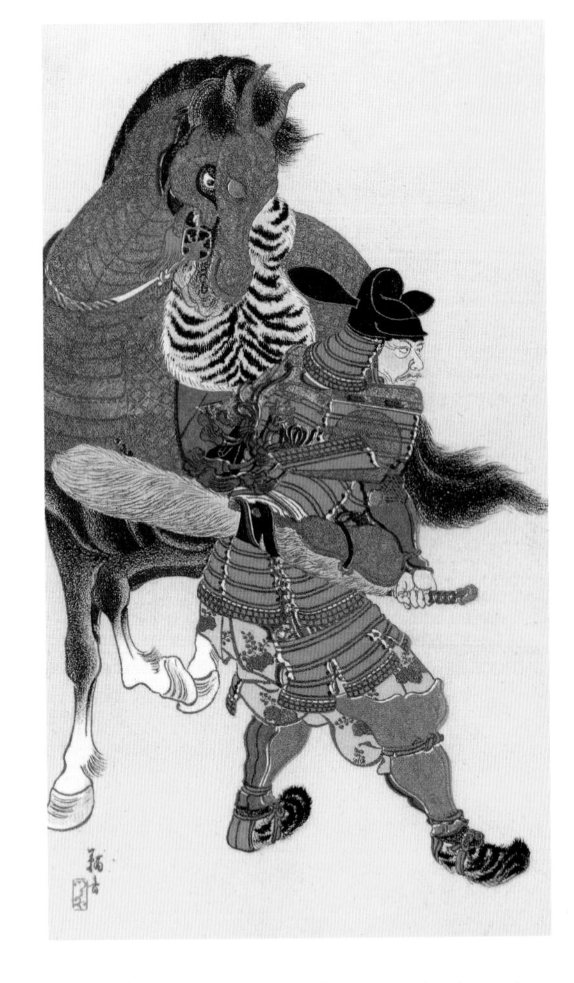

Before Christianity reached Korea, religious and philosophical inspiration came from animism, Confucianism, Buddhism, and Daoism. In the last decade of the sixteenth century, Japan invaded Korea, and Jesuit priests ministered to Korean Christians on the peninsula. In Japan at the beginning of the seventeenth century several Korean Christians were martyred along with Japanese Christians. During the next two and a half centuries, the Korean emperor maintained barriers around the "Hermit Kingdom" to keep travelers, traders, and missionaries at bay. However, in Peking (Beijing) Jesuits baptized Koreans during the annual diplomatic missions. In 1784, while participating in a diplomatic mission from Korea to Peking, Korean scholar Lee Seung-hoon discovered Christian books written in Mandarin by the seventeenth-century Jesuit Matteo Ricci and his companions. He was impressed by the exposition of Christianity he found. Father Jean de Grammont baptized him, and he accepted the Christian name Peter.

Founding Christianity

In 1784, Peter returned to Seoul with Christian writings and instructed his friends and baptized them, Lee Byok as John Baptist and Kwon Il Shin as Francis Xavier. Through Peter the Christian community was firmly re-established in Korea. Christian evangelism continued, converts were baptized, and the community held prayer services and expanded. The laity expanded the communities of the Korean Catholic Church but in 1794, concerned by the lack of educated clergy, the bishop of Peking sent James Chu, a Chinese priest, to assist the community. A growing Christian community of 4,000 welcomed him. For the continuity of the community, the Holy See asked the Paris Foreign Missions Society (*Missions étrangères de Paris* or MEP) to minister to the emerging Korean Church.

Below: An example of religious freedom, seen in today's multi-religious Korea, is the Daoist practice of burning joss sticks and making offerings to various deities during Daoist festivals.

Persecutions

Despite these auspicious beginnings, the Korean Church was to suffer severe persecutions in the years 1791, 1801, 1839, 1846, 1866, and 1869, and during these times around 8,000 Christians were executed. The community grew, but in 1801, seven years after Father Chu's arrival, he and 300 other Christians were put to death for their faith. Three priests arrived from the Paris Foreign Missions Society and were martyred in the persecution of 1839.

The first Korean priest, Andrew Kim, was ordained near Shanghai in 1845 and arrived in Korea with a bishop and a priest from China. Andrew knew his father had suffered martyrdom in 1839, and prepared himself for the same fate. He objected to an accusation of treason by saying: "If I have held communication with foreigners, it has been for my religion and for my God. It is for Him that I die. My immortal life is on the point of beginning." In 1846, at 25 years of age, Andrew Kim was tortured and beheaded.

Above: The founder of Christianity in Korea, Lee Seung-hoon, was so impressed by the Jesuits during his travels in China that he converted and baptized many nobles on his return to Korea.

A second Korean priest, Thomas Choi, arrived in 1849. The term "Korean martyrs" today refers to two groups canonized by the Catholic Church: 79 executed in various fashions between 1839 and 1846 were beatified in 1924; 24 more were beatified in 1968. These 103 Christians were canonized in 1984. They included both Korean men and women, and a few clergy from the Paris Foreign Missions Society who were beheaded, strangled, tortured to death, or died in prison from neglect. Despite persecution, the struggling Korean Church community grew to 7 priests and 15,000 laity in 1857, and 12 priests and 23,000 laity in 1866. The Korean martyrs represent the fourth largest group of martyrs in the Catholic Church.

Religious freedom

The persecutions ended in 1883 when, by diplomatic agreement, Korea was opened to the world, and religious freedom was accepted. Diplomatic pressure saw the French missionary and bishop Félix Ridel released from a Korean prison to build a viable church. He sent Korean seminarians to Malaya to study for ordination as Catholic priests, built a cathedral in Seoul and churches elsewhere, and opened his own seminary in Seoul in 1891. After 1885, a number of American Presbyterians and Methodists came to Korea; following World War II they were joined by several other Protestant denominations (discussed in Part Seven).

At least two Korean families' Catholicism can be traced back to the early seventeenth century. Three archdioceses and twelve suffragan dioceses guide the South Korean Catholic Church. North Korea has one Catholic church in Pyongyang, but no clergy to minister to an estimated 3,000 Catholics. Catholics in South Korea publish a daily and weekly newspaper and several periodicals. Despite a strongly Catholic history, South Korea's Christians are mostly Protestant; Christians make up around 40 percent of the population of 49 million, and Buddhists represent 23 percent of the population. Since World War II, Catholic evangelization has greatly increased the Catholic presence in Korea.

CALIFORNIA MISSIONS

Above: Not until Russia began to express its territorial ambitions toward North America did King Philip V of Spain feel the need to establish missions in this part of his empire.

It was the long reach of the Russian Empire that first prompted Spain's King Philip V to extend control over his holdings in New Spain (the Caribbean, Mexico, and southwestern North America). By the 1740s it was clear that the Russians were gradually heading south, via Alaska and the American west coast. They reached Fort Ross in California's present-day Sonoma county by 1812. To counter this threat, Philip ordered colonial expansion into northern or Alta California (in contrast to Baja California in what is now Mexico).

The "Mission Trail"

The result of King Philip's order was a 600-mile (966-km) string of mission stations up the west coast of California. The northernmost outpost was San Francisco Solana (in Sonoma), established in 1823. It was the end run of a string of 20 mission stations about 30 miles (50 km) apart that began with San Diego de Alacalá in the south, founded in 1769. In the history of California, the "mission period" falls between these two dates. The stations were placed along the coast, partly because this was the most fertile region and partly because ships were the only way to transport heavy items. In time the string of missions became known as the Mission Trail, with the explicit purpose of providing safe rest stops for travelers overland; the missions were a long day's horseback ride apart. Many of the cities in California today, such as San José, Santa Cruz, and Santa Barbara, take their names from these Spanish missions.

With Bible and sword

Colonial expansion and missionary activity went hand in hand. The task of colonizing was entrusted to the Spanish Franciscans for Alta California; the Dominicans were given control of the peninsula of Baja California. The monks set out on foot, traveling by twos, following Jesus' command to the disciples to travel in pairs. A company of soldiers went with each pair to protect them against unfriendly natives.

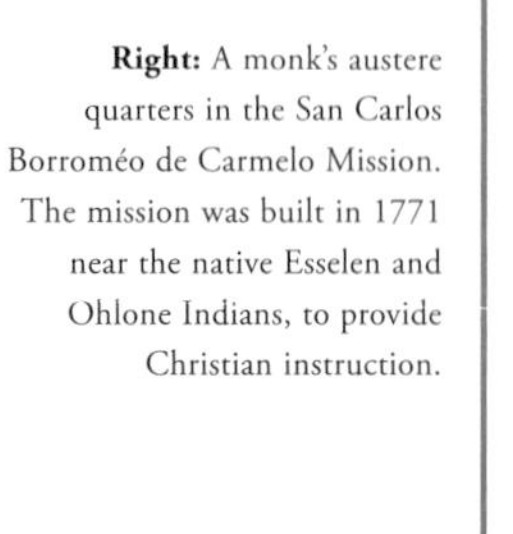

Right: A monk's austere quarters in the San Carlos Borroméo de Carmelo Mission. The mission was built in 1771 near the native Esselen and Ohlone Indians, to provide Christian instruction.

How does one convert an indigenous population? Preaching and calling for people to admit their sins and turn to God was not a favored option. Baptism was seen as the key. However, baptism (for adults) first required catechism, or teaching the fundamentals of the Christian faith. The missionaries might have simplified the complex course of catechism to a few basic ideas, but the need for teaching remained. The problem, then, was how to encourage the local people to stay long enough in order to be taught. The solution was the mission station.

Life on a mission

The mission station served to draw the local population into one place so that they could be taught the catechism.

Mission stations usually had a chapel and separate accommodation for monks, single males, single females, and married couples. They had fields for cultivation and for cattle, as well as workshops, since everything had to be made on site. The missions were protected by a *presidio* (garrison), but they had to supply all the *presidio*'s needs. The farms grew crops of cereals and fruit (such as oranges, apples, pears, peaches, and figs), as well as olives, grapes for wine, and even tobacco. The animals included cows, sheep, goats, mules, and pigs—all brought north from Mexico.

Conversion obviously meant far more than committing one's life to God. Missions were popularly known as *reducciones* (reductions) or *congregaciones* (congregations) and their purpose was to "reduce" the local population from its "unfree" and "uncivilized" status to properly civilized people. If you were a Native American, that meant acquiring European ways, including dress, work rhythms, foods, and customs. Once baptized, you were a convert and you lost your freedom. You were expected to work a full six hours a day (carefully regulated by bells) without pay on the farms, in the workshops, or in building programs. Each day Mass was held; attendance was compulsory. Many became disillusioned and fled, and the monks had limited success in finding them. If you were single and were interested in a boy or girl, you could conduct courtship on the Spanish model: Under the watchful eye of a monk, you would talk with your prospective partner through bars. Once married, you moved from the single male or female quarters to a hut for married couples.

European living conditions brought European problems and diseases. In 1806, for example, around a quarter of the mission Indian population died during a measles epidemic. Although unsanitary conditions in the living quarters resulted in thousands of deaths, at their peak there were more than 20,000 people living at the various missions. In 1833, the missions were secularized (confiscated) by the Mexican government, the Franciscans were expelled, and their work came to an end.

Below: A statue of St Barbara on the pediment of an adobe building at Santa Barbara Mission. Today the mission is home to a community of Franciscan friars.

Left: Santa Barbara Mission was established in 1786 by Spanish Franciscans. Its purpose was to convert the local Chumash Indians, and teach them agriculture and various trades.

ANGLICAN BEGINNINGS IN AUSTRALIA

In Australia, Anglicanism arrived with the new British penal colony. It was unthinkable that the services of the so-called "established church" would not be required in the new venture, not just for the sake of the convicts and their keepers, but because the Church of England was then still an integral part of the British state.

Anglican pioneers

A chaplain, the Rev. Richard Johnson (c. 1756–1827) was appointed to sail with the First Fleet. His exact responsibilities were unclear. So too was his status: His was a military chaplaincy under the authority of the governor. Although Johnson enjoyed some advantages—a lack of competition, the provision of 400 acres (160 ha) as glebe lands, and the enforced attention of the convicts every Sunday—his mission did not prosper. Official indifference was the main obstacle. Religion was regarded as a necessary adjunct of the state, and perhaps useful for the convicts but not a first-order concern in a young, imperiled, and frequently violent penal colony. Johnson built the first church in 1792, largely with his own labor and resources. Convicts promptly burnt it, perhaps not distinguishing the church's spiritual function from Johnson's role as a magistrate.

The arrival and appointment in September 1795 of the evangelical Anglican Governor John Hunter did improve the Church's standing somewhat, and it was Hunter himself who appointed the extraordinary Samuel Marsden (1765–1838) as chaplain upon Johnson's return to England.

Building a church

Johnson is entitled to his status as the pioneer of Australian Anglicanism, but it is Marsden who dominated its early history. This is not surprising because between 1788 and

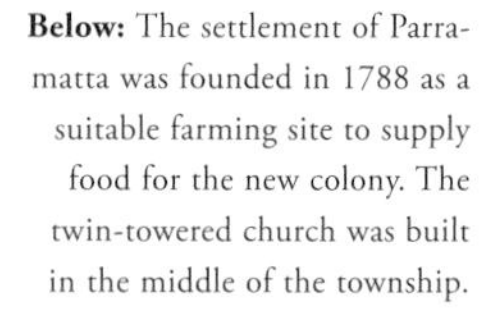

Below: The settlement of Parramatta was founded in 1788 as a suitable farming site to supply food for the new colony. The twin-towered church was built in the middle of the township.

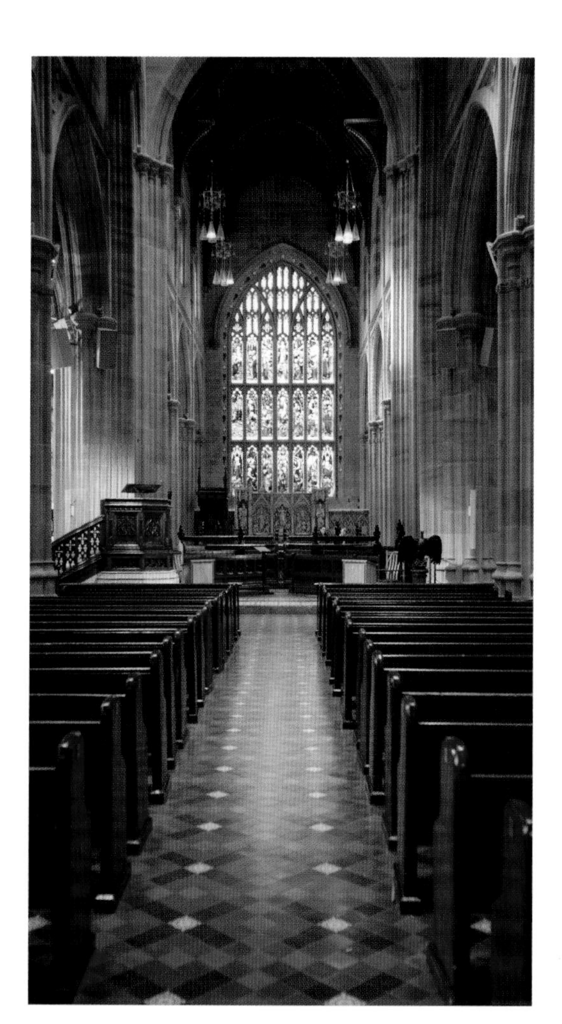

Left: The interior of St Andrew's Cathedral in Sydney features a harmonious arrangement of Perpendicular Gothic architecture. It seats the Anglican Archbishop of Sydney.

1820 only twelve Church of England ministers (including Johnson and Marsden) served in New South Wales. By sheer force of will, Marsden created a proper ecclesiastical infrastructure that could provide (if often only just) for the growing population of convicts and, increasingly, free settlers—although not yet many Aborigines. His cause was advanced in 1798, when retreating members of the London Missionary Society's Tahitian mission chose to remain in Sydney. Although many of these evangelical Protestants were non-Anglicans, the Anglican Marsden worked with them. In the 1810s and into the 1820s, Marsden encouraged a level of inter-denominational Protestant cooperation that would have been quite unthinkable in England.

Replicating the English Church Establishment

As New South Wales grew, so too did the Church of England. It became necessary to decide exactly what role the English established church would have in Britain's newest colony. In 1810, Marsden converted his military chaplaincy into a civil commission, which secured him at least some independence from the governor. But a hierarchical church needs a hierarchy, particularly when aspiring to be an integral part of the state. An important move in this direction was taken in 1824, when the clergyman Thomas Hobbes Scott (1783–1860) was appointed the first archdeacon of Australia. Scott and his Church were privileged by the state: The archdeacon was granted a public rank behind only the governor and lieutenant governor, and appointed *ex officio* to both the Legislative and Executive councils. Anglican clergy were made the sole legal registrars of birth, death, and marriage, and were granted effective veto power in the licensing of public houses. In 1826, the government created the Church and Schools Corporation, and one-seventh of all crown lands were granted to provide for Anglican school and church building.

Equality

This replication of the English established church in what was already a religiously diverse colony met with fierce opposition, both in New South Wales and Britain. Scott himself did not help matters with his unbending churchmanship and reluctance to continue Marsden's policy of pragmatic cooperation among Protestants. The situation changed in 1829. Scott returned to England, to be replaced by the High Church (but pragmatic) William Grant Broughton (1788–1853).

The Church and Schools Corporation was suspended in 1829, and in 1833 it was terminated. Although Broughton tried to maintain his Church's near-established position, it was a losing battle—despite his appointment in 1836 as the first bishop of Australia. That same year, the British Government decided to directly fund all religious denominations in New South Wales. As it was numerically the largest, the Church of England did quite well, but it was now only first among legal equals. Broughton's 1846 resignation from the New South Wales Executive Council only registered the inevitable.

The early Anglican churchmen failed in their desire to become the established Church. However, the early history of Anglicanism in New South Wales is, like the new colony itself, one of endurance in the face of incredible odds.

Below: The Anglican Church set up missions within Aboriginal tribes to convert them to Christianity, but to no avail. Nineteenth-century missions were more successful, and today more than half of Australia's Aborigines are Christians.

PROTESTANT MISSIONS TO INDIA

Above: The British East India Company's presence in India was initially as a trade outpost. By the end of the eighteenth century the company held a military stronghold over southern India.

The arrival of the two Lutheran Pietist missionaries, B. Ziegenbalg and H. Plütschau, on July 9, 1706, marked a watershed in modern education in India. These missionaries were well acquainted with the educational models of the Pietists in Halle (Saale) in Germany. Mother-tongue education was imparted in age- and gender-specific group contexts, and children of all social status were introduced to the study of art and sciences in their natural environments. Artefacts collected from various parts of the world and displayed in child-friendly cabinets kindled intellectual curiosity.

Ziegenbalg also wished to understand the local people. He quickly concluded that the Malabrians were very intelligent and not "barbarians," as was believed in Europe.

Missionary work in Tranquebar

The missionaries transferred the Pietist educational models from Germany to Tranquebar, a small Danish colony on the Coromandel Coast of southeastern India. In their attempt to deepen indigenous learning, they founded the first public schools for girls as early as 1710. It was a revolutionary step in sociocultural development. They collected Tamil palm leaf manuscripts and created accessible libraries. Their European successors and their Indian co-workers laid the foundation for the emergence of modern lexicons and grammars in Tamil, Telugu, and other Indian languages. Missionaries like C.F. Schwartz encouraged the local rulers to adopt an educational system that featured the best practices found in India, Germany, Denmark, and Great Britain.

Consolidations

After the British East India Company (EIC) had agreed to establish Anglican bishoprics in Kolkatta (Calcutta), Mumbai, and Chennai in 1813, several English missionaries served in India. They spread the best English education available at the time.

Twenty years later the EIC permitted Protestant missionaries from Western Europe, North America, Australia,

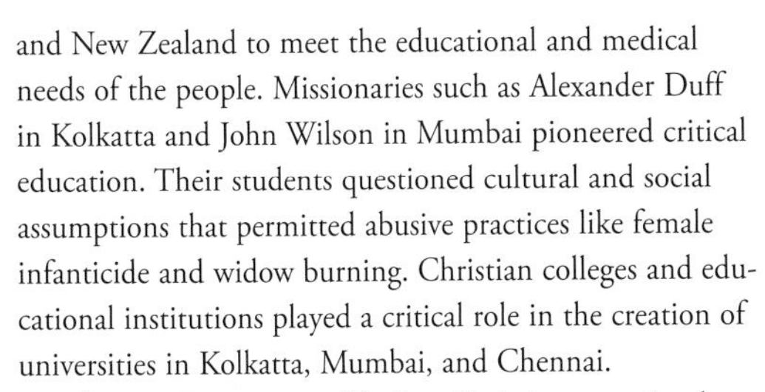

Above: British power and influence grew in India during the eighteenth century. Skilled workers, traders, and ship builders migrated to Bombay, which had become a hub of industry.

and New Zealand to meet the educational and medical needs of the people. Missionaries such as Alexander Duff in Kolkatta and John Wilson in Mumbai pioneered critical education. Their students questioned cultural and social assumptions that permitted abusive practices like female infanticide and widow burning. Christian colleges and educational institutions played a critical role in the creation of universities in Kolkatta, Mumbai, and Chennai.

Likewise, European and Indian Christians associated with the Basel Mission commenced vocational training institutes that taught tile-making, carpentry, and weaving and contributed to the mechanized production of affordable goods and the improvement of lifestyle. However, many schools established by Protestant missionaries made use of what was known as Wood's Educational Dispatch (1854); giving in to pressure from the EIC, it asserted that education should be carried out in English not local languages.

Expressions

The First War of Indian Independence (1857) led to Indian educators becoming extremely weary of English political, civil, and penal laws. These leaders did not differentiate between the European colonialists and European Christian missionaries, seeing them as part of the total colonial endeavor. Animosities between the Europeans and the Indians came to a head. Protestant missionaries had attempted to challenge caste structures and to uplift marginalized peoples, especially females. They were involved in the "Upper Cloth Controversy," trying to boost the self-esteem of oppressed women in southern India and enable them to work toward social betterment. However, the missionaries' efforts also engendered hatred.

Growing nationalism spurred a few Protestant Indian Christians to establish indigenous missionary movements. Among these, V.S. Azariah's Indian Missionary Society (1903) and National Missionary Society (1905) were the most well known. Indian missionaries went to remote villages, improved the health of their inhabitants, opened sanatoria for patients afflicted with tuberculosis and leprosy, introduced new forms of agriculture and animal husbandry, and educated the people in a holistic manner.

Under leaders such as Vedamanickam Maharajan, Ditt, and Venkayya, Christian relief work, was provided during times of famine and other natural catastrophes, as well as in the ordinary lives of Indian Christians. Their work brought about large-scale conversions of people from the lowest social strata or castes. Christianity was seen as a way of breaking out of the caste system because it encouraged converts to give up debasing "jobs" such as scavenging. Christian literary societies and Sunday school organizations produced and disseminated vernacular Christian literature.

Some Protestant leaders roused the missionary zeal of ordinary Christians in India who cultivated the habit of regularly praying for the salvation of India, conversion of fellow Indians, and education of tribal children, and who gave money and time to meet these goals. Missionaries belonging to various, sometimes competing, mission agencies like the Friends Missionary Prayer Band and Indian Evangelical Mission, or belonging to the Baptist and Presbyterian churches in northeastern India, provided primary and secondary education in villages, tribal communities, and among marginalized peoples in cities.

Above: The Lutherans were the first Protestant missionaries to arrive in India, at the Danish port of Fort Dansborg in Tranquebar. Moravian missionaries arrived in India shortly after.

MORAVIANS

In the early 1700s, several people fleeing religious persecution in Moravia (the southern part of the Czech Republic) found refuge on the estate of German nobleman Count Nikolaus Ludwig von Zinzendorf (1700–1760). Initially Zinzendorf, who shared the religious Pietism of these spiritual descendants of John Hus, found himself sheltering ten refugees. Within four years that number had grown to ninety and kept climbing. To the dismay of his neighbors, Zinzendorf gave the Hussite Moravians some of his land, on which they built a self-sustaining village they named Herrnhut.

Change of focus

Those Moravian refugees had fled northward to Saxony looking for a safe haven. However, within a decade they started turning their attention away from cultural and religious survival to becoming a zealous force in global evangelism. How did that turnabout happen? How did a group of refugees turn into trailblazers for the Protestant global outreach movement?

A key factor in that paradigm shift was their host, Count Zinzendorf. Culturally and economically, Zinzendorf was very different from the Moravians he protected; however, the Herrnhut community soon relied on the Count for advice and counsel.

On a visit to Copenhagen in 1731 to attend the coronation of King Christian VI, Zinzendorf met an African man who, after being freed from slavery in the West Indies, had heard the Gospel message and become a Christian. The former slave, named Anthony, traveled with Zinzendorf from Denmark back to Saxony to visit the Moravian community. At Zinzendorf's invitation, Anthony met with the Moravians and recounted many stories about his own horrifying ordeal as a slave and about his friends and family who were slaves in the Caribbean and who had never heard anything about the Gospel.

Their important encounter with Anthony inspired the Moravian community with an urgent sense that they needed to get involved, so within a year they sent forth two members as missionaries to one of the West Indies islands. That trickle of missionaries grew into a stream. Before too long, around ten percent of the Moravian community served as foreign missionaries, principally in the Americas (including Labrador in Canada), and in India.

Moravian strategy

Though Western missionaries have sometimes been accused of being tainted by the colonial/imperialist attitudes of their home countries, this was not true of the Moravians. Some of the early Moravian missionaries went so far as to become almost slaves themselves in order to be able to minister to the slaves working in the sugarcane fields of the West Indies. Many of those first Moravian missionaries died within a couple of years after arriving on the mission field. However, as news of Moravian missionary deaths

reached Europe, rather surprisingly, even more willing evangelists came forward to replace them.

Because the Moravians were entrepreneurial and self-directed, their missionary activity was reminiscent of the Celtic *peregrini* of earlier centuries. At Herrnhut the Moravians were tradesmen who worked with their hands. When they went out as missionaries, they continued using those skills to support their ministries. Thus, they would today be called "tent-making" missionaries (after the Apostle Paul whose tent-making skills at least partially supported his missionary band on their journeys around the northern rim of the Mediterranean).

The Moravian movement had a profound effect on John Wesley, founder of the Methodist movement. Wesley encountered some Moravian missionaries during his brief stint as a missionary to the indigenous peoples in the colony of Georgia in the 1730s, and maintained contact upon his return to England. In even a cursory reading of Wesley's written works one can see ways in which his thinking was shaped by his contact with the Moravians. While Wesley personally had no success in Georgia as a cross-cultural missionary, it is interesting to speculate that Moravian influence may in some measure have led Methodism to eventually become a global missionary force.

William Carey, sometimes known as the "father of the modern missionary movement," was also greatly influenced by the missionary zeal of the Moravians. In his classic booklet, *An Inquiry into the Obligation of Christians to use Means for the Conversion of the Heathens*, Carey referred to the Moravian experience as a model of what communities of faith should be doing to evangelize the world. About a decade later, Carey authored a covenant for Christian community living, the "Serampore Compact," in which he held up what the Moravians had done as an example.

Above: Slaves in the West Indies prepared manioc (cassava) flour as an important food staple. The plant must be soaked, cooked, and fermented to prevent it from causing illness.

Opposite: Within 20 years of starting their missionary movement, Moravian volunteers were evangelizing natives in all parts of the world, including North and South America, the Caribbean, Africa, and the Far East.

MISSIONARY SOCIETIES

For the first two hundred years after Martin Luther posted his 95 theses, the Protestant movement did very little in the way of cross-cultural missionary work. That might seem puzzling, given that foreign missions work is now such an integral part of Protestant tradition and practice.

Religious orders rejected

Scholars have speculated that a principal reason for Protestantism's slow start in developing global outreach was because Martin Luther and other early Reformers emphatically rejected the use of religious orders like those of the Roman Church (Luther himself had been an Augustinian monk). Those orders of the Western Church—which began with the Benedictines in the 500s—were by the 1200s the primary structures through which the Roman Church launched and carried on global missionary outreach. When Protestant leaders rejected the celibacy of those organizations, it was somewhat akin to "throwing out the baby with the bathwater" because it left them without a structure with which to do global missionary outreach.

Protestantism began to get involved in worldwide mission outreach in a significant way with the origination of "missionary societies." These somewhat independent organizations were not only concerned with sending missionaries. The Protestant missionary societies also served as promotional arms that raised consciousness among believers regarding global needs, facilitated the collection of funds, and solicited prayer support.

The first Protestant missionary societies were organized with a focus on the indigenous peoples of the New World. In this vein, the Society for the Propagation of the Gospel in New England came into being in 1649. That was less than 30 years after the Pilgrims landed at Plymouth Rock

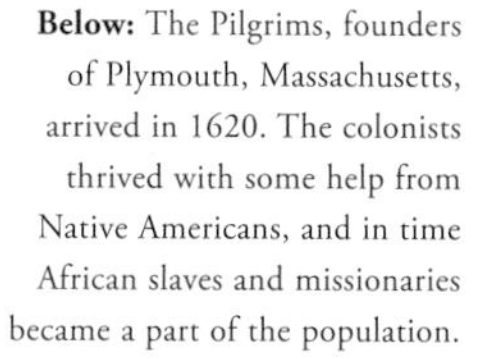

Below: The Pilgrims, founders of Plymouth, Massachusetts, arrived in 1620. The colonists thrived with some help from Native Americans, and in time African slaves and missionaries became a part of the population.

to establish their colony in what is now Massachusetts. At about the same time, Baron Justinian von Welz began writing tracts calling for Protestantism to respond to the Great Commission. Within a few decades the Christian Faith Society for the West Indies and the Society for the Propagation of the Gospel in Foreign Parts were organized; both focused on evangelizing the peoples of the New World.

Inspired by Captain Cook's travelogues

About a century later, a bi-vocational Baptist pastor named William Carey read Captain James Cook's graphic *A Voyage Round the World* (1777). Carey was gripped by Cook's descriptions of the societies he had encountered who had no knowledge of the Christian Gospel. Carey felt his church ought to be doing something to reach them, but his attempts to get his denominational leaders to act were in vain. So, Carey and some of his friends organized the Particular Baptist Missionary Society for Propagating the Gospel Among the Heathen, and in 1792 the small group appointed Carey and his wife to India as its first missionaries.

"Father of modern missions"

Carey was a mobilizer who quickly became more than just a missionary focused on the immediate area in which he was trying to minister. Carey's society became a conduit for the booklets and sermons he published aimed at inspiring individual believers and churches, and for encouraging the formation of other missionary societies. As a direct result of Carey's inspirational writings, the London Missionary Society was formed in 1795. Within less than a decade, ten more Protestant missionary societies had been organized in the British Isles and on the European continent.

Some of these societies were denominational arms, while others were totally independent. In 1810 Congregational Church leaders set up the first North American missionary society: The American Board of Commissioners for Foreign Missions. Another group of missionary society start-ups was established in the mid-1800s. As had happened a half-century earlier, the inspiration for starting these new societies came from a pioneer British missionary. This time it was a man by the name of J. Hudson Taylor, founder of the China Inland Mission, which was for some time Protestantism's largest missionary-sending organization. Those societies inspired by Taylor's vision for moving beyond the coastal cities to China's interior often followed his model of using "interior" or "inland" in their titles.

The Great Century

The wave of missionaries that Protestant missionary societies in Europe and North America sent forth in the nineteenth century was so great that historian Kenneth Scott Latourette referred to the period from 1793 to about 1914 as the "Great Century" of missionary outreach. By the end of the nineteenth century, European ideas and principles had spread everywhere, and Christianity was part of this.

The Great Century of outreach that turned Protestantism into a truly global movement probably would not have happened without those dedicated missionary societies that functioned within, alongside—and sometimes very separate from—denominational structures. Such organizations continue to proliferate today, waxing and waning depending on leadership and a variety of other factors.

Above: Captain James Cook was an English explorer who made several voyages to the Pacific Ocean. His descriptions of the places he visited contributed to European knowledge of the area.

Below: In 1778, Captain Cook arrived in the Hawai'ian islands, during the Makahiki season when all conflicts ceased. Seeing Cook as a representative of the god Lono, the natives honored him with gifts.

ORTHODOX CHRISTIANITY IN ALASKA

As a result of Russian Orthodox missionary work in Alaska in the eighteenth and nineteenth centuries, the indigenous people of the Aleutian Islands, other islands nearby, and western Alaska (the Unangan, or Aleuts as the Russians called them) are primarily Orthodox to this day. The Russian mission, one of the furthest outposts of missionary activity by the Orthodox Church, was the culmination of a great expansion across Siberia to the eastern reaches of Russia. The Unangan, part of the circumpolar peoples, inhabit the Aleutian, Pribolof, Shumagin, and Kodiak Island archipelagos.

Below: The Unangan are the indigenous people of the Aleutian Islands of Alaska. Following the arrival of missionaries in the late eighteenth century, many joined the Russian Orthodox Church.

Herman of Alaska

The story of Russian missions in Alaska begins with Herman of Alaska (c. 1756–1837). A robust constitution and simple living enabled Herman to live for more than 40 years on Kodiak and Spruce islands. He had already learned to live as a monk in cold conditions during his time at the Valaam monastery, on an island in Lake Ladoga in northwestern Russia. It was to Valaam that Gregory Shelikov, head of the Golikov-Shelikov company, came to inquire if some monks would be willing to assist with commercial expansion into North America by undertaking a mission. Eight monks were chosen, Herman among them.

They arrived on Kodiak Island by ship on September 24, 1794, and settled among the local Unangan people. Harsh conditions, illness, occasional arrests, threats, and abuse by traders meant that Herman was soon the last man standing among the missionaries. But he was not alone, for in 1784 the company had established a colony to hunt and trade in seal and sea otter fur. Herman was a persistent gadfly in the colony, complaining about the exploitation and often slavery of the Unangan in the service of commercial interests. He established a hermitage on Spruce Island, along with a school, chapel, and guest house. But he retained the ways of a monk; his missionary work was low-key; he preferred his small cave for meditation and prayer.

Innocent and translations

Herman was a simple, if persistent, monk, but the other saint of Alaska was a scholar and leader. Eventually canonized as Innocent of Alaska (1797–1879), his name was originally Ivan Popov, but it was changed to Ioann Veniaminov when he was ordained a priest. He was another robust, energetic, and fit man who lived to be 81 years of age. Hailing from Irkutsk in central-southern Russia, he progressed from being a simple deacon at the age of 20 to metropolitan of Moscow. During his long life his work spanned the vast extent of Russia. This included a decade (1824–1834) in the Aleutians as parish priest of the island of Unalaska, as well as the nearby Pribolof and Fox Islands. He had the habit of rowing a fragile canoe through rough seas between the islands of his parish. His travels throughout the islands enabled him to master the local dialects. Eventually he became bishop and then archbishop of a vast stretch of territory that included Yakutsk, Kamchatka, the Kuril Islands, and the Aleutian Islands.

It was Innocent's impressive gift with languages that became perhaps his greatest legacy. He managed to pick up half a dozen dialects while in Unalaska, and then the complex language Tlingit (or Koloshi as the Russians called it) when he was on Sitka Island (1834–1838). He wrote some scholarly works, including *Notes on the Kolushchan and*

FACT OR FICTION?

There is a rather intriguing story about Peter the Aleut, a native of the Aleutian Islands who supposedly was martyred by the Spanish in northern California. Although formally recognized as a saint and with some churches dedicated to him, some people have questioned whether Peter really existed.

Kodiak Tongues and *Other Dialects of the Russo-American Territories, with a Russian-Kolushchan Glossary*. However, he is best known for his translations into Unangam Tunuu (Aleut) of parts of the Bible, especially the Gospel of Matthew, selections from the other Gospels and the Epistles, sermons, teaching materials, and hymns.

Translating the Bible is difficult enough when you are working in a language you have learned. In Innocent's case, the difficulty was even greater, since he found no written language. So, his first task was to produce a written form of Unangan using Cyrillic, the script of the Russian language. Once he had done that and sorted out the grammar, he had to teach the Unangan how to read. Finally, he was able to translate from one written language to another. It is an intensive task that takes a high level of linguistic skill, and it helps to have a native collaborator. Innocent was lucky enough to have Ivan Pankov, an Unangan leader with whom he worked closely, as well as St Jacob Netsvetov, who had worked for Innocent when he was bishop.

Above: An Orthodox church at Karluk on Kodiak Island, Alaska. The Russian missionary, Herman of Alaska, endured the harsh conditions here and on nearby Spruce Island for over 40 years.

Left: A native of Unalaska Island. Forced relocation by the commercial fur seal industry, and the 1836–1840 epidemic of chickenpox, whooping-cough, and measles, reduced the island's Unangan population from over 3,000 to around 400.

PART SEVEN

GLOBAL MISSIONS
1801–1900 CE

MISSIONS TO AFRICA

Below: Born in Yorubaland in modern-day Nigeria, Samuel Ajayi Crowther (c. 1809–1891) was the first Anglican bishop of African descent. He translated the Bible into the Yoruba language.

Nineteenth-century evangelical enthusiasm for personal conversion and social transformation produced a confident Protestant missionary movement motivated by Jesus' "Great Commission." The work of Catholic orders was bolstered by a missionary revival in the 1840s and the development of new religious orders for Africa.

The impact and effectiveness of the missionary work varied depending on resources, ideologies, and locations as well as other factors like the mortality rate of early missionaries and the decision to either work with chiefs or create segregated villages of converts. Africa's predominantly Muslim north raised different challenges to those presented by racial segregation in South Africa, or slave-trading on the east and west coasts, or engagement with educated, Christian, freed slaves in Sierra Leone.

Early missions

Early nineteenth-century evangelical Protestants emphasized the international and ecumenical nature of their missionary endeavor. German Lutherans, like Samuel Gobat and Christian Kugler, who went to Ethiopia in the early 1800s, provided the Anglican Church Missionary Society (CMS) with its first missionaries. An anti-slavery stance was indicative of the broader Enlightenment concerns of progress through liberation, education, equality, and civilization. Missions blended these with the belief that Bible preaching and translation enabled true progress.

Most missionaries avoided political issues except where they prevented Christian improvement. John Philip of the London Missionary Society (LMS), recognizing the virtual slavery of the Khoi in South Africa, declared that all humans were savages who could change if given liberty, a liberty he understood as fulfilled through Christianity.

Self-determination

Voluntarism gave to Protestant missions an independence that encouraged self-determination among the indigenous Christians. Converts were initially few, but by mid-century they joined the task of evangelizing. Bible women of the Transvaal or young men of the Buganda court spread the Gospel. Some were employed by mission societies to preach, teach, and plant churches. William Koyi, a Xhosa of the Livingstonia Mission, worked among the Ngoni of

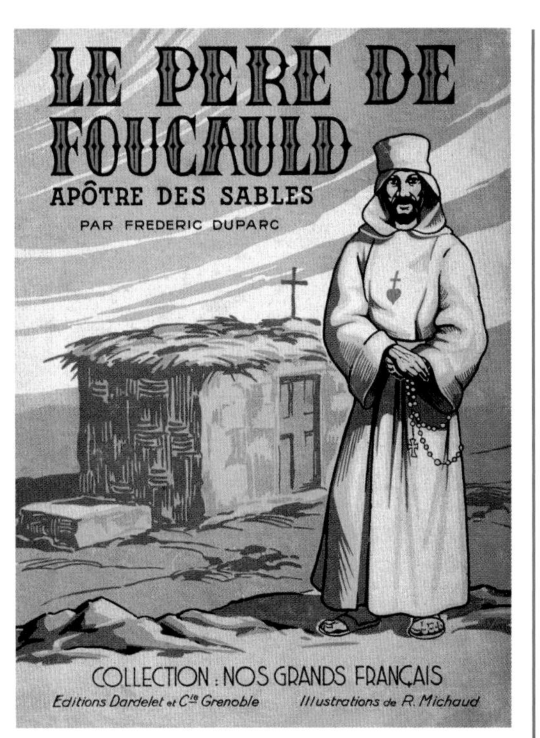

Previous pages: Nineteenth-century Protestant missionaries set out from churches like this one in New Hampshire, USA, as well as from churches in European countries such as England, Wales, Scotland, France, and Germany.

Left: Charles de Foucauld (1858–1916), a French missionary priest in Algeria, inspired the founding of communities known as Little Brothers of Jesus and Little Sisters of Jesus.

Above left: An engraving from John Campbell's *Travels in South Africa* (1822). The book details Campbell's second journey into Africa's interior, undertaken at the request of the London Missionary Society.

Nyasaland from 1876. Samuel Ajayi Crowther's life of preaching, itineration, translation, and eventual consecration as Bishop of Upper Nile demonstrates the great extent of his influence on the CMS.

Though the *Propaganda Fide* in Rome (the congregation for evangelizing people outside of Western Europe) had greater control over Catholic missions, the new orders found that they had some local autonomy. In 1867 Daniel Comboni established the Verona Fathers, which aimed for "the regeneration of Africa by Africa," and Charles Lavigerie established the White Fathers and Sisters, which emphasized the study of African languages and customs.

Imperialism and the missions

Colonialism took hold in Africa during the latter part of the century. At times missions fulfilled the cultural expectations of the colonial powers. The favor shown to missions that were Belgian and Catholic in the Belgian Congo and the attack on Samuel Ajayi Crowther by young, zealous, and imperialistic missionaries both illustrate the pernicious effect imperialism could have on missions. Yet the complex interweaving of mission theory, mission practice, local issues, and colonial administration in any one location could lead to empowerment of individuals in one circumstance, but subservience in another situation.

David Livingstone's call for commerce, civilization, and Christianity was originally intended to encourage the autonomy of African peoples but was often used to support the economic influence of white settlers and mining companies. Likewise, instruction in domestic tasks that was undertaken by women missionaries might be given in a spirit of empowerment by Americans with a frontier mentality, yet Europeans, imbued with a long-held sense of class, might consider themselves to be preparing servants. Mary Slessor of Calabar (now Nigeria) championed the causes of the poor in part through her role as Vice Consul for the British colonial administration.

High colonialism coincided with a growing skepticism about the task of civilization, articulated by a new wave of "Faith missions" from 1878. The Livingstone Inland Mission, the Sudan Interior Mission, and others were influenced by the Holiness Movement and the Student Volunteer Movement. The missions emphasized dependence on God for financial support, and simple preaching of the Gospel. Believing that such preaching would hasten Christ's second coming, they wished to take the Gospel into the interior of Africa, unencumbered by the responsibility of schools and hospitals such as those established by the previous generation of missions.

MISSION CONVERSIONS

In Africa, Western missionaries usually provided converts with a template of their own spiritual tradition. Anglicans followed the prayer book, and Methodists were guided by the hymns of Charles Wesley. African Christians themselves, aided by the rapid translation of the Bible and other Christian texts into African languages, began to develop a spirituality that melded these innovations into their own religious worldview and produced indigenous expressions of Christianity inside and outside the mission churches.

PROTESTANT MISSIONS TO CHINA

Above: Carved during the Ching Dynasty, this is an ivory sculpture of the Buddhist Bodhisattva (divine being) of compassion, Guan Yin. Christian missionaries in China found Guan Yin to be similar to Jesus.

Below: The number of Christians in China increased quickly in the early part of the twentieth century. Chinese pastors of that time usually maintained their traditional Chinese raiment.

Christianity came to China in several stages: Nestorians during the Tang Dynasty (618–907), Nestorians and Catholics during the Yuan Dynasty (1271–1368), and Catholics during the Ming and Ching (Qing) dynasties (1368–1644 and 1644–1912). The fourth wave of Christian missions to China was Protestant.

Introducing Protestant Christianity

Protestant Christianity was introduced to China at the beginning of the nineteenth century, when the Ching Dynasty, China's last dynasty, started to decline in the face of domestic revolutions and foreign intrusions. Christianity had been banned since 1720, mainly due to the ill-famed Rites Controversy over ancestor worship. In 1807, the Reverend Robert Morrison (1782–1834) of the London Missionary Society became the first Protestant missionary to China when he arrived in Macau, which was then under Portuguese control. To secure his stay in China, from 1809 Morrison worked for the East India Company, which was notorious for the opium trade. The Opium Wars and other foreign interventions exacted successive unequal treaties, which opened China to the West as well as to Christianity and thus consolidated the unhappy association of Christianity and imperialism.

In the first half of the nineteenth century, missionary work was severely limited and missionaries could contact only a handful of the Chinese who were significantly associated with missions. This was the beginning of the long-standing mission control of the Chinese Church. Some missionaries, especially Catholic, asserted themselves as the guardian of national Christians, claiming extraterritorial rights for both themselves and Chinese Christians, and this accelerated the foreignness of Christianity, on the one hand, and the dependence of the Church on missions, on the other hand. It was against this backdrop that John L. Nevius (1829–1893) introduced his Nevius Method, which he described as the New Method against the Old Method; it heavily relied on missionary money. Like other proponents of the "three-self principle," such as Henry Venn and Rufus Anderson, Nevius emphasized the vital importance of self-propagating, self-supporting, and self-governing in church life. This idea, which was later radicalized by Roland Allen (1868–1947), was to signal the beginning of local control in the Church, pave the way for the foundation of a united national church, the Church of Christ in China in 1927, and finally come into full bloom in the People's Republic of China in an unexpected way.

Breaking a deadlock

In the latter part of the nineteenth century, although treaty ports were crowded with missionaries and other Western expatriates, missions hardly penetrated into the hinterland of China. J. Hudson Taylor (1832–1905), who was previously commissioned by the Chinese Evangelization Society, returned to China in 1866 as leader of a new, radically innovative mission called the China Inland Mission. Established only in the previous year, it later became the Overseas Missionary Fellowship. Its goal was to break the missionary deadlock in China.

Christianity and Chinese nationalism

Besides foreign encroachment, the Ching Dynasty rulers were harassed by continuous domestic rebellions and revolutions. Of these, the Taiping Revolution (1850–1864), led by Hong Xiuquan (1814–1864), was most interesting in terms of the Christian mission. The Taiping Revolution was a mixture of anti-foreign nationalism (in this case, anti-Manchu) and pro-Christianity, as illustrated by the fact that the name of the new empire, Taiping Tienkuo, was the compound word of the two traditions (Chinese "Great Peace" and Christian "Heavenly Kingdom"). During its tumultuous developments, foreign governments took a neutral position between the Taipings and the court, while missionaries were more concerned with whether or not this movement was genuinely Christian. At any rate, because of its messianic or utopian message, especially its emphasis on equality in gender and class during its early stages, some scholars regard it as a forerunner of the indigenous communist movement.

The later years of the nineteenth century saw the growth of a number of nationalistic movements, which were now anti-Western or anti-Christian rather than anti-Manchu. This anti-foreignism to a large extent checked the growth of Christianity, despite the large-scale investment of personnel and money the missions had made. It even resulted in heavy casualties on missionaries and Chinese Christians, especially during the Boxer Rebellion of 1900. It was not until the turn of the century that Chinese Christianity for the first time grew rapidly.

THE CHINA INLAND MISSION

Founded by J. Hudson Taylor, the China Inland Mission had some distinctive features: It emphasized absolute dependence on God for financial support; it claimed the leadership of mission field over home base; and it later played a role as an advocate of evangelical or fundamental groups in Chinese Christianity.

Left: Suspected of aiding Chinese rebels, French Jesuit missionary Père Auguste Chapdelaine was arrested and tortured to death by Mandarin guards in Guangxi Province, China, in 1856.

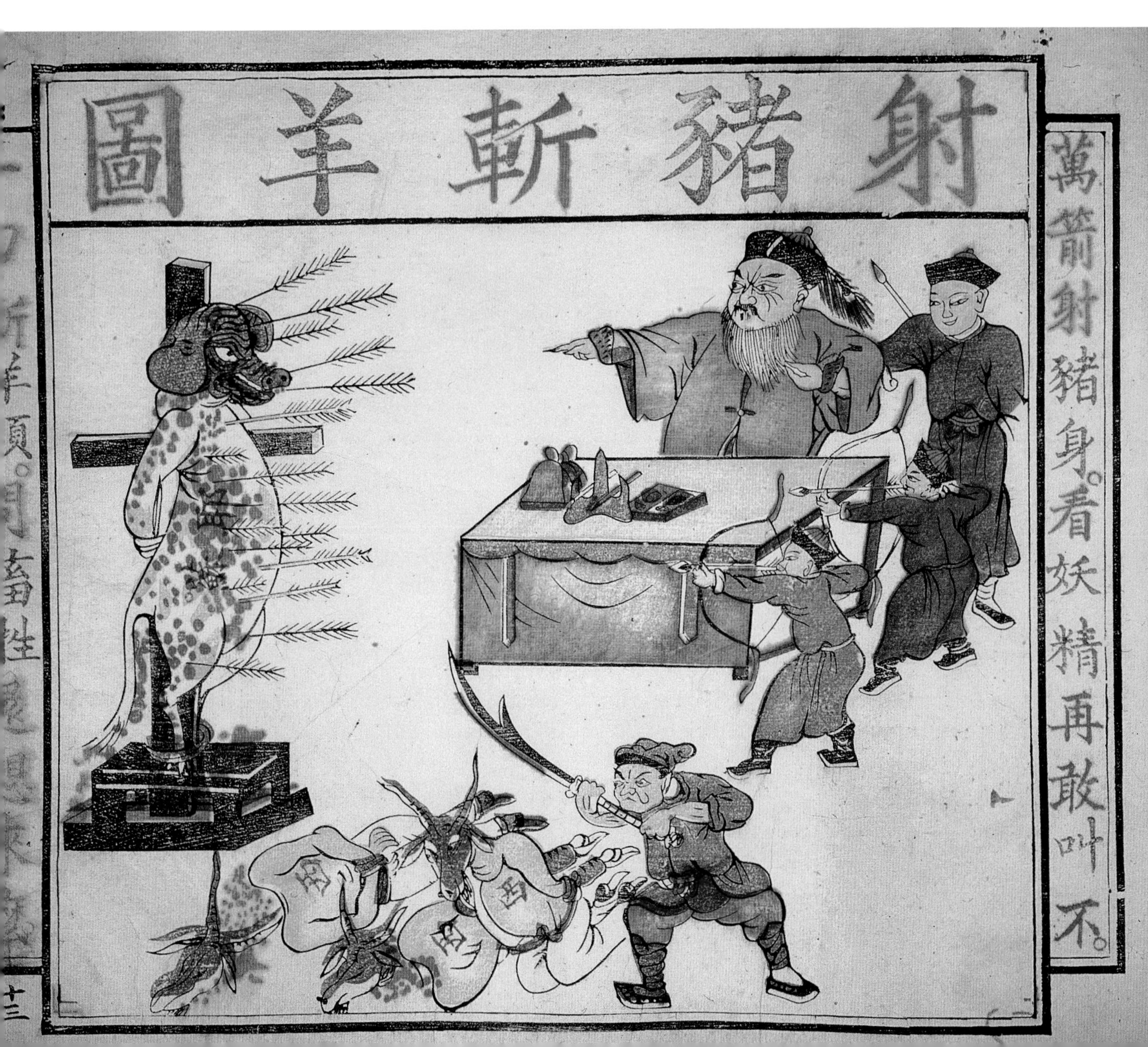

Below: A c. 1890 Chinese woodcut clearly reflects the anti-Western and anti-Christian atmosphere of the time: Both the pig (representing Jesus) and the sheep (symbolizing Christians) are being slaughtered.

RELIGIOUS PERSECUTION IN KOREA

In 1884, when the first Protestant Christian missionaries entered Korea (a century after the Catholic convert Peter returned from China and began baptizing fellow Koreans), the country was culturally remote from the West, not least because of its religious and cultural traditions of Shamanism, Buddhism, and Confucianism. Regarding itself as a "small China," Korea actually adhered to the Confucian tradition more strongly and for a much longer period than China did, steadfastly believing that all Westerners were political intruders. Korea had turned against all foreign contacts, was known in the West as the "Hermit Nation," and remained the last Asian country to open its doors to the West when the Shufeldt Treaty of 1882 between Korea and the USA was negotiated.

Below: Nineteenth-century Christian martyrs in Asia—such as Robert Thomas, who was the first Protestant to die for his beliefs in Korea—were celebrated in the West as pillars of piety.

The first Protestant martyr

Protestant missionaries had already shown an interest in working in the country. Robert Thomas (1839–1866), a Welsh Congregationalist missionary to China, made the first serious attempt to begin Protestant missionary work in Korea. In 1863, Thomas met two Korean Christian

refugees who possessed rosaries, crucifixes, and medals, but no Bibles. They were sent back with Chinese Bibles to begin a Protestant mission. In 1865, Thomas traveled along Korea's west coast, heavily disguised in Korean clothes, and learned Korean with the help of Catholics.

In 1866, Thomas sailed again for Korea, on the *General Sherman*, an American schooner loaded with glass and tin-plate. In that year, Roman Catholics in Korea faced great persecution because of their refusal to practice Confucian ancestor worship and accusations that they were conspiring with Western imperial powers. The ship entered the mouth of the Daedong River below the city of Pyongyang. On the way upriver, a group of Korean Catholics boarded the vessel, and Thomas gave them Chinese Bibles. The governor of Pyong'an province warned the ship to leave since he did not want foreign trade. The vessel, however, pushed up the river until it reached a place close to the city. There the ship became stuck in the mud. A firefight with the Korean army ensued; the ship's whole crew of 23 men was exterminated and the vessel burned. Thomas was killed by a soldier on the shore and became the first Protestant martyr in Korea.

Pioneer missionaries

In the 1882 Treaty negotiated with Korea, the USA included a clause promising protection for American residents in Korea, and in 1884–1885 the first pioneer Protestant missionaries arrived in the country: Dr Horace Allen and the Reverend Horace Underwood of the Northern Presbyterian Church, and Dr and Mrs Scranton, his mother Mrs Mary Scranton, and the Reverend and Mrs Henry Appenzeller of the Northern Methodist Church.

The Reformist party's bloody coup, *Kapsin chongbyon* (Kapsin Coup), which occurred at the banquet celebrating the completion of the postal office building on the night of December 4, 1884, provided a breakthrough for Western missionaries. During the coup, the queen's nephew, Prince Min Young-Ik, who was then the commander of the royal bodyguard, was seriously injured by an assassin's knife. Allen provided meticulous care for three months and saved the prince's life. This gave the king confidence in Western medicine and trust in an American alliance. As a result, in April 1885, the government hospital called Kwang Hye Won (later the known as the Severance Hospital) was opened, sponsored by the Korean court and under the charge of Allen. Thus the groundwork of resident missionary work in Korea was established.

To some degree both authorities and common people remained hostile to and afraid of foreigners and their religion. In 1888, an incident with the Catholic Church led to a ban on Christian mission work. Even after missionaries were able to propagate Christianity publicly, local authorities continued to oppress Christians. In the summer of 1894, the Pyong'an province governor imprisoned a Methodist deacon, a Presbyterian preacher, and other Christians, and tortured them severely because they spread an "evil" doctrine and science. In some districts, authorities expelled preachers from their villages and prevented Christians from doing farm work. Incidents of beating Christian women and the cutting of their hair by their own family often occurred, as Christianity opposed Korean conventional customs, especially things related to Confucianism's ancestor worship.

Above: Confucius (551–479 BCE) devised the ethics-based belief system known as Confucianism that has long been practiced in numerous Asian countries including Korea.

THE 1888 BAN

The Korean government banned both the open propagation of the Gospel and the convening of religious meetings in 1888. This incident was caused by the Catholic Church's insistence on building a cathedral on a site close to both the royal palaces and Jongmyo, the shrine dedicated to the royal ancestors, and their refusal of the king's request for the site of the cathedral to be changed. While the prohibition was mainly directed against the Catholic Church, it also impacted the Protestant community.

THE PROTESTANTS ARRIVE IN JAPAN

Above: Sister Iwasaki survived the atomic bomb blast that rocked Nagasaki on August 9, 1945. At the time she was working as a chambermaid in the Otsugé-no-Maria convent, founded by a French mission.

Below: Despite their warrior nature, many Samurai—the military elite of Japan—followed Zen Buddhism. The *Samurai* died out as a social class in the late nineteenth century.

During the seventeenth century Japan prohibited Christianity, expelling Europeans living in the country and killing many Christians. Worship was suppressed until the nineteenth century.

Christianity is reintroduced into Japan

Like other countries in East Asia, Japan was later opened to Christianity via unequal treaties with Western powers. The United States–Japan Treaty of Friendship in 1854, which was signed one year after the arrival of Commodore M.C. Perry, was the first of its kind, and thus it can be said that the cross followed the flag. The ban on Christianity among foreign residents in Japan was lifted in 1858, and the notice boards banning Christianity were finally withdrawn in 1873. During this transitional period, Protestant and Russian Orthodox missionaries landed on the island-nation from 1859, and Roman Catholic missionaries arrived on their heels in 1860.

Much to the surprise of Roman Catholic expatriates, after 1865 Japanese Catholics who had kept the faith over more than two centuries in the disguise of traditional religions such as Buddhism and Shintoism (underground Christians, *Senpuku* or *Kakure kirishitan*) emerged to rejoin the Roman Catholic Church. These so-called resurrected Christians (*Fukkatsu kirishitan*) left a minority who were determined to stay underground and adhere to their ancestors' radically indigenized faith. After initial considerable growth, the Russian Orthodox mission faced a number of ordeals, such as the Russo–Japanese War in 1904, and had to satisfy itself with modest development. Various Protestant missions including Presbyterian and Reformed, Congregational, and Methodist, flocked to Japan, and it was these missions, predominantly American, which took the lion's share of the newest Christian mission.

Growth of the Japanese Church

Together with imperialistic association, the fact that the re-entry of Christianity took place in the midst of Japan's national transformation from a medieval feudal society to a modern nation-state fundamentally, if not totally, characterized the trajectory of Japanese Christianity. Although missionary works were strictly limited until 1873, the first Protestant churches had already emerged from 1872, mainly through the encounter between missionaries and other foreign advisers who were de facto lay missionaries, and the sons of ex-Samurai (the military elite). They were the most victimized and marginalized group during the period of the demise of feudalism in Japan, and they hoped to find a way to realize their nationalistic aspiration in Christianity.

In the 1880s Japan showed great openness to the West, and the Church's first impressive growth was indebted to this change. However, the Japanese government was eager to put religions, including Christianity, under its control; for example, the new Constitution of 1889 granted freedom of religion but with the proviso that religions should not disturb peace and order. Furthermore, when the Japanese gradually realized that modernization did not necessarily mean Westernization, or Christianization, the

A NATIONALISTIC CHURCH

The Japanese Christian Church tried to stand with nationalism and the government. It supported the government's war effort, the submission to Shinto Shrine worship, and imperial ideology. Its own foreign missions were initiated as a religious tool of Japanese imperialism, and the government even sponsored the union of churches into the United Church of Christ in Japan (*Nihon Kirisuto Kyodan*) in 1941.

role of Christian missions as transmitters of Western civilization, especially in education, was reconsidered. In the 1890s when Japan's relations with Western powers grew unfriendly, especially due to the delay of the revision of the unequal treaty, expatriate missions as well as churches were viewed as suspicious or even traitorous.

The legacy of nineteenth-century Japanese Christianity

To maintain the balance between nationalism and internationalism, the Church generally put nationalism before internationalism in the nineteenth century and the first half of the twentieth century. The Church began to keep itself away from foreign missions, challenging missionary Christianity in various ways: Some opted for ecumenism instead of denominationalism, some claimed strong national leadership against missionary control. Japanese Christian evangelists like Uchimura Kanzo (1861–1930) even denied the institutional structure of the Church, commencing the *mukyokai* (non-Church) movement, an ingenious form of indigenized Christianity. In various ways the Church chose to stand with the government, while struggling to prove itself as a legitimate national institution.

It must be remembered, though, that there were Christian dissidents and martyrs in wartime Japan. The postwar Japanese Church, which is no longer under the pressure of missions and the government, has served the society in its capacity as a dissenter and pacifist, in spite of its meager size. Nowadays, alongside the United Church of Christ in Japan (UCCJ) and other traditional denominational churches, indigenous Christian movements endeavor to shape Japanese spirituality in a new way.

Below: Heads are covered during an Easter vigil at a Catholic church in Amakusa, Japan. By the year 2000, less than two percent of the Japanese population classified themselves as Christian.

PROTESTANT MISSIONS TO INDIA

The origins of Christianity in India are pre-colonial. Traditionally, it is claimed that Thomas, an apostle of Jesus Christ, established the first Christian churches (52–72 CE). Later, Syriac-speaking Christians from Persia migrated to various parts of the west coast and made India their home. They thrived until Portuguese traders arrived in 1498. With them came the Padroado Agreement, in which the pope gave the king of Portugal the mandate to establish Roman Catholicism in his overseas colonies.

Accordingly, the king authorized different orders of the Roman Catholic Church to send their representatives to India. They opened order-specific "mission stations" in places with newly established Portuguese colonies, such as Goa. After 1663 the papal institute of *Propaganda Fide* sent their missionaries, who disagreed with the Padroado missionaries. The prolonged conflicts among the Padroado and Propaganda missionaries drained their energy and resources. Later missionaries, associated with the French East India Company, continued the legacy of the Roman Catholic Church in places like Pondicherry.

Below: Brightly painted in blue and gold, the church of St Sebastian in Kerala, southern India, is representative of the colonialism and Christianization of India.

Protestants on the horizon

Protestant missionaries learned much from the experiences of the Roman Catholic missionaries. Dutch preachers, like Abraham Roger and Philipp Baldaeus of the Dutch East India Company, served in the Dutch colonies of Palaverkadu and Nagapatnam. Their work did not last long. In contrast, German Lutheran missionaries, sent by the Danish monarchs to work among the Tamil people who lived in the Danish colony of Tranquebar on the Coromandel Coast (1619–1845), were instrumental in the emergence of an indigenous Protestant Christianity. They and their Indian converts suffered at the hands of Danish colonial authorities, however, who felt the success of Christianity would jeopardize their colonial and economic enterprise. Nevertheless missionary work resulted in the formation of several Tamil Christian congregations in and beyond Tranquebar. Their translations of the Bible into Tamil and Telugu, and attempts to incarnate Christian faith into the cultural idioms of the Tamil, bore fruit.

The British East India Company also frowned on missionary activity, opposing William Carey's work in Kolkata and that of his successors. The company's colonial policy had little or no place for missionary activity. Eventually, under enormous pressure in England, the company revised its charter, first in 1813 and then in 1833. European and American Protestant missionaries were allowed to provide educational, vocational, and medical services to Indians as long as they were free. The company still resisted the conversion of Indians and remained focused on commercial and political gains, although some of their employees, including chaplain Claudius Buchanan, British Resident Colonel John Munro in Travancore, and commissioners David Scott and Francis Jenkins in Assam, fully supported missionary work. Thus it was that Anglican and Baptist churches appeared in many regions of India.

New wave of missionaries

After Queen Victoria became the Empress of India in 1857, European and American missionaries of various denominational persuasions rushed to India. Soon they realized the importance of cooperation and organized interdenominational meetings in Benaras (1857) and Ooty (1858). Their decennial meetings in Allahabad (1872), Kolkata (1882), and Mumbai (1892), along with their cooperative work in theological education and medical services, were quite successful. Their relationship to colonial authorities, however, remained ambiguous. As citizens they enjoyed colonial protections; as missionaries they suffered discrimination.

Throwing off the missionary yoke

The formation of the Indian National Congress (1885), growth of Indian nationalism, rise of Hindu and Muslim fundamentalism, and the inability of national leaders to provide a coherent vision for communal and religious harmony convinced Indian Christians not to rely uncritically

on European and American models of theology, Church organization, and worship. Leaders like V.S. Azariah appreciated the dedication and self-sacrifice of European and American missionaries, yet questioned their paternalism and arrogance. Indian Christian leaders like Jesudasan pioneered Christian ashram movements. The Re-Thinking Group reinterpreted the Christian faith within the contexts of *Advaita*, *Bhakti*, and popular spiritualities. Many groups worked toward Church unity, such as the South India United Church of 1908 and the national council of Protestant churches in 1912. Indian Christians associated with the YMCA and YWCA became more sensitive to Indian cultures. Simultaneously, the impact of World War I and the Great Depression affected Indian Christianity negatively.

In August 1947, British India was divided into India and Pakistan. Indian Christians quickly inaugurated the Church of South India (September 1947) by merging Presbyterian, Anglican, and Congregational churches into a single body that has its own challenges. Indigenous Protestant movements in post-independent India, especially in relation to Dalit and tribal theologies, continue to question European and American theologies and Church structures. They consciously seek alternate ways of developing an authentic Indian Christian theology and ways of being religious.

Above: The flower market in Kolkata (formerly Calcutta) is a flurry of color and movement. English Baptist William Carey began his missionary work in Kolkata in November 1793.

Left: This nineteenth-century stipple engraving shows the missionary William Carey with Brahmin Pundit (Mritunjaya). Carey was opposed to the caste system in India.

MISSIONS TO BURMA AND THAILAND

Opposite: The interior of a Catholic church in Mandalay, Burma's second-largest city, is much more brightly decorated than Western houses of worship, reflecting local artistic customs.

Below: King Chulalongkorn with his son, Prince Vajiravudh. On October 8, 1878, the king's viceroy issued the Edict of Toleration, which protected Christian rights throughout Siam (Thailand).

Below: Despite the tireless work of early Christian missionaries, 89 percent of today's Burmese population are Buddhist. Boys often train to be monks from a young age.

Culturally, the Southeast Asian region of present-day Burma (Myanmar) and Thailand (formerly Siam) is very diverse, with several language and ethnic groups found in common in both countries. Most of the earliest inhabitants worshipped various spirits (*nats*) and honored ancestors. Among the majority people (Bamars in Burma and Thai in Thailand) Theravada Buddhism has been the dominant faith, often mixed with the older *nat* worship.

Burma

Persian Christian monks traveling to the Far East in the seventh to ninth century may have reached the region, but the first recorded missionary work began with the arrival in Burma of the French Franciscan Pierre Bonfer in 1554.

Burmese Buddhism was resistant to Christian outreach. Bonfer's mission was short-lived and missionaries after him needed military protection to ensure residence in Burma. Even the Portuguese fort established near Pegu in 1600 lasted only 13 years. Missionary martyrs were more common than missionary heroes. Some missionaries were sewn into sacks and thrown in the river. Nevertheless, important translations into Burmese—including prayer books, catechisms, and language primers—aided later Protestant and Roman Catholic work.

By the nineteenth century the British had become the regional colonial power in South Asia, and missionary work in Burma was accordingly less risky. Felix Carey (the son of William Carey, the pioneer English missionary in India) was the first Protestant to arrive, in 1807. The Congregational convert to Baptist theology, Adoniram Judson, is the best-known pioneer in Burma. Missionaries, both Catholic and Protestant, were caught up in the colonial wars in Burma, the final annexation taking place in 1885. Anglican chaplains did some work, but American Baptists did the majority of the Protestant work.

A Burmese Bible was printed by 1840, and this aided greatly in missionary work throughout the country. The majority Bamar people were always less receptive, but other groups such as the Kayin (Karen) responded heartily, in part because of their own mythology of a "lost book" that would be returned to help them to get to know God. The Bible was brought, translated, and taught, and the Kayin converted at a rapid rate. Methodists arrived in 1878, and Presbyterians (coming in from India) arrived in the early twentieth century. Baptist and Catholic missions expanded their work under the British colonial presence, setting up a network of schools, hospitals, clinics, and churches. However, it was among the Kayin, Kachin, Chin, Shan, and Mon minorities rather than the Bamar ethnic majority that Christianity had its greatest impact.

Thailand

The first missionaries to arrive in Ayutthaya (Thailand) were the Portuguese Dominicans Jeronimo da Cruz and Sebastião da Canto in 1567. Following them were the Franciscans. The Jesuits began to arrive in 1607. Although Roman Catholic missionary orders were often in conflict with one another, under the progressive Thai King Narai (1656–1688) Christianity began to grow: A seminary was built, local priests were trained, and a hospital was built. Later, however, Christian missions faced a greater problem: French colonialism moving in from the east (Annam and Cochin China) was seen as a Christian imperial threat by the Thai rulers. The Christian community grew slowly during the eighteenth century; much of the growth was among South Asians of Portuguese blood and refugees from Annam (Vietnam) and from Cambodia. By 1800 fewer than 3,000 Christians lived in Thailand.

Siam was a buffer state between the French in Indo-China and the British in India and Burma. Because Siam was a relatively independent region, missionaries did not have the protection of a colonial government, and thus cooperation with the Thai king was necessary. The Roman Catholic Church grew steadily, but most of the growth was among Annamese refugees and the ethnic Chinese. Under the leadership of Jean-Louis Vey (1875–1909), the Roman Catholic Church grew and built several new churches, chapels, schools, and a hospital. Protestant missions began in earnest with the arrival of American Baptists (1833) and Congregationalists and Presbyterians (1834). The reign of both king Mongkut (Rama IV, 1851–1868) and king Chulalongkorn (Rama V, 1868–1911) brought modernization to Siam and, in 1878, an Edict of Toleration for Christianity in the royal realm. Baptists, Disciples of Christ, Presbyterians, and Roman Catholics all established churches and schools, but the greatest response continued to be among the Chinese and tribal peoples outside the country's center. A state caught between regions of French and British colonialism, Thailand remained a Buddhist realm with cautious toleration of Christianity.

COME LORD JESUS

MISSIONS TO THE OTTOMAN EMPIRE

The early nineteenth century saw a resurgence of missionary activity across the area covered by the Ottoman Empire. Several Catholic orders reinvigorated their endeavors, particularly French orders of Capuchins, Jesuits, Lazarists, Sisters of Charity of St Vincent de Paul, Sisters of St Joseph of the Assumption, and Sisters of Nazarene. Newly organized European and American Protestant missionary societies also began work in the region.

From the Balkans to Baghdad

Among the Protestant missionary societies, the London-based Church Missionary Society working in the eastern Mediterranean was prominent early on, but it was soon eclipsed by the Boston-based American Board of Commissioners for Foreign Missions, an interdenominational organization that was dominated by Congregationalists and Presbyterians. After a subsequent split, the Congregationalist American Board focused its activities in Anatolia and southeast Europe; Presbyterians directed their efforts toward the Arab provinces, and also outside the empire to Egypt and Iran. Catholic and Protestant missionaries alike built churches, schools, convents, hospitals, orphanages, translation bureaus, and publishing houses. Their operations extended from the Balkans to the Bosphorus, and from there to Baghdad.

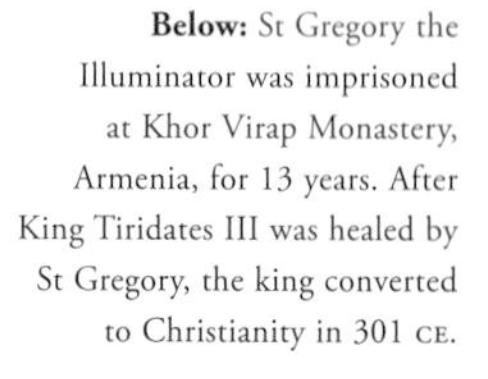

Below: St Gregory the Illuminator was imprisoned at Khor Virap Monastery, Armenia, for 13 years. After King Tiridates III was healed by St Gregory, the king converted to Christianity in 301 CE.

In the footsteps of St Paul

There was great rivalry between Catholic and Protestant missionaries for Ottoman souls. Catholic missionaries worked to bring the Eastern churches back into communion with the Roman Church. Inspired by the enthusiasm of evangelical revivalism, and the idea of traveling in the footsteps of St Paul, Protestant missionaries initially expected to convert Muslims and Jews. They soon learnt that neither was interested in becoming Christians. Tolerant of all religions, the Ottoman state organized religious communities under their own administrative units (millets), and Jews and Christians were mostly left to their own devices. Still, the relationship between the Ottoman state and Islam favored Muslims, who were unlikely to convert to what they perceived to be an inferior religion. Muslims also had an incentive not to convert: Capital punishment was the penalty for apostasy until the mid-nineteenth century. Protestant missionaries turned their attention instead to the people of the Eastern churches, among them Armenian Gregorians, Greek and Bulgarian Orthodox, Nestorians, Chaldeans, Copts, and Maronites. They planned a modern-day Protestant reformation of the Eastern churches.

Christ and culture

The work of all missionaries was facilitated by a period of Ottoman civil reform known as the Tanzimat, beginning in

Left: A nineteenth-century Bulgarian fresco depicts God the Father in glorious gold. Missionaries to Bulgaria had great success in converting the Eastern Orthodox Bulgarians to Protestantism.

1839. The reforms proclaimed, among other things, freedom of religion. Missionaries engaged in the process of reform through their discussions about religion and education. Protestant missionaries disagreed among themselves as to the balance they should adopt between evangelizing and educating, but they were pushed into education by local conditions. The Armenians, Greeks, and Bulgarians among whom they came to work most closely wanted modern translations of the Bible and as much education as they could get. Because the availability of the scriptures in the vernacular was indispensable for a reformation of the Eastern churches, translation work was essential. Some missionaries believed education should be restricted to basic vernacular literacy; others worked to establish high schools and colleges.

Although missionaries succeeded in establishing small Catholic and Protestant communities across the Ottoman Empire, they are most remembered for their educational achievements. Over the course of the nineteenth century, an estimated 100,000 students had studied in the nearly 500 French (mostly mission) schools across the empire. In Anatolia, in the one year of 1909 alone, over 20,000 students were enrolled in more than 300 schools operated by the American Board. Prominent missionary institutions included: Robert College (now Bogazici University, Istanbul); Syrian Protestant College (now the American University in Beirut); the Jesuit-founded Université St Joseph, also in Beirut; and the American College for Girls (renamed Robert College, Istanbul).

Perhaps the greatest changes wrought by Catholic and Protestant missionaries were in the sphere of women's education. Missionaries did much to popularize the idea of female education in Ottoman domains and inspired many communities to improve educational opportunities for girls. In their institutions of higher education, missionaries provided an international environment where students from all faiths and nationalities were welcome. By the early twentieth century, Christians, Jews, and Muslims studied together in American and French educational institutions in the Middle East.

Below: Selim III reigned as Ottoman Sultan from 1789 to 1807. Influenced by the French, he undertook a series of reforms that were opposed by the Janissaries (infantrymen) and the ulama (religious scholars).

PROMINENT MISSIONARY FAMILIES

Elias and Martha Jane Riggs worked for more than 50 years throughout the Ottoman Empire. Elias Riggs (1810–1901) supervised translations of the scriptures and hymnals into several languages, including Armenian and Bulgarian. Martha Jane Riggs (1811–1887) wrote *Letters to Mothers,* an advice manual for women that was translated into a number of languages including Armenian, Bulgarian, Greek, and Turkish, and contributed to discussions about the changing contributions of women to Ottoman society.

PROTESTANTISM IN LATIN AMERICA

Protestantism made a relatively late start in Latin America, making slow inroads into traditionally Catholic areas. James Thompson, an agent for the British and Foreign Bible Society, distributed some Bibles in 1817. Missionary work began in different areas: Presbyterians in Colombia (1856); Baptists and Methodists in Argentina (1864 and 1867); and Baptists in Cuba (1898). Justus Henry Nelson and his wife Fannie Bishop Capen Nelson established the first Protestant church in Amazonia in 1883. But it was not until 1890 that an organized Protestant mission was undertaken—the Central American Mission.

Below: Tilaco Mission in Sierra Gorda, Mexico, was founded in the mid-1700s by Father Juan Crespi, a Franciscan missionary from Spain. Up until the nineteenth century, Catholicism was the predominant form of Christianity in Latin America.

From scandal to mission

Central American Mission was the brainchild of a complex man, Cyrus I. Scofield (1843–1921). His early life was given over to fighting with the Confederates in the American Civil War, Republican Party politics in Kansas, prison for forgery and shady financial dealings, alcoholism, and divorce. Then he converted to evangelical Christianity. He devoted the rest of his life to evangelistic campaigns, founding Bible colleges, ministering to Congregational and then later Southern Presbyterian churches, and working with missionary organizations. At a meeting of the Niagara Bible Conference (or Believers' Meeting for Bible Study) in 1888 he met the well-known J. Hudson Taylor, founder of the China Inland Mission. Taylor was known for his strong evangelicalism and sensitivity to Chinese culture—he took to wearing Chinese clothes. Scofield was deeply impressed, and within two years he established the Central American Mission (CAM) with the help of three businessmen.

Scofield's other claim to fame is the *Scofield Reference Bible*, an annotated study Bible published in 1909. The *Reference Bible* provided the most thorough description of "dispensationalism"—a theory that the history of the world is divided into seven stages, the last of which precedes the final judgment. The key to this final stage is a series of recognizable signs of the coming end, such as the establishment of the state of Israel. It has profoundly influenced the development of fundamentalist Christianity in the USA.

Into "Samaria"

Scofield's study of the Bible led him to interpret Acts 1:8 in a distinctive fashion. The text reads: "But you will receive power when the Holy Spirit has come upon you; and you shall be my witnesses in Jerusalem, and in all Judea and Samaria, and to the ends of the Earth." Scofield felt that "Samaria" meant the countries next door, and for someone in the USA that meant Central America. He believed it had long been ignored as an area for Protestant missions.

Central American Mission took on a life of its own after Scofield's initial work. It is an organization driven by a similar evangelical ideal, and, like J. Hudson Taylor's China Inland Mission, it draws its members from any Protestant church as long as they agree to its basic position.

CAM's first act was to send the McConnell family with their three children to Costa Rica in 1891. They were ably assisted by two Canadian women—Mrs Ross and Mrs Lang—who were the wives of coffee plantation owners living in San José, Costa Rica. As for many missionaries, the major adjustments for the young family were to both language and culture. These were small beginnings indeed. It was five years before the next missionaries, Albert E. Bishop and his wife, went out, this time to Honduras. They were so zealous that they set out without arranging for anyone to meet them, without knowing what to do, and without applying to CAM until after they arrived. CAM was all too pleased to add their second missionary endeavor to the movement. Within the next decade, missionaries spread to Guatemala (the Bishops moved there due to health concerns) and El Salvador. In those ten years, five missionaries died from tropical diseases, but seventeen others remained in the field. In the twentieth century, CAM missionary work spread to Nicaragua, Panama, Mexico, and Cuba, and even to Spain and the US Hispanic communities.

THE BIBLE FOR THE WHOLE WORLD

Perhaps the most important development within the Central American Mission (CAM) was the establishment of the Robinson Bible Institute in 1929 in Guatemala, led by Albert Bishop and William Cameron Townsend. Townsend would go on to create two of the major Bible translation organizations in the world today, the Wycliffe Bible Translators and the associated Summer Institute of Linguistics. Out of those two organizations, the dominant model of Bible translation developed, known as "dynamic equivalence" or meaning-based translation. Gaining experience from widespread translation activity, the purpose of this approach is to create a fluid, accesible translation rather than a literal translation.

Below: Nineteenth-century Mexican artists were often inspired by the Bible stories told by Protestant missionaries. Juan Urruchi's 1853 painting depicts Lot and his family leaving Sodom.

MISSIONS TO INDONESIA

Above: An illuminated cross on a headland near the city of Jayapura, the capital of Papua Province, Indonesia. Christianity was established in the region as part of Dutch colonialism.

The year 1799 marked a turning point in the story of Christianity in the Indonesian archipelago (known as "the Dutch East Indies"). After two centuries of controlling the islands, the Dutch East India Company (VOC) went bankrupt and the Dutch state took over the company's assets. One of the first acts by the Dutch government was to declare freedom of religion in its new colonial territories.

Controlled by the company

This step was a major break with the past; under VOC control missionaries had been kept on a tight leash, and the remnants of Roman Catholic missions, introduced by the Portuguese and Spanish in the sixteenth and seventeenth centuries, had been taken over. East Timor and Flores remained Catholic, but the other islands came under Reformed Protestant influence. Since the clergy, the missions, and the churches were entirely reliant on VOC money, resources, ships, and food, they had little choice but to do the bidding of the hand that fed them. This meant that the missionaries had to neglect commercially unimportant islands, which were left to their own devices without ministers, and concentrate on areas vital for VOC's commercial interests—especially Ambon and surrounding islands.

Church ministers had to be from the Netherlands. Indigenous people were not permitted to be ordained, administer the sacraments, or be on church governing bodies. The result was that by the end of the eighteenth century there were 55,000 Reformed Christians in the Indonesian archipelago, but not one local leader.

Missionary explosion

The change in 1799 was dramatic. Roman Catholic priests returned after 200 years of absence, the Reformed churches were reorganized as the Protestant Church in the Netherlands Indies, and wave after wave of missionaries spread over the islands. Now the Dutch government supported both Roman Catholic and Protestant missions.

Above: An 1826 French lithograph shows the village of Cayeli, on the island of Buru, Indonesia. Buru was occupied by the Dutch East India Company, and later came under Dutch government control.

The government soon found that support was costing far more than it had planned for, since missionary societies began to spring up like mushrooms after rain. From Holland there came the Netherlands Missionary Society, and then new bodies such as the Netherlands Missionary Union and the Utrecht Missionary Union, which had been established as a result of theological differences back in Holland. From Germany the Rhenish Missionary Society—the largest German organization of its kind—turned up in the archipelago, along with the Basel Mission. Even the Dutch Mennonites put their hand out for assistance, along with Baptist, Methodist, and Congregational missions.

Government support came with a catch. Based on its experience in the Netherlands, the government wisely tried to avoid religious conflict and competition. Its solution was to give each missionary group a monopoly over a certain area. This was all very well in theory, but some regions had been Muslim for quite a while and they were relatively resistant to Christian conversion.

The Christian missionaries made little headway in Java, where there was a well-established Muslim presence. In the non-Muslim areas they had far greater success. In Sumatra among the Batak people, the German Rhenish mission under the leadership of the energetic L.I. Nommensen (1834–1918) established a large church. Other Protestant groups were successful in Sulawesi (Celebes), the Moluccas, Kalimantan, and Sumba, and in the region known as Netherlands New Guinea. The Catholics reinvigorated their long-term presence in East Timor and Flores. As a result of all this energy, in Indonesia today Christians make up 10 percent of a population of 240 million—more than the total population of Holland.

Conversion and independence

Missionaries soon began producing Bible translations in many local languages. The missionaries also changed their approach to conversions. Instead of mass baptisms of people after little instruction, they aimed at individual conversion—following the missionary organizations' Pietistic emphasis on individual piety and a vigorous Christian life. They felt that individual conversion ensured people were genuine about their faith.

However, the missionaries were very careful about giving the new churches independence. The missionary groups kept each new congregation under close supervision, trying to ensure that there was a great depth of knowledge and understanding about the Christian faith before passing the congregations over to local leadership.

TRANSLATING THE BIBLE

Although the Bible was translated in the archipelago in 1733, it was available only in one language, Malay; yet the Indonesian islands have no less than 737 living languages, so one of the first changes brought about by the ninetennth-century missionaries was to use local lan guages instead of insisting on Malay. In a process that continues today, Bible translation projects were begun, usually of the Gospels and the New Testament first before including the rest of the Bible.

Above: Carlos Felipe Ximenes Belo (born 1948) is a Catholic bishop in East Timor. Colonized by Portugal in the 1500s, East Timor was part of Indonesia from 1975 until its sovereignty was declared in 2002.

MISSION TO THE JEWS

The concept of a "Mission to the Jews" arose during the early years of the Reformation. Martin Luther thought that many Jews would become Christians if they were presented with a reformed version of the faith. This did not happen. Two centuries later, the spiritual movement of Pietism also expressed a keen interest in converting the Jewish people. By 1728 German Pietists had founded a missionary center called *Institutium Judaicum,* for training evangelists and producing literature to convert the Jews; however, it closed in 1791. German interest in evangelizing the Jews was revived by the impact of British missionary endeavor in the late eighteenth century; the Berlin Society for the Promotion of Christianity Among the Jews was established in 1822, and gave rise to many similar societies.

British missions

Both England and Scotland showed a great interest in converting the Jews as a nation. The fervor aroused during the English Civil War saw the first increase in prayer for the Jews to join with the Christian nations. Calvinists promoted defending the Protestant faith against what they saw as the evils of popery and the Ottoman Turks. Coupled with the belief of living in the "last days," this brought great attention to the conversion of the Jews during the 1600s and set the stage for later evangelical missions.

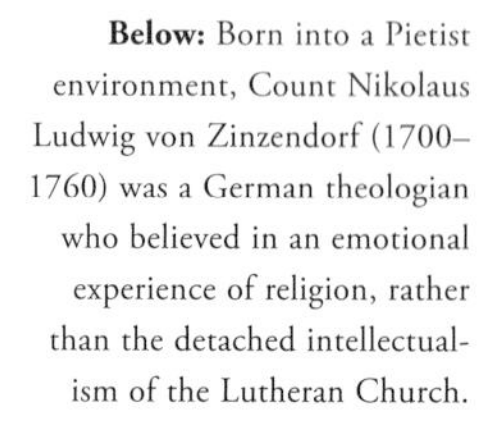

Below: Born into a Pietist environment, Count Nikolaus Ludwig von Zinzendorf (1700–1760) was a German theologian who believed in an emotional experience of religion, rather than the detached intellectualism of the Lutheran Church.

In the British Empire there was an unprecedented interest in evangelizing the Jews. The Calvinist idea of being elected to improve the world was reflected in the religious outlook of the British people. A self-perception of being chosen for a mandate, taking part in the "end times" events, fighting to demolish the "evil" Ottoman Empire, undermining the role of Catholicism, and converting the heathen were all imperatives for evangelical Protestants to proselytize among the Jews. They strongly believed that the conversion of the Jews together with the fulfillment of the number of pagans would hasten Jesus' second coming, precipitating the millennial, paradise-like state. British, and later American, missions to the Jews related to God's preordained plan to convert the Jews. While this often aroused anger within Judaism in different countries, it stimulated a variety of responses to identity questions stirred by romantic nationalistic ideas. Messianic Judaism, Zionism, Communism, Neolog-Reform, and Hasidic Judaism, as well as the Hebrew Christian movement, saw their roots in the fertile nineteenth century.

At the same time, the first Protestant missionary societies were established—the Baptist Society for Propagating the Gospel Among the Heathen (BSPGH) in 1792, the London Missionary Society (LMS) in 1795, and the Church Missionary Society (CMS) in 1799. Jewish mission grew out of the context of a larger missionary fervor. British Protestantism produced the most active organizations, such as the London Society for Promoting Christianity Among the Jews (1808), and the London-headquartered society was named the Mildmay Mission to the Jews (1822).

Scotland also harbored fervent missionary attitudes toward the Jews. Besides the parachurch organizations, the Church of Scotland sent missionaries across Europe, Asia Minor, and Palestine from 1839 onward. The Irish Presbyterian Church joined the missionary efforts.

THE LONDON JEWS' SOCIETY

Established in 1808, the London Society for Promoting Christianity Among the Jews, commonly known as the London Jews' Society, enjoyed the support of both nonconformist and Church of England believers. It grew out of the London Missionary Society (LMS) into a separate organization. Over the years the name of the society changed, and it is now known as the Church's Ministry Among Jewish People.

American missions

On the other side of the Atlantic, the American Society for Meliorating the Condition of the Jews was founded in 1816. Influenced by British evangelism, "Dispensationalism"

Left: The missions to the Jews carried out by the Presbyterian Church of Scotland were sent by its various councils, whose offices are situated in Edinburgh.

(which included a belief in the "end times") saturated the religious life of American people, and interest in evangelizing the Jews flourished. From the 1870s through the 1920s, almost 50 Jewish mission societies were established; they employed hundreds of missionaries. The most significant of the twentieth-century Jewish mission societies are the American Messianic Fellowship, until 1953 called the Chicago Hebrew Mission; and the American Board of Missions to the Jews, which altered its name in 1983 to the Chosen People Ministries. Similar to Great Britain, many Protestant ecclesiastical bodies, like the Southern Baptist Convention and the Presbyterian Church in the USA, set up independent mission departments for converting the Jews.

Evangelizing efforts often arouse ire on the part of Jews, who see them as one more attempt to eliminate Judaism. Since the 1960s, interfaith dialogue has led many mainline Protestant churches to abandon attempts to convert Jews. Conservative evangelical churches, however, persist. The best-known mission to the Jews in the last half century is Jews for Jesus, founded by Moishe Rosen in 1973.

Below: A Hasidic Rabbi at the door of a synagogue in Safed, Israel. Hasidic Judaism was founded by Israel ben Eliezer in Eastern Europe in the 1700s, and defied Christian proselytization to spread across the world.

BIBLE SOCIETIES

A Bible society is a nonprofit organization that exists in order to translate, publish, and distribute the Bible. Usually ecumenical in their outlook, Bible society translations do not include notes or commentary on any texts. Rather, the primary aim is to supply copies of the Bible in different languages in order for the Bible to be read and studied.

The need for translations

Bible translations are needed whenever the people's language is not the same as the language of the scriptures. The earliest known example is the Septuagint, the translation of the Hebrew Bible into Greek for the Greek-speaking Jews of Alexandria who were no longer fluent in Hebrew. Latin eventually replaced Greek in the western Roman Empire, and Latin translations of the Bible were made, culminating in Jerome's version (completed c. 405 CE). Missionary work also prompted translations: Ulfilas translated sections of the Bible into Gothic c. 360 CE. In the ninth century, Cyril and Methodius translated the Gospels and sections of the Old Testament into Slavonic. English and Czech Bibles appeared in the fourteenth century. By this time, the Church hierarchy was trying to suppress translations into vernacular languages, but they would not succeed. Latin was no longer the language of the people, so the time was ripe for translation of the Bible into various European languages. Martin Luther made his own translation of the Bible into German; other Reformers made translations in French, Finnish, and Italian, as well as a number of other languages. In 1710, a group of Pietists in Saxony formed a society for the distribution of the Bible. Believing that small group Bible study was essential for a vital Christian faith, they wanted to see Luther's edition of the Bible reproduced and more widely distributed. By 1722, they had expanded their work to include several other European languages.

In the eighteenth century in England, various groups that emerged out of the evangelical movement took an interest in the distribution of scripture, among them the Society for Promoting Christian Knowledge Among the Poor (1750) and the Society for the Support and Encouragement of Sunday Schools (1785). In 1780, a group called the Bible Society was formed, but as its work was limited to seamen and soldiers, the name was later changed to the Naval and Military Bible Society.

The British and Foreign Bible Society

In the nineteenth century, Bible societies were formed in response to the need to make the Bible available to all. The first modern Bible society, the British and Foreign Bible Society, was formed in 1804 to make more Bibles available

Above: Martin Luther translated the New Testament into German in 1522, and the Old Testament in 1534; the translation was based on Erasmus' Greek New Testament (2nd ed., 1519).

in the Welsh language. A proposal for the society was brought by the Reverend Thomas Charles of Bala to a group known as the Religious Tract Society. Inspired by the story of a Welsh girl, Mary Jones (1784–1864), who walked 25 miles (40 km) to obtain a copy of the Bible in her native tongue, it was agreed that a new society should be formed with the sole purpose of encouraging: "a wider circulation of the Holy Scriptures, without note or comment." The society's work expanded to include the publication of Bibles in other languages.

Controversy over translations

Through the years, the British and Foreign Bible Society has experienced several controversies over issues related to circulation and translation. Although it was perceived to be Protestant, it was ecumenical in outlook and, by 1813, had Bibles printed that included the Apocrypha. This broadly ecumenical outlook was not supported by more conservative Protestants or by the Roman Catholic Church. In 1831 the Trinitarian Bible Society was started by Protestants who did not wish to include Apocryphal books in the canon of scripture. The Catholic Church did not officially endorse vernacular translations until Vatican II in the 1960s. Initially, the British and Foreign Bible Society could not circulate copies of the scriptures in English other than King James' Authorized Version of 1611, though this was eventually changed to include the Revised English Version.

Over the years, the British and Foreign Bible Society extended its work to England, India, and Europe. As the work spread, separate Bible societies were established in numerous countries around the world. Today their work is coordinated under the banner of the United Bible Societies (UBS), which is the name for a fellowship of 145 individual Bible societies working in over 200 countries and territories. Bible societies are not affiliated with any one Christian denomination. They work to serve all Christian churches, and today have extended their mission beyond Bible translation and distribution to include literacy programmes for those who cannot read, and audio material for people with impaired vision.

Above: This fifteenth-century illumination depicts a monk teaching children using the Historical Bible, a thirteenth-century French translation of the Bible with commentaries that characterized scripture as a historical record.

Opposite: In his Vulgate Bible, St Jerome used Hebrew texts to translate the Old Testament into Latin, rather than the Greek Septuagint that had been the basis of previous translations.

WOMEN MISSIONARIES

Below: In 1621, Mother Jerónima de la Fuente founded the first Catholic Monastery in the Philippines. She welcomed any Filipino woman with a genuine desire to pursue the Franciscan lifestyle.

From the beginning, mission and evangelism has been a primary concern of Christians. Believing that they had been commissioned to go out into all the world to proclaim the Gospel, both men and women engaged in the task of telling others "the Good News of Jesus Christ." The mission field for women, however, was more limited than for men; women were often confined to the private rather than the public sphere.

While missionary activity has always been an important feature of the life of the church, Protestant missionary work did not begin in earnest until the seventeenth and eighteenth centuries. The Pietists in Germany were among the first to send out missionaries to far-flung places. Moreover, a number of societies were formed in Britain in an attempt to reach out to the American colonies. Some examples were: The Society for the Propagation of the Gospel in New England (chartered in 1649), the Society for the Propagation of Christian Knowledge (1699), and the Society for the Propagation of the Gospel in Foreign Parts (1701). It may be argued, however, that the growth of the modern missionary movement was due in considerable part to the religious fervor generated by the evangelical revival that had spread in Britain, Germany, and the North American colonies during the eighteenth century.

The modern missionary movement

In 1792, the well-known British Baptist minister William Carey published a treatise entitled *An Enquiry into the Obligation of Christians to Use means for the Conversion of the Heathen.* As a result, the Particular Baptist Society for the Propagation of the Gospel to the Heathen—later known as the Baptist Missionary Society (BMS)—was formed in the same year. Although Baptist in name, the society gained wide support from across many denominations, even receiving donations from Anglican priests.

The first missionaries sent to India in 1793 by the society were all men. Although wives accompanied the men to the mission field, it was clear that the Missionary Society did not appoint women or even consider them missionaries.

As early as 1796, however, William Carey, who had gone to India as one of the first missionaries, claimed that women were needed to "communicate the gospel...in a situation where superstition secludes all women of respectability from hearing the word unless from their own sex." Wives of the missionaries engaged in the work alongside their husbands and were involved in translation, education, and even agriculture. As the mission work grew, the society occasionally noted the need for women to serve as teachers, but still did not appoint women as missionaries. As other missionary societies were formed in Britain and in America in the nineteenth century, a policy of the non-acceptance of women seems to have generally prevailed. Eventually women who were widows were sent to the mission field,

Right: Though the Pietists were one of the first religious groups to send missionaries to non-Christian areas, female Pietists such as these women were never considered missionaries.

"SHE COULD GET THE DEVIL TO JOIN THE CHURCH"

By the close of the nineteenth century, the majority of missionaries worldwide were women. In China, almost two-thirds were single women. Mary Slessor of Calabar lived for many years in what is now Nigeria, in the midst of tribes labeled "murderous" by colonial officers. Not only was she unharmed, she was appointed as a judge to resolve tribal disputes. Mary Collins, another single woman, was a missionary to the Lakota on the northern plains of North America. She lived with Sitting Bull's band, and the renowned warrior respected her opinions. After Sitting Bull was killed, Mary Collins stayed with his people and accompanied them to the reservation. The Unitarians and Universalists accepted women ministers earlier than most other denominations. Milma Lappala and her husband, Risto, were missionary ministers to the Finnish Americans in northern Minnesota, North America. Milma was such an eloquent preacher that some people declared: "She could get the devil to join the church if she tried hard enough."

though the boards in Britain and America did not appoint single women who had never been married.

Women's missionary societies

Since missionary societies were reluctant to appoint women, in 1867 a group of women in Britain formed their own society in order to train and appoint women as missionaries; in the following year women in America did the same. The women's societies proved the key to opening the door for women who wished to serve as missionaries. The male-dominated denominational societies tried to hold tightly to what they believed to be the true ideal of womanhood, perhaps fearing that the appointment of women as missionaries might be construed as support for women's suffrage or women's rights. Meanwhile the societies that were controlled by women got on with the work of appointing teachers, nurses, and doctors to the mission field.

Although they often had to confront objections from their families and find ways of gaining the necessary qualifications of training and education, many single women applied for service. Not surprisingly, the women who were appointing female missionaries did not seem to have the same apprehensions as their male counterparts about sending unmarried women into service in foreign lands. In fact, single women often appeared far more able than their married counterparts in tackling the work required.

Although the female missionary societies eventually ceased to operate as separate entities, they succeeded in opening the way for both married and single women to serve as missionaries by proving that they were effective in mission work. Single women especially gained a new sense of freedom, and there was great recognition of women for taking on tasks not only on the mission field but when they returned home, too.

Above: This hand-colored illustration depicts the arrival of the suffragettes in London, England, in September 1908. The suffragette cause was greatly assisted by the success of early female missionaries.

NEW ZEALAND RECEIVES CHRISTIANITY

Right: Churches in New Zealand are often decorated with indigenous art. This Maori wood carving can be seen in St Faith's Church, an Anglican institution in Ohinemutu.

The first Christians probably sighted New Zealand (Aotearoa) in 1642, from a boat commanded by Dutch explorer Abel Tasman. A conflict with the native Maori resulted in several deaths and it would be 127 years until Christians returned, and a few more years until any stayed.

The early religious history of New Zealand was shaped by several important factors, not the least of which was the question of which of the marauding and competing European states would establish itself as the colonial power. Christianity in early New Zealand is best seen as operating in a sort of religious "bazaar." Within a religious and political free market, different denominations ministered to their own people, while they competed with each other for the attentions of the Maori.

First missions

The whaling, seal hunting, and flax trades drove early European settlement. From the 1790s many thousands of sailors from many nations set foot in New Zealand, but few chose to settle there. Their interactions with the Maori were largely commercial, violent, or sexual. No doubt some were Christians, but there was no organized religious provision, either for the Europeans or the Maori. In 1814, the Church of England minister Samuel Marsden (who was based in Parramatta, NSW, Australia) established the first Christian mission station at Rangihoua, Bay of Islands, on the North Island. The Anglican Church Mission Society (CMS) sponsored the station, but Marsden expended much of his own time and money, although not entirely without personal recompense. By the mid-1820s the CMS had three stations in the Bay of Islands region. They were quickly joined by the Wesleyan Missionary Society. Through the 1820s, the missionaries were largely confined to the Northland, where they preached with limited success to both Europeans and Maori. The often rough Europeans—many were former convicts—were hardly fertile ground, and there were as yet few Maori conversions.

Below: Located on the east coast of Northland, the Bay of Islands is the birthplace of modern New Zealand. It was here that Christian missionaries first came into contact with the Maori.

The Maori, the Bible, and literacy

The Maori were inevitably affected by the encounter with Europeans, including missionaries. As elsewhere, evangelically minded Protestants were concerned to make their hosts aware of the good news of the scripture through the translation and distribution of the Bible—which in New Zealand meant the creation of a written Maori language and a concomitant effort to spread the ability to read it. As in Polynesia, literacy was instrumental in attracting Maori people of New Zealand to the new faith.

Mission expansion

The 1830s saw a rapid expansion of both the European population and of missionary activity. In this decade the number of Europeans living permanently in New Zealand

grew from an estimated 300 to 2,000. The first real successes in evangelizing the Maori took place and, perhaps not coincidentally, the first mission press was established in 1834, and a Maori New Testament had appeared by 1837.

Power rivalry and the Catholic mission

As in the Pacific Islands, early Christianity in New Zealand was shaped by European power rivalries, particularly that which occurred between Protestant Britain and Catholic France. In 1838, the first Catholic mission was established. Its leader was Jean Baptiste Pompallier, a young French member of the Society of Mary (the Marists). He was consecrated in 1836 as vicar apostolic of western Oceania, a territory encompassing most of the South Pacific. Pompallier set out almost immediately with a small group of French Marists, eventually settling in the Hokianga region of the Northland. In a sign of the sectarianism that was all too real a part of New Zealand's early history, the missionaries were promptly attacked by a mob inflamed by the local Wesleyan mission station.

The first bishop of New Zealand

The French presence, and domestic pressures, helped to motivate the British into taking a closer interest in New Zealand. On February 6, 1840, the Treaty of Waitangi was signed between the British Crown and several Maori chiefs. Significantly, the treaty was translated into Maori by the CMS missionary leader Henry Williams.

The establishment of British sovereignty, and the imminent plans of the New Zealand Company to settle the islands with British colonists, demanded a more formal religious establishment. In 1841, George Augustus Selwyn was appointed the first bishop of New Zealand. His salary was paid equally by the British government and the New Zealand Company; his churches were subsidized by the latter. The arrival of Pompallier, the Treaty of Waitangi, and the appointment of Selywn marked the establishment of both European sovereignty and European Church institutions in New Zealand. Both would grow, and later settlements such as Canterbury and Otago would have distinctly religious characteristics (Anglican and Presbyterian, respectively).

Above: The Church of the Good Shepherd has overlooked stunning Lake Tekapo since 1935. It was built to commemorate the first Pakeha (European) settlers of the South Island's Mackenzie Basin.

CHRISTIANITY IN THE PACIFIC ISLANDS

Above: Captain James Wilson was known as the "Missionary Captain." His ship, the *Duff*, carried a group of British missionaries to the Pacific, arriving in Tahiti on March 6, 1797.

Opposite: This c. 1895 photograph shows the mission students at Olal, on the Isle of Ambryon, New Hebrides, Melanesia. Literacy in the Pacific Islands developed as a result of missionary activity.

The evangelization of the Pacific Islands did not necessarily follow the expanding empires of the European powers. However, it was inspired by Europe's explorers, not least of them Captain James Cook. Cook's journeys, his shocking death in Hawai'i, and above all his published *Voyages*, inspired a generation of missionaries fascinated (and appalled) by the beautiful and savage lands he described. In 1795, the newly founded London Missionary Society decided to make the Pacific its first mission territory. The British were already active in the area—the First Fleet had brought white settlers to Australia in 1788—but the Pacific Islands were as yet unclaimed by the European powers.

First encounters

In 1685 a Roman Catholic prefecture was established at Manila for the Pacific region. However, in most instances the London Missionary Society and other evangelical Protestant missionaries made the first sustained attempts to convert the diverse and widely separated Pacific Island communities. In March 1797, twenty-nine British missionaries (only five accompanied by their wives) arrived in Tahiti. Some stayed there, others went on to Tonga and the Marquesas Islands. They were grossly unprepared; many quickly retreated to rapidly growing Sydney, leaving only a handful on Tahiti. Polynesian religion hardly impressed the missionaries, many of whom saw in it only primitive nature-worship, licentiousness, and brutality. For their part, the Christian God made little sense to Polynesians accustomed to visible, active deities, whose stories were told in a rich oral culture and through communal activities such as singing or dancing, not through the mysterious medium of a printed book. Nor was the Christian God's extreme prudery easily understood, or appreciated.

Literacy and conversions

Despite hardships and mutual misunderstanding, some of the early missionaries persevered. With time, they began adjusting to the requirements of their mission. They recognized the intense Polynesian interest in the written word—

a particularly congenial discovery to evangelical Protestants focused on the centrality of scripture. In fact, in much of Polynesia and later Micronesia, a desire for literacy seems to have been the strongest bond between the missionaries and their hosts. In 1801 a catechism appeared in Tahitian; by 1810 a substantial portion of the Bible had been translated and published, which necessarily required the creation of written Tahitian. It was not simply a desire for literacy that drove the steady success of the missionaries, however. The emphasis placed within the Polynesian religious system on sacred powers and taboos provided an opening for Christians: If a missionary could violate taboos with impunity, surely the God who protected him must be great?

Beyond Polynesia

After their hesitant start, the British missionaries, utilizing both the Polynesian desire for literacy and a policy of targeting chiefs and other local elites, made many conversions. One of the most important local chiefs, Pomare II of Tahiti, requested baptism in 1812, and was granted it in 1819. By the 1820s, Tahitian converts began to go out as missionaries, carrying *lotu* (Christianity) to other Polynesian islands, thus marking the beginning of a distinctly indigenous understanding of the Christian faith. Other Protestant missionary societies also entered the field: The Wesleyans successfully established themselves in Tonga; the Anglican Church Missionary Society in New Zealand; an American group in Hawai'i; and the London Missionary Society extended its reach to, among other places, New Caledonia and the New Hebrides. Not all were successful. The first Protestant mission in Micronesia, an 1839 expedition to Vanuatu, resulted in the death and possibly the consumption of the missionaries. Despite the setbacks, many Protestant Christian missionaries enjoyed enormous success across the Pacific region.

Catholic competition

The Roman Catholic Church was not prepared to leave the Pacific Islanders to what they saw as religious error. Just as the majority of the Protestant missionaries were British, the vast majority of the Catholic missionaries were French, thus extending Old World political rivalries into Oceania. In the early 1830s, members of the Society of Mary (the Marists) and other French orders spread out across the Pacific, from New Zealand to New Guinea and Samoa. From 1838, a series of conflicts erupted between the Catholic missionaries and the Tahitian authorities (egged on by the British). This resulted in the establishment of a French protectorate over Tahiti, and subsequently the rest of the Society and Marquesas Islands; other territories were soon added. Direct conflict was avoided, but the British responded with their own territorial acquisitions. Christianity, in both its major Western European forms, was now well established across the Pacific, and both Catholic and Protestant Polynesians, Micronesians, and Melanesians began the long process of making a new faith their own.

Below: From 1768 to 1779, Captain James Cook made three voyages to the Pacific region, paving the way for the first Christian missionaries in the late eighteenth century.

DEVELOPMENTS IN WESTERN EUROPE

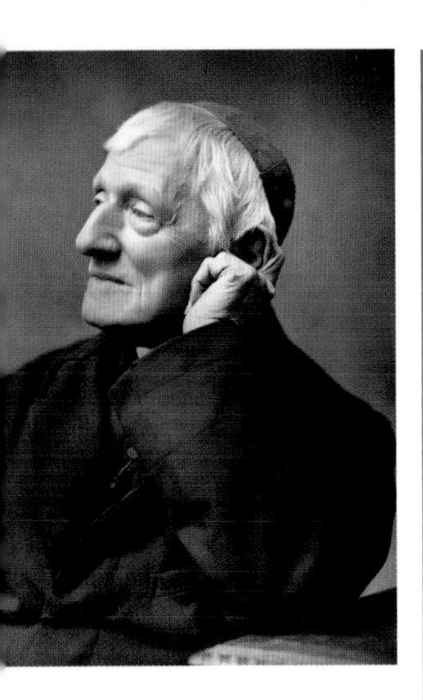

Above: John Henry Newman converted from Anglicanism to Roman Catholicism in 1845. He went on to write numerous persuasive theological tomes, including *Grammar of Assent* (1870) and *Development of Religious Error* (1885).

The French Revolution changed the religious face of Western Europe. The framework of long tradition was irreparably damaged by those bent on eliminating Christianity and monarchy as barriers to progress. The efforts of unbelievers brought them into prolonged collision with the churches, most notably the Catholic Church.

Legacy of the French Revolution

In the nineteenth century, writers in France, Germany, and the United Kingdom were the leading proponents of unbelief, provoking responses from defenders of Christianity. In the early part of the century, defenders tended to retreat from strict demonstration of the truth of Christian teachings to recommending them as fulfilling the needs of individuals and of societies. One need was for beauty, so the beauty of Christian belief was extolled by, for example, Chateaubriand (1768–1848). Another need was for civilization—a society in which intellectual progress and beneficence flourish. Frédéric Ozanam (1813–1853) praised Christianity for these effects in his *History of Civilization in the Fifth Century*. Christian apologists appealed to feelings. Friedrich Schlierermacher (1768–1834) persuaded many that belief in God is warranted by a profound feeling of dependence.

The French Revolution polarized believers and unbelievers in continental Europe, and provoked churches to act. Up to about 1870, Britain and France saw big increases in the number of church buildings and attenders, and in membership of religious orders. Christianity flourished in other European nations. The Catholic Church promoted a warmer emotional piety, fuelled by devotion to Mary and pilgrimages to sites of her apparitions, such as Lourdes.

Nevertheless, rejection of belief in fundamental Christian doctrines, including belief in God, was voiced by numerous influential thinkers and leaders. This viewpoint spread everywhere, including South America.

Scientific and historical arguments

There were many different reasons why belief in Christian doctrines declined. Two are noteworthy: The high valuation of the scientific method, and lack of historical evidence for important Biblical episodes such as the exodus from Egypt.

Regarding the emphasis on science, the educated class had come under the influence of Descartes and Kant, with the result that standards of proof and rationality became stringent. The other side of this movement was a rise in the level of skepticism. Much of what had been widely accepted as common sense and hallowed by tradition was reclassified as doubtful. One answer to this was empiricism, the notion that observation and experience were the tests for truth. The number of scientific discoveries in the century was astounding. These brought benefits to humans, such as improved health and fast communications. Christian faith lacked cogency—it could not be confirmed by observation. Charles Darwin's *On the Origin of Species*, 1859, provided an explanation for much in the universe without reference to God. Karl Marx analyzed history "scientifically" to argue that religion, though an illusion, was a capitalist tool for exploiting workers. Religion was not to be tolerated.

Where history-based arguments were concerned, Christianity's origins and support came mostly from the Bible; but the Bible's historical reliability was thrown into doubt, principally by German scholars. They had new resources in improved knowledge of ancient languages,

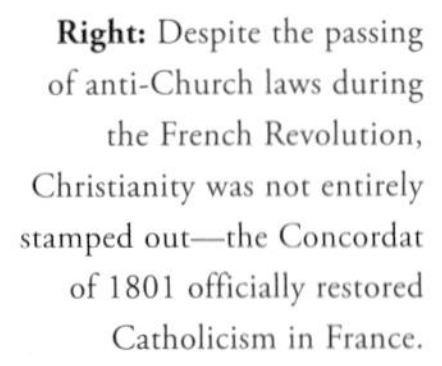

Right: Despite the passing of anti-Church laws during the French Revolution, Christianity was not entirely stamped out—the Concordat of 1801 officially restored Catholicism in France.

Previous pages: Pope Pius IX opened the First Vatican Council on December 8, 1869. One of the major discussion points was papal infallibility, an idea the German bishops in particular found to be controversial.

Above: Encouraged by the Catholic Church, pilgrims undertook arduous journeys in order to reach important religious sites in Europe, such as Lourdes in France and Santiago de Compostela in Spain.

collections of inscriptions, archeological findings, and studies in comparative religion. In his *Life of Jesus Critically Examined* (1835), D.F. Strauss, a German theologian and writer, examined the Gospels minutely and came to the conclusion that the picture of Jesus therein is mythical and incredible. His book caused a sensation, and in 1846 it was translated into English by the novelist George Eliot (Mary Ann Eliot). Other scholars arrived at the same conclusion as Strauss. These writings persuaded many clergy and theologians, and "liberal" Christianity was launched.

The Oxford Movement

Acutely aware of the challenge of liberal Christianity was John Henry Newman (1801–1890). One of the great prose writers of English, he argued insightfully for the justification of religious faith and the fact of divine revelation. Along with E.B. Pusey, John Keble, and others, Newman inaugurated the Oxford Movement within the Church of England, which led to numerous Anglicans adopting Catholic practices and theology. Despite their endeavors, and those of others, many Europeans rejected Christian claims and, further, became convinced that Christianity was a barrier to social reforms.

The Catholic Church was aware of these trends. Pope Pius IX responded by summoning bishops to the First Vatican Council (1869–1870), which issued dogmatic decrees, binding on Catholics, affirming the reliability of the Bible, the fact of divine revelation, and the rationality of belief in God and divine revelation. Most bishops thought a declaration of papal primacy and infallibility would strengthen the Church, so the council defined the doctrines as binding. The Church experienced unprecedented unity, but unbelievers repeatedly took control of governments that acted to reduce the influence of religion.

RELIGIOUS CONFLICT IN CANADA

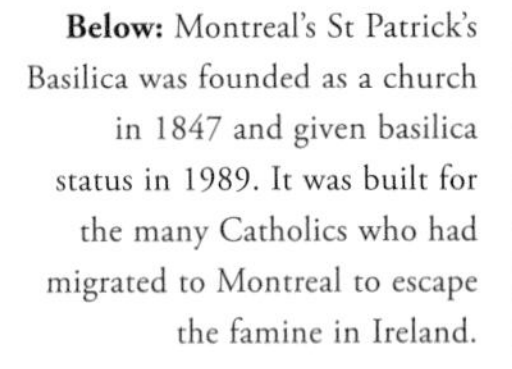

French Catholics in Canada enjoyed 150 years of rustic solitude until 1754, when the struggle between the British and the French for control of the territory west of the Appalachian Mountains erupted in the French and Indian War. The French forces were overwhelmed by the numerical superiority of the British troops and American militia. After the capitulation of Montreal and Quebec a peace was restored when the Treaty of Paris was signed in 1763, and the colony was surrendered to the British Crown.

The victory of the Protestant Crown over Canadien Catholics might have led to the Canadiens' expulsion and the imposition of the British penal laws, but this did not happen. The British commander, General James Murray, wanted Quebec to become a secure English bastion in the north against the revolutionary spirit of the American colonists to the south. As a temporary measure to gain their good will, General Murray allowed the Canadiens to practice their religion, use their language, and exercise their laws.

In the meantime, the Church of England military chaplains arrived with the occupying forces, and soon Anglican bishops Samuel Seabury and Charles Inglis were appointed. The British political, military, and religious strategy was to anglicize the Canadiens; despite this plan, the concessions continued under the governor, Sir Guy Carleton. The *Quebec Act* of 1774 confirmed the concessions, inviting Canadiens into the government and adding western lands to the conquered colony.

Two solitudes

The Empire Loyalists settling to the west of the Canadiens in the St Lawrence valley led to the Canadian Constitution of 1791, which gave the English their own province of Upper Canada, along with their language and religion, while confirming concessions made to the Canadiens in the province of Lower Canada. The "Clergy Reserves" were established, committing one-seventh of all crown lands of the Canadas for the support of Protestant clergy.

Below: Montreal's St Patrick's Basilica was founded as a church in 1847 and given basilica status in 1989. It was built for the many Catholics who had migrated to Montreal to escape the famine in Ireland.

The provinces of Nova Scotia, New Brunswick, and Prince Edward Island followed suit and established the Church of England in their jurisdictions. In Lower Canada, the "Château Clique" formed the government, and in Upper Canada the "Family Compact" formed the government. The Anglican hierarchy was part of these governing circles. It was expected that the strong Protestant establishment, along with the military, would ensure public order, instruct the youth, and provide education for the elite.

English Protestantism would grow and prosper in Upper Canada, as would Canadien Catholicism in Lower Canada.

Denominational competition

The influential Canadian churchman, John Strachan, became rector of the Anglican Cathedral of St James and was consecrated as the first bishop of Toronto at Lambeth Palace in England in 1839. A number of ecclesiastical provinces were formed: Canada (Atlantic provinces and Quebec) in 1860; Rupert's Land (the western prairie lands of the Hudson Bay Company) in 1875; and Ontario and British Columbia, added later.

The establishment of the Anglican Church lasted about 75 years, until the *British North America Act* in 1867 brought it to an end. Although the Church of England remained influential in Canadian social and business life, its privileges were dramatically reduced and it was introduced to a world of denominational competition.

THE CLERGY RESERVES

The *Constitutional Act* of 1791 established the Clergy Reserves, tracts of crown land designated to provide permanent funding for the Church of England. During the nineteenth century other Protestant denominations (Presbyterians, Methodists, Baptists, and Mennonites) entered Canada. The Church of Scotland was the first (but not the last) to challenge the fact that revenues from the Clergy Reserves went exclusively to the Church of England. In 1854 the Clergy Reserves were secularized by Parliament. The remaining revenue was distributed for municipal development and railway building.

Anglican theological differences

Anglo-Irish bishops in nineteenth-century Canada had theological differences with established Anglican thought. The ideological conflict between the High Church and the Low Church remains visible at the University of Toronto, where the High Church Trinity College sits directly across the street from the Low Church Wycliffe College.

In 1955, the name of the Church of England was changed to the Anglican Church of Canada, and seven years later the *Book of Common Prayer* was revised. In 1965, with numbers decreasing, Pierre Berton published *The Comfortable Pew*, a critical assessment of Anglican Church polity as complacent and unengaged. After this, the Church's theology was renewed, women were ordained, contraception permitted, the divorced remarried, and homosexuals welcomed for the first time. However, during the late twentieth century, Caribbean and Asian Anglicans who proposed a "moral and gender conservatism" pushed against these trends in Anglican thought.

The Church still operates residential schools for the First Nations and continues to advocate rights and land claims for indigenous peoples. Today, Anglicans represent 6.9 percent of the Canadian population.

Above: Fought in Pennsylvania, USA, in 1775, the Battle of the Monongahela was an early engagement of the French and Indian War. Despite the French victory in this battle, the British soon conquered Canada.

Below: Sir Guy Carleton (1724–1808) was made governor of Quebec in 1768. Devised with his guidance, the *Quebec Act* of 1774 was seen by the British settlers as pro-Catholic.

CHRISTIANITY IN THE USA

Above: Thomas Jefferson (1743–1826) was influential in the development of American Christianity. As well as advocating the separation of Church and state, in 1779 he wrote the Virginia Statute for Religious Freedom.

American Christianity derived a good deal of its distinctive character from the atmosphere that it breathed, becoming in turn egalitarian, competitive, and expansive.

A new Christian world, 1801–1850

In an 1802 letter to the Danbury Baptist Association, President Thomas Jefferson gave metaphorical power to the First Amendment to the Constitution's clause, "Congress shall make no law respecting an establishment of religion, or prohibiting the free exercise thereof," when he wrote of a "wall of separation" between Church and state. The American rejection of state religion and three additional parameters laid out an unprecedented playing field for Christian churches. First, in establishing democratic government, the new republic promoted an egalitarian culture, particularly in the Jacksonian era, where many older social distinctions no longer mattered. Second, capitalist economics touted competition as the hallmark of American business. Third, the frontier provided an expansive proving ground for the legal, governmental, economic, social, and religious principles enshrined by the new nation, as well as a place for people to create their own identities and lives.

The Second Great Awakening

The Methodists and the Baptists, the primary beneficiaries of these changes, increased in numbers to become the largest Protestant groups. Methodist circuit riders and Baptist farmer-preachers embodied much of nineteenth-century American Christianity, in that they mostly originated from among the people, they contended for converts, and they traversed or inhabited the frontier. Evangelization of the western states was boosted by a series of lively camp meetings at Cane Ridge, Kentucky, in 1801, in tandem with the revivals led by Charles G. Finney, who boasted of his reproducible "means" to salvation. The phenomenon was referred to as the Second Great Awakening.

New varieties of Christianity, both orthodox and heterodox sectarian groups, emerged. The Scots-Irish immigrant Alexander Campbell illustrates orthodox sectarianism. Campbell uneasily affiliated with the Baptists from 1812 to 1830, but his restorationist theology and assertive personality created a rupture in the relationship. Campbell and Barton W. Stone joined together in 1832 to form the Disciples of Christ, despite Campbell's foresworn anti-denominationalism. On the other hand, Joseph Smith's Church of Jesus Christ of Latter-day Saints illustrates a peculiarly American kind of heterodox "Christianity." Smith claimed that the angel Moroni revealed golden tablets that, when translated, constituted the Book of Mormon, which Smith and his followers regarded as inspired scripture additional to the Bible. After a hostile crowd shot Smith in 1844, the Latter-day Saints migrated to Utah, where they established their own Mormon society that included allowances for polygamy.

Below: M. Jackson Jr.'s 1863 wood engraving for the *Illustrated London News* depicts a white South Carolina family worshipping alongside the black slaves who work on their plantation.

Christian America fractured and reunited, 1850–1900

By mid-century, the northern and southern states disputed a host of issues, most conspicuously slavery, with implications for American Christians. Amid much rhetorical jostling and frequently bitter quarreling, the Methodists (1844), Baptists (1845), Presbyterians (1857–1861), and Lutherans (1861) divided into northern and southern bodies. Of the major Protestant denominations, only the Episcopalians remained united. Full reunions were not forthcoming for many years after the war, and in the case of the Baptists, never came. Christian leaders fought over slavery vociferously, with some calling for its abolition, and others defending it scripturally and theologically.

The Civil War began in 1861, with clergy on both sides claiming God's support. President Abraham Lincoln, who came from a predestinarian Baptist background before identifying himself as a "doubter" of orthodox Christianity, possessed great sensitivity and morality, and throughout his presidency struggled to align himself with God's hidden will. Mercifully, the brutal war ended in 1865; however, tragically, Lincoln was murdered and the nation deprived of his postwar leadership. Reconciliation between the estranged northern and southern Protestant groups was protracted, and southern Protestantism began developing distinctive forms that would become unusually influential into the twentieth century. Reconstruction and the period thereafter saw greater prominence of existing Black churches such as the African Methodist Episcopal Church and new autonomous groups such as the National Baptist Convention.

Denominational parameters began to matter less in the last quarter of the century, as seen in the parachurch cooperation to facilitate the evangelism of Dwight L. Moody, and the unity between conservative Christians opposing the theories of Karl Marx and especially Charles Darwin, whose book *On the Origin of Species* (1859) suggested that creation was entirely explainable by evolution. Immigration to the United States, mainly from Europe, continued throughout the century, drastically changing the character of American Christianity. Irish, German, Polish, and Italian immigrants established enclaves retaining Catholic loyalty, making Catholicism the largest Christian group in the United States. Protestants could no longer regard the nation and its culture as exclusively theirs.

Below: Joseph Smith (1805–1844) founded the Church of Jesus Christ of Latter-day Saints (Mormon Church). Due in part to his promotion of polygamy, he was assassinated by a group of non-Mormons at 38 years of age.

Left: Sunrise casts a golden light on the Latter-day Saints Temple in Logan, Utah. Led by Brigham Young, the Mormons settled in Utah and founded the capital, Salt Lake City, in 1847.

ORTHODOX REVIVAL IN RUSSIA

Opposite: During the reign of Tsar Nicholas I (1796–1855), a state policy of "Autocracy, Orthodoxy, and Nationality" required adherence to the Russian Orthodox Church; other "non-Russian" religions were quashed.

Almost all spheres of Russian life experienced a revival during the late seventeenth and eighteenth centuries, especially culture, literature, architecture, and religion.

From west to east

The cultural dimension was part of the rise of nation-states. As people gained a greater sense of their national identity, there was a greater interest in their past. Older literature, ancient religious practices, and architecture became the focus of those uncovering this past. Geographically, Russia had become a vast unified country after the reforms of Peter the Great (reigned 1682–1725). Even today it takes a week to cross the country by train or ten hours in an airplane. In the late eighteenth century it took much longer. Gradually the Russian Orthodox religion spread across the whole country. By the beginning of the twentieth century it had reached well into Siberia, the eastern provinces, across the Aleutian Islands, into Alaska, and down what is now the western Canadian coast. Remarkable figures led this expansion, such as the untiring St Innocent of Alaska (1797–1879), who set up Orthodox missions in Alaska and Siberia.

Places to worship

In terms of architecture, the revival of the nineteenth century led to what is known as the Russian revival style. It was actually a creative blending of Byzantine, old Russian (pre-Peterine), romantic, and modern elements. It owed much to a wider movement in Europe that was very interested in revitalizing older national styles in light of new developments. One direction, pushed by Tsar Nicholas I, stressed the religious and architectural connections with Byzantine Christianity. The architect Konstantin Thon was responsible for some of the great cathedrals built during this time, such as the Cathedral of Christ the Savior in Moscow, as well as cathedrals in Rostov-on-Don, Krasnoyarsk, Yelets, Sveaborg, and Tomsk. Perhaps the most famous structure designed by Thon is the Grand Kremlin Palace. Another direction was to draw from Russia's unique heritage of domestic building styles. It was fed by a romanticist sense of the importance of Slavic identity, and churches built with this in mind had a tented roof structure. A further line of this revival turned away from Western influences and even church design altogether, drawing on peasant traditions of wooden construction.

Below: First built between 1839 and 1883, Moscow's Cathedral of Christ the Savior was demolished by Stalin's forces in 1931. A replica of the original building was erected on the same site in the 1990s.

New holy men

Inside the churches there was an internal revival in both spirituality and theology. A major stimulus was the addition of the Ukrainian Church to the jurisdiction of the Russian Church. Millions of new believers and thousands of priests stirred up renewal. The spiritual revival was focused on the *staretz*. A translation of the Greek word *gerōn*, or "elder," it designates someone who is sought out as a spiritual counselor because of his exceptional holiness. The *staretz* is usually a monk who focuses on prayer (Hesychasm), self-discipline, and denial. He is widely believed to have been granted extra spiritual gifts, such as healing, prophecy, and the ability to see into one's soul and thereby give effective guidance. A *staretz* is unique, since he is not appointed by any authority; instead, he is recognized by the people. They travel great distances to seek his advice, which the *staretz* gives when not in seclusion and in prayer.

The revival of the *staretz* first took place with Paisius Velichkovsky (1722–1794). He was born in the Ukraine, studied on Mt Athos in Greece, and settled in the Optina Monastery in Russia. His major act was to translate some crucial spiritual Greek texts into Russian, especially the *Philokalia*, a collection of texts by masters of the Hesychast tradition. Velichkovsky was the first of the "Optina Masters," but the greatest *staretz* was Seraphim of Sarov (1759–1833). Among the writers who sought advice at Optina were Nikolay Gogol and Leo Tolstoy.

Theology also surged. There was the highly educated and liberal Platon II of Moscow (1737–1812), writer of *Orthodox Doctrine: Or, A Short Compend of Christian Theology* (1765), in which he drew on rationalism to give a distinct modern sense to orthodox ideas. Lay theologians also emerged, such as Aleksey Khomyakov the poet, who criticized both capitalism and socialism as signs of Western decadence, and championed the idea of *sobornost* ("togetherness" or "symphony"), which stressed the need for cooperation between people. As Ivan Kireevsky, another proponent, put it, *sobornost* is when "the sum total of all Christians of all ages, past and present, comprise one indivisible, eternal living assembly of the faithful, held together just as much by the unity of consciousness as through the communion of prayer." The great model was the *obshchina*, or peasant communities in which everything was held together.

CHRISTIAN INTELLIGENTSIA IN RUSSIA

The Church as a tyrant and the traitor of Christ, salvation as a free gift from God to the poor, the denial of Christ's divinity, and the moral teachings of the Sermon on the Mount—in Imperial Russia these new religious ideas were put forward by the towering literary figures Fyodor Dostoyevsky and Leo Tolstoy.

They became part of the great revival of Russian culture in the eighteenth century. That revival permeated Russian life, especially in architecture, missionary expansion, the recovery of spirituality, and new directions in theology. Some theologians were quite orthodox, such as Platon II of Moscow with his defense of orthodoxy, or Aleksey Khomyakov and Ivan Kireevsky, who recovered an idealized communal peasant life and saw it as the basis of a distinct Russian political and religious life. Others were far less orthodox, especially Dostoyevsky and Tolstoy. The former barely avoided execution for revolutionary activities, while the latter was excommunicated.

Freed from death row

In 1850, Fyodor Mikhaylovich Dostoyevsky was condemned to death for taking part in revolutionary agitation. For months he expected death each morning, only to be saved from that fate at the last minute and sent to Siberia for four years of forced labor. Yet that sense of imminent death made a profound impression on him, influencing his religious beliefs and writings.

Now renowned as a novelist, Dostoyevsky was actually known as a journalist in his lifetime. He also spent some time in the army, suffered in an unhappy first marriage, loved to gamble, and was incompetent as a money manager. Eventually he held a job as editor of the newspaper *Grazhdanin* and married for the second time. Meanwhile he wrote some impressive novels: *Memoirs from the Underworld* (1864), *Crime and Punishment* (1866), *The Idiot* (1869), *The Possessed* (1872), and *The Brothers Karamazov* (1880). As a novelist, Dostoyevsky had an uncanny ability for uncovering the hidden processes of the human mind and emotions. The heroes and heroines in his works live purely by their emotions, which are far more powerful than reason, but they are also redeemed through the strongest emotion of all—unlimited compassion.

Dostoyevsky's theology was expressed in his novels. He argued that: We cannot know God through our reason or our will, and God is certainly not revealed through the pomp and ceremony of the Church; since we are all weak, miserable, and sinful, we can never reach up to God or cooperate with God for our salvation; instead, we rely entirely on God's compassion, love, and grace. Dostoyevsky had little time for the Church. In *The Brothers Karamazov* there is an extraordinary passage called "The Grand Inquisitor." The Inquisitor is none other than the Church, which has falsified Christ's teachings and become a tyrant. The parable suggests that if Christ came to earth again the Church would not hesitate to crucify him.

Below: Leo Tolstoy was inspired by Jesus' idea of turning the other cheek (Matthew 5:39, Luke 6:29). His pacifist writings greatly influenced later historical personages, such as Gandhi.

A hatred of hypocrites

Leo Tolstoy (1828–1910) hated hypocrites, so much so that he sought to live out his beliefs. He fought his whole life for social reform and alleviating the plight of the peasants. He supported persecuted religious groups like the Doukhobors—a communist peasant Christian movement that lives in agricultural communities and rejects the idolization of the Bible, ritual, icons, sacraments, and dogma regarding Christ's divinity (they escaped persecution by migrating to Canada). Tolstoy had traveled widely in Europe and studied new educational methods and Enlightenment ideas. When he returned to Russia he established a community, refuge, and school on his estate in Yasnaya Polyana.

However, even this was not enough. Although he wrote some of the world's great novels—*War and Peace* (1869), *Anna Karenina* (1877), and *Resurrection* (1899)—Tolstoy gave up his literary work in later life and devoted himself to propounding his religious ideas, especially in his short work, *A Confession* (1882). He was deeply struck by Jesus' teaching in the Sermon on the Mount. He gave up his property (although his wife, Sophia Behrs, held on to her part of the estate for their many children) and the happiness of family life, took up manual labor, and espoused pacifism. He was a great believer in love, which he saw as the fulfillment of God's commands. Love would overcome evil and establish the kingdom of God on earth.

TOLSTOY'S FIVE COMMANDMENTS

In *What I Believe* (1884), Tolstoy summarized what he regarded as the essential teaching of Jesus:

1. **Suppress all anger, even righteous anger, and live in peace.**
2. **Sex is for marriage only.**
3. **All oaths are wrong.**
4. **Evil should not be resisted and one should not act as judge or police officer.**
5. **Unreserved love of one's enemies is the way to overcome evil.**

Left: Tolstoy's religious views were molded by Jesus' famous Sermon on the Mount: "Love your enemies [and] do good to those who hate you" (Luke 6:27) because "[b]lessed are the peacemakers" (Matthew 5:9).

Below: In 1899, the Doukhobors—religious dissenters who opposed both governmental militarism and the Russian Orthodox Church—migrated from Russia to Canada to lead a more peaceful life.

DEVELOPMENTS IN LATIN AMERICA

Above: Blacksmiths, carpenters, and other peasants were roused into action against the Spanish authorities by Miguel Hidalgo y Costilla, a Catholic priest who is known as the Father of Mexican Independence.

Opposite: Pilgrims in Juazeiro do Norte, Brazil, participate in the Festa do Padre Cícero, an annual pilgrimage to the statue of Father Cícero, the priest who founded the town in the 1920s.

Latin America began the nineteenth century in revolutionary ferment. During the years 1810–1825 the Spanish and Portuguese colonies fought for and attained independence one after the other. Once independence was achieved, the most pressing question was how to relate to the Roman Catholic Church, which had converted most of Latin America in the sixteenth century. The Church owned immense lands. It had taken care of education and the sick, it had been a banker for the wealthy, and it still expected allegiance.

For many people in Latin America, especially the liberals, the Roman Catholic Church was a reminder of the old order that had been overthrown. These liberals wished to make a new start and take over all the Church's former functions. When they were in power, the liberals closed monasteries, established state-sponsored education and hospitals, and sought to limit the Church's power. By contrast, conservatives felt that the Church was a bastion of morality in a rapidly changing society. In many ways, the history of Latin America has been the history of this struggle.

Death to the Spaniards!

The story unfolded very differently in the various Latin American countries. In Mexico, the war of independence had been inspired by the rebel priest and theologian Miguel Hidalgo y Costilla (1753–1811), with the inspiring cry of "Long live Our Lady of Guadalupe, death to bad government, and death to the Spaniards!" Uttered at the doors of his parish church (Dolores) just before dawn on September 15, 1810, it was the cry that led to the uprising and then, after ten years, independence.

Despite these fiery beginnings, after Mexican independence the Church still held most of the political, social, and financial strings. It took the liberals 30 more years to realize their secularization program. Finally, in 1858, a liberal reformer and Zapotec Indian became president—

Benito Pablo Juárez García (1806–1872). For the next 14 years he oversaw a massive program of reform: Abolition of Church lands; separation of Church and state; disenfranchisement of nuns, monks, and priests; and civilian control of the military (which was significant for the Church because the Church and the military were political allies). Many of Juárez's anti-clerical reforms were inscribed in the Mexican Constitution of 1917. They remained so strong that diplomatic relations with the Vatican were restored only in 1992.

Religious melting pot

Brazil followed a comparable path to Mexico, although secularization took a little longer to arrive. Independence from Portugal came in 1822, but the country passed through a unique period as the Empire of Brazil before the Republic was finally formed in 1889. Here, too, the liberals wanted to see the end of the privileged status of the Church and the tendency of the clergy to look to Rome (called Ultramontanism). The new Republic separated Church and state, and it ceased to cover the Church's costs.

More importantly, freedom of worship was guaranteed. In part this was due to the influx of Protestant European immigrants and missionaries after the abolition of slavery in 1850, but it also had much to do with some distinctly Brazilian changes. One was the new type of religion that resulted from the combination of African and Brazilian beliefs. The many African slaves in Brazil had brought their own beliefs and practices, which were put into the mixing pot with indigenous and Christian elements, creating something new. Popular religious movements also came out of the dirt-poor northeast. One was led by Antonio Conselheiro (1828–1897), a wandering preacher who established a new city for the poor in Canudos. Another was the mystic Padre Cícero (1844–1934), whose visions and ministry led to an influx of people to the town of Juazeiro (in Ceará state).

The Church holds on

By contrast, in Argentina and Chile the Roman Catholic Church maintained a strong hold even after independence. In Chile the Church remained both protected and state-subsidized after 1818, keeping a close relation with the powers that be (Church and state were not separated until 1925). At the same time, other religions were tolerated, especially in light of the push by Protestant missionaries from the United States.

In Argentina, despite a strong current of opposition, Roman Catholicism remained the state religion following independence in 1816 (and until 1994 even the president had to be a Roman Catholic). However, by the middle of the nineteenth century European Protestants began immigrating and establishing churches. Many church groups remained very small, such as the Baptists, Methodists, Presbyterians, and Anglicans. However, there was one exception. A steady stream of blond, blue-eyed Lutherans from Germany and Scandinavia led to the growth of a small but significant Lutheran Church.

Below: Founded by Franciscans in 1663, the Church of San Diego in Guanajuato, Mexico, is an exceptional example of a colonial edifice. It faces the Jardín Unión, the social hub of the city.

CATHOLIC BEGINNINGS IN AUSTRALIA

Above: Built in 1836–1837, the nondenominational church at Tasmania's Port Arthur penal colony was never consecrated. Convicts were required to attend the Sunday service because the authorities sought to reform them through religion.

The first European settlers brought Christianity to Australia in 1788, on the First Fleet. Among the prisoners and keepers were many Roman Catholics. However, Great Britain was a Protestant state, and made no provision for alternative religious needs in its newest and roughest colony. In the early years, convicts were expected to attend Church of England religious services, whatever their own confession.

Keeping the faith

Probably some lay Catholic convicts kept up their faith, but they left little record of their activities. Some early free settlers—notably the lay Carmelite James Dempsey—did their best to preserve and protect their own religion and that of other Catholics. Official religious provision was erratic. In 1803, an Irish convict priest named James Dixon was permitted to celebrate Mass, partly as an act of official tolerance but also, no doubt, with a view to testing the efficacy of organized Catholicism as a means of social control over the restless (and often Irish) Catholic population. The experiment was abandoned in 1804, after a number of Dixon's congregants attempted an insurrection.

British opposition and Roman indifference

Between 1804 and 1817 there was no open Catholic religious provision in Australia, although transported priests probably said Mass in secret. This was partly the consequence of British opposition, but also of Rome's inattention to regular appeals to send a priest, due to the perilous state of the Holy See during the Napoleonic Wars.

Finally, in 1817, Father Jeremiah O'Flynn appeared in New South Wales. O'Flynn had the approval of Rome but not of London for his mission, but in Sydney he claimed both. When his deception was discovered in 1818, he was expelled. But as the penal colonies and the associated free settler communities of New South Wales and Van Diemen's Land (now known as Tasmania) grew, it was time for the

Right: Arthur Phillip, Governor of New South Wales, inspects some of the 732 convicts of various religions who survived the voyage as part of the First Fleet from England to Sydney Cove in 1787–1788.

British to stop shutting out the Roman Catholic Church, which numbered perhaps 15,000 adherents by 1820. In that year, the decision was taken to appoint the first Roman Catholic convict chaplains.

Founding generation

The first generation of Australian Catholic priests included some extraordinary figures. Men like J.J. Therry and Philip Connolly traveled vast distances, ministering to a flock that ranged from prosperous free settlers to degraded and abused convicts, while trying to build the basic infrastructure of their Church in the colonies. Unchecked, these men created their own empires and some, such as Therry, became powerful figures, with interests that ranged far beyond the merely spiritual. It was not until the 1832 arrival of the English Benedictine William Bernard Ullathorne that there was any ecclesiastical discipline. Ullathorne's status as vicar general, although it gave him some power, was clearly not adequate. The hierarchical Roman Catholic Church required a bishop. In 1834, another English Benedictine, John Bede Polding, was appointed Bishop of Sydney, a diocese that in fact encompassed the entirety of Australia.

John Bede Polding

Polding's long episcopate (he died in 1877) marked the real beginning of the institutional history of the Roman Catholic Church in Australia. He was often frustrated by willful priests and the fractious Irish, and ultimately thwarted in his desire to build a Benedictine Abbey-diocese in Sydney. Nevertheless, Polding was a tremendous success. Against long odds he organized the infrastructure of the Roman Catholic Church in Australia, founding many parishes and schools, and introducing religious orders to run both. As bishop, Polding covered vast distances, ministering to both the free and convict populations. His 1843 visit to Brisbane was probably the first by any priest. He was an important advocate for the humane treatment of both convicts and Aboriginals. Polding's agitations did much to secure the closure of the notorious prison on Norfolk Island, and he encouraged the Passionist Fathers to begin missions to the continent's indigenous population.

Growth and consolidation

Australia was too vast—and growing too rapidly—for it to remain a single diocese. In 1842, Polding was made Archbishop of Sydney, and new sees were created at Hobart and Adelaide. Perth became a diocese in 1845, and Melbourne in 1847; more would follow. Despite this institutional growth, the early years of the Australian Catholic Church were ones of hardship and clerical shortages. In Tasmania, for example, Philip Connolly celebrated the first Mass in 1821, but in 1844 the English bishop Robert Willson arrived to find some three priests ministering to a Catholic population that numbered perhaps 5,000. Still, by Polding's death in 1877, the Roman Catholic Church had grown to some eleven dioceses, encompassing hundreds of parishes, priests, and religious people, and Catholics had fully entered almost every aspect of Australian life.

Below: In March 1788, a small group of convicts and free men arrived on Norfolk Island; by the time the large penal colony was disbanded in 1855, it was regarded as Britain's most brutal settlement.

PART EIGHT

UNITY AND CONVERSION
1901–PRESENT DAY

EDINBURGH MISSIONARY CONFERENCE

Above: Some 1,200 representatives of various Protestant groups descended on Edinburgh, Scotland, in June 1910 for ten days of discussion and debate about the future of Protestant missions.

Preceded by four missionary conferences in Europe and in the United States, Edinburgh became a cornerstone for the modern missionary and ecumenical movements. Under the leadership of John Raleigh Mott, a Methodist lay leader and its chairman, and the wise theological diplomacy of its secretary, the Scot John Oldham, the World Missionary Conference held in Edinburgh in 1910 took missionary discussions to a different level.

"The evangelization of the whole world in this generation"

Seen by many as both the culmination of nineteenth-century Protestant Christian missions and the formal beginning of the modern Protestant Christian ecumenical movement, the Edinburgh Conference focused on eight different themes through its discussion of reports from missionary circles all over the world. These reports addressed the issues of taking the Gospel to the non-Christian world; the Church in the mission field; education as it was related to Christianizing national life; the missionary message and its relation to non-Christian religions; the missionaries' preparation and formation; the home base of missionary work; the relationship between mission work and the state; and the urgency for cooperation and unity among missionaries and mission work.

The early preparation of the reports and the logistics of the conference facilitated dynamic interaction between participants. Daily papers and plenary, in a space conducive to debate and discussion, provided a pedagogical environment. The Edinburgh Conference reflected the desire of missionary activity at the time to see "the evangelization of the whole world in this generation" and was both a detailed assessment of missionary work in most of the non-Christian world and a generative event which signaled the dawn of the vitality of the Christian religion in the "missionary lands." Edinburgh became the conference where the term "younger churches," referring to the vitality of Christian communities in the non-Christian world, slowly took ground.

It became evident that missionary endeavors had a common purpose—to develop self-governing, self-propagating, and self-supporting churches in every missionary region. From a world perspective, Edinburgh claimed that the heart of the Church is mission. This theme would recurrently come to heated debates as the modern missionary movement explored the relationship between Christian mission and ecclesiology.

Previous pages: During a 2006 visit to Istanbul, Turkey, designed to bring Catholicism and Eastern Orthodoxy closer, Pope Benedict XVI (left) and Ecumenical Patriarch Bartholomew I were photographed together, hands clasped in unity.

Notwithstanding these achievements, Edinburgh was predominantly a Western conference. There were very few Christian leaders from India, China, or Japan, and none from Africa and Latin America, and no observers from Eastern Orthodox or Roman Catholic missionary organizations. Edinburgh did not address the complex missionary terminology of "Christian lands" or "completely missionized lands," and "new missionary territories." In fact, Latin America was excluded from Edinburgh in order to minimize the theological and ecclesial disputes of what should be considered "Christian lands" and the geo-political and ecclesial discussion of legitimate missionary work in "completely missionized lands." The exclusion of Latin America, however, was only official. In a subversive manner, US missionary leaders conducted meetings that would later result in the Latin American Missionary Conferences of Panama 1916, Montevideo 1925, and Havana 1929.

The missiological debates also raised questions about both the character and purpose of mission work. Scholars note that Edinburgh's missiological language was fueled by imperial and militaristic metaphors and images. Perhaps one of the most eloquent reactions to this kind of language came from Indian Christian leader V.S. Azariah, who challenged the missionary boards to send "friends" to the missionary field. Although he clearly appreciated the missionaries' dedication in the field, he also recognized the ethnic and religious arrogance and cultural imposition of so many that deeply hurt missionary work.

Cooperation and unity

Edinburgh also addressed the urgent issues of cooperation and unity in the missionary field and among missionary boards. With theological and ecclesial wisdom, the organizers of this conference brought together a vast variety of Protestant missionary endeavors—different missionary strategies, reports, theological positions, and interpretations. As a result of the incredible spirit of cooperation and missionary urgency, a Continuation Committee was established, which later became the International Missionary Council (IMC). Out of the work of the IMC, other missionary conferences were held, up until the IMC was integrated into the World Council of Churches, under the Mission and Evangelization Unit.

Edinburgh set the scene for the development of ecumenical leaders who guided the creation of the later world conferences on Faith and Order (held at Lausanne in 1927), and Life and Work (held at Oxford in 1937). Edinburgh's legacy is the grounding to the modern missionary and ecumenical movements.

Finally, Edinburgh represents, perhaps with the exception of Vatican II, the turning point that recognized the world character of the Christian community.

Above: Havana, Cuba, held the Latin American Missionary Conference in June 1929. Organized by Latin Americans rather than North Americans, this gathering was an important step in defining a Protestant Latin American identity.

Above: In addition to directing the 1910 World Missionary Conference in Edinburgh, Scotland, John Raleigh Mott was awarded the Nobel Peace Prize in 1946 for his leadership of the YMCA.

VATICAN II

Above: Pope John XXIII called the Second Vatican Council in 1959, but succumbed to peritonitis related to stomach cancer at the age of 81 before the completion of the council.

Below: Reigning as pope since April 19, 2005, Benedict XVI is pictured here offering members of the Roman Curia—administrators of the Holy See—his 2006 Christmas greetings.

The Second Vatican Council was one of the most significant events in twentieth-century Christianity. It shook the Catholic Church and reverberated among many Christians.

The agenda

In January 1959, Pope John XXIII unexpectedly made the announcement that a second Vatican Council would be held (the first was held in 1868), the reason being that it was "time to open the windows of the Church to let in some fresh air." There seemed to be no apparent crisis facing the Catholic Church, although the pope shared a widespread sense that the Church was out of touch with the modern world. Others within the Church felt that there was no need for change.

Church "Fathers" were invited to submit items for inclusion in the agenda. Many made no submission, others proposed trifling changes to things such as canon law, indicating that, for many, expectations were low. They were content with the Church as it was. Leaders of the "Rhine group" (Germany, Netherlands, Switzerland, Belgium, France) were outstanding in that they contributed detailed proposals based on modern theological research and they wanted changes. They soon dominated proceedings. Various commissions, consisting largely of members of the Roman Curia (the central governing body of the Roman Catholic Church), began preparing an agenda and documents for consideration and adoption.

The council met in four sessions in St Peter's Basilica in the Vatican from September to December in 1962, 1963, 1964, and 1965. Its members, called "Fathers," were bishopsas well as the heads of male religious orders. Nearly all who were able to attend did so, and 2,540 members took part in the opening session. Attendance thereafter ranged from about 2,200 to 2,400, with all documents and speeches made in Latin.

The council showed up the long-standing tension between those who wished to keep all decision-making power with the pope and the Roman Curia and those who wanted a stronger role for councils—known as the conciliar movement. Pope John tended to the conciliar side, and so encouraged the council to operate largely free of his control. He also invited other churches to send observers. As soon as the council opened, the energetic Rhine group—with strong conciliar tendencies—moved successfully to overthrow the dominance of the Curia and establish the primacy of the council. Pope John died between the first and second sessions and was replaced by Pope Paul VI, who exerted much more control. Significantly, he withdrew consideration of the subject of contraception, reserving a decision to himself on its morality, with major consequences.

The council's decisions

Vatican I had concentrated mainly on the authority of the bishop of Rome (the pope). Vatican II produced the first conciliar teaching on the nature of the Church, according authority to the bishops and spelling out their relation to the pope. A document discussing divine revelation clarified some basics of Catholic theology, giving high authority to the Bible and promoting its study.

The decisions of the council are mostly contained in the 16 official documents it produced. Pope John had said he wanted no definitions of dogma, and there were none. He did want the Church's teachings presented in a manner that was clear and accessible, and the documents reflect this. The Pastoral Constitution on the Modern World (*Gaudium et Spes*), by far the longest document, made a significant advance on the tradition of "Catholic social teaching" concerning issues of capitalism, socialism, family and social matters, and the rights of workers for fair conditions. Widely noted was the *Declaration on Religious Liberty*, which condemned governments that restrict freedom of religious expression.

Two of the most important documents—on the Church (*Lumen Gentium*) and on divine revelation (*Dei Verbum*)—exhibit the success of the Rhine group in winning the support of the majority of the Fathers with the concomitant defeat of the theology espoused by the Curia.

The dynamics of this council have fascinated historians. The bishops had become accustomed to not having much say in

teachings or disciplinary decisions coming from popes and Curia. Once congregated as the council, and led by bold and learned bishops, they began to exert their authority.

The aftermath

Ordinary Catholics were most affected by changes in the liturgy, but they discovered they had a voice—as did everyone else. During Vatican II, a wide range of new ideas and opinions hit the Church. Progressives were encouraged, especially liberation theologians in Latin America, the women's movement within the Church, and lay leaders. Catholic theologians began to enter mainstream theological discussions. Conservatives were less impressed, feeling that the authority of the pope and Curia had been undermined. Since the council, conservatives have sought to reassert the traditional authority of the Curia.

Above: Pope John XXIII is carried ceremoniously to St Peter's Basilica for the inauguration of the Second Vatican Council, the twenty-first Ecumenical Council, which supported the reunion of all Christians under the Church of Rome.

GLOBAL EXPANSION OF REVIVAL FAITH

There is a predictable pattern about Christianity: It moves from revival to stagnation and to revival again. The specific reasons may vary from age to age, but the nature of those revivals is remarkably similar—they seek to renew the inner life of faith. Two of the major forms of revival in the twentieth century have been evangelicalism and Pentecostalism (or the Charismatic revival); they both stress one's personal walk with God, especially through time set aside each day for prayer and Bible reading.

What's in a name?

"Evangelical" comes from the Greek word *euaggelion,* meaning "gospel" or "good news." Evangelicals seek to base their lives on the Bible, especially the gospel about Jesus. The word has been used this way for over 500 years, beginning with the Reformation of the sixteenth century. At this time evangelical actually meant Lutheran and was used to distinguish Lutheran Protestants from Reformed (or Calvinist) Protestants. Eventually it came to be used to refer to all of the Protestant churches in Germany. In England, the word had a different sense: In the eighteenth century, evangelicals stressed personal piety and tried to reform the Church of England from within, where they still form a significant branch.

The early English evangelicals were social reformers. For example, William Wilberforce (1759–1833) led a group in Parliament that succeeded in abolishing slavery. He and many others were keen on missionary activity, and evangelicals were behind many of the missionary movements. In the nineteenth century, evangelicals in the USA also combined a zeal for missions with social reform. They were involved in the abolitionist, feminist, and temperance movements.

Here come the Americans

The dawn of the twentieth century brought a change of direction for evangelicals. They were influenced by the rise of American "fundamentalism," a movement which tried to maintain the fundamentals of the Christian faith in the face of new currents in science and education: Evolutionary theory was gaining ground, as were modern Biblical-critical and liberal forms of theology. From its beginnings, evangelicalism has held to five main points: The inerrancy of the Bible; the bodily resurrection of Jesus; the virgin birth of Christ; Jesus' death as atonement for our sins; and the physical return of Christ at the end of history (Judgment Day). As American influence spread across the world, fundamentalism went with it, influencing older movements in England, Australia, Canada, and elsewhere, and providing new impetus to existing missionary movements.

The gift of the Holy Spirit

Although evangelicals and fundamentalists have often been suspicious of Pentecostalism, they are all elements of the same pattern of revival. Types of Pentecostalism have been seen throughout history, with a focus on the direct role of the Holy Spirit, speaking in tongues, prophecy, healing, and exorcism. The name itself refers to the story of Pentecost in Acts 2 and the gift of the Holy Spirit to the first followers of Jesus, who were then able to perform many miraculous acts. The first wave of modern Pentecostalism arose in the early twentieth century in the United States. It stressed a vivid personal experience of God, and "baptism in the Spirit," an idea which spread very quickly and soon reached England. The movement rapidly developed into individual churches, the largest of which are the Assemblies of God, with more than 280,000 churches and outstations in over 110 countries,

and the Church of God in Christ, a black Pentecostal institution that has churches, schools, missions, and medical clinics in nearly sixty nations. Other groups, however, remained within their own churches, calling themselves Charismatics to distinguish themselves from Pentecostals.

To the ends of the earth

Both evangelicals and Pentecostals lay great emphasis on personal conversion and the reality of heaven and hell, which led to a great concern with converting as many people as possible. Since many in these movements believe that the end of the world is coming soon, the need to convert is urgent. So evangelicals and Pentecostals are behind many of the missionary movements throughout the world, whether in medical or educational capacities, or in Bible translation. Traditionally missionaries were sent out to remote parts of the world, but in recent years, with the decline of religious observance in Europe and North America, these regions too have become mission fields.

Its focus on the world of spirits has made Pentecostalism very appealing in places with spirit-influenced religious traditions. Africa, South America, and indigenous peoples in Australia and North America have been fertile grounds for Pentecostal advances. In many cases these people have taken their own initiative, heard the spirit speaking to them and developed their own missionary movements.

Below left: The Tuomiokirkko is an Evangelical Lutheran cathedral in Helsinki, Finland, featuring statues of the Twelve Apostles on its roof. In 2008, over 80 percent of Finnish people said they were Evangelical Lutheran.

Below: Detail from Rogier van der Weyden's polyptych *Last Judgment*. The reality and the significance of Judgment Day is an important theme among evangelical, Pentecostal, and fundamentalist Christians.

CHALLENGES FOR WESTERN EUROPE

Above: Roma (gypsies) were persecuted by the Nazis because they were considered "racially inferior" to the Aryans. Up to half of the one million Roma in Europe during World War II were killed.

Opposite: On November 9, 1989, Germans celebrated the demise of communism in their country with the symbolic fall of the Berlin Wall that had divided socialist East Germany from West Germany since 1961.

Below: Auschwitz-Birkenau was the most infamous Nazi concentration camp of World War II. The horrors of the war led to a change in the relationship between churches and governments in Western Europe.

Secularism, socialism, two world wars, fascism, Shoah (the Holocaust), the rise of Islam—these have been the main challenges for twentieth-century European Christianity.

From secularism to socialism

Back in 1850, the redoubtable George Holyoake, who had just finished a stint in prison for blasphemy, coined the word "secularism" to describe a new movement that had arisen in England. Drawing on the Latin *saeculum*, meaning "this age" or "this world," for him secularism meant that we live our lives purely in terms of this age and this world, not in terms of a world above or an age to come. The new movement soon split. Holyoake argued that secularism was not necessarily opposed to religion, but that there were more pressing matters of concern such as education, medicine, ethics, and government. Others felt that secularism was at heart an anti-religious position—this second meaning has become dominant.

Over the following decades the churches throughout Europe gradually withdrew from everyday life, and church attendance dropped dramatically. One by one, traditional church roles were taken over by the state—education, medical care for all, care for the aged, sport, marriage, and death. Secularism led to the separation of Church and state in one country after another. This had happened in France after the Revolution in 1789, but in the twentieth century more followed. These developments have led the churches to take on an increasingly prophetic and critical voice, rather than supporting the status quo.

Furthermore, spurred on by the principles emerging from the communist East, socialism gained immense ground in Western Europe. Socialism was strongly anticlerical—it opposed Church involvement in the ruling classes—but not always anti-religious, since its basic platform was freedom of religion. Socialism's position was strengthened when radical traditions reasserted themselves within Christianity, and thus we find Christian socialists and communists joining forces with secular movements.

Fascism and genocide

When the true horror of the attempted genocide of the Jews, the Roma (gypsies), and a good number of communists in the fascist concentration camps first became known, Europe was shocked and disbelieving. How could this take place in the midst of supposedly civilized and secular Europe? The fact that a good number of churches initially supported the Fascists made the matter worse. The Christian school of thought that opposed these developments, initially led by the Confessing Church in Germany whose leaders included Dietrich Bonhoeffer, Karl Barth, and Martin Niemöller, eventually convinced many people that the Church should never be too closely connected with political movements. This was another impetus for the churches to take on a critical role against governments.

With God on their side

This critical stance was enhanced by the experience of two world wars. Traditionally the Church of one's own country would bless the armed forces and pray for victory in battle. However, when enemies attempt to slaughter one another, with both sides claiming God's blessing, either cynicism or a critical distance develops. The cynics said that God was always on the side of the largest battalions, while the critics began criticizing war itself. Even the old theory of a "just war" went into eclipse in the face of two world wars and the atomic bomb. During the wars churches were full, for people realized that life could end at any moment. But after the wars the nature of church prayer changed, as more and more began praying for an end to all war.

A Christian West?

Another after-effect of World War II was the political divide between a communist East and a capitalist West. Here Christianity also was divided. While the conservative wings of the Western churches longed for the end of "Godless communism," others began what is called the Marxist–Christian dialogue, which came to its peak in the 1970s.

With the rolling back of communism after 1989 and the fall of the Berlin Wall, these antagonisms faded. In their place many perceived a new threat: Islam. During the 1970s and 1980s many Western European countries were happy to encourage cheap labor from the Middle East and North Africa. At the same time Islam began to revitalize, and many of these countries suddenly realized that they had large Muslim populations in their midst. Once again the churches were divided—some argued that the West is deeply Christian and Islam has no place in it, while others acknowledged the deep common areas between the two religions and sought to bridge the gap. The lengthy coexistence of Christianity and Islam in Eastern Europe provides a model that those promoting harmony seek to follow.

LONG LIVE
THIS

DRAMATIC CHANGES IN THE USA

The Catholic Church and the United States have sustained a complex historical connection, and although Catholic missionaries were on American soil well before the Protestant English planted their colonies, Catholicism has frequently seemed like an alien ideology at odds with the nation's traditional values and institutions.

Backlashes: 1900 to 1950

As the twentieth century began, the Church was growing ever more irritable toward many in its American flock. In his 1895 encyclical to the American Church, Pope Leo XIII, while criticizing the separation of Church and state as well as the conduct toward Native Americans and blacks, complimented the United States. Not long after that encyclical, though, Leo would have difficulty maintaining his favorable opinion, as so-called "Americanism" began causing trouble for him. Americanism, like the related liberal movement of "modernism," called for the Catholic Church to re-evaluate its dogma in light of contemporaneous intellectual and cultural developments. Leo's subsequent condemnation of Americanism signaled a hardening of Catholic attitudes, and despite his successor, Pius X, in 1908 offering full recognition to the American Church, which had been a "mission church," the new conservatism meant that American Catholicism entered a period of intellectual retreat in the early century.

Below: In 1889, Pope Leo XIII's apostolic letter *Magni Nobis Gaudii* formally inaugurated the Catholic University of America. The university's location, Washington, DC, was chosen because of its political importance.

Two early twentieth-century Protestant movements, Pentecostalism and fundamentalism, uncovered spiritual and scriptural power for many marginalized people. Pentecostalism emerged from the work of the Holiness evangelist Charles Parham, who oversaw the first instance of speaking in tongues in 1901. After meeting Parham in Houston, William Seymour went to Los Angeles, where in 1906 he led a three-year revival at the Azusa Street Mission, which is usually acclaimed as the launchpad of modern Pentecostalism. Fundamentalism appeared when Christian conservatives, frustrated with the modern world, coalesced into a militant movement. *The Fundamentals*, a series of booklets published between 1910 and 1915, gave the movement a name, and a list of non-negotiable truths—Biblical inerrancy, virgin birth, substitutionary atonement (that Jesus died to atone for our sins), Jesus' bodily resurrection, and literal second coming of Jesus—gave them fighting orders. The fundamentalists were convinced that their nation and religion had failed, and assailed such trends as the Social Gospel, an advocacy of Protestant ministries associated with the Progressive Movement, that fed and sheltered people as a first priority and precondition for evangelism. Both Pentecostalism and fundamentalism endured abuse from their enemies yet earned great importance in American Christian history.

Newfound power: 1950 to 2000

After a history of invisibility to white Christians, black Christianity by mid-century began exhibiting remarkable potency, particularly in leading the Civil Rights Movement. In 1955–1956 the Baptist pastor Martin Luther King, Jr. emerged as the leader of a black boycott of city buses in Montgomery, Alabama, after Rosa Parks refused to give up her seat to a white passenger. King's organizational talent and electrifying oratory propelled him to national prominence, and his "I Have a Dream" speech at the 1963 March on Washington inspired many people to seek racial justice. His assassination in 1968, like Abraham Lincoln's a little more than a century earlier, can reasonably be regarded as an American martyrdom.

After the fundamentalists disappeared from public view following the embarrassment of the Scopes Trial in 1925, evangelicalism arose, reorganized, and embraced education during the 1930s and 1940s. A group of intellectuals appeared, none more important than the theologian Carl F.H. Henry, whose scholarship imparted respectability to the developing movement. As editor of *Christianity Today*, he displayed a unifying and reasonable temperament. The radio evangelist Charles E. Fuller desired to see an educational institution that was better than the usual Bible college; he began assembling a capable faculty, so that when Fuller Seminary opened in 1947 it quickly earned a reputation for offering high-quality education. Evangelist Billy Graham, whose preaching "Crusades" used the classic methods pioneered by George Whitefield, Charles Finney, and D.L. Moody before him, converted innumerable persons and became the most commanding leader of evangelicalism.

In the latter part of the twentieth century, Episcopalians, Methodists, Presbyterians, and Lutherans all witnessed their numbers shrink alarmingly and their power surpassed by other groups. To many observers, mainline Protestants appeared indolent when compared to the transdenominational charismatics, whose "baptism in the Spirit," manifesting in "praise and worship" and, commonly, speaking in tongues, signified a new course for Christianity. A few innovative Protestant pastors envisaged contemporary worship and plenty of impressive amenities in churches that would be central in people's lives. The trendsetting "megachurches" that resulted from this vision, such as Willow Creek Community Church (Illinois), Saddleback Church (California), and Lakewood Church (Texas), significantly altered American Protestantism.

Left: Billy Graham (born 1918) was ordained as a Southern Baptist pastor in 1939. He founded the Billy Graham Evangelistic Association (BGEA) in 1950, which still uses various media forms to conduct its ministry.

Below: Martin Luther King, Jr. ended his "I Have a Dream" speech with the words of an old Negro spiritual: "Free at last! Free at last! Thank God Almighty, we are free at last!"

THE UNITED CHURCH OF CANADA

Below: During World War II, Canadian factories employed women in small arms ammunition production. One aim of the United Church of Canada was to offer factory workers more useful religious guidance.

Opposite: Members of the Pentecostal Church—not part of the United Church of Canada—raise their hands in prayer at the start of their week-long conference in Montreal, which began on September 15, 1958.

Below: Constructed by Methodist missionaries in 1875, McDougall Memorial United Church at Morleyville Settlement in Alberta was restored in 1951 by the United Church of Canada.

In 1902, at the Presbyterian General Assembly in Winnipeg, Principal William Patrick of Manitoba College presented greetings to the Methodist General Conference meeting in the same city and spontaneously advanced a plea for the organic union of the two churches. The Methodists responded, suggesting that as the Presbyterian, Methodist, and Congregational churches already shared spiritual unity, organic unity should also be pursued. In 1908, a joint committee was appointed to prepare a Basis of Union. The Anglicans and Baptists were invited to join the committee as well, but declined.

The Congregationalists approved the document in 1910 and looked forward to unification. The Methodist Church also approved the Basis of Union and gained from their congregations overwhelming support. Oddly, it was the Presbyterian Church that went through tumult to reach agreement. Initially the Church's General Assembly approved the Basis of Union by a majority vote in 1910, but a plebiscite among the congregations revealed a cleavage of 67 percent in favor and 32 percent against. Discussion continued during World War I but remained inconclusive. Then, in 1921, the General Assembly felt compelled to act to avoid a schism. A solid majority decided to go forward with church union and appointed a Joint Committee on Law and Legislation to do the legal preparation. The General Assembly of the Presbyterian Church enacted the legislation in 1925.

Union achieved

The Methodists, Congregationalists, and 70 percent of Presbyterians agreed to form the United Church of Canada on June 10, 1925. The new church hoped to cope more adequately with the urbanization of Canada, the growing immigrant population in the western prairies, and missionary activities. By sharing their resources, they believed they could better meet the social and spiritual needs of the factory workers in the cities. By combining their ministries in rural areas, they felt that fewer churches could serve more congregants at less cost. More missionaries and funding would enable the church to make a larger impact when the Gospel was carried to northern Canada and foreign shores.

The foundational document, the Basis of Union of 1925, provided information to congregants, and its initial theology was expanded by the Statement of Faith in 1940. The United Church believed that the Bible was the keystone of Christian belief and stressed the usefulness of Christian tradition. Within these founding principles, a wide variety of personal interpretation of both scripture and tradition was permitted. By embracing the Social Gospel, it was hoped to achieve social equality, the abolition of capitalism, and to extinguish denominational disharmony. Spokespersons such as J.S. Woodsworth, Salem Bland, Ralph Connor, and Nellie McClung preached optimistically for a better Christian future. The United Church strengthened the Lord's Day observance, Christian temperance activities, child welfare, public health, model housing, and urban beautification.

The General Council of the United Church meets every two years, and a moderator is elected for this period. The first lay moderator was elected in 1968, the first woman moderator in 1980. Under the General Council are eleven territorial conferences, made up of three or four hundred ministers with an equal number of laypersons. Below the conference is the presbytery, which maintains oversight of pastoral charges, and grants licenses to ministerial candidates and supervises their education. The Church tries to keep a balance between local autonomy and central authority, and theologically between Calvinism and Arminianism. Sharing the different traditions, those approved for ordination are asked to state their belief in Christ, a divine call, and the scriptures. A congregation retains the right to call a minister, but the settlement committee appoints the minister. The first woman was ordained in 1936, but only since 1970 has this practice become common. Recent controversies have included the ordination of homosexuals and the settlement of the Indian residential school issue. The United Church is the largest Protestant church in Canada.

Presbyterians continue

While the United Church in 1925 was working out a new theology and ministry program, the Presbyterian Association organized to keep its church continuous and asked the law courts to block church union. Despite these efforts, the parliamentary bill establishing the United Church of Canada received royal assent in July 1924. The Presbyterian Association asked congregations to vote for continuing in the Presbyterian tradition, and assets were then divided between the United Church and the 30 percent who preferred to remain Presbyterian.

Left: Christian churches in Canada not only had to contend with the issue of unity among themselves, but also with the traditional religious beliefs held by the indigenous or Aboriginal peoples.

CHRISTIANITY IN AUSTRALIA

Above: To mark the centenary of Australia's constitution in the year 2000, the Anglican Archbishop of Brisbane Peter Hollingworth and Aboriginal didgeridoo player Richard Walley participated in a service at Westminster Abbey, London.

Australian Christianity entered the twentieth century by gradually identifying as "Australian" or, rather, taking part in defining what being Australian actually meant. It was a slow process and the ties to national origins of the various churches remained strong. For example, during World War I the Church of England and the Presbyterian, Methodist, and Congregational churches supported the British Empire, seeing the war as a struggle for civilization and Christianity. By contrast, some Irish Roman Catholics questioned the support given to the Empire, and Archbishop Mannix from Melbourne was strongly opposed to conscription. At the same time, more and more Australian-born clergy appeared on the scene, and the churches began establishing their own theological colleges to train those clergy. The Uniting Church of Australia was formed in 1977 by the union of Methodists and most Congregationalists and Presbyterians, and in 1981 the Church of England changed its name to the Anglican Church of Australia.

Looking to the outback

Another sign of growing interest in Australian concerns was a change of perspective. The churches looked less overseas to their origins and turned their gaze inland. From their coastal bases, they began pondering effective ministry to the outback. The Anglican Bush Brothers, especially the Brotherhood of the Good Shepherd (1903–1972), undertook long-range ministry by horse, car, and then airplane. The best known ministry is the Australian Inland Mission (AIM), which was formed by the Presbyterian Church in 1912. Minister and aviator John Flynn (1880–1951), known as"Flynn of the Inland", put his significant skills to work in forming a network of ministry and medicine, leading to the famous Flying Doctor Service.

The churches also established Aboriginal missions, and debates began about the social and economic disadvantage faced by many indigenous people. Flynn's own tensions over this matter mirrored those in the churches—he felt that the AIM's task was not to deal with such concerns, but he also realized the churches had much to learn about Aboriginal needs. It was not until the later twentieth century, when indigenous ministers became more numerous, and when independent church bodies such as the Uniting Aboriginal and Islander Christian Congress were formed, that the churches realized the vital importance of land rights, self-determination, and social justice.

Below: Presbyterian minister John Flynn founded the AIM Aerial Medical Service in 1928, which is known today as the Royal Flying Doctor Service and is still a vital part of outback life.

From conflict to cooperation

The intense rivalry, sometimes leading to protests and riots, that characterized nineteenth-century Australian Christianity gradually eased. In the twentieth century, two world wars and the intervening Great Depression era brought to light deep social problems. The churches established social justice departments that became very active in practical programs and policy statements regarding unemployment, health, working conditions, and immigration. The churches began cooperating, forming councils of churches in each state to address important questions of public morality and

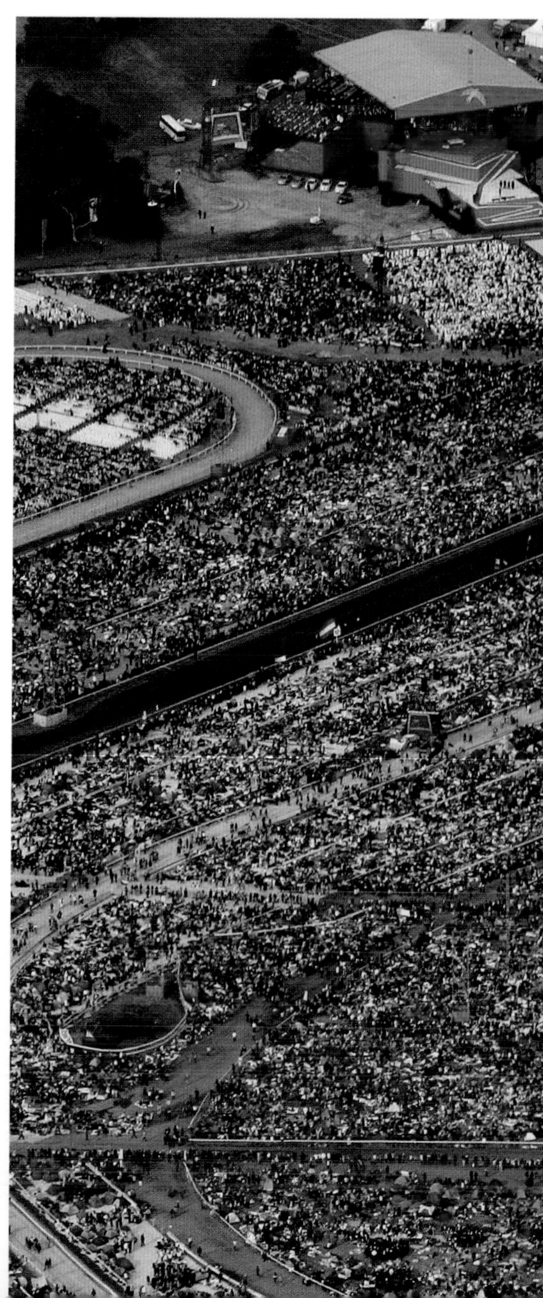

social need. At a local level, cooperation led to joint services at significant events such as Anzac Day and Carols by Candlelight, and invitations to join in each other's worship regularly. By 1977 they were able to produce together an *Australian Hymn Book*.

The aftermath of World War II saw a large increase in immigration from a Europe that was struggling to rebuild. New churches formed, and others were strengthened, such as the Orthodox churches with immigrants from Greece, Russia, and the Middle East—3 percent of Australia's population now identify as Orthodox. The largest number of immigrants came from Italy. Joined by people from other Roman Catholic countries like the Philippines and the southern Netherlands, the Catholic Church began to change from a church of Irish heritage to one with greater diversity. It became the largest church, with 26 percent of the population identifying as Catholic by the end of the century. At the same time denominational loyalties diminished, with young people "church hopping" in search of a church that better suited them. It is in this context that the Charismatic and Pentecostal churches, with their upbeat worship styles, have attracted many new members.

Internal struggles

While conflicts between denominations declined, internal struggles increased. There were political debates, such as the anti-communist wing of the Catholic Church in relation to trade unions, as well as the push to make the Australian Labor Party more Christian democratic than social democratic. The ordination of women became the major issue from the 1970s onward; some churches (Uniting, Anglican, Churches of Christ, and Lutheran) decided to ordain women, while others resisted (Catholics, Presbyterians, and Pentecostal churches). At the end of the twentieth century and into the twenty-first century the most important struggles concern indigenous, environmental, and gay and lesbian issues. In each church, smaller and larger groups are slowly working to bring about change.

Below: Approximately half a million Catholic pilgrims from around the world gathered at Randwick Racecourse in Sydney to take part in the final Mass of World Youth Day in July 2008.

CHRISTIANITY IN NEW ZEALAND

Below right: Raetihi Whare Whakamoemiti is a smaller version of the original Ratana Temple constructed near Wanganui in 1927. The Ratana movement combined *Ture Wairua* (spiritual works) and *Ture Tangata* (secular works).

As the twentieth century opened, the various churches in New Zealand were still basically immigrant churches rather than emerging local churches. There was no established church of New Zealand, and sectarianism was characteristic of the overall community. Christianity in New Zealand today, however, is a richly diverse reality.

Falling numbers

Declining church attendance in the early twentieth century did little to diminish sectarianism prior to World War II. This was often due to antipathy between Protestants and Catholics over the Catholic Church's identification with the Irish struggle for political independence, or over the lack of government financial support for Catholic parish schools. Theologically, most Pakeha churches were committed to conservative doctrinal positions, and there was little emphasis on the Social Gospel, although women from most churches were engaged in various social ministries to poorer groups in society. (Pakeha is the Maori word for New Zealanders of European ancestry.) Some younger Protestants attributed the fall in church attendance to a lack of attention on the part of the churches to contemporary issues, and believed this could be remedied by toleration of greater theological diversity. This led to a reworking of some important theological emphases, particularly by the Student Christian Movement (SCM) in the interwar years.

Maori Christian numbers rose and fell over the years. The Ratana Church, formally established in 1925, was a significant religious and political force. However, other specifically Maori religious groups—such as Ringatu, Pai Marire, and Wairua Tapu—experienced a drop in numbers between the 1930s and 1950s.

Post-World War II developments

There were many significant changes in the churches after World War II: In the Protestant churches triggered by the establishment of the World Council of Churches (WCC) in 1948, and later by the growth of Pentecostal churches; in the Catholic Church by the Second Vatican Council (1962–1965). Societal changes such as the march toward political independence on the part of former colonies, the impact of the United Nations' Decade of Development in the 1960s, and the increasingly secularized nature of New

Below: Christ Church Cathedral has been a living house of Christian worship for Anglicans since it was completed in 1904, some 40 years after the cornerstone was laid.

Zealand society also contributed. Church attendance continued to decline among the mainstream churches, although the significant increase in numbers of Polynesian Catholics has prevented the falling levels in the Pakeha Catholic community from being obvious.

Declining numbers, however, should not be equated with a loss of religious consciousness. Pastoral directions offered by the WCC and Vatican II provided a theological mandate for positive responses to societal shifts. These included solidarity with Maori in their struggle for economic and cultural justice. The impact of the women's movement also affected church life and structures, and in 1989 the Anglican Church ordained Dr Penny Jamieson as Bishop of Dunedin, the first woman in the world ordained as head of an Anglican diocese. Members of the mainstream churches were and are active in various peace and environmental movements, personally and at an institutional level.

The changing face of the churches

The Pakeha churches responded in very different ways to the immigration of Polynesian Christians after World War II. The Anglicans encouraged structures that allowed for cultural particularism grounded in unity in Christ, which explains the threefold structure of Tikanga Maori, Tikanga Pakeha, and Tikanga Pasifika (*tikanga* means "custom," "convention," or "practice"). Catholics favored Polynesians being integrated into the existing parish structure. There are independent Congregational and Methodist Polynesian churches, and in 1971, Pacific Islanders in the Presbyterian Church of Aotearoa New Zealand established the Pacific Islanders' Synod within the church.

The most recent census (2006) indicated that a third of New Zealand's population professed no religious belief, and that Catholic attendance figures had almost overtaken those of Anglicans. Perhaps the most surprising development was the increase in the numbers of religious communities to which people were affiliated—up from 10 at the end of the nineteenth century to 127 at the time of the census.

Perhaps the most significant developments are the extraordinary growth of Pentecostal churches such as the Assembly of God, and particularly of the smaller independent Pentecostal churches, the impact of Pacific Islanders on the mainstream churches, and the emergence of religious movements or churches in which Maori dominate, such as the Rastafarian movement (which attracts disaffected Maori youth) or the fundamentalist Destiny Church. Established in 1998 by Brian Tamaki, Destiny Church's unambiguous approach to contemporary ethical and theological issues found a receptive audience among Maori initially, and subsequently among Polynesians and a smaller number of Pakeha.

Below: To attract Maori to Christianity, the Church of England and the Catholic Church both ordained Maori elders to official church positions. Christian prayer (*karakia*) is often heard at Maori gatherings.

PACIFIC ISLAND CHURCHES

Above: Mormon missionaries evangelizing in Funafuti, Tuvalu. Although around 90 percent of Tuvaluans belong to the largely Congregational-based Church of Tuvalu, Mormons actively seek new members for their church.

Right: White Sunday is celebrated in Samoa during the second weekend in October. Children dress in white and recite Bible verses (*tauloto*) for their relatives in church.

To understand the post-World War II histories of the Pacific Island churches it is important to appreciate the ongoing impact of their nineteenth-century histories, particularly the legacy of denominational divisions and sectarianism. The first church established in a particular nation or area continues to be the dominant church.

Ecumenical initiatives

Churches established by the London Missionary Society (LMS) were and still are dominant in Tahiti, the Cook Islands, Samoa, and the southern part of Papua; Methodists are numerically the strongest in Fiji, Tonga, and the Western Solomons; Anglicans elsewhere in the Solomon Islands; Presbyterians in Vanuatu; and Lutherans in former German-controlled New Guinea. Catholics are large or small minorities in much of the Pacific apart from New Caledonia, where they are a majority group given that country's status as a French overseas department.

The denominational division observable prior to World War II began to change, especially during the war, as Christians in Papua New Guinea and the Solomon Islands found common ground in their struggle against the Japanese. Influenced by European ecumenism, also a legacy of World War II, it is not surprising that in 1966 a Pacific Conference of Churches comprising Melanesian, Micronesian, and Polynesian churches was established. Membership of the conference does not include those churches that arrived later, such as the Church of Jesus Christ of Latter Day Saints (Mormons) and some independent Pentecostal groups.

World War II ushered in a number of other important changes. Leadership became the responsibility of the local church rather than the foreign missionary organizations. Interestingly, except perhaps in the case of New Caledonia, where the large French population influenced the Catholic Church, church leaders were often at the forefront of independence movements. This was particularly true of Vanuatu, where the independence movement was led by Walter Lini, an Anglican priest, and Fred Timakata, a Presbyterian minister.

In pre-Christian Pacific cultures, women were largely excluded from religious activities, but the ecumenical movement has encouraged them to move into the public domain in church and society. Their involvement as ordained ministers is still minimal, however, apart from some ordinations in the United Church of Papua New Guinea and the Solomon Islands from 1976 onward, and a few in exceptional circumstances in some other islands.

Post-World War II missionary activities

Even before World War II, indigenous missionaries from one island were often sent to another island along with European missionaries, a practice that has accelerated since the mid-twentieth century. The older mission-sending

LOCAL THEOLOGICAL COLLEGES

One of the more interesting developments in the Pacific Islands has been the effort to contextualize the Christian faith within the many different cultures. This process depends to a significant extent on the ability of a particular church to train potential ministers in their own schools. The ecumenical Pacific Theological College (established 1966) and the Catholic Pacific Regional Seminary (1972), both located in Suva, Fiji, and the Catholic Holy Spirit Seminary (1963) at Bomana, Papua New Guinea, encourage their students to contextualize their theology and their liturgical practices. The development of local theological colleges has continued in most of the island nations.

agencies of Europe, both Protestant and Catholic, now involve Pacific Christians extensively in their missionary outreach. Generally their missionary activities adhere to the style of Social Gospel (applying Christian ethics to social problems) rather than evangelizing (preaching the Gospel in an attempt to convert people to Christianity).

Overt evangelization is generally carried out by the new churches and sects that have moved into the Pacific. Because most Pacific nations, apart from Fiji with its large Hindu and Muslim Indian population, are Christian, these new arrivals direct their proselytizing efforts toward members of existing churches, much to the consternation of their leaders. The Mormon Church has been helped in its evangelizing work by its significant involvement in primary and secondary education. Students are encouraged to bring their families along to Mormon services, and this approach has contributed to church growth—25 percent of all Samoans are now Mormon, and in Tonga, where Methodism is still the religion of the majority, Mormons have become the next largest group.

Several environmental issues have encouraged ecumenical approaches, hence the opposition of the churches to the French nuclear testing that took place in the Pacific between 1966 and 1996. Ecological issues are now demanding an even more united approach as small Pacific nations cope with overfishing, deforestation, the dumping of nuclear waste, and, perhaps most significantly, climate change, which is already having a clear impact on low-lying islands.

Above: A British Royal Marines officer greets Father Walter Lini in mid-July 1980. More than 200 soldiers had arrived in Port Vila, Vanuatu, to quell rebellions in the colony before its July 30 independence.

PACIFIC CONFERENCE OF CHURCHES

In 1961, the Protestant Pacific churches and missions, encouraged by the World Council of Churches (WCC), explored how they might engage ecumenically with one another. In 1966 the Pacific Conference of Churches (PCC) was formally established, and has met at five-year intervals since. The grassroots ecumenism of the war years was now complemented by structures that would facilitate a more formal approach to ecumenism. In 1976, the Catholic Episcopal Conference of the Pacific became a full member of the PCC, and there are currently over forty member churches.

The PCC's mandate

Although financial shortfalls have affected the PCC—funding for the organization mostly comes from outside the Pacific—these have not definitively curtailed its activities. In 1981, PCC activities were grouped under three headings: Mission, Unity, Renewal, Witness, and Dialogue; Justice and Development; and Ecumenical Relations.

Ecumenically focused theological education was identified as a priority, and saw the establishment in 1966 of the Pacific Theological College in Suva, funded through the WCC's Theological Education Fund. Catholic seminarians are educated at the major seminaries in Port Moresby and Suva. There are good relations between these Protestant and Catholic colleges, particularly the two Suva-based institutes, which carries over into village life when ministers return home to their island nations. In some parts of the Pacific, ecumenical cooperation lay behind the successful translation of the Bible into the vernacular, and to greater women's involvement and participation in the life of the Christian community.

Since 2004, the PCC has been part of the campaign against HIV/AIDS, particularly through its efforts to raise awareness about the disease. This has allowed church members to arrive at a better understanding of the pastoral, social, and economic issues associated with HIV/AIDS and to identify appropriate pastoral responses.

Above: Colonel Sitiveni Rabuka (born 1948) led two military coups in Fiji in 1987. His aim was to oust the ethnic Indian-dominated government and replace it with an ethnic Fijian administration.

PCC involvement in justice and ecological issues

From its inception, the PCC has taken its mandate to bring about cultural, economic, political, and ecological justice seriously. Thus the Pacific churches have sought to ensure that their liturgies were expressed in culturally appropriate ways. Additionally, Church leaders were mandated to resolve conflict in different parts of the Pacific. For example, the PCC asked the Catholic bishop of Tonga and the bishop of the United Church of the Solomon Islands to help resolve the violent land disputes over the Australian-owned copper mine at Panguna on Bougainville—but though their efforts were endorsed by Bougainville's Catholic and United churches, the two leaders were denied entry into Bougainville. Nor were the Fijian Council of Churches or the PCC able to effect any positive change when Lieutenant Colonel Sitiveni Rabuka, a Methodist lay preacher, overthrew Fiji's legally elected government in 1987. The Methodist Church, which accounted for 90 percent of the country's Christians, was divided on the issue while other churches, particularly the Catholic Church, were outspoken in their condemnation of the coup.

The traditional pre-colonial close relationship between political and religious leadership persisted in the post-colonial era, and meant that Church leaders were often at the forefront of movements for political independence, as the example of the Anglican priest, Father Walter Lini, in Vanuatu demonstrates. Ecological issues are emerging as significant for the future of the Pacific region, and the PCC is often at the forefront of protests that seek to call attention to threats to the people's way of life.

At the institutional level, the ecumenical work of the PCC has contributed to overcoming the sectarian and denominational rivalry that was characteristic of the

Christian churches in the Pacific prior to World War II. However, four major problems face the PCC today. First, since the early 1960s, the influx of "new" churches into the Pacific, and their proselytizing work among the established churches, has become a source of tension. The older churches resent the success these "new" churches enjoy, particularly among the youth. Second, important theological and doctrinal differences can be ignored in the interests of an inclusivity that fails to respect those differences. Thirdly, the PCC is sometimes accused of an excessive preoccupation with justice and peace issues, human rights, and ecological concerns, and its apparent anti-government bias can alienate politicians. Finally, most churches are struggling to achieve some sort of financial autonomy.

Perhaps the PCC's most important contribution to the lives of people living in the Pacific Islands is that in the event of regional and national crises, the churches can generally speak with one voice through the national councils. That this did not happen in the case of Fiji's military coups is considered an aberration rather than the norm.

Above: A splash of local color is evident at church services in Fare, Huahine. The Pacific Conference of Churches ensures that the needs of all Christians in the region are met.

Left: Mining on Bougainville Island—part of Papua New Guinea—by a Rio Tinto Group subsidiary was halted in 1989, but land disputes continued into the 1990s; the PCC attempted to bring peace.

DEVELOPMENTS IN LATIN AMERICA

Above: By 2001, almost 80 percent of Bolivia's population classified themselves as Catholic, despite the lack of an official state religion. The next most popular church group is the Evangelical Methodists.

Below: Before the revolution, Mexican president Porfirio Díaz declared: "Without its religion, Mexico is irretrievably lost." The revolutionaries disagreed, and relations soon cooled between Mexico and the Vatican.

Tense standoffs between Church and state, revolutionary Christianity and a frowning Vatican, huge inroads by Pentecostal missions—these are just some of the features of Christianity in twentieth-century Latin America.

The Church, the ruling class, and the liberals

At the turn of the century, Latin America was overwhelmingly Roman Catholic, but that did not mean it was always easy for the Church. Many people, especially those who considered themselves political liberals, saw the Church as the bastion of conservatism. Often the Church hierarchy was bound up with the ruling class, whom the Church felt would maintain order and Church privileges.

This was certainly the case in Chile, which did not separate Church and state until 1925. In Argentina the Catholic Church was even more closely tied in with the state, gaining protection and support—what is called "ecclesiastical privilege." Argentina struggled to find a middle way between exclusive support for the Church and a secular state with religious freedom. The reality is that the Church is closely meshed with the state—to the point that the arrangement has the status of a concordat, or international treaty, with the Vatican. Toward the other end of the scale is the strong separation of Church and state in Brazil, and even more so in Mexico, where the constitution of 1917 (after the revolution of 1910–1917) banned the Church from owning land and influencing the state in any manner. Needless to say, relations between Mexico and the Vatican have long been cool. Only in the 1990s did they resume formal diplomatic connections.

Winds of change: Marxism and Christianity

Back in Rome, the winds of change of the 1960s began to blow through the Vatican. The quiet Pope John XXIII surprised everyone when he called the Second Vatican Council (1962–1965), which was to have profound effects with its opening up to the secular world.

In Latin America the 1960s had their own effect, most especially in the voice of the poor. Priests who had worked among the poor were inspired by Vatican II to challenge the hypocrisy highlighted by Archbishop Dom Hélder Câmara of Brazil in his statement: "When I give food to the poor, they call me a saint. When I ask why the poor have no food, they call me a communist."

The response to that important challenge was liberation theology, which flowered in the 1970s and onward. By analyzing society and economics using Marxist methods, liberation theologians argued that poverty was due to exploitative economic relations, especially between the wealthy nations of the Northern hemisphere and those of the South. However, that is where the Marxist analysis stopped. The solution was not to be found through armed revolution, but through the grace of God, which would

bring liberation as part of salvation. Liberation theology's central tenet is "the preferential option for the poor"—in both theology and society.

The strength of liberation theology came from tens of thousands of "base communities"—small groups of the poor who met to read the Bible, pray, affirm their traditional faith, and help one another wherever possible. These communities have had a profound effect on Latin American politics, lying behind the success of left-wing political parties in the early twenty-first century in Brazil, Venezuela, and Bolivia.

This tentative engagement with Marxism, highlighted by the occasional priest joining insurgents' groups, was too much for the Vatican. It began to call the theologians to account, stressing the tradition of Catholic social teaching, and replacing radical bishops with conservative ones. The problem was that the bishops who had become radical were originally very conservative; their experience of working among poor people had radicalized them—and so, after a dip in the 1990s, liberation theology is now on the resurgence in Latin America.

Wildfire of the Spirit

However, by the 1980s another form of Christianity had spread like wildfire throughout Latin America: Pentecostalism. Initially the Pentecostal missionaries came from the United States, but soon the movement took on a life of its own. One reason for its success was the low level of religious observance among Roman Catholics. No matter how important their politico-social effect, the "base communities" remained a small percentage of the population. One reason for this is a persistent shortage of priests. In 2001, the USA had one priest for every 1,325 Catholics, while Latin America had one priest for every 7,176 Catholics. Pentecostal growth is also favored by the preaching of the "prosperity Gospel" (the belief that God gives material prosperity to those he favors), and by the willingness to use native, lay ministers who are not required to have the extensive theological training of a Catholic priest.

Above: Designed by Heitor da Silva Costa and sculpted by Paul Landowski, *Christ the Redeemer* is a 120-ft (37-m) high statue that has towered over Rio de Janeiro, Brazil, since 1931.

Left: A leading preacher of Latin American liberation theology, Leonardo Boff, presides over a 1986 service in Bacabal, Brazil. The promotion of direct social action for the poor lies at the heart of liberation theology.

BOOM IN AFRICA

Above: Since William Wadé Harris traveled through Ghana in the early 1900s, converting a large number of people, the Christian population in Ghana has risen to almost 14 million.

Below: The government policy of apartheid enforced in South Africa between 1948 and 1994 led to numerous violent protests in black townships across the country. Most churches disapproved of racial segregation.

Although Christianity has been present in Africa since the first days of the early Church, it reached the interior only in the last quarter of the nineteenth century. Since then there has been phenomenal growth. In 1900 there were 8.8 million Christians; by 2004 there were almost 383 million, most in southern Africa. A number of factors have influenced such growth.

Farewell to the missionaries

The "Scramble for Africa" by European colonial powers in the late nineteenth century was followed by an influx of missionaries. Bush schools, catechism, and translations of the Bible and hymns made an initial impact. By the 1890s, however, people began throwing off missionary control and forming their own independent churches. Sometimes these arose as the result of a charismatic leader or "prophet," the best known being "Prophet Harris" (William Wadé Harris, c. 1860–1929) and Simon Kimbangu (c. 1889–1951).

The independent churches kept on growing, subdividing, and spreading. There are now many thousands of them, of all sizes. They vary, but usually emphasize spiritual healing and accept traditional views of sickness in terms of spirit possession. At the same time, mainline Protestant churches—Methodist, Baptist, Congregational, and Anglican—all experienced splits, which produced churches with local leadership but which otherwise resembled the original church.

Farewell to colonial powers

The greatest impetus to church growth was the wave of anticolonial movements in the 1960s and 1970s, which saw one state after another became independent. The churches underwent a shift from white missionary to black indigenous leadership at the same time, and their memberships exploded. For example, by 1990 there were over 350 Roman Catholic African bishops and more than 150 Anglican African bishops. In many countries, such as Zaire, Roman Catholics are the most numerous. In South Africa there is a wide range of denominations, with no one church being dominant. In the north Orthodox Christianity dominates, especially in its traditional centers such as Egypt.

Another sign of independence was the growth of a distinct African theology, with leaders like John Mbiti, Bolaji Idowu, Kwesi Dickson, and John Pobee challenging the denigration of traditional African religions in missionary work. They have sought to reconcile African beliefs in spirits and ancestors with Christian doctrine. In 1989, Mercy Amba Oduyoye formed the Circle of Concerned African Women Theologians. With a focus on feminist concerns, the group has attracted hundreds of women theologians, among them such significant scholars as Musimbi Kanyoro, Isabel Phiri, and Fulata Moyo. Another important development has been the Institute for the Study of the Bible, directed by Gerald West at the University of Kwazulu-Natal in Pietermaritzburg. Here a process of soliciting insights from ordinary readers of the Bible from independent churches and worker movements has opened new ways of interpreting its words.

The struggle against apartheid

In the long struggle to end racial segregation (apartheid), which finally happened in 1994, churches in South Africa were split for decades. The various branches of the Dutch Reformed Church in South Africa supported, although not without disagreements, "separate development" for white and black South Africans. All the other churches, especially the thousands of independent churches, were opposed to the policy of the state, and their leaders often suffered imprisonment and deportation. The center of opposition was the Christian Institute in Johannesburg, established by Beyers Naudé in 1963. It provided a stimulus to black theology, which focused on liberation of the poor and oppressed, and included figures such as Basil Moore, Allan Boesak, and the Biblical scholar Itumeleng Mosala. It remains a focus of progressive theology in South Africa.

AFRICAN PROPHETS

The Liberian, William Wadé Harris, was called to prophecy through a vision of the angel Gabriel; he donned a white robe and a cross, took up a Bible, and gathered a group of women singers. He traveled throughout Liberia, the Ivory Coast, and Ghana, converting tens of thousands, urging them to join the mission churches, and, where there were none, starting new churches with local leaders. He stressed immediate conversion, the imminent end of the world, and combat with spiritual powers. Though harassed by colonial governments and the missions, he became the inspiration for many independent churches. Simon Kimbangu, too, had a visionary calling; he began preaching in the Belgian Congo (now Zaire). Imprisoned within six months for sedition, he spent the rest of his life in prison. But the movement grew to become the Church of Jesus Christ on Earth by His Special Envoy Simon Kimbangu, which now has almost two million members.

Above: Each year, Ethiopian Orthodox followers gather in villages across the country to pray and celebrate during the Timkat Festival, Ethiopia's Epiphany celebration.

Left: Following his release from prison in 1990, anti-apartheid activist and African National Congress leader Nelson Mandela (center) met with Archbishop Desmond Tutu (left), the first black South African Anglican Archbishop of Cape Town.

THE ORTHODOX WORLD

Previous pages: Orthodox priests and monks chant hymns during Easter celebrations at a monastery on Mt Athos—an autonomous monastic state in northern Greece—on April 19, 2009.

The political changes of the last two centuries in Eastern Europe, including events such as the liberation of Greece from the Ottomans, the collapse of the Ottoman Empire, and the rise and fall of communism in Russia and its satellite states, affected the Orthodox world in multiple ways.

Collapse of empires

The nineteenth and early twentieth centuries saw the establishment of national Orthodox churches at a time when their natural spiritual center (Constantinople) was still subject to the Turks. After the liberation of Greece, the Church of Greece declared its autocephaly and its administrative independence from the Patriarchate of Constantinople in 1833.

The autocephaly of the Church of Romania was achieved in the years 1872–1885, the Serbian Patriarchate was re-established in 1920, and the Church of Bulgaria became autocephalous in 1945, as did the other churches of the Balkan world in the early part of the century. The Orthodox world thus saw its former ecumenical character compromised by the rise of churches that identified themselves in national and ethnic terms. Even later, the fate of the Church in the Balkans was often influenced by national interests, as exemplified by the schismatic Church of Ohrid and Macedonia, which broke away from the Serbian Church in 1959, and whose canonicity remains unrecognized by any other Orthodox church.

Under communism

Survival for the Russian Church was also difficult. After the ascent to power of the communists, many Russian intellectuals fled to the West, mostly to Paris and New York. The Soviet state's attempts to control and subjugate the Church led in 1927 to a schism between the Church in Russia and a significant portion of the Church abroad, known thereafter as the Russian Orthodox Church Outside of Russia (ROCOR), which restored its communion with the Patriarchate of Moscow only in 2007 with the signing of the *Act of Canonical Communion*. Religion under Soviet rule was openly opposed. Many churches were closed, and many religious leaders exiled. Yet, even in the gulags of Siberia the Christian tradition was preserved. This difficult period was experienced as something very similar to the era of persecution of early Christians, so that many speak of a "catacomb Church" during the Soviet years. The Soviets also exacerbated the problem of Uniatism (churches that follow the Orthodox tradition of worship but are in communion with the Roman Catholic Church) by forcibly placing some Eastern Catholic churches under the Moscow Patriarchate. After communism collapsed, these churches

Below: Asen's Fortress near Asenovgrad, Bulgaria, dates back to before the eleventh century. The best-preserved section of the fortress is the twelfth-century St Mary Petrichka church, complete with original frescoes.

Above: Metropolitan Kirill of Smolensk and Kaliningrad conducts a service in Moscow's Christ the Savior Cathedral on January 27, 2009, after his election as patriarch at the Russian Orthodox Church Local Council.

Left: Built in the 1860s during the reign of Russian Emperor Alexander II, who was also the Grand Duke of Finland, the Eastern Orthodox Uspenski Cathedral in Helsinki is dedicated to the *Theotokos*.

returned to their affiliation with Rome, adding to centuries-old tensions between the Orthodox and Catholic churches.

Christianity was opposed to various degrees in countries under Soviet influence. In places such as Bulgaria and the USSR the state was hostile to religion, and attempted to use it as part of its control mechanisms, but did not unleash open persecution. The Church was allowed to exist in Romania, apparently unharmed, but was infiltrated to a great extent by the state. Albania, however, proclaimed an officially atheist state and allowed no religious activities.

The Orthodox Church in the West

The exodus of Russian theologians after the communist revolution, following the path of the Greek Orthodox exodus in the late nineteenth century, saw the emergence of many Orthodox parishes in Western Europe and America. A problem the Orthodox Church still faces in Western Europe and North America is that instead of an overarching structure there are often several parallel structures administratively independent from each other (yet usually in full communion), identified by ethnic heritage rather than faith. Often discussed among the leaders of the Orthodox churches, this problem has not yet been resolved.

Nevertheless, the foundation of Orthodox theological institutions in Western Europe and North America, such as St Sergius in Paris, St Vladimir's Seminary in New York, Holy Cross in Boston (and many others), and the increased integration of immigrant groups into the culture of the host country, has made it possible for Orthodox Christianity to spread beyond ethnic boundaries and its traditional Eastern European cradle.

The Orthodox Church in formerly communist countries

Following the collapse of the communist bloc, the Orthodox churches in the former communist countries have re-emerged, sometimes without much difficulty but sometimes, as in the case of Albania which had to be re-founded from the ground up, with a completely new generation of priests and bishops. In most of these countries the Church was one of the few institutions that people could trust and respect through the difficult years of suppression and change, and its return to power has been dynamic and most impressive.

THE CHINESE CHRISTIAN CHURCH

Opposite: During an Easter service at Liuhe, Shanxi Province, robed catechumens line up to receive the holy sacraments. Today, with over 6,000 Catholics, Liuhe parish is one of the largest in mainland China.

After almost a century of stagnation, Chinese Christianity showed remarkable growth at the beginning of the twentieth century, when a pro-Western spirit took hold in China as the people struggled to resuscitate the country by adopting the Western pattern of modernization.

Pre-1949

During the period 1900 to 1920, the Christian churches tripled their membership, from around 100,000 to a figure in the vicinity of 300,000 followers. This growth, however, came to an end as the missions faced various new challenges. First, due to the resurgence of anti-foreign feeling, in the 1920s Chinese Christianity found itself harassed by a number of movements such as the nationalistic and socialistic Anti-Christian Movement. Second, indigenous leadership was on the rise; internationally, Chinese Christians participated in the World Missionary Conference in Edinburgh in 1910, which signaled the emergence of non-Western church leadership, and domestically they took over leadership from foreign missionaries of churches and Christian institutions, especially schools. Third, Chinese Christians were now playing a major role in ecumenism—for instance, in 1927, when a united national church, the Church of Christ in China (*Chung-hua Chi-tu Chiao-hui*), was established, 66 of the 86 commissioners were Chinese; only 22 were Westerners. Fourth, numerous indigenous churches, in most cases with Pentecostal outlooks, came into being in this period, among them the True Jesus Church, the Assembly Hall or Little Flock, the Jesus Family, and the Spiritual Gifts Church.

Another significant challenge for Chinese Christianity was that many missions were divided over issues of theology, especially in the 1920s and early 1930s. Theological feuds in their home countries, particularly the United States, such as the modernist–fundamentalist controversy, were subsequently reflected in the mission field. Equally, strife in China was felt in the home churches, reflected, for instance, in the publication of the controversial layperson's report, *Re-Thinking Missions*, in 1932, and the volte-face of former missionary Pearl S. Buck, who refuted the traditional way of mission.

Right: Deng Xiaoping (1904–1997) is remembered as an influential and active leader. His policy of cultural freedom allowed Christianity to rekindle, and his industrial reforms transformed China into an economic powerhouse.

Opposite: Villagers flee during the Chinese Civil War. In 1949, the Communist Party emerged victorious and Mao Zedong proclaimed the People's Republic of China. Religions including Christianity were soon restructured by the new government.

Church revival

Immediately after the Communist Party victory in 1949, the new government rigorously reorganized Christianity and other religions, emphasizing their dissociation from foreign intervention and patriotism. Thus it was that the Three-Self Principles (self-propagation, self-support, and self-government) evolved from a missionary policy that was meant to safeguard ecclesiastical independence to a political policy that is more or less intended to harmonize religious loyalty and nationalistic loyalty. Protestant Church leaders drafted the "Christian Manifesto," which was approved by Premier Zhou Enlai in 1950; this was followed by a similar Catholic manifesto in the same year. Protestants started the Three Self Patriotic Movement (TSPM) in 1951 (officially in 1954), and Catholics began the Three Autonomies of the Catholic Church in 1950 (later the Chinese Catholic Patriotic Association, or CCPA). Many Christians, both Protestant and Catholic, chose to remain underground. During the Great Cultural Revolution of 1966–1976, however, even these government-sponsored Christian organizations were closed down.

It was only under the open policy of Communist Party leader Deng Xiaoping in the late twentieth century that Christianity, particularly Protestantism, revived. In 1980, alongside the TSPM and CCPA, which had dealt with the relationship with government, Protestants and Catholics formed new umbrella organizations for all churches to handle intrachurch matters: The China Christian Council and Chinese Catholic Bishops' Conference (and the Chinese Catholic Church Administrative Commission), respectively. The phenomenal growth of the Church, both official and underground, from 1980 raises questions about the efficacy of missionary Christianity in pre-1949 China and also about the resilience of religion.

The Church under communist rule: An oxymoron?

The ever-present question of whether the Christian Church can exist under communism has repeatedly been raised in

relation to the Chinese Church, which is now the largest national church in absolute terms. As of now, the answer is a cautious "maybe." After the Cultural Revolution, power passed to more moderate leaders. The 1978 Constitution allowed freedom of religion. Five religions—Buddhism, Daoism, Catholicism, Protestantism, and Islam—are recognized by the state, though the government continues to ban some other religions such as Falun Gong. While religious belief is more acceptable now, it remains incompatible with membership in the Communist Party of China (CPC), and party membership is necessary for advancement in many careers and government positions.

Meanwhile, Chinese Christians have struggled to adjust to the changed context. Though Catholics played the role of antagonist in the mid-twentieth century, the Vatican recently attempted to normalize relationships with the incumbent government. Protestants, who were relatively free of foreign connections, have collaborated with the government more actively, and theologians such as Bishop K.H. Ting (Ding Guangxun), CCC president, are endeavoring to develop nondenominational theology in the communist context.

CHRISTIANITY IN KOREA

Opposite: Worshippers at the Yoido Full Gospel Church in Seoul. The church's first service, held at the base of a mountain on May 18, 1958, was attended by Pastor David Yonggi Cho and five Christians.

Opposite bottom: The Presbyterian Church of Korea has more members than any other Presbyterian group in the world. Suh Sang Ryun founded the first Presbyterian church in Hwanghae Province in 1884.

Below: A priest and nuns amid a group of children from Maryknoll Kindergarten in Seoul, Korea. Education was a prime focus of the Christian mission in Korea in 1946.

Christianity is said to have come to Korea in 1784 when Lee Seung-hoon (Peter) was baptized a Catholic in China and returned home to baptize his countrymen. Catholicism in Korea is thus a century older than Protestantism; Protestant missionaries first entered the country in 1884–1885.

Missionary activity

Methodist and Presbyterian missionary societies played prominent roles in the development of modern Korean Christianity. Evangelism, and then education, was their primary focus. Christians needed to be able to read the Bible, so primary schools were established along with churches. These schools eventually developed into high schools and colleges, where a variety of modern Western subjects were taught. Missionaries also spread the use of *han'gul* (Korean script) by translating, publishing, and distributing Korean Bibles.

Medical missionaries established hospitals, and medical and nurse training schools. The benefits of modern education and medical services generated great respect for Christianity, and the schools and hospitals became invaluable evangelistic tools. Missionaries introduced farmers to modern agricultural methods and established social-evangelistic centers for women and children. Many mission schools, hospitals, and social centers have evolved into major institutions such as Severance Hospital, Yonsei University, Ewha and Baewha Woman's Universities, and Tai Wha Social Welfare Foundation.

Christian resistance to Japanese rule

Japan controlled Korea from 1910 to 1945. The colonial government subjected church services to police surveillance, imprisoned Christian leaders, and forced Christian organizations to adjust to governmental rules. Protestants were particularly active participants in the nationalism movement, and almost half of those who signed the 1919 Declaration of Independence from Japan were Christians. Between the early 1930s and World War II, many Christians clashed with the government because they resisted worship at Shinto shrines. By 1940 foreign missionaries had been evacuated, and there was a dramatic decrease in the number of Christians.

North Korea

Christianity was stronger in the north than in the south before 1940; however, after World War II and Korea's division, many Christians from the north moved to the south to escape persecution. Those who remained in the north were severely repressed. In 1983, the North Korean communist government allowed limited religious freedom; however, the handful of government-recognized churches remain under surveillance, and the actual number of Christians and house churches is unknown.

South Korea

After the Korean War (1950–1953), foreign aid organizations, including Christian mission agencies, poured into South Korea. The churches played a significant role in relief efforts and providing spiritual guidance to the poor, and became a vital democratic force. Programs of industrial and army chaplaincy, begun by Protestant and Catholic churches in the 1950s, continue to be important agents of evangelistic work. Effective propagation and social services saw spectacular church growth take place from the 1960s. In the 1970s, the churches translated the Bible for common use, and began to emphasize mass communication as a means of evangelism.

By the end of the twentieth century, Christians comprised one-third of South Korea's population, and there were 230 different Protestant denominations across the country, including Presbyterian (the majority), Methodist,

MINJUNG THEOLOGY

Although Korean Christianity was unconsciously influenced by Shamanist, Buddhist, and Confucian beliefs, the majority of Protestants are evangelical-conservative and do not interact with other religions. In the 1970s and 1980s, under the military regime, progressive theologians developed a Korean version of Latin American liberation theology for the oppressed, appropriating folk cultural elements from Shamanistic arts and rituals: This "Minjung theology," is now more familiar abroad.

Baptist, Holiness, Pentecostal, Salvation Army, Nazarene, Seventh Day Adventist, Lutheran, and Anglican. Nearly 10,000 Korean missionaries were active in 119 countries, making it the world's second greatest missionary force. One of the most explosive groups was the Pentecostals, the Yoido Full Gospel Church being the largest congregation in the world, with over 750,000 members. Along with historical and social elements, spiritual factors contributed to the growth of the churches, including emphasis on prayer, revivals, church attendance, and sacrificial giving.

Catholic growth lagged behind Protestant growth for several reasons, including memories of the long-term persecution of the Church in 1801–1867 and the celebration of Mass in Latin by foreign priests until the 1960s. Since then, however, Catholicism has experienced impressive growth due to the elevation of a Korean archbishop to cardinal, an increase of the number of Korean priests, Catholic leaders' active involvement in human rights and democratic movements against the military regime, and in 1997 the election of the Catholic Kim Dae-Jung, "Korea's Mandela," as President. In 1984, Korean Catholics celebrated their bicentennial. Pope John Paul II was present at the celebrations, during which he canonized 103 Korean martyrs.

POSTCOLONIAL SOUTHEAST ASIA

Below: Cao Dai priests pray in their temple. Caodaism is a Vietnamese religion that combines elements of Hinduism, Buddhism, Confucianism, Daoism, Judaism, Christianity, Islam, and the Vietnamese religion called Geniism.

The colonial era in Southeast Asia spanned almost four centuries, from the arrival of the Portuguese in Melaka in 1511 to the British in Burma in 1885. In between those years we find colonization by the Dutch (East Indies), French (Indo-China), Spanish (Philippines), Portuguese (Timor, Melaka, Macau), British (Burma, Malaya, North Borneo), and, in the twentieth century, by the Japanese.

Colonial policies toward religions set the context for the nature of religious life in the postcolonial era (after independence). For the most part the British were pragmatists, supporting missions if it meant schools for training civil servants would be established, but also restricting Christian missions from work among Muslims (Treaty of Pangkor, 1874) if the government feared religious strife. The French supported the Roman Catholic Church and resisted Protestant missions in Vietnam. The divisions of nation-states in Asia, the toleration of religions, and the cooperation of governments with "missions" and churches were all established by European governments in the colonial period.

Liberty, liberation, and realignment

The period of postcolonialism in Southeast Asia began with the crushed hopes of the Filipinos—they exchanged one colonial power for another, Spain for the USA. Filipino scholars studying in Europe in the nineteenth century had picked up themes of liberty and national independence. The independence movement gained the support of the USA, and Spanish control was crushed in 1898. However, America stayed and continued ruling as a modern colonial power (promoting Protestant missions) until the Japanese invasion. After 333 years of Spanish colonialism and Roman Catholicism, it is no surprise that Philippine Christianity continue to be Catholic (81 percent); Protestants have gained a foothold (about 6 percent). In the postcolonial

Opposite: Catholics in the Philippines joyfully take part in parades and dancing during the Ati-Atihan Festival, held every January to mark the Feast of the Holy Child (Santo Niño).

Left: After a lengthy procession, Catholics in towns and villages in parts of Indonesia re-enact Christ's crucifixion. They call this passion play the drama of Jalan Salib.

era missionary work continues, but most of the missions come from Korea and other East Asian countries.

In Indonesia liberation from the Dutch (and from the Japanese) eventually came, but a national identity quickly needed to be formed. Indonesia was a conglomerate of about 13,000 islands, 300 ethnic groups, and 250 languages that were brought together by the Dutch. After independence was declared in 1945, the new government created five principles (*Pancasila*) to guide the country. The five principles include belief in God, humanity, national unity, consultative democracy, and social justice. Although Indonesia is mostly Muslim, it has developed as a tolerant and pluralistic country, giving a certain amount of protection and space for Christian development.

Religious revivals, secular ideology, and Asian missions

Three major themes have dominated the postcolonial period. First, the region has experienced religious revivals of Islam (Indonesia, Malaysia, and southern Philippines) and of Buddhism (Taiwan, Singapore, and Malaysia). These religions have been supported, at times, by local governments, making Christian life more restricted.

However, secular ideologies have also competed for the hearts of the people and the minds of the rulers. The spread of communism from China, and then from North Korea, has had a tremendous impact on the development of Christianity. The crushing of a communist coup d'état in Indonesia in 1965 is viewed by some people as an impetus to the growth of Christianity.

A similar result occurred in Malaysia during and after the Emergency, which began in 1948 and lasted until 1960. People were uprooted and resettled in an effort to reduce the influence of Chinese communists and, in the midst of uncertainty, the "new villages" became places where Christian missionaries found many converts.

In Vietnam, the communist opposition to Christianity reflected suspicion of the close links between Christian missions and European colonialism. After the reunification of Vietnam and victory of the communists in 1975, churches were closed, seminaries were shut down, and many Christian leaders were imprisoned. However, by the 1990s, when Vietnam was finally stabilized after many years of anti-colonial wars, the government began to allow new freedoms, including limited freedom of religion. In this new environment, Christianity has been able to expand.

Similarly in Cambodia, where there are newer freedoms (although without the economic vitality of neighboring countries), Christianity has grown rapidly, primarily through the missionary work from other Southeast Asian nations (Malaysia, Singapore, Indonesia, and Korea).

And this is the third theme of the postcolonial period. The overwhelming majority of missionary work in Southeast Asia is done by other Asians. Malaysians working in Vietnam or Thailand or Cambodia seem to understand the cultural contexts more easily, and they also pick up the languages more easily than Westerners. Postcolonial Southeast Asian Christianity is a matrix of Asian religious vitality in the midst of growing economies and healthy religious communities of Islam and Buddhism.

Above: Catholic missionaries brought Christianity to the Cambodian region as early as 1660; Protestantism followed in 1923. Today, almost all Cambodians are Buddhists, with Christian missions carrying out much humanitarian work.

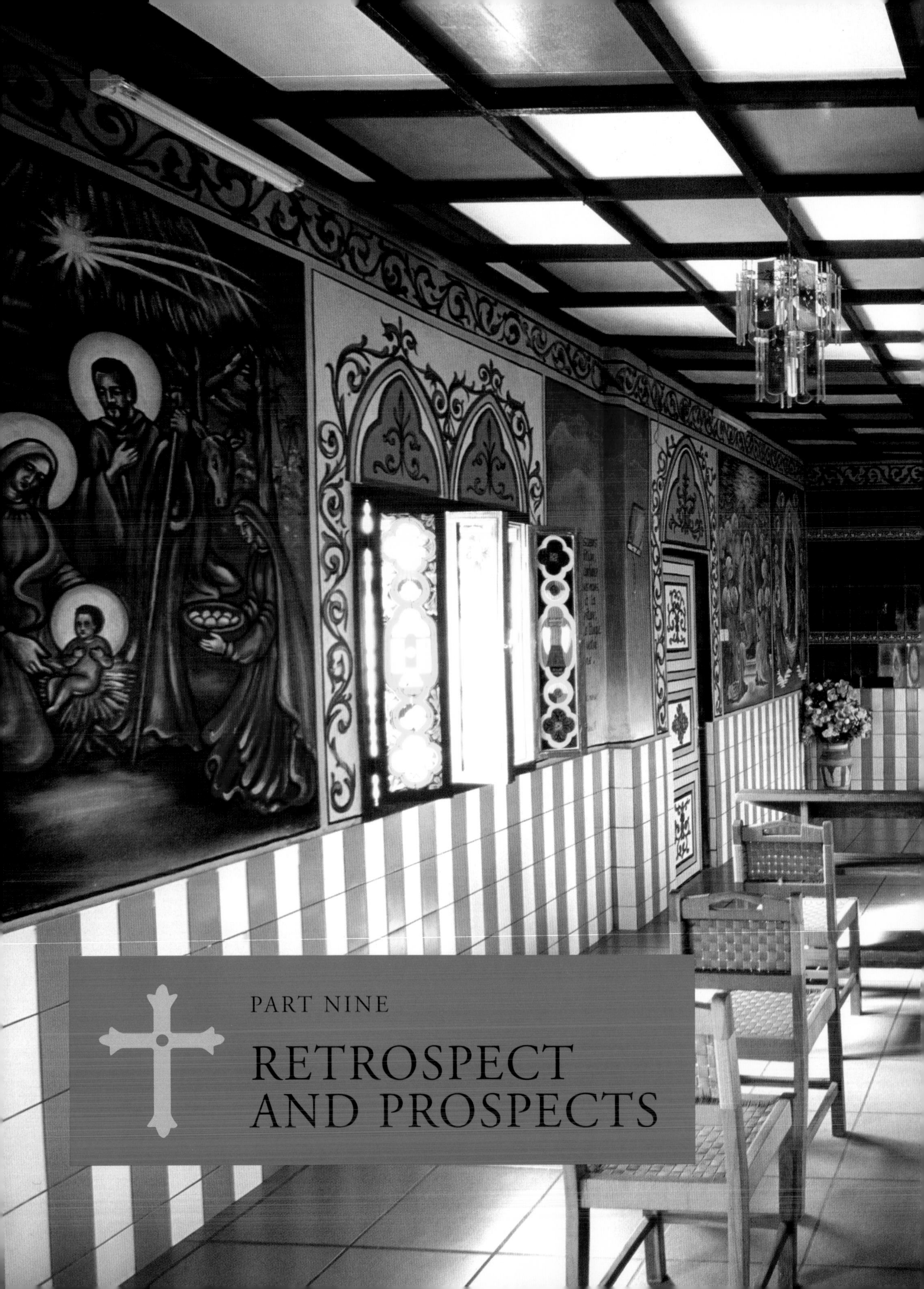

PART NINE

RETROSPECT AND PROSPECTS

CHRISTIANITY AND OTHER RELIGIONS

Above: The apostle Andrew is said to have been crucified by the Romans around 60 CE. Like many early Christians, he was martyred for his beliefs.

Like other religions, Christianity points toward a universal truth. What should be the relationship between different religions, each making a claim to universal truth? We can imagine at least three possibilities: Confrontation, coexistence, or finding common ground. In this section, we examine the various historical and contemporary Christian responses to religious pluralism.

The early centuries

Christianity began as a minority Jewish sect. The first Christians did not see themselves as a new religion; they viewed themselves as faithful Jews for whom Jesus Christ was the promised Messiah. However, after they were expelled from the synagogue in around 90 CE Christians were forced to decide whether to view Judaism as a "false religion." Even though Christians believed that those who rejected Jesus had rejected the Messiah, the Christian Church decided to retain the Jewish scriptures. With this action, the early Church declined to pronounce Judaism a "false religion."

The split with Judaism coincided with the decision to spread the Christian Gospel "beyond Israel." Christians found themselves confronted by Jewish, Greek, Roman, and other Mediterranean peoples espousing diverse religious systems. How did they react? Early Christians believed they had a superior message, but they did not universally assume a negative view of other traditions. The Word, Wisdom, and Spirit of God were evident in creation, words of prophets, and wisdom-writers, and among the nations. The apostle Paul praised the religious spirit of the people of Athens.

In the early centuries, Christians were a marginal group within the Greco-Roman Empire. They created a problem for the Roman system of government because they did not worship any of the many deities tolerated by Rome, nor did they participate in the rituals honoring the Roman gods and rulers. They were often persecuted, even martyred, for their beliefs. They were on the defensive.

Below: Detail from *Battle of Constantine and Maxentius* by Peter Paul Rubens. Constantine greatly altered the lives of early Christians when he declared their faith legal throughout the Roman Empire.

How Christianity related to other faiths

All this changed in the fourth century when the Emperor Constantine legalized Christianity in the Roman world (c. 312–313 CE). While Constantine did not make Christianity the state religion (his policy was one of toleration), Christianity grew rapidly and by the end of the fourth

century it had become the state religion. Christianity's new, dominant role sometimes implied a more negative, at times militant, attitude toward other religions. This was especially evident after the eighth-century clash with Islam and in the growing denigration of Judaism.

Nonetheless, in medieval Europe, Christian hostility to other religions was not universal. Christians like Hildegard, Aquinas, Eckhart, and Francis engaged in positive dialogue with Muslims and Jews. Another exception is medieval Spain where Jews, Christians, and Muslims lived together in harmony for several centuries.

Following Columbus and the colonization of the New World, Christianity saw itself as the world's civilizing power. Non-European cultures and religions were considered to be exotic, inferior, and temporary. With rare exceptions, the Christian attitude toward them was, at best, patronizing.

Significant events of the twentieth century—two world wars, a billion deaths, and postcolonial independence movements—challenged European imperialism and the Christian claim to superiority. Religions of the East and indigenous traditions grew in authority and confidence. Christians were forced to reassess their own identity and attitude to other religions within a radically changing world.

Christianity and religious pluralism

The majority of Christians no longer live in Europe, but in Asia, Africa, and Latin America. Like other religions, Christianity is confronted by internal divisions and the

Previous pages: The interior of this church in Togo reflects the country's West African heritage. Traditional Christian scenes, such as the nativity, have been rendered in an African style.

Below: This statue of Thomas Aquinas adorns a basilica in central Italy. Aquinas respected the views of Muslim and Jewish thinkers, and quoted them in his writings.

Above: Worshippers outside a church in Gonder, Ethiopia. Africa is home to a very large number of Christians; around 60 percent of Ethiopians are Christian, mostly Orthodox.

rise of fundamentalist movements. The real question is no longer about the Christian attitude to other religions; rather it is who speaks for Christianity in the context of religious pluralism?

The member organizations of the World Council of Churches (WCC), including Orthodox, Catholic, "mainline" Protestant, and some Evangelical churches, are committed to "dialogue" among peoples and religions of the world. Their aims are to overcome divisions and prejudice; foster mutual understanding; and work together for peace, social justice, and moral values. These churches now reject an approach that limits grace and salvation to the Christian religion. Agreeing that other religions are also carriers of truth and goodness does not thereby assume the sameness or equality of religions. Some Christians still affirm a certain priority of their own tradition while recognizing each religion has its own spiritual insights and vision to share.

Religious dialogue does not occur in a vacuum. There is little hope of genuine dialogue without acknowledging past guilt. Many Christian leaders have expressly asked forgiveness from Jews, Muslims, indigenous peoples, and others for past injustices. World religious leaders have gathered a number of times in Assisi, Italy, to pray for world peace. These initiatives demonstrate that interreligious understanding is happening.

Among the fruits of Christian dialogue with Muslims and Jews is a growing awareness that all are followers of Abraham and believers in the one, same God. From the classical religions of the East, Christians are able to learn meditation practices, moral precepts, and spiritual truths that enhance our human experience of the divine mystery. From indigenous traditions, Christians are introduced to a heightened sense of the sacredness of creation. Through dialogue with other religions, Christians discover they are not alone—a generous God is present throughout creation and in the spiritual traditions of humankind.

However, not all Christians agree that dialogue should be the main form of Christian interaction with other religions. Many conservative theologians and ministers take a more exclusive position with respect to religious truth, holding that Christianity is the only true religion. These Christians believe that the teachings of the various religions of the world are mutually incompatible, and therefore we are forced to make a choice regarding which one we will believe in. It is not possible, these Christians argue, to believe in mutually exclusive truth claims. Therefore, argumentation and debate, not dialogue, are the most appropriate forms of interaction with other religions.

What does the future hold for relations between Christianity and other faiths?

Which form of interaction between Christianity and other religions will prevail in the future? Will dialogue flourish, or will increasing numbers of Christians assert that Christianity has an exclusive claim to religious truth? This question is hard to answer because Christians themselves are divided on the issue, and currently neither side is strong enough to overpower the other. The pressure applied by other religions also tends in different directions: Some want to dialogue with Christians, others want to confront Christianity, and still others want neither dialogue nor confrontation but simply peaceful coexistence.

Left: Chief spiritual leader of Tibetan Buddhism, His Holiness the Fourteenth Dalai Lama of Tibet. He has written a book called *The Good Heart: A Buddhist Perspective on the Teachings of Jesus.*

Below: Pope John Paul II talks with a Jewish leader, one of the representatives of 12 religions at the first Day of Prayer for Peace in the World, held in Assisi, Italy, in 1986.

INDIGENOUS CHRISTIANS

Above: The church of the Mission San Xavier del Bac, south of Tucson, Arizona, was founded by a Jesuit priest in 1700. It features a blend of Byzantine, Moorish, and Mexican architectural styles.

Opposite: Catholics in Antigua, Guatemala, take part in *Semana Santa* every Easter. Their unique way of celebrating Holy Week involves a re-enactment of Christ's Passion, Crucifixion, and Resurrection.

Below: Ivorian tribal leaders attend the consecration of Our Lady of Peace Basilica in Yamoussoukro, Cote d'Ivoire, by Pope John Paul II, in 1990.

Questions regarding cultural adaptation have accompanied Christianity's expansion since the beginning. The first followers of Jesus were Jewish, but they soon carried the Gospel to Gentiles (non-Jews). How much of Jewish law and mores would Gentiles have to adopt? It was easily agreed that they would need to avoid idolatry and visiting prostitutes, but what about the entire framework of Mosaic Law that shaped the day-to-day life of Jews? Paul of Tarsus argued against forcing Gentiles to adopt Jewish law, and prevailed.

Colonial missions

By the time European colonial expansion began in the fifteenth and sixteenth centuries, Paul's argument was forgotten. Like the Greeks and Romans before them, Europeans had come to identify Christianity with their own culture and civilization. So, as they traveled under the aegis of first the Spanish and Portuguese empires, and later with the Dutch, German, French, Italian, Danish, Russian, and English empires, to places as distant as Brazil, South Africa, New Zealand, and Greenland, they assumed that their mission entailed the bringing of European civilization as much as it entailed the gift of the Gospel.

Missionaries in a bind

Indigenous peoples were made to live in European-style settlements, wear European clothes, submit to European law codes, learn European manners, and speak only the language of the colonial power. "Civilize first; then convert" was the motto of the Catholic missions in South America or California, the Orthodox missions in Siberia and Alaska, and the Protestant missions in Greenland, the Pacific, or Australia.

However, some missionaries could see a contradiction in this process. Lancelot Threlkeld (1788–1859) in Australia defended the Awabakal people from exploitation by colonists while he translated the Bible. Herman of Alaska (c. 1756–1837) protested against the mistreatment of the Aleuts on Kodiak and Spruce Islands. Matteo Ricci (1552–1610) in China developed the idea of accommodation, patiently learning Chinese culture and adapting Christianity to Chinese beliefs. These and others believed that Christianity can only transform cultures by becoming a part of them, not by substituting one culture for another.

Atoning for the past

Despite their best efforts, there were all too many cases where missionaries broke up the old patterns of indigenous life, attacked indigenous belief as coming from the devil, and worked too closely with colonial governments and troops. At the same time, indigenous peoples became Christians. As the old saying put it, "When the missionaries came, we had our land and they had the Bible. They told us to look to heaven to find God. When we looked down, they had our land, but we had the Bible." Once they had the Bible, indigenous peoples made it their own and developed new forms of Christianity.

The rise of political consciousness among indigenous peoples in the 1960s and 1970s brought a new phase. Indigenous Christians began to ask difficult questions about their treatment in the past, and many churches struggled to answer them. Gradually those churches began to apologize and make recompense for events of the past such as breaking up families and putting children into orphanages, destruction of traditional social structures and ways of life, and heedlessly infecting indigenous peoples with deadly European diseases. Churches with colonial origins in Canada, USA, Australia, South America, Africa, and Asia sought to atone for the past.

Looking to the future

Indigenous peoples are now overwhelmingly Christian, but they have taken Christianity and made it their own. Attend any worship service in Africa, central Australia, or northern Canada, and you will see how distinctive they are. The distinctions may be evident in indigenous art, dance in worship, unique songs, or new ways of expressing belief.

The World Christian Gathering of Indigenous People (WCGIP) meets bi-annually to worship using indigenous dance, music, and arts, and to participate in workshops and discussions on issues of concern to the indigenous peoples of the world. These issues include illiteracy, malnutrition, poverty, and a lack of roads, schools, and doctors. WCGIP's founders, Monte and Linda Ohia, are Maori from New Zealand. The first gathering was in Rotorua, New Zealand, in 1996. In 1998 the WCGIP met in Rapid City, South Dakota (USA), at the base of Paha Sapa (the Black Hills), sacred to the Lakota people. Australia's Aborigines hosted the WCGIP in Sydney in 2000. The conference met in Hawaii in 2002. The 2004 meeting in Kiruna, Sweden, was hosted by the Saami of northern Scandinavia. Mindanao in the Philippines was the location of the 2006 meeting. The seventh WCGIP convened in Israel in 2008, allowing delegates to visit the places where Jesus lived.

MI REINO NO ES DE
ESTE MUNDO
Sn. Juan
18

CHRISTIANITY AND WOMEN

Above: In 1989, Barbara Harris of the Episcopal Church, USA, became only the second female bishop in the global Anglican Communion. Penny Jameison, former Bishop of Dunedin, New Zealand, was the first.

"So God created humankind in his own image, in the image of God he created him; male and female he created them." This verse from Genesis 1:27 embodies a tension within Christianity over gender. Here we find "he" and "him" used in a way that makes it clear that God is pictured as male. Yet we also find the statement that both male and female are created in God's image. The first sense is the way Christianity has operated for centuries—with a male God and male leaders. The second sense has been taken up since the late eighteenth century as an argument for both sexes having an equal role in the Church.

Only men in frocks?

The most obvious struggle has been over women taking on leadership roles, especially as priests and ministers. In the very early Church there is evidence to show that important women (usually of high social standing) took leadership positions. But by the second century when the threefold office of bishop, priest, and deacon was established, women were noticeably absent. Until the nineteenth century, skilled women were kept on the margins, given special positions such as deaconess (with care for other women and the sick) or occasionally leader or abbess of a nunnery. Whenever these women became too influential, their positions were closed down; deaconesses ceased to function by the eleventh century (the role was revived at a later time).

The first women's rights convention was held in Seneca Falls, New York, USA, in 1848. The springboards to this early form of modern feminism were abolitionism and evangelicalism. As women worked on behalf of slaves, they began to reflect on their own lack of rights. Evangelical associations gave women a chance to work and preach outside the home, and sometimes to assume leading positions in organizations.

By the last years of the nineteenth century, the suffragettes were agitating for the right to vote, Elizabeth Cady Stanton published *The Woman's Bible* (1895), and in some isolated cases women were ordained in the Congregational, Baptist, Methodist, and Lutheran churches. It was not until the 1960s and 1970s that the issue of women's ordination re-emerged. Most mainstream Protestant congregations debated and then agreed to ordain women. However, women bishops are still exceedingly rare, and the Catholic, Eastern Orthodox, and Oriental churches continue to resist the ordination of women, citing tradition and some Biblical injunctions against women.

Informal leadership and the life of faith

In many cases the churches that ordained women were recognizing the reality that women already carried out many informal ministerial roles. In any remote parish it was not uncommon to find women preaching, planting new churches, teaching catechism, providing religious education in schools, and leading organizations. Here were talented women willing to exercise ministry without formal recognition. Eventually some of the churches caught up.

This informal leadership reflected a reality of the membership of many churches where women outnumbered men. In the traditional arrangements of family life, religion was seen to be a woman's role—the woman was responsible for nurturing the children, which included some instruction in religion. Religion was also seen as a matter of private conviction and one's inner life, and so belonged to the private sphere, while the role of men lay in the public sphere. As social expectations changed, churches began to recognize the public roles of women's leadership.

A new movement in theology

A noticeable shift since the 1960s has been the development of feminist theology and Biblical studies. The generation of pioneers, such as Elisabeth Schussler Fiorenza (1938–), Rosemary Radford Ruether (1936–), and Dorothy Soelle (1929–2003), has provided the basis for thousands of feminist theologians and Biblical scholars working today. Their work has changed perceptions of the history of Christian origins, where it is now agreed that there was a significant circle of women. It has drawn attention to the presence of women in the Bible, the contradictions of patriarchy, and way the Bible has been used to marginalize women for more than two millennia. It has also shown how perceptions of God are not limited to one gender; in fact, God is beyond such perceptions. In challenging the way theology had been an exclusively male world, it has provided far more space for both women and men within Christianity.

As a sign of the influence and maturity of feminist theology, it has begun to interact with and draw upon other important streams. These include gay and lesbian theology, the legacy of colonialism (called postcolonial theology), liberation theology, and environmental concerns in what is known as ecotheology. Theology has changed and will continue to be enriched by these interactions.

Previous pages: Members of the Soweto Gospel Choir perform at the Live Earth concert in Johannesburg, South Africa, in 2007. These Christian women are singing to help raise awareness of environmental issues.

Opposite: In 1926, in Boston, Massachusetts, USA, the Rev. Robert Watson ordained the first female deacons of Presbyterian churches. Left to right: Mrs A. MacPherson, Lily Johnathon, Martha Smerer, and Mrs Jenni Miller.

Above: A reverend greets one of her parishioners in Los Angeles, California, USA. Women now have greater access to leadership roles within the Church, though significant resistance remains both at the institutional level and within local congregations.

Left: In 2006, Katharine Jefferts Schori (center) was installed as the twenty-sixth Presiding Bishop of the Episcopal Church, Washington, DC, USA. Most provinces of the Anglican Communion ordain women to the priesthood, but none had ever elected a woman to their most senior position.

MAIN EVENTS IN CHRISTIAN HISTORY

c. 4 BCE Birth of Jesus.

c. 27 CE Jesus begins his ministry.

c. 30 Jesus is crucified.

c. 36 The name "Christian" is first used in the city of Antioch.

c. 46–64 First documents of Christianity written: The letters of Paul.

c. 47 Thomas establishes the Church of the East in Persia.

64–68 Persecution of Christians in Rome under Nero; deaths of Paul and Peter.

c. 67–78 Linus is bishop of Rome.

70–90 Gospels of Mark, Luke, and Matthew written; Acts written.

90–100 Gospel of John written. The earliest known fragment dates from 117 CE.

c. 100: Epistle of Barnabas written; the beginning of Christian literature that would not be included in the canon.

100–150 Remaining documents of the New Testament written.

107 Ignatius, third bishop of Antioch, is the first to refer to Christians as "Catholic" and advocates Sunday for worship. He is fed to lions in Rome.

135 Christmas instituted as a Feast day by Bishop Telesphorus.

136 Hyginus, bishop of Rome, assumes the title "pope."

166–174 Pope Soter moves Easter from Nisan 14 (Jewish calendar) to the following Sunday and opens rift with Eastern churches.

202–210 Persecution under Emperor Septimius Severus (reigned 193–211).

249–275 Persecutions of Christians by emperors Decius, Valerian, and Aurelian.

285 St Antony of Egypt, the first of the Desert Fathers, retires to the desert to become a hermit.

285 Roman Empire divided into Western and Eastern empires.

303 Death of St George; he later becomes patron saint of England and several other countries.

310 Armenia becomes first Christian state; persecution of Christians under Persian King Shapur II (reigned 310–379).

312 Constantine converts to Christianity before crucial battle of Milvian Bridge to win control of the Western empire.

325 First Council of Nicaea called by Constantine to come to agreement on the divine/human nature of Jesus.

380 Emperor Theodosius I proclaims Christianity the sole religion of the reunited Roman Empire.

397 Council at Carthage (the eighth in a series from 251 to 424) ratifies the canon of the New Testament as we know it now.

400 Jerome translates the Bible into Latin; this becomes known as the Vulgate (common language) Bible.

425 Augustine writes *The City of God*, one of the most influential texts in Christian history.

530 Cassiodorus, the Benedictine monk, encourages monks to copy manuscripts of the classics.

533 Mercurius is elected pope and takes the name John II, the first pope to change name upon election.

563 Columbanus founds the monastery of Iona off the coast of Scotland, which became the center of the Columban school.

600 Pope Gregory I, the last "Latin doctor," reforms the liturgy, promotes the doctrines of purgatory and penance, and popularizes the teachings of Pseudo-Dionysius.

636 Muslim Arabs capture Jerusalem; they allow Jews to return in 638.

680 At the Sixth Ecumenical Council in Constantinople, called by Emperor Constantine IV, the pope is declared the head of Christianity.

711–718 Muslim Arabs conquer southern Spain.

726–843 Controversy over icons in the Eastern Orthodox Church.

800 Pope Leo III crowns Charlemagne emperor and thereby establishes the Holy Roman Empire.

988 Vladimir of Kiev converts to Orthodox Christianity and commissions the creation of religious icons and architecture.

1000 Iceland decides at the national assembly (*Thing*) to become Christian.

1009 Caliph al-Hakim sacks the Church of the Holy Sepulchre, and the tomb believed to be Christ's is hacked down to bedrock.

1054 The patriarch of Constantinople and the pope in Rome issue mutual excommunications and begin the Great Schism.

1071 The Turks capture Jerusalem.

1073 Hildebrand becomes Pope Gregory VII and begins a monumental reform of the Church: Celibate clergy, papal supremacy, infallibility of the pope.

1095 Pope Urban II calls for a crusade against the Muslims after a request from the Byzantine emperor Alexius I Komnenos.

1098–1099 Crusaders capture Antioch and Jerusalem.

1187 Saladin recaptures Jerusalem.

1206 Francis of Assisi renounces wealth and adopts a life of absolute poverty.

c. 1207–1282 The mystic Mechthild of Magdeburg, one of the first woman writers in Christian history, describes her visions of God in *The Flowing Light of the Godhead.*

1210 The pope recognizes the Franciscan order of mendicant friars.

1215 The Dominican order of mendicant friars is established in Languedoc, France.

c. 1250 Hadewijch of Brabant, one of the earliest female Christian voices, writes stunning works of poetry and mystical visions.

c. 1263 Thomas Aquinas publishes the *Summa Contra Gentiles*, using Aristotelian philosophy to reshape theology.

1396 John Wyclif (also spelled Wycliffe) completes the first English translation of the Bible, but it is declared heretical.

1439 At the Council of Florence, a treaty is signed to unify the Roman Catholic Church and the Eastern Orthodox Church under Roman terms; it defines seven sacraments.

1453 Both Constantinople and the Eastern Orthodox Church fall to the Ottomans; Constantinople is renamed Istanbul.

1484 Pope Innocent VIII orders the persecution of magicians and witches.

1492 Granada falls to Christian troops; Jews and Muslims expelled from Spain.

1492 Christopher Columbus departs from Spain and crosses the Atlantic.

1498 Vasco da Gama arrives in India and finds the Thomas Christians, who have been there for over a millennium.

1516 Erasmus publishes a Greek text of the New Testament.

1517 Martin Luther nails his "95 Theses" to the church door at Wittenberg in Germany, arguing against the Catholic practice of selling indulgences.

1519 Ulrich Zwingli breaks with Rome and becomes leader of the Swiss reformation.

1526 Martin Luther publishes his German translation of the Bible.

1534 The *Act of Supremacy* recognizes King Henry VIII as Supreme Head of the Church of England.

1536 First edition of John Calvin's *Institutes of the Christian Religion* is published just before he settles in Geneva, Switzerland. It becomes a major theological statement of the Reformation.

1540 Ignatius of Loyola founds the Society of Jesus, or Jesuits.

1542 The missionary Frances Xavier arrives in Goa, India, and makes it his base for mission work as far east as Japan.

1547 Council of Trent meets in response to Protestant reformation and begins Counter-Reformation.

1582 Pope Gregory XIII introduces the Gregorian calendar.

1589 Moscow becomes a patriarchate.

1611 King James' Authorized Version of the Bible is published in English.

1618–48	Thirty Years' War between Roman Catholics and Protestants in the Holy Roman Empire.
1620	English Puritans aboard the *Mayflower* land at Plymouth Rock on Cape Cod, Massachusetts, North America.
1622	Pope Gregory VI establishes the Sacred Congregation for the Propagation of the Faith in order to better coordinate mission activity.
1641–1651	English Civil War (Puritan Revolution).
1708	Peter the Great fails to appoint a new patriarch to the patriarchate of Moscow.
1710	Society for the Propagation of the Gospel is formed: The first British missionary society.
1726	Beginning of the "Great Awakening" in North America.
1738	John Wesley begins the outdoor preaching that would later lead to the formation of Methodism.
1775–1783	American Wars of Independence.
1789–1799	French Revolution and attacks on Roman Catholic Church.
1791	The First Amendment to the American Constitution prohibits government promotion of religion, and government restriction of religious freedom.
1793	William Carey, the first English missionary, arrives in India.
1794	Herman of Alaska arrives on Kodiak Island and begins Russian missions to Alaska.
1848	Pius IX sends the "Epistle to the Easterns" to the Orthodox churches, requesting communion with Rome; in reply, the "Encyclical of the Eastern Patriarchs" points out theological differences and questions papal supremacy.
1869–1870	First Vatican Council asserts dogma of papal infallibility.
1905	French Parliament passes the bill separating Church and state.
1910	First World Missionary Conference (Protestant) held in Edinburgh.
1910	William Wade Harris establishes the first independent African church in Liberia.
1910–1915	The 12-volume *The Fundamentals,* published by the Bible Institute of Los Angeles, marks the beginning of Protestant fundamentalism.
1917	The Russian Revolution and restoration of the Russian patriarchate.
1929	Italy and the Holy See sign the Lateran Treaty, creating the Vatican and also re-establishing the sovereignty of the pope after 60 years of tension.
1948	World Council of Churches formed.
1962	Pope John XXIII convenes the first session of the Second Vatican Council.
1971	Liberation theology emerges in Latin American countries.
1978	Karol Wojtyla from Poland is elected as the first non-Italian pope (John Paul II) in over four centuries.
1988	Barbara C. Harris is first woman bishop of the Episcopal Church of the USA.
1997	World Council of Churches releases *Towards a Common Date for Easter.*
2005	John Paul II dies; his funeral is the largest gathering of world leaders in history.
2007	Reunification of the Russian Orthodox Church after 80 years of schism.

Following page: The Hill of Crosses is one of Lithuania's most symbolic religious pilgrimage sites. For centuries it has signified Lithuanian Catholics' peaceful resistance to oppression.

Below: This icon of "The Sleeping Virgin" is held at the Museum of the Orthodox Church in Finland. On May 17, 2007, Patriarch Alexy II of Moscow and All Russia and Metropolitan Laurus of the Russian Orthodox Church Outside of Russia signed the *Act of Canonical Communion.*

INRI

CHRISTIANITY AROUND THE WORLD TODAY

THE MIDDLE EAST AND AFRICA

Opposite top: St Catherine's Monastery, or Holy Monastery of the God-trodden Mt Sinai, in Egypt is the oldest continuously inhabited Christian monastery. It houses ancient manuscripts, books, and icons.

The churches of the Middle East and North Africa were responsible for the first expansion of Christianity, but a series of invasions—Arab, Mongol, Crusader, and Ottoman—greatly diminished their numbers. The twentieth century brought further decline: Millions of Christians were killed as the Ottoman Empire disintegrated. Palestinian Christians were ousted along with Palestinian Muslims when Israel was created. Christians emigrated due to violence in the region, repressive governments, and fear of Islamist groups. Fifteen percent of the population of the Middle East was Christian in 1953; today the figure is less than 2 percent.

Christians in Muslim majority states

Many Middle Eastern Christians belong to non-Western churches—Coptic, Maronite, Orthodox, Eastern Rite Catholic, Chaldean, and Assyrian. The largest group, the Copts, are estimated to make up between 8 and 16 percent of the Egyptian population.

Lebanon has the highest percentage of Christians (30 to 40 percent), with Maronites being the largest group. No census of religion has been taken there since 1932, when Christians were in the majority, for fear of upsetting the political agreement by which the president is always a Christian, the prime minister a Sunni Muslim, and the speaker of parliament a Shiite Muslim.

Right: These three boys were sent by their families to the Debre Damo monastery, an important monastic and educational center for the Ethiopian Orthodox Tewahedo Church. Females are forbidden from entering the monastery.

Opposite bottom: Russian pilgrims inside a rock-cut cave church at the foot of the Mount of Olives in Jerusalem. They have come to pray at the Tomb of the Virgin Mary.

Syria is 5 to 10 percent Christian. The secular Ba'ath Party provides political safety for Christians, who make up a disproportionately high percentage of its membership. Christians who leave Syria do so for economic reasons, or because of the generally repressive regime in power there. Christians entering Syria today are fleeing Iraq.

The Chaldean and Assyrian churches of Iraq were strong supporters of the Ba'ath Party. Under Saddam Hussein (ruled 1979–2003), many teachers, doctors, and engineers were Christians. However, with the economy devastated by two wars and the ensuing sanctions, those who could do so left Iraq. Professionals, among whom Christians were well represented, had the best chance of emigrating. After the US-led invasion in 2003, attacks on Christians rose sharply, and an estimated 40,000 to 60,000 fled.

About 9 percent of the Arabs in Israel are Christians. Israel allows freedom of worship, but Israeli Christians suffer from discrimination against Arabs.

In the West Bank and Gaza, Christian decline (5 percent of the population in 1970, less than 2.5 percent today) is due to violence, poverty, and low birth rates. Christian–Muslim relations are good, and many Christians have risen to high ranks in the Palestinian Authority. Jordan, which is 3 to 4 percent Christian, also enjoys peaceful Christian–Muslim relations.

Iran's Christians (less than 1 percent of the population) belong mainly to the Armenian and Assyrian churches. Iran's constitution guarantees such traditional Christian groups freedom of worship and representation in the parliament, but newcomers, notably evangelical Christians, do not share these rights.

Saudi Arabia and the other Gulf states prohibit public expression of non-Muslim religions. Presumably there are no Christian citizens, but among the large numbers of expatriate workers there are many Christians. Expatriates have freedom of worship in private; however, they may not attempt to convert Muslims.

Sub-Saharan Africa

With the exception of Ethiopia, sub-Saharan Christianity began with mission churches (Protestant and Catholic) established by Americans and Western Europeans between the late fifteenth and nineteenth centuries. Beginning in the late nineteenth century, these mission churches were joined by African independent churches (AICs), Christian churches which were founded by Africans and function independently of European or American oversight. Some AICs differed from mission churches only in having African leadership, while in others there was a strong admixture of African customs like polygamy and belief in witches. Today most AICs resemble American Pentecostal churches.

The Ethiopian Orthodox Tewahedo Church was part of Egypt's Coptic Orthodox Church until 1959, when it received its own patriarch. With over 40 million members, it is the largest Oriental Orthodox Church.

Sub-Saharan statistics

Christianity is the dominant religion in sub-Saharan Africa. Countries with the largest Christian majorities are Congo (50 percent Catholic, 38 percent Protestant), Democratic Republic of the Congo (55 percent Catholic, 30 percent Protestant), Equatorial Guinea (87 percent Catholic, 6 percent Protestant), Namibia (8 percent Catholic, 10 percent Lutheran, 71 percent other Protestant), and Rwanda (50 percent Catholic, 44 percent Protestant). Although Nigeria is only 40 percent Christian, it currently has the largest Christian population in Africa (over 60 million).

Phenomenal growth

The approximately 10 million Christians living in Africa in the year 1900 became about 380 million by the end of the century. In 2005, Africa still had fewer Christians than Europe (which was home to 26 percent of the world's total Christian population) or Latin America (24 percent) did. However, by 2025 Africa and Latin America are projected to be tied for first place, each with approximately 24 percent of the world's Christians. By 2050, Africa will have the largest number of Christians of any region in the world (29 percent of the global total).

EUROPEAN CHRISTIANITY

Above: Many thousands of pilgrims gathered at the Fatima sanctuary, Portugal, in 2007 for the ninetieth anniversary of the first apparition of the Virgin Mary to three shepherd children on May 13, 1917.

Europe's Christian landscape is interesting and varied. Orthodox Christians predominate in Eastern Europe: Greece is 98 percent Orthodox Christian, Romania 87 percent, Serbia 84 percent, Bulgaria 83 percent, Montenegro 74 percent, and Macedonia 65 percent.

There is a cluster of predominately Roman Catholic countries in the southern half of Europe, including Italy (88 percent), Luxembourg (87 percent), Croatia (85 percent), Portugal (84 percent), Slovenia (82 percent), Spain (76 percent), Belgium (75 percent), Austria (72 percent), Hungary (56 percent), France (54 percent), and Slovakia (49 percent).

The United Kingdom is 63 percent Protestant. Germany is 34 percent Protestant and 34 percent Catholic. The northernmost tier of countries is predominantly Lutheran (Denmark 95 percent, Sweden 87 percent, Norway 86 percent, Iceland 86 percent, and Finland 84 percent).

All of this is as it has been for centuries. However, other statistics seem to show an alarming change.

Puzzling statistics

Only about 20 percent of Europeans say that religion is very important in their lives. In several countries less than half of the population claims any religious affiliation. In most of Europe less than 20 percent attend church weekly. While 95 percent of Europeans were Christian in 1900, that measure had dropped to 75 percent by 1970.

Several hypotheses have been put forward to explain this decline. Secularization theory predicts that populations become less religious as modernization progresses. Since Europe modernized early, it is not surprising (according to

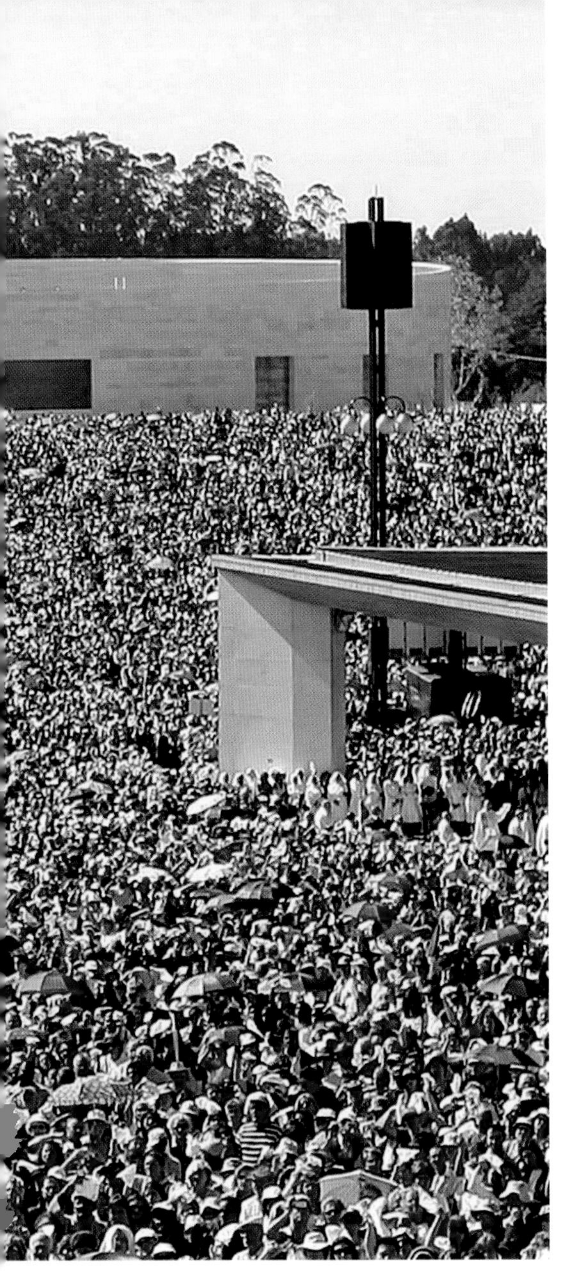

Above: The Urnes Stave Church in Norway was built around 1050 CE. The Vikings erected more than a thousand "Stav" churches—designed to resemble their ships—across Scandinavia.

Left: Polish Christians celebrate God's day (the Sabbath; *Sobadah* in Polish). Participants usually wear traditional costumes for this religious procession to a number of altars.

this theory) that it is one of the first areas to lose interest in religion. Another theory associates vibrant churches with religious competition and the availability of alternative religious choices for "consumers." This free-market model links the decline in religious participation to the persistence of national churches in Europe. A third hypothesis suggests that Europe has abandoned institutional religion in favor of a diffuse spirituality. All of these hypotheses assume that the death of European Christianity is imminent, but consider these two cases.

Even though church attendance has been low for generations in the Scandinavian countries, Lutheran pastors and bishops continue to play a significant public role in cultural and political affairs. They openly criticize proposed government policies in the media, and Scandinavian governments have adopted many of their proposals. In a sense, the media offers a larger pulpit than even a mega-church can provide.

In the colonial period in America, no more that 10 to 20 percent of colonists belonged to a church. Even in New England only 20 percent of the population had a religious affiliation in 1776. Yet the USA consistently produced religious revivals and new forms of Christianity in the following centuries. It is far too soon to say what the statistics for Europe really mean.

New immigrants

Europe is home to increasing numbers of Muslim immigrants from North Africa and the Middle East, in some countries giving rise to alarmist talk of an "Islamic invasion." Europe's Muslim population may rise to 15 to 20 percent by 2050. At the same time, however, Europe is experiencing an influx of Christian immigrants from Asia and Africa. Neither immigrant population is expected to cause a noticeable change in the percentages who identify themselves as Christians. In 2005, 76 percent of Europe's population was Christian. Projections indicate that 77 percent of Europeans will be Christian in 2025, and that the figure will be 76 percent in 2050.

CHRISTIANITY IN ASIA

Right: A priest blesses a Christian fisherman and his boat at Amakusa, Japan. The Blessing of the Fleet ritual is performed in many countries around the world to pray for a safe and bountiful fishing season.

As in no other region of the world, Asian Christianity finds itself in the midst of a large number of major religions such as Islam, Hinduism, Buddhism, smaller religions like Daoism, Sikhism, and Jainism, and local collections of indigenous beliefs. Currently Asia is 9 percent Christian; that is projected to increase to 11 percent by 2025. If the projection holds, Asia would then be home to 19 percent of all the Christians in the world.

Few Christian majorities

The largest concentrations of Christians are found in the Philippines (87 percent Christian), South Korea (26.3 percent), and Indonesia (8.7 percent). In these three countries missions have been able to work for long periods of time with relatively little opposition.

Countries with smaller but still significant groups of Christians include Singapore (14.6 percent), Brunei (10 percent), Hong Kong as a special administrative area within China (10 percent), Malaysia (9.1 percent), Vietnam (7.2 percent), Sri Lanka (6.2 percent), Taiwan (4.5 percent), and India (2.3 percent). Even though Christianity is clearly a minority religion in India, the size of the population means that there are more Christians here (approximately 25 million) than in many other countries.

In some Asian countries, resistance to missions is exceptionally strong, and Christians remain small minorities. In Afghanistan, Bangladesh, Cambodia, and Thailand they are less than 1 percent; in Laos and Pakistan less than 2 percent; in Japan and Mongolia they make up 2 percent of the population; and Burma is 4 percent Christian.

China is perhaps the most interesting Asian country in terms of Christianity. Officially 3 to 4 percent of China is Christian, but that statistic is notoriously unreliable due to the high number of "underground" churches. These churches are not officially sanctioned by the government but, at least for now, they are permitted to exist and grow.

Below: A Pakistani Christian on Easter Sunday. Christians are a persecuted minority in Pakistan—many live in an enclave in Gojra city—and their numbers are dwindling.

Above: In 1964, Pope Paul VI attended the 38th International Eucharistic Congress in Mumbai, India. Most Indian Christians live on the Malabar coast, in what is now the state of Kerala.

Not just in China, but in any nation of the world in which Christians are seen as culturally foreign and "outside the mainstream"—whether that mainstream is Buddhist, Muslim, or communist—Christians are vulnerable to discrimination or even persecution.

Changing landscape

Until the last two decades the Philippines (which is mainly Catholic) as well as South Korea and Indonesia (both mainly Protestant) have been the main strengths of Asian Christianity, largely due to successful missionary work in the eighteenth and nineteenth centuries. The Philippines had been the center for Spanish interests in the Pacific since the sixteenth century; with them they brought Catholicism. In Indonesia the Dutch ensured Protestantism became the dominant form of Christianity, while in South Korea the Presbyterians were by far the most successful.

However, the situation is changing rapidly, especially in China. Although some modern Chinese Christian families go back at least five generations, the numbers of Chinese Christians are now expanding rapidly. So-called "underground" churches spring up daily. The increasing number of underground seminaries struggle to keep up with the demand for training of clergy and theological study. Estimates put the number of Christians in China at anywhere between 20 and 100 million; census statistics are not the most reliable guide, since many will not list Christianity as their religion. A more reliable indicator may be sales records, which show a strong demand for Christian printed materials. A press will publish 10,000 copies of a translation of a work on theology or the Bible and it will sell out in just four or five months.

POST-SOVIET RELIGION

Right: Each year, over half a million pilgrims visit Our Lady Gate of Dawn sanctuary in Vilnius, Lithuania, to view the portrait of the Blessed Virgin Mary of Ausros Vartai.

At its height, the Union of Soviet Socialist Republics (USSR) covered one-sixth of the earth's land surface. Communist opposition to religion was manifested in the seizure of churches and monasteries, which were destroyed or converted to non-religious uses. Religious organizations lacked access to schools, media, book publishing, and workplaces. Some churches were permitted to remain open, but attendance could impede career advancement.

Religion's return

After the USSR collapsed in 1991, in most cases the people of the former Soviet republics returned to their traditional religion. Such was the case in Armenia and Georgia, countries with unique forms of Christianity that originated in the fourth century. Moldova and Belarus returned to their Orthodox roots, as did Russia and Ukraine, although Russia remains about 50 percent atheist, and Ukraine about 20 percent. Albania, the only member of the USSR to declare an officially atheist state, while now allowing freedom of religion is still 70 per cent atheist. Azerbaijan, Kazakhstan, Turkmenistan, Uzbekistan, Tajikistan, and Kyrgyzstan experienced Islamic revivals.

Lithuania is once again openly Roman Catholic. The Evangelical Lutheran Church (ELC) returned to prominence in Estonia and Latvia, but the Soviet era lingers in Estonia, where 72 percent are religiously unaffiliated and the ELC, though the largest religious organization, claims only 14 percent of the population.

Opposite: The colorful spire of the Church of the Resurrection of Jesus Christ. Citizens of St Petersburg call it the Church of the Savior on the Blood because it is sited where Alexander II was fatally wounded in 1881.

Religion and government

In an effort to reinvigorate national identities submerged during the Soviet era, many countries extended special honors and privileges to the faith(s) most central to their cultural identities. This benefited traditional, established churches, and hindered newly arrived denominations and sects. While the constitutions of the fifteen former Soviet republics state that they guarantee religious freedom, and equality of religions before the law, this is in tension with the special importance given to the national Orthodox churches and other "traditional religions."

Governments may require religious bodies to register in order to receive benefits and privileges such as state support and access to local and national officials. It is more difficult for a "non-traditional" or "foreign" religion to be registered. An unregistered religion may still be allowed to operate, but it misses out on the benefits of registration.

Islam has not received special governmental privileges in the Central Asian republics, despite these countries' Muslim heritage. The emphasis has been on the secular nature of the new republics. The goal was to avoid attempts to create Islamic states, and this has helped to create a more open and plural religious environment, benefiting Orthodox Christians and other minorities.

Below: Ukrainian Orthodox Church followers at the celebration of the 1,020th anniversary of Kievan Rus' Christianization in 988. They are awaiting the arrival of Alexy II, Patriarch of Moscow and All Russia.

Restrictions on religion

In the late 1990s, the former Soviet republics began to pass laws that restricted all religions, but especially Islam and "foreign" religions. The concerns that gave rise to these laws include fear of radical Islamic groups; fear that "foreign" religions might destabilize culture and society; and fear of psychologically damaging groups that demand total authority over the lives of their members ("cults"). The restrictions that have been imposed in one or more countries include: Pre-screening sermons, banning missionaries, censorship of religious literature, outlawing religious political parties, and granting governments the right to make clerical appointments. Those most impacted by the new laws (beyond specific target groups) are Muslims, Protestants, and such Christian sects as the Jehovah's Witnesses and the Church of Jesus Christ of Latter-day Saints (Mormons).

RELIGIOUS CHANGE IN LATIN AMERICA

Below: Mandolin players on a pilgrimage to the shrine of Our Lady of Guadalupe, patron saint of Mexico. Each year, millions of worshippers visit this Catholic shrine in Mexico City.

Latin American Christianity is in ferment, with a dwindling Catholic majority and a vigorous Protestant minority. At stake is a region that is projected to tie with Africa by the year 2025 for the world's largest Christian population (24 percent of the global total).

Shake-up in the Catholic Church

For centuries, the Catholic Church in Latin America was an authoritarian religious body that was operating in an authoritarian sociopolitical setting. It shocked both politicians and bishops when, in the 1970s, liberation theologians started to address the poverty of the people with a praxis that worked from the bottom up instead of from the top down. Laypeople met in "base communities" to read the Bible and apply it to their lives; liberation clergy saw serving the poor as central to their vocation. However, Pope John Paul II, citing worries about Marxist influences, dismantled liberation theology in the 1980s and early 1990s. Latin American governments had begun to suspect

anyone associated with liberation theology, or even with Catholicism, of being a political revolutionary.

Pentecostal explosion

The silencing of Catholic liberation theology was deafening; spiritual leadership was desperately needed in the face of the social and economic changes that were occurring. But another religious revolution was already underway. Protestants, mainly Pentecostals, were growing at an astonishing rate. Growth has recently leveled off, but the gains are impressive. El Salvador, Guatemala, and Honduras are about one-third—and other Central American countries are somewhere either side of one-fifth—Protestant. Protestants make up between 4 and 16 percent of the populations of most South American countries. Mexico is 88 percent Catholic and 6 percent Protestant.

Can Pentecostals bring about positive change?

Unlike the Catholic churches, the Pentecostal churches were not suspected of harboring political revolutionaries. They intended to change society by a different route. Lives were turned around, and former social outcasts began to exercise leadership and responsibility.

While there is considerable evidence that Pentecostalism supports personal transformation, Bolivian lawyer and International Coordinator for the Rutherford Institute, Pedro C. Moreno, himself a Pentecostal, worries that the Pentecostal explosion might not bring about desperately needed economic and social changes. Moreno believes Pentecostals draw too sharp a line between the religious and the secular, with the result that family, work, and social life are deprived of any religious meaning. In addition, the emphasis on the closeness of the Second Coming of Jesus Christ leads to a mentality in which politics, economics, engineering, and law seem unimportant. Moreno is afraid that, with attitudes like these, Latin American Pentecostals are not well positioned to change society. However, James W. Dow, Professor Emeritus of Anthropology at Oakland University, argues that Protestantism facilitates the removal of barriers to the market economy, enabling peasants to become mini-capitalists.

Liberation theology regroups

Avoiding public attention, liberation theologians continue their work. Unlike Dow's Protestant vision, their hope for Latin America does not involve more capitalism, which they link with consumerism and materialism. What these theologians seek is a society where the life and needs of people come before profits and possessions. What has changed since the 1970s and 1980s is the means to the end: Today's liberation theologians do not want a socialist state, but rather more grassroots organizing.

Above: A cross on the shores of Lake Atitlan in Santa Catarina Palopo, Guatemala. The Central American Mission took Protestantism to Guatemala in the early twentieth century.

Below: A Honduran woman and her elaborate home altar. Pentecostal movements in Central America spread from El Salvador to Honduras and Guatemala, then to Nicaragua.

CANADA AND THE UNITED STATES

Both the Church of England and religious dissenters were well represented in the early days of the American colonies. But many Anglicans fled north to Canada in the wake of the War of Independence (1775–1783), strengthening the Anglican presence there and the proportion of dissenters in America.

Canada

The population of Canada is 77 percent Christian (43.2 percent Catholic, 29.2 percent Protestant), 6.8 percent religious minorities, and 16.2 percent unaffiliated. The largest Protestant denominations are the United Church of Canada (an amalgam of Methodist, Congregationalist, Evangelical Brethren, Presbyterian, and other Protestant denominations; 10 percent of the Canadian population) and the Anglican Church (6.9 percent).

The Catholic, United, and Anglican churches are not, technically speaking, established churches; however, they do form the unofficial religious establishment. Alliances between these three churches and the state discourage religious innovation and experimentation in Canada, and therefore encourage religious stability.

The ecumenical nature of the United Church represents a degree of Protestant unity that is not found in the USA. The reason may be, as Seymour Martin Lipset argued in *Continental Divide*, that US values are highly individualistic and competitive by comparison with the more corporatist and cooperative values of Canada.

In 1971, Canadian Catholics outnumbered Protestants for the first time (46 percent versus 44 percent). Today, the difference is 14 percentage points. The loss of the Protestant majority is the result of changes in immigration patterns, however, not competition between the churches, for Catholics have been the largest faith group within each new wave of immigrants since the 1960s.

Immigration patterns also contributed to the growth in those reporting no religious affiliation (less than 1 percent prior to 1971, now 16.2 percent). One-fifth of immigrants in recent decades have been unaffiliated; many are from the People's Republic of China, Hong Kong, and Taiwan.

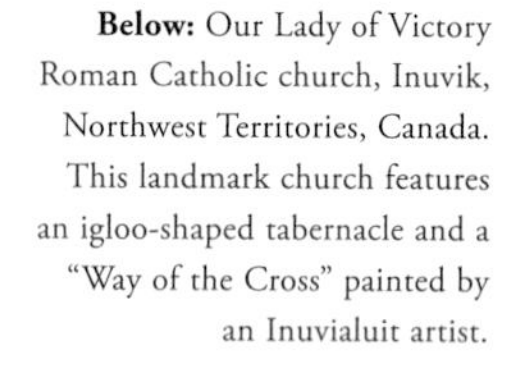

Below: Our Lady of Victory Roman Catholic church, Inuvik, Northwest Territories, Canada. This landmark church features an igloo-shaped tabernacle and a "Way of the Cross" painted by an Inuvialuit artist.

The United States

The US population is 79 percent Christian, divided among Protestants (50 percent), Roman Catholics (24 percent), and others (5 percent). The largest Protestant denominations are Baptist (16.3 percent)—quintessential dissenters—and Methodist (6.8 percent). On surveys designed to measure fundamentalism, Americans score higher than any other Western nation.

Compared to Canada, the USA has lower percentages of Catholics (24 percent versus 43.2 percent) and Anglicans (1.7 percent versus 7 percent), higher percentages of evangelicals (26 percent versus 7 percent) and fundamentalists, a higher percentage of Baptists (16.3 percent versus 2.4 percent), and a similar percentage of unaffiliated persons (16 percent versus 16.2 percent).

American Protestant Christians are divided among evangelical churches (26.3 percent of the total population), mainline churches (18.1 percent), and historically African-American churches (6.9 percent). Unlike the Canadian Protestant churches, these three groups display substantial ideological differences.

The US religious scene is characterized by great fluidity; people are constantly moving in and out of all the religious options. For example, the Catholic Church has claimed 25 percent of the population for the past several decades, giving the illusion of stability. In reality, this church has lost more members than any other. The difference is made up by the large percentage of Catholics among recent immigrants (46 percent versus 24 percent Protestant).

The unaffiliated group is growing faster than any other option, but it also has one of the lowest retention rates. More than half the people who were unaffiliated with any religion as a child join a religion as an adult.

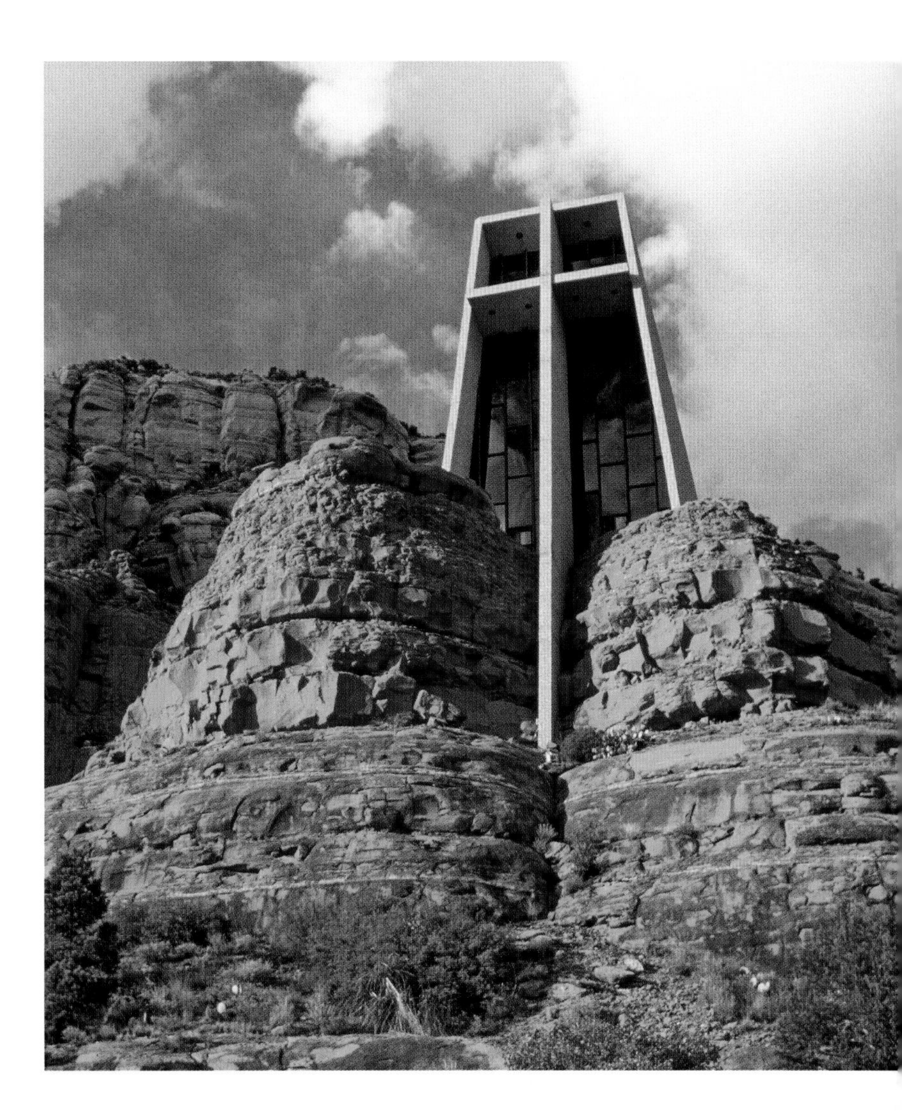

Above: The Chapel of the Holy Cross near Sedona, Arizona, USA, was built by a disciple of American architect Frank Lloyd Wright. It serves the Roman Catholic diocese of Phoenix.

Left: In the US today, many who grew up in non-religious households have chosen to become Christians. Numerous adult baptisms are performed across the country each year.

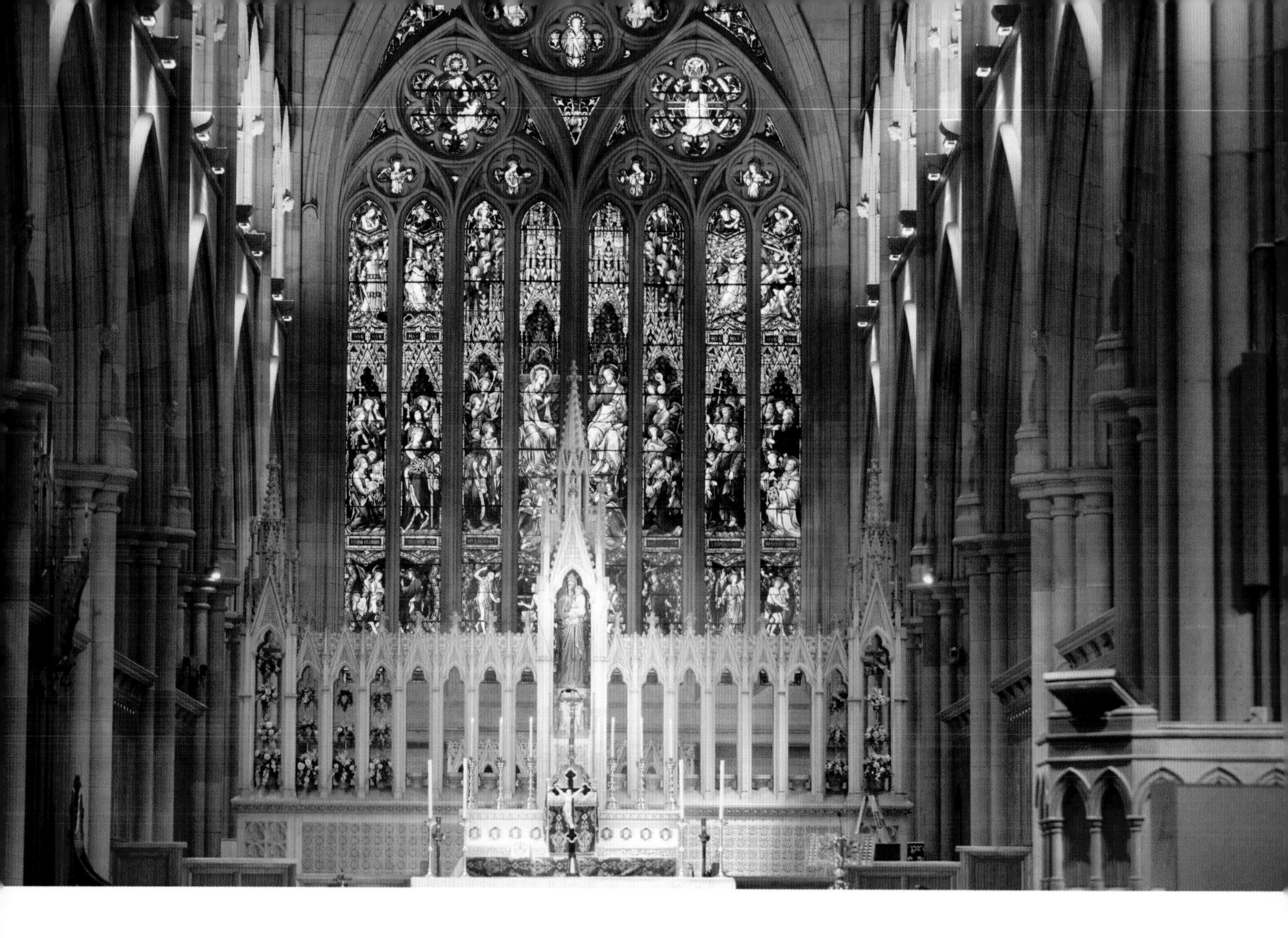

CHRISTIANITY ACROSS OCEANIA

Above: Interior of St Mary's Cathedral, the spiritual home for Catholics in Sydney. Built on the site of the first Catholic chapel in Australia, this cathedral replaces the one destroyed by fire in 1865.

Oceania (Australia, New Zealand, and the Pacific Islands) has by far the smallest population of any of the earth's regions, only a little over 1 percent of the global total. Around 80 percent of Oceania's population is Christian, but it is home to only 1 percent of the world's Christians.

Christian diversity in the Pacific

At the census of 2006, 63 percent of Australians identified themselves as Christian (though many of these are nominal; that is, non-active members of the church) and 30 percent reported that they were not affiliated with any religion. The census results showed that 25.8 percent indicated they were Catholic, 18.7 percent Anglican, 5.7 percent Uniting Church, 3 percent Presbyterian and Reformed, 2.7 percent Eastern Orthodox, and 7.9 percent of Australians chose the "other Christian" category.

In New Zealand, Protestants outnumber Catholics. The country's population is 14.9 percent Anglican, 12.4 percent Catholic, 10.9 percent Presbyterian, 2.9 percent Methodist, 1.7 percent Pentecostal, 1.3 percent Baptist, and 9.4 percent belong to the category "other Christians." The most popular choice was "unaffiliated"; 53 percent of New Zealanders do not identify with any religion.

There is a great diversity of churches on the Pacific Islands, most of which are Protestant. The Island nations range from almost completely Roman Catholic—such as Guam (85 percent)—to the Protestant monopoly of the Congregational Church of Tuvalu (97 percent). Other significant Protestant churches include Tokelau Congregational Christian Church (70 percent), Cook Islands Christian Church (55.9 percent), Nauru Congregational Church (35.4 percent), the Samoan Congregational Church (34.8 percent), and Methodist Church of Fiji (34.6 percent). In many cases Seventh-Day Adventists attract significant numbers: Solomon Islands (11.2 percent), Vanuatu (10.8 percent), Papua New Guinea (10 percent), Cook Islands (7.9 percent), Fiji (3.9 percent), and Tuvalu (1.4 percent).

Two examples illustrate the diversity of Christianity in the Pacific. Papua New Guinea is 27 percent Catholic, 19.5 percent evangelical Lutheran, 11.5 percent United Church, 10 percent Seventh-Day Adventist, 8.6 percent Pentecostal, 5.2 percent Evangelical Alliance, 3.2 percent Anglican, 2.5 percent Baptist, and 8.9 percent belong to a myriad other Protestant churches. The Solomon Islands report the following breakdown: Church of Melanesia (32.8 percent), Catholic (19 percent), South Seas Evangelical (17 percent), Seventh-Day Adventist (11.2 percent), United Church

Left: Sapapali'i in Western Samoa is the historic birthplace of Christianity for both Western Samoa and American Samoa. Today the Church is known as the Ekalesia Fa'apotopotoga Kerisiano o Samoa (EFKS).

Below: Mennonites, who practice a version of Anabaptism, are a minority Christian group in New Zealand. They follow a simple, pious way of life.

(10.3 percent), Christian Fellowship Church (2.4 percent), and other smaller Protestant groups (4.4 percent).

Growth in small, new churches

Australia is evenly divided between Catholics and Protestants. Over half of those who identify as Christian do not participate in the institutional life of their church. The most substantial growth is in newer Christian movements, such as the many Pentecostal and Charismatic churches.

In New Zealand, Anglican, Presbyterian, Congregational, and Reformed Churches have all declined in the last decade. Only the Catholics and Methodists have seen small increases. But the smaller Christian groups like Eastern Orthodoxy, as well as Pentecostal and Evangelical churches, have experienced relatively substantial gains (almost 38 percent among Orthodox Christians, mainly through immigration).

On the Pacific Islands, religious beliefs are very important to individuals and to entire societies. The dominance of one church or another—Catholic in Kiribati, Methodist in Fiji, Presbyterian in Vanuatu—is a result of significant success by missionaries. Above all, they have an extraordinary variety of Christian churches, including new churches, successes by the Mormons and Seventh-Day Adventists, and fascinating groups such as Bukot nan Jesus in the Marshall Islands.

"McChristianity"

Some Pacific Islanders view fundamentalist or Pentecostal churches of US origin as Trojan horses for neo-liberalism and neo-conservatism. It has been said that their emphasis on financial contributions exacerbates poverty, and their use of the media and mega-churches to deliver their message undercuts local Christian communities. The term "McChristianity" suggests these churches, like McDonalds, have spread their unhealthy fare around the world.

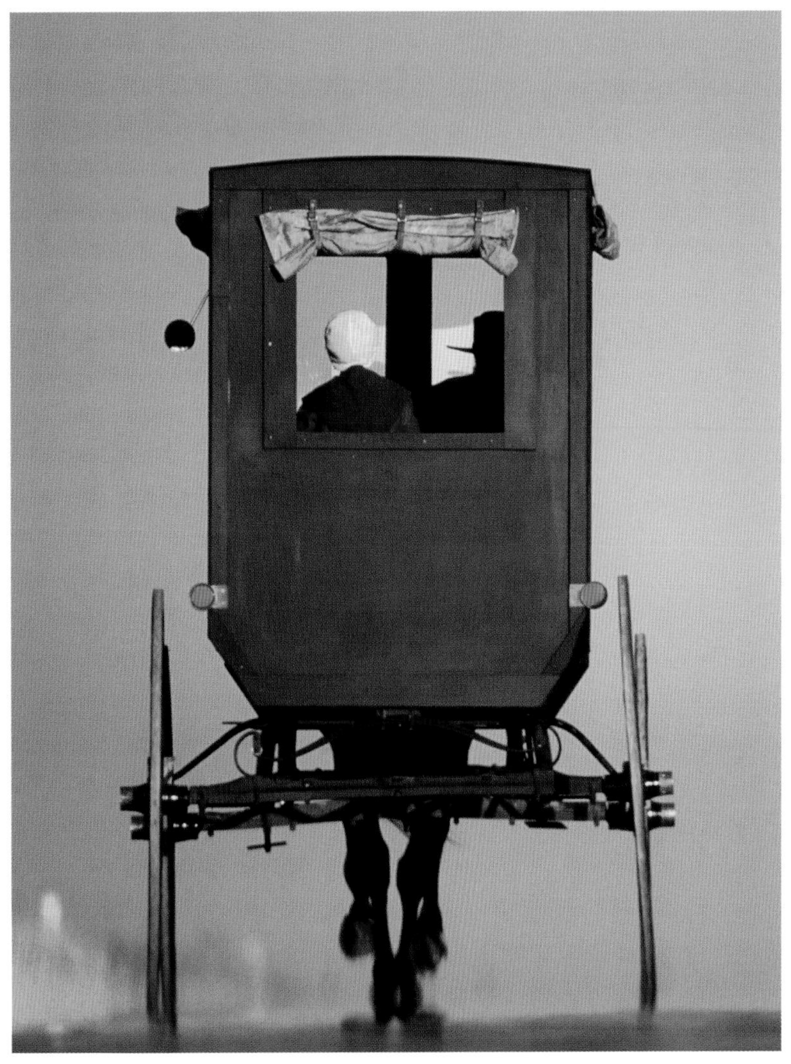

In the beginning

c. 4 BCE Birth of Jesus.

c. 4 BCE The Star of Bethlehem guides the three wise men (magi) from the east in their search for the newborn "king of the Jews" (Matthew 2:1–2). When they find the baby, the magi offer him gifts of gold, frankincense, and myrrh.

c. 4 BCE According to Luke's Gospel (2:1–6), Joseph and his heavily pregnant wife, Mary, travel from Nazareth to Bethlehem to take part in a census. Unable to find accommodation, Mary gives birth to Jesus in a manger.

0–99 CE

c. 26 CE	John the Baptist begins his missionary work.
c. 26–36	Pontius Pilate is governor of Judea.
c. 27	Jesus begins his ministry.
c. 29	John the Baptist killed by Herod Antipas in Tiberius.
c. 30	Jesus is crucified.
c. 30–70	Period of oral tradition among early Christians.
c. 36	The name "Christian" is first used in Antioch.
c. 46–49	First missionary journey of Paul and Barnabas spreads the word of Christianity.
c. 46–64	First documents of Christianity written: The letters of Paul.
c. 47	Thomas establishes the Church of the East in Persia.
c. 50	The Council of Jerusalem deals with the question of Jewish and non-Jewish Christians.
c. 50–53	Paul's second missionary journey to Asia Minor and Greece after split with Barnabas.
c. 52	Possible founding of Thomas Christians of India by Thomas.
c. 53–57	Paul's third missionary journey to Asia Minor and Greece.
c. 59–60	Paul arrested and requests to go to Rome.
62	James the Just, brother of Jesus, stoned to death in Jerusalem for breaking the Jewish law.
63	Traditional date for missionary journey of Joseph of Arimathea (who bore the cross of Jesus) to Glastonbury, England.
63–107	Simeon is leader and bishop of Jerusalem Church after James the Just.
64–68	Persecution of Christians in Rome under Nero; deaths of Paul and Peter.
66–73	Great Jewish Revolt; Romans lay siege to Jerusalem and destroy Temple built by King Herod.
c. 67–78	Linus is bishop of Rome.
c. 69–107	Ignatius is bishop of Antioch.
c. 70	First Gospel, by Mark, written.
71	Traditional date for foundation of Christianity in Egypt by Mark the Apostle.
75–90	Gospel of Luke and Acts written.
80–90	Gospel of Matthew written.
90–100	Gospel of John written. The earliest known fragment of the Gospel dates from 117 CE.
93	Emperor Domitian orders persecution of Christians.

c. 26 CE St John the Baptist preaching in the desert. Part of his mission was to encourage Jews, including Jesus, to confess their sins and allow him to baptize them in the River Jordan.

c. 30 CE *Father Forgive Them*, by Gustave Dore, illustrates Christ's crucifixion. The artwork's title refers to Jesus' defence of his killers: "Father, forgive them: for they do not know what they are doing." (Luke 23:34)

c. 46–57 CE Over a period of 12 years, St Paul leads three evangelical missions. He establishes churches in numerous places, including Antioch on the Orontes in Syria.

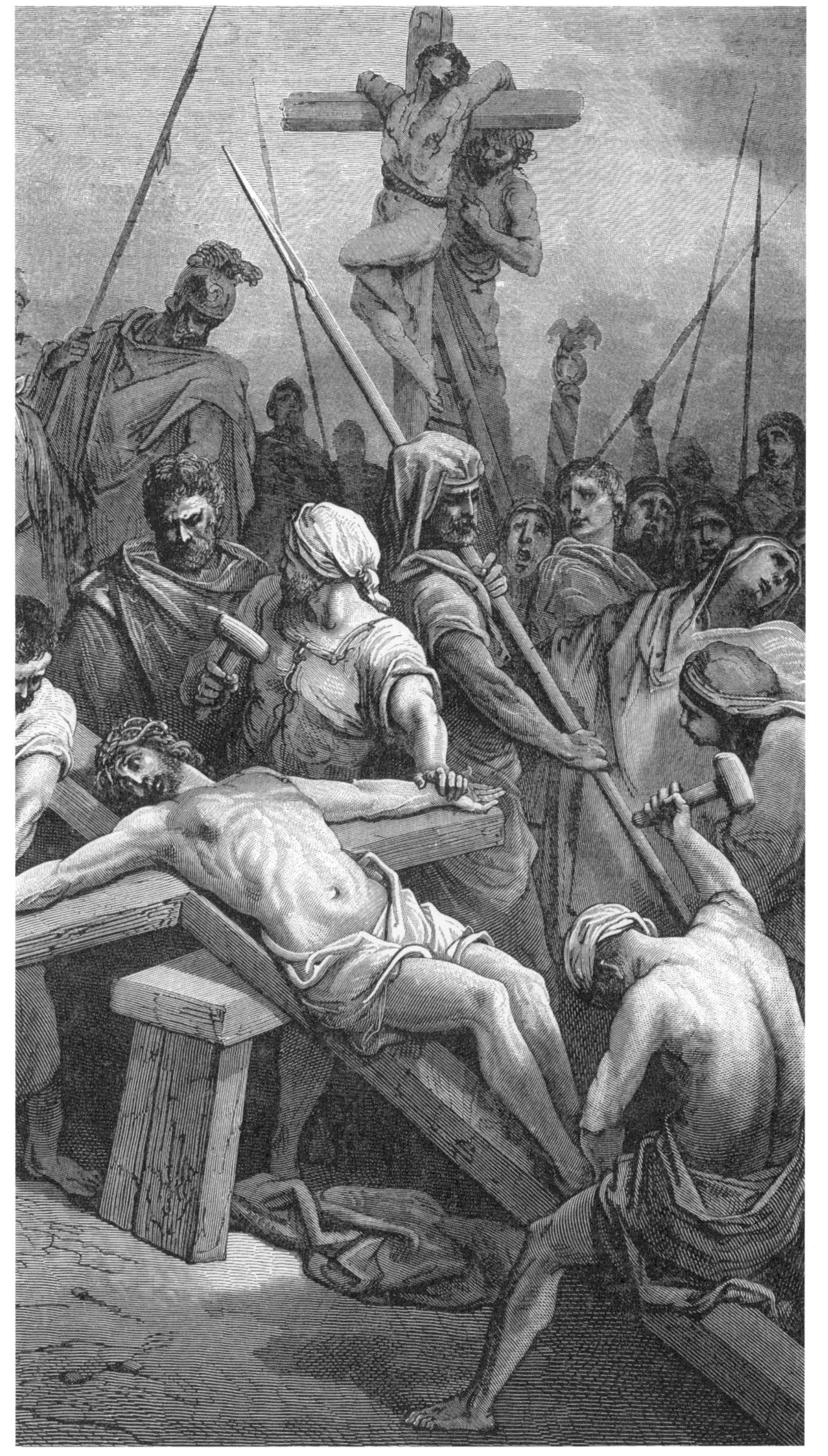

c. 178 CE Irenaeus is appointed bishop of Lyon. In this role he was pastor, missionary, and writer. Most of his writings criticized the heresy of Gnosticism, including his famous *Against Heresies*.

177–180 CE Roman Emperor Marcus Aurelius, a Stoic, persecutes Christians. During this time Stoic philosophers and Christian teachers were rivals for the role of spiritual guide to the people.

100–199 CE

c. 100 Epistle of Barnabas is written; the beginning of Christian literature that would not be included in the canon.

100–150 Remaining documents of the New Testament written.

100–150 Non-canonical Christian documents written and used in churches: Secret Book (Apocryphon) of James; Gospel of Mary Magdalene; Infancy Gospels of Thomas and James; Secret Gospel of Mark; Gospel of the Egyptians; Apocalypse of Peter.

107 Ignatius, third bishop of Antioch, is the first to refer to Christians as "Catholic" and advocates Sunday for worship. He is fed to lions in Rome.

108–124 Persecution of Christians under Emperor Trajan, continuing under Emperor Hadrian.

125 Date of Papyrus 52: Oldest extant fragment of the New Testament. Contains John 18:31–33, 37–38.

125–136 Bishop Telesphorus of Rome martyred.

130 Beginning of writings by Christian Apologists against non-Christian religions: Justin Martyr, Athenagoras, Aristides, Theophilus of Antioch, Tatian, Quadratus, Melito of Sardis, Apollinaris of Hierapolis.

130 Bishop Papias of Hierapolis (Asia Minor) writes *Expositions of the Sayings of the Lord*, widely quoted at the time but now lost.

132–135 The final Jewish revolt against Rome, led by Bar Kokhba, crushed; Jerusalem renamed Aelia Capitolina.

135 Christmas instituted as a Feast day by Bishop Telesphorus.

136 Hyginus, bishop of Rome, assumes the title "pope."

140 Letters of Marcion (one of the first "heretics") outline a significantly smaller canon without the Old Testament; it includes an edited Gospel of Luke and ten letters of Paul.

c. 150 Valentinius (Valentinus), one of the most famous Christian Gnostics, narrowly loses election for pope.

c. 150 Tatian produces the Diatessaron, a "harmony" of the four Gospels.

155 Anicetus is the first pope to come from Syria.

156 Beginning of the Montanist movement under Montanus in Hierapolis (Asia Minor); Montanus declared a heretic by Anicetus.

160 Polycarp, bishop of Smyrna, martyred at 86 years of age.

166–174 Pope Soter moves Easter from Nisan 14 (Jewish calendar) to the following Sunday and opens rift with Eastern churches.

170 Debates over different versions of the Gospels. Letters of Irenaeus, future bishop of Lyons, refer to versions of the Gospels that are later described as "Western."

170 Letters of Dionysius, bishop of Corinth, claim Christians were altering his own letters just as they had altered the Gospels. Controversy begins over different versions of Gospels.

177–180 Persecution under Emperor Marcus Aurelius.

188–231 Demitrius is bishop of Alexandria.

185 Muratorian canon provides the first list of New Testament books. It excludes Hebrews, James, 1–2 Peter, and 3 John, but includes Wisdom of Solomon and Apocalypse of Peter.

189–198 Pope Victor I is the first Latin pope; he excommunicates Eastern churches for continuing to observe Easter on Nisan 14.

190 Christian council held to determine "official" date of Easter; the Quartodeciman controversy remains unresolved.

190 Pantaenus founds the Coptic Catechetical School at Alexandria.

200–299 CE

200 Bishop of Antioch notes Gospel of Peter being used in Cilicia (southern Turkey).

202–210 Persecution under Emperor Septimius Severus.

c. 205 Origen, a major early theologian, reportedly castrates himself as a young man in Alexandria.

206 King Abgar IX of Edessa converts to Christianity.

c. 210 Hippolytus, one of the Church's great theologians and last Greek-speaking bishop in Rome, writes *Refutation of All Heresies* and *Apostolic Tradition*.

215 Conversion of Tertullian of Carthage to Montanism.

217–236 Hippolytus elected the first of many rival popes ("antipopes") against Zephyrinus, whom he accuses of heresy and lax discipline.

220 Bishop Clement of Alexandria makes use of what is called an "Alexandrian" textual tradition of the New Testament.

223 Tertullian makes use of a "Western" textual tradition of the New Testament.

227 Origen of Alexandria begins his *Commentary on Genesis*, and completes his work on *First Principles*.

230 Christian council in which Demetrius, bishop of Alexandria, condemns Origen.

235–238 Emperor Maximinus Thrax institutes persecution, exiles the feuding Pope Pontian and Antipope Hippolytus to Sardinia, where they soon die.

c. 240 Origen writes *Hexapla* (comparison of six different Hebrew and Greek versions of the Old Testament).

c. 246 Paul of Thebes becomes first Christian hermit in Egypt.

248 Origen writes in *Against Celsus* that God had ordained the Roman Empire.

248–264 Dionysius is bishop of Alexandria.

249–275 Persecutions of Christians by emperors Decius, Valerian, and Aurelian.

251–258 Novatian is antipope; he states that forgiveness for sins is not granted after baptism.

254–257 Pope Steven I involved in major schism concerning the rebaptizing of heretics and apostates.

258 Letters of Cyprian, bishop of Carthage, make use of the "Western" textual tradition of the New Testament.

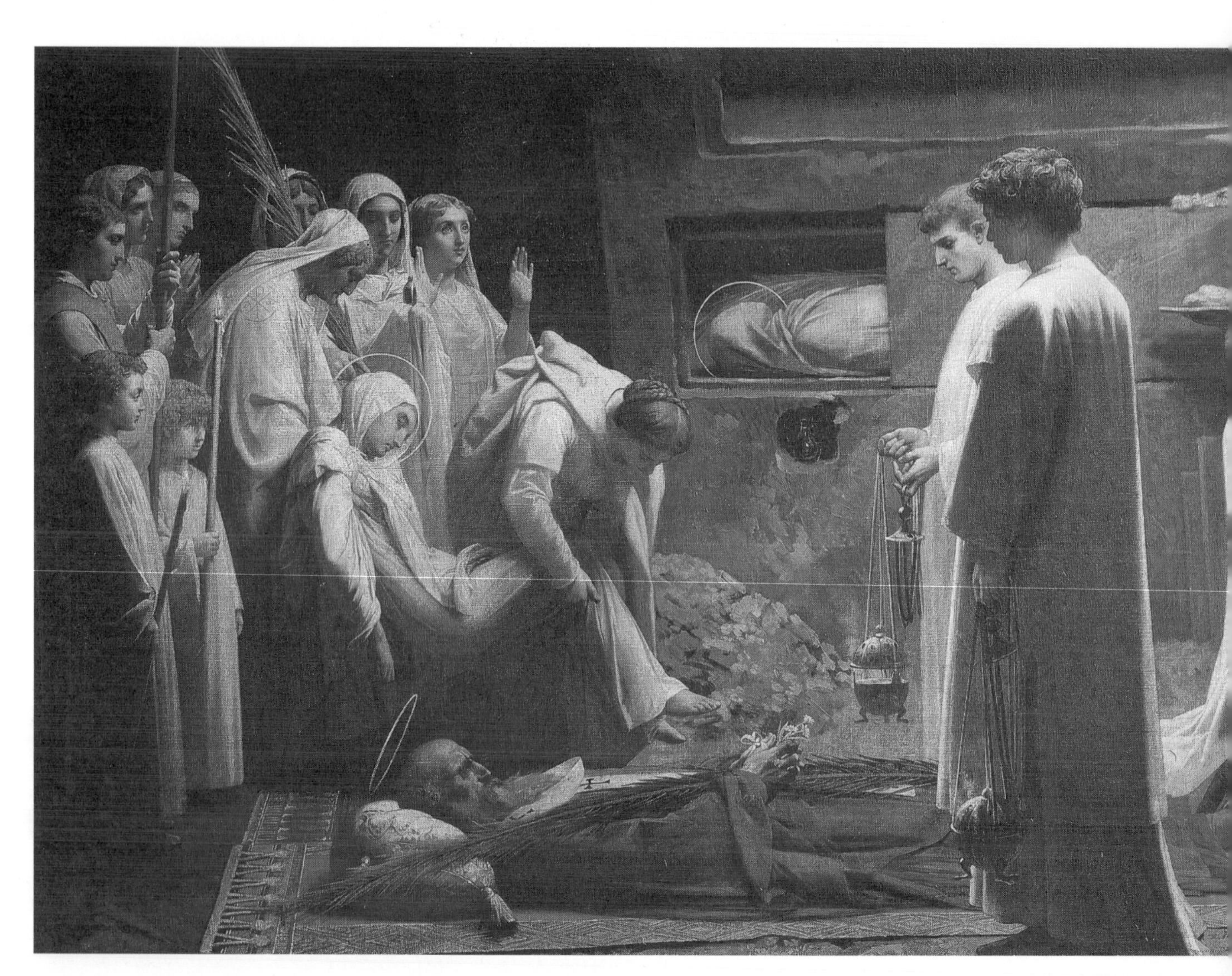

260	Paul of Samosata, bishop of Antioch, begins preaching against the divinity of Christ.
264	Paul of Samosata deposed as bishop of Antioch.
264–268	Synod in Rome condemns Paul of Samosata's position that Jesus only became divine when he was baptized ("Adoptionism").
265	*Homoousios* ("of one substance") first used to describe relation between the persons of the Trinity.
275–283	Eutychian is pope; he decrees that only beans and grapes be blessed at Eucharist.
276	Mani, founder of Manichaeanism, is crucified in Persia.
285	St Antony of Egypt, the first of the Desert Fathers, retires to the desert to become a hermit.
285	Roman Empire divided into Western and Eastern empires.
296–304	Marcellinus is pope; he lapses and offers pagan sacrifices for Diocletian during persecution.

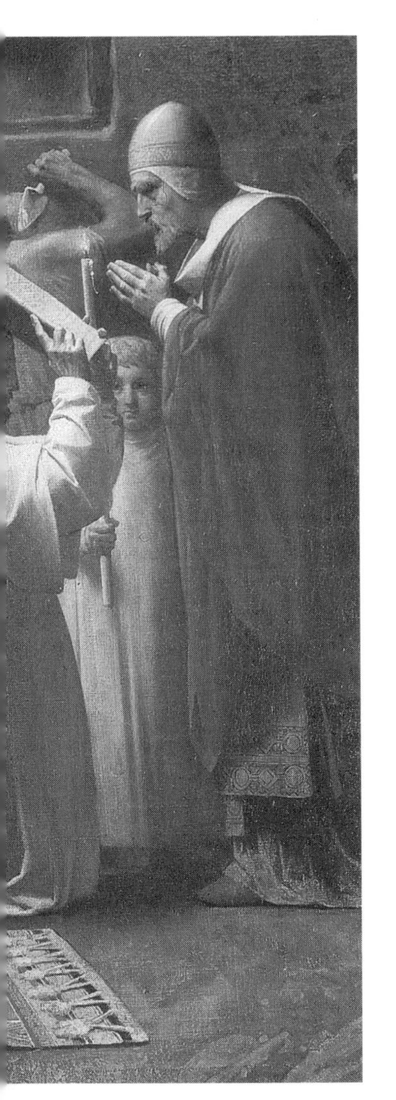

c. 202–c. 275 CE Numerous martyrs, including popes, are buried in the catacombs of Rome. These underground Christian burial places were outside the city walls. Pope Sixtus II, who suffered persecution under Emperor Valerian, is buried in the Catacombs of St Callixtus.

285 CE Antony of Egypt, pictured here with Paul the Hermit, retires in solitude. St Antony is known as the first Christian hermit. He lived for twenty years inside an old fort on a desert mountain in Egypt without seeing another human face.

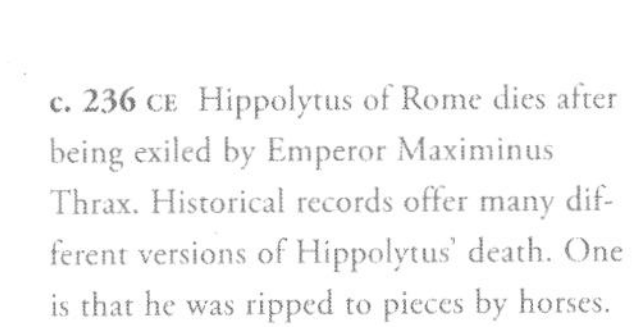

c. 236 CE Hippolytus of Rome dies after being exiled by Emperor Maximinus Thrax. Historical records offer many different versions of Hippolytus' death. One is that he was ripped to pieces by horses.

300–399 CE

301 Traditional date for conversion of King Tiridates III of Armenia by Gregory the Illuminator (actually 314).

303 Death of St George; later becomes patron saint of England and several other countries.

303–312 Last great persecution under Emperor Diocletian; martyrs and burning of Scriptures.

304 Victorinus, bishop of Pettau (modern-day Poetovio in Slovenia) and writer of Biblical commentaries, dies a martyr.

304 Pope Marcellinus repents of lapsing and dies a martyr.

c. 306 Synod of Elvira (Spain) bans relations between Christians and Jews; imposes severe penalties for apostasy and adultery; institutes celibacy for clergy.

310 Armenia becomes first Christian state; persecution of Christians under Persian King Shapur II (310–379).

311 Emperor Galerius issues Edict of Toleration, ending persecution of Christians in his part of the Roman Empire.

311 Donatus and others rebel against the appointment of the bishop of Carthage and claim that the people should determine the worth of a priest.

312 Lucian of Antioch, founder of the Antiochian School of theology, is martyred.

312 Constantine converts to Christianity before crucial Battle of Milvian Bridge to win control of the Western empire.

313 Emperor Constantine and Licinius, the Eastern ruler, issue the Edict of Milan to end persecutions.

313 A cathedral is built in Edessa.

314 Donatism in North Africa spreads; condemned as heresy.

318 Arius preaches in Alexandria that Jesus was human and not divine ("Arianism").

318 Pachomius, a disciple of Antony, organizes the first monastery made up of ascetics at Tabennis in Egypt.

320 Eusebius of Caesaria, first church historian, regards unified Christian empire as a divine goal.

320 Arius is expelled by the patriarch Alexander of Alexandria, but on his travels through the Eastern Roman Empire he converts more bishops.

323 Emperor Constantine orders a church to the apostle Peter be built on the Roman cemetery where the martyr is buried.

325 First Council of Nicaea called by Constantine to come to agreement on the divine/human nature of Jesus.

330 Constantine renames Byzantium as Constantinople and makes it the imperial capital.

334 First bishop appointed in Merv, Transoxania (modern-day Uzbekistan, Tajikistan, and Kazakhstan).

335 Emperor Constantine builds the Church of the Holy Sepulchre in Jerusalem.

339 Athanasius of Alexandria visits Rome with two Egyptian monks, Ammon and Isidore (disciples of Antony), and introduces the idea of monasticism.

340 Conversion of the Goths to Arian Christianity and translation of the Bible into Gothic by Ulfilas.

340 The first monastery in Persia is founded by Aphrahat at Mar Matti near Mosul.

345 Pachomius of Egypt dies, leaving behind eight monasteries and hundreds of monks.

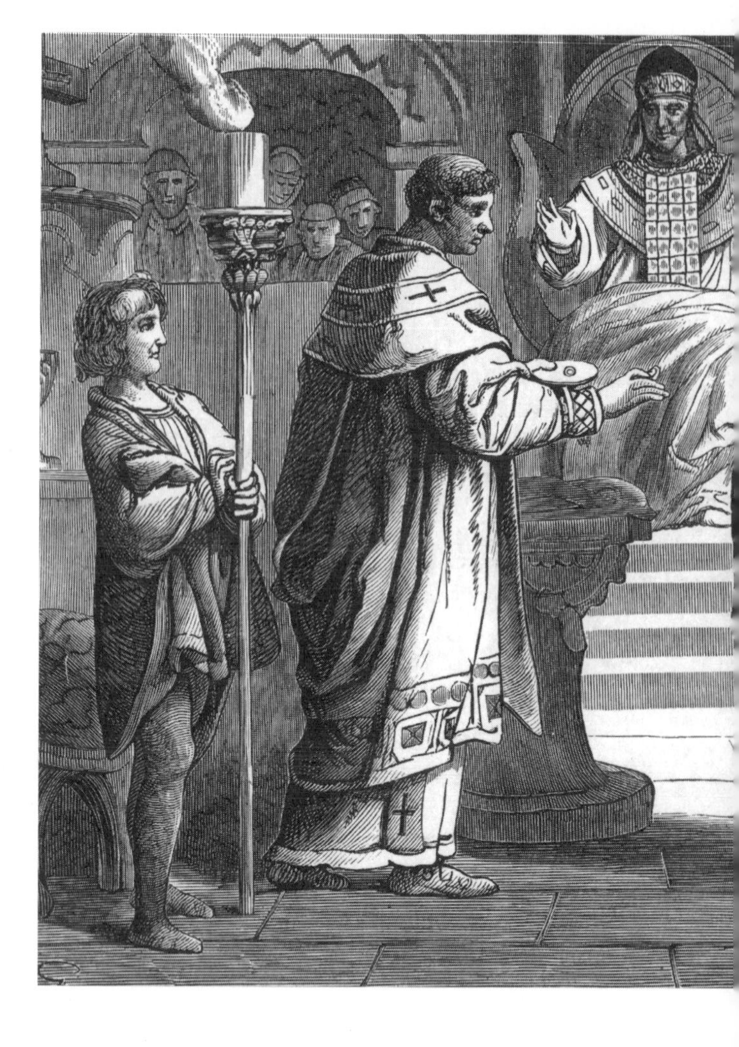

c. 350 Ninian the missionary establishes the church of Candida Casa at Whithorn in Galloway, Scotland.

358 Basil establishes the monastery of Annesos in Pontus, which becomes a model for Eastern monasticism.

360 Martin, future bishop of Tours, establishes the first French monastery at Ligugé.

360 The Vandals convert to Christianity.

361–363 Roman Emperor Julian the Apostate attempts to ban Christianity.

363 Persia gains Nisibis from the Romans and the theological school of Nisibis moves to Edessa.

371 Martin of Tours converts non-Christians in what is now France.

374 Ambrose is elected bishop of Milan, which becomes a theological center.

376 Visigoths, Vandals, Suevi, Burgundians, Herals, and Ostrogoths are converted to Arian Christianity by Goths.

379 Arianism banned in Roman Empire.

380 Emperor Theodosius I proclaims Christianity the sole religion of the reunited Roman Empire.

381 Second Ecumenical Council called by Theodosius I in Constantinople.

386 Jerome establishes monasteries in Bethlehem.

397 Council of Carthage (the eighth in a series from 251 to 424) ratifies the canon of the New Testament as we know it now.

380 CE Roman Emperor Theodosius I is baptized by the Catholic bishop of Thessalonica, Ascholios. Here we see Theodosius officiating at his niece's Catholic wedding.

312 CE Constantine the Great converts to Christianity before the Battle of Milvian Bridge. Legend has it that he looked up to the heavens and saw a cross and the words: "In this sign, thou shalt conquer."

400–499 CE

c. 405 Jerome translates the Bible into Latin; this becomes known as the Vulgate (common language) Bible.

410 The Persian Church at the Council of Seleucia declares its independence from Antioch and Rome.

410 The Visigoths sack Rome.

410 Maron, an ascetic monk from Syria, founds the Maronite movement, which holds to a Monothelite Christology (Christ has "one will").

410 The Synod of Seleucia (in modern-day Iraq) declares the bishop of Seleucia-Ctesiphon, Mar Isaac, primate and "Catholicos" of the Persian Church.

415 The Celtic monk Pelagius is accused of heresy at the synod of Jerusalem for arguing that the soul has free will and may take the first step to salvation.

423 St Simeon the Stylite begins his 36 years living atop a pillar near Aleppo in Syria.

424 The Synod of Dadyeshu, held in Markabata, declares the Persian primate supreme authority of the Persian Church and not subject to any other authority.

425 Augustine writes *The City of God*, one of the most influential texts in Christian history.

425 First bishops appointed in Herat (now in Afghanistan) and Samarkand (now in Uzbekistan).

428 Nestorius appointed patriarch of Constantinople. He argues that there are two persons in Christ, human and divine.

431 Palladius is sent by the pope as first bishop of Ireland.

431 Third Ecumenical Council of Ephesus declares there is only one person in Christ and condemns Nestorius.

432 The Roman missionary Patrick is taken prisoner to Ireland.

445 Monastery of Armagh in Ireland is founded.

445 Emperor Valentinian III decrees that all Western bishops must obey the pope.

449 Second Council of Ephesus, often called the "Robber Council" (Latrocinium), adopts the monophysite position (Christ has one divine nature) of Eutyches of Constantinople and Dioscurus, patriarch of Alexandria.

450 First British monasteries established in Wales.

450 Marcian is the first Roman emperor to be crowned by a religious leader—the patriarch of Constantinople.

451 The Fourth Ecumenical Council of Chalcedon overturns decisions of Ephesus (449), condemns Dioscurus of Alexandria, and affirms that Jesus was one person of two natures (both human and divine).

457 The monophysites of Alexandria reject the decisions of Chalcedon (451) and found the Coptic Orthodox Church.

481 Emperor Zeno of Constantinople closes the Nestorian school of Edessa, causing Nestorian scholars to flee to Nisibis in Persia.

484 Synod of Beth Papat in Persia declares Nestorian doctrine (two persons of Christ) as the official theology of the East Syrian Church, centered in Edessa.

493 The Arian Ostrogoth, Theodoric, becomes ruler of Italy and tolerates both Catholic and Arian Christianity.

496 Clovis converts the Franks to Catholicism.

496 CE As king of the Franks, Clovis wins a battle against the German Allemanni at Tolbiacum (Zülpich) and, crediting God with his victory, converts to Catholicism. Clovis' Catholic wife, Clothilde, had greatly influenced his eventual conversion.

c. 405 CE St Jerome uses Hebrew and Aramaic texts to translate the Bible into Latin. His Vulgate Bible, which includes several of the Apocrypha, becomes the standard version for Catholics.

500–599 CE

500 Pseudo-Dionysius writes mystical works called *Corpus Areopagiticum.*

525 Christian monk Dionysius Exiguus argues that the birth of Jesus took place in the year 753 from the founding of Rome.

527 Constantinople enforces anti-Jewish laws.

529 Benedetto (Benedict) of Nursia founds the monastery of Monte Cassino and writes the rules of Western monasticism with a focus on absolute power of the abbot.

529 Council of Orange in southern France condemns the Pelagian heresy and accepts Augustine's doctrine of salvation.

530 Cassiodorus, the Benedictine monk, encourages monks to copy manuscripts of the classics.

533 Mercurius is elected pope and takes the name of John II, the first pope to change name upon election.

534 Roman armies destroy the Arian kingdom of the Vandals.

537 Justinian builds the church of Hagia Sophia in Constantinople.

541 Jacob Baradaeus, bishop of Edessa, organizes the Monophysite Church in western Syria (the "Jacobites").

c. 551–628 Babai the Great establishes main theological pillars of Church of the East, following Nestorian (two-person) Christology.

553 The Fifth Ecumenical Council is held at Constantinople.

563 Columbanus founds the monastery of Iona off the coast of Scotland, which becomes the center of the Columban school.

580 The Benedictine monastery of Monte Cassino is sacked by the Lombards and the monks flee to Rome.

587 Reccared, Visigothic king of Spain, converts from Arianism to Catholicism.

590 For the first time a monk, the Benedictine Gregory I, becomes pope.

597 Pope Gregory I sends Augustine to England with forty monks.

580 CE Benedictine monks flee to Rome after the Lombards sack their Monte Cassino monastery. Pope Pelagius II accommodates the monks in a monastery next to the Lateran Basilica.

635 CE A monastic community is established on the tidal island of Lindisfarne (later called Holy Island), off the northeast coast of modern-day England. The buildings were eventually abandoned and fell into disrepair. Wilfrid of York began his monastic life at Lindisfarne.

601 CE Augustine baptizes King Ethelbert of Kent at Canterbury. Ethelbert was the first Anglo-Saxon to convert to Christianity; within a few months, thousands of Anglo-Saxons had followed his lead and become baptized.

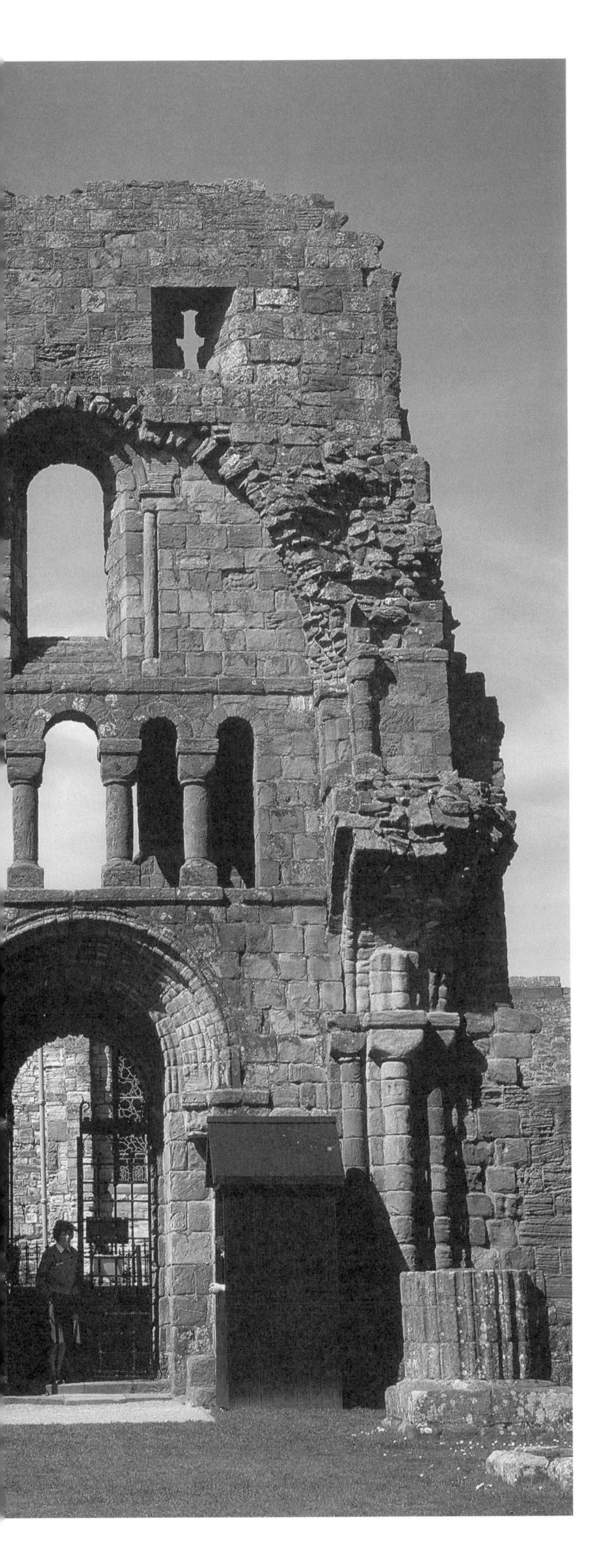

600–699 CE

600 Pope Gregory I, the last "Latin doctor," reforms the liturgy, promotes the doctrines of purgatory and penance, and popularizes the teachings of Pseudo-Dionysius.

601 Augustine converts King Ethelbert of Kent, establishes the see of Canterbury, and becomes its first archbishop.

603 The Lombards convert to Christianity and move their capital to Pavia in Italy.

604 Pope Gregory I dies.

612 Sisebut, Visigothic king of Spain, forces the Jews of Spain to release all slaves and convert to Christianity.

615 Colombanus dies in Italy.

627 Paulinus converts King Edwin of Deira and Bernicia (now Northumbria) and becomes archbishop of York.

635 Aidan, a bishop of Iona in Scotland, establishes a monastic community on the island of Lindisfarne off the coast of modern-day England.

635 Cynegils, King of Wessex, converts to Christianity.

636 Muslim Arabs capture Jerusalem.

638 Muslim Arabs allow the Jews to return to Jerusalem.

639 Muslim Arabs conquer Syria (mainly Nestorian) from Constantinople.

642 Muslim Arabs conquer Egypt (mainly monophysite) from Constantinople.

647 Amadeus, bishop of Maastricht, carries out missionary work in Frisia (Holland) and among the Slavs.

650 Arianism disappears after the Lombards convert to Catholicism.

663 Constans II is the last Eastern Roman emperor to visit Rome.

664 Synod of Whitby brings the Celtic (English) church into conformity with Rome.

664 Wilfrid, a monk from Iona, is appointed bishop of York.

668 Theodore, a monk from Tarsus (in modern-day Turkey), is appointed archbishop of Canterbury.

670 Caedmon, a monk from Whitby in England, translates the Gothic Bible into Germanic vernacular (ancient English).

678 Wilfrid converts people in Frisia (Holland).

680 At the Sixth Ecumenical Council in Constantinople, called by Emperor Constantine IV, the pope is declared the head of Christianity.

685 John V is the first of a series of Greek and Syriac popes under the influence of Constantinople.

690 English missionary Willibrord evangelizes in Holland and Denmark.

698 Muslim Arabs capture Carthage.

700–799 CE

711–718	Muslim Arabs conquer southern Spain.
716	Iona in Scotland conforms to Roman doctrine and practice.
719	Pope Gregory II sends the Anglo-Saxon Benedictine monk Boniface (Wynfrid) to evangelize in Frisia.
726–729	Eastern emperor Leo III issues a series of edicts against the worship of images (icons).
731	The Venerable Bede writes the *Ecclesiastical History of the English People.*
732	Muslim Arab conquest of Europe is halted by the Franks at the battle of Tours in France.
732	Pope Gregory II appoints Boniface archbishop of the Franks.
739	Boniface reforms the Frankish Church.
751	King Aistulf of the Lombards conquers Ravenna in northern Italy from the Eastern (Byzantine) Roman Empire and indirectly releases Rome from the influence of Constantinople.
754	Boniface is killed by the Frisians.
754	Pope Stephen II anoints Pepin III king of the Franks.
754	Eastern emperor Constantine V orders all iconic images destroyed.
756	Pepin III defeats the Lombards and conquers Ravenna but leaves the conquered territories to the pope; papal state founded with temporal power for the pope.
769	The Lateran Council decides that only cardinals can become popes.
775	The patriarchate of the Church of the East moves from Seleucia-Ctesiphon to Baghdad.
787	Second Council of Nicaea restores the use of icons and decrees that visual artists should work for the Church and be faithful to the letter of the Bible.

719 CE The missionary Boniface follows Pope Gregory II's instructions to "go forth to preach the word of God to those still enslaved in paganism… [and] imbue them with the Old and New Testaments in a spirit always of love and moderation."

804 CE Alcuin, Abbot of St Martin at Tours, dies. The eminent educator, theologian, and scholar is pictured here being received by Emperor Charlemagne.

863 CE Rastislav of Moravia asks Emperor Michael III to send him missionaries. The brothers Methodius and Cyril, an expert linguist, are chosen. They are pictured here with an example of the Slavic alphabet they invented.

800–899 CE

800 Pope Leo III crowns Charlemagne emperor and thereby establishes the Holy Roman Empire.

817 Benedict of Aniane in France achieves reform of the monastic movement at the Synod of Aachen, where his constitution of Benedictine monasteries is approved.

822 Mojmir, prince of Moravia, converts to Christianity.

826 Harald Klak of Denmark converts to Christianity.

843 The "Restoration of the Images" under Methodius, Patriarch of Constantinople, ends the iconoclastic controversy.

845 The Irish theologian Johannes Scotus Eriugena takes over the Palatine Academy in France.

846 Muslim Arab armies attack Rome.

849 Caliph al-Mutawakkil deposes the patriarch of the Church of the East and persecutes Christians.

858 Pope Nicholas I asserts the independence of the Church from temporal authorities.

862 Boris of Bulgaria converts to Christianity.

862 Rastislav of Moravia converts to Christianity.

863 Cyril and Methodius from Constantinople translate the Bible into Slavic and in the process create Glagolitic, the first Slavic alphabet.

870 The Serbs convert to Christianity.

883 Muslim armies burn the monastery of Monte Cassino.

885 Mt Athos in Greece is granted independence as a religious retreat by Emperor Basil I.

900–999 CE

904 Sergius III is elected pope as a result of aristocratic feuding and the support of a powerful Roman noblewoman. He fathers a son who will become Pope John XI.

912 The Normans convert to Christianity.

922 Dirk I, the Viking ruler, establishes the Egmont Benedictine monastery of Haarlem in Holland.

948 Grand Prince of the Magyars converts to Christianity.

950 The church and monastery of Holy Luke (Hosios Loukas) are established at Stiris in Greece.

c. 955 Archbishop Oda of Canterbury rebuilds Canterbury Cathedral in Kent, England.

963 Athanasius of Athos establishes the Great Lavra (monastery) on Mt Athos in Greece.

965 Harald Bluetooth (Harold I) converts the Danes to Christianity.

966 Duke Mieszko I of Poland converts to Christianity when he marries Dabrowka of Bohemia.

988 Vladimir of Kiev converts to Orthodox Christianity and commissions the creation of religious icons and architecture.

995 Olaf Tryggvason, king of Norway, converts the Vikings to Christianity.

996 Gregory V is the first German to be elected pope.

999 Holy Roman Emperor Otto III appoints Gerbert d'Aurillac as the first French pope, who takes the name Sylvester II.

912 CE The Viking leader Rollo (Rolf), Duke of Normandy, is baptized. Many Normans also convert to the Christian faith. Legend has it that Rollo died a pagan about twenty years later.

c. 955 CE Canterbury Cathedral in Kent, England, is rebuilt. Archbishop Oda lengthened the cathedral's nave. Augustine was the first Archbishop of Canterbury; he established his seat there in 597 CE.

1000–1099 CE

1000 Iceland decides at the national assembly ("*Thing*") to become Christian.

1001 Cathedral of Ani in Armenia is constructed.

1008 Sweden becomes Christian.

1009 Caliph al-Hakim sacks the Church of the Holy Sepulchre and the tomb believed to be Christ's is hacked down to bedrock.

1012 Romualdo founds the Camaldolese Benedictines, an order of hermits in Italy modeled on the tradition of the Egyptian Desert Fathers.

1017 King Canute of Denmark converts to Christianity.

1018 Bishop Hildebrand establishes the monastery of San Miniato al Monte near Florence in Italy.

1022 The Cathari (Albigensians)—who believe that matter and the body are evil—spread to France from their origin in the Balkans, where they are known as Bogomils.

1032 A teenager is elected Pope Benedict IX, the last of the "dynastic" popes.

1036 Giovanni Gualberto, a noble Florentine, establishes the monastery of Vallombrosa near Florence in Italy.

1037 Construction of St Sophia Cathedral in Kiev (Ukraine) begins.

1039 Odilo, an abbot from the Cluny monastery, leads reform of the Benedictine Order, centralizes control and spreads its influence throughout Europe.

1045 Pope Benedict IX marries and sells the papacy to his godfather Gregory VI.

1045 Holy Roman Emperor Henry III pressures Gregory VI to convene the Synod of Sutri to reform the papacy, and calls all three current popes to attend—Gregory VI, Sylvester III, and Benedict IX. They are replaced by Clement II.

1050 The Camaldolese hermit Pietro Damiani publishes a book denouncing the moral and sexual corruption of the Church.

1050 The ascetics Anthony and Theodosius establish the Monastery of the Caves in Kiev.

1054 The patriarch of Constantinople and the pope in Rome issue mutual excommunications and begin the Great Schism.

1070 Lanfranc, an Italian lawyer, becomes Archbishop of Canterbury and ensures that Canterbury overshadows York as the primary see in England.

1070 Hospital of St John is established in Jerusalem by Amalfi merchants.

1071 The Turks capture Jerusalem.

1073 Hildebrand becomes Pope Gregory VII and begins a major reform of the Church: Celibate clergy, papal supremacy, infallibity of the pope.

1075 Pope Gregory VII tries to end the habit of "lay investiture" in which kings appoint bishops.

1075 Cathedral of Santiago de Compostela built; it becomes the most popular site of Christian pilgrimage after Jerusalem and Rome.

1076 Gregory VII excommunicates the Holy Roman Emperor Henry IV.

c. 1076 Order of Grandmont established in Normandy.

1084 Bruno establishes the Carthusian Order at Grande Chartreuse near Grenoble.

1085 Toledo in Spain is recaptured from the Muslims by the Christian king Alfonso VI.

1085 Henry IV invades Italy and drives Pope Gregory VII out of Rome.

1088 Christodoulos of Patmos founds the monastery of St John the Theologian on Patmos.

1088 A monk from the powerful monastery of Cluny is elected Pope Urban II.

1093 Anselm becomes Archbishop of Canterbury.

1095 Pope Urban II calls for a crusade against the Muslims following a request from the Byzantine emperor Alexius I Komnenos.

1098 Robert of Molesme founds the Cistercian Order at Citeaux in Burgundy.

1098–1099 Crusaders capture Antioch and Jerusalem.

1018 CE San Miniato al Monte monastery in Italy is established. It is named for St Minias (Miniato), the first Christian missionary and martyr in Florence, who lived as a hermit in a nearby cave.

1099 CE Godfrey of Bouillon and his men are the first crusaders to break through the walls surrounding Jerusalem. The soldiers massacre many Jews and Muslims living in the Holy City.

1070 CE The Hospital of St John in Jerusalem is founded by pious merchants from the Italian republic of Amalfi. They set up the hospital to care for sick and injured pilgrims visiting the Holy Land.

1112 CE Tancred, Prince of Antioch, dies at Antioch. The Christian crusader knight played a significant role in both the siege of Antioch in 1098 and the capture of Jerusalem in 1099.

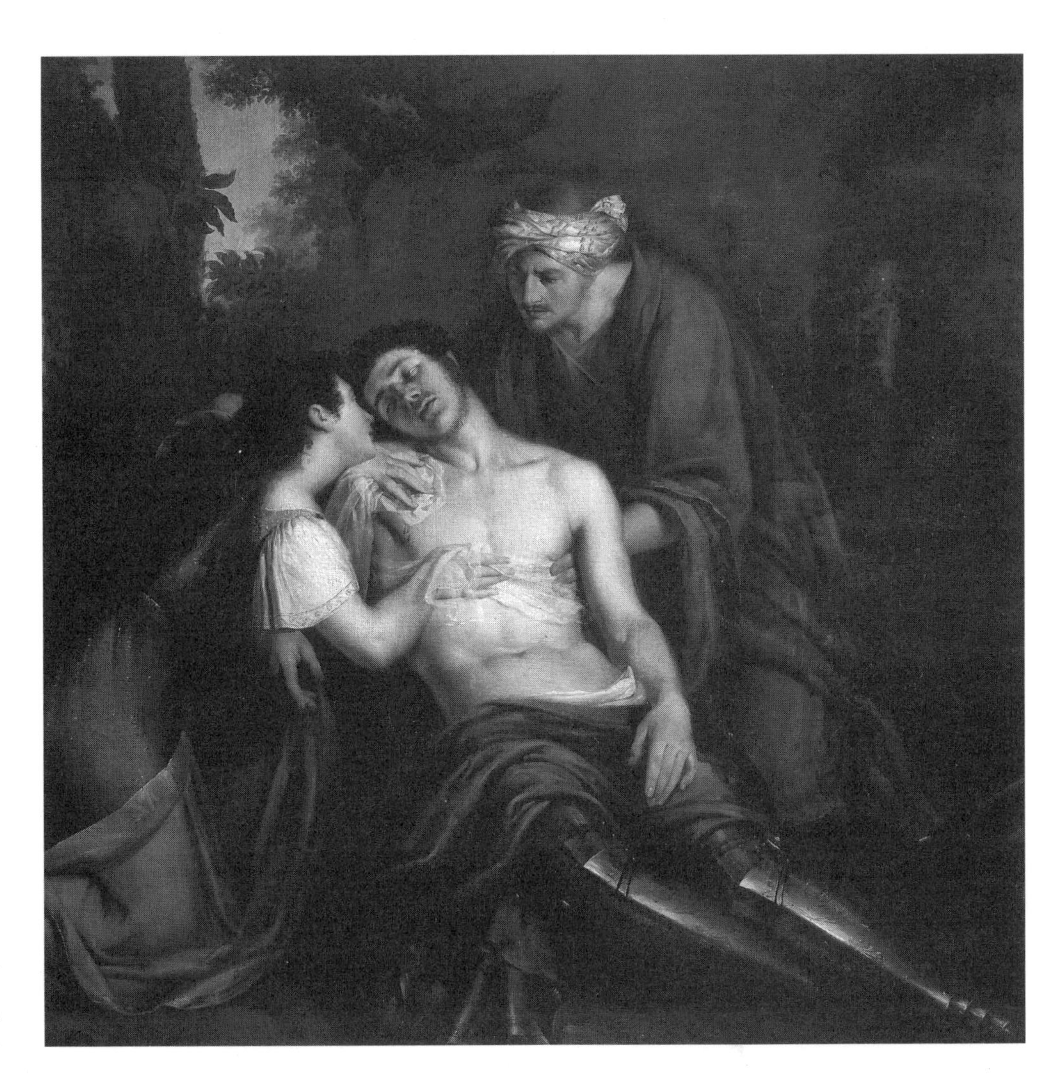

1163 CE Building work commences on Notre Dame Cathedral in Paris, France. The Gothic cathedral dedicated to the Virgin Mary overlooks the River Seine.

1100–1199 CE

1100 King Henry I of England struggles with Pope Paschal II concerning lay investiture.

1107 Concordat of London finds a compromise between Henry I of England and Pope Paschal II on the question of lay investiture.

1113 Paschal II recognizes the Hospital of St John as a separate monastic order, called the Hospitallers, with headquarters in Acre in Palestine.

1115 Bernard of Clairvaux establishes a Cistercian monastery at Clairvaux and begins a campaign against the influence of Cluny.

1118 Hugh de Payens founds the order of warrior monks, the Knights Templar, at the Temple Mount in Jerusalem in order to protect pilgrims traveling to the Holy Land.

1120 The very strict Premonstratensians Order is established by Norbert at Prémontré in northern France.

1122 Pope Calixtus II and Emperor Henry V sign the Concordat of Worms that resolves the "investiture controversy" by giving the emperor veto power over the Church.

1137 The Benedictine monk Suger rebuilds the cathedral of St-Denis in a new style now known as Gothic.

1141 Pierre Abelard, jointly famous with his former lover, the abbess Héloïse, for their theological writings, is condemned as a heretic and his books are burned.

1144 Bernard of Clairvaux calls for a second crusade to relieve the siege of Jerusalem; the crusaders are defeated by Muslim armies.

1160 Alexander III excommunicates the Holy Roman Emperor, Frederick I "Barbarossa."

1162 Frederick I raids Rome and Milan.

1163 Construction of Notre Dame Cathedral in Paris, France, is begun.

1170 Archbishop Thomas Becket is murdered in Canterbury Cathedral.

1177 Frederick I recognizes Alexander III as pope and is forgiven.

1184 First Episcopal inquisition to extirpate heresy established.

1184 Pope Lucius III excommunicates Peter Waldo, founder of the Waldensians (the "poor men of Lyons").

1187 Saladin recaptures Jerusalem.

1189 The Third Crusade is led by King Richard I (Lion-Heart) of England, King Philip II of France, and Frederick I, who drowns on the way.

1190 The Teutonic Knights are established to fight in crusades, and establish their capital at Acre.

1200–1299 CE

1204	The Fourth Crusade sacks Constantinople.
1206	Francis of Assisi renounces wealth and adopts a life of absolute poverty.
c. 1207–1282	The mystic Mechthild of Magdeburg, one of the first woman writers in Christian history, describes her visions of God in *The Flowing Light of the Godhead*.
1208	Pope Innocent III launches a crusade against the Cathari (Albigensians) and the Waldensians.
1210	The pope recognizes the Franciscan order of mendicant friars.
1212	Spanish victory at the Battle of Las Navas de Tolosa marks the beginning of the end of the Almohad grip on Spain.
1215	The Dominican order of mendicant friars is established in Languedoc.
1216	Innocent III dies.
1217–1221	Fifth Crusade fails in Egypt.
1219	Francis of Assisi preaches to the Sultan of Egypt.
1226	The Order of Carmelites is founded.
1228–1229	Holy Roman Emperor Frederick II succeeds in regaining Jerusalem by negotiation in the Sixth Crusade.
1234	Pope Gregory IX issues papal decretals, which invest the doctrine of perpetual servitude of the Jews with the force of canonical law.
1238	Valencia in Spain is recaptured.
1244	Jerusalem falls once again to Mamluk Turks.
1248	Seville in Spain is recaptured by Ferdinand III.
1248–1254	Seventh Crusade fails in Egypt.
c. 1250	Hadewijch of Brabant, one of the earliest female Christian voices, writes some stunning works of poetry and mystical visions.
1250	Eusebius of Esztergom establishes the Order of St Paul the First Hermit and unites all the hermits in Hungary and Croatia.
1252	Pope Innocent IV issues a papal bull approving the torture of heretics.
1261	Constantinople is recaptured from the crusaders.
c. 1263	Thomas Aquinas publishes the *Summa Contra Gentiles*, using Aristotelian philosophy to reshape theology.
1270–1271	Eighth Crusade peters out when its leader, Louis IX, dies in Tunis.
1271	The newly elected pope Gregory X institutes the conclave of cardinals to elect popes.
1291	Last Western holdings in the Middle East fall to Mamluk Turks.
1291	After the fall of Acre, Hospitallers and Templars move their headquarters from Acre to Cyprus and Teutonic Knights move their headquarters from Acre to Venice.

1206 CE After experiencing a vision, Francis of Assisi rejects his wealthy upbringing and takes on a life of poverty and simplicity. He was inspired by the life of Christ, who was born in a manger.

1300–1399 CE

1300 Boniface VIII announces the first Jubilee Year, when special indulgences are granted.

1303 French king Philip IV (the Fair) captures Pope Boniface VIII over the right to tax the French clergy.

1309 Archbishop of Bordeaux becomes Pope Clement V and moves the papacy to Avignon in France.

1309 The Hospitallers capture the island of Rhodes and move their capital there.

1312 Pope Clement V abolishes the order of the Knights Templar at the instigation of Philip IV of France and seizes their assets.

1312 The Hospitallers are awarded the Templars' possessions in Western Europe, Cyprus, and Greece.

1314 Jacques de Molay, the grand master of the Templars, is burned at the stake in Paris.

1321 Jordanus, a Dominican monk, begins a Christian mission in India.

1321 William of Ockham is excommunicated for arguing that Pope John XXII was a heretic and that the Church should not own property.

1324 Marsilius of Padua publishes *Defender of the Peace*, arguing that the pope is a human leader and the state is independent of the Church.

1327 Marsilius of Padua is excommunicated.

1328 Holy Roman Emperor Louis IV invades Italy and appoints Antipope Nicholas V (1328–1330).

1329 Pope John XXII condemns writings of Meister Eckhardt.

1337 Gregory of Palamas writes his *Triads in Defense of the Holy Hesychast* in response to the Calabrian monk Barlaam.

1347–1351 The Black Death (bubonic plague) decimates Europe.

1350 Sergius of Radonezh establishes the Monastery of the Holy Trinity (at Sergiev Posad), which becomes a new center of Russian Christianity.

1377 Pope Gregory XI moves the seat of the papacy from Avignon back to Rome.

1378 Pope Urban VI undertakes a campaign against corruption.

1378 The cardinals return to Avignon and elect Pope Clement VII, generating the Western Schism, which lasted until 1417.

1378 John Wyclif, the Oxford theologian, argues that the Church has fallen into sin, that it should give up all its property, and that the clergy should live in complete poverty.

1385 Lithuania converts to Christianity and is unified with Poland.

1396 John Wyclif completes the first English translation of the Bible, but it is declared heretical.

1350 CE Sergius of Radonezh establishes a monastery in the forest of Radonezh. Born Barfolomey Kirillivich in 1314, some say he had a religious vision when he was a boy. He was tonsured a monk in 1337 and took the name Sergius.

1309 CE Pope Clement V moves the papal capital from Rome to the French city of Avignon. He is the first of seven popes to reside at Avignon until the papacy moves back to Rome in 1377.

1400–1499 CE

1414	The Council of Constance (1414–1418) assembles to settle the problem of having three popes: Gregory XII, Benedict XIII, and John XXIII.
1415	Jan Hus burned at the stake at Constance for opposing the sale of indulgences and claiming that the Church is a human invention.
1417	The Council of Constance dismisses the three rival popes and elects Cardinal Odo Colonna as Pope Martin V, thus ending the Western Schism.
1420	Pope Martin V arrives in Rome to find the city in ruins; his first task is to restore order and prosperity.
1420–1434	The power of the Church is challenged as the Hussite Wars are waged in Bohemia.
1439	At the Council of Ferrara–Florence, a treaty is signed to unify the Roman Catholic Church and the Eastern Orthodox Church under Roman terms; it defines seven sacraments.
1447	Nicholas V becomes pope and begins to gather the Vatican Library of ancient Latin and Greek classics.
1450	Nicholas V oversees the restoration of many of the glories of Rome for the jubilee; millions of pilgrims come to Rome.
1453	Constantinople and the Eastern Orthodox Church fall to the Ottomans; Constantinople is renamed Istanbul.
1456	Rodrigo Borgia, a nephew of Callixtus III, becomes a cardinal.
1471	Sixtus IV becomes pope and adds one thousand books to the Vatican Library.
1478	The Spanish Inquisition inaugurated to seek out Jews, Muslims and heretics.
1484	Pope Innocent VIII orders the persecution of magicians and witches.
1492	Granada falls to Christian troops; Jews and Muslims are expelled from Spain.
1492	Rodrigo Borgia becomes Pope Alexander VI.
1492	Christopher Columbus crosses the Atlantic.
1493	Alexander VI appoints his son Cesare Borgia a cardinal and weds his daughter Lucrezia (aged 13) to Giovanni Sforza.
1494	Treaty of Tordesillas, sanctioned by the pope, divides the newly discovered lands outside Europe between Spain (the Americas and west) and Portugal (Africa and east).
1498	Leonardo da Vinci completes *The Last Supper.*
1498	The Dominican monk Girolamo Savonarola is excommunicated, tortured, and burnt as a heretic.
1498	Vasco da Gama arrives in India and finds the Thomas Christians, who have been there for over a millennium.

1498 CE Leonardo da Vinci finishes his vast painting, *The Last Supper.* The mural, which he began in 1495, covers a large wall of the refectory at the Convent of Santa Maria delle Grazie near Milan, Italy.

1571 CE Anneken Hendriks, an Anabaptist, is burned alive at Amsterdam, Holland. Although she was tortured, she refused to name any fellow Anabaptists, and was sentenced to death for heresy.

1521 CE Martin Luther defends his reformist views before Emperor Charles V at the Concordat of Worms, Germany. Luther refused to retract his "95 Theses" and other teachings and was outlawed.

1500–1599 CE

1500	Alexander VI appoints 12 new cardinals in return for massive payments.
1500	Cesare Borgia leads the Papal Army to recapture the old papal states.
1501	Lucrezia Borgia, daughter of the pope, marries Alfonso I d'Este.
1506	Pope Julius II decides to rebuild the Basilica of St Peter and leads an expedition to recapture the papal states.
1506	The Swiss Guard is formed to protect the pope.
1508	Michelangelo begins painting the ceiling of the Sistine Chapel. He completes the composition four years later.
1509	Desiderius Erasmus publishes *In Praise of Folly*, advocating a return to the values of early Christianity.
1513	Giovanni de' Medici, the last non-priest to become a pope, is elected Pope Leo X.
1516	Erasmus publishes a Greek text of the New Testament.
1517	The Ottoman Empire takes Jerusalem from the Mamluks.
1517	Martin Luther nails his "95 Theses" to the church door at Wittenberg, arguing against the Catholic practice of selling indulgences.
1519	Ulrich Zwingli breaks with Rome and becomes leader of the Swiss reformation.
1521	Martin Luther is excommunicated by Leo X.
1525	Peasants Rebellion under Thomas Müntzer is crushed with much difficulty by German princes.
1526	Martin Luther publishes his German translation of the Bible.
1528	Matteo Bassi establishes the Capuchin order of friars.
1530	The Hospitallers are defeated at Rhodes by the Turks and move to Malta under the king of Spain.
1534	Michelangelo paints *The Last Judgement* on the altar wall of the Sistine Chapel.
1534	An Act of Parliament recognizes Henry VIII as Supreme Head of the Church of England.
1535	Radical Anabaptists engage in the Münster Rebellion and establish a short-lived theocracy.
1536	First edition of John Calvin's *Institutes of the Christian Religion* is published just before he settles in Geneva. It becomes a major theological statement of the Reformation.

1536 William Tyndale is burned at the stake for his translation of the Bible into English.

1536 The Radical reformer, Menno Simons, joins the Anabaptists in Holland; his followers become known as the Mennonites.

1536 Portuguese Inquisition established.

1540 Ignatius of Loyola founds the Society of Jesus, or Jesuits.

1541 Franciscans establish first missions in Baja California.

1542 Pope Paul III establishes the inquisition into Protestantism.

1542 The missionary Frances Xavier arrives in Goa, India, and makes it his base for mission work as far east as Japan.

1547 Council of Trent meets in response to Protestant reformation and begins Counter-Reformation.

1549 Jesuit missionaries arrive in Brazil.

c. 1550 Congregational movement begins in England.

1553 Mary I, daughter of Henry VIII and Catherine of Aragon, takes the throne and sets about re-establishing Roman Catholicism in England.

1555 Peace of Augsburg provides for the subjects of each land to follow the religion of their rulers, whether Roman Catholic or Lutheran (but not Calvinist).

1564 Michelangelo dies after designing the dome of St Peter's Basilica.

1567 The forces of Mary, Queen of Scots, are defeated by the Protestant lords.

1571 Pope Paul IV issues the *Index Librorum Prohibitorum*, a list of banned books.

1571 Mexican Inquisition established.

1582 Pope Gregory XIII introduces the Gregorian calendar.

1583 Jesuit missionary Matteo Ricci arrives in China.

1589 Moscow becomes a patriarchate.

1598 The Edict of Nantes allows religious freedom to French Huguenots after years of persecution.

1506 CE Pope Julius II appoints Donato Bramante to be the architect in charge of rebuilding St Peter's Basilica in Vatican City. The original fourth-century basilica was built on the site that held the relics of the Apostle Peter.

1600–1699 CE

1600	The philosopher Giordano Bruno is executed as a heretic in Rome for claiming that the universe is infinite.
1609	John Smyth establishes Baptist Church in Amsterdam among English exiles.
1611	King James (Authorized) version of Bible published in English.
1618	Thirty Years' War between Roman Catholics and Protestants in Holy Roman Empire begins.
1620	English Puritans aboard the *Mayflower* land at Plymouth Rock on Cape Cod, Massachusetts.
1622	Pope Gregory VI establishes the Sacred Congregation for the Propagation of the Faith in order to coordinate mission activity.
1626	Construction of St Peter's Basilica in Rome is completed after 120 years.
1636	The rebellion of Christians in Shimabara (Japan) ends in the slaughter of over 30,000 rebels.
1641–1651	English Civil War (Puritan Revolution).
1648	Treaties of Hamburg, Osnabrück, and Münster end the Thirty Years' War.
1666	John Bunyan writes *The Pilgrim's Progress* while in prison.
1679	First steps in developing the "Mission Trail" in Alta California.

1632 CE Italian scientist Galileo Galilei appears before the Holy Office of the Inquisition in Rome. He is charged with heresy for supporting the doctrine that says the sun is at the center of the universe.

1664 CE Armand-Jean la Bouthillier de Rance becomes the abbot of La Trappe Abbey in France, which he owns. He founds the austere reformed Cistercian order, known as Trappists.

1721 CE Russian Emperor Peter the Great institutes his "Spiritual Regulation," which abolishes the patriarchate and replaces it with a Holy Synod. Members of the synod can be appointed and dismissed by the emperor at any time.

1797 CE Napoleon Bonaparte and Pope Pius VI sign the Peace of Tolentino, thus ending Napoleon's recent invasion of the papal states. Napoleon takes the legations of Bologna, Ferrara, and Ravenna.

1700–1799 CE

1700 Following the death of Patriarch Adrian, Peter the Great fails to appoint a new patriarch to the patriarchate of Moscow.

1710 Society for the Propagation of the Gospel formed: The first British missionary society.

1721 Peter the Great abolishes the patriarchate and appoints a ten-member Holy Synod to head the patriarchate of Moscow.

1721 Hans Egede establishes a Danish mission in Greenland.

1726 Beginning of the "Great Awakening" in North America.

1728 Irish Catholics lose the right to vote.

1732–1733 Moravian mission to West Indies and Greenland.

1738 John Wesley begins outdoor preaching that would lead to formation of Methodism.

1775–1783 American Wars of Independence.

1784 Roman Catholicism is reintroduced in Korea and spreads after first being introduced in 1593.

1788 First Fleet of convicts arrives in Australia with a Church of England priest.

1789–1799 French Revolution and attacks on Roman Catholic Church.

1791 American Constitution includes the First Amendment, which establishes freedom of religion and prevents the state from supporting religion.

1793 William Carey, the first English missionary, arrives in India.

1794 Herman of Alaska arrives on Kodiak Island and begins Russian missions to Alaska.

1795 London Missionary Society formed.

1797 "Second Awakening" begins in North America.

1799 Wave of Dutch and German Protestant missions to Indonesia after the Dutch Government takes it over as a colony from the Dutch East India Company.

1800–1899 CE

1804 The British and Foreign Bible Society formed, the first of many to follow.

1812 Adoniram Judson is the first Protestant missionary to Burma.

1814 Reorganization of the Jesuits.

1814 Protestant missionaries arrive in New Zealand.

1822 Thousands are slaughtered by Turkish invaders in the Agios Minas monastery in Chios, Greece.

1828 The *Catholic Emancipation Act* is passed in England.

1828 Plymouth Brethren movement formed.

1828 Karl Gütslaff of the Netherlands Mission Society arrives in Thailand.

1832 Prussian union of Reformed and Lutheran churches; Old Lutherans not tolerated.

1834 Spanish Inquisition formally abolished.

1834–1838 Innocent of Alaska translates parts of the Bible into Unangam Tunuu (Aleut).

1845 Southern Baptist Convention formed in Augusta, Georgia.

1848 Pius IX sends the "Epistle to the Easterns" to the Orthodox churches, requesting communion with Rome; in reply, the "Encyclical of the Eastern Patriarchs" points out theological differences and questions papal supremacy.

1851–1864 Taiping Rebellion at Thistle Mountain (Guangxi, China), begun by Hong Xiuquan, self-proclaimed younger brother of Jesus Christ, causes 20–30 million deaths.

1854 The missionary J. Hudson Taylor arrives in China.

1858 Benito Juárez becomes president of Mexico, abolishes Church lands, separates Church and state, and dismisses clergy.

1859 Protestant missionaries first arrive in Japan.

1865 William Booth founds the Salvation Army.

1869–1870 First Vatican Council asserts dogma of papal infallibility.

1870 Italy declares war on papal states, which cease to exist.

1878 Pope Pius IX dies after a reign of 32 years, the longest of any pope.

1884 Bible Students movement is founded by Charles Taze Russell; renamed Jehovah's Witnesses in 1931.

1889 Republic of Brazil established with separation of Church and state.

1890 Formation of the Central American Mission.

1897 CE The Klondike goldrush in Yukon Territory, Alaska, begins. Within several months, around 30,000 miners have arrived at the goldfields. Intrepid missionaries, like those pictured, soon follow.

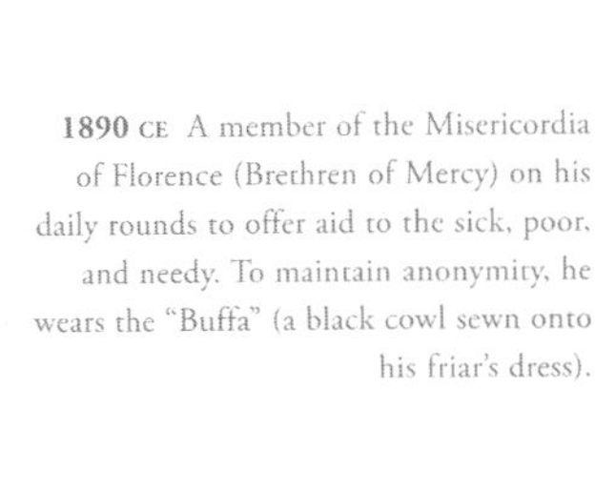

1890 CE A member of the Misericordia of Florence (Brethren of Mercy) on his daily rounds to offer aid to the sick, poor, and needy. To maintain anonymity, he wears the "Buffa" (a black cowl sewn onto his friar's dress).

c. 1895 CE A Roman Catholic girl poses in her Holy Communion outfit—the dress, veil, and gloves are white to symbolize purity. She is ready to receive the sacrament of the Eucharist for the first time.

1992 CE In Ireland, many thousands of Catholic refugees from Belfast in the north flee to the southern city of Dublin to escape sectarian violence.

1955 CE Rev. C. Lloyd Lee, pastor of Tremont United Methodist Church in the Bronx, New York, welcomes a worshipper to the Sunday drive-in chapel service. Many Christian churches now offer this convenient way of worshipping God.

1900–1999 CE

1903 After nine years of conflict between Church and state, the government of President Combes of France closes monasteries.

1903 Pope Leo XIII dies, aged 93, after a 25-year pontificate that has seen him work toward unifying Christendom.

1905 French Parliament passes the bill separating Church and state.

1907–1912 Nicholas of Japan is archbishop of the Japanese Orthodox Church.

1910 Soldiers of the Portuguese Royal Army revolt, King Manuel II flees to England, the monarchy is abolished and all nuns and monks are expelled.

1910 First World Missionary Conference (Protestant) held in Edinburgh.

1910 William Wadé Harris establishes the first independent African church in Liberia.

1910–1915 The 12-volume *The Fundamentals* is published by the Bible Institute of Los Angeles, marking the beginning of Protestant fundamentalism.

1917 A new constitution is adopted in Mexico. It provides for universal suffrage, separation of Church and state, and a bill of rights.

1917 The Russian Revolution; end of rule by tsars allows for restoration of the Russian patriarchate.

1922 Pope Pius XI sets out to be an international peacemaker.

1925 St Thérèse of Lisieux, who died in 1897, is canonized by Pope Pius XI.

1925 Scopes "Monkey Trial," concerning the teaching of evolution in schools in the USA.

1927 Leaders of the Cristero War in Mexico, a reaction to government seizure of Church property, are executed, and rebellion brutally suppressed by President Calles.

1929 Italy and the Holy See sign the Lateran Treaty, creating Vatican City and re-establishing the sovereignty of the pope after sixty years of tension.

1930 The Church of England reluctantly accepts that members of their congregations can use contraceptives.

1930 Sarah E. Dickson is ordained in Cincinnati as the first female Presbyterian elder in the USA.

1930 The papal encyclical *Casti Connubii* reaffirms the Roman Catholic ban on artificial birth control.

1942 Women are allowed into church in the UK without hats.

1945 A library of early Christian Gnostic texts is discovered at Nag Hammadi in Egypt.

1946 The first American saint is canonized: Mother Frances Xavier Cabrini.

1947 The Dead Sea Scrolls are discovered near Qumran.

1948 World Council of Churches formed.

1950 Mother Theresa establishes the Missionaries of Charity in Calcutta, India.

1951 Pope Pius XII cautiously sanctions the use of the rhythm method as a natural form of birth control.

1954 Wording in Pledge of Allegiance in the USA changed from "one nation, indivisible" to "one nation under God, indivisible."

1962 Pope John XXIII convenes the first session of the Second Vatican Council (1962–1965).

1963 The Supreme Court of the USA rules that the Lord's Prayer and Bible recitation should be banned from public schools.

1964 Pope Paul VI visits the Holy Land, meeting the patriarch of the Greek Orthodox Church, the first such meeting for more than 500 years.

1966 Pope Paul VI meets Dr Ramsey, Archbishop of Canterbury. It is the first meeting for 400 years between the heads of the Roman Catholic and Anglican churches.

1966 Pacific Conference of Churches is established.

1971 Barbara Ward is the first woman to address a synod of Roman Catholic bishops.

1971 Liberation theology emerges in Latin America.

1972 Seven nuns are arrested at St Patrick's Cathedral, New York, for disrupting a Mass in an anti-war protest.

1976 One of 48 extant copies of the *Gutenberg Bible* is sold at auction for US$2 million in New York. It is the most expensive book on record.

1978 Karol Wojtyla from Poland is elected as the first non-Italian pope (John Paul II) in over four centuries.

1978 American Episcopal priest Mary Michael Simpson is the first woman to preach at Westminster Abbey.

1980 Queen Elizabeth II visits the Vatican, the first British monarch to do so.

1981 Pope John Paul II survives an assassination attempt.

1988 Pope John Paul outlines two "particular dimensions of the fulfillment of the female personality" as virginity or motherhood, in an apostolic letter on the Dignity and Vocation of Women.

1989 Dr Penny Jameison from Dunedin, New Zealand, is the first woman in the world to be ordained a bishop in the global Anglican Communion.

1997 World Council of Churches releases *Towards a Common Date for Easter.*

1997 Roman Catholic Church and Lutheran World Federation release *Joint Declaration on the Doctrine of Justification.*

1998 Sister Edith Stein, a victim of the Holocaust, is canonized by Pope John Paul II.

1986 CE Christian missionaries pray with homeless children in South Africa before sharing a meal with them. Liberation theology—which says that serving the poor must take priority over evangelizing—has become a significant movement in South Africa (they call it contextual theology) in this time of aparthied.

2000–2009 CE

2002	Sexual assault claims engulf the US Catholic Church; the pope issues an apology to victims of pedophile priests.
2004	June Osborne becomes the most senior woman in the Church of England after she is made Dean of Salisbury Cathedral.
2005	John Paul II dies; his funeral is the largest gathering of world leaders in history.
2005	German cardinal Joseph Ratzinger becomes Pope Benedict XVI.
2007	Reunification of the Russian Orthodox Church after 80 years of schism.
2008	Conservative evangelical Anglicans establish a rival church, the Anglican Church of North America.
2009	The Codex Sinaiticus, the world's oldest Bible, is digitally reassembled and available to be read online at the British Library website.

2007 CE Patriarch Alexy II of Moscow and All Russia (center) and Metropolitan Laurus of the Russian Orthodox Church Outside of Russia (left) listen to President Putin following the signing of the *Act of Canonical Communion* to reunify the Russian Orthodox Church.

GLOSSARY

A

Abbot The official title in the Western Church of the head of a monastery.

Absolution The formal forgiveness or remission of one's sins by a priest.

Advent A Latin word meaning "coming;" the season of preparation for Christmas.

Affusion Pouring or sprinkling water over a person's head at baptism (contrasts with **Immersion**).

Allegory Beginning in Alexandria, a method of interpreting the Bible that found up to four layers of meaning.

Anabaptists Various groups of Christians that hold to the baptism of believers rather than children.

Antinomianism The belief that, since we are set free by grace, we do not obey any moral law.

Apostles' Creed A major early statement of Christian belief from the fourth century, although not actually written by the apostles of Christ.

Apostolic succession The claim that bishops stand in a continuous line from the first apostles.

Aquinas, Thomas (1225–1274) Extremely influential theologian, who used the Greek philosophy of Aristotle to reshape Christian thought.

Arianism An early heresy, which argued that Christ was created by God and then granted the status of Son of God.

Asceticism Practices of self-discipline and self-denial that allow a person to focus on God.

Athos, Mt In Greece; the center of monasticism for Eastern Orthodoxy.

Augsburg Confession Dating to 1530, it is the major statement of belief for Lutheran churches.

Augustine of Hippo (354–430 CE) One of the world's most influential theologians, who argued for original sin, predestination, and complete reliance on God's grace.

B

Baptism A central rite, involving either affusion or immersion, for admitting a person to the Christian Church.

Baptists A large Protestant body established in 1609 by John Smyth that advocates baptism for conscious—usually adult—believers.

Beards, clerical Clerics of the Eastern Churches have worn beards since apostolic times.

Bede (Venerable) (673–735 CE) Father of English Church history and an influential Biblical scholar.

Benedict, St (480–550 CE) Founder of Western monasticism, after whom the Benedictine Order is named.

Bible From the Greek word *biblia*, meaning "books," and originally plural, it now refers to a collection of holy scriptures.

Bishop One translation of the Greek word *episcopos*, meaning "overseer;" the bishop is the highest office in churches with a priesthood.

Bogomils A medieval Balkan sect for whom the material world and the body were of the devil.

C

Calvin, John (1509–1564) Major systematic theologian of the Protestant reformation.

Canon From the Greek word meaning "rod" or "measure," it refers to the list of books in the Bible, and is part of the Catholic Mass and Church law.

Canonization The final statement in both the Catholic Church and the Orthodox Church that declares a dead person a saint.

Canterbury The most ancient center for Christian worship in England (from 597 CE).

Cardinal Originally the clergy of Rome, cardinals have become the pope's counsellors and electors.

Catacombs Early Christian burial places located below ground, which were used as places of refuge during times of persecution because Roman law regarded tombs as sacrosanct.

Catechism A manual for teaching the basics of the faith.

Cathedral A church containing the *cathedra* or throne of a bishop.

Catholicism *see* **Roman Catholicism**.

Cenobite Member of a religious order that follows a cummunal way of life.

Chalcedon, Council of (451 CE) A crucial assembly of church representatives, which decided that Christ has two natures in one person.

Christian socialism A nineteenth-century movement aimed at reforming society through Christian principles.

Christmas Originally a pagan festival of the winter solstice, it celebrates the birth of Christ.

Christology The study of the nature of Christ, with a focus on the union of divine and human natures.

Church A religious building, the people who worship in it, and the universal body of Christians.

Cloister An enclosed space usually in the middle of a monastery.

Confirmation The completion of baptismal vows and full admission into the membership of the Church as an adult.

Counter-Reformation A revival of the Roman Catholic Church in the sixteenth century in response to the Protestant reformation.

Creed A concise formulation of doctrine binding on Christians.

Curia The court of the pope, which administers the government of the Catholic Church.

D

Deacon The office in the Church below priest and bishop, which focuses on almsgiving and care for the poor.

Deism Developed in the seventeenth century, it is the belief that God created the world but has not intervened since.

Deposition The removal of Jesus' body from the cross after his crucifixion.

Devil Traditionally understood to be the chief of the angels who sinned and were banished from heaven.

Dispensation Permission granted by the Church to undertake an act that is otherwise illegal under Church law.

Dissenters Those who separate from the established Church of the land, such as Baptists, Presbyterians, and Congregationalists in England.

Docetism Found in the early Church, the belief that Christ's humanity and suffering were illusory and not real.

Donation of Constantine A forgery from the eighth or ninth century that claimed Emperor Constantine gave all power to the pope.

Donatists A fourth-century breakaway group in North Africa that sought strict discipline for those Christians who lapsed during persecution.

E

Easter Originally a pagan fertility festival, it is the oldest feast in the Church and celebrates Christ's resurrection.

Eastern Orthodox churches Concentrated in Eastern Europe and the Middle East, a series of independent churches sharing the same faith and in communion with each other.

Ecclesiology From the Greek word *ekklesia,* meaning "church," and referring to the theology of the Church.

Ecumenical council From the Greek word *ecumenon,* meaning "world;" an assembly of bishops and other Church leaders representing the whole world.

Ecumenical movement A twentieth-century campaign aimed at achieving cooperation between all believers in Christ.

Ecumenical patriarch The title of the patriarch of Constantinople since the sixth century.

Edinburgh Conference (1910) The forerunner of the ecumenical movement and the impetus for worldwide Protestant missionary work.

Election The theological doctrine specifying the way that God chooses some people for salvation and to carry out special tasks.

Epiphany The feast on January 6 celebrating the visit to the infant Jesus of the wise men from the East.

Eremite A Christian hermit or recluse.

Eschatology The theological doctrine concerning the end of the world and Christ's return.

Eucharist From the Greek word meaning "thanksgiving;" the celebration of Christ's last supper with his disciples.

Evangelicalism From the Greek word *euaggelos,* meaning "gospel," it refers to both the German Lutheran Church and a conservative movement within English-speaking Protestantism.

Excommunication Censure by the Church that excludes a person from communion with the Church but does not prevent one's union with God.

Exegesis The practice of interpreting the Bible.

Exorcism The expulsion of evil spirits by prayer and formulas.

F

Faith Both a belief in God and a statement of that belief.

Fast Self-denial of food, sleep, and comfort in order to focus on God.

Feasts (or festivals) Apart from Sundays, the main events or observances (such as Christmas and Easter) of the annual Church calendar.

Florence–Ferrara, Council of (1438–1445) An assembly of Church representatives that established a short-term union between the Greek Church and the Western Church; the union lapsed in 1453.

Francis of Assisi (1181–1226) Founded the Franciscan Order in 1209.

Fundamentalism A twentieth-century Protestant movement that was originally established in response to evolutionary theory and modern Biblical criticism.

G

Gallicanism A doctrine originating in France that asserts the freedom of Roman Catholic churches from the authority of the pope.

Gnosticism A complex movement in the early Church that emphasized the secret knowledge (*gnosis*) required for salvation.

Good Friday The Friday before Easter, which celebrates—usually with prayer and fasting—Christ's death.

Grace The doctrine concerning God's gift (*gratia*) of salvation and sanctification ("making holy").

H

Halo A circle of light around the head or (rarely) the whole body.

Hebrew The Semitic language in which almost all of the Old Testament was written.

Hell A translation of either the Hebrew word *Sheol* or the Greek word *Gehenna,* it traditionally refers to a place of suffering for the souls of those who remained unsaved at death.

Heresy From the Greek word *hairesis,* meaning "choice," it refers to deviation from established doctrine.

Hermeneutics The theory or science of Biblical interpretation (see **Exegesis**).

Hesychasm The practice of inner, mystical prayer in the Eastern Church.

Hierarchy The ordered sequence of bishops, priests, and deacons.

Holy Spirit The third person of the Trinity, equal to and one with the Father and the Son.

Homoousion Meaning "of one substance;" an early Greek term used to describe the unity of the Father and the Son.

Huguenots French Protestants who followed the teachings of John Calvin.

Hymns Sacred poetry set to music as part of worship.

I

Iconography Christian art characteristic of Eastern churches, usually depicting Christ in a stylized manner.

Immersion Submerging a person in water during baptism (contrasts with **Affusion**).

Immortality Although not restricted to Christianity, it is central to the Christian hope for eternal life.

Incarnation From the Latin phrase *in carne,* meaning "in the flesh;" refers to the belief that Jesus Christ is the union of human being and God.

Indulgence The reduction or remission of penalties on earth or in purgatory for sins committed.

Inquisition A Church court charged with the task of prosecuting heretics.

J

Jansenism A Roman Catholic movement of the seventeenth and eighteenth centuries that stressed the sinfulness of human beings and the total reliance on God's grace.

Jesus Christ The Greek form of the Hebrew *Joshua Messiah*—Joshua the Baptized One.

Justification From the Latin phrase *justificatio,* meaning "purging, cleansing;" the moving of a believer from a state of sin to a state of righteousness as a result of Christ's death.

K

Kiss of Peace Originally a kiss given to one another during the Eucharist, it is now usually a handshake.

L

Lambeth Conferences A meeting of all bishops of the Anglican Church that occurs about once a decade under the presidency of the Archbishop of Canterbury.

Lectionary A compilation of selections from the Bible that are to be read during public worship.

Liberal theology Preference for freedom and openness in theology rather than restriction to traditional doctrines.

Liturgy Both the written and established orders of public worship, and (in the East) the Eucharist.

Luther, Martin (1483–1546) The first significant figure of the Protestant reformation.

M

Magnificat Named for the first word in the Latin version of the text, these are the words Mary spoke on hearing that she was pregnant with Jesus (Luke 1:39–55).

Manichaeism The Gnostic system of belief, as taught by the Persian religious leader Mani (216–276 CE), that sought to release particles of divine light trapped in the human mind.

Marcion A second-century heretic who preached a Gospel of Love without the Law and who rejected the Old Testament.

Martyr From a Greek word meaning "witness;" soon came to refer to anyone who had been persecuted for their faith.

Mennonites Followers of Menno Simons (1496–1561) from Friesland, the Netherlands, who preached pacifism and believer's baptism.

Messiah A Hebrew word meaning "anointed" (equivalent to the Greek word *Christos*), and applied to a person given a special task by God.

Miaphysitism/Monophysitism The belief that Christ has one divine nature into which his human nature is absorbed, in contrast to the teaching that Christ has a double nature.

Millenarianism The belief that Christ will return at the end of history and reign over a glorious kingdom on earth for a thousand peaceful years.

Mysticism The immediate knowledge and experience of God, often through prayers, trances, visions, and ecstasies.

N

Natural theology Knowledge about God that may be attained through reason and not revelation.

Nestorianism The doctrine that Christ was two persons, divine and human, and not one person with two natures.

Nicaea, Council of (325 CE) The first "ecumenical" (worldwide) assembly of bishops and other Church leaders called by Emperor Constantine to provide uniform doctrine.

Nicene Creed Both the original statement of faith from the Council of Nicaea and the longer version, with additions, used in worship services.

O

Oblations From the Latin word *oblatio,* meaning "gift;" the bread and wine offered for the Eucharist.

Old Catholics A group of national churches that has separated from the Roman Catholic Church over matters of doctrine, especially the issue of papal infallibility.

Oratory A place of worship other than a parish church in Catholicism and the Church of England.

Ordination Appointment to a specific task or position within the Church.

Oriental Orthodox churches Those that follow a Miaphysite/Monophysite Christology, rejecting the decisions of the Council of Chalcedon (451 CE); they include churches in Ethiopia, Egypt, Lebanon, Armenia, Syria, and India.

Origen (185–254 CE) One of the most influential theologians from the early Church, who pioneered the use of allegory to interpret the Bible.

P

Palm Sunday The Sunday before Easter, celebrating Christ's entry into Jerusalem on a donkey.

Papal infallibility The doctrine that the pope is protected by divine guidance from making errors when instructing on faith or morals.

Parable From the Greek word *parabole,* meaning "short story;" a brief narrative that uses an example from nature or everyday life to make a spiritual point.

Paradise A word of Persian origin that refers to a park or pleasure ground.

Parish An area under the spiritual care of a clergyman.

Passion The suffering and crucifixion of Christ.

Passover A Jewish festival celebrating the Exodus from Egypt that features the killing and eating of a lamb; it has been taken over by Christians at Easter to designate Christ's sacrifice.

Patriarch From the sixth century, the title of the bishop of the main centers of Christianity; it is now used for the heads of national Orthodox Churches.

Paul, St The first Christian theologian and missionary, whose letters are collected in the New Testament.

Penance A series of acts that one must undertake in response to the forgiveness (absolution) of one's sins.

Pentecost From the Greek word meaning "fifty;" celebrates the descent of the Holy Spirit upon the Twelve Apostles fifty days after Christ's crucifixion.

Pentecostalism A modern movement that believes Christians may experience the same gifts of the Holy Spirit that the Apostles were given at Pentecost.

Pharisees From the Hebrew word meaning "separated ones;" popular leaders who appear as opponents of Jesus in the Gospels.

Pietism Beginning in the seventeenth century, a movement in the German Lutheran Church that advocated spiritual renewal through prayer and Bible reading.

Pope Meaning "father;" originally applied to any Western bishop but later came to refer only to the bishop of Rome.

Predestination The doctrine that God chooses those who will be saved and that Christ's death was for them alone.

Presbyter From the Greek word meaning "elder;" refers to a body of leaders in a church who were originally the same as bishops but later became a separate group.

Presbyterianism A system in which presbyters, not bishops, govern the Church.

Priest Common to many religions; in Christianity, the priest is the parish leader in Orthodox, Catholic, Anglican, and Lutheran churches.

Prophet From the Greek word *prophetes;* refers to one who delivers God's word to the people.

Protestantism Derived from a *protestatio* (protest) against Roman Catholic dominance; a form of Christianity based on the Reformation.

Psalms From the Greek word *psalmoi;* refers to songs accompanied by stringed instruments.

Purgatory In Roman Catholic doctrine, a place where those who have died in a state of grace go to await final absolution for their sins, and to be admitted to heaven.

Puritans Calvinist Protestants in England and North America, who sought purification of the Church from corrupt and unbiblical practices.

R

Redemption Common to many religions; in Christianity, the desire to be free from sin and death and to be united with God.

Reformation The extensive reform and return to the model of the early Church during the fifteenth to seventeenth centuries that led to Protestantism.

Resurrection The rising of Christ and then all who believe in him from the dead.

Revelation Both God's act in communicating with human beings and the written records of those teachings.

Roman Catholicism That part of the Christian Church which maintains a continuity with the early, undivided Church and which owes allegiance to the bishop of Rome, the pope; also referred to as Catholicism.

S

Sacrament The outward sign of God's gift (grace).

Sacrifice An act of giving God a gift, especially a living one.

Saint A human being who has been canonized after death due to their exceptional sanctity during life.

Scholasticism Beginning with Thomas Aquinas, the use of human reason to understand revealed truth.

Sin Voluntary disobedience of God's will.

Social Gospel Advocated by Protestant ministries in the late nineteenth and early twentieth centuries, a movement that fed and sheltered people as a priority and precondition for evangelism.

Soul Although long held to be the part of ourselves that goes to heaven, Christian doctrine does not teach the separation of body and soul.

Synod A Church council.

T

Temptation From the Latin word *temptatio;* refers to a trial or proof.

Theodicy The effort to reconcile God's goodness and power with the existence of evil in the world.

Thomas Christians An ancient body of Christians in India that dates from at least the fifth century, if not earlier.

Toleration The act of allowing and not judging beliefs and practices that are different from one's own.

Transubstantiation A Catholic doctrine that the bread and wine change into the substance of the body and blood of Christ when blessed during the Eucharist.

Trinity The doctrine that God has three persons—Father, Son, and Holy Spirit—yet is one God.

U

Ultramontanism Meaning "over the mountains" (to Rome); refers to the centralization of Roman Catholic authority in the pope.

V

Vatican The main residence of the pope in Rome.

Vestments The clothing worn by the clergy when acting in an official capacity for the Church.

Vulgate From the Latin word meaning "common;" the Latin translation of the Bible made by St Jerome (345–420 CE) and used widely in the Western Church.

W

Wesley, John (1703–1791) English founder of the Methodist movement.

Y

Yahweh Along with El and Elohim, it is the main Hebrew name for God in the Old Testament.

Z

Zwingli, Ulrich (1484–1531) Leader of the Swiss reformation.

INDEX

Page numbers in *italics* refer to an illustration, photograph, or map

A

B

C

D

E

K

L

M

T

PICTURE CREDITS

pp. 1 to 9 Copyright Corbis Australia
10–11 Steven Weinberg/Stone/Getty Images
12–13 The Art Archive/Musée de l'Hospice Villeneuve-les-Avignon
14 bottom left Copyright Corbis Australia
15 bottom right Copyright Corbis Australia
16 bottom left Copyright Corbis Australia
17 top right Copyright Corbis Australia
17 bottom right Copyright Corbis Australia
18 top left Copyright Corbis Australia
18 bottom left Copyright Corbis Australia
18–19 center Copyright Corbis Australia
19 top right Copyright Corbis Australia
20 top Copyright Corbis Australia
21 bottom right Copyright Corbis Australia
21 top left Copyright Corbis Australia
21 top right Copyright Corbis Australia
22 bottom The Art Archive/Musée du Louvre Paris/ Alfredo Dagli Orti
22–23 center Copyright Corbis Australia
23 top right Copyright Corbis Australia
24 top left Copyright Corbis Australia
24 bottom left Copyright Corbis Australia
24–25 center Copyright Corbis Australia
25 center right Copyright Corbis Australia
26 top left Copyright Corbis Australia
26 bottom Copyright Corbis Australia
27 top Copyright Corbis Australia
28–29 Photo Scala, Florence
30–31 The Art Archive/University Library Messina Sicily/Gianni Dagli Orti
32 The Art Archive/Museo della Civilta Romana Rome/Gianni Dagli Orti
33 bottom right Copyright Corbis Australia
33 top The Art Archive/Culver Pictures
34 top Copyright Corbis Australia
34 bottom left Copyright Corbis Australia
34 bottom right Photo Scala, Florence
35 bottom Copyright Corbis Australia
36 bottom left The Art Archive/Musée des Beaux Arts Nantes/Gianni Dagli Orti
36–37 center The Art Archive/Queretaro Museum Mexico/Gianni Dagli Orti
37 top right Copyright Corbis Australia
37 middle right Copyright Corbis Australia
38 bottom Photo Scala, Florence
39 bottom right Copyright Corbis Australia
39 top right Photo Scala, Florence
40 bottom left Photo Scala, Florence
41 top Photo Scala, Florence
41 bottom The Art Archive/Museo San Marco Florence/Gianni Dagli Orti
42 bottom left Photo Scala, Florence
43 The Art Archive/Museo del Prado Madrid/Gianni Dagli Orti
44 top The Art Archive/Musée des Beaux Arts Tours/ Alfredo Dagli Orti
45 top right Photo Scala, Florence/Fondo Edifici di Culto, Min. dell'Interno
45 bottom left The Art Archive/Galleria degli Uffizi Florence/Alfredo Dagli Orti
46 bottom White Images/Scala, Florence
47 top The Art Archive/National Museum La Valletta Malta/Gianni Dagli Orti
47 bottom right The Art Archive/Saint Sebastian Chapel Lanslevillard Savoy/Gianni Dagli Orti
48–49 center The Art Archive/Museo di Castelvecchio Verona/Alfredo Dagli Orti
50 bottom Copyright Corbis Australia
50 top right Photo Scala, Florence, courtesy of the Ministero Beni e Att. Culturali
51 top right The Art Archive/Cathedral Treasury Aachen/Alfredo Dagli Orti
51 bottom right The Art Archive/Gianni Dagli Orti
52 top right Photo Ann Ronan/HIP/Scala, Florence
52 bottom left The Art Archive/Cathedral of Monreale Sicily/Gianni Dagli Orti
53 The Art Archive/Museo Diocesano Bressanone/ Gianni Dagli Orti
54 bottom left The Art Archive/Gianni Dagli Orti
54 top right The Art Archive/Museo Tridentino Arte Sacra Trento/Alfredo Dagli Orti
55 The Art Archive/Galleria d'Arte Moderna Venice/ Alfredo Dagli Orti
56–57 Copyright Corbis Australia
58 bottom right Photo Scala, Florence, courtesy of the Ministero Beni e Att. Culturali
59 top Photo Scala, Florence
59 bottom left The Art Archive/Palazzo Leoni-Montanari Vicenza/Gianni Dagli Orti
60 top The Art Archive/Gianni Dagli Orti
61 top right Photo Scala, Florence
61 bottom right The Art Archive/Gianni Dagli Orti
62 bottom left The Art Archive/Tempio di Canova Possagno/Alfredo Dagli Orti
62–63 center Photo Austrian Archive/Scala, Florence
63 top right Copyright Corbis Australia
64 bottom left Copyright Corbis Australia
65 top left The Art Archive/National Gallery London/Eileen Tweedy
65 center right Photo Scala, Florence
66–67 Photo Scala, Florence/Mauro Ranzani
68 bottom The Art Archive/Gianni Dagli Orti
69 top left Copyright Corbis Australia
69 center right The Art Archive/Goreme Cappadoccia Turkey/Alfredo Dagli Orti
70 top Photo Scala, Florence/HIP
71 top right The Art Archive/Sant Agostino Gubbio/ Gianni Dagli Orti
72 bottom left The Art Archive/British Library
73 center right Copyright Corbis Australia
73 bottom Copyright Corbis Australia
74 top Photo Werner Forman Archive/Scala, Florence
75 bottom right The Art Archive/Monastery of Saint Catherine Sinai Egypt/Gianni Dagli Orti
76 bottom Copyright Corbis Australia
77 top The Art Archive/Armenian Museum Isfahan/ Gianni Dagli Orti
78 bottom right White Images/Scala, Florence
79 top Copyright Corbis Australia
79 bottom right Photo Scala, Florence/HIP
80 top right Photo Scala, Florence/HIP
80 bottom Copyright Corbis Australia
81 top left Photo Ann Ronan/HIP/Scala, Florence
81 center right The Art Archive/Suermondt Museum Aachen/Alfredo Dagli Orti
82 bottom left Photo Scala, Florence
83 top left Photo Scala, Florence
83 center right Photo Scala, Florence, courtesy of the Ministero Beni e Att. Culturali
83 bottom left The Art Archive/Pinacoteca Nazionale di Siena/Gianni Dagli Orti
84 top right Photo Scala, Florence
84 bottom left Photo Scala, Florence, courtesy of the Ministero Beni e Att. Culturali
85 Photo Scala, Florence/HIP
86 bottom left Copyright Corbis Australia
87 top right Photo Scala, Florence
87 bottom Photo Scala, Florence, courtesy of the Ministero Beni e Att. Culturali
88 bottom Photo Scala, Florence
89 top left Photo Scala, Florence
89 center right The Art Archive/Musée Baron Martin Gray France/Gianni Dagli Orti
90 bottom left Photo Scala, Florence, courtesy of the Ministero Beni e Att. Culturali
91 top Copyright Corbis Australia
91 bottom left White Images/Scala, Florence
92 bottom left Photo Ann Ronan/HIP/Scala, Florence
93 top The Art Archive/Private Collection/Alfredo Dagli Orti
93 bottom center The Art Archive/Roger Cabal Collection/Gianni Dagli Orti
94 bottom Photo Scala, Florence
95 bottom right Copyright Corbis Australia
95 top left The Art Archive/Diozesanmuseum Trier/ Alfredo Dagli Orti
96 bottom center Photo Scala, Florence/HIP
96–97 center Photo Scala, Florence
97 top right Photo Scala, Florence
98–99 Photo Scala, Florence, courtesy of the Ministero Beni e Att. Culturali
100 top Copyright Corbis Australia
101 bottom right Copyright Corbis Australia
101 top left The Art Archive/Unterlinden Museum Colmar/Gianni Dagli Orti
102 top left Photo Scala, Florence
102 bottom left Photo Scala, Florence/BPK, Bildagentur fuer Kunst, Kultur und Geschichte, Berlin
103 Photo Scala, Florence
104–105 Copyright Corbis Australia
106–107 center White Images/Scala, Florence
108 bottom left The Art Archive/Cathedral Treasury Aachen/Alfredo Dagli Orti
108 bottom right The Art Archive/Château de la Verrerie/Gianni Dagli Orti
109 top Photo Scala, Florence
110 top left Copyright Corbis Australia
110–111 center Copyright Corbis Australia
111 center right The Art Archive/National Gallery Budapest/Alfredo Dagli Orti
112 bottom left The Art Archive/Gianni Dagli Orti
112–113 top center Copyright Corbis Australia
113 top The Art Archive/Museo del Prado Madrid/ Gianni Dagli Orti
114 bottom left Copyright Corbis Australia
114–115 bottom center Photo Scala, Florence
115 center right The Art Archive/Chapelle Royale St Louis Dreux/Gianni Dagli Orti
116–117 top center Copyright Corbis Australia
117 top right Photo Ann Ronan/HIP/Scala, Florence
117 bottom right Photo Werner Forman Archive/ Scala, Florence
118 top left Copyright Corbis Australia
118 bottom left The Art Archive
119 bottom right The Art Archive/Bibliothèque de l'Arsenal Paris/Marc Charmet
120–121 Copyright Corbis Australia
122 Photo Scala, Florence
123 top right Copyright Corbis Australia
123 center right Copyright Corbis Australia
124 bottom left Copyright Corbis Australia
124–125 top Copyright Corbis Australia
125 bottom right Copyright Corbis Australia
126 bottom left Copyright Corbis Australia
126 top right DeAgostini Picture Library/Scala, Florence
127 The Art Archive/Palazzo Leoni-Montanari Vicenza/Gianni Dagli Orti
128–129 Photo Scala, Florence
129 center right Copyright Corbis Australia
129 top right Copyright Corbis Australia
130 bottom left Copyright Corbis Australia
131 top left Copyright Corbis Australia
131 bottom right Copyright Corbis Australia
132 bottom left Copyright Corbis Australia
132–133 center Copyright Corbis Australia
133 bottom right Copyright Corbis Australia
133 center right Copyright Corbis Australia
134 top left Copyright Corbis Australia
134 bottom left The Art Archive/Gianni Dagli Orti
134–135 bottom Copyright Corbis Australia
136 bottom Copyright Corbis Australia
137 bottom right The Art Archive/Palazzo Leoni-Montanari Vicenza/Gianni Dagli Orti
138–139 Copyright Corbis Australia
140 top left The Art Archive/Turkish and Islamic Art Museum Istanbul/Alfredo Dagli Orti
141 top Copyright Corbis Australia
142 top Copyright Corbis Australia
142 bottom center Copyright Corbis Australia
143 top right Copyright Corbis Australia
143 bottom Photo Spectrum/HIP/Scala, Florence
144 bottom Copyright Corbis Australia
144 top right The Art Archive/Bardo Museum Tunis/ Gianni Dagli Orti
145 top Photo Scala, Florence
145 bottom center Copyright Corbis Australia
146–147 Copyright Corbis Australia
148 bottom Copyright Corbis Australia
149 center The Art Archive/National Palace Museum Taiwan
150–151 Leandro da Ponte Bassano/The Bridgeman Art Library/Getty Images
152–153 The Art Archive/Thyssen-Bornemisza Collection Madrid/Kharbine-Tapabor/Coll. Bouquig.
154–155 top Copyright Corbis Australia
155 top right Copyright Corbis Australia
155 bottom right Photo Scala, Florence
156 bottom left Photo Scala, Florence
157 bottom right Copyright Corbis Australia
157 top right Photo Scala, Florence
158 bottom center Copyright Corbis Australia
158 center left Photo Scala, Florence
159 The Art Archive/Galleria Sabauda Turin/Gianni Dagli Orti
160 bottom left Photo Scala, Florence, courtesy of the Ministero Beni e Att. Culturali
160–161 center Copyright Corbis Australia
161 right The Art Archive/National Gallery London/ Eileen Tweedy
162 top The Art Archive/Kharbine-Tapabor/Avant-Demain
162 bottom right The Art Archive/San Gennaro Catacombs Naples Italy/Gianni Dagli Orti
163 top right Photo Scala, Florence/HIP
163 top left Photo Scala, Florence/HIP
164 bottom left The Art Archive/Cathedral Treasury Aachen/Gianni Dagli Orti
164 top right The Art Archive/Museo Civico Bologna/Gianni Dagli Orti
165 Photo Scala, Florence, courtesy of the Ministero Beni e Att. Culturali
166 top The Art Archive/Musée du Château de Versailles/Gianni Dagli Orti
167 top right Copyright Corbis Australia
167 bottom right Photo Scala, Florence, courtesy of the Ministero Beni e Att. Culturali
168 bottom left Photo Scala, Florence
169 top right Copyright Corbis Australia
169 bottom left The Art Archive/Museo di Castelvecchio Verona/Gianni Dagli Orti
170 top The Art Archive/Musée du Louvre Paris/ Alfredo Dagli Orti
171 top right Copyright Corbis Australia
171 bottom right The Art Archive/Musée du Louvre Paris/Alfredo Dagli Orti
172 bottom right Photo Scala, Florence
172 center left Photo Scala, Florence
173 top right Photo Scala, Florence
173 top left The Art Archive/Biblioteca Nazionale Palermo/Gianni Dagli Orti
174 bottom Copyright Corbis Australia
174 top left The Art Archive/Museo Civico Sartorio Trieste/Alfredo Dagli Orti
175 top left The Art Archive/National Museum Damascus Syria/Gianni Dagli Orti
176 bottom Copyright Corbis Australia
176–177 top center Copyright Corbis Australia
177 bottom Photo Ann Ronan/HIP/Scala, Florence
178 top left Photo Ann Ronan/HIP/Scala, Florence
178 bottom right Photo Scala, Florence/HIP
179 bottom right Photo Scala, Florence
179 top right The Art Archive/University Library Istanbul/Gianni Dagli Orti
180 top left Photo Ann Ronan/HIP/Scala, Florence
180 bottom left The Art Archive/Topkapi Museum Istanbul/Gianni Dagli Orti
181 The Art Archive/Musée du Louvre Paris/Gianni Dagli Orti
182 left center The Art Archive/Nicholas J. Saunders
182–183 bottom Photo Scala, Florence
183 top right The Art Archive/Alfredo Dagli Orti
184–185 Photo Scala, Florence
186 bottom left White Images/Scala, Florence
187 The Art Archive/Museo di Capodimonte Naples/Gianni Dagli Orti
188 top left Photo Scala, Florence/HIP
188 bottom left The Art Archive/Musée des Arts Décoratifs Paris/Alfredo Dagli Orti
189 bottom left Copyright Corbis Australia
189 top Photo Scala, Florence
190 top Copyright Corbis Australia
191 bottom left Copyright Corbis Australia
191 top right The Art Archive/Bodleian Library Oxford
192 top left Photo Ann Ronan/HIP/Scala, Florence
192–193 center The Art Archive/Museo del Prado Madrid/Gianni Dagli Orti
193 top Copyright Corbis Australia
193 bottom right The Art Archive/Real Collegiata San Isidoro Leon/Alfredo Dagli Orti
194 bottom Copyright Corbis Australia
195 bottom right Copyright Corbis Australia
195 top right Photo Ann Ronan/HIP/Scala, Florence
196 top left The Art Archive/Private Collection/ Philip Mould
196 bottom left Photo Ann Ronan/HIP/Scala, Florence
197 bottom right Photo Scala, Florence/HIP
197 top The Art Archive/Musée Eucharistique du Hiéron/Gianni Dagli Orti
198 top left Copyright Corbis Australia
198 bottom left The Art Archive/University Library Heidelberg/Gianni Dagli Orti
199 Copyright Corbis Australia
200 bottom left Photo Scala, Florence, courtesy of the Ministero Beni e Att. Culturali
201 center right Copyright Corbis Australia
201 top left Copyright Corbis Australia
202 top left The Art Archive/Gianni Dagli Orti
202–203 top The Art Archive/Gianni Dagli Orti
203 bottom right Photo Scala, Florence, courtesy of the Ministero Beni e Att. Culturali
204–205 top Photo Scala, Florence
205 center right Photo Scala, Florence
205 top center Photo Scala, Florence, courtesy of the Ministero Beni e Att. Culturali
206 bottom left The Art Archive/Carmelite Convent Beaune/Gianni Dagli Orti
206–207 top center Photo Austrian Archive/Scala, Florence
207 top right Photo Scala, Florence
208–209 Copyright Corbis Australia
210–211 top Copyright Corbis Australia
211 center bottom Photo Scala, Florence
211 top right Photo Scala, Florence
212 top Copyright Corbis Australia
213 right Copyright Corbis Australia
213 bottom left Photo Scala, Florence/HIP
214 bottom left The Art Archive/Kharbine-Tapabor /Cheuva

215 bottom center Copyright Corbis Australia
215 top Martin Gray/National Geographic/Getty Images
216 bottom left The Art Archive/Turkish and Islamic Art Museum Istanbul/Alfredo Dagli Orti
217 Benjamin Constant/The Bridgeman Art Library/Getty Images
218 bottom left The Art Archive/Biblioteca Nazionale Marciana Venice
218 bottom left Photo Scala, Florence
218–219 center Copyright Corbis Australia
219 center right Photo Scala, Florence/BPK, Bildagentur fuer Kunst, Kultur und Geschichte, Berlin
220–221 Photo Scala, Florence/HIP
222–223 Copyright Corbis Australia
224–225 Photo Scala, Florence/BPK, Bildagentur fuer Kunst, Kultur und Geschichte, Berlin
226–227 center The Art Archive/Bibliothèque Nationale Paris/Marc Charmet
228 top right The Art Archive/Palazzo Barberini Rome/Alfredo Dagli Orti
228 bottom Photo Scala, Florence
229 bottom right The Art Archive/Galleria d'Arte Moderna Rome/Gianni Dagli Orti
230–231 top center Copyright Corbis Australia
230 center left The Art Archive/Galleria degli Uffizi Florence/Alfredo Dagli Orti
231 bottom left Photo Werner Forman Archive/Scala, Florence
231 top right White Images/Scala, Florence
232–233 center The Art Archive/Musée du Louvre Paris/Gianni Dagli Orti
234 top right Copyright Corbis Australia
234 bottom left The Art Archive/Stei am Rein Switzerland
235 center left The Art Archive/Bach House Leipzig/Alfredo Dagli Orti
236 bottom The Art Archive/University Library Geneva/Gianni Dagli Orti
237 top left The Art Archive/University Library Geneva/Gianni Dagli Orti
237 bottom right Copyright Corbis Australia
238 top right The Art Archive/Bibliothèque Universitaire Geneva/Gianni Dagli Orti
239 bottom right The Art Archive/National Gallery Budapest/Alfredo Dagli Orti
239 top left White Images/Scala, Florence
240 bottom left The Art Archive/Musée du Louvre Paris/Gianni Dagli Orti
241 bottom center Copyright Corbis Australia
241 top left The Art Archive/Burnley Art Gallery
241 center right The Art Archive/Pinacoteca Nazionale di Siena/Gianni Dagli Orti
242 bottom left Photo Ann Ronan/HIP/Scala, Florence
243 Copyright Corbis Australia
244 top left The Art Archive/San Nicola Basilica Tolentino/Gianni Dagli Orti
244–245 top center Copyright Corbis Australia
245 bottom center Photo Scala, Florence, courtesy of the Ministero Beni e Att. Culturali
246–247 top Photo Scala, Florence, courtesy of the Ministero Beni e Att. Culturali
247 top right Photo Scala, Florence
247 bottom right The Art Archive/Museo de Santa Cruz Toledo/Gianni Dagli Orti
248 bottom left White Images/Scala, Florence
249 bottom left Copyright Corbis Australia
249 top right The Art Archive/Academia BB AA S Fernando Madrid/Alfredo Dagli Orti
250 top Copyright Corbis Australia
251 bottom right Copyright Corbis Australia
251 top center Photo Ann Ronan/HIP/Scala, Florence
252 bottom right Copyright Corbis Australia
252 top left Photo Scala, Florence/HIP
252 top right Photo Scala, Florence, courtesy of the Ministero Beni e Att. Culturali
253 bottom right Copyright Corbis Australia
253 center The Art Archive/Carmelite Convent Beaune/Gianni Dagli Orti
254–255 Getty Images
256 bottom left The Art Archive
256–257 center Photo Scala, Florence
257 top right Copyright Corbis Australia
258–259 top Millennium House
258 bottom left The Art Archive/Museo de America Madrid/Gianni Dagli Orti
259 bottom left The Art Archive
260 bottom Copyright Corbis Australia
261 bottom right The Art Archive/Museu Historico Nacional Rio de Janeiro Brazil/Gianni Dagli Orti
261 top White Images/Scala, Florence
262 bottom left Copyright Corbis Australia
262 top left Photo E&E Image Library/HIP/Scala, Florence
263 Photo Scala, Florence
264-265 top Copyright Corbis Australia
265 center right The Art Archive/National Gallery London/Eileen Tweed
265 center The Art Archive/University Library Istanbul/Gianni Dagli Orti
266-267 Gavin Hellier/Getty Images
268 bottom Copyright Corbis Australia
269 bottom center Copyright Corbis Australia
269 center right The Art Archive/Russian Historical Museum Moscow/Alfredo Dagli Orti
269 top left Photo Scala, Florence
270–271 The Art Archive/National Palace Mexico City/Gianni Dagli Orti
272 top left Copyright Corbis Australia
272–273 center Photo Scala, Florence/HIP
273 center left Copyright Corbis Australia
274 top left Copyright Corbis Australia
274 bottom left Copyright Corbis Australia
274–275 center The Art Archive/National Palace Mexico City/Gianni Dagli Orti
276 Photo Scala, Florence/Fondo Edifici di Culto, Min. dell'Interno
277 top right The Art Archive/Museo Tosio Martinengo Brescia/Alfredo Dagli Orti
278–279 bottom The Art Archive/Musée des Beaux Arts Lyon/Gianni Dagli Orti
279 top right Copyright Corbis Australia
279 bottom right Copyright Corbis Australia
280 top left Copyright Corbis Australia
280–281 center Photo Ann Ronan/HIP/Scala, Florence
281 center right Copyright Corbis Australia
282 bottom left Copyright Corbis Australia
282 top left Copyright Corbis Australia
283 top The Art Archive/Galerie La Tour Camoufle Louvre des Antiquaires/Gianni Dagli Orti
284 top left Copyright Corbis Australia
284 bottom Copyright Corbis Australia
285 center right The Art Archive/Kharbine-Tapabor
286 bottom left Copyright Corbis Australia
287 bottom right Copyright Corbis Australia
287 top right Photo Ann Ronan/HIP/Scala, Florence
288 bottom right The Art Archive/Musée Départemental des Vosges Epinal/Gianni Dagli Orti
288–289 top The Art Archive/Reproduced with the permission of the Trustees of Wesley's Chapel, City Road, London/John Wesley's House/Eileen Tweedy
290 top left Copyright Corbis Australia
290 bottom right The Art Archive/Private Collection
291 top The Art Archive/Garrick Club
292 bottom left The Art Archive/Byzantine Museum Athens/Alfredo Dagli Orti
292–293 center Photo Scala, Florence, courtesy of the Ministero Beni e Att. Culturali
293 center right Copyright Corbis Australia
294 bottom left Copyright Corbis Australia
294–295 Copyright Corbis Australia
295 top right Copyright Corbis Australia
296 bottom left Copyright Corbis Australia
296–297 top Copyright Corbis Australia
297 bottom right The Art Archive
298 Copyright Corbis Australia
299 bottom center Copyright Corbis Australia
299 top right Copyright Corbis Australia
300 top The Art Archive/National History Museum Mexico City/Gianni Dagli Orti
301 top right Copyright Corbis Australia
301 bottom left Copyright Corbis Australia
302 bottom left The Art Archive/Bibliothèque des Arts Décoratifs Paris/Alfredo Dagli Orti
303 top right The Art Archive/Victoria and Albert Museum London/Eileen Tweedy
303 top left The Art Archive/Private Collection/Gianni Dagli Orti
303 bottom left The Art Archive/Bodleian Library Oxford
304–305 Louis Charles Auguste Couder/The Bridgeman Art Library/Getty Images
306 bottom left Photo Scala, Florence
306–307 center Copyright Corbis Australia
307 top right The Art Archive/Russian Historical Museum Moscow/Alfredo Dagli Orti
308 bottom left The Art Archive/Chateau de Blerancourt/Gianni Dagli Orti
309 Photo Scala, Florence
310 bottom left Photo Ann Ronan/HIP/Scala, Florence
310–311 center Copyright Corbis Australia
311 top right Copyright Corbis Australia
312–313 Copyright Corbis Australia
313 top right Copyright Corbis Australia
313 bottom right The Art Archive/Chateau de Blerancourt/Gianni Dagli Orti
314 bottom left The Art Archive
314 top left The Art Archive/United Society for Propagation of Gospel/Eileen Tweedy
314–315 bottom Copyright Corbis Australia
316–317 The Art Archive/Musée des Beaux Arts Tours/Gianni Dagli Orti
318–319 center White Images/Scala, Florence
319 bottom right Copyright Corbis Australia
319 top right White Images/Scala, Florence
320–321 center Copyright Corbis Australia
320 top left The Art Archive/Reproduced with the permission of the Trustees of Wesley's Chapel, City Road, London/John Wesley's House/Eileen Tweedy
321 bottom right Copyright Corbis Australia
322 bottom left Copyright Corbis Australia
322 top right The Art Archive
323 top Copyright Corbis Australia
324 center right Copyright Corbis Australia
324 bottom center Copyright Corbis Australia
324 top left The Art Archive/Museo del Prado Madrid
324–325 center Copyright Corbis Australia
326 bottom Copyright Corbis Australia
327 top left Copyright Corbis Australia
327 bottom right The Art Archive
328–329 top Photo Scala, Florence/HIP
329 bottom right Copyright Corbis Australia
329 top right Copyright Corbis Australia
330 bottom right Copyright Corbis Australia
330–331 top The Art Archive/Private Collection/Marc Charmet
332–333 center Copyright Corbis Australia
333 top right Copyright Corbis Australia
333 bottom right Photo Scala, Florence/HIP
334 bottom left Copyright Corbis Australia
335 bottom center Copyright Corbis Australia
335 top Copyright Corbis Australia
336–337 Copyright Corbis Australia
338 bottom left Copyright Corbis Australia
338–339 top The Art Archive/Geographical Society Paris/Gianni Dagli Orti
339 center right The Art Archive/Private Collection/Marc Charmet
340 top left Copyright Corbis Australia
340 bottom left Copyright Corbis Australia
341 top left Copyright Corbis Australia
341 bottom The Art Archive/Church Missionary Society
342–343 bottom Copyright Corbis Australia
343 top right Photo Scala, Florence/HIP
344 top left Copyright Corbis Australia
344 bottom left White Images/Scala, Florence
344–345 bottom Copyright Corbis Australia
346 bottom left Copyright Corbis Australia
347 top Copyright Corbis Australia
347 bottom right Copyright Corbis Australia
348 center left Copyright Corbis Australia
348 bottom left Copyright Corbis Australia
349 Richard Ross/Lonely Planet Images/Getty Images
350 bottom Copyright Corbis Australia
351 top left Copyright Corbis Australia
351 bottom right Photo Scala, Florence/HIP
352–353 bottom The Art Archive/Gianni Dagli Orti
353 bottom center The Art Archive/Queretaro Museum Mexico/Gianni Dagli Orti
353 center right The Art Archive/Bibliothèque des Arts Décoratifs Paris/Gianni Dagli Orti
354–355 top Copyright Corbis Australia
355 top right The Art Archive/Kharbine-Tapabor/Coll. Jean Vigne
355 bottom right Copyright Corbis Australia
356 bottom left Photo Ann Ronan/HIP/Scala, Florence
356–357 center top Copyright Corbis Australia
357 bottom right Copyright Corbis Australia
358 top right Copyright Corbis Australia
358 bottom Copyright Corbis Australia
358 bottom The Art Archive/Bibliothèque Mazarine Paris/Kharbine-Tapabor/Coll. Jean Vigne
359 top Copyright Corbis Australia
360 center left The Art Archive/Museo del Prado Madrid
360–361 bottom Copyright Corbis Australia
361 top right Copyright Corbis Australia
362 bottom left Copyright Corbis Australia
362 top right Copyright Corbis Australia
363 top Copyright Corbis Australia
364 top The Art Archive/School of Oriental & African Studies/Eileen Tweedy
365 bottom The Art Archive/Kharbine-Tapabor/Coll. S. Kakou
365 center right Photo Ann Ronan/HIP/Scala, Florence
366–367 The Art Archive/Museo Pio IX e Pinacoteca d Arte Sacra Senigallia/Gianni Dagli Orti
368 top left Copyright Corbis Australia
368 bottom The Art Archive/Musée des Beaux Arts Lyon/Gianni Dagli Orti
369 top Photo Austrian Archive/Scala, Florence
370 bottom Copyright Corbis Australia
371 top Copyright Corbis Australia
371 bottom right Copyright Corbis Australia
372 top left Copyright Corbis Australia
372 bottom left The Art Archive
372–373 center Copyright Corbis Australia
373 center right Copyright Corbis Australia
374 bottom left Copyright Corbis Australia
375 Copyright Corbis Australia
376 bottom left Photo Scala, Florence
377 bottom Copyright Corbis Australia
377 top left The Art Archive/Galleria d'Arte Moderna Rome/Alfredo Dagli Orti
378 top The Art Archive/National History Museum Mexico City/Gianni Dagli Orti
379 bottom right Copyright Corbis Australia
379 bottom left Copyright Corbis Australia
380 top Copyright Corbis Australia
380 bottom right Copyright Corbis Australia
381 bottom Copyright Corbis Australia
382–383 Copyright Corbis Australia
384–385 top Copyright Corbis Australia
385 top right Copyright Corbis Australia
385 bottom right Copyright Corbis Australia
386 top left Copyright Corbis Australia
386 bottom left Copyright Corbis Australia
387 top Copyright Corbis Australia
388 bottom left Copyright Corbis Australia
388–389 bottom Copyright Corbis Australia
390 top left Copyright Corbis Australia
390 bottom left Copyright Corbis Australia
391 Copyright Corbis Australia
392 bottom left Photo Scala, Florence
393 bottom Copyright Corbis Australia
393 top center Copyright Corbis Australia
394 bottom Copyright Corbis Australia
394 center left Copyright Corbis Australia
395 top center Copyright Corbis Australia
395 bottom Copyright Corbis Australia
396 top left Copyright Corbis Australia
396 bottom left Copyright Corbis Australia
396–397 bottom Getty Images
398 to 419 Copyright Corbis Australia
420 bottom left Copyright Corbis Australia
420 top left The Art Archive/Humor Monastery Moldavia/Alfredo Dagli Orti
420–421 bottom Copyright Corbis Australia
422 top Copyright Corbis Australia
423 bottom Copyright Corbis Australia
423 top right Copyright Corbis Australia
424 top left Copyright Corbis Australia
424 bottom left Copyright Corbis Australia
425 Copyright Corbis Australia
426–427 Copyright Corbis Australia
428 top Copyright Corbis Australia
428 bottom left Photo by Steve Liss/Time Life Pictures/Getty Images
429 bottom left Copyright Corbis Australia
429 center right Copyright Corbis Australia
431 bottom right Copyright Corbis Australia
431 bottom Copyright Corbis Australia
432–433 Copyright Corbis Australia
434 to 447 Copyright Corbis Australia
448 left Copyright Corbis Australia
448–449 Photo Scala, Florence
450–451 Copyright Corbis Australia
452 The Art Archive/Gianni Dagli Orti
452–453 Copyright Corbis Australia
454 The Art Archive/Musé d'Orsay Paris/Gianni Dagli Orti
455 top Photo Scala, Florence/Mauro Ranzani
455 bottom Copyright Corbis Australia
456 to 469 Copyright Corbis Australia
470 The Art Archive/Gianni Dagli Orti
471 to 474 Copyright Corbis Australia
475 The Art Archive/Museo Civico Sartorio Trieste/Alfredo Dagli Orti
476–477 Copyright Corbis Australia
478 Photo Scala, Florence
479 to 483 Copyright Corbis Australia
484–485 The Art Archive/Musée du Louvre Paris/Alfredo Dagli Orti
486 to 496 Copyright Corbis Australia